D1285272

WITHDRAWN
WRIGHT STATE UNIVERSITY LIBRARIES

DIARIES
of
William Souder Hemsing

An Intimate Look at Souderton, Pennsylvania

1885-1888, 1902-1906, 1918

INDIAN VALLEY PRINTING, LTD.
Souderton, Pennsylvania
1987

Copyright © 1987 by Union National Bank and Trust Company of Souderton.
10 West Broad Street, Souderton, PA 18964

All rights reserved. No part of this book may be reproduced without permission.

Published by Union National Bank and Trust Company of Souderton

Printed by Indian Valley Printing, Ltd., Souderton, PA

Photographic Reproductions by Phil Ruth.

Cover Art by Arthur F. Skwierzynski, taken from an original drawing
by William Hemsing of North Main Street, Souderton.

Library of Congress Catalog Card No.: 87-50462
ISBN 0-9618393-0-9

Dedicated to the memory of
William S. Hemsing
by his home community in celebration
of the Borough of Souderton's
one hundredth anniversary.

Contents

Introduction

Foreword

Contents, continued

Appendix

Introduction

In 1885 William Hemsing, son of Henry and Mary Souder Hemsing, was a 19-year-old bank clerk living on Main Street in Souderton, Pa. What set William apart from the other young men of his time? Maybe it was his thirst for knowledge. He read every good book that he could get and was keenly aware of what was happening around the world as well as in the Souderton area. But most importantly, William kept a daily diary in which he put down on paper the important events of his time, his observations about life, and his innermost thoughts and desires.

William Hemsing kept a diary from 1885 to 1888, 1902 to 1906, and in 1918. What of the missing years? We do not know if he kept diaries through those periods; perhaps he did so and they were somehow lost. It seems unlikely that he kept one so faithfully for years, then stopped for several years and started again with no explanation. But all efforts to locate the missing diaries, if indeed there are any, have been to no avail.

Still, we must be deeply grateful for the daily journals that we do have access to. Because of Will Hemsing's efforts we now have a window to the past through which we can look and understand what life was like in the late 1800s and early 1900s. Through his words we come to understand, for instance, why the weather was so important a factor in daily life. Without paved roads, rain turned everything to mud and travel became very difficult. Heavy snow, of course, could be removed only by shoveling by hand.

It is almost impossible to read the diary from 1902 without shedding a tear and feeling the pain caused by the terrible diseases so common at that time. Diphtheria, scarlet fever, spinal meningitis, chicken pox and tuberculosis threatened the population, especially the young children.

The diaries provide an explanation of the reasons Souderton became a borough, and the politics involved in selecting the first borough council and school board. We learn of the people who helped shape our town. Great and tragic moments in our country's history are also described: the East Coast earthquake, the blizzard of 1888, France's gift of the Statue of Liberty to the United States, the great ice storm of 1902, Russia's efforts at dominating other countries, General Grant's death, and the end of World War I. From the trips to New York in search of immigrants to employ as domestics, we learn the importance of the railroads in everyday life. The reader can almost feel the cold wind in his face as he reads of racing over snow-covered roads in open sleighs. He can nearly smell the smoke from the great Telford fire.

But the most important lesson we learn from the diaries is that in the most essential ways, life in Souderton has changed very little over the years. Young men and ladies are still reluctant to let their true feelings for each other show.

We still lose patience and get angry with our friends. The borough council and school board still experience infighting and politics. The weather still concerns us, though for somewhat different reasons. Sickness and death are always with us, although older folks are now confronted with the greatest problems in that area.

As this unique book was being prepared for you and other readers, we tried to be as true as humanly possible to the original diaries and to copy them word for word. Spelling and punctuation are presented as it was written by Will Hemsing. When we could not decipher a word, we presented our best collective guess within parentheses with a question mark or noted it as "illegible." The years missing from the diaries were researched in back issues of the *Souderton Independent* and the important items and events were added to the appendix of the book, in order to keep the reader abreast of the chain of events.

Many people shared the responsibility of bringing these diaries to print. Thanks to William Hemsing, for writing the diaries, and to his grandson, William S. Hemsing and family, for making them available; to Floyd "Jake" Frederick for his aid; to the Souderton Centennial Commission for supporting the project; to Kit Romanoski, for securing the ladies to type the diaries from the original manuscript — no easy job. Those transcribers included Shirley Flick, Gloria Furezyk, Nancy Greshock, Nita Harris, Pat Kenworthy, Martha Moody, Ruth Mortimer and Mary Schnable. Thanks to Dr. John Ruth, Phil and Beth Johnson Ruth and Charles Grasse, Jr. for their help and guidance; to Charles Hoeflich, Chairman Emeritus of Univest Corporation of Pennsylvania and Merrill Moyer, President and Chief Executive Officer of Union National Bank and Trust Company for underwriting the project. And last but by no means least my family: Emily, Terri, GiGi, Lance and Tara, for all their help in reading, assorting, translating and sharing of my time while I worked on this project.

There is one thing we all have in common with William Hemsing: the fact that we find Souderton a great place to live and grow up in and we are all working to keep it that way.

Ted Boyer
Chairman of Historical Data
Souderton Centennial Commission

Foreword

Trying to imagine the history of a country railroad stop evolving into a town often becomes a matter of reading patient chronologies of business ventures and the minutes of borough secretaries. This husk of records seldom contains the kernel of interiority. There will be dates aplenty, the names of officials, school board notes, specifications for buildings, genealogies, reports of deep snow-falls and spectacular fires, the pronouncements of passing politicians and impressive clergymen, and records of a church's switching from coal to oil heat. But the sense of life itself?

To get the breath of intimate thought on the backs of our necks, to feel what it was like to be conscious on a particular porch on a particular evening in a particular conversation with a particular person in a particular culture — for this we need diaries, and not just diaries that tell what the weather was. Such a document is the personal record of William Souder Hemsing. Living among neighbors who were mostly inarticulate in English (he complains that "Henry Hackman hasn't enough language to explain even what he knows"), Will Hemsing himself could readily get into words a broad range of feelings and sensations. Thus, though linguistically atypical of his townspeople, this scrupulous young man was speaking, all unknowingly, for them all.

The prosaic, cigar-making Pennsylvania Dutch village of Souderton, midway between Philadelphia and Bethlehem, was already in its third generation when Will Hemsing, grandson of the town's founder, wrote the diary presented here. Three decades before his first entry the North Penn Railroad had passed (1853-57) between the lands of two Mennonite families belonging to the nearby "Gehman's" (Rockhill) congregation: those of lumber dealer Henry Souder and farmer-carpenter Jonathan Hunsberger. Both the Souders and the Huns-bergers had begun at once to exploit their favorable economic location with stores, factories, hotel and sales of real estate. The third generation provided Will Hemsing with his peers, such as his cousins Horace and Uriah Souder, living next door, or Jonathan Hunsberger, from the eastern side of the tracks. The rivalry between Hunsberger and Souder clans is evident in the diary.

Among other families drawn to the same new economic nucleus was that of Daniel Hemsing, a Reformed cooper of Huguenot ancestry, who took up residence in the string of houses along the dirt lane that was rapidly becoming Main Street. Daniel's son Henry married a daughter and was taken into the business of lumber dealer Henry Souder, the chief entrepreneur in the village.

Henry and Mary Souder Hemsing, parents of one surviving child — the William (b. 1866) of this diary — retained their parental religions. Henry fellowshipped at "Leidy's" Reformed Church just next to "Souder's Station," and Mary continued to go to the Mennonite communion at "Gehman's," near the "Derstines" stop on the railroad just beyond Telford. By 1879, when young

Will was thirteen, there was also a Mennonite Meetinghouse in Souderton just a block back (west) from the Hemsing home on the west side of Main Street near Chestnut. It is important to notice that when Will attends Mennonite services he records himself as going to "meeting," whereas when he attends Reformed or Lutheran worship he goes to "church." This is but one example of the innumerable nuances this diary registers from the interweaving cultures Will inhabited. He himself identified with his father's Reformed faith, becoming a key leader in the emerging "Zwingli" congregation on Main Street.

Perhaps the most impressive aspect of this record is its moving on so many levels, in a milieu so unlikely to be represented in written history. There is business, in which we see Will moving from his grandfather's rough lumber-sawing into a planing mill, and finally into the making of very fine furniture — influenced, according to neighbors' recollections, by Hemsing's visits to museums in Philadelphia and New York. Eventually we see Will Hemsing building whole sections of Souderton on his grandfather's original farm. There is social life, with its quaint "entertainments," courting, sleighing, an "apron and necktie party," weddings and gossip. There are Italian immigrant workers in a homogenous Pennsylvania German neighborhood. There is politics, with its voting blocs, rivalries, and a term for Will as Burgess. There are Phila-delphia newspapers, amateur plays, and an endless series of novels. A year after reading **David Copperfield,** Will still finds it "the height of enjoyment to think of it." There is social interaction with people from the surrounding stagecoach villages, the registering of the coming of the telephone and the automobile, and the notation that one day a young fellow in the town went about "hatless." There is bankruptcy, alcoholism, and a robbery-shooting followed by an operation on a kitchen table that looked "like butchering."

There is religion: visiting preachers among the Mennonites, and the Mennonite Sunday School Will assists with, helping his crusty neighbor on Main Street, miller Herman Godshall, nicknamed "the Governor." Will comes home from a Sunday School session disgusted with himself for his "worldly-mindedness," then cheers his "moodiness" by turning to Shakespeare. There is the persistent Methodist pastor trying to get a foothold in Souderton, and the Reformed minister being told by a member that he did not "preach sharp enough."

There is the cautious courting of Jennie Moyer ("J."), daughter of conservative Mennonite hay-merchant Jonas Moyer living directly opposite from the Hemsings, on Front Street on the Hunsberger side of the tracks. Will quite modestly describes the first approach in German. There are the first kiss, the lovers' tiffs, and, in the later diaries, Jennie's puzzling and obsessive religiosity as she is first influenced at a tent meeting of the "Mennonite

Brethren in Christ" and then baptized near Silverdale by the "River Brethren." The unbearably poignant deaths of two Hemsing children are also here in detail.

Whether or not Will Hemsing was a memorable personality to his neighbors, he will certainly become one to the readers of his diary as it unfolds like a story. Here is familiar access to the mind of a person moving between village and world awareness, sectarian and secular mind-sets. Though surrounded by a racially homogenous society, Will was nevertheless a person living, as most of us do today, in a transitional culture. Most of his children did not stay home, but continued in the movement their great-grandparents had begun in transferring from the countryside. One of them spent a lifetime in Alaska. It was through Will's son Henry, depicted in these pages as a stubborn little fellow, that the diary was saved, and through the kindness of Henry's son that permission was granted for publication.

Souderton is to be congratulated on having someone like Mr. Ted Boyer who could recognize the worth of this document for us all, and go after it. The town is also fortunate in receiving the support of the Union National Bank and Trust Company, for whom Will Hemsing once clerked, and for whom the sponsoring of this publication is not its first investment in the region's heritage. These benefactors have given the descendants of a modest community exceptional access to its memory. Publication in the Borough's centennial year of both this diary and a companion book of visual history, **Seeing Souderton,** as well as the appearance of a video review of the Borough's history, raise for it an unexpected but significant profile on the historical horizon of southeastern Pennsylvania. In the words of Souderton's thoughtful diarist, "much valuable history" has here been kept from being "lost."

John L. Ruth
Lower Salford
March 12, 1987

DIARIES
of
William Souder Hemsing
An Intimate Look at Souderton, Pennsylvania
1885-1888, 1902-1906, 1918

William Souder Hemsing (1866-1940)
Photograph taken 1887.

*Decides against studying medicine—follows Gordon's
exploits in the Sudan—spies on a pair of lovers—a second
Sunday School begins in town—the death of Ulysses S.
Grant—cyclones—an outing to "the Rocks"—Dutch bands
serenade local newlyweds—organizes drive for a library*

1885

Thursday, January 1, 1885. The year 1885 was ushered in with more
ceremony than usual. Last evening shots were fired till late into the night. The
band, which had been engaged for the skating rink to have been opened last
night, but which proved a failure as the bosses did not come, went and
serenaded Old Tremper who gave them a 10 Dollar bill for their trouble. They
then serenaded the druggist and so on till late. About 12 O'clock, some fellows
(they were Horace, Heins & Will Benner I think) took our old wagon and
Wm's horse and took three large bells and laid or hung them on two pieces
Setlg. (Scanantling) laid lengthwise on the wagon. They then drove through the
town making a great noise awakening nearly everybody. I myself slept on as
soundly as if all were silent. Andrew tried to awaken me, pushing me and
wishing me a Happy New Year, but all to no purpose, for without knowing it I
in my sleep told him to shut up.

Friday, January 2, 1885. I was up to see Dr. Loux yesterday on business. He asked me if I had not yet made up my mind to study medicine. I told
him I had not. He asked me this same question some time last summer. At first
it pleased me well but other thoughts had entered my head and I had almost
forgotten the circumstances. So when he asked me again I was still undecided.
I told him I was afraid of it. If I could only see into the future I would not
hesitate. He said, if a person liked the profession, and was determined to win,
success would be almost certain. He said that, to all appearances he will have
employment for another doctor though he would not promise. That he needed
an assistant in many operations where now he must get the aid of a regular
physician. That he would pay much attention to a student. That there was a
wide field open for good physicians. He estimated the cost of studying to be
about 400 a year for three years. The usual doctor's fees for students was 100
Dolls. He offered me his books to study in.

And when I left he asked me to consider over the matter.

Saturday, January 3, 1885.   When on my way to dinner, I met Dick Young staggering down the middle of the road. When he saw me he came over on the pavement and stopped me, "Let the bank man go to h_____", were his first words. "I am all right now. I got that money. Kulp gave me the money. I know Moyer. He says I forged my sisters' names. It's my money. What did you hear? Tell me. You won't? I hired a horse and buggy. It's my money. Heard something else? Tell me. I'm Dick Young. You can tell **me**. I'm Dick Young. I can lick any man in this place. You go home. Go when you please? will you? You go to _____, you go home." Here I told him he was a little drunk. "Certainly," said he giving me a parting kick.

This Dick Young is one of the most depraved specimens of man. He is seemingly well educated, was once a J.P. But drink ruined him. He is continually drunk, and, so it is said, has sometimes practised the art of stealing.

Sunday, January 4, 1885.   Today is Sunday. As the Sunday School closed last Sunday, I will have nothing to do but stay at home. It is rather lonely in having to stay at home. When one gets used to something, as soon as it is taken from him, he will miss it. It is very pleasing to think that, by teaching a class of little boys, you can perhaps, impress upon their minds some great truths. That perhaps they may get a glimpse of eternity. You come to love them, and you hope that they may perhaps love you a little. To be conscious of being loved by someone will, I believe, have a very agreeable influence on a person. He will cultivate the good opinion of others. He will cease to make enmities. He will try to heal old grudges. He will work himself into a new being.

Monday, January, 5, 1885.

Thursday, January 8, 1885.   This evening while discussing the uses of History, its influence on the character etc, father suddenly asked me if I had found in history any authority for a decent person to shrug his shoulders, deform his figure and in short act the buffoon. I told I had not and that I hoped he meant not me, secretly however in my thoughts comparing myself with some great men in history and seeing the contrast. This I fear has been a great fault of mine for sometime. When away from home I flatter myself I behave decently. But sometimes when I come home from work I want some fun and so start up something by moving all kinds of figures. This, though I by no means mean any ill, if sifted to the bottom would leave little more than a clown in the sieve. If I could only leave it but it comes so easy that I hardly think of it. But it must be done away with.

Friday, January 9, 1885.   It is not often that I find anything more touching than Carlyle's account of the death of Mirebeau. Carlyle is surely a great author, and although very deep, he cannot fail to interest you. He has such a masterly way of description. He holds the story in his hands, picking the actors in the drama out of the thousands and following them on through their careers, And then what is best in him, his hatred of all falsehood, of all skepticism, of all irreligion. His admiration of firmness, honesty, sincerity, earnestness which can even elevate mean [illegible]

A man honest and sincere and in earnest, must and will be firm. The poor heathen worshipping idols, if he is sincere he is in earnest, and is a hundred-fold better than the Christian knowing that there is a God who created us, but does not worship him in earnest, Who is not sincere in his worship. Who worships by formulas or more likely does not worship at all merely affects to do so. Thin-coated Hypocrisy! Double sin!

"And thou Capernaum which art exalted unto heaven shalt be brought down to hell: for if the mighty works which have been done in thee, had been done in Sodom, it would have remained to this day. But I say unto you that it shall be more tolerable for the land of Sodom in the day of judgement than for thee."

Saturday, January 10, 1885.   Tomorrow I will be nineteen. Thus far have I lived in this lower world. Not a very long time and yet it is a long time. Perhaps the happiest part of my life is already spent. The future has nothing for me but struggles, temptations, troubles. It is all dim. But the Past is all before me. Many a happy day has passed since the day I saw the light. Days that are gone, never to return. How great an opportunity had I to gain knowledge. How did I neglect this opportunity. How many boyish friendships did I form? Did not I also have a case or two of boyish love? Forgotten already. How many acquaintances are no more. Perhaps many of them already forgotten. It is sad to think that perhaps many who are now my friends will perhaps become enemies. I hope not. It is more sad to think that perhaps some of my friends will be forgotten in the future and others, who are present entire strangers to me, take their place. Such future friends do seem at present like usurpers.

But will not I also be forgotten? Why should I not? But still it is hard to leave a friend. There are many of my former playmates who are now long dead, the memory of whom is already growing dim. But I hope to meet them all in a better land where we may never separate. How many such are already in their graves. With whom many happy hours were spent. Many too are now alive whom I see and talk to often. Pleasant times we have together. Whom I write to, visit, hear of, and speak to. Will I meet these also elsewhere? I hope so. There are perhaps some who knew me in my childhood carried me in their arms, but who in my manhood know me not, will not know me in this life. Such also do I hope to meet again.

Sunday, January 11, 1885.   The day is come. It will soon be gone again never to reappear. Other days will come and go. The world will move on — on till the end of time. It will drag me along and I have to open my eyes to the fact that I am approaching manhood. When the struggle of life will begin. Hitherto it has been mere play, all joyous longing for the time when I will be a man. But woe to the man who finds himself unprepared for the struggle. For there will be struggles, times when you know which way to turn. Times when black clouds overspread the horizon. When the Fates seem to conspire against you.

Steady must the course be. "To dare and again to dare, and without end to dare" etc. Danton said, This with God's help will carry me through. The sky may seem bright now overhead, not a cloud visible. But this is no proof that clouds will not come. Clouds will come. Will come and hide the heavens. So that the Sun is not visible. Then comes the trial, and not till then. Why not win? No cloud changed day into night. The knowledge of the fact that the clouds will disperse is enough. So it is, or ought to be in real life. Is not there a God who made us who will take care of us in storm or calm. I have nothing to fear if I be stedfast. Perhaps I will not live to see another birthday if it should please God to take me away. All creatures are in the hands of God. He cares for all.

Monday, January 12, 1885.   Tonight we have to cipher over a house which Mr. Schoch is going to build on a lot he bought of Tobias Nice. Tiresome work, but let them build. We are ready for the conflict. We have about three jobs assured us in Harleysville only one which has as yet been ordered. W D Hunsberger is going to put up a 3 story stone building 40 x 50 just above his house. It is said to be intended for a hardware store. I don't know how that is. One thing I do know, that it will be a nice job for the one who gets it. Another thing is apparent. That there are not enough dwelling houses in the village. Every Spring there is a rush for houses to rent. The demand exceeding the supply. A dozen more decent houses could be disposed of without trouble. Why don't somebody with the money invest in this way. Tenants are very troublesome especially the lower class. Of this we have case or two at the present time. But did not I say decent houses? and get decent people to live in them. There are many beatiful sites for building in this town if they were not too high-priced. That is what is keeping this village back, as it would improve a great deal faster if land were more cheap.

Tuesday, January 13, 1885.   I am very busy these two weeks. Work is crowding on me everywhere. Bills innumerable to make out, letters to answer, milk to fetch, books to read and everything else. Tonight Chas Roberts will start a skating rink. They say there will be splendid fun to see them tumble. I cannot go. Am too busy. I rece'd a letter from Ed. Danley today. He wishes me "increased prosperity for 1885 and years hereafter". He wants to come over here one evening to the rink. They have none in Doylestown. He was 18 years old on Friday the 9th. Little Florence writes that Mrs. Hunsberger is sick and that they can not come up till she gets better. She says, Lidy may come along up.

It is a warm day for winter. The roads are very muddy. It became colder toward night.

All the old Directors were re-elected at the stockholder's meeting today.

Wednesday, January 14, 1885.   The Board today raised my salary to $400. for this year. The skating rink turned out pretty well last night. I was not there. It is said all the skates were in use and many others there besides. Several ladies were there. Bought a ticket today for $1.00 of IG Gerhart. I did it more for a favor than anything else. It will admit me free every evening of the fair. Also 25 prizes to 200 tickets will be chanced off in value fr. 2 Dolls to 25¢. Got an invitation today to attend a party given in honor of J.G. Leidy's 40th birthday. I don't yet know whether I'll be there or not. Emma is going to get married on Saturday. She has been writing letters everywhere all week publishing it although at home it is to remain a secret till they are off. I'm to act as hostler, Andrew is going to waylay them somewhere and make them pay. Mr. Detweiler has hired himself to Slifer. So I guess they will not move out of town.

Thursday, January 15, 1885.   Have a touch of the toothache today. If it gets too far I'll have the monster pulled.

Heard today that Mr. Schoch was worthless and that he drinks. So it does not matter much whether we get the job or not.

Schuyler Colfax late Vice President of the United States died yesterday of heart-disease.

Mlle Nevada (Miss Wixom) made her debut yesterday night in Philada. She made a great success.

Dr. Loux talked to mother about that matter again yesterday. He seems to be in earnest, but I can not go.

There was a small snowfall this morning but rained the greater part of the day.

Friday, January 16, 1885.   It is still raining. Dick Young came to bank today and had a five dollar bill changed. He wanted to make up with Mr. Moyer. He did want him to have any ill feelings against him.

I cannot go to the party tonight.

I sent an order for the Phila Weekly Press today.

Saturday, January 17, 1885.   This morning it is clearing off. It is very windy all day. The party last night was attend by something over twenty persons. The orchestra furnished the music. Today Emma is to be married. Mr. D is expected at one o'clock. Accordingly she gets ready by that time. Dressed in a dark brown suit with black velvet all the way down front, she did not look as if she were dressed for a wedding. I had quite a different idea of a wedding dress. One o'clock came and half past one still he had not come. I began to get impatient as it was high time to go to bank. Time passed slowly round till two o'clock when he at last arrived. I held the horse till they came out. Andrew stopped them at the door for which trouble he got fifty cents. I also got fifty cts for my valuable services. They then drive off no one knows whither. They will be home on Monday. This evening I told Dr. Loux that I could not accept his offer. I did not suit him, but I can not help it. After this I went to the skating rink. To see them fly round seemingly without effort, I could hardly wait till one was done, the skates being all in use, so that I could try it myself. I soon found myself tumbling round in a very ungraceful manner. I did not get over this fit the whole evening. It is warm work. I was sweated all through.

Tuesday, January 20, 1885.   John did not seem to be pleased very much when he found the history goes only over the space of seventeen years. But when he had read a little he said it read like Blaine's Letter of Acceptance.

Those who have not yet hauled their ice would better go at it now as they may not have another chance. It is said to be about three inches thick.

Mr Wm M Evarts received the nomination for United States Senator from New York from the Republican caucus of that state. This will elect him.

I must try and learn short hand writing some time or other. I have a notion that it might be useful to me in the future.

Wednesday, January 21, 1885.   It is a noteworthy fact that at present trade seems to be very slack all over the country. Prices are sinking or else have already touched bottom. The stockmarket is unsettled and in general stocks sell very low. Iron is very cheap. Iron screws have been selling lower than at any time before. Sugar is lower than ever. Mr. Becker says his business has to suffer with the rest. Women engaged in csty tailoring which at present is very slack, and as flour is very cheap, do their own baking. Thousands of people have been and are now out of work through out the country. This depression is partly owing to over-production and partly to lack of confidence in the future policy of a Democratic Administration.

Thursday, January 22, 1885.   Today Mr. Becker filled his icehouse about half. The day is very cold. The ice is about five inches thick. He had to haul it up from Hockertown. There were four teams. Andrew had one of them. He had on three coats and two pair of mittens in which he managed to keep quite warm.

I was at the skating rink tonight. There was quite a crowd of onlookers. I did not skate. It was fun to see a greenhorn skate. His performances resembled those of a drunken man. The "Lady Jane" was there escorted by her fellow. She did not stay long but left early.

Friday, January 23, 1885.   Today we had Annie Frederick to help in baking till noon. When I came home I had to help myself. I cleaned the porch and other outside work.

Andrew tried and is going to learn bookkeeping. I am to help him. Have no notion that he will learn it. At present there is a railroad war and rates are cut so that an emigrant ticket from New York & Phila to Chicago, St Louis, all points in Penna and Ohio reached by the Penna R R Co, for One Dollar. The steerage rates on steamers it is said are only six dollars from Hamburg to New York. You can go to Antwerp and return for 20 Dolls. This is getting too cheap.

Saturday, January 24, 1885.   Was at the skating rink tonight again. I can skate a little better, that is, I don't fall so often as I did last Saturday night. The trouble with me is I can't make the turns right at the corners. Then I run too much on one leg and push myself with the other. This has a tendency to make one a little lame. I took notice of several ladies who were there. Some were dressed fashionably in the extreme. It made a sorry sight. Some used more reason in their attire. They were dressed fashionably enough no doubt, but more simply. It would be queer if a woman could not combine beauty with simplicity in her dress. I can't for the life of me see why at the waist a corset must be used to press in those parts to make it slender while below the waist a bustle must be used to expand the skirt so as to make a monstrous shape for a human being. It is to me inconceivable, why the shape in which woman was created, should now be altered by pressure where too full, and stuffing where not full enough to meet the fashionable fancies of the age. I do hope that the time will come when corsets hoops bustles and other feminine foolishness will no longer be in vogue.

Sunday, January 25, 1885. I am at home all day. No meeting or anything going on. I read for the most part Tom Brown's School Days at Rugby. This a very interesting and instructive book. It makes me form a very high opinion of Dr Arnold the great and pious instructor of that school. So much so that I am going to read his History of Rome some time if I can afford to buy it.

Father was away today for a maid. He was down to Hagey's but did not get one. He afterwards went for Hannah Roth and got her. She will come on Tuesday.

Monday, January 26, 1885. On Saturday a dastardly attempt was made to blow up the Houses of Parliament. The first explosion took place in Westminster Hall. A man and woman noticed suspicious looking object lying on the steps leading to the crypt. They called the attention named Cole, who picked up to carry it away. He had not carried it far when he dropt it and it exploded knocked him down much wounded, tearing great holes in the floor. It also tore off the great iron gate from its hinges. The second explosion took place a few minutes afterward under the Peers gallery of the House of Commons. Had Parliament been in session it is estimated that about two hundred members would have been instantly killed including several of the ministers. It is a notable fact that the chair which Mr Gladstone usually occupies was blown to atoms. The third explosion occured in that portion of the Tower of London which is called the White Tower. This was used as an arsenal and the muskets that were in it were turned and twisted into every shape. The people are greatly excited over the outrages.

Tuesday, January 27, 1885. A man by the name of Cunningham has been arrested. The ruins have been photographed. Nobody is allowed to enter the Tower or Westminster Hall except officers examining the ruins. The Queen has ordered Windsor Castle to be closed to visitors. On Sunday a Socialist meeting was held in Chicago at which a colored woman presided. One speaker said that private property had to be abolished if it took all the dynamite there is and 99/100 of the population of the world had to be blown in the air. This is carrying this thing too far. It seems that all the rascality of the earth rejoices at this event. It seems that they are linked together by a state of common depravity. Had these explosions been aimed at something, if it had been intended to kill the ministers or anything that would show a purpose. But to expose the lives of innocent women and children for an aimless nothing is inexcusable. If there were in all probabilities a chance that Ireland could be freed thereby were an excuse. But instead of accomplishing this it has the opposite effect, for already it is rumored that in England Irishmen will be discharged and thus thrown out of work. Nor does it surprise me. These men are hardly to be trusted with anything. Were I a king or ruler I would rule with a strong hand too tyranical I'm afraid but I couldn't help it.

Wednesday, January 28, 1885. Last night Morris Zendt's daughter Stella died of Diphtheria. She was about six years old. She will be buried on Saturday. On Sunday night Dr. Loux performed an operation on her throat which greatly relieved her. She was Mr Zend's only child living. Tommorrow Chas. Godshall's wife will be buried. She died on Saturday. A few days ago news came that Gen Stewart in command of a division of the army which has been sent by England to the relief of Gen Gordon at Khartoum, had encountered an army of Arabs numbering about 10000 men at Abu Khlea Wells and had defeated them. This was on the 17th. The Arabs lost 800 killed 800 wounded. The British lost 65. No further news have been received from Gen Stewart and it is feared that he has been surrounded. Were it not for the greater excitement of Dynamite outrages there would be great anxiety for Gen Stewarts safety. Last Saturday by a singular coincidence Sen Edmunds introduced a bill against the manufacture and use of dynamite for criminal purposes.

On Monday the Liberty Bell arrived at New Orleans. Jeff Davis made a speech.

Thursday, January 29, 1885. I was over in Funkes shop this afternoon. He has it fixed right snug. He has a jig saw, a boring machine, and a circular saw. He has two man at work besides himself. They are Newboldt and a German from Phila. W talks as big as usual. Talking about the dynamiters, Mr Funke declared himself to be an enemy to England. England's conduct towards us during the rebellion, her refusal to alleviate (redress) Ireland's wrongs, her greed for empire were all denounced by him. He was not in sympathy with the dynamiters and the wanton destruction of human life. But the inability of the Irish to cast off their yoke caused a deep feeling of revenge which found its outlet in this way. He is opposed to Senator Edmund's bill now before the Senate. Socialism instead of being crushed by such a law gathers new strength from oppression. I called his attention to the Chicago meeting. He said these were no Socialists. They are Communists. Socialism was only directed against monopolies rich men such as Vanderbilt. There is enough and more than enough food for everybody in this country. And yet do not many suffer hunger. This country at the present moment is suffering from over production. Now if too much work is finished in ten hrs a day let them only work eight hrs. The labor saving machinery instead of being a help as it should be is thus made a curse to the laboring man. He advocated governmental control of all the railroads and telegraph. Such are the doctrines of Socialism. Mr. Funke it appears is a Socialist. There is some good in it. I certainly am opposed to monopolies but I can note take up the doctrine of Socialism. With Socialism is too often coupled the doctrine of Atheism which also will not bring any good.

Friday, January 30, 1885.   Yesterday Mr J G Gerhart was married to Miss Angeline Hackman. It was all done in high style and after it was over the pair started on a trip to New Orleans. Gen. Stewart has routed the Arabs near Metemneh. He has now reached the Nile and is in communication with Gordon. The latter sent three steamers from Khartoum to meet him. The pecularity of the fighting in the Soudan is that instead of forming into one continuous line, the army is formed into a square the non-combatants being placed inside of the square and are thus in as great danger as the soldiers themselves. Two newspaper correspondents were killed in this battle. This forming a square is necessary because the Arabs being in greater numbers surround the army which has thus to repel their attacks from all sides.

Saturday, January 31, 1885.   Slifer had sale this afternoon. Mrs. Slifer got suddenly ill day before yesterday of cholera morbus. She is better today.

Emma came over here today and mother seeing her asked her to come down right away, but which she said she would not do because of "the boys". She was afraid she'd get teased a little. She must have changed her mind for in the evening she brings Mr. Detweiler and they stay over night.

Sunday, February 1, 1885.   I was at the singing school in the meetinghouse in the forenoon. There were not many there. I was at meeting in the afternoon. We expected that Rev Isaac Moyer would preach but as he did not and as Rev. Jacob Moyer preached instead we were a little disappointed. He is very unfortunate as a preacher.

It is amusing to see these Franconia fellows file in in an almost endless line and bound every one of them for the back seats. I happened to sit on one of these benches when in pours the stream of Franks pressing me in an uncomfortable manner.

Monday, February 2, 1885.   Yesterday occurred the first malicious explosion of dynamite in this country. It happened in Grand St New Yrk. A dry goods firm had discharged a clerk for not bolting a door right at night. He belonged to the Dry Goods Clerks' union. The union demanded his reinstatement. The firm refused. A strike was ordered and the firm was left without clerks. They employed non-union men. The Union now began a series of persecutions to compel the firm to employe their clerks. Men were stationed on the sidewalk to persuade intending purchasers not to buy. They smashed the show case with a stone. All of no avail, and now on Sunday they resorted to the cowardly act of blowing them up with dynamite. The damage done is about $2500.

Tuesday, February 3, 1885.   Yesterday a woman by the name of Mrs Dudley shot and wounded O'Donovan Rossa the famous Irish dynamiter. Rossa is wounded in the shoulder.

Though Rossa by his example brought this on himself. But still it should not be. A supposed traitor to the dynamite cause is stabbed and half killed and now a noted dynamiter is shot by an enemy of that article. With already one explosion, this thing, if allowed to go on will bring anarchy into the land. Laws will have to be made not only for the protection of foreign countries but for our own. If allowed to grow it will become the greatest evil that ever existed.

There is snow on the ground. The crossroads are well fitted for sleighing while the other roads do not so well being almost bare. Some boys are coasting with big sled on the pike.

Wednesday, February 4, 1885.   We were very busy during the day getting through about four o'clock. The directors complained that their room was not warm enough. I am in fault of this as I did not open the register in their room till this morning expecting it would warm up in time and also that it would make it too cold for Mr. Greaser in the night. After this I must open it on Tuesday evening and I think the room will be warmed during the night.

I finished reading "Vicar of Wakefield" this evening. When I first read it I thought it was intended to be humorous and that it was covered with fine irony all through. But after reading it a second time I find all the humor is directed against that which is false. On the whole it is written in an earnest manner and contains much valuable instruction.

Thursday, February 5, 1885.   This morning early when I came to bank Mr. Beans was there talking about their debating society. John had spoken to him before about getting up some kind of literary society here and now he (Mr Beans) said he had spoken to some teachers belonging to their society, would be willing to come down. John did not say much about this plan but he told me afterwards that he did not approve of it. I agree with him. It is not well to have too many outsiders. Mr Beans continuing said there subject for discussion next Tuesday evening was, "Resolved, that Gen Grant should be placed on the retired list" etc. Hereupon a discussion ensued in which Mr Beans and John were for retiring him whilst Mr. Landis and Mr. Borneman during the discussion were against it. I was silent all through though I am surprised at it as I am on Grant's side and very prone to take part even where I am not directly concerned.

Friday, February 6, 1885.   On Jan 28 Col Wilson with three steamers reached Khartoum. As they approached the city they were surprised to find themselves fired on from both banks of the river. They however pushed on. When an island in the river also gave fire it became more serious. Still they pushed on. When they were near the city they were again fired on from the town and citadel. No flags were flying and both town and citadel appeared to be in the hands of the rebels. Being unable to learn anything of the fate of

Gen. Gordon he steamed back to Metemneh, wrecking two of his steamers on his way back. It was learned however that he had come just two days too late as Khartoum had surrendered or been captured on the 26th. It appears that Gordon sent too many of his troops up the Nile to meet Gen Stewart and that he thus weakened had been attacked by the Madhi and compelled to surrender. Some say that one of his Pashas had opened one of the gates and let in the Madhi. However it be it is not known whether Gordon is alive or dead. Most army officers believe that he is dead.

Saturday, February 7, 1885. There is great excitement in England over the news of Gordon's capture. This may bring England into great difficulties. Wolseley will now have to act on the defensive until he is reinforced. He will have to change his whole plan of campaign. He will have to stay down there all summer while the heat is fatal. The Madhi will gain new strength. This person who claims to be a prophet has hitherto had various success. First Hinds' army was massacred. Next Tewfish Pasha's suffered nearly the same fate. Gen 'Chinese' Gordon was next sent to calm the storm but he could do nothing. He offered to make the Madhi Sultan of Khordofan. He allowed the slave trade to be again carried on, but all of no avail. The Madhi seems bound to spread his doctrines power over the whole Mohammedan world. Gordon was now shut up in Khartoum which he has defended for almost a year against the power of the Madhi. Last winter or Spring Gen Graham obtained a great victory over Osman Digna the Madhi's lieutenant. Last Aug. Gen Wolseley with about 15000 men was sent to bring away Gordon and Stewart. The latter with his crew was massacred by the natives on his steamer which had grounded Abuhomet about ten days before Wolseley had arrived at Wady Halfa on Oct 5. Since then he has been slowly moving up the Nile and arriving just two days too late to save Gordon. This may cause the fall of the Gladsone ministry. The Madhi will have to be smashed and England's honor maintained whatever the fate of Gordon.

Sunday, February 8, 1885. We got up late this morning. Andrew is going to take Emma or rather Mrs. Detweiler over to her parents and then he will visit Tyson's with whom he lived a year. I got a letter from Florence last evening saying she has got up in school and that Mrs. Hunsberger is better that she sits up but has no appetite. After breakfast I am sent after Hannah Roth to take Emma's place.

Sit around all day reading a life of Washington in German. After dinner I take a nap and when I awake the sun is shining so bright on the white snow and everything seems so pleasant that I feel like taking a walk. After I come out there is noticable silence. No birds are singing and I am reminded that it is still winter. That the snow still covers the ground. I find myself at a loss where to go so I return to the house. Grandfather and grandmother Souder spend the afternoon with us. I notice they are both getting old. In the evening I go up to grandfather Hemsing to return a book he wanted me to read. I get introduced to Amelia's beau Mr. Coar. After sitting in their company awhile I go home and to bed.

Monday, February 9, 1885. On Saturday President-elect Cleveland visited Mr. Tilden at Greystone. They said Cleveland seems to be trying to be trying to get all the good advice he can. Has called to himself the best representative Democrats such as Randall, Carslisle. He seems to be a good listener chosing what is best for himself. As yet it is a secret who will become members of his cabinet. The day is rainy. There was sleet in the morning which made it very slippery. Mr. John Stover a brother of Jacob D. Stover was buried today.

It is said that Mr. Danley wants to come back again. I believe he has asked William to rent the spoke factory again.

Tuesday, February 10, 1885. 'Rain and snow followed by colder clearing weather' read the Signal Service bulletins. And they hit it too. It did get cold as I found out when I took hams up to Hangey's to smoke, with no overcoat on. Alice Gross left for the West today. She goes with her sister and husband who live in South Bend Ind. Before leaving, she said would stand at the car window and wave her handkerchief when they would pass this place on the 9 P.M. train. When Andrew came home he told me he had seen her wave her handkerchief as the train rushed by. That was the last that was seen of her here. I can't help recalling many incidents with which she is connected. Although only about eleven years old and not at all in my company, yet I feel that I shall miss her from among the young folks of the neighborhood. How much more must her companions feel it. It calls to my mind how unhappy I was after the last day of school. When I was separated from my schoolmates until the next school term. And then some of them were always missing. Some though far, far away, were still living, while others were no more. But especially on the last 'last day' did I feel sad. For this was to be my last school day. The last day that I would see all the old familiar faces together. With what ardor did I take a part almost sadly in that long, though too short two hour dinner. How loath were we, after the school had been let out, to go home, and so played another game of 'Copenhagen' in the school house cellar. The teacher only staid back to desire us to lock the door after we were through and not to make too much noise. How we played on till the sun began to sink in the western sky and how I, heated and huffing and sad went slowly home.

Wednesday, February 11, 1885. It is now almost certain that Gen Gordon has been killed. Col. Wilson has returend to Korti. He received his information from the natives. One treacherous Pasha let the troops out of the city on the side of Omdurman while another opened the gate at the other end of the city and let in the Madhi's soldiers. Gen Gordon was stabbed in the back as he came out of the Palace to learn the cause of the tumult. A horrible massacre followed. Gen. Chas. George Gordon was 52 yrs of age. He must have been a great heroic man. I could not help to admire his actions and so do I lament his death.

It is a very cold day. Most people say it is the coldest day we have had this winter. Old Wenhold came into bank this afternoon and swore it was the coldest day in his life. But his statements must not be taken at par. It was 9°

below zero in some places this morning.

I went up to see Mr. Bergeys stocking factory this afternoon but did not see much as they had nearly all gone skating, it being too cold to knit.(?) Mr. Bergey has 7 or 8 machines running. He pays 18¢ per doz for making. Some can make about 5 doz. They turn out about 25 doz a day.

Thursday, February 12, 1885.   Mr. Francis Frederick was buried today at the Goshenhoppen church yard. He died last Friday. He was 77 years old. He was an uncle of Chas. F. Hendricks.

Friday, February 13, 1885.   There was an insurance agent around today. He tried with all his might to insure father but couldn't. Father is opposed to life insurance and so am I. There is only one good in them as Mr Moyer says and that is when a young man has no money and wants to be educated he can obtain money by insuring his life and giving the policy as security to the lender until such time as he can pay the loan. This afternoon as I was sitting in Hen's office Mr. W. D. Hunsberger came in to talk about the coming election for school directors etc. They formed a plan to elect a school director each for Souderton and Telford. They decided to call a meeting on Monday evening and form a ticket to vote solid for it against the township. This is as yet secret.

Saturday, February 14, 1885.   It is snowing fast. If it keeps on long enough we will have more sleighing. Today is Valentine day. I think I must send valentines to the little girls in the city as I am sure they will expect it. I was in the store to look at them but as I could not see any and the store was crowded I put it off till Monday. Today we went over the discounts. This is always a tiresome job. We found them about $95 short. But there may be error some where as we found them usually a little long. It is almost impossible to copy off upwards of 1300 notes without an error. It would be well to go over them again before April.

Sunday, February 15, 1885.   It quit snowing. Enough has fallen for sleighing. Andrew wanted to go home today, so he asked for the horse and sleigh but did not get it. So after dinner he started to walk home all the way to L--. Father said I could have the sleigh to take him down which I, intending to remain at home, refused to do. And so all the blame of this will hang on me. Father and mother went up to grandfather H's with the sleigh whither I about two o'clock, followed, Taking with me Sallie and little Penrose we took a long sleigh ride which we enjoyed very much. The day was clear and the sun shone warm enough to melt the snow a little. It was a little rough in some places where the runners cut through to the ground. We drove down the Cowpath to near Hatfield station then over to the County Line at Hockertown. Penrose amused himself by counting the dogs we met or who took the trouble to bark at us. There were ten if I remember aright. Amelia and Maggie expected their beaux would give them a ride but were badly disappointed. We were much amused at their expense.

Monday, February 16, 1885.   Tomorrow will be the election. This morning, circulars were distributed calling a meeting tonight to form a Union ticket to elect a school director for Souderton and Telford. At the regular convention on Saturday evening three were nominated, insuring the defeat of one of the villagers. There will be a hot time tomorrow.

It is raining and it looks as if the snow will have to go.

Was at the store for a V-- [Valentine] but found only poor trash so gave it up. Received a V from Philada presumably from (illegible).

I notice Mr Beans accompany Miss Jane into the house today. Don't believe there is anything wrong but think it was wiser for her not to do it. I know him well enough. This will be food for the scandal-mongers which they should not have.

Tuesday, February 17, 1885.   The weather has changed. Become very cold. The melted snow has all frozen and the ground is covered with ice.

Mr Godshall is much dissatisfied with last night's action. Mr. Landes opposed him. Mr. G. said the township would take another man on their ticket and defeat both Leidy & Moyer. This would leave four schools in and near S---- and two in T---- without anybody to look after them. If this thing keep on at this rate the towns will have to separate from the township. The hatred and envy which the township shows against the villagers is ridiculous. All along since the school house was built they resisted every attempt of the villagers to elect a school-director. Such a man, whoever he might be was distrusted. They were and are afraid of six months school. Five mos long enough. About noon reports came in from the Square, Goettler says the Union men are scratching every name but Leidy's to run him ahead. Borneman thinks it's a dead shot. The people don't all go. Business considerations. Farmers greatly excited. Are sending in every man.

Wednesday, February 18, 1885.   Jas Y Hendricks and A H Leidy were elected School Directors yesterday. Nice & Fretz were reelected Supervisors. Wm H Moyer had 89 votes for school director. The Souderton men abandoned him and voted for Leidy only whose majority over Jacob D Stover was 8 votes. The township did everything to defeat Leidy. Here there would have been great dissatisfaction had he been defeated.

Sleighing is spendid.

Mr Wm E Strohl one of the famous Strohl family, has formed a company for himself consisting of himself his wife, Mr Wm J & Lotta J. Mayo & two little boys about 13 years old. They performed here tonight. The seats were only half taken. Mrs. Alice Strohl who led the orchestra, was in my opinion the best artist. She is a good violinist and gave a cornet solo so clear and well that I wished Uriah had been there. Her singing to me approached perfection. W E Strohl played 'Last Rose of Summer' with two cornets. He sings well. On the whole I think it did not equal the Strohl's. Charlie was particularly missing. The childlike singing of Mamie and Esther was also lacking.

Thursday, February 19, 1885. The board of school directors is now tie on the six months question. Three being for and three against it. Woodward one of the former is President of the board. He is to resign and one of the five months men is to be put in his place. This would leave the six months men in a majority of one on the question. This is the plan proposed by Aaron H Leidy and the newly elected member.

Mr. Allen M Fretz was married this afternoon to Miss Ella Hartzel formerly of Harleysville and now of Telford. They were Dutch banded in the evening.

Friday, February 20, 1885. There was a great fire on Chestnut St Phila that did damage to the extent of 500000 Dollars. The Corn Exchange Nat Bank had a narrow escape.

I hear this morning that Mr Beans was drunk last night again. It is said that this happens about once a week.

Mr Beans is the most curious person I know. He practices dissimmulation. If Mr. Landes is with him he is very sincere and seems down on liquor. He 'sees the monstrosity of tobacco chewing' and when among a crowd of roughs he is as bad as any of them. I have not always known him. I used to think a great deal of him. He knows how to hold the veil before your eyes. He will turn out bad if he keeps on this way.

Saturday, February 21, 1885. Gen. Herbert Stewart died of the wounds received in the engagement with the Arabs. The Washington Monument will be dedicated today. It is 573 ft in height if I remember aright. Last evening Uriah came for me again to help at the fair. I had not intended to do it this time but finally promised to help this evening. When I came up they had everything fixed splendidly for me having a writing desk and easy chair belonging to Goettler. I had quite a nice time of it, so much so that I have broken my resolution not to do it any more. Fairs are not quite legitimate and there are many reasons why I should not help them. But then I will be wanting to go anyhow and I might as well be their and at work as there expending money, and coming in contact with bad company. When I came home from the fair, I found on passing the window that there were two persons in the room. I could not help stopping to watch them through the window, the lemon tree inside shielding me from their view. There, on the settee sat a young man, half-dozing, with his right arm about Hannah who was lying most contentedly with her head against his side. This thing so surprised me, having never seen or heard of anything like it before, that I waited to see what would happen next. So did they sit apparently half asleep, when, with a swaying movement pressed himself against her as he meant to kill her. Then, swinging suddenly back again they resumed their former positions. This seemed to be about the whole performance excepting only when he took a fresh hold about her waist when I verily thought he would break through the isthmus and thus seperate forever the upper and lower parts of the body or break her corset or that some other direful calamity would happen. This programme was repeated often enough. I now began to desire means how to get into the house honestly without discovering that I had been watching. So I sneaked back to the street aided by the silent tread of the rubber shoe and the drowsy state of the lovers. I now returned making much noise to give notice of my approach. I tried to get in at the kitchen door but finding it locked I was ushered into the presence of the amourous pair. I was introduced to Mr. Wampole. I believe that he was drunk. I got off to bed.

Sunday, February 22, 1885. This morning Uriah Souder and I drove down to Leidy's church in the sleigh. Rev Abel Horning preached in Rev Mr Dengler's stead. On our way home we drove a little round for a ride. The road is getting bare in many places. In the afternoon we all attended meeting. Rev. Joe B Detweiler was there. He spoke a few words. He does right well for a beginner. I like to see preachers of different denominations come together. They throw aside all their differences and embrace as brothers. Rev Abel Horning preached the sermon. Cousins Maggie & Amelia were with me after the meeting. Maggie wears specks on account of her weak eyes. She is going to join the Church.

Monday, February 23, 1885. Yesterday morning the house of Mr King in Pine St Phila [burned] whereby five lives were lost.

My uncle Henry Souder bought the hotel at Quakertown station. He paid 12050 for it. Wonder if this is a wise step. He has been looking round for such a place a long time. His parents were much opposed to this. Taking nothing else into consideration, if the 500 license bill will become a law with only one hotel for every two hundred voters, it might not go well with him. He will take care of himself.

Mr. Reideman is here over night.

Tuesday, February 24, 1885. This evening Andrew is studying bookkeeping. He has learnt some definitions, ruled some paper, and is now engaged in copying off the Day Book in the first set Double Entry. I have some doubts of he will carry it far. He has so far not done much in this direction and his two years are almost up. He had splendid opportunities to read and study every book that I own. He did begin to read about three but left them afterwards.

Wednesday, February 25, 1885. There was a sale of seven Souderton and three Sellersville bank stock at the bank this morning. Souderton sold at 142.50 — 141. — 141.50, while Sellersville sold at 135. This latter is quite out of reason as Sellersville has only 9000 surplus and pays 5% dividends. Souderton was high enough but cheap in comparison to Sellersville. This stock has sold at 149, Surplus 20,000.

At the fair this evening I had the good fortune not to have any money with me, for I would certainly not have brought any home. As it was, I was tortured and had to talk myself to pieces in self defense. Receipts 43. on Saturday and 17[00] tonight.

Thursday, February 26, 1885.   Andrew and I took a sleigh ride after supper. It is not very cold and I fear the snow will not last much longer.

After our return I went down to Jesse Kline to pay my toll. This poor fellow was cheated out of his accordian on which he is an adept ? by a peddler who took it along to fix it for him. The simpleton was easily imposed upon and now he mourns its loss.

Friday, February 27, 1885.   The ingrain carpet weavers being on a strike in Phila. their former employers fetched new men from Boston in their stead. This excited great discontent among the strikers. Those also who refused to take part in the strike are in great danger. Over four hundred policemen were employed in clearing the streets in Kensington and escorting Walter Cameron a loom fixer who did not take part in the strike, home. His house is guarded by policemen during the night.

Saturday, February 28, 1885.   It is now so warm that by this afternoon very little snow was left on the ground. The sleighing was splendid this week again but I fear this was the last.

The Sellersville Band was at the fair here tonight. The fair was well attended through there was no crush, Receipts $68.28. This is the first evening that it cost me anything.

Uriah escorted Miss J-- home tonight. I believe he had her out sleighing last Sunday night. I wish them much joy.

Horace & M Bergey did not behave too well I hear. I am afraid they will get spoilt.

I got a new pair of shoes today.

Sunday, March 1, 1885.   The weather today was cloudy with a little rain in the afternoon. Uriah and Katie were here in the morning. Grandfather H- in the afternoon and also C Hunsberger. I was reading Shakespeare's 'All's well that ends well'. I had almost forgotten all about it.

I was very sleepy all day owing to the late hour at the fair last night.

We are expecting Emma home today.

I believe Amelia and Maggie were coming down here this evening with their male companions but they did not come.

Monday, March 2, 1885.   Emma came home late last night. President-elect Cleveland has taken a decided stand on the Silver Question. A few days ago Congress defeated a bill for stopping the coinage of the Silver dollar. It is thought that if this goes on this rate Gold will soon be at a premium. To prevent this the Sil Dollar coinage must cease. Bank examiner Drew was here today. He expects a red mouth democrat in his place. Gen Grant is reported to be very near his end. He is afflicted with cancer. He is working on his book.

Drew says that his heart is broken. Congress should pass the retirement bill.

Mr. Gladstone has been sustained in the English Parliament by a vote of 312 to 288. At a cabinet meeting it was decided by the ministers not to resign. The Conservative policy is the annexation of the Soudan.

Tuesday, March 3, 1885.   President-elect Cleveland with Manning and Lamont left for Washington last evening. It is said that he has never been in Washington before. Who will compose his cabinet remains as yet a secret though everybody pretends to know. Bayard Garland Lamar Manning are most mentioned.

Gen Grant is reported to be better.

Mother does not feel at all well today. She has for some time past not been well as could be wished.

Wednesday, March 4, 1885.   It is a very nice day for the inauguration. Today was a great day at Washington. The People flock there from every part of the country. Andrew N Leidy went down from here. I'll bet he won't see much. The hotels in Washington have been full a week ago and last evening the railroads carried many to Baltimore to pass the night. Cleveland arrived in Washington yesterday morning. The evening papers say that the House on motion of Mr. Randall to suspend the rules, passed the Grant retirement bill at 11³⁵ A.M. The bill was signed by Pres. Arthur who nominated him as General on the retired list and unaminously confirmed by the Senate. This is a mere act of justice and should have been done long ago. Mother is not at all better, and she remained abed all day.

The fair was not well attended Receipts only 7.72

Thursday, March 5, 1885.   Yesterday Grover Cleveland was inaugurated President of the United States. It is estimated that there were over one hundred thousand strangers in Washington. The city was very gaily decorated, 25000 men marched in the procession which was reviewed at the grand stand by Pres. Cleveland and Ex Pres Arthur. The inauguarl address was Short. The oath was administered by Chief Justice Waite. Mr. Arthur will be the guest of Mr Frelinghysen for the next three weeks. He took leave of the Diplomatic Corps, the members of the Supreme Court on Tuesday.

In the evening was the great ball attended by about 12000 persons. This was held in the new Pension building. Admission 1⁰⁰. Pres Cleveland held a reception. A grand display of fireworks finished the business. Cleveland's allusion to civil service reform in his inaugural address fell rather flat.

Friday, March 6, 1885.   President Cleveland yesterday sent the following names to the Senate for confirmation.

Thos F Bayard	Sec State	of Delaware
Dan. Manning	" Treas.	" N.Y.

Wm C. Endicott	" War	" Mass.
Wm. C. Whitney	" Navy	" N.Y.
L.O.C. Lamar	" Interior	" Miss.
Wm F. Vilas	" P.M.G.	" Wis.
Aug Garland	Att'y General	" Arkansas

Mr. Riddleberger objecting to Mr. Bayard the whole business was laid over till today.

Mother was up again the greater part of the day.

I do believe that a business man if he be credulous to the extent that Mr. J Wenhold is, will if he live long enough, die a poor man. Mr. W- thinks if he has a man's name on a note that that is all that is necessary even if such person is worthless.

Saturday, March 7, 1885.   Yesterday Grover Cleveland was inaugurated President of the Uni March 5.

The nominations sent in by Pres. Cleveland were yesterday unaminously confirmed by the Senate.

Mr Will Yocum is at present sponging on his father here and is sitting round doing nothing. He is now about 30. What a fine promising lad he was when he left home loved by all. I remember him well when he came round with milk every morning. That was over 13 years ago. Now he returns to sponge on his father. Has a very nice wife and child but is divorced from her. He drinks too much. Three times did he almost lose his life and yet has not mended. Hope he will yet. At the fair in the evening F Crouthamel and he cut up the former being drunk.

The fair was not very well attended. Receipt 31.58 The Chalfont Band was expected but did not come.

Sunday, March 8, 1885.   Andrew's younger brother Wilson came up last evening and staid til this evening. I was at home all day except in the evening when I walked up to the station. In the afternoon cousins Amelia, Maggie, and Martha and Kate Souder all came in body. Had a pleasant time. Mag is a good girl. She and Martha are very quiet. Martha is only about 15 now but I expect her to become a very sensible lady. Amelia can sing very well although too loud. Katie is wild as she ever was. She and Andrew acted up a little too much.

Mr Isaac Freed Sen, was buried today. None of us got to the funeral.

Mr. F. G. Detweiler was here today. They took a ride in the afternoon. He says he can't stand it at home.

Monday, March 9, 1885.   At present the relations between England and Russia are very much strained owing to the Russian advance upon

Afganisthan. Both countries have appointed commissioners to arrange the dispute. It is said the Russians are sending troops toward Afghanistan and that their object is to occupy Herat. The Germans too have hauled down the British flag in Africa and raised their own. Bismark coarsely insulted Lord Granville during the last week. France too is opposed to England. In Egypt has concentrated all his troups at Korbi. He addressed the troops on Saturday. He expects to enter Khartoum before the year is out.

Tuesday, March 10, 1885.   Andrew got some new tools today. They were a fore-plane, jack-plane and smoothing plane and a plane a saw, hammer hatchet and square. He did not get any chisels or augurs. Father got them for him. He had promised conditionally to do so. He seemed to be not quite satisfied. I think he expected more. I think he ought to have had some more tools. He gets fifty Dollars too but he says this will go to his mother. He will stay next summer and go to school next winter. He has not yet made a bargain with father. Uriah Stover will come here too in April. He will probably board here and sleep at home.

Wednesday, March 11, 1885.   The board today decided to buy trade dollars at 80 cents from today. They will probably decide to sell those we have next week. They sell at between 83 and 85 cents. The bank has over 6700 of them, 2500 at par, 737 at 88¢ and 3558 at 85 cents, and about 2600 sold at 86 or 87. The Trade Dolls fell about Sept 1883 and we had about 5100 at that time. With Int and everything I believe the bank will lose over 1200 Dollars. They had better been sold right away next morning when we were offered 92. John thinks Congress will redeem them but I wouldn't risk much on Congress.

I will not go to the fair tonight.

Thursday, March 12, 1885.   I hear Jonathan Umsted is with Dr. Loux to study medicine. I think he will suit pretty well. Dr. Loux is building an addition to his house for the drug store which he has bought out of Schimmel. John Frederick moves in the house he bought of Yocum today. Yocum moves to Telford. Mr. D. W. Kratz moved into the house he bought of Frederick.

The weather is cold for the middle of March. Some snow still remains on the ground and the ground is frozen.

Friday, March 13, 1885.   Cleveland has so far sorely disappointed the office-seeking Democrats. He has appointed nothing more than his Cabinet and filled a few other offices that were vacant. Only two nominations were sent to the Senate Wednesday and yesterday none were sent. This threw these fellows in a rage and profane words were used. If they are not relieved today it is probable that many will give up in despair.

Pres. Barrios of Gautemala has decreed the union of the Central American States and assumed command of the army. San Salvador Costa Rica and Nicarauga will oppose him. Pres Diaz of Mexico has warned him to desist.

Saturday, March 14, 1885.   Mr. & Mrs. Jos Benner with their little daughter Maggie were here over supper. They have been living in the city coming next spring five years. Miss Maggie who is eleven years old talks German but I thnk prefers English. Isaac is in a drug store. Pete is a decorator of glass. He wants to become an artist I understand. He attends school in the (two) evenings a week. Joseph is in a grocery store. They are all smart boys. Mr. John Benner fetched them away here.

The Zeiglersville band was at the fair tonight. They do not play as well as our band does. They have a long trip. Miss L.M.Z. was at the fair tonight for the first time. W. H. Souder had his'n. I'm tired of this thing.

Sunday, March 15, 1885.   It is raining slightly this morning. Uriah came down for the team for grand father H's to go to uncle Joe Derstines. We went along up to and found cousins Henry & Penrose Hunsberger there with the rest. Elwood and Henry dressed up in ancient garments and made quite a funny show.

In the afternoon I attended meeting. Rev. Isaac Moyer preached the sermon. He said he did not expect to come here again. In the evening while at the station Mr. Landis came in to telegraph for Mrs. Gardiner as her father Mr. Tremper who has been ill all week had broke down and was not expected to live till morning. Amelia and Maggie with their gentlemen followers paid me a visit. We talked mostly about horses and stock of knowledge about the animal was about exhausted. Mr. Davis is in the employ of Tyson the horse jockey.

Monday, March 16, 1885.   Mr. Tremper is still living this afternoon. Grand father was out to see him and he thinks he will not live till tomorrow. Mr. Landes was there nearly all last night. He said he was delirious, talking most of the time, praying, spelling a word counting and other expressions. His daughter Mrs. Gardner has not yet arrived although she is expected with the 5 o'clock train. Young Frank Greaser is reported said that they expect the house where he lives.

Today was a partial eclipse of the sun which was visible here from about twelve to three. We viewed it through a piece of smoked glass. It appeared on the west side of the sun and gave it the shape of a half moon. It (the moon) covered about one fourth of the sun's surface.

Thursday, March 19, 1885.   This morning we shipped 7000 trade dollars to J Walsh & Son 5 Wall St New York, who pay 84-3/4. There were ten bags of 700 each. We had 2650 par 737 — 88 and 3558 — 85 — 29 — 80. This mades 6974. J S Ruth 187 and I H Moyer 30 were also sold so that we have now 189 on had which we take in the a/cs at 80. We did not find one bad or bland in the 6974. We found 2 Blands in J.S. Ruth's. Mr. Tremper was buried today at Woodland Cemetery Phila quite private. Messrs Zendt & Slifer acted as pall bearers.

People are more curious to learn about Mr. Tremper and there propably more gossip going about than about any body else. All the talk is Tremper. The fact of our shipping the Trades started a rumor that Mr. Tremper had had an immense am't of money and that half a ton had been taken away. People would like to find out how much he was worth. They would like to know the contents of the will. It's said Mrs. Gardiner gave Heim the big revolver, Lucetta the chickens and silver teapot. Mrs. Gress the wash tubs tc. She (Mrs. Gardiner) will go home and return in three weeks when she wants to settle up. She is going to rent the house.

Friday, March 20, 1885. It has been and still is very cold. The thermometer has been near zero nearly all week. Tomorrow Spring begins according to the calendar but according to the weather it would seem that spring were a month off yet.

Saturday, March 21, 1885. Dan. Hunsberger came up from the city today. He went with me to the fair. He was here over night. He is learning the bricklayer's trade. He has been in the city since last June. He is boarding with M Hunsberger's. I think he will turn out well.

This was the last evening of the fair. Receipts 132.61. Entire Receipts 387.00. Goettler and a fellow from Hatfield fought. Nobody hurt. Goettler lost a ring. Good for him. M Shellenberger drew a berry set. Uriah Stover drew a nice hanging lamp. Told Clint I wasn't going to help next year. The Chalfont Band was here. They have fine uniforms. Our band want to get new uniforms out of the proceeds of the fair.

Sunday, March 22, 1885. Still cold. Don Hunsberger left here after dinner.

This afternoon Misses Ella and Annie Fretz, second cousins to me, came to our place to make a short call. During their stay here the three o'clock train on which they had intended to go home passed by and left them back. So they staid for supper. There were present Ella & Annie Fretz Martha & Katie Souder Harry Hunsberger who dropped in during the afternoon and who had taken the girls to a Dunkard meeting in the forenoon. After supper we all went up to uncle Henry Souder's. We had a very pleasant time. The Fretz girls intend to go home tomorrow. Ella is going to Blooming Glen Hotel. Annie is by far the most agreeable. She is only about sixteen.

Monday, March 23, 1885. Heins and Lucetta are reported to have been married on Saturday evening. They were at the fair awhile late. It is a good thing if they are married.

Was at the auction tonight. It is reported that a watch chain charm and four rings were stolen during the fair. Many more articles were probably stolen which will never be noticed but it is a shame that there are such people. Nobody should have been allowed back of the counter.

Rufus came back from West Chester this evening. He is suffering from rheumatism for the last two weeks.

Tuesday, March 24, 1885.

Wednesday, March 25, 1885.

Thursday, March 26, 1885.   Today there has been much moving. Every body is moving. G. F. Schwenck, Isaac Fellman, Wm. Hochman, Tyson the new hotel keeper above here, Mahlon Stover all moved about. Mr. Frank Detweiler too had his things moved over to Slifer's. In the evening we carried over some carpets and canned fruits etc. We drank a glass of wine.

Friday, March 27, 1885.   The weather has become milder. The ice has nearly all disappeared. There was a little rain in the afternoon. Many roads had dried off but now I expect them to get muddy. Received a letter from Ed. Danley this evening. They will move on Tuesday on a farm near the Delaware River. He says he is coming over when the festivals commence. He will bring his 'mash' along who he says is an acquaintance of mine. I have not the slightest idea who it is unless it's a North Wales girl.

Saturday, March 28, 1885.   There was a slight snow this afternoon. The band went up to serenade Mr. Tyson the new landlord.

Mr. & Mrs. Detweiler went over to Wentz church this afternoon. They will not return till tomorrow evening.

Was up at grandfather S- this evening. Grandmother showed me a picture whereon was Ellis when about eight or nine years old with Milton then fat little boy of 3 or 4 years. She showed me also another picture of Ellis taken last Fall. There is not the least resemblance of the one to the other. We talked so much of relations of ours that I have come to think it a good plan to make a chart of the Hemsings Fredericks Souders and Hunsbergers.

Sunday, March 29, 1885.   During the night a snow fell 4 or 5 inches deep. Now for muddy roads.

Uriah and I were down to Landes's today. We had promised to come and see them for 2 or 3 yrs. It is a shame that I don't get to see them oftener. Ed's school closed on Friday. He is going to work on the farm. He would like to become a telegraph operator. Morris wants to go west. He would like to have a partner. Ed is much taller than I and weighs 169 pounds. We found them all well. Ed seems to be fond of music. He plays well on the melodeon and clarionet. Henry has a fife.

Monday, March 30, 1885.   Today we were quite busy. It savoured a little of April. Money is commencing to move a little.

I was out this afternoon. Stopped at W. Bilger's and wanted to leave Edelman's order there to collect but his wife who I thought was very foolish refused to keep it saying he would not accept any orders but I hunted him up in Barnd's hay house and he promised to give preference to this one outside of those for his own house. Barndt's are cutting hay. It is very dirty work as well as unhealthy.

Tuesday, March 31, 1885. In consequence of the defeat of the French forces in Tenquin; where the Chinese recaptured Longson and it is said are advancing upon the French positions a 100,000 strong. Gen. Negrier, was badly wounded. About one fourth of the French were left on the field. Jules Ferry the French prime minister asked for 40,000,000 dollars for the Tenquin campaigns which was lost and the Ferry ministry immediately resigned. There was great excitement in Paris. Jas M Slifer was down today. He did not come in bank. I spoke a little with him. He was down for money for the new bank. Today was Andrew's last day as 'prentice. He will stay all summer. Uriah Stover will come tomorrow. We expected Susie Daub too but now Mr. Freed won't let her come till Thursday evening. Emma is not at all pleased.

Received my shoulder braces this morning from Ed Danley. They cost $7⁰⁰ and postage. I put them on right away. It feels a little queer.

Wednesday, April 1, 1885. We were very busy today at bank. Every body wanted money and we do not have much money remaining here. The deposits ran up to 196,700 and something. Bills Dis are 189,000. This was the last time that A.S. Heany will come.

This was Uriah's first day. How he felt about it I do not know.

Gen. Grant felt better yesterday.

Am very sleepy. Must go to bed.

Thursday, April 2, 1885. Gen Grant sank rapidly yesterday. It was thought he was dying. He was not expected to live 24 hrs.

It is reported that the city of Aspinwall has been reduced to ashes by insurgents.

M de Freycinct has been asked to form a new cabinet.

Miss Susie Daub came here today. Mrs. Freed did not like to give her up so she kept her as long as she could.

Emma was here the last time this morning. Helped to haul up her things in the evening.

Friday, April 3, 1885. Today was Good Friday. The bank was nominally closed. We were all in in the forenoon. I assorted the checks etc. I told Levi Meyer on Wednesday the bank would be closed today for the reason he comes every legal holiday. But this morning Mr. Meyer was one of those that came. Several other persons came in. On Decoration day I'll fix him, if Mr. L. & M. will go away. I'll send him home with his money. It is only to earn ten cts or so that he does it. That has been a very nice day. The roads have dried off a great deal today.

Gen. Grant was thought be dying at five yesterday but during the day he rallied and It was expected he might live 3 days.

Horace is not going West. It was all a sham. Morris Landis was up for him on Monday. Rufus says he heard him ask his father to go and not at once receiving a favorable answer he asked for a team if he were to stay here.

Saturday, April 4, 1885. A very heavy rain fell last night. I think the frost ought to be out of the ground by this time although it is not. It is so deep. It is said to average 18 inches deep. Gen Grant was still living this morning. He is however reported to be liable to die at any moment.

Our deposits are now up to 204000.

Andrew went home this evening. Think he has April settlements to make. Uriah will stay over night.

Sunday, April 5, 1885. Cool and clear. Rufus and 'Bubby' Moyer came in after dinner and together we went to meeting. Rufus with Jonathan and John Hunsberger and Jane Moyer will start for West Chester tomorrow morning. Jonathan I understand (intends) wants to teach. Rev. Henry H. Rosenberger of the River Brethern preached the sermon. His text was Gal. III-1. There was a full house. He preached a very forcible sermon. Uncle Cornel's and Aunt Sarah stopped in after meeting. Maggie Amelia Uriah Souder staid for supper. Maggie and Calvin will join the church. Jonathan and John Hunsberger and Newboldt were in here awhile in the evening. Harry Dettry is here. Is an operator on the Penna Railroad. Goody Frick was up today. He is now named Charlie for short Godshall being too long. He signs his name Chas G. Frick.

Monday, April 6, 1885. Gen. Grant was still living according to the latest advices. He says he is going to die and is willing to die.

Most people are keeping holiday today and so find time to do their bank business.

Helped to load part of the car that will carry H. Souders HH goods to Quakertown tomorrow. Vinie and Mary were in here to bid goodbye.

"Butcherly" was around here this afternoon the boys treated him unmercifully.

Tuesday, April 7, 1885. M Brisson has formed a cabinet for France. This includes M de Freycinct who failed in the same task.

It is reported that Barrios of Guatemaula is dead.

Gen. Grant is still about the same.

Henry Souder's moved to Quakertown today. Grandmother, Mrs. Ed, Mrs. Fred, Mrs. Ellis Aunt Kate, mother and Katie Souder all went along up. Ellis took a load up with their team. Jonas Freed and Will Ruth are up yet. Mother says the children are highly delighted with their new home. Lillie especially could hardly wait till the train came to take them off.

Wednesday, April 8, 1885. Today was probably the busiest day we will have for some time. We did not get out till six o'clock. The deposits rose from 192000 yesterday to 207000 today. There were 5200 in deposits including 9000 discounts while against this were charged 3700 checks. If I rember aright 4500 dep. and 2500 cks were the highest last year. Bills Dis are 194000, and 16000 lear Trusts.

Gen Grant is sinking after a violent fit of coughing he had an arterial hemorrhage when he lost about two ounces of blood. His end is near.

Mrs. Gardner is down again. They wanted Mr. Landis to go along to Norristown today but he did not do it. They will go tomorrow. Mr. L. and Mr. Borneman are the witnesses to Mr. Trempers will which is to be filed tomorrow.

Thursday, April 9, 1885. We were not at all busy today with outsiders. Mr. Landes went to Norristown to attend to the Tremper will as witness. From there he went to Phila. and came back at three. I was just done with my part of the work except the mail which Mr. La got ready. It is now understood that Mrs. Haines (Lucetta Young) will get a 1000 4% Gov. Bond and Mrs. Greaser $700. This will square a mortgage Mr. Tremper had against Mr. Greaser. A lady in Sellersville probably Annie Raudenbush will get $2000.

It is supposed that this woman was a little too intimate with Mr. T. Our girl still talks about changing places with Hannah Roth who is at the hotel and who would like to come here.

Friday, April 10, 1885. Gen. Grant continued to improve yesterday. There was a fight between the Russians and Afgans in which the latter were defeated. It is rumored that the Russians have occupied Rendjeh which is in Afgan Territory. This occurrence may lead to war between Russia and England. There is a very warlike outlook.

We unloaded a 17000 car lumber from Moyer of Perkasie. E H. Souder C S Moyer, Chris Freed & Fen Crouthamel and Andrew did it. There was a little bit of a fire in the shop this forenoon by a box getting hot but it was put out before the flame reached the woodwork. We are having new envelopes printed for the bank; with Goettler.

Saturday, April 11, 1885. The weather today was unpleasant. There was snow falling all the afternoon melting as it came down. But this evening I notice the snow has whitened the ground. Young Clinton Becker was in mother's care today Mrs Becker being with her mother who is very sick.

Money is very slow coming in. Father has still a great many bills to collect and many will not be paid at all this spring some parties having given notice to that effect. At the bank money is not so scarce. The deposits are going down fast however being only about 185000, this afternoon.

Sunday, April 12, 1885. Was at home all day. Grand-father H was down in the forenoon. He has an order for 12500 stakes to fasten tents which he has agreed to furnish for $275. This is a little too cheap I think.

Emma Nace was here this afternoon. Katie Souder Henry Hunsberger and Henry Souder were here in the evening. Susie brought her sister in also.

Monday, April 13, 1885. Gen Grant is growing weaker. He had several severe spells of coughing Saturday and Sunday.

Ex. Secretary Frelingshuysen is dying in Newark of hardening of the liver. It is reported that he may not live more than 48 hours.

I was up at the shoemaker's this afternoon and on my return I walked in to see how far the doctor's building was. Jonathan Umsted called me in and I remained awhile looking over the books. He says he likes it.

A H Leidy's little girl will be buried tomorrow. She was 5 yrs. old.

Tuesday, April 14, 1885. War between England and Russia grows more probably. Both countries are preparing for ware.

Ed. had a fall out with old Herman yesterday about the new toll gate the Turnpike is going to build.

It is about time to start up the Sunday school. Mr. G. has not said a word about it. He wants us to run after him and then he would dictate terms. Must see him about it soon. John is going to resign. Can't see who will take his place. Had my shoes soled today. Stopped in at Grandfather. He has cancelled the 275 order. Stopped in to see grandmother S. this afternoon. She is not at all well.

Wednesday, April 15, 1885. It has been reported today that C G Barndt & Son have made an assignment. E. C. Beans is the assignee. This morning the Sellersville letter contained the following line "C. G. Barndt & Son's etc. are in notary's hands but will hold a day under promise of payment." This has not been unexpected. They way they did business selling cheaper and paying higher prices for hay than any of the others could not last long. Mr. Borneman says that H E Wampole and Eli Cassel have each endorsed a 1000 note for them. If Wampole will have to pay this it will ruin him. In this case Father would lose about a $100. He is going up tomorrow to get a judgment from him if he can. Borneman was chased out of bed at three o'clock on account of this.

Thursday, April 16, 1885. Today seemed more like Spring. The day was warm and decidedly different from yesterday when the snow fell all the forenoon. Wampole this morning confessed judgment for 101.42 Father had it entered through Danl. instead Being not altogether safe as whoever pushes first is ahead in personal property So this evening he and William who has claim against him of about 55 went up to buy lumber. He was up at Sellersville and tomorrow he will come down. The Sellersville Bank I understand feels very sore. It is reported that Wampole & Cassel for a 1000. Kistner 3000 and L Gerhab 1300. Some of these notes are weak enough and they will probably lose some money. It is reported that Ben could not raise bail enough. Susie is still unsatisfied. She will go home on Sunday and act accordingly. Mother said this morning she believed we would lose her.

Friday, April 17, 1885.   No fresh news from Telford. Isaac Gerhart did not know much about the party affair. It is said that Mr. Beans the Assignee has not been able yet to furnish the amount required of him. It was reported that Borneman had joined him but it is not true. He denies it. The Sellersville Bk fellows have promised to give Wampole all the time he needs. The Barndts too promise to fix it all right for him. He has not yet had his wifes judgment entered. He feels secure. He was down today at bank. Whitey the switch man has been on a spree since yesterday. He was kicked out at Leidy's store and at Kratz's. He then went home and got a gun. He wanted to shoot Gehman.

Monday, April 20, 1885.   The day was very warm. Most people began plowing today. We intended to dig the garden but found it too wet. After I came home from bank I straightened the fences and fixed up the pavement along the pike in front of the house.

Abner Kindig was sheriffed by Elias Shellenberger for 7000 Dolls. if I remember aright. 2500 is right.

Gen. Grant still continues to improve. Both the Russians and the English are actively preparing for war. They are both buying and building vessels. Turkey has decided to remain neutral and to close the Dardanelles should war ensue.

Tuesday, April 21, 1885.   Much warmer than yesterday.

Uriah and I dug part of the garden this afternoon but gave it up the ground being too wet.

Susie was pasting pictures in her scrap book. She wanted to go to Freed's but Andrew kept her back. She goes there too often for her own good.

It is rumored that Barndt & Son had 1400 over drafts. If this proves true the Bk will lose near 7000.

Wednesday, April 22, 1885.   Worked again in the garden this afternoon dug another part but it is still too wet. Am tired of it.

Oliver found a number of coins which were hid away in one of the Trempers out buildings. He found them in a cupboard behind a false back in the upper shelf. They consist mainly of eagle cts which were were put up in bags of 100 each labelled and marked C.L.D. for Lotta Bollow to whom he willed all of his coins. They were also two Chinese or Japanese coins together with several Blands Trades etc. England has received Sir Peter Lumsden's reply to Gen. Komaroff's statement in regard to the battle with the Afghans. Sir Peter contradicts nearly every statement and where he does not he places the blame on the Russians. In my opinion war will ensue sooner or later.

Thursday, April 23, 1885. I noticed this morning Jas Slifer's little boy running about in the yard. Soon after I saw his mother at the window. She was out for a walk in the evening and stopped in front of our yard to speak to me. She says James coming down Saturday eve. At noon Mr. Godshall spoke to me in regard to the Sunday School. He said he had waited for us to speak. He seems to be in favor of having it only every two weeks and of putting away the Quarterlies so as to make teaching easier. The idea! This would put away with teaching altogether. He says he would start up the old way if we would not help. He asked concerning John whom he said he expected felt a little sore over the last.

Friday, April 24, 1885. Finished the first bed of garden this afternoon. Still too wet. Godshall was up at bank this morning to hear how the others were minded on the Sunday School. He did not receive much satisfaction. Jno told him he would resign as Asst Supt as soon as a meeting was being held. Herman did not say much about but soon tried to get Jake to take John's place. But he did not do it. Godshall flattered him in every way but all in vain. He intends however to call a meeting on Monday eve to discuss the question.

War is now believed to be inevitable between Eng. and Russia. Another dynamite occurred in London yesterday in the admiralty office. Windows broken and a stair case shattered.

Saturday, April 25, 1885. Today was the Tremper sale. John and I went out at three and I bought a flute. This was all I had intended to buy although afterwards I was sorry I did not bid on Washington's picture which Dr. Gope got for 50 cts. There was an immense amount of stuff and the sale commenced at twelve oclock. We closed our accounts in bank before noon so as to let Jake off.

Wrote out a report of the Sunday School last evening.

Jas Slifer arrived in town tonight.

Tobias Swartley's barn burned down last night. A tramp who was in the barn narrowly escaped gave the alarm and rescued nine cows. The horses were saved. About 12 cows were burnt. It was insured for how much I do not know.

Sunday, April 26, 1885. There was rain in the forenoon. Under its beneficient influence the fields turned green. Every thing soon will be benefitted thereby. Os. Kline came last evening. He went with me to meeting. He works for Geo. B. De. Keim. He went down again at 6.19. I was to meet him again at the depot but on account of a late supper I missed the train and so did not see him.

Amelia and Maggie were here.

J M Slifer, wife, and little Walter were here after supper. He is full of the bank they are going to start at Topton. Tomorrow they are going to commence selling stock.

Nothing came of the singing school which was to have commenced this evening as the teacher didn't come. They was plenty drinking however I believe. Have a notion that H. Freed will not keep a first class hotel.

Monday, April 27, 1885. This evening there was a meeting in the school-house to re-organize the Sunday School. Of the old officers Jno. D. Moyer, Israel Klein and Ed H Souder resigned. I. S. Borneman was chosen in John's place. P.C. Barndt was chosen in Israel Klein's place. J.C. Landes was chosen Treasurer. Milt. Moyer was chosen Ass't Sec. Old Herman was not present. He received a telegram this morning to come down to the city as Susan his daughter had rheumatism. He went down but did not return. He sent word up to do just as we would if he were here. I must say I had great fears that nothing would come of this meeting but so far it has been all right.

Tuesday, April 28, 1885. It is been raining this evening. Everything growing finely. Have not found not whether Herman came back from the city or not. Found out today that he supposed we had made up that 1.45 between us and paid John off. He would have found out his mistake last evening had he been there. I expected a row for this meeting and perhaps there would have been one had he been there. As it is now he won't say any thing probably.

This afternoon we fixed Jno Mininger, poor fellow, who had brought two notes to bank for discount tomorrow with F.B. Geyer and Jno D. Yoder's names forged on. Mr. L. went and fetched him back from the train and he came and took the note along again.

I hear Fritz Cumora is in jail for unbecoming conduct to a girl.

Wednesday, April 29, 1885. Very windy. Many old fences blown down. I expect some old trees have been blown down. A counterfeit ten dollar bill was taken by one of us today. It is very poor Webster's face looking as if decomposition had set in and as though worms were eating.

Gen. Grant is getting stronger daily. He takes a drive every afternoon. He believes he will get well.

The situation in Europe remains unchanged. War seems to be imminent. It is said that Gen. Middleton has been defeated by Reil in battle.

Thursday, April 30, 1885. It is supposed by some that Mr. Zendt has sold out to Hunsberger & Bros. He was propably forced to take this step or he would have been sold out some other way. It is reported that he owes Hunsberger's 2000 and that he had no settlement with them since he has been here. Chas Schwenck has 1300 in it too. Mr. Zendt's father is supposed to have about 1500 in the concern. If I am not mistaken his stock a/c amted to 3000. He has been very unwilling to give security to his creditors and this is the cause why Chas Schwenck has been plying him so hard. Yesterday Zendt's note of

150 endorsed W.D. Hunsberger was due at bank and protested without expense however. This made Zendt mad but cooled off again. Hunsberger ordered the note to be charged to his a/c. Don't see what will come of it yet. Sowed some grass seed under the maples this afternoon. Pres. Cleveland is making a great many appointments in the diplomatic service. Middleton is reported defeated by Reil.

Friday, May 1, 1885.   Cold, windy and rain.

Mrs. Gardner withdrew her bal from bank. She also took the coins along which Heins found and which had been left at bank. She was accompanied by Gustie Gardner a grand-daughter of Mrs. Gardner's husband. She is said to be a great favorite with Mrs. Gardner. In about three weeks she will return again and pay the bequests in this neighborhood. Mr. Greaser and Lucetta have to pay 5% state tax on their legacies. Miss Raudenbush 5% state tax and 5% com to the exec. Mrs. Gardner having waived the latter in Greaser's case. Dr. Gillmer must be soft. He is said to have asked Mr. Zendt's advise in regard to a wife. He wants one who is healthy stout and who can work. But what is just as soft is that the above seem to flatter themselves that he meant something by it. And they seem to try their best to draw him in.

Saturday, May 2, 1885.   Mrs. Bilger and Sarah were here last evening. The History of Montg. Co. was delivered today. H.K. Godshall, H. R. Loux and E. H. Souder each received one. I saw Godshall's. It contains the portraits and biographical sketches H. R. Loux and J. Tremper.

I have not yet received my instruction book for the flute. I know not what's the matter.

The reports of the Anglo-Russian difficulty are now of a more peaceful nature. It is believed that Russia will withdraw her troops pending the decision of the boundary commission.

Sunday, May 3, 1885.   Today was communion at Leidy's church. The sunday school commenced today. Nothing was done but arranging the classes and that has not been done satisfactory. There are many boys that did not come. No teachers have as yet been appointed. Mr. Borneman the new Sup't, who has been connected with Sunday Schools before says they never used the quarterlies. He thought at first they were not of much use. But finding everybody in favor of retaining them he gave orders to send for them at once. Schwenk & M.L. Moyer had their new teams there. H.G. & Dan Bilger's with the boys, were here for supper. They came late as we were about through eating our supper. I and the boys went up to Amelia and there Will acted like everything. But he has always been so. The old folks go home in the morning the boys evening.

Monday, May 4, 1885.   The bank today bought 20000 Car Trust Bonds as an investment. These added to 16000 now on hand makes 36000 now held by the Bk. J. M. Slifer was in bank today. He says they have 5 Directors and will pay in their first installment on June 1st. He and his family went up to Pennsburg this afternoon but will return again tomorrow evening. I today sent for quarterlies etc for the Sunday School. They will cost about 17.39 and including 1.45 due to Jno D. Moyer makes the SS 18.84 in debt. The Bilger boys went home with the five o'clock train. Christ Moyer seems to be very fond of carpentry as he works at it every now and then. He worked in the shop today.

Tuesday, May 5, 1885. Mr. A. S. Heany of the late firm of W. S. Heany & Bro but who have moved to Norristown called at the bank today and withdrew his deposit. He has bought a property in Norristown where he will go into the store business. He was messenger for the bank from Tylersport ever since his brother Will got sick about a year or more ago. He has a habit of repeating his own so often that you get tired of it. This he again did today in asking us to come and see if we come to N. to such an extent that he came near missing the train. Of course he was in earnest and if I get to N. I must see him. I cut down an apple tree in the yard which insects had killed.

Wednesday, May 6, 1885. This afternoon it was once reported that the sheriff had paid Mr. Zendt a visit but it turned out to be an agent who was making collections. The fact is everything is so hot that the arrival of a stranger is enough to start a commotion. It is now said that Chas Schwenck will leave there about the 18th and that Zendt is selling out. Received my flute instructor today. Father and Andrew are away putting up a hand rail and will not be home till about one oclock AM.

Russia and China are getting into trouble. England and Russia are going to fix matters up. The Conservatives are indignant at the out come and say England has surrendered every point to Russia.

Thursday, May 7, 1885. Rained fast most of the day. I am trying to make a new flute if I can.

Gen Irwin McDowell perhaps the most unfortunate soldier of the late war died yesterday.

Wm Hartzel will be buried tomorrow. He died on Sunday having been sick a long time.

Friday, May 8, 1885. Weather: Rain followed by clearing weather.

The German Quarterlies and Lämmerweide arrived. There are 50 Quarterlies and 25 Lämmerweide. I only order 35 Quarterlies These cost 5.72.

I attended meeting this evening. A minister from Canada preached the sermon. His chest is so compressed and his body so bent that his head seemed to rest on his shoulders. His voice in consequence was so weak that it was sometimes inaudible.

The house was not quite filled.

Sir Peter Lumsden the British Boundary Commissioner has been recalled.

Saturday, May 9, 1885. Henry Souder and Preston were down this afternoon. They say they like it up there. Preston says Lillie cried to come along too. Hen. hired Rosa daughter of Paul Schmidt to help at the hotel.

There were slight rains during the day and occasionally a peal of thunder was heard.

The ground is wet too wet for the farmers who will be delayed I expect by the rain. This season commences late and many things will have to grow double quick. Many crops it is expected will be failures this year. Farmers have been used to having good crops.

Monday, May 11, 1885. Today the English Quarterlies for the Sunday School arrived. We can accommodate over 150 Scholars with the Quarterlies Eng & Ger. Lesson Paper Lämmer etc. Felt very churly part of the day. Don't know the reason. Felt half made all the time. Frank Detweiler did our plowing today. I believe it must be too wet, yet he went at it. Charlie Roberts had his girl here yesterday. Chas. Schwenck is going to leave Zendt on the 18th.

Tuesday, May 12, 1885. Frank Detweiler plowed our land and this afternoon we planted our potatoes. We planted nearly eleven rows.

Mrs. Hannah Slifer and her boy Walter were here this afternoon and evening.

This evening when father came home he saw a fire west-north west from here. We got up on the roof but could see nothing more than on the ground. We could not form an idea where the fire was.

Young Clintie Becker is calling Andrew, "Benny", as for instance, 'Benny not here', 'Benny wash Gindie' etc.

Wednesday, May 13, 1885. It is raining a little this evening. I planted lima beans, soup beans sweet corn cucumbers etc. this afternoon.

The road machine passed through here today.

The plasterers are already at work on Dr. Louxs addition to his house. J. G. Leidy is putting up a frame building to keep furniture in.

W. D. Hunsberger is digging the cellar for his store. It is to be 48 x 50. It is said that he has received a car lumber from up country, and I believe that he will get his mill work at the same place.

Wm. H. Moll has already opened a tinshop in the house in which he lives.

Thursday, May 14, 1885. This morning the news arrived that old Michael Alderfer a man in the neighborhood of eighty had hung himself. Later news proved it's truth. He was many years President of the Farmer Perkiomen Nat Bank and still was up to his death. No cause is yet known. Mr. Landis says no one would hang himself who is in his right mind. Mr. Jno Alderfer held than no Christian could commit suicide.

The fire we saw last evening was up near Boyertown.

Friday, May 15, 1885.　Dug the remaining piece in the garden this afternoon. It is now reported that W. D. Hunsberger will start a lumber yard. Quite a number of carloads will arrive in a few days. M. Alderfer who hung himself Wednesday was 82 years old.

Saturday, May 16, 1885.　Owing to a mistake that I made in putting away a note I had to go to Hatfield to see Jno. Mininger. A note had been sent here fr. Schwencksville signed J. Mininger Due May 7. I took this for May 17 and put it away accordingly. Today the note was found. I ran up to Borneman's but he had gone to Boyertown this morning. I was then sent down and got a judgement from him. He wants to pay it Wednesday. If he dont there'll be a crash.

I'm making the Sunday School stuff ready for tomorrow. It is late and must to bed.

Sunday, May 17, 1885.　Today was communion day at Gehman's. Father & mother both were there. Uriah was here in the morning so that I was a little late for sunday school. Today the Bible class was started with J.D. Moyer Jr. Kate Slifer, Mrs. Emma Detweiler, Amelia Stover Maggie Hunsberger. The Eng Quarterlies were first distributed today. Two new classes were formed. Teachers are scarce. We have 30 officers and teachers on the roll. Was in meeting this afternoon but was so sleepy that I could hardly stand it. Rev Mr Loux preached. When I came home I laid myself on the bed till supper and took a nap which did me much good. After supper took a walk with Uriah to see the new lumber yard of Hunsberger's, and also the cellar for his new hardware store. It is 46 x 50. From there we went to the school-house where Rev. Mr. Van Ommern was announced to preach. When we came down many people were standing about and could [not] get in as the key to door on the second floor was with the teacher in Lansdale. As the lock was on the outside of the door we fetched a screw driver, took it off and let them in. There was wretched singing, there was nobody to lead. Mr. Van Ommern is a good preacher and his fire is very distinct.

Wednesday, May 20, 1885.　As John Mininger did not put in an appearance today the judgment I got from him on Saturday will be tomorrow put on record and a writ issued. He can now blame nobody for this but himself. He promised to pay it today and did not ask for more time. Under the circumstances the bank is compelled to push him at once.

It is very likely that there will soon be trouble with Wenhold. The board refuses to discount all notes not absolutely safe or which are unknown to them and no amount of talking has so far helped his case. But yet there are too many weak notes of his in bank. He has taken out money on notes signed by his sons and brothers. These notes are likely to make the trouble as very little is paid on them when renewed.

Thursday, May 21, 1885.   The women are nearly done house cleaning. They were at it since last week.

Rev Moses Godshall who preached at M. Alderfer's funeral is severely critisized for his plainness of speech.

This morning I had the belly ache severely so I went to Freed's took a glass of brandy and it soon left me.

Mr. Jno. S. Ruth today returned from his trip to Berks and Lehigh Counties selling road machines. He stopped in at the bank this morning on his way home. He bought a horse on his trip paying 136 for it. C. F. Schwenk is still at Zendt's as the Zendt have sold out in the store to Hunsbergers on Monday.

Friday, May 22, 1885.   Am working at a small table for the kitchen. Ex. Sec of State F. T. Frelingshysen is dead aged 68 yrs.

Saturday, May 23, 1885.   Was at the festival tonight. The band has new uniforms. They look well in them. Jonathan and John Q. Hunsberger are back from West Chester. They say they are well satisfied with the school. There was quite a crowd at the festival. I did not play. Nothing in it for me. Ed. Delp L Garner and one Reichenbach tried raise a fuss but it was 'mostly blow and a little beer'.

Sunday, May 24, 1885.   Milt. Moyer was down here this morning to help me with Sunday school work. He saw my flute and grew fond of it. He wants to buy Morris Hunsberger's and learn to play it too. The sunday school was well attended. There must be about 125 scholars on the roll.

Was at singing school this evening. This was poorly attended. Cal. Hunsberger said that Will Billger was in jail for six months for stealing tickets from the railroad office to come in here to attend communion services. It has often been prophesied that he would get there some day and now he is there already.

Monday, May 25, 1885.   Most people around keep holiday today, yesterday being Whit Sunday. I had my measure taken today for the suit I bought last week. I measure 36 in around the chest. I weighed myself the other day and weighed 160 lbs.

Was up at grand fathers tonight. Took Amelia and Maggie along down and treated them on ice creame at Beckers'. Afterwards accompanied them home again. Most people think that six mos. will do Will. Bilger good. I believe that if he repents and resolves to do better he may get some good of it. But on the other hand if he believes that he is played out anyhow etc it will do him much hurt.

Tuesday, May 26, 1885.   Today they have been making an appraisement at Zendt's store. Mahlon Moyer of Perkasie and Allen Reiff of Franconia Square were employed on it besides C. F. Schwenck W. Hockman S. D. Hunsberger W.D. Hunsberger & M.D. Zendt. This selling out is said to have cost one of Zendts family some tears. Do not know whether it will reach for Schwenck or not. He and Hockman are to tend the store. Schwenck is probably expecting the post office. Milt. Moyer is trying to buy Morris Hunsberger's flute and learn to play on it. He had it down here and we tried it. Rec'd a letter fr. E.N.D. He says the girl he has been going to see was Ida Snyder but he had stopped. He is going to get a pleasure boat. They have their corn all planted.

Wednesday, May 27, 1885.   Warm today.

Destructive worms are already destroying currant bushes. I put some stuff on them that will probably kill them. It is called slug shot, costs 6 cts a pound. I wet the bushes and sprinkle it on dry.

The railroad company changed their time table. No important changes were made.

The directors came early today and by half past nine they had all left. The body of Victor Hugo has been removed to the Arc de Triomphe where is lying in state.

Friday, May 29, 1885.   I cleaned the safe and vault this afternoon.
Worked at it from half past two to half past seven and did not leave the bank till after eight o'clock. It was very dirty. It was not thoroughly cleaned since the bank was built. Jas Slifer washed out the floor but I took down every thing and tried my best to banish the dust. It was not fit anymore. Wenhold was down this afternoon.

It is expected that there will be a great strike after June throwing 100000 men out of employment. The men are willing to accept 10% reduction but the manufrs. want more.

Saturday, May 30, 1885.   Today was Decoration Day. Cleaned the
bank today. Wm Freed's barn burned down this morning. He was in the city and one cow was burnt. I do not know if it was insured or not. There was nobody at home but a little boy and the women. Dan Umsted burnt his hands in trying to save a wagon. I saw the smoke from Moyer's third story.

Gov. Pattison yesterday vetoed the Apportionment bill passed by the Legislature, giving the Reps. 21 and Dem 7 Congressmen.

The Shackamaxon Bank yesterday suspended on account of overdrafts by W. Bumm & Son and one Conklin supposed to am't to over $200,000. which the cashier allowed them to make. Bank examiner will go over the accounts today. They are all in a muddle.

Sunday, May 31, 1885.   This morning Father Andrew Rewb and I
drove over to see the burnt barn. Mr. Freed is to be pitied. Every thing was burned and he had no tools to go to work with. Two cows and a calf were burnt. The Sunday school was well attended. Mr. Van Ommeren had intended to preach here in the school house but nobody came because it had been but

imperfectly announced and so he went home again. Jane Moyer is home today. Milt. Schwenck & Uriah drove out tonight.

Susie is just about crazy for W. T. Hunsberger. He runs after her and she after him. She is on the road half the time. She goes with such little girls as Lerra Souder and such. Tonight she and some others went up to Telford. Father is out of humor about her and I guess she'll get a scolding tomorrow morning.

Monday, June 1, 1885.   Frank Detweiler and wife were here on a visit last evening. Mr. D. has bought W. B. Slifer's share in the butcher business. As soon as I heard it I guessed that Bill was going to give his whole attention to the Phila. business. He was closeted again with Mr. Landis this morning. Grand father S. was also present. I don't know how Slifer liked it. That thing looks a little dark.

Mother was down stairs today again. It is now near time for the 17 yr. locusts. I have not seen any yet.

Godshall began tearing out his south wall for the new bay window today.

Tuesday, June 2, 1885.   Hearing the sound of rattling hoofs on the pavement we went out and look and found it to be Moyer & Detweiler's horse who had run away from Mr. Moyer. He began to run over on the county line lost the wagon at Slifers ran on Landis ect. porch and broke the window and then ran down the sidewalk till the bank fence stopped him. Mr. M. was only a little scratched. Shortly afterwards another horse broke loose from the store and ran off. Amelia has been sick since Sunday. She must be worse today for Uriah is gone for the Doctor.

Victor Hugo the French Poet was yesterday conveyed fr. the Arc de Triomph to the Pantheon his final resting place. No riots occurred as was expected. The Communists carried red banners in the procession. The Gov. yesterday vetoed the Water Supply bill. Over 65000 men went on a strike in the western part of the state. 10 out 38 manufs. accepted the scale.

Wednesday, June 3, 1885.   Fully a million people are believed to have been present at the funeral of Victor Hugo. The middle and lower classes kept the day as a holiday. The Manhattan Bank of NY. has again been robbed this time by its paying teller who absconded with $160,000 of the banks funds.

I mowed the yard this afternoon after the scythe had been sharpened by father. It is true but I cant see into it for I cant mow. Last evening I tried with a dull scythe but it wouldn't do. Mother declared she could beat me were she stronger. I lost patience and left it. Last year everybody laughed at my mowing. Mr. Zendt is said to be not very well pleased with his sale to Hunsberger & Bro. Mrs. Gardiner wants 4000 for her house and 1000 for the lot adjoining. J. H. Moyer had bid 3000 for the whole thing. Dr Loux is going in very big. I fear it wont hold out.

Thursday, June 4, 1885. It is a puzzle to me how Dr Loux intends to get himself out of his seemingly embarrassing situation. His notes come due at bank and he does not look at them. In the latter part of April he gave a judgement note he held against G. H. Swartz for collateral to waive protest on a 200 note then due, promising to pay it next week. He was not in the bank since and today we discounted the 500 judgment note and paid another note of 208.91 due today. There is another note coming due on Monday. If this thing go on at this rate he cant last long. Meanwhile he is building a drug store fixing it up the finest and if this is the way he attends to his money affairs he can not avoid getting into trouble.

Friday, June 5, 1885. An earth quake occurred in Cashmere India some day during the last week doing great damage.

Susie has been getting very troublesome because of her running about evenings. Last evening she got a scolding from mother for coming late. I cannot understand her. There's no use talking to her, all the answer one of us gets is "none of your business" or such like.

W. B. Slifer is I hear going to take the Phila business into his own hands. H. Ward Beecher is preaching a series of Evolution Lectures the second of which was delivered on Sunday last.

Saturday, June 6, 1885. The number of men who are thrown out of work by the great strike is 60,244, as reported in beginning 100 iron mills and 34 rail factories have shut down. No change in situation. Christ Moyer predicts hard times. France and China have at last signed a treaty of Peace. Eng. & Russia are ready to submit their difs. to an arbitrator. It is believed that war will only be averted for a time.

Saw the first locust yesterday which Paul Schmidt had brought into the shop in a box. This morn Christ Moyer brought a whole lot up to the bank. They were weak yet. He says the chickens eat them. The right name for them is not locust. Scientific men say cicada. One of these Prof. had a breakfeast of them. Uriah told me last evening that he has been encouraged in regard to becoming teller in the Topton Bank. This bk was to have been opened June 1. Among those who bo't stock in this neighborhood Henry Souder 2000 W Souder 2000 JS Ruth 1000. Jno B. Moyer 500. Mr. Landis has not much faith in Jno N. Jacobs. Ellis insulted me a little this afternoon. He affected to be surprised at the fine clothes I wore saying it was to be something big. Mr. Zendt had auction this afternoon of such articles as were not taken by SD Hunsberger & Bro.

Sunday, June 7, 1885. Sunday School was held in the forenoon owing to the meeting. The attendance was good but teachers were not at all here, as they should have been. It is reported that Van Ommeren will start another Sunday School here in the hall. If he does I don't think much of it. Some think it won't hurt our school much while others believe the contrary. We have now 138 scholars on our roll, and 34 teachers. Christ Allebach and a man fr

Dauphin Co. preached here this afternoon. I believe that C. Allebach is an honest man and that he is in earnest.

Jos. F. Derstein's and Henry Schreck's were on a visit today.

Monday, June 8, 1885.   This morning we had a heavy shower. It awoke me and that is a thing that does not often occur. Last evening we played a trick on Susie. Uriah Souder and Andrew were in it. Susie came home last night with Elemer Souder. She did not take him in yet. It is almost time to vote on the Press Prize Questions. Have not yet decided on all of them.

Tuesday, June 9, 1885.   The Deisingers moved into Trempers house yesterday. They are ten in all. The case they are having with Jos Derstein speaks not well for them. Joe thinks it must be done to get money out of him. They charge him with saying they kept a disorderly house. He says he never said any such thing.

The English ministry was yesterday defeated on the second reading of the budget by a vote of 264 to 252. It is rumored that Mr. Gladstone will tender his resignation today. The Parnellites voted with the majority. At the announcement of the vote Mr. Parnell and Lord Randolph Churchill jumped on their seats and waved their hats.

Wednesday, June 10, 1885.   Ben. Alderfer was after me last evening to join the choir at Leidy's church. Of course I will do no such thing.

Mr. Gladstone yesterday resigned and the House of Lords and Commons were adjourned til Friday. It is not known whether the Conservatives will accept office or not. They themselves probably don't know what to do about it. The Gladstone Ministry came into power in 1880 and passed through great crisises and is now defeated by proposal to increase the tax on whisky and beer. The Amerr of Afghanistan is reported to have been assassinated. The President has appointed Gen W T Rosencrans to the office of Register of the Treasury in place of Blanche K Bruce the colored ex-senator from Alabama.

Thursday, June 11, 1885.   Heard the locusts sing for the first time today. They did sing but this is the first time I heard them. I sent in my vote on the Press Prize Rolls today. It is as follows

1	Favorite living story writer,	Wm Black
2	Favorite poem	Paradise Lost
3	American Orator	D. Webster
4	American Statesman	H. Clay
5	Most useful invention (Amer)	Telegraph
6	Greatest happiness	Liberty
7	Woman suffrage	No
8	Eng. & Russia	Russia
9	Best state to live in	Penna
10	Light wine substitute	No

Several of the above were selected at random I not having given such matters any thought. Amelia is not well yet.

Friday, June 12, 1885.   Fixed up my old saddle again this evening. I must ride out one of these evenings. It would give much exercise.

Mrs. Becker meddles too much between our girls and their bakers. Such was the case with Emma Nace and Fritz Cumora. Now she is trying it on Susie. She is constantly trying to get them together. Jacob handed her a letter this morning containing an invitation to go with him to Hatfield festival. Whereupon Mrs. Becker urged Susie to go with him and being anxious to carry the answer back to him. These things show not well for a married woman to take hold of.

Saturday, June 13, 1885.   Went out riding this afternoon. Had a fall off while riding past Ed's lane. The horse wanted to turn in there while I was trying to button my coat. I landed on my feet but Martha and her mother saw me and there's the shame. Was at Zendt's auction later. He was trying to sell men's clothes. They went very low.

The Queen has summoned the Marquis of Salisbury to Balmoral in connection the formation of a new ministry. Mr. Gladstone announced the resignation of the Cabinet and that the Queen had accepted the resignations. The House was adjourned till Monday.

Sunday, June 14, 1885.   Chas G Frick (Goody) was up from the city today. He will have vacation in the latter part of July. He is clerk in a Phila factory.

Was at sunday school this afternoon. Attendance good. Artie Jordan a fellow from Yardley who was bro't here by the Bilger's boys was over here to see his girl Sarah Detweiler. He bro't news from Wm Bilger who says he is very lonely and that he can't see how he can stand it six months. He is assistant to the cook at the prison. Was at the church held by Van Ommeren. Attendance slim. He intends holding meetings regularly every two weeks. He intends starting a sunday school next Sunday. I do not think it will hold long as most people are prejudiced against him. And he does not seem to act in the right way to accomplish anything.

Monday, June 15, 1885.   The weather today and yesterday was the warmest this season so far. It is dry we need rain. The grass will be a failure probably.

J C Landis' horse ran away with Henry Hunsberger on Saturday afternoon. He is now afraid of everything and it may be that he will not forget it soon.

The Marquis of Salisbury is to form a Cabinet.

Got a coat and vest made of something like linen. I paid $1.65. I think they are cool.

Tuesday, June 16, 1885.   It was very warm today. I hoed corn and potatoes this afternoon and it was almost too much for me as the heat was so great.

Frank D. Hartzel son of Andrew S Hartzel drew the prize for the best essay on Wm Penn in the Freshman class of the University of Pa. They used to live here in Souderton. Frank was a very serious fellow. He used to keep a store which delighted in robbing. He was the sheriff among us boys and when he tried to sell me out we laughed at him and chased him off as the charge was bogus. He wants to take the whole course his father says. Jos F. Hackman's ran off but did not get far.

Wednesday, June 17, 1885.   Weather was cool owing to the rain last night.

Gen. Grant was removed to the Highlands yesterday.

It is very late and I must go to bed, it is a quarter of eleven. I go to bed entirely too late. It is half past ten almost every evening.

Thursday, June 18, 1885.   The steamship Iseri bearing Bartholdi's statue of Liberty enlightening the World arrived at New York last evening after a voyage of 27 days. In the Central News Perkasie there appeared this week the following news item from a Souderton correspondent. "Hon Herman K. Godshall our worthy bank president

Friday, June 19, 1885.   Gen. Grant is said to be slowly sinking and his end is probably near. His moving away from the city seems to have had a bad effect on him. He has lost his voice and is unable to speak. Lord Salisbury is said to have formed a ministry but is said to be negotiating with the Liberals to have their support. If this can not be pledged Lord Salisbury will refuse office it is said.

Gen. Von Naanteuffel died Wednesday aged 76 years.

The masons (bricklayers) got through with Schoch's house today. Walked up in the evening and stopped awhile at Uncle Cornels'.

Mr. R. L. Priester is in trouble. Wenhold took three horses away that had not been paid. Priester is in Phila and nobody knows where he is. Stever and C N Frederick went down this afternoon to find him. He has been down over a week. He was up once but did not go home to his family.

Saturday, June 20, 1885.   Gen Grant is reported to be a little better than Thursday. Tremper's pictures and plates arrived today. Mr L. retained one of his pictures for himself. The locust make a great noise down at the woods. Am going to study them up. Zendt and Hunsberger's have settled now. He received some 1100. after paying. Hunsberger's and C F Schwenck. They now buy at Landis & Co. It is warm out in the sun but cool in the bank building. There is a festival going on at Telford and a musical entertainment here at

Freed's. Andrew went to the festival and Susie to the concert and I to the Store to buy a new summer hat.

Sunday, June 21, 1885.   Was in Sunday school this afternoon. There was no perceptible difference in the attendance that was owing Van Ommeren's Sunday School which opened this morning. I have not been able to hear anything how it turned out. The attendance was very small however. Was out after supper to hunt locusts coming out of the shell. Was out at Jane Landis', but did not see any. It is too late for that. Took a long walk up along the brickyard and down that way home. Uriah who has been at Topton yesterday and today called. He chances for speedily beoming teller are not so excellent as he at first thought. Hufnagel and Lillie M. went tin at Becker's for ice cream. We went in too when Huffy who was in the inner room slammed the door shut. I think he was angry with us for coming in too.

Monday, June 22, 1885.   Mr Godshall does not seem to be to me as he used to. He must have an idea that somehow we in the bank are connected with that epigram or he must think that we enjoyed it immensly as we certainly did. He does not come to the bank so often nor does he talk more than is necessary.

I am going to make a hanging book shelf. I have no room for all my books.

Wrote to Ed Danley today.

Tuesday, June 23, 1885.   Mrs Salome Freed my mother's aunt was here for supper together with grand father Souder's.

It was decidedly cooler today than yesterday, It is expected that Lord Salisbury will announce his Cabinet today. The obstruction in the Suez Canal has been removed and it is again open for traffic.

Wednesday, June 24, 1885.   The vote on the Prize Polls of the Press was announced today. I missed five of the questions. The following received the highest number of votes. No 1. Harriet Beecher Stowe 113, my vote Wm Black 4th 65. No 2 "Evangeline" 125, my vote 6th "Paradise Lost" 40. No 3 Daniel Webster 521. No 4 J G Blaine 248 my vote 3rd H Clay 163. No 5 telegraph 370, No 6 Religion 279, my vote Liberty 8th 22. No 7 No. 537. No 8 England 516, Russia my vote 515. No 9 Penna 670. No 10 No. 881. There were 1065 ballots cast. Mr. Moyer had four right out of ten. He had 'Hope' for No 6 which received only 9 votes. On most of the other questions I was ahead of him. The ticket that won the prize had 9 right out of ten. The mistake she made was in the first question where she voted for Wm Black. Her name is C M Temple.

Thursday, June 25, 1885.   R L Priester made an assignment yesterday. Chas. N Frederick is the assignee.

Took Salome Freed home to get some things as she wants to go to Phila. Mother & Susie went along, Susie stopped at A.G. Reiffs till we went home.

Commenced a hanging shelf for my books today.

Gen. Grant has lost his voice for over a week.

Gov. Pattison has signed the marriage license bill which will take effect Oct 1 of this year.

J.M Landis & wife started for South Bend Ind. this evening. They intend to bring Alice Gross along back.

Friday, June 26, 1885.   The locusts form a great topic of conversation just now. Every other man is turned into an entomologist for the present at least.

A new bank has just been organized in Philada. and will be called the Ninth National.

The Eng. Parliament has been adjourned till July 6.

Lord Salisbury has accepted office. The members of his cabinet will be announced at the next meeting of Parliament.

Saturday, June 27, 1885.   It is a very warm day. Irwin Moll's wife died last night in Philada where they had gone on a visit. She was a daughter of Rev J W Langley. She died of Bright's disease.

Jonas Moyer is going to build an addition to his house and a French roof on the whole.

The new toll house at Five Points is to be built of brick.

Got my new suit this evening. It cost 25⁰⁰. I must not wear it every Sunday.

Sunday, June 28, 1885.   The Sunday School this forenoon was poorly owing mostly to a slight rain.

Godshall was not present as he was at the funeral of Mrs. Jno G Godshall of Lansdale. Was at home all afternoon. Miss Mamie Dettry formerly of Souderton and now of Lancaster is here visiting.

A strip out at the county line and over at Bloming Glen had plenty of rain yesterday afternoon while we had none.

Monday, June 29, 1885.   This morning with the 5.15 train Will Benner left Souderton. Some say he went to Williamsport others to Canada and Wisconsin. I saw him last evening on Becker's porch. He spoke hardly any-thing. It is said he lay all night in the station house and in the morning bo't a satchel went home fetched his clothes and boarded the train. The money he obtained from Wm Souder by whom he has been employed for some time. He got 20 Dollars on Sat eve saying it was for paying a suit of clothes. He had an appointment with E B Slifer to have his measure taken on Saturday but did not make his appearance. He has always been a wild sort of fellow. Yet I don't know what his motives can be. He is said to have gone to his uncle in Oskosh Wisconsin.

Tuesday, June 30, 1885. Today closes the half year. The bank added to its surplus 1000 making it 21000. pays a dividend of 2/2 per cent. amounting to 2250. took off from Premium a/c 250. and charged off worthless notes to the extent of 1368. The expenses for the half year amounted to about 3000. After all deductions the undivided profits amt to about 492.

Last evening the boys found a locust just crawling out of its shell. It was the first I had ever seen. As I had nothing to put it away in I sent it to J D Moyer who wants one to put it into alchol. He thinking it would soon die left on a log till morning when no trace of it was left. It had opened its wings and gone. There is bound to be some trouble over that Afghan affair. There is now in progress a rebellion against the Ameer which the Russians are accused of aiding or encouraging.

Wednesday, July 1, 1885. Yesterday was Mr. Levi Moyers last day as mail carrier bet. Soud. & Blooming Glen, and today Franklin Hunsberger made his first trip. He gets only 239 a year, Moyer got 446. He will soon get tired of it is the general opinion. But he is responsible for four years.

Mrs. Yseult Dudley who attempted to shoot O. Donovan Rossa was acquitted yesterday on the ground of insanity.

Gen. Grant is slowly sinking. His physician says that his removal to Mt. McGregor was a great benefit to him and that he would probably not be alive any more had he remained in New York.

Mr. Godshall is troublesome again. He is after Ed on account of the new toll house. He has a dif plan for it making a queer appearance to which Ed and almost everybody is opposed. He is getting a little mad about it.

The weather yesterday and today was very cool, so cool that thick clothes felt comfortable. It is very cool for hay making.

Thursday, July 2, 1885. Water is getting scarce. Our well at the house is empty and we have to draw the water from the well at the barn. The well at the bank supplies water for the Hardware Store, H Hangey Jno Smith's Funks and Wm Souder's. A regular highway has been made from the street through the yard to the pump.

C.G. Rosenberry has failed or the next thing to it. His partner M.H. Henry took all the stock away.

Friday, July 3, 1885. This afternoon E H Moyer's child died of scarlet fever. He will be buried at the meeting house cemetery. Horace and Morris Wile are the grave diggers. Uriah Souder asked me to join the 'Sons of America' this afternoon. I told him I had no such wish. He said he was and then he talked on its merits, etc I don't care. There are none of these questions that can not be satisfactorily answered to my mind. First they are selfish affairs. They allure people in becoming members because they will be cared for when he is sick. Such persons are either very selfish or they belong to a class with whom I would not like to associate. These characters will sooner or later spoil the whole thing as nobody respectable wants to be connected by a brotherhood with such fellows. Tomorrow is the Fourth.

I have a notion to go to Yardley tomorrow.

Saturday, July 4, 1885. This morning I left for Yardley at 7.44. Expected to go alone but was half mad when I saw Sarah Detweiler on the platform. I saw the first wheat cut and sheared this year some where below North Wales. At Jenkintown I got on an excursion train from Phila to Neshaminy Falls. The conductor was in fault here as he told everybody to go to the rear cars. I did so and soon afterward the train parted in the middle and the fore part left leaving us and fifteen cars behind. But there was one consolation Sarah Detweiler was on the first train. These cars were crowded with young pleasure seekers bound to get away from the heat of the city. After backing around for about an hour passed a wreck train loaded with broken coal cars and broken engine the results of an accident on Yardley bridge. When we stopped at Neshaminy all on board left the train with lunch baskets in their hands prepared for a day of pleasure. It was here I learned that it was an excursion train. I went to the conductor who was kind enough to take me and three others to our destination. When we came to Yardley the train whirled past over the bridge to Trenton Junction. On their way back they left me off. James met me at the station and took me to a neighboring wood where a picnic was in progress. Here under some tall trees beside an old school house looking more like a primitive loghouse than a public school. Here under these trees two or three very officious looking women were spreading the tables, who I afterward learned were not of the best character. Took dinner at Bilger's. Walked over the bridge with Mr. Bilger in the afternoon. Talked to me about Will who he said had been very disobedient to him but that he saw it now and that was going to do better. The Yardley Cornet Band of which 3 of the Bilger boys are members furnished the music. In the evening was at the same picnic.

Sunday, July 5, 1885. About nine oclock started for the river. James had the boat ready. Seven of us got in. They were Henry James Artie Gordon, Archie, Irwin, Josie and myself. Henry had the oars. He took us across the river above the bridge. We carried the boat to a kind of canal called the water power. Here we rowed to a place where a hanging willow shielded us from the sun and where we could watch the wrecking train in their work of raising the debris of last Thursday night. A crushed passenger car lay under the bridge. This they burned. The iron they raised to the top of the bridge and took away in the morning. In this work they were engaged all Sunday. While on the river the train on which I had intended to go home with, passed over the bridge. It was twelve oclock when we went home. The said bridge is 7/8 of a mile long and 70 ft high over the water. The middle part is of iron and stands on piers. In the afternoon we went to Sunday School. After Sunday School we walked out to young Henry about 1½ miles from Yardley where we staid for supper. We played several games of croquet. He is farming this land. In the evening we went to church. Yardley is a place about the size of Souderton is very dusty the soil sandy part of the streets well shaded frame buildings some low but the new ones mostly cottage style.

Monday, July 6, 1885.   Came near missing the train this morning again. James went to work this morning at seven. Saw J Steelman at Jenkintown. He works at Hatboro at painting. I was in a hurry to get home now. At last I got home with the train a quarter of an hour later. This brings me late in my work and I didn't get done. Andrew was down at Lansdale Park over Sunday. We had a nice rain here yesterday.

Enos H. Moyer's little son was buried at the meeting house today. He was 15 mos. old.

Tuesday, July 7, 1885.   We had a very nice rain about noon today but it did not last long.

I feel very tired yet. I was half asleep today while adding and this is very vexatious. It wastes time to find yourself dreaming when you come near the head of a column of figures.

I fell back today and will not get quite through with all my work today. These are the evil results of going from home a few days. I must go to bed a little earlier than usual so as to rest a little. It would not do for me to go to sleep tomorrow.

Wednesday, July 8, 1885.   Very warm today.

Amelia and Maggie were down this evening. They were not very well satisfied with me for not saying something to them when I went to Yardley. I told them I did not know myself that I was going till Friday evening. Isaac H. Moyer did not come till this afternoon. We thought there must be something wrong with him but he had a business in the forenoon that he could not come. He talks as if the new pike were to be built by the company itself and that they would commence work in a few weeks.

Thursday, July 9, 1885.   Weather was very warm today. In John Smith's shop it was 96°. Went with Horace and Milt Moyer to Hunsbergers quarry and took a bath. Mr. J.H. Moyer commenced hauling bricks and stone to build an addition to his house.

The Pall Mall Gazette is to be prosecuted for publishing or exposing the traffic in young girls going on among the rich. The sale of the newspaper was forbidden by the police but there was a demand for them everywhere and the papers commanded a premium. The Pall Mall is defiant. Money is very plenty. Our deposits are higher with the exception of 1881 before the Sellersville Bank was started, than ever before. They am't to about 170,000.

Friday, July 10, 1885.   Rufus, Jno. L. and Jennie Moyer arrived home from West Chester this evening. Jonathan did not come. He will stay in the city till tomorrow or Sunday. I forgot to mention yesterday that the Harleysville baker's team ran away from SDH & Bros' Store and ran into Herman Godshall's fence breaking it. None of the horses were hurt.

Borneman had a dispute with C M Tyson about some money which the latter claimed he had given to him to put in bank, and which he claimed was not done. The money was put in bank all right but Borneman to settle the matter gave Tyson his ck for 65.50. This was for his license. So B. paid Tyson's license for this year. He is not very well pleased.

Saturday, July 11, 1885.   Brought in my book shelf which is still unvarnished and filled it with books just to see how it looked.

Amused ourselves with a telephone out in the woods this afternoon. We had it stretched a distance of at least 250 ft. and carried on a not disagreeable conversation through it. And several songs which little Henry sung at one end were plainly audible at the other end words and tone.

Walked to Stever's festival with Uriah Souder this evening after nine. Met Oswin Kline there who had come up from the city to stay over Sunday.

Hiram Hackman caught hold of Leera Souder 13 or 14 yrs old and who ought to have been in bed. Abe Stover laid hands on Norah Hunsberger.

Sunday, July 12, 1885.   Henry Landes' who with the two younger children had come for a visit to Ed's but found them not at home came to our place on a visit. They say Morris likes his trip West right well but is coming back in the Fall when no plans have yet been made what he will do in the future. The Sunday School was well attended. Os Kline was in Sunday School. Miss Lizzie Gerhart daughter of IGG was also present.

Oswin went home with the 6.19 train. We had a little music together after Sunday School.

In church this evening the Deisinger family were present. One of them furnished the music. They are very stuffily dressed. Sam Benner is struck on one of them to the extent of blacking his moustache.

Monday, July 13, 1885.   Nothing worth noting happened today.

Tuesday, July 14, 1885.   Cherries are very scarce this summer. They are nearly all gone already. We wanted to buy some but did not get a chance. We found out that Pete Hunsberger had some trees that were full. So Susie and I had to go and pick some. We got 11 quarts. Old Pete is very accommodating. He helped me with the ladder and did not charge anything for the cherries. Was on the hall to hear the band play.

The Pall Mall Gazette is daily publishing letters approving their course in publishing or exposing the scandulous practises of the rich in London.

Wednesday, July 15, 1885.   Work will commence on the new pike next Monday. They will commence at this end. Have solved two other puzzles which I am going to send down tomorrow. Am getting to be quite a solver. Those last week I had correct but I don't know yet about the prizes. Andrew has bought an old telegraph instrument of Morris Weil.

They have torn down the old school house at Rosenbergers and are building a new one.

There is only one school house remaining in the township which has not been rebuilt and that is the one at Five Points. It seems to be the policy of the directors to tear down all the old contract built school houses, and to build new ones which are substantial.

Thursday, July 16, 1885.   The masons have finished their part of the work on the new toll house at five points. J.H. Moyer's addition to his house is almost ready for laying the joists etc on the first floor. The new stocking factory is to be pushed on now too. The Examinations are in progress and Jonathan & Jane Moyer yesterday were at Lederachville and today at Kulpsville to see how the thing goes. They say they are having a hard time of it. The Moyer family must be in favor of having Beans again as teacher here as Milt said tonight that Van Ommeren was crowding himself in on the people. There is to be a meeting in the school house Saturday evening to vote who (which) is to teach the school next winter. A H Leidy got up this arrangement. Goettler tried to get up a tribe of Red Men but could not raise enough members. Now he is trying to start a base ball club.

Friday, July 17, 1885.   Today was decidedly one of the hottest days of the season. At the Hardware Store the thermometer stood at 98° at Landis Store 96° and at Moyer & Bros. 104°.

I do not think anything came of the meeting called by the would be Sons of America. The speakers did not come. We made our hay today. We got two loads.

Jos. Taylor was hanged in Phila for the murder of his keeper Michael Dorner. Onofri Murderer of Lotta Cook has been granted a new trial. The cholera has been making great havoc in Spain. As high as 1600 new cases have been reported in a day with over 600 deaths. The Eng. Home office has decided not to prosecute the Pall Mall Gazette.

It is reported that Russia has made another move and seized Zulzificir Pass.

Saturday, July 18, 1885.   The weather today I thought was warmer even than yesterday.

Jas. Bilger arrived this afternoon from Yardley. After supper Rufus and I went up to Harr's dam to take a bath. Mr. Moyer, Horace and Haines the night operator also went up. There were about twenty there. Moyer had his horse in the water. There were two others horses in. The water was nice and warm. We arrived home about 9.30 o'clock. We went to the festival here. We enjoyed ourselves very much. I didn't get home till one o'clock.

Sunday, July 19, 1885.   Jas. Bilger was here over night, Sunday School was in the forenoon. The attendance was not very good on the part of the teachers.

There was an election in the school house to decide who is to teach the school next winter. There were only two candidates, Bean and Van Ommeren. There were 29 votes cast and one arrived late which would have made it a tie. Bean received 15 and Van Ommeren 14 votes. This was the method School director Leidy took to decide the matter. It is not right that a man who has a character as Bean has should get the school. But he went round the village yesterday morning. He has some friends who will stick to him. Mr. Landes among them. Was at singing school in the evening.

Monday, July 20, 1885.   Yesterday it was a year since Ella Slifer died. It is not a long time and yet how long it seems since we last felt her presence among us. When it happened I thought I would never forget her. And now only a year has passed and my memory of her is already dimmer. I think it is too much the same way with many of her companions. John Roach the ship builder made an assignment on Saturday. The Gov's rejection of the Dolphin with the Boston Chicago and ＿＿＿＿＿＿ are said to be the cause of his embarrassments.

Work was today commenced on the Dublin & Souderton Turnpike, Jonas F. Nace the Sup't. About ten men commenced work. The masons are through with J.H. Moyer's house.

Sir Stafford Northcote is now Lord Iddesleigh. There is a boom in the stock market the past few days. J D Moyers and I talked about getting up a public library in the village.

Tuesday, July 21, 1885.   The weather today was again so warm as to be almost unbearable. The thermometer registered 98 at Landis & Co and 109 at Hunsbergers store. The election in the school house for teacher did not give the best satisfaction after all. There was too much democracy? in it. The party that was defeated are not at all satisfied. Those who were in favor of Van Ommeren are all down on Bean while those who voted for Bean defend their man as best as they can. Godshall who was by no means a friend of Bean's, but who was so afraid of the Methodists took this opportunity to take or keep him from supporting himself in this place, and over-looked his objections to Bean, on that account. Hunsberger's were just as hard against Bean.

Wednesday, July 22, 1885.   The school matter seems not to be settled yet. W D Hunsberger had got up petition or remonstrance against Bean. They are getting signers.

Gen. Grant is reported getting weaker and weaker. Dr. Douglas said that he had known patients in his condition to survive two days.

John D Moyer is reported to draw a prize of a handsome book in the Press of this week. He has not yet received the book.

This evening we unloaded a car of lumber after supper. It contained over 14000 ft ¼ in. Most of them were very wide and were difficult to handle. It was past twelve oclock when we went home.

Thursday, July 23, 1885.   The weather today and yesterday was warm but not quite so unbearable as the fore going days.

Gen. Grant is believed to be dying this morning and very probably tomorrow morning we will hear of his death. It was not expected that he would live longer than 4 o'clock this morning.

He has been removed from his chair to his bed. He will probably not leave it any more. Drs. Sands Shrady and Douglas are prepared any time to be called to his death bed!

This afternoon grandfather S asked me to help haul in a load of oats. I was on the wagon. It was the first load of oats I had ever loaded and accordingly a portion at one corner fell off. We hauled it in on a load and a half. I'm to help tomorrow evening. I scratched my hand awful.

Friday, July 24, 1885.   Gen. Grant died yesterday morning at 8.08 oclock. As is usual when anything happens we did not get the Ledger this morning. So I went over to the station and got the Times. I will preserve the paper.

He died of exhaustion. He had been suffering from this disease for about nine months. Most cities are draped in mourning. Pres. Cleveland in a proclamation announcing his death ordered all departments closed on the day of the funeral, all public buildings to be draped in mourning and all flags to be displayed at half mast in respect to memory of Gen. Grant. Messages of sympathy have been rec'd from all parts of the world. He was undoubtedly the greatest American of his day.

Queen Victoria's youngest daughter Beatrice was yesterday married to Prince Henry of Battenburg. She is 28 years old. He has been created a Knight of the Garter.

Saturday, July 25, 1885.   Gen. Grant is to be buried on Aug. 8 in Central Park New York City. President Cleveland had sent Adj. Gen Drum with a note offering the Soldier's home Washington D.C. as a place for burial. But New York City had already been decided upon. For my part I think it would be much more fitting if he were buried in Washington. C G Frick came up this evening. Rufus Reuben Hangey and I together went to Harrs dam to swim. When we came back Uriah Souder wanted me to sleep with him in the hammock.

When we came down here Katie and Martha were here and kept us about two hours. At last we tried to sleep but no none of us couldn't. The mosquitoes wouldn't let us. And I was really glad when drops of rain camd down through the leaves, to find an excuse for going to bed. Uriah too had to give up. So we went into the house where was Uriah in the darkness trying to gather his things together for home. He got everything except his hat and went home in the rain. This was at 2 o'clock.

Sunday, July 26, 1885.   Slept all fore noon to make up what I lost last night by (sleeping) in the hammock. Went to Sunday School in the afternoon as usual. I miss Leidy's boys very much in my class this year. It is not the class it was last year. The Leidy boys are under J T Moyer now and are doing first rate.

Was at the station after supper. Saw Jonathan there. He says he was in B. Junior in Arithmetic, Reading Spelling History Geography, while in Grammar and some others he was in A Preparatory. He says he would like to graduate.

It is raing slowly if it only would keep on till tomorrow evening.

Monday, July 27, 1885.   The selection of Central Park New York as Gen Grant's burial place has awakened much criticism. All the papers exclaim against it as well as other public men. And all seem to be agreed that the national capital would be the most fitting resting place of the great soldier. The family services will be held at Mt. McGregor on Aug. 4th. Rev. J. P. Newman will officiate. The cottage where he died will never again be used by anybody and will be presented by its owner J W Drexel to the state or nation. El. Mahdi is reported to have died on about June 28 of small pox. There is no certainty in it. The weather is cool today after the rain. It ought to rain more.

Tuesday, July 28, 1885.   The papers this morning announce that the site of Gen Grant's burial place has not yet been selected. Col Fred & Jesse Grant were in New York yesterday and viewed Central & Ridgeway Parks. Col. Grant said that it would be left to his mother to decide the spot. The new pike has been finished as far as W. D. Hunsbergers house.

They are getting the stones at Gehman's quarry. We were down there this evening. There is a great heap of stones there. They can not get enough teamsters. They pay 1.75 a day, and 1.10 for other labor. The stones come loose very easy.

Today John made the first effort in regard to getting up a library. Last evening he talked to C Moyer and Borneman about it and this morning to Edmund and Ben Barndt. They all seemed to be in favor of the scheme.

Wednesday, July 29, 1885.   Riverside Park has been selected as the burial place of Gen. Grant. This is said to be not quite as objectionable as Central Park, but is not as it should be.

Bergey the book peddler was around this afternoon trying to sell a Life of Gen. Grant. We asked him if it were the book the Gen. had written himself and he said he supposed it was. But the title page gives one Col. Herman Drick the 'well known' author. It is one of those cheap gotten up things 'to take' when people are excited. We looked at the pictures and told him we didn't want it. This afternoon witnessed a peculiar phenomena different from anything I had seen. The eastern sky was all over cast with dark clouds. Towards the south east a white conical shaped cloud seemed to hang down and connect itself with the earth like a string as it were. We made that it must be a cyclone or something. On the roof of J.H. Moyer's house they saw it take away the roof of a barn supposed to be Leonard Schidts. Also a barn door at Dover's on the County Line where it commenced.

There was rain south and west of us.

Thursday, July 30, 1885.   The cyclone of yesterday did considerable damage. It consisted of whirlwind about 33 ft wide, which started near Telford went down the County Line over beyond Lexington along the Neshaminy Creek and there dissolved. It took Leonhard Schmidt's roof off his barn C Himly's off the house and barn tore out the corn and left no traces of tore out trees and took them along. On Saml Detweilers land an apple tree land which they did not know where it came from. Sir Moses Montefiore the Jewish Philanthropist over a 100 yrs old died Tuesday. Gen Grant's body has been placed in the casket. The hardening has commenced. The body will remain about 6 mo in its present condition. Gen. Hancock is making great preparations. Was up at grandfather Hemsing's to hunt up the old family papers. Am preparing a kind of family history.

Friday, July 31, 1885.   Maud S. trotted a mile in 2.08 3/4 yesterday at Cleveland O. 10000 people were present. This beats her previous record by ½ second.

The Salvation Army marched through London yesterday to the House of Commons with a monster petition signed by 500000 persons, and 1½ miles long praying for an amendment to the criminal law raising the legal age of girls from 13 to 18 yrs. These signatures were obtained in 17 days. The President at the request of Mrs. Grant has named the following gentlemen as pall bearers at the funeral. Gen. Sherman, Lt Gen Sheridan, Admiral Porter, Vice Adm. Rowan, Gen Jos E Johnston, Gen. S.B. Buckner, Hamilton Fish, GS Boutwell, GW Childs, John A Logan, Geo. Jones, Oliver Hoyt. The Pres. and Cabinet will attend the funeral. Jno Cadwalader has been appointed as Collector of the port of Phila to succeed Gen Hartranft. Had a humorous experience I got from Mr Moyer to read. I bro't it in and mother asked me what it was. I did not tell her and had a job to explain. We had a nice rain after supper. Peter Benner and a young man he brot along were here over night. He works in glass factory, and is studying art. This was the first time he was with me since they moved to the city.

Saturday, August 1, 1885.   Father was in the city today. He bought moulding cutters and planing knives. Received of Funk & Wagnalls new book entitled Mentor a book on manners.

Went over the Bills Discounted today. They am't at present to 145950. We have at present 1273 notes averaging 114.61 each.

Today was examination day. I hear Jonathan Hunsberger got a certificate. Did not hear about Jane Moyer. They were a little anxious about it as he took them very rough on arithmetic.

Andrew and I in our team and Rufus Morris Weil and Mahlon Alderfer were at Harr's dam this evening. We expected get wet as it looked very threatening. We got home all right though.

Sunday, August 2, 1885. 'Charley' Frick came over this morning about 9 oclock. Walked around with him all day. Walked up to the station to get the paper the Sunday Item his favorite. From there we went up to Stover's to see the Kansas horses brought there by some kind of a cowboy. There are 46 of them. As fat as a board. Nasty colors and nothing nice about them. We went back through the town, wanted to get soda water but nobody at home. So we got ice cream instead. In afternoon we went to Sunday School. Got more ice cream and in evening to the station and to church in meeting where Reiter preached. As the result of yersterdays examination, J M Hunsberger gets Franconia Square, Jennie Moyer the Primary, C.N. Gerhart the Grammar, Bean Indian Field, J.H. Leidy Five Points, Bergey Rosenberger's and so on. Am glad Bean didn't get the Grammar. He is not a fit person for it. Susie had a fellow in the front room tonight and when Andrew went into the room a second time and asked him what he wanted any how, he mumbled a few inarticulate words and fled.

All bash was done to fool me.

Monday, August 3, 1885. Gov. Pattison has appointed Saturday as a legal holiday in commemoration of the death of Gen. Grant. Accordingly all notes must be protested on Friday evening. Today was the last day that the remains will remain at Mt. McGregor. The body was to lie in state this afternoon. It is expected that 75000 men will take part in the parade. Another tornado passed near this place shortly after twelve o'clock. So far as I know it spread its ravages from below Hatfield through Franconia. Jos. Proctor's house and barn were unroofed the house so badly shaken that the furniture was taken out and the house will probably have to be torn down if this is true. Every tree was uprooted. Stan Kinsey's barn was also unroofed. From there it went on till it reached Levi Hunsberger's barn about one third of which a roof was blown off and the barn moved about 3 inches from its foundation. Everything between the house and barn is a wreck. Corn crib, pig sty, Grape arbors, fruit trees, fences all lie scattered confusedly in the garden and the neighboring fields. The house was also battered. Blowing away fences trees great and small excepting only such as bent down to the earth under its fury. Blowing down three large cherry trees standing side by side. It laid low the corn potatoes &c and reached Jos. Stover's orchard and made havoc with about 20 of his best trees. It blew away the back roof of his barn leaving only a few of the rafters standing. From here it went up across the fields entered Wm Gerhart's woods blew down almost every tree in its path and blew the roof off John N. Souder's barn. This is all the extent I am informed of as yet. Was over at Levi Hunsbergers and Jos Stovers this evening. At Hunsbergers dead chickens stray the grounds. It has been raining all day. When it clears off I am going over the track. I did not see nor hear it. I was in bank. Many people here heard it. They said it made a noise like the letting off steam of a locomotive. Jos. Stover said it made a noise as if the earth were breaking into pieces.

Tuesday, August 4, 1885. The storm yesterday was general east of the Mississippi River. At Chicago the rain fall was 5.58 in. Great damage was done by water. At Reading and other places great damage was done by water. There were several tornados like the one in our neighborhood, one passing through Camden and Philada in which 5 lives lost and propally as many as a hundred injured. 400 houses were unroofed in Camden alone. It came up as far as Kensington and there dissolved. There was another in Salford which tore away a porch and barn roof. Another in Berks Co, another in Delaware. The weather today was clear, Stover and Hunsberger are at it repairing the damage down them.

A.D. Wagner's barn is said to be about demolished. Levi Hunsberger not insured. Jos Stover will do no good as it is only for Fire.

Planted celery this evening. Gen. Sherman arrived yesterday at Mt McGregor to take charge of the funeral services.

Wednesday, August 5, 1885. Gen. Grant's body was today removed from Albany to New York. Yesterday the family had their funeral. Dr. Newman preaching a panegyric on his life. His text was taken from Matt. XXV-21. The body was taken in a funeral train car on the Hudson River RailRoad.

Tornadoes are all the talk now. I notice in the Press that I have taken a prize on a puzzle solved on July 8. The book I get will be 'Ivanhoe.' J.D. Moyer got his 'Scottch Chiefs' all right one day this week. Chas G Frick has to leave the city tomorrow. He did not intend to go till Friday but on account of the Holiday on Saturday he has been summoned down by the firm by whom he is employed. Was about with him this evening. Ben. Hackman and Irishman who works on the pike were in a spree tonight. The pikemen got their pay today and now they are spending it. We witnessed the Irishman's efforts to take him home. Ben was in hardest and about all he knew was that he didn't want to go home.

Thursday, August 6, 1885. Charley Frick went down today. He did not intend to go till tomorrow. He promised to write. I did not see him today. Mr and Mrs Oliver Heins were today presented with a boy.

The remains of Gen Grant were yesterday removed from Albany to New York where they arrived at 3 P.M.

Susie's cousin Miss Susan Kent is staying with her tonight.

Dr. Loux narrowly escaped being run over by a coal train. He jumped out of the wagon and saved himself. Three wheels were broken and the horse bruised.

Friday, August 7, 1885. People are streaming in day and night to view the remains of Gen Grant. Yesterday at one time they pushed them through at the rate of 170 a minute. The arrangement for the procession has all been completed.

It is raining at present. Received a letter from Ed Danley. He has the Chills and Malaria and was in bed on Monday and Sunday.

Saturday, August 8, 1885. The remains of Gen Grant were today buried in Riverside Park. It was probably the most splendid funeral ever held on this continent.

It is estimated that more than 300000 persons viewed the remains in the City Hall during the past few days. The President and his Cabinet left Washington yesterday to attend the funeral.

Mr Moyer is getting tired of 'Scottish Chiefs'. He says it contains blasphemy.

We have made a plan to go to the Rocks tomorrow and from there to the Camp meeting. We hired Hen. Freed's cab and will take our horse and Jake Wile's. Morris & Elmer Weil, Andrew Rufus Jonathan and myself will compose the party.

Sunday, August 9, 1885. This morning we started gaily off at the appointed hour eight o'clock. We took along oats for the horses, one watermelon, ½ lb. butter, 2 lbs. sugar 4 lemons 1½ doz eggs 2 loaves bread, 1 Doz cakes, salt and pepper. We also provided ourselves with a kettle, dishes, knives forks a glass, table cloths, 2 hammocks. When we came to Benner's where Andrew used to live he undertook to take us down a lane a short cut to the rocks probably. Before we were half through we repented of having tried it. But the lane was too narrow and we could not go back. At last we came to a wood but this only increased the danger. This lane had probably not been used for years. At last we reached one of those narrow roads which take delight in winding over hills around immense rocks. We passed over the Ridge well and reached a one story house where a woman had just got her wash ready to dry. We asked to put our horses in the stable which she allowed if we took the cow stable which we found to our dismay bore a close relation to a pig pen. The peoples name was Heffentrager. We took up our things and started for a high hill to the south east which we surmounted, when Rufus and Jonathan and Cassel and Elmer Weil started in quest of a chicken and potatoes respectively. While Morris kept watch over the things I started to select a camping ground. This was two large rocks on the crest of the hill one of which we erected a stove on the other we spread the table. R & J soon came in with an old hen which they had bought for 55 cts. The hen was ready for cooking at 12.05. A & E came in with potatoes which were done before the hen. At about two o'clock dinner was ready. So we sat and laid down Eastern fashion and tore everything to pieces. At 3.15 we started for the camp meeting where we arrived before 5 o'clock. We started for home 7.20 and arrived home before nine. The whole expense of the party amounted to 3.02 which came 50 cts on the man. I took a book along to while away the time. A party of rocksers showed us around the hill showed us the Indian Rock. The only mistakes were made in stealing the potatoes and the language of the party was not at all time decent.

Monday, August 10, 1885. On Saturday Gen Grant's body was laid to rest with probably the most imposing funeral cermonies ever held on this continent. The procession was nine miles long. There were 800 carriages in line. These passed on four abreast. Maj. Gen. Hancock and staff headed the procession which started at 9 o'clock and consisted of detachments of the regular army, marines, National Guards, Grand Army Posts civic and other organizations. The President, his Cabinet, Ex-Presidents Hayes & Arthur, Vice Pres. Hendricks, members of Grant's Cabinet and many others were in line. First came the military, the funeral car and then the civic bodies. The funeral car was drawn by 24 black horses each led by a colored groom. They arrived at the tomb at half past five. Mende [?] Post Phila performed the Grand Army service, Dr Newman performed the last religious service. The body was laid in a temporary tomb about twelve feet square and riveted into a steel case.

One of my wisdom teeths is coming on the left upper jaw. This is the first to arrive.

Tuesday, August 11, 1885. Am reading the Scottish Chiefs at present. I find it very fascinating, although Mr Moyer does not like it. But it draws me and keeps me at it. Received a letter from Chas G Frick. He says he does not know anything to write but nonsense.

Andrew was much displeased at father at the dinner table because he told him it was not all fun to steal potatoes and that one who will not mind to steal potatoes will not mind to steal something more than potatoes. The poor fellow took this hard but it was not he alone that did it. We were all in for it. I was ashamed of it all day yesterday for Mr Moyer when I told him the circumstances said it was a shame. And I felt it too.

Wednesday, August 12, 1885. The Cholera in Spain is increasing. The new cases are now more than 4000 daily and 1600 deaths are often reported. It has also got a foothold at Marseilles again.

Harvey Frederick and Morris were down this evening. I had often told them to come and I would help them with their lessons. Some how or other my class does not it seems to me take the same interest in their lessons as they did last summer. Surely the cause there of must all rest with me. Did I pray more then? Did I give myself up as the teacher of these boys to my best.

It must be so. For wherever the teacher is in earnest the scholars will soon catch his spirit and do likewise.

Thursday, August 13, 1885. Finished reading the Scottish Chiefs this evening. Wm Wallace is here described as the most perfect of men. It is a most charming book to read. Many people went to the campmeeting this morning with the 9.06 train. Susie went up on the 3.03 train.

They were a little disturbed as it began to rain in the evening. Most of them returned on the 8.00 o'clock train.

The President is seeking repose in the Adirondacks where will remain for about a month.

Friday, August 14, 1885.   Have been writing letters to Chas G Frick and Ed Danley. Mr Frick promised to write to me when he left and he did so.

Mr Moyer has offered me 50 cts and The Scottish Chiefs for my Goodrich's History of England. I would do it right away but I asked Newboldt to buy his but he does not sell.

Saturday, August 15, 1885.   Weather was very cool today. Chas G Frick came up again this afternoon. He was sorry he couldn't go to the Rocks last Sunday. There was harvest meeting at the meeting house this afternoon. There were many people the house being more than filled. The Telford S. School had their celebration this afternoon. Susie was up their. The band from here was also there.

Sunday, August 16, 1885.   Got me the Press this morning from the milk train. The Press is the earliest of the Sunday papers. Went up to the station with Frick but just missed the train. A great many city people come up to Leonard Schmidt's I think they must board there. Uncle Henry's from Quakertown are down. They were here for dinner.

Jacob Barnes were also here. This was first time the former were down since they moved away. Lillie is almost as tall as Preston. After the Sunday School and after Supper we spent the time lounging around the station as we always do when he is with me.

Monday, August 17, 1885.   Frick left for the city with the early train. The railroad company it is said will immediately commence to lay double track from here to Quakertown.

I today subscribed for the Personal Memoirs of U S Grant, cloth $7.00, through Mr. Bergey. Although the price is high I want to have it as it is the genuine work. The first volume will be ready Dec. 1 the second March 1.

Was up at grandfather H's to arrange that family record.

Wrote Ed Donley a letter this evening. Rec'd from Os Kline. Kline over here the driver is sick of Typhoid Fever. It came upon him quite sudden.

My cousin Sallie Stover was thirteen today.

Tuesday, August 18, 1885.   An attempt was made to blow up the steamboat Fenton on the Delaware yesterday with dynamite or something of that kind. No one was killed but many were injured.

Received Ivanhoe from the Press this morning. It is a nice book.

As Greaser is away to attend the funeral of his grand niece I had to watch this night I think I did right well.

Wednesday, August 19, 1885.   Mrs Liz Hunsberger and little Florence came here today. She is as fat as any time. We took our potatoes home this evening. We got about eight or nine bushels. The early potatoes this year have been a failure owing to the drought. There is a better chance for those planted later.

Thursday, August 20, 1885.   Hoed the celery plants this afternoon. This used to be Em's work but Susie does not get done. Mrs. H is still here. There is always pretty much racket when she is here.

The county tax had to be raised very perceptibility. Grandfather S had to pay 21 Dolls more than last year.

I G Gerhart started today for the West.

Friday, August 21, 1885.   Mrs Hunsberger this afternoon went to her uncle Enos Hunsberger.

There has been a general advance in the stock market during the last week.

Germany has taken possession of the Caroline Islands which belong to Spain and whose king to show his displeasure of this act, has resigned the colonelry of an Uhlan Regiment which was bestowed upon him on the occasion of his visit to Germany.

Am reading Ivanhoe.

Saturday, August 22, 1885.   Gared, J C Landes' brother and his family are up from the city. Liz came down from Enos Hagey's to spend the night.

There is some talk as if Kline the sick man next door will be married next month to Lydia Leidy. Some people think there will be a rush for it before Septemb Oct. 1 when the License will appear.

Sunday, August 23, 1885.   Finished reading Ivanhoe this evening. At first I thought I did not care as much for it as for Scottish Chiefs but soon I was hanging on to it murmuring even when it was time for meals. This afternoon I did not like to go to Sunday School. Rev. Mr. Godshall from Deep Run addressed the Sunday School in German. English is more easy for him to speak. The child of David Moore (Hannah Yoder) was today buried at Franconia Meeting House. The child was about 9 mos old.

Liz is today up at grandmother's.

Tomorrow school will be opened again F.G. Wile as teacher.

Monday, August 24, 1885.   Russia has agreed to abandon all claims to the Zuficar Pass. The secures peace. W.B. Slifer is now in all probability ruined. Ruined by a brother who it seems would not have stopped with him who would have robbed the bank and anybody had not his operations been discovered and checked. Early in March I noticed that one of the notes indorsed by Slifer & Co was signed Agt. I called the attention of Mr.

Landes who in turn showed it to Mr. Slifer and Uncle Ed. This caused an investigation into Slifer & Co's account when it was found to am't to over 16000. No one was more struck than Ed., who now believed that there was more behind. Bill now took hold of the business himself and found gradually one by one of that he had been most grievously robbed by the brother he trusted. It seems now that he will close up the business. It is hard for man who has made a fortune [to] lose it and to go to work in the beginning. Chas. Godshall has taken unto himself a wife after his wife has been dead 7 mos.

Tuesday, August 25, 1885.   The rail road commenced work today. They are cleaning out the cut.

Mother grandmother and Lib were down at Henry Landis'. They came home through the rain.

A great effort is now to be made to push the library scheme. Beans was down and we hit upon a plan how the money of the school can be transferred to the Association. The book was prepared and I S Borneman heads the list with 2 shares or 10 Dolls. Mr. J B Wolf has now been appointed PM at Telford.

The weather made a great change today. This morning was very warm but this evening as cool. In Minnesotta the ther. was down to 26° yesterday.

Wednesday, August 26, 1885.   The weather today is very cool. A Sorver officiated today in Gerhart's place. Howard brought the deposits from Telford. He is even worse than his father to laugh and talk. Jas M Slifer sent a statement of the Topton Natl Bk. They have 25000 Discounts 18000 Deposits, Real Estate 1000, Circulation 18000, Premiums paid 4412.50 Expense 621, P & F 192. Discount 504 &c. I think this is doing right well for only two mos. business in a neighborhood where the people are opposed to bks and in the fall season of the year. He wants to have a statement of our deps. increased the first two yrs.

Dan'l Beideman and wife and Gertie arrived here this evening (afternoon). After Supper they went up to Slifers. Gertie is now a tall grown girl of 21. The first time I saw her was at Ocean Grove in 1882.

Thursday, August 27, 1885.   The Beideman's were here over night. This forenoon grandfather took them to Aunt Kitty's. For Dinner and this afternoon they were at grandfather's. They left for Custer Station with the market train this afternoon. They were not at Ocean Grove this summer. Gertie is a teacher in a Female Academy in Reading. I never knew her hair was as black as it is. I think Mrs Beideman is as sensible a woman as I ever met. She is a good talker.

When I came to bank this morning I found John thoroughly discouraged with the Library business. He was convinced that nothing could be done. I also believe that. We made out to see what we could do so as to have a basis for the future. The Austrian and Russian Emperors met and visited each other at Kremsier for the last two days. Spain is greatly excited over the action of

Germany in seizing the Caroline Islands. There was a run on the Spring Garden Bank yesterday caused by rumors. The Bank announced that they would continue payments today. When asked for a statement of the banks affairs said that none had been made out since Jan 7th. This looks a little suspicious. I am anxious to learn how they made out today.

Friday, August 28, 1885.   The run on the Spring Garden Bank continued yesterday but so far the bank has continued to pay out. On Aug 19 Miss Marietta Gerhart daughter of I G Gerhart and Mr Wm H G Godshall son of A C Godshall Lansdale were married. The first time I heard of I took it for mere rumor and so took no notice of it.

Father and mother and Cornelius's intend to go to Yardly tomorrow. This is the first time they are over there.

I today exchanged Goodrich's His. of Eng for Scottish Chiefs and 25¢. So I sent immediately for Keightheys His. Eng. 5 vols clo 16m to Leary's. Mr Landes also took a set. They are cheap. Only 1.00 for the five vols.

Saturday, August 29, 1885.   The Spring Garden Bank got through all right so far. Father and mother with Cornelius's went down to Yardley this morning. C Frick came up this afternoon. We went up to the Stocking factory which is ready for work on Monday morning. From there we went to Tyson's Hall to hear Frank L Murphy of Norristown make a speech. He talked about one thing and another without much sense in it but abounding with fun. We went home. Went up to the station and found my books had arrived. Took these home and went up again. They were playing Copenhagen and so for the great sensation tonight is that Enos Frederick is married to Cecilia Stellman. This is a great mistake.

Sunday, August 30, 1885.   We rose very late this morning. It being about 8³⁰ when we got up. There was not a soul in the house save ourselves and so all restrictions were removed. The Sunday School being in the forenoon Frick came over and accompanied me to the Sunday School. After dinner I had to come over to his house. Mr. G. was trying to get him to attend Sunday School by hint of a 12 Dol. book. We went to Meeting afterwards but no preacher came and so Deacon A D Clemmer made a short speech instead without rising. He could preach pretty well.

This evening after walking about from one place to another Frick seemed to change a little looking frequently at his watch. He then wanted to bid us good night but thought he was only in fun. When actually he left us and walked in the direction of Zendts'. How he got hold of her I can't say.

Monday, August 31, 1885.   Sullivan and Mcleaffrey had a sham fight in Cincinnatti. Sullivan was declared the winner. An absurd story comes from Paris to the effect that Prince Bismark had no object in view when he seized the Carolines. It is said that he has had an eye on Cuba for a longtime and it was to secure an understanding with the United States in regard to Spanish possessions. The United States was to have the Phillipines while Germany occupied Cuba. This story is absurd and untrue. The U.S. would never allow another power to occupy Cuba.

It is now believed that Gen Gordon is still alive and that he escaped to the Equator.

Tuesday, September 1, 1885.   This evening I was out trying to sell Library Stock. I sold a share to B C Barndt. M B Bergey promised to take some. J B Frederick wants to consider. I L Gehman and S.X. Swartley each took a share. So far it amounts to $50. Mr Barndt thinks it can not be got up. I don't know how it is.

Wednesday, September 2, 1885.   Mr Isaac H Moyer who is the treasurer of the D & S Turnpike Co. today collected or tried to collect the second installment on the stock in this neighborhood. The directors came in very slow today and no quorum was present at any one time.

John Frederick and Reuben were over to Jersey yesterday for peaches. They got 24 baskets. We took three at 85. They stopped at Danley's. They were about one week too early. Ed has the chills. Andrew wants to go over soon.

Thursday, September 3, 1885.   The weather at present is cool. Mr Jacob G Barndt a brother of Isaac G Barndt hanged himself this morning. Have not heard a reason.

They have put a new gravel train on the lode today. Yesterday they did not work.

Leidy has a new store keeper. His name Musselman from Hatfield.

Friday, September 4, 1885.   About 150 miners out in Wyoming made an attack on the Chinese quarter of a town and made them clear out. They then fired some volleys after them killing 15 of them and burned their houses 100 in number.

We had a little rain this afternoon.

Silver and most kinds of change are very scarce. We do not have half enough for our customers. I expect however that we will be flooded with in a short time as the Treasury is paying Silver to save the gold. The 1 and two Doll Bills have been recalled and this may be a cause of the trouble.

Saturday, September 5, 1885.   It is rumored that Miss Mary Freed was married today to Mr Mahlon Derstine. They must be afraid of Oct. 1st. It is also rumored that Andrew got the sack from L.M.Z. Don't know this but probably true. Mr. Landes went to Norristown and Phila to file a judgment again W B Slifer. The banks has more or less reason (cause) of suspicion on Mr. S. that the above was done as a precautionary measure.

I still get in my head to leave this place. I don't see why I should not some time in the future. John B Beck and family are said to have left for parts unknown.

Sunday, September 6, 1885.   Uriah and I walked up through the cut and back and along the course of the new pike. Sunday School in the afternoon. In the evening I walked up to the station and there met Haines. We took a walk throught the place. He tackled every girl he met.

We came back to Uriah, where we staid awhile Haynes singing songs and had a merry time altogether. It being after nine o'clock We came home. I finding the front door open we all entered at first supposing nobody was in the room. After a while a match was struck disclosing to our view Morris Weil and Susie sitting side by side on the lounge. With a spring Haynes and Rufus rushed to grab him them and forthwith Haynes went to the organ and sang several songs emphasizing, "I love my Love in the night". We had a great racket Andrew came down stairs after awhile and back again. We sat all the while without a light.

Monday, September 7, 1885.   We saw Haynes and Rufus to forbid them to say anything of last night's episode. There is great excitement in Spain at the occupation of the Island of Yap by Germany on the 24th August. A Spanish vessel has been there to occupy it since the 21st. The Germans being quicker. When this news reached Spain a mob attacked the German Ambassy and wrecked it compeletely. It is thought this will either end in war or in a revolution.

The rumor that Mary Freed was married on Saturday is untrue but Amanda Hunsberger was married on that day to a certain Swartley. Mr J C Landes' horse ran away last evening throwing him and Rufus out of the wagon. He wants to sell him now.

Tuesday, September 8, 1885.   President Cleveland has returned to Washington. It is now thought that the difficulty between Spain and Germany can be adjusted. So it is every time. There is talk of arbitration but is probably unfounded. Saw Oliver Kline for the first time today since he was sick. He walked up to the watchmakers today but complains of weakness in his legs.

Hannah Borse is quite low with typhoid fever. The cholera in Spain is subsiding. It is reported that Will Benner is in government employ on a ship for a period of seven years.

Wednesday, September 9, 1885.   The race between the Puritan and the Genesta was declared off on account of an accident by which the Puritans main sail and the Genestas bow skirt was carried away. The Puritans sailing master thought he could run ahead of the Genesta the accident happened. People were greatly disappointed as the wind was splendid. No race can possibly take place before Friday. The race was to have taken place on Monday but both yachts wer becalmed. Rufus, Cassel and I have a talk about going over to Danley's on Sunday, and to take Charley Frick along. I am to write to him about it.

Thursday, September 10, 1885.   Hannah Borse died this morning. She has been sick from typhoid fever. She is said to have got wet at the camp meeting and hence the fever. She must have been about 20 yrs of age. Little did she think a week or more ago that she today leave the land of the living. Her death should a warning to all young persons who feel too secure of life.

Mrs Ellis was down here this evening. We picked most of our grapes this afternoon. Mother made ketchup. Was up at grandfathers and finished the Hemsing side.

Friday, September 11, 1885.   In consequence of the excavations up at the cut and the new pike the town is at present full of Irish Germans &c who are at work here or who are here for work. Today two new ones a negro and an Irishman graced the town. Hardly a day passes now without one or two of these drunk. Funke has five or six of these boarders. A Prussian and a Switzer taking the French side disputed and came near fighting from this national emnity. These poor fellows when they go on a spree will continue to drink sometimes one or two weeks doing without food rather than deny themselves the poisonous drug.

Heard from Frick today, says he can not go along. We must get somebody else.

Saturday, September 12, 1885.   This evening is all bustle and preparation for tomorrows drive. I washed the wagon greased it and fixed a shaft to it. Andrew was at the reunion. He is at Telford this evening at the festival. We asked for Ben Barndt's double harness. Morris Weil refused to go along. Rufus is down here for the night. Andrew is to wake us up and feed the horses. This evening as we were walking up the pike we saw a light in Moyers feed store. I crawled up a window and looked in and saw a lantern standing on the scales. We went over and woke up Jonas who came along over and took it home. He said the lantern had been extinguished or was supposed to be.

Sunday, September 13, 1885.   This morning we started at 4.12 A.M. for Danley's. In the night Andrew had arranged with Mahlon Alderfer to go along. We passed through Lawndale, Blooming Glen, Deep Run, Meeting House Pipersville, Wormansville through Deep Dark Hollow up the River. We got over about half past eight. They had been looking for us. They were just ready to go to a baptismal in the river at Frenchtown. A & Ed wasn't ready so they went awhile and we didn't get there. We went out under a tree and ate all the watermelons and cantelopes we wanted. We walked around to the canal to Uhlersville. Back of the canal there is a steep ascent parts of it showing the bare rock about two hundred feet high. We walked half way over Frenchtown bridge. After dinner, we went over to the island and bought each a monster cantelope. At ten min past four we left for home and arrived home at 15 min past eight we having promised Mahlon to put him into Souderton by eight o'clock, as he had an engagement to fulfill. He sees Mary Shellenberger. We were at Singing School in the evening.

Monday, September 14, 1885.   About four marriages are expected to take place shortly. They are Schwenck but I don't believe it. Maria Roudenbush Sallie Alderfer Emma Leidy & Wm H Sellers.

Hannah Borse was buried yesterday at Schlichter's Church.

On Saturday W B Slifer sold his Phila. Property for 2100 and received a 1000 on acc. But ere he gave possession the sheriff was on him and now probably all his property will be sold.

It is very hard for him but it is so and all account of his own brother. Mother is doubtful if the strain is not too great for him.

Tuesday, September 15, 1885.   Slifer thinks this morning that his sale will hold out. He says the others were just ten minutes too late. He is not quite certain yet.

The worry and trouble he has gone through are beginning to show on him. Chas. Frick saw it in the paper on Sunday and he cut it out and sent it up to old Herman who already knew part of it and he lost no time in coming up to the bank to find out about it.

I began talking about going away to sound them. At first she only made fun of it, but soon I was made to understand that they did not think much of it.

Father went out and did not listen to it.

Wednesday, September 16, 1885.   Today another race will be sailed between the Puritan and Genestra. Should the Puritan be successful the races will be at an end. If not another race will be sailed.

Hauled in a wheel barrow load of dirt to transplant the flowers with Grandmother H & Aunt Sarah were down this afternoon on a visit. Grandma walked down. I took them home this evening in the carriage. Cousin Kate and Polly were here this evening. Took Kate and Susie out for a short ride.

The weather is a little cooler than the past few days. The roads are very dusty.

Thursday, September 17, 1885.   In the great international yacht race the Puritan beat the Genestra by 1 min and some seconds. The race was over a course of 40 miles 20 miles to leeward and 20 miles to windward. So the matter is ended, the Puritan having won two races a third is not necessary. So the America's cup stays in America.

This afternoon I applied myself to book binding. I bound a volumne of the Guardian and cut the edges of which work so far I am very proud. The next I will have to go for the covers.

This evening there was a large meeting in the meeting house on the occasion of two Russians preaching. The house was full. They are excellent preachers. They speak German beautifully. Rev. Van Ommeren and wife sat together among the audience. Rev. Jos B Detweiler was also there.

Friday, September 18, 1885.   Slifer said this morning that he was living in constant misery. That his creditors in the city torment him continually. That his brother Dan said that there was money enough here to pay everybody, this making it appear that Bill came down to the city for the purpose of swindling them. This was too much for Bill. He says it must be stopped somehow or he couldn't stand it much longer. He is looked upon as a rogue in the city while Dan the author of all the mischief is not blamed.

Mr. Landes advised him to have his lawyer draw up a statement of the facts and send to each of his creditors and thought this might relieve him. If I were to have such a brother I would never want to see him.

Mr. Slifer thinks a similar case can never have happened. Dan the thief the forger ought to be hung or else the next thing to it.

Saturday, September 19, 1885.   The Genestra yesterday took part in the annual race of the N Y Yacht's Club. There were 11 entries. There were two cups one by J G Bennet for schooners and one by W H Douglas for cutter sloops.

The Genestra won early and will have something to console her for her ill success against the Puritan.

Barnum's great elephant Jumbo was killed by the cars on Tuesday evening.

Vinie Ruth is down this evening. This is the first time she was down since they left here. She had a fit at Gentsch's. She did not have anything or much of this as long as they lived down here.

Sunday, September 20, 1885.   This morning I was ready early to go to Sunday School. Chas Frick who came up last evening sometime came over and we went together. The attendance was slight. Indeed I don't know whether Van Ommeren is gaining on us or what. We were at meeting in the afternoon.

We went up to meet the train as usual and loitered around the station house when about 8 o'clock, Frick having told me that he had an engagement for the evening, declared he must go. I now believe that he is going to follow it up for a while at least. Took a walk through town did not get home till the singing school people all were home when I found Susie had one. Andrew came home just then and I pretending I were gone to bed while he made

(There is more text but it's unreadable.)

Monday, September 21, 1885.   Andrew and Morris came home this evening about eight with about 14 baskets of peaches and some watermelons. It is thought that the Roumelian revolution is the outcome of the Kremsier interview and that Russia had a hand in it. The Porte [the Ottoman Turkish government] has addressed a note to the Powers for aid to suppress the rebellion. But is probable that they will not interfere.

A road was laid out between here and Leidy's somewhere commencing at H Souders land and ending at J R Moyers land. It is feared that the station will yet be moved away here to. Priesters and Telford and Souderton consolidated. The course of it is said to be Christ Hunsberger's moving out of his fence into the road leaving not enough room for the business of the station. The news is said to come of a high railroad official. If so it would be too bad.

Tuesday, September 22, 1885.   The revolution in Phillopolis may cause some trouble yet. This province lies inside the Balkan frontier it is believe by some that the Porte will never consent to lose this last defence or barrier of Constantinople. If the Powers stand together she will not attempt this. It is a little early yet to speak about it.

Have been working at my books this evening again.

Wednesday, September 23, 1885.   Today it was very windy and cold. It would have been a comfort had the room been heated. But I think we are all right for the winter as the heater has been repaired a few days ago and we shall probably not have to suffer as much from the cold as we did last winter. I have a very bad cold. I wish I was rid of it.

This afternoon I cut the grass in the yard with a lawn mower. This evening after supper we made cider on Wolford's cider press.

Thursday, September 24, 1885.   The weather was warmer again today. Yet we made a fire or Greaser I mean made a fire into the heater.

Godshall is a little suspicious of young Frick that he has some connections with some girl as likes to come up much better that he did before. Also his coming so late. He told me about but I did not enlighten him about it.

The Republican State Convention yesterday nominated Ira P. Davenport for Governor of NY.

The Puritan was sold at auction yesterday, to her builder Biergess for 13500. The Genesta yesterday won another race a 200 mile one, from Newport to New York with the Dauntless. The wind was blowing a gale at the time.

Friday, September 25, 1885.   The Democratic State Convention of New York yesterday renominated Gov. David B Hill for Governor.

This afternoon Uriah cut off his third finger on the right hand at the second joint. He did it working on the rabbeting machine. He ran toward the door where father who had seen that something was wrong met him and took him to the house bandaged it and took him to the doctor for treatment. He gave him ether and amputated the third finger, the second finger was cut from the first to the second joint scraping of some of the bone. The first finger too was cut but only the fleshy part. When under the influence of ether he was in a trance and called out, 'Hello boys,' several times and, 'The moulding machine' Father fetched a buggy and took him home. He was still under the influence of ether and complained of being very tired.

In the evening I visited him and he greeted me with his accustomed nod. He said he did not have any pain but his hand felt tired. I promised to bring him books to while away the time. He said that while he was under the ether he imagined he was out hunting the boys and called them. Then he heard a man calling him miles away. He did not suffer any pain during the amputation.

Saturday, September 26, 1885. Roswell P Flower has received the Democratic nomination for Lieut. Gov. of N.Y. The Mugwumps will probably go back and support Davenport. The N.Y. Times and Evening Post both papers against Blaine last year declare against Hill. This constitutes a factor in so great a state as N Y where the parties are so nearly balanced.

I cleaned the yard this afternoon. Took up a book for Uriah to read.

This was working late at Sunday School Quarterlies.

Sunday, September 27, 1885. Worked very late last night at the quarterlies for the Sunday School. So I laid in bed till nine o'clock. Went to Sunday School in the afternoon. Mr. Zendt a kind of an address. No doubt it pleased him well. Andrew was up to see Uriah. He saw the finger that was taken off. It is put in a bottle and sealed. Uncle Cornelius' were here this afternoon. It is reported that Aaron Hartzel has another baby. Cal Hunsberger had had his teeth pulled. He was here a few minutes this afternoon. Uriah, Haynes and I were together this evening. Haynes teased the girls with a cane as they passed our yard.

The picnic in Raudenbush's grove turned out to be a humbug as I expected. No Strohl Family no balloon ascension, no band no nothing. Uriah has stopped going to J.

Monday, September 28, 1885. Andrew got his photographs this morning. He looks a little sober quite unlike him when there is fun about. But undoubtedly it is his settled look. It is the face of one not in entire health. But yet he never said anything or nothing.

Roswell P Flowers has declined the nomination of Leut Gov of N.Y.

The weather was quite warm today and yesterday.

J M Slifer and wife were down yesterday, I did not see him. Their deposits amt to about 20 or 21000. Mr Oliver Kline and Lydia Leidy were married. This evening a band started out to furnish the music.

Father hurt himself in the face today at the circular saw by a piece of wood flying in his face. His face is much swollen. It might cost him an eye had the missile struck him there.

Tuesday, September 29, 1885. The 'Dutch' band last evening did not make out very well. After playing about five minutes Mr Leidy asked them if they knew the law which frightened them so that they cleared out. They say they are going to do it over. Just now about 10.15 lusty tones of another Dutch band can be heard. The present one is in honor of Mary Freed who was married to Mahlon Derstine today. As we went out to listen to them I could not help wishing to be with them.

The only time I ever was with such was in the case of Will Hackman 3 yrs ago.

Mr. Jno S. Fluck has made an assignment to Jonas D Moyer of Dublin. Mr. Moyer is largely interested in Mr. Fluck.

Wednesday, September 30, 1885. Mr. Isaac Gerhart came down today again. He looks somewhat bronzed. He gained five pounds in weight. We had a kind of quilting today. Two comforts were turned out complete. At four o'clock it was all over. Grandmother Mrs. Fred Ed. and Ellis, Cousin Kate Souder and Annie Gernhardt Becker's girl.

Was up this afternoon to see Uriah. I saw the finger that is bottled up. Saw his hand too. It is much cut up. He has no pain. He had on Sunday and Monday. It is poulticed.

This evening another 'dutch band' was got up to serenade Lydia Leidy. We heard them here at home. Father and mother had gone to bed and were listening through the window. Andrew and I went over and approached them. A number of dark forms kept moving up and down the road blowing horns ringing sleighbells dinner bells drumming hollering and altogether making a horrible din. We came away unobserved. They split. Some went home. The others are still there!!

Thursday, October 1, 1885. They are after poor Lydia again tonight as can be heard plainly. They are going to keep it up all week.

It is said that the old woods must go. They must make room for building lots which are at present scarce.

The discovery has been made that Turkey's army is in a delapidated condition. Some regimen is being without shoes and short in clothing.

Friday, October 2, 1885. It is raining a little this evening. Rain would be very welcome. It might spoil the fun for tomorrow however.

We this afternoon cleaned out the well at the house. There is about 2 ft 6 in water in the other one yet.

Saturday, October 3, 1885. This morning it was raining and the prospects for the reunion were poor when however it cleared off and so the reunion was suffered to be. The Sellersville and Souderton Bands were present. This evening however when the real fun was to begin it rained heartlessly. This rain is very welcome. Water was getting very scarce. I did not get out as I did not feel like it and the evening there was too much rain. O S Kline is home they say.

Sunday, October 4, 1885.   We had very much rain yesterday and today. Lightning is said to have struck into Geller's warehouse at Kulpsville. The fire was seen from here. Was in Sunday School this afternoon. Took a walk with Uriah and Os. Kline through the cut and down the pike. They are very near done with the digging.

Went, this evening with Haynes down to see Uriah and Haynes went in very unceremoniously when Kate opened the door. We got to singing when a loud rap was heard at the door. Haynes followed Kate to the door supposing it to Uriah and hollered 'hello' as loud as he could. Finding it was Mr. Bean he came back and we played again. Uriah came in afterwards. We went back to the station and there had more fun.

Monday, October 5, 1885.   Rainy part of the day. We are getting enough rain now when it comes.

Mr Landes sold his horse yesterday though it was Sunday to Frank P Hering of Phila who has a hostler stand and who furnishes teams to the market men in the city. He sold him for 148 Dolls. He paid about 161 for the horse. And under the circumstances he did pretty well. I picked all the Clinton grapes this afternoon.

I am working at the third set in bookkeeping.

Tuesday, October 6, 1885.   Still raining slowly all day. Respecting the Roumelian situation not much can be said. But the end of the matter will probably be the Sultan will be required to recognize the union of Bulgaria and Roumelia. The latter two to remain under the suzerainty of the Sultan.

Wenhold is reducing his account at bank at present in a very satisfactory way. He has reduced over 7000 since May last and over 1200 since Sept 5. At this rate Wenhold's trash would be a thing of the past in the near future. We make him waive protest on every note he alone is endorser. There are two other accounts which are far more threatening than the above.

Wednesday, October 7, 1885.   In the French elections the Conservatives have made large gains on the Republicans. It is thought many of the Cabinet will have to resign failing to be reelected. The Conservatives include the Royalists Orleanists Bonapartists and if they were to unite with the Radicals might effect the overthrow of the Republic.

It was intended to fire the mine with 375000 lbs dynamite at Hell Gate New York today. But it was thought that it will have to be postponed. But it will come off between now and Saturday.

Priester's hotel is said to be sold to Mrs Kulp and Geo B Hunsicker for $5600.

Thursday, October 8, 1885.   The subscriptions for the library amount to $90 with $5 promised and $30 belonging to the school would make $125 leaving $75 to be raised. Whether this can be done or not is a question. C D

Hunsberger is anxious that we should get it up.

Intended to go up to the dentists to have a tooth filled, but glad to take the wet weather as an excuse I did not go. So I went up to the store and bought me an overcoat paying $4 for it.

This evening went to meeting. A preacher was here from Lansdale named John Landis and also a deacon. He holds that the outer actions, garb etc are a type of the inner person. He also laid much stress on the 'defenceless' character of their sect, etc.

Friday, October 9, 1885.   Mr Landes' opinion of last evenings sermon was that it was mostly old Fogeyism. He told old Herman so, Herman agreed with him.

Mr Godshall intends to light his street lamp all winter if A.G. Stover will extinguish it when he goes home. He began last evening. There are at present more lights in town than was the case sometime ago. Mr Wolford intends to put one up too. Moyer & Detweiler have one the doctor and J G Leidy Old Mr Moyer has one too.

Mr Landis & Co have a good one. It is self extinguisher, will die out at about eleven oclock.

Saturday, October 10, 1885.   Today at Eleven is to have been the great explosion at Hell Gate NY. Some people expected something unusual.

Charley Frick is up again. Every body knows what he us up for.

Am too sleepy must go to bed.

Irwin Sellers was around today. He is on the lookout for a job but must have a thousand dollar bond signed first if he can.

Sunday, October 11, 1885.   Got to Sunday School pretty late this morning. Were up with Uriah all afternoon. Haynes was there awhile.

This evening were around the station and when Chas started to go Haynes Uriah started with him. He did not like this and probably thought that Haynes was full. So he told him that he did not like to take anyone in his condition. This makes Haynes a little mad for he really was innocent. He does not understand our ways around here, Haynes especially.

The Flood Rock explosion took place yesterday at 11.15 and was ignited by an electric button by Miss Mary Newton daughter of Gen Newton who did the same thing at the other explosions nine years ago. The explosions is it believed at present were highly successfull.

Monday, October 12, 1885.   F & M were down at J K Clemmer's. The weather yesterday was very pleasant. Today it is colder and more wind. Arch deacon Forrar preached in Phila yesterday. He will lecture in Newark N J on Dante soon.

Was up to see Jonas Fredericks new house. It will make a nice home. Is a very nice place to build as the whole town is in view. The rail roads were yet at work in the cut. There now sloping down the sides very neatly.

Becker's have a new maid. She is a sister of Ed Watte. She looks,

————————————.

The force of Saturday's explosion threw up three columns of water to the height of one to two hundred feet. Only a slight tremor was noticed throughout the city. I will preserve the paper in which the description is given.

Tuesday, October 13, 1885.   Today is the Ohio State election. The Rep. and Dem. candidates had a joint debate at Toledo a week or so back. Hoadly speaking for an hour Foraker following with an hour and a half and Hoadly closing with half an hour. The Prohibition vote is expected to decide the contest. The Dems. expect that Dr Leonhard the Prob. candidate will receive 30000 votes. The Dems. are in favor of License against Temperance, Low License against High License. The Reps favor the Scotts Con. Today was to have been a husking at Freed's but owing to the rainy weather all day nothing came of it.

Wilson the self confessed murderer of C Daly brought to Norristown from Chicago on Sunday has been committed for trial.

Becker's have a new girl a sister of Ed Watts to take the place of Gunheimer. This one is a very devil. This is only the second day and she has already acted in a most beastly manner toward Jacob Nase. Her words, actions, and appearance are most foul. She is men crazy. The first time I saw her she made an unhappy impression upon me.

Wednesday, October 14, 1885.   The Republicans yesterday carried Ohio by from 12 to 20000!

Wenhold is reducing his act somewhat. He was down today and seemed proud of it. He says he has used more oaths than the whole thing is worth.

Was up to see Haines tonight. There is still a coolness between him and Frick.

Thursday, October 15, 1885.   The returns of the Ohio election are not yet all in but they indicate the election of the Republican ticket. Several Amendments to the Constitution were also voted on and carried one of which is to change the State election from October to November.

It is said that the Porte has rejected the Union of Bulgaria and Roumania, that King Milan must abdicate or declare war and that he has decided on war. The problem now for Bismarck is to prevent Russia and Austria from fighting.

There was a quilting at Williams today. Artie, Fred's little boy has pants now. Today was the first time I saw him in them. He is big enough for them.

This evening there was to have been a dancing party but nothing came of it. No girls there willing to dance.

Was up and saw Uriahs' finger. It is not healed up yet.

Friday, October 16, 1885.   The funeral of Cardinal Mcloskey took place today.

The Ohio Legislature is probably Republican by a small majority on joint ballot thus insuring the reelection of John Sherman to the Senate.

Fred was after me this afternoon to report for the 'Lansdale Reporter.' At first I didn't want to accept it now although I do not feel equal to it and will cause much trouble.

Mother was boiling soap this afternoon.

It is expected the Servian troops will soon cross the frontiers.

Saturday, October 17, 1885.   The Servians yesterday crossed the frontiers into Bulgaria. King Milan is in command. It is believed that they will speedily capture Sofia the capital of Bulgaria. Austria has sent a warning to Servia leaving them to their fate. The King of Greece has called out the reserve.

Father this afternoon contracted the two toll houses of the D & S Turnpike Co for $697 a piece. Gerhab gave in $720, but father special arrangements with Musselman and was able to beat old John. W D Hunsberger said they could be built for $675 and that they should let it awhile yet. But the rest did not agree with him. I guess he would have preferred to have furnished the lumber. But that's all bosh. Gerhab makes his work for the store and that spoils it. Mr J D Moyer is planning a house in secret. He would like to build one next September. Jonas Fredericks' is now being plastered. Andrew is off to some husking.

Sunday, October 18, 1885.   Went to Sunday School this afternoon Godshall was not present. He and A.D. Clemmer started for Lancaster County yesterday morning and intend to stay a few days. Borneman was in Sunday School in his stead. The girls led the singing. There were six of my class present today.

Uriah and I drove up to Sellersville this evening. We took our horse their's being sick and Uriah's carriage. We stopped at Nase's hotel. The majority seem to stop at Kern's this fact alone makes me prefer the other place. I hate great crowds at Hotels. We attended church. Rev. Mr Dengler preached in the English language. Services were held in the basement the other part of the church being under repairs. Out in the cemetery we saw a great monument obelisk shaped, which O H Nase has erected to his own memory when he dies. Milt Moyer and Horace were up too. The former escorted a Miss Leidy to church. Wonder whether he intends to run it double. Saw the Sellersville Bank for the first time. This was the first time I have been in Sellersville Church.

Monday, October 19, 1885.   Wrote my acceptance to the Lansdale Reporter as correspondent. Wrote also to Brummer of North Wales about Andrew.

A Patent Medicine man calling himself Dr Cram of Phila. He is an excellent talker as are all of his craft. Ready to pick up any incident to talk on. An array of poetry was at the end of his tongue.

Tuesday, October 20, 1885.   The weather today was such that the 'husking' at Freed's this evening. This is the second failure. There will be one at S.W. Zeigler's tomorrow afternoon. Mahlon Alderfer will take a load of girls along over. I intend to go too if I can get off.

W.B. Slifer and Fred are out West in Ohio or somewhere. I learned this from Mr. Landes yesterday morning but saw from his manner that their purpose was secret. I asked mother about and she said that Fred wants an Agent out there who is to buy up hay and cut it. Slifer is to do this and if they find anything, they will move out there in about six weeks. They are to be pitied but so it is. I said this evening it is a case very similar to the Grant & Ward business though not quite so disastrous.

Wednesday October 21, 1885.   The weather today was rainy but cleared off this afternoon and tonight is it getting much colder. Two huskings were spoiled by the rain. I had intended to go to one. But still it does not matter.

Received an answer from Dr Andrews of the Lansdale Reporter. He will furnish the stationary and twenty 20 cts a letter. I felt a little put off on reading this letter. I felt that I had accepted before being really asked.

But Fred was to have asked me and I had nothing to do but accept.

Thursday, October 22, 1885.   Was up at the Dentist's this afternoon about my tooth. He will put in a gold filling next week.

Went to grandfather H and staid till near six o'clock. He was repairing a sausage machine. Sarah was clearing the garden.

There were nine huskers at Freed & Price's Husking. There were considerable more. We all had lots of fun. Haynes spent the greatest part of the evening here. Miss Jennie Moyer was there too. She was walking about with Miss Anna Lapp most of the time. I talked with her about the prospective Library. She says she has no names as yet but several promised. She would like if it were got up. She says she prefers 'Bingo' playing to Copenhagen. I could, had I tried, have made my mark.

Friday, October 23, 1885.   Fred came home this morning. He always comes very unexpected I think. Always a little before the time set. Slifer did not come along. This afternoon when at the Barber Shop Ben Alderfer that the sheriff was here after Slifer's goods. I went out to Mr Landes's and told him about it. He said it was all fixed. Was at Mrs Detweiler's. I had not been up there since they moved. This evening I am going to a regular old fashioned husking at Fred Hunsberger's. The corn is to be husked in the evening. Hearing there was a husking at C N Leidy's Milt Moyer, Horace and Harry

Hunsberger walked went over. There were only a few there, but we had some fun. I got acquainted with Miss Lovina Hunsicker a sister of Em's. At 8.45 over a dozen of us started for Hunsbergers. We got there about half past nine. We helped to husk till they stopped. There was now a crowd beseiging the door waiting for supper. When the door opened in they rushed till the table was full. Mr Hunsberger got mad about it and wanted those who did not husk corn to clear out. We got in near the last. Our table got a special scolding because of the non-workers. Harry Smith was chased from the table. I gave him a piece of cheese, cake and that was all he got. The others were Irwin Bean Rufus, Horace, Jonas Freed Mathias, Frederick Josiah Clemmer Jr Calvin Groff and Isaac &c. Miss Jennie was there also. About half past twelve I started for home all broke up.

Saturday, October 24, 1885. Felt very sleepy this morning when I got up and afterwards. WB Slifer came home last evening. The Sheriff was here again today. Got my overcoat this afternoon.

There is another husking at Kuhn's hotel Telford. Andrew and Susie are up but I am happier at home I am very very tired and sleepy.

Sunday, October 25, 1885. Lay in bed all morning till almost noon. Andrew did the same. We thought to make up for loss of sleep the previous evenings.

Was at Sunday School. Got thoroughly disgusted with it. There were six of my scholars present and therefore so much more inattention. It sometimes seems to me that there is no use in the whole thing. A person should either be more in earnest with or leave it altogether. I know I am too worldly minded and think not on what I would teach and here lies the whole fault.

Went home and began to read Shakespeare's Henry IV to cheer up my moodiness. Uriah was down. We intended to go to Sellersville but didn't get the horse.

Monday, October 26, 1885. On Saturday the sheriff found only about 140 or 160 worth of goods and so could not proceed. He took Sam D Hunsberger along as an appraiser but Slifer objected to him. I think it made Sam, or displeased him.

Mr & Mrs Gardner were in bank today. He is about 6 ft 2 or 3 in tall. They are transferring the Gov. Bonds to the legaters.

In the conference about the Bulgarian difficulty, Russia Germany & Austria voted to restore the status quo while England France and Italy voted to recognize the Union of Bulgaria and Roumelia. William intends to put a wheel factory, brick, BOX 40 this fall yet. B D Alderfer also wants to build a house. Wrote my first letter to the Reporter. Will send it tomorrow. Have not seen Fred about it.

Tuesday, October 27, 1885.   Sent in my first letter to Lansdale Reporter this afternoon. Took it to Fred at noon who made a few corrections. Mr & Mrs. Gardiner were at bank today again. Frank Detweiler wanted to know of Slifer's case if he were in any case secure in his business. He talked of perhaps buying it (the property).

Was at the Strohl family's entertainment this evening. I didn't expect very many but when I came it was full and some took a reserved seat. The girls have new dress. Their color is red. It was a very pleasant evening to me. Little Rosa received much attention. Charley is as good as ever. Wish I could play the flute as he can. But the cornet is his instrument. Alice the wife of W.E. is along too. Her singing is excellent. Charley played two cornets at the same time. So did W.E. and Alice his wife, Little Rosa had the big drum. Mr & Mrs Gardner, Mr & Mrs Slifer were up. The former seemed to enjoy themselves while on the latter could be plainly seen the marks of the great misfortune that has befallen them.

Wednesday, October 28, 1885.   This morning John S Ruth asked me to clerk his Apple Sale this afternoon. I did not like to promise as it was Wednesday and we were very busy. He said he would not commence till near three o'clock. A little before three the sale commenced. H Robinson Auct. The entire carload 164 bbls were sold at an average price of $1.69 per bbl, each containing 3 bus.

Father bought 13 bbls for himself and the shop men. He got one bbl of Kings for 2.10 which are elegant. This was the highest price reached. There were Premium, Eng Streak King Greening Spitzberger Waldo, Seek No Further Russet, Gilliflower, &c.

Thursday, October 29, 1885.   At last a postmaster has been appointed, WKShellenberger is the man. Most people are glad he has it. If Leidy had got it it would have been too far removed from the lower part of the town. Schwenck who was also an applicant was set up by Hunsbergers. The great question now is where will be removed. To Shellenberger's house is too far away. There was talk of the Hardware Store, the tailor shop, but these are inadmissible as it must be in a building occupied by the P.M. or his deputy.

So this very important thing is still a burning question. Hunsberger's it is said are doing all they can to prevent it being placed in Landis & Co's store. But if they will make a separate space for the Post Office their place is not objectionable.

Friday, October 30, 1885.   Gen Geo B Mclellan died suddenly yesterday morning of heart disease. He was born 1826 and was in the 59th year of his age. His home is in Orange N.J. He leaves a wife and two children a son about twenty years of age a student at Princeton. MClellan doubtless was one of the great generals of the war and he has been meanly used.

We have a fine joke in progress for Uriah.

Tomorrow I will send with Isaac Gerhart a letter for Uriah to be mailed in Phila. It will contain a $1000 Saicremoc Valley R.R. Bond sent as a sample to the bank and mark specimen. The signatures are mine. It will be accompanied by a brokers letter which I wrote last evening and copied by John. It is signed J.R. Seligman & Co. Philade

Saturday, October 31, 1885.   The funeral of Gen. Mclellan will take place on Monday. He will be buried at Trenton. No military rites and display will take place at the funeral in accordance with the wish of the deceased during life. His disease is believed by some to have been caused by excessive smoking.

It now turns out that he could have become a member of Pre't Cleveland's Cabinet and that he could probably have been appointed Civil Service Commissioner.

Barnes & Frederick had an apple sale here this afternoon.

Sunday, November 1, 1885.   Was in Sunday school this morning and in church this afternoon. Rev. S.D.Detweiler preached assisted by Rev. M R Moyer. Mr Eph Stover and wife were here on a visit. This afternoon Uriah told me he'd had something to show me and I knew at once what he meant. The $1000 had arrived. He showed it to me and asked my opinion of it. He seemed to be surprised at being trusted with so much money. I persuaded him to lock it up in the safe. He will show it to Mr Landes tomorrow.

Monday, November 2, 1885.   Uriah came this morning and showed the bond to Mr Landes. As he seemed to be so completely deceived and already written an answer to the letter he could not find it in his heart to deceive him more so he told him it was worthless. Uriah who was satisfied had gone out. I went after him and told him all.

Miss Zendt & Miss Tyson were here this afternoon in regard to getting up an entertainment on New Year's Day. They want me to join.

Schools were opened today. Mr Chas N Gerhart has taken Bean's place.

I heard something that Ida Souder will have to marry Enos Freed. The story may be without foundation.

Tuesday, November 3, 1885.   Today is election day. A director of the Poor will be voted for in Montg. A sheriff and City Treasurer in Phila. A State Treasurer for Penna. A Governor for New York Virginia and other states. The above are the most interesting.

Everything is quiet here. Most people go to the election. Horace and Milt Moyer who are both now of age did not go although it was so intended at first. Mr Shellenberger said this morning it was now decided where the Post Office would be moved. Hunsberger's wanted $50 rent not including fuel for which he would get the front room in their store where the tailor shop used to be. Landis etc offered everything for nothing accordingly the latter place was chosen.

Shellenberger's daughter Mary is to be deputy post master. Father Reuben and Paul Schmidt are at work tonight making the necessary changes in the store.

Andrew who is going away on Monday is making a tool chest in the evening. He told me this evening that as he did not like to come here so he does not like to go away.

Wednesday, November 4, 1885. Quay was elected yesterday State Treasurer by about 33000 majority. David B Hill was elected Gov. of New York by about 10000 plurality. Virginia went Dem. 12000 or 15000. FitzHugh Lee nephew of R.E. Lee travelled round the state in his uncle's saddle with battle flags flying. Philada elected the Rep. ticket. Even Rowan who is probably not fit to hold office was elected by about 12000 while the others rec'd 22,000.

A company of gipsies or something of that kind filthy in appearance with little red caps on their heads, three families with 2 wagons full of children and three performing bears passed through here today. One woman had her baby in a kind of papoose on her back. Grandmother H sprained her arm on Monday by a fall. I was up there evening. She has it shingled. Father worked till near three o'clock last night. It is said Mr Shellenberger has been reported at Norristown for having been drunk the other day.

Thursday, November 5, 1885. Mr Shellenberger received his commission as postmaster today. He has not charge of it yet.

Was along up to Tyson's this evening. Went up because I wanted a Literary Society. Didn't care much about an entertainment. There were 7 gentlemen and 5 ladies present. They were Moyer, Horace John Q. Jonathan, Penrose Schwenck, Mr Musselman of Leidy's store and myself. Misses Tyson, Zendt, Kate Souder Jane & Annie Moyer. I was chosen chairman and began to talk of a Literary Society. The others seemed agreed but wanted to talk of the entertainment first. It was finally decided to proceed with the entertainment and go on with the Society afterwards. I had determined not to go on the stage nor will I. After it was over I escorted Miss Zendt home. She told me about Frick being much out of humor with us at the time.

Friday, November 6, 1885. The post office was this forenoon removed from Hunsberger's store to J M Landis & Co. The all absorbing talk at present is about the post office. It is said Shellenberger has been reported for drunkeness. It is believed that Hunsberger's would rather see the post office go up to Leidy's than be kept where it is. Geller of Lansdale sent a man up to help him along. This evening Miss Shellenberger was out for the first time assorted the mail.

I was up at the dentist's yesterday to have my tooth filled but did not get it done yet. I am to come next week at noon.

Father will have to work late again tonight.

Saturday, November 7, 1885. The Bulgarian question is at present considered very critical. The Servians under King Milan have for a long time been making war preparations and now the Bulgarians are ready to capture Belgrade the capital of Servia. No one knows what will become of it.

Father, Reub and Paul worked all night to finish the post office. They did not get to bed at all. Andrew had his tool chest neatly painted by John Smith. He moved this afternoon. He will go home on Monday morning I think. He wanted me to go along this afternoon but I did not get through in time. He worked till Noon and this will have been his last day.

Sunday, November 8, 1885.   Today it rained very much.

We were very uncertain in regard to the Sunday School. We went out and found three girls and about a dozen little boys with Mr Godshall. Soon after more arrived there were enough there to have some good singing. We did not recite. Meeting by a Virginia preacher who had been a prisoner during the war was announced for Tuesday evening night. This comes on the 'Society' meeting night and the girls will make efforts to have it postponed as we would like to go.

Andrew talked as if he were going down this evening and Susie took steps to prevent it by hiding his hat &c. He does not like to go, that's plain, and we don't like to see him go that's certain. After having been used to him so long it is but natural to regret the approaching time of parting.

Monday, November 9, 1885.   This morning we got up at five o'clock

and Andrew was ready to go with the 6.06 train. So saying goodbye to the others I accompanied him up to the store where he found out the train was 50 m. late. He sat around and didn't talk unless spoken to. When Mr Landis came for the mail I gave him my hand and said good-bye. He asked me to come down and I told him to come up. He said he would. So I left him. He went down with the milk train at 6.50. He will be up about every two weeks to attend Sunday School.

Mr Landis was down to the city today. Hunsberger's have about 100 names who get their mail at their place and now to deprive Mr Shellenberger of a part of his salary instead of bringing this mail to the post office they put it direct into the car thus depriving Mr. S. of all benefit of part of the P.O. This shows how mean they can act when they wish to do so.

Tuesday, November 10, 1885.   John McCollough the actor died on

Sunday afternoon at his home in Philada. His disease was blood poisoning and his mind had been giving way for some time. He was removed from the Bloomingdale Asylum a few weeks ago.

The English political campaign is at its height. All the great men are out Mr Parnell, Lord Salisbury Lord Randolph Churchill Mr Chamberlain Mr Gladstone and others. The last had been ill for some time but has recovered and spoke at Edinburgh the other night.

We put up the stove in the sitting room this evening. Got a note from Miss Zendt this morning that would meet after meeting. Was at meeting. Rev Beery of Virginia preaching in English. After meeting was up at Tyson's hall. Milt Moyer got out of patience with on my continued refusal to go on the stage. After I had explained he seemed satisfied.

Wednesday, November 11, 1885. The weather today was excellent. It reminded one of Spring.

War has been declared between the Indian Government and Burmah. The trouble arose about trading King Theebaw who is a licentious bad man failing to give a satisfactory explanation. War vessels and troops are proceeding to Mandelay the capital of Burmah.

Uriah has come down today. I believe father had a talk with him about it. He did not seem inclined to come very much.

J D Moyer was a little impatient this evening. He was trying to buy land of W D Hunsberger and also to sell Library Stock in both of which he was not successful.

Thursday, November 12, 1885. Cal. Hunsberger was at work this afternoon repaving our pavement. He is about half done. Becker should fix his too.

Rec'd of D C Cook 50 in stamp.

Mr Gladstone made another speech in Edinburg. The speech lasted 80 min.

Had my tooth filled today. It cost a dollar. It does not feel over pleasant. He says it ought to last 20 years. It seems to be not airtight. I don't know though.

Friday, November 13, 1885. The weather this morning was pleasant but rained a little this afternoon.

Mr Moyer got a little restless about bookbalancing. He wants to exchange it for charging up notes. I am not so foolish as to do this. I must help him balance books however else it won't go.

The car time was changed on Sunday.

Wenhold was down today. He had the butcher team. Mr Kline his son in law being on a bear Hunt.

Saturday, November 14, 1885. Servia has declared war against Bulgaria. Meanwhile the Balkan Conference is to decide the fate of the Roumelian Union.

A great fire in Galveston on Thursday night destroyed over 400 house and rendered 1000 families homeless. Riel is to be hanged on Monday. Great excitement prevails in all parts of Canada.

There was to have been a party at C M Tyson's tonight again. Owing to the total absence of girls the boys went away again.

Rec'd an invitation from Misses Tyson and Koffle for Mrs R S Gerhart's Surprise Party. Declined.

Chas Frick is up again I hear. He has Lillie over at Moyer's this evening. Wonder if he is cross yet.

Rec'd a letter from Andrew. He says he likes it as well as he expected and has a good teacher.

Sunday, November 15, 1885. Chas Frick was over this forenoon. Uriah was down too. Mr Gentch was here and wants to have his old shop moved and converted into a house.

Went to Sunday School this afternoon. The Sunday School is not so well attended any more. Van Ommeren's is slowly taking some of our scholars away and it is now felt as his Sunday School is in the afternoon too.

After S.S. Frick was over Martha and Katie were here and so was grandmother S. Slifer's now came and all the others went home. Frick will go down this evening.

Uriah wanted me to go along to Sellersville but I didn't do it. Slifer's spent the evening here and seemed to be cheerful. William was also down a part of the evening.

Monday, November 16, 1885. There was a little court held at grandfather's on Saturday evening regard to the Slifers. Slifer who had transferred a 1000 judgment note to the bank had retransferred it to Wm Delp, and she is said to be the chief instigator for him to do so.

Milt Moyer told me he was going to back out of the entertainment business. I guess it'll go to nothing.

Tuesday, November 17, 1885. The Bulgarians were again defeated. The Dragoman Pass has been captured by the Servians and the road is now open to Sofia.

Horace will start for West Chester tomorrow. He was 21 in Oct. and now he begins to go to school. It's too bad with this boy. He had chances enough to go to school before but he would not take them. Instead of going to school he led a dissipated life and will probably continue to do so. He associated with the lowest characters, and took delight causing others trouble. He had no respect for his father. He had already done that which would have seated him in jail. He often repented but these were of no force. He borrowed money wherever he could and probably will forget to pay his debts. Rufus too is not doing well. He was full two successive Saturdays and does not seem to have any respect for himself.

Was up at Tyson's Hall. The entertainment is as dead as a mackerel. Milt Moyer and four others were not there. Miss Tyson looked mad the other girls didn't say anything and so we went home without doing anything. Milt had a spat with his sister and got stubborn.

Wednesday, November 18, 1885.   The Servians have won another victory. It seems as if they were sweeping all before them.

The President has appointed a Mr Harrity Postmaster of Phila instead of H S Haidepoper suspended.

The first couple in this part of the country to make use of the new license was Josiah Clemmer Jr and Lydia Ella daughter of Levi Hunsberger. We made our Sauerkraut this evening.

Father is not home yet. He is working entirely too hard and it will do no good.

Thursday, November 19, 1885.   News from the seat of war are so conflicting and so hard to understand that I will have to clip the whole from the news papers. The news today do not say definitely whether there was a Servian or Bulgarian victory.

Horace did not get off to school yesterday. He will start on Monday.

We got a new stove today. It is a range and cost 15 Dolls. It is larger than the old one and is very handsome. The old one was a Niagara no 6 and cost 24 Dolls when new. But it has been that long in use almost.

Mr Moyer and Landis both would like to buy land from Mr Gehman. The one for building and the other for speculation. G. wants 300 an acre along the pike.

Friday, November 20, 1885.   There seems to be some lying about the Eastern wars. Thus far it was all in favor of the Servians. It is also noteworthy that all reports received thus far come from the Servians who did not allow any war correspondents with the forces. The most likely is that the Servians were defeated at Slivnitza by Prince Alexander. That prince was in the thick of the fight all along.

They are working very late in the shop. They have put up a new stove in the shop which looks like a giant.

Greaser thinks he will go away tomorrow, and then I will have to be watchman.

Saturday, November 21, 1885.   It has turned out to be true that the Bulgarians have driven the Servians from their positions and they have been fighting since in which the Bulgarians had the advantage.

Greaser went away this morning on a visit to Donley's. Oswin Kline came up this evening.

We expected Andrew to come up but he did not come. Don't know what's the matter with him.

Have to be watchman tonight in Greaser's place. Got Horace to go along in Uriah Souder came in later on. Got some books from Horace which we looked over.

Mrs Ellis and Mrs Landis were down this evening.

Today we had the first snow of the season. Very little of it reached the ground.

Sunday, November 22, 1885.   Went home about half past seven this morning. Did not sleep a bit till three o'clock. Did not mind it much. Went to Sunday School in the morning. Teachers very scarce.

Did not go to meeting this afternoon.

Was in the hardware store toward evening where we talked over reminiscenses of school days &c.

Greaser did not come home and so I must work another night.

Did not get till about nine o'clock. The night is cold and stormy. Some rain has fallen.

Monday, November 23, 1885.   Got to bank about half past seven. Fought another battle with the Carthuginians without knowing peace had been declared.

Greaser did not get home till this afternoon. I think he is in the bank tonight. This morning snow covered the ground two inches. This will make it very muddy.

The great scandal of the hour is about Squire Beans. He is said to have had unlawful intercourse with the wife of a banjo player living at Telford known as black Philip. Black Philip went to hunt his wife with a shot gun and Beans also is said to have armed himself with the same weapon. There are different stories in regards to the matter. Some believe it, some don't. But the character of the man is not above suspicion. His conduct toward Miss Durrin was inexcusable and I believe Miss Durrin had abundant reason for shunning this monster.

Tuesday, November 24, 1885.   This morning there was a fresh snow on the ground. This evening it commenced snowing again. This is bad weather for building. Ben. Alderfer's house is not yet under roof while the toll house near Lawndale is only one story high. W D Hunsbergers Monsard roof is also in an unfinished state. There is not much more than the frame of it yet. Horace will go tomorrow. The Servians have evacuated all their positions. Widdin has been bombarded and is on fire. Great preparations are under way for the bombardment of Slivnitza. Prince Alexander has given up Eastern Romelia.

Hunsberger's still continue putting their mail into the car. If it can be stopped it will take an end some time.

The B & O is said to have obtained a road to N Y by leasing the Staten Island road and building fourteen miles.

Wednesday, November 25, 1885.   Still snowing at different times. Greasers commenced cleaning in the directors room this afternoon, I am to help tomorrow.

Uriah wants me to go to Quakertown with him on Saturday evening. I have not yet decided to go.

The Servians are still in retreat. The main army is now on Servian territory. King Milan has summoned the Landsturn and at the head of this he will make a final attack on Bulgaria. It is rumored that King Milan will have to resign or rather abdicate. How the tables are turned.

The King of Spain is so seriously ill that he is not expected to live long. The English elections are in progress. So far the Conservatives seem to have made again.

Thursday, November 26, 1885.   Thos. H Hendricks Vice President of the United States died very suddenly yesterday at 4.45 P.M. He was in the 66th year of his age. It is thought that his disease was paralysis. He was sick during the day but the doctor who did not suspect any danger had left him and was down stairs receiving a caller and when he returned he was dead.

The President has directed all flags on all public buildings &c to be at half mast.

King Alfonso XII of Spain died yesterday. He was only 28 yrs old. His disease was consumption aggravated by dysentery. This will leave the throne to a five year old girl. The queen has been appointed Regent. It is thought that attempts will be made to change the government to a republic. The Powers have directed King Milan and Prince Alexander to cease fighting. The Bulgarians carry of the honor of the war. Their loss so far was 200 killed 2000 wounded 250 prisoners.

Friay, November 27, 1885.   The funeral of Vice President Hendricks will be on Tuesday. The President and his Cabinet and also a delegation from the Senate will attend the funeral.

It is now said that Prince Alexander has invaded Servia at the head of 50,000 men.

Mr Gladstone is deeply chagrined at the results of the English elections. The Tories continue to gain in the same ratio as previously reported.

There may be trouble ahead in Spain. The Anarchists have already been at work and the Carlist chiefs are awaiting the commands of Don Carlos. Senor Zorilla has left for Spain. He is a republican. A hundred thousand troops are on duty to overawe a rising.

The weather has cleared off at last. Forgot to mention yesterday we cleared the bank. School were closed. All business and bustle elsewhere. Today was a busy day especially at the feed store. They put the roof on Alderfer's house today.

Funk at Leidy's was married to Miss Koffle last evening. He went to Camden to get married. Last evening they dutch banded them at R E Gerhart's house. Many people couldn't sleep.

Saturday, November 28, 1885.   Heard this morning that Freed and Ida Souder were to be married today. Saw Freed this afternoon in his everyday suit looking about as usual. It made me mad to think that some old gossip had again been at work.

Went up to Quakertown with the 6.40 train. Just when I got on the train I saw Andrew come off. As the train passed I told him I was sorry but could not help it.

When we came up we saw Hartzel at the station and then walked over to the Bush House. We found them all well. We took a walk through the east end of the town. Uriah wanted to go to Shultz but he was not at home. We returned to the house and tried our hand at the piano. Vinie came home and introduced us to a Miss Trumbore Lillie hung about me all evening. She is growing fast and is a very smart little girl.

Uriah went over to the station awhile I had to go over for him and then we went to bed in a room in the third story.

Sunday, November 29, 1885.   We were awakened this morning by a bell that kept ringing on for a quarter of an hour. In the forenoon we were over at the station with Aaron Hartzel. He has a nice large room and is very busy. He was here all night yesterday and today.

After dinner we in company with Miss Vinie and Miss Trumbore took a walk through the town and came back about three o'clock. We sat about the bar-room till supper. Henry has a very nice place. Everything is quiet and is very handy. They all like it very well. They have two maids usually but at present one has left. We took the 6.19 train for home. When I came home I found Andrew had not left. He could not come up last Sunday as he was sick. Heard that Ida Souder was married after all last evening. The band serenaded them afterwards.

Monday, November 30, 1885.   Helped Mr Godshall to assort the samples for buying new books for the Sunday School. He is very tight and wants to save money every where. It is all right enough if the books bought do not come too low a quality.

Slifer's are making preparations to move to Phila where he will go in the Hay business. They are already loading the car with furniture and father & mother were up this evening. Father helped to pack goods. I believe they are glad to go. I'm sorry for them. Bertolet one of the men who gave note was at the bank this afternoon. He scolds about it and said he would not pay unless compelled to.

Tuesday, December 1, 1885.   Today a jury went over the new D & S turnpike road to award damages. Some fellows have heavy claims. It was expected they would have stormy times.

Slifer made his final preparations to leave tomorrow morning. C H Moyer will go into business with him.

Geottler was about today and wanted to sell a picture of Grant engraved for 2.50. He is always in want of money.

The President had decided not to go to Hendrick's funeral because of the danger there may be in his going. Should Pres. Cleveland die, there would be nobody to succeed him. And so it will not do to take risks.

Wednesday, December 2, 1885.   The Czar of Russia has issued an order thanking Maj. Gen. Prince Contacuzene Bulgarian Prime Minister for his services to his country. On the other hand Austria is ready to enter Servia to defend it and these powers may yet find something to quarrel over.

The funeral of Vice President Hendricks took place yesterday in Indianapolis, Ind.

Thursday, December 3, 1885.   Turkish troops are entering Eastern Roumelia as to take possession of the Balkans should Austria enter Servia and Russia enter Bulgaria.

The weather today was clear interupted in the morning by a violent gust of snow which lasted but a short time.

The filling in my tooth came loose today and I went up to Tyson's to have it fixed but Saylor wasn't down today and so I will have to wait a week. It made me impatient at first.

John Newbold and Harvey Souder are building a shop to manufacture cigar boxes and furniture. I have no high opinion of the new firm.

Tomorrow the standing timber in the old woods is to be sold. This will throw some new lots in the market.

Friday, December 4, 1885.   King Theebaw has surrendered to the British. Gen Prendegorst was sent to Rangoon from whence he will be transported to Calcutta. Mandalay the capital of Burmah has been captured.

The Roumelians have refused to dissolve the union and Prince Alexander promised the Roumelians officers to do all he could in defence of the Union. It is my opinion that there will be a muddle out there yet Russia will stand by Bulgaria Austria by Servia and Turkey will try to recover Roumelia.

This afternoon all the standing timber in grandfather's wood on the Chestnut St side was sold in 20 lots amting to $237.50. Williams bought all except 3 lots.

It is said C H Moyer has a notion to go to the city into partnership with

Slifer. If he should do this he will not get at building a house next summer of which he is already tired.

Saturday, December 5, 1885.   This afternoon I got Vol I Grant's Memoirs. The agent sold 15 in this township. I rec'd it more promptly than I expected. The work was published on Dec 1 true to the announcement. The next Vol. is to be ready Mch 1st.

The papers say that so far 325000 of the first volume have been sold. Mrs Grant is said to get 70¢ per vol. This would make her about 455000 Dolls.

At first mother thought I had not asked to subscribe for it but I convinced her.

This evening Uriah Stover came to me at the barber shop and asked me if I had any objections to his staying overnight with Pres. Crouthamel. He had promised father not to go there again and I gave him to understand what he thought of it but still he staid with him.

Sunday, December 6, 1885.   This morning mother found out that Uriah was not in bed last night and I told her not to say anything to father about it. Afterwards I spoke with him how this thing could not go on what he should do and what he must not do, he gave no answer and if he heed it not I think the last of it be not yet heard. He is acting too much as he pleases and this will not hold out.

Uriah brought down grandmother H with the team. Grandfather and Sarah afterwards followed. Uncle Fred's were here this afternoon and evening.

Having been reading Grant all day. Is very interesting speaks plain no fuss and seems to have had no very high opinion of himself at first.

Monday, December 7, 1885.   Made ready for winter this afternoon for surely winter is already here. Today it was very cold down to 14 in the early part of the day.

William is already at work felling trees in the woods and soon none will remain.

Received from Alden the Pilgrim's Progress for which I had sent. The other did not yet arrive.

Tuesday, December 8, 1885.   Made a list of Sunday School books ready with old Herman this morning. He will go to the city tomorrow and buy them himself this time. With John out of the way and myself offering no opposition he can have his own way.

John was grumbling about Lewis Keller's book all morning and so I helped him this afternoon till near five o'clock.

Elwood is sick with pleurisy. Uriah was up this evening.

We were at work lay stone pavement till half past ten o'clock this evening. Ed came down to see it and told us Ellis had a little daughter. I afterwards came up to the store where I saw Ellis smiling and smoking a cigar. I told him I was sorry I had not brought the library Subscription book along. He said 'that's right. Make your hay while the sun shines.' He is not often seen smoking.

Wednesday, December 9, 1885.   Wm H Vanderbilt died suddenly yesterday of paralysis caused by the bursting of a blood vessel at the base of the brain. Mr Vanderbilt was worth about 200,000,000 and was the richest man in America and probably in the world. His income amt'd to 20,000,000 a year. He leaves 8 children. He was in his 65th year.

Was up in the store this evening selling Library Stock. Ellis took a 55 Dollar share. Jonas Landis and Fretz refused to take a share.

The President today sent his message to Congress. It is a very long document and is looked upon in all other respects as a strong document. He is against the further coinage of Silver Dollars. He wants them heavier so as to contain a Dollars worth of silver.

Thursday, December 10, 1885.   Herman was in the city today. He brought the sunday school books along. In the evening he fetched me over to see them. The best ones have very fancy covers and look well on the outside but the inside is very little account. On the average those bought last year by John were better than these for the price. The books cost $18.97 one cent more than in the hands of the treasurer.

Elwood is sick of typhoid fever instead of pleurisy as it was at first said. Uriah goes up every evening. He was no better at last accounts.

Katie was here this evening and it got very late. She forgot to take along the yeast for which she had come.

Friday, December 11, 1885.   The Servians have rejected Prince Alexander peace proposals and fighting will probably commence today. This evening my Byron arrived all right. It is a very pretty book. Have been reading Grant's Memoirs to the exclusion of some necessary work.

Was up to the dentist again yesterday and he says I must come to Quakertown tomorrow afternoon where he has the proper machine to do his work.

Heard today that Chas Godshall was not in his right mind. He was but recently married. His mother was the same way long before she died.

Isaiah Leidy's of Line Lexington is dead. He was suffering from bronchitis.

Saturday, December 12, 1885.   W D Hunsberger is building a steeple or cupola on top of his store to be about twenty four high. It is said this will afford an excellent view in every direction. There was some talk that Charley Schwenck would furnish a telescope but this is propably only bluster.

Got on the 3.03 train for Quakertown. At Telford saw Frank Gerhart the cowboy get off the train. He had on a gray stock hat and a belt around his waist. This was the first time I saw him since he had come back. Went to Saylor who refilled my tooth and made a better job of it, smoother a better polish. He did not bore it as I expected. As I came back Mary & Vinie both popped out their heads of a window each. I went in and up stairs where the room was where I spent a few minutes till it was time for the train.

Sunday, December 13, 1885.   Sunday School in the forenoon. Andrew came up in a team but left after the school was out. He will come up over Christmas.

Miss Moyer came to me and asked about the Literary Society. We must meet somewhere and talk over it. When on my way to Sunday School it commenced to rain a little and it has been raining since almost all day.

Finished reading Grant's Memoirs this afternoon.

Vanderbilt has left $10,000.00 to each of his 8 children. The widow gets the house paintings and stables $500,000 absolutely and 200,000, a year. The house &c after the widows death will go to his son George. About $1,100,000. goes to charities. W.H. son of Cornelius gets 100,000, Cornelius 2,000,000 in addition to other bequests, and the balance is to be equally divided between Cornelius and Wm. K.

Monday, December 14, 1885.   C H Moyer went to the city today. Slifer was up on Saturday. He said he had sold two carloads for this week already.

Father was up at grandfather's this evening. Elwood is a little better but Sallie is not better. Mrs Saml Young is not expected to live over the night. Rev. Mr Clemmers has been sent for to administer the rite of baptism. Six little children must look to a worthless father for support.

Uriah went up to the stocking factory tonight to work.

Tuesday, December 15, 1885.   R. E. Gerhart's little girl died today of scarlet fever. Their remaining child is also sick of the same disease. Goettler's little boy also has scarlet fever.

Got my new suit ready now. The coat fits very well.

Father and three of his men are to go to the city tomorrow to put up a hay cutter for Fred. Uriah is to go along. He never was in the city yet.

Wednesday, December 16, 1885.   Chas. Godshall was at bank today. His Son-in-law, Swartley accompanied him. He is not as crazy as people would make it appear. But he has for a long time been very queer. His is different now, looks like melancholy.

Father and the others went down to the city today and Uriah forgot to take their dinner along. He is the forgetfulest of human beings. He has not his mind on his work or what he is doing. He left him down at Jos Benner's overnight.

All the rest came home. Father won't go down if he dosn't feel well. He is much out of order just now and should take good care of himself.

Thursday, December 17, 1885.   Was up at grandfather's to see the sick folks. Elwood is better. The fever has I think left him and he is only very weak. Sallie was at no time as low as Elwood. She was sleeping most of the time.

We did not expect our folks to come home tonight as they had missed the seven o'clock train but about half past nine they arrived after a good walk up from Lansdale.

John is trying to get the Library business through. There is about $165 raised and the question is how to get the rest. I am getting to be very busy with the books closing the Sunday School, getting or trying to get up the Literary.

Friday, December 18, 1885.   Tomorrow they will all go to the city again. Mother will go too, and she is making preparations to go. Uriah went to work in the stocking factory this evening.

If I am not mistaken the Hoar bill providing for the Presidential succession was passed today in the Senate. The bill provides in case of the death of the President the Sec. of State shall succeed and after him the Sec. of the Treas. and so on. This will keep the same party in power where as it is, the Pres't pro tem of the Senate is a Republican.

Saturday, December 19, 1885.   Mother went to the city with the 1.26 train with Fred.

There was a shooting match over at Tyson's by J W Koffel. All the marksmen in the vicinity were there. Christ Hunsberger did pretty well.

Enos B Slifer talked to me about selling the organ and giving the proceeds to the Library Association. This would make very near enough money. I don't know how this would take, but the organ would soon be ruined anyhow and the money would be well used.

Sunday, December 20, 1885.   Was all alone most of the day. At Sunday School in the afternoon. Sam'l Sell was in my class for the first time since the accident happened to him. There was a good attendance it being the second last time. Harvey Frederick has the most credits in my class and consequently he gets the Pilgrim's Progress I had promised.

Miss Moyer says she has $40 for the Library and more promised. This will almost make the Library a success. A meeting about the literary society is to be held some day next week.

In the evening was with Haynes and took a walk with him. There was singing school tonight. Its a splendid moonlight night.

Monday, December 21, 1885.   Father and Mother came home this evening. Mother must be very tired. She staid at Slifer's till this morning when she came to Mahlon Hunsbergers'. She bought three fine linen handkerchiefs one for Andrew, Uriah and me. Susie got a pair of gloves.

We are now making preparation for a meeting of Library share holders on New Years eve.

I expected to hear from Miss Moyer today in regard to the Literary but did not as Milt did not see her.

Had promised Herman to assort the sunday school books this evening but could not do it as I could not get ready with the writing.

Tuesday, December 22, 1885. Rec'd the transfer from Bean signed and all right. Morris Weil Rufus Souder M L Moyer signed this evening.

Was over at Herman's this evening. Milt Moyer was already there and we assorted the books for the Sunday School.

Tried to buy a new diary today but was too little and he wanted 75¢. Paid 90¢ for this. Ellis says diaries are dead stock. But he had no business to bring me such a little one. Uriah has a xylophone, only a common one though but we played one piece on it.

Wednesday, December 23, 1885. Today was a very warm day for the season. Tried to sell a share Library Stock to Aaron Hartzel but could not do it. He talked as if he would do something when we were at Quakertown. He says he is too poor. And what could I say. It was so there was no use of my denying it. Watched for Jonathan and missed him too. Got W T Hunsberger to sign the paper.

Landis & Co have made a great improvement in their gas lamps at the store. They have placed fancy chimneys over the gas etc.

News came that Ed's had a little daughter yesterday. This is their eighth child.

Thursday, December 24, 1885. There is a raffling match going on at Freeds' this evening.

Have been reading Byron's Don Juan. The poem is more or less licentious. It made me wonder if the poet was really guilty of so many escapades as he mentions. He must have been a wild reckless young fellow.

Belsnikel's are getting rare on Christmas. There were only a few around this evening. I did not see any.

The band is practicing this evening. Anders is here giving lessons.

Friday, December 25, 1885. Passed Christmas Day at home. C G Frick came up with the nine o'clock train. He came over soon after. And was over again this afternoon bringing Uriah with him. He is dressed in a dress coat reaching almost to his knee, and has a gold watch and chain which his father gave him as a Christmas present.

Amelia and Maggie with Penrose were here this afternoon. Little Hannah was here too. She says their little baby's name is 'Saida Irene,' named by Martha.

Have been reading Don Juan most of the time.

Saturday, December 26, 1885.   Andrew came up with the 8.53 train.

Saw Horace this afternoon. He came home the other day. He likes West Chester. What seems very strange he and Rufus seem to be good friends. They tease each other and they can take it all. This is very different from what it used to be. They were always fighting and would scarcely look and talk to each other.

Milt Moyer settled 'Butcher' once this afternoon. The little boy had been teasing him and he went for Milt who told him he would knock him down if he struck. This settled him.

Sunday, December 27, 1885.   This morning Charley Frick came over. They are having company but he could not get anything out of a girl at home so he came over. I had intended to come over to him. Miss Kate and Miss Lillie came in and made a short stay. We had a little music.

This afternoon was the last day of the Sunday School. It was crowded. Every teacher was present who started in the Spring except two who married viz Mary Freed & Miss Musselman. I gave Harvey Frederick who had 1702 credits, the highest in my class, Pilgrims Progress. Some of the others gave theirs Xmas presents. Mine expected some too but I had not thought of it. Os Kline was up today. I got some to sign the Library Transfer.

This evening Miss Landis Becker's girl was here for the first time since I was at home.

Monday, December 28, 1885.   Andrew went home this morning. He bought the diary I refused to take. He will keep a good account of his cash at least. He was down at North Wales week. He will start in next Monday. He will study bookkeeping and grammer with reading and spelling.

Ordered another diary like this this evening.

Mr. Moyer saw Miss Jennie Moyer about the Library this afternoon. I notified several about the meeting on Friday night.

Listened to some war anecdotes by Funk, William and others. Some real good ones.

Got Horace's signature to the Library transfer in the store.

Prince Alexander has returned to Sofia in triumph.

Tuesday, December 29, 1885.   County Superintendent Hoffecker was in bank at noon giving advice about the library. He left a list of books which he thought were suitable. He gave some hints as to buying and said if he were not too busy he would go along to buy the books.

Miss Moyer was here this evening to see me. She has sold 40 Dolls worth of Stock. She will get 5 more and this would make $195. We can sell the other share some where yet.

M. Grevy was yesterday reelected President of France for the term of 7 years.

The Silver Question is much agitated. The West and South are almost solid for silver while the east is for suspension of coinage. The house is believed to be in favor of unlimited coinage.

Wednesday, December 30, 1885. Was up to C S Hunsberger to sell Library Stock this afternoon. He did not refuse and said he might take share but wants to wait. Went up to Moyer & Detweiler's this evening. Milt Benner who had promised to take a half share backed out. The others refused to take a share. And so I could do nothing at all.

The Hunsberger's have published a letter in their defense in the Norristown 'Herald'. They try to shift all the blame on Schwenck and figure as an innocent party.

Not a word do they say about the meanness of depriving Shellenberger of a part of his salary.

Thursday, December 31, 1885. A rainy day followed by clearing colder weather in the evening.

Today the year is up. The bank added a thousand to its surplus making it now 22000.

This evening as I came into the hardware store I saw Enos Frederick beside another man I did not know. Shortly afterward I found out he was handcuffed and the person who had him in charge was constable Rosenberger of Lansdale. He came up with the three o'clock train beastly drunk went out to Steelman's threatened to commit suicide etc. Lizzie Steelman telegraphed for the constable who arrested him after a short resistance in Jonas Hackman's house and handcuffed him. This sobered him. But still he was not ashamed but talked and joked as if nothing had happened. He shook hands with grandfather Souder. Father talked to him awhile. It is sad to see him go away in this way. He went down to Lansdale with the 8 o'clock train.

Day Day 1885   11.06 P.M.   Good bye 1885.

*A newlywed and a runaway husband are killed by trains—
library opens—anarchists and socialists demonstrate in
Chicago—contributes to a history of Franconia—begins
calling on Lillie Zendt—a picnic with the girls—writes to
Jennie Moyer and "Countess Vere de Vere"—begins
reading Dickens—breaks off with Lillie*

1886

Friday, January 1, 1886.   Last night and this morning many shots could be heard more so than has been the custom of late.

Helped to take stock account. Got through about two o'clock, went with father over to the new toll houses. On the way over went over the new pike. It is very rough. It is not stoned over about Holly's J. Derstine's for about a mile. The toll houses are very snug affairs.

H.G. Bilger's were here for supper and overnight. We had a turkey for supper. Went down to the school house to the Library meeting, not nearly all the members were present. Mr. Moyer was made chairman, Dale Barndt & S. R. Swartley Secretaries. I. L. Gehman, Jennie Moyer and myself were appointed a committee to make out a list of books suitable and report at the next meeting. Mr. Moyer, S. R. Swartley and W. F. Goettle on the Constitution. We then adjourned till next Friday evening.

Saturday, January 2, 1886.   Was late at Bank this morning, were very busy today.

Annie Gross was married today to Andrew Benner. Alot of youngsters assembled this evening to band them but they were away.

G. F. Schvenck bo't the Reliance Hotel.

Have been at work on the books this evening, don't have them done yet.

Elwood is worse again or was last evening. I suppose there were too many people in the room with him.

Saw Miss March today. She was in bank with her mother. Mr. Landes says she is an excellent musician. They will move to Reading.

Sunday, January 3, 1886.   Was at home all day except toward evening went to see Elwood who had a relapse a few days ago. When I came up Clara Detweiler was just ready to go away Coz. Katie was also there. I asked how Elwood was and they said he was in a critical condition. I went up and saw him, He talked quite freely. He told me his pulse was 120 the other day and 88 yesterday. He is very weak but I can't believe he is as low now as they make it.

They showed me his arms and legs, These look like a skeleton.

Was at work making out a list of books for the Library. This is tiresome though pleasant at first. Did not get to meeting. Mother wanted me to go but I had no time. F & M went up to grandfather's this evening, Uncle Joe's were also down.

Monday, January 4, 1886.   Weather rainy all day. Roads muddy, warm, little or no frost. Was working on the books all evening. Yesterday was Emperor William's 25th anniversary of his accession to the throne of Prussia.

Prince Alexander and the Turkish envoy have agreed on the union of Bulgaria and Roumelia.

Tuesday, January 5, 1886.   Jonas H. Freed still wants to back out of the Library. He says his father scolded him for doing it and that he said he wouldn't pay it. I can't leave him off as I have nothing to do with it.

Was up to see Elwood this evening. They made a rope in the new bed I helped to carry it up stairs. He is still very weak. Wrote in reply to the Hunsberger letter in the Lansdale Reporter.

Wednesday, January 6, 1886.   Owing to the bad roads many of the directors came very late and so we did not get through till a late hour.

Was over at Moyer's this evening Mr. Gehman was already there. We read over great list of books which will be submitted on Friday evening. I wish the thing was done as I am tired of it.

Thursday, January 7, 1886.   Talked with Milt Moyer awhile this evening. He would like to get away from here west or any thin-settled country. He says there is not much money to be made here. I suppose he wants to get rich quick but he may be disappointed.

Heard Morris Landis is about to marry Miss Emma Hackman a sister to Mary Hackman! Didn't think he'd get married yet.

The other Planing Mill is advertised for sale on Feb.13 by I. T. Borneman Agt. I think it won't sell.

Friday, January 8, 1886.   Weather cold and this evening stormy with some snow.

Becker's have a little girl named Emma born yesterday.

Was at the Library meeting this evening.

Dr. Loux wanted an expensive cyclopedia for a reading room. Appenzeller did not want a book like Gibbon's Rome wanted a cyclopedia books of travel and adventure. Finding their views to coincide Loux and Appenzeller seated themselves together. I spoke against excluding biographies in favor of a cyclopedia and got almost stuck. John smiled a little while I spoke because I told him today I would not speak.

Our committee is now to make a selection of books limited to the amt of money we have subject to the approval of the committee society. We will [meet] at Moyer's on Wednesday eve Gehman will stay here. Next meeting on Thursday night.

Saturday, January 9, 1886.   Last night it was very stormy accompanied by snow. The roads are almost impassable. Gehman and Swartly went home last evening. Becker went out this morning with the wagon but returned and took the sleigh. It doesnt go well with the sleigh as the ground is almost bare at some places.

At the sale of the bank this afternoon Souderton Bank Stock sold at 149½ and 146, Lansdale 199½ and 199, 4% bonds 122½ City Loans 1895. 124½ &c. The above belonged to the estate of Isaac T. Freed with the exception of the Lansdale stock which was sold by Mr. Godshall.

Heard this morning that Haynes nearly lost his life the other day. He slipped and fell on the connecting rod which threw him forward against the cylinder. His clothes were torn but he was unhurt. It frightened him.

Sunday, January 10, 1886.   Was at home reading all day. We let in the black cat for the first time last evening. She did not know how to act. The other two were shot by Milt Moyer last week.

Was up at the station at train time this evening. Saw Haynes. He says it happened on Wed morning. He was walking on the platform, which had been rendered slippery by snow and handed a despatch to the conductor who was standing on the front of the engine when he slipped and fell backward toward the engine against the cylinder. His clothes became entangled with the connecting rod which must have thrown him back upon the platform. The train was stopped but he was not hurt except a gash in the knee. His coat was all torn. He says he can't see how it was that he wasn't all cut up but his time wasn't up. Went to Grandfather's after ward. Sallie has still some fever but Elwood is doing well and the fever has left him.

Monday, January 11, 1886.   Weather very cold. At one place on the Northern Pacific Railroad the cold reached 51° below zero. It was as cold down in Texas as it is here and in Florida the oranges froze.

Today has come the great day which comes around only once each year. Today I am no longer in my teens and am nearing the time when I shall have to act for myself. It is but a short time left to me and as I have so far left many things undone. I should be earnestly employed in preparing myself for the great struggle which I shall have to go through. Many years have I misspent but there is no use in looking back. May God strengthen me to resist any and all temptations which beset mortals.

Tuesday, January 12, 1886.   Today was the coldest of the year so far. It registered zero on our thermoter which is in a protected place. Wolford's which is more exposed registered 9 below. We could not get it warm at the bank till about 10 o'clock although to me it was not unbearable, but John had his overcoat hanging over him all morning. He is balancing Hunsicker's book. Today was the stockholders meeting at the bank. All the old directors were reelected. Not very many votes were cast.

Mrs. H. B. Sell had a stroke of apoplexy on Saturday and her case is quite serious. J. B. Frederick, K. Leatherman, L. G. Barndt were the election officers today. I. G. Gerhast was also down.

Wednesday, January 13, 1886.   Said to have been colder today than yesterday, 4 below zero on our glass.

All the directors were sworn in today except Henry Ruth. A. Thomas came this afternoon, T. S. F. Leidy's discount business is to be stopped that is new notes are to be accepted for old ones and no notes coming due are to withheld from protest on new notes not endorsed by Thos. Leidy.

I. L. Gehman came this afternoon having walked down from Telford. After supper he went over to Moyer's and there made out a list of books. We worked on them till about half past ten. It is past eleven o'clock now. I asked Mr. Gehman to stay again tomorrow evening and I think he will.

Thursday, January 14, 1886.   Mr. Gehman came down with the 515 P.M. train. Went out to the school house at 7.30. We had to write the title of every book on our list on the black board. Dr. Loux made a long speech in favor of a reading. Mr. Moyer and Mr. Gehman spoke against it. Appenzeller spoke in favor but said if our finances would not admit of it it would be better to leave it for a year or so. The vote stood 4 for 4 against and several not voting. Mr. Moyer as chairman decided against. The constitution was then adopted. They then went after our book list, Dr. Loux was called out about this time, Cruden's Concordance was stricken off Fred the Great, Joan of Arc etc. The rest were adopted. The next meeting is on tomorrow two weeks.

Received an invitation to attend a surprise party for Jennie & Annie Moyer from Misses Zendt & Tyson. I must go this time.

Friday, January 15, 1886.   Was up at grandfather's this evening and wrote a letter to Matthias H. Wile to find out about his mother a sister of grandfather. She has been sick for a long time and he has been unable to hear from her. Matthias was in Penna in 1876 and seemed to be a nice young business man and was much more likely to reply than any of the others. Elwood and Sally are both getting better and Elwood is a little stronger, although he is still much like a skeleton.

Got to talking about the shape of the earth and so on when grandfather gave his theory of the earth on the principle of an egg the yolk representing the earth. I did not oppose his opinion.

Saturday, January 16, 1886.   The party which was to have come off at Moyer's this evening was postponed indefinitely. Miss Zendt met me when coming home for dinner and told me none of the gentlemen invited had promised to come except myself. Charley Frick had intended to come up but she says he is sick. The Presidential Succession bill has been passed in the lower house.

The Silver question is uppermost in the minds of Congressmen. Senator Beck a few weeks ago made a speech attacking the President for his attitude on this question. So far as is known the majority in Congress is against suspension.

Sunday, January 17, 1886.   Last night's sleet having rendered the pike quite smooth the little boys were out with sleds and skates this morning. Uriah Souder and I took a few rides with them. Walked down to church with Uriah Rister preached from John IV 13-14 verses. The church members are to meet on Thursday two weeks to consider the advisability of building a church here at Souderton. B. D. Alderfer is back of the scheme.

Was at the singing school this evening. This was the last evening. The boys at the depot were playing dominoes.

Miss Kate Bayard daughter of the Sec. of State was found dead in bed yesterday. She died of heart disease.

Miss Kate Louder daughter of H. N. Louder was married to I. O Roth and Miss Kate Alderfer was married to his brother A. O. Roth yesterday.

Monday, January 18, 1886.   The husband A. O. Roth of Kate Alderfer who were only married on Saturday met with a sad end this afternoon. While driving across the railroad near Sellersville the wreck train without warning came along struck his team and he was instantly killed. Peter Rotes who was with him in the wagon is living but how serious his wounds is not known. His horse is also dead and his wagon broken to pieces. This must be a sad stroke for his young wife who is thus changed into maid wife and widow in two days time.

Enos Frederick today received his trial. He has to furnish bail for $200 and pay her 1.50 a week. In default of bail he was taken back to jail. He did not want to go back but there was no way for him.

Tuesday, January 19, 1886.   The funeral of A. O. Roth killed yesterday is to be on Saturday. Peter Rotes is said to be better though it is not known whether he will recover as he has received internal injuries. The wreck train was on its way from Lansdale to Sellersville and didn't whistle at Telford nor where the accident occurred. They must have been going at a great speed.

Harry Hunsberger had a fainting fit at school. He sank into the snow. The

Doctor says it is heartdisease and that he must leave the band and not work very hard.

A snow fell last night but it is thawing a little by tomorrow sleighing will be splendid.

Wednesday, January 20, 1886.   Mr. Moyer who had asked to have his salary raised is disappointed as we were all reappointed at the present salary.

As sleighing is very good I took Reub's sleigh as our one is not yet taken down and took Amelia and Maggie along. We had a long ride.

We stopped at Derstine's in Telford and staid an hour. Then we started again and came home past ten o'clock. The roads are very good and have all been opened except in a few places. We got into deep snow in one of these places and were glad when we were out.

Thursday, January 21, 1886.   Rainy and the snow is going.

Milton Stover of Dublin was married to Emma K. Moyer of New Britain on Jan 16. This must be Eph Stover's son a second cousin of mine. He has about my age.

It is said that Amos Senft the husband of Laura Dettry and who was operator here a long time has left his wife and has left for parts unknown.

The other evening a speaker from Ohio spoke on Liberty Hall in the interest of the P.O.S. of A. I did not hear him.

The band will play at the Hatfield fair on Saturday evning.

Friday, January 22, 1886.   Parliament was yesterday opened by the Queen in person. She was driven to WestMinster in an open carriage drawn by eight horses.

John spoke to me about his salary this afternoon. He has given up the project of building a house and he is glad he has not commenced it. He is very much displeased that they took no notice to his letters. He asked for 600 dollars. He spoke to Ed about it. Does not know whether he will write another letter to the board. He really takes it as an insult. He feels exactly as I felt two years ago. He thinks my salary is too high in comparison to his. I think if he tries right hard they will raise his salary.

Wrote to Andrew and Frick this evening.

Saturday, January 23, 1886.   Today was young Roth's funeral. He was buried at Gehman's He was twenty four years old. Haynes, Alonzo, and Old Herman were up. It was an immense funeral. The house was crowded every available inch. And a sufficient number to fill the house again were unable to find shelter from the cold and so many went home. The youthful widow who exactly a week ago put on the bridal dress now followed her husband's body to the grave. Little did she think what great things could come to pass in a week.

She was accompanied by her brother Mahlon.

This evening I went over to the station and staid rather late, two o'clock in the morning.

Sunday, January 24, 1886.   Slept all forenoon. Got a lesson from father for my last night's lateness. Mother scolds awful long when she begins. Went to meeting in the afternoon.

Uriah came down in the afternoon and wanted me to go along to Sellersville. We had old Kate in Reuben's sleigh. We overtook Jonathan and Cal near Telford. They had their old white horse who was so slow that we couldn't go faster than a walk all the way. It was biting cold and Uriah who was imperfectly clad suffered from it. We arrived in church about 8 o'clock. We there found Haynes with Miss Jennie Schwenck and Miss Annie Moyer, Milt Moyer was also up alone. Cal has a girl named Flora Scheetz somewhere in Sellersville. I think saw her in church. Dengler preached. Deacons and elders were installed. Elias Shellenberger is one of the former. On the way home Uriah had his muff fixed and we drove ahead and all went well. I had a kind of tooth-ache owing to the cold. We did not see anything of Jonathan and Cal this evening anymore.

Monday, January 25, 1886.   Yesterday Becker's black horse died. Black Bunker as Clinton used to call him. Miller of Sellersville fetched him this afternoon.

This morning John Jake Ben Barndt and others made out it would be well if some one would go down to Leary's and buy secondhand books. He wanted me to go but I didn't do it. So he made ready and went with the 1.25 train. Should he not be able to make the train, I was to meet him at Lansdale at 8.50. I went up to the station and was very glad to see him come and save me a long ride. Because of the inclement weather.

He bought 53 vols. at a cost of 31.77 and had his fare paid. He has an 8 vol. edition of Shakespeare for 8.00. This must be an excellent edition.

Heard this evening that Frank Yocum had left his wife. Old Chas. Daub had an attack of apoplexy several days ago.

Tuesday, January 26, 1886.   Heard today that Frank Yocum who left his wife and child some time ago was killed in the act of boarding a train last night. A telegram arrived here from Summit Missouri where it happened. It is supposed by some that Senft is or was with him.

Having rec'd invitation to a sleighing party to Quakertown I made ready to go. Sleighing was just splendid this morning but it melted so fast that it threatened to disappear before evening. I had to run round for Uriah and mother began to interfere. I was angry and would almost have given it up. We assembled at Freed's some time after four and were ready to start. H. B. Freed and Miss Bergey, Jno Smith, Miss Raudenbach, Haynes, and Jennie Schwenck and Annie, Dean & Kate Will. Ruth and Miss Slifer and myself and Martha. Just before we got to Sellersville Hayne's horse fell and broke the shaft. He was all covered with mud on one side. We stopped at Kerns. We started again and came to Quakertown about half past seven. Milt Moyer had gone up on the train.

We had a fine supper, Music afterwards by Haynes and myself. Dancing afterward with 2 fiddlers. They charged 2 Dolls apiece. We started for home at half past twelve. I was second last Haynes coming after me. My horse being tired could not keep up with the others and we lost them soon. We upset on a snowbank but nobody was hurt. We almost lost our way one time but came all right again. I got to bed at four o'clock. The roads were hardly fit.

Wednesday, January 27, 1886.   The body of Frank Yocum is to be brought home. It is sad to remark the fate of these boys. Milt Souder was killed five years ago in his 18th year. Yocum died the other night a violent death a 1000 miles away. Hartzel is married, 3 children, and is at work at Quakertown. Willie Stover died soon after Milt. Harvey Snyder has had his adventures. Two of them became operators, the other two cigar makers. Milt worked in Fred's mill.

The sleighing is entirely dead.

It is raining this evening. The others got home about three o'clock.

The Salisbury Ministry was yesterday defeated in Parliament. Matilda Hangey died this afternoon after a brief illness of typhoid fever. She was married on or near Christmas.

Thursday, January 28, 1886.   The books from Leary's arrived this morning. Some of the books are nearly new while others are well worn. The total cost of 53 vols. for 32.02. There is a splendid set of Shakespeare in 8 vols among them. Ed made an offer and I think will be accepted to give his Hist. of Montg. Co in exchange for shares.

Matilda Hangey will be buried on Monday.

Frank Yocum will arrive on Saturday and will be buried on Sunday.

Friday, January 29, 1886.   It is not yet known whether the Salisbury ministry will resign. It is thought that Lord Hartington will be called upon to form a coalition Ministry. Prince Bismark made a long speech in the Prussian diet. yesterday on the Polish question. S. D. Yocum was in bank this morning. He said Frank was out there 4 months and 2 weeks at this place. He will arrive some time tomorrow.

The Library association met this evening. Did not go down till late on account of my toothache. J.D. Moyer Pres. Jennie Moyer Sec. Rufus Landes Treas. W.S. Hemsing Librarian, J.G. Appenzeller and I.L. Gehman Managers were the officers elected. A committee was appointed to buy the remaining books. The book case was awarded to father for 15 cash and one share of stock.

Saturday, January 30, 1886. The Salisbury Ministry has resigned and the Queen has summoned Mr. Gladstone for consultation and probably to form a Government.

Last night Haynes heard a message that Yocum's body started at St. Louis last evening. This evening I was up there and he caught up another message as follows. "Frank's body will come over the B&O utterly impossible to get him up before Monday. Adams Express Co will hand over the remains to 9th & Green instantly upon its arrival. I am going home this evening." 'Harry'.

Arrangements have been made to hold the funeral tomorrow but what will be done now I do not know. Slifer's came up this evening.

It was snowing nearly all day, very muddy. My toothache or neuralgia has abated.

Sunday, January 31, 1886. Mrs. Samuel Young died today. She had been languishing for a long time but had been gradually growing weaker.

Was up to grandfather's to get Sallie and Elwood's signatures on the Library transfer. They were over at Drey's for dinner. Yesterday they worked up their hog yet. They received a reply to my letter to Matt H. Wile written by Mina Wile wife of David Wile. Anna Wile sister to grandfather has been confined to her room (i.e. consumption) for two years and is unable to help herself not even comb her hair. She wants pictures of my grandparents. Isaac Wile is in Indiana, Danl H. Wile is in Michigan where he lives on a small farm. Benj. Wile Jr. is working at his brother Matt's store and is not in good health.

Mary Shellenberger was there on a visit. W.B. Slifer and wife and Miss Ellie Slifer were here for supper. They went down with the train this evening.

Monday, February 1, 1886. Frank Yocum's body arrived on the fast line at 10 o'clock or thereabouts. It is said Howard went to Phila. to hunt him and so he was not at home when the corpse arrived. Had he been at home he would without doubt have been buried with Matilda Hangey. Under this impression I walked down to the church along with many others who went for the same reason. Revs. Dengler & Horning conducted the service. She was 30 yrs. and 5 mos old at the time of her death. She was married on Christmas to a man named Kelley. It was announced that Yocum would be buried tomorrow. Many people are going up to see him. He is said to be much mangled and scarely recognizable.

This evening the comittee met at Moyer's and enlarged the list of books. They were Moyer, Swartley, Appenzeller, Miss Moyer and myself. Gehman was not present.

Tuesday, February 2, 1886. This morning at ten o'clock the funeral procession of Frank Yocum passed through here. I did not get to see him. Mr. Landes was up last evening. He could not recognize him. Howard says he would not know him except for his ring. The whole expense for bringing in the remains was in the neighborhood of 60 Dollars. The verdict of the jury was that he was accidently killed near station between mile posts 52 and 53. The upper part of his head was cut off and a cloth was laid over it to hide it from view. The eyes were not visible. One arm is supposed to be cut off. He was dressed in his best suit including overcoat.

Mr. Landes went over to Blooming Glen to buy a sleigh. It is rumored that A.B. Godshall wants to open a store at Midway shortly. M.B.Bergey's stocking factory was entered and some stockings stolen.

Wednesday, February 3, 1886.   Weather colder, has been snowing all day, no drifting.

Jacob Nase left Becker's on Saturday. Do not know yet whether he gets a new baker or not.

The family of Samuel Young is to be broken up tomorrow. His wife will be buried tomorrow. H.G. Barnes will take two of his boys. Mrs. Hannah Fritz will take another. What will be done with the remaining one I am not informed. Sam is to be pitied. He will have to leave his home his children scattered his wife dead. Dreary outlook.

Thursday, February 4, 1886.   The great snow storm of yesterday and last night has ended. A north wind came up today and the snow has drifted very much. Many roads are blocked up.

Mrs. Samuel Young was buried today. Hen. Barnes' will take two of the little boys till they can get a place.

John Souder and family were on their way home but as the train was late it being too late for them to go home they came back here and will stay till tomorrow. They have three children.

Friday, February 5, 1886.   Today the new bank examiner was here. His name is Robert E. James. He is, as Jno Ruth said a very handsome man. He has a commanding figure with black hair fast turning into gray. Long jet black whiskers and a moustache. His finely formed soft hands show that he never did any hard work. He arrived with the nine o'clock train and left at three. His smile is like that of Dr. Slifer. His method of counting money show that he had not been employed by a bank. He is doing well for the time he is at it.

Saturday, February 6, 1886.   No Library meeting last evening because of the severe weather. Swartley had a notion to go today and buy the books. But he did not go.

It is said Charley Frick is up. I have not seen him. Andrew came this afternoon. They moved to North Wales last week. He likes the school. Brunner has 43 scholars. He has an assistant named Miss Steoer. He has seven in the bookkeeping class. The only ones remaining of the time I went are Carrie Shearer, Charley Stetson and Grant Sexton.

Sunday, February 7, 1886.   Charley Frick did not come over today. I saw him this evening when the train went down. He said he felt too bad to come over. Took a sleigh ride this afternoon with Andrew. We got into deep snow once. Father & Mother were up at grandfather's with the sleigh.

Allie Slifer came up from the city last evening and brought me a nice silk scarf which mother had ordered. She evidently came for a sleigh ride. Every body seemed to be out today sleighing. The weather was not very cold. But the snow is not quite settled. Alice Hendricks was up from Lansdale. She went down this evening.

Monday, February 8, 1886.   The snow is fast giving way. The roads will become very bad if this kind of weather continues. For at many places the snow is so deep that it will lie for weeks yet. Many roads are not open. Many will soon have no snow at all.

Mr. Seidel a farmer made an assignment last week. Much money will be lost by him. He seems to owe everybody. He is in at the bank for about 1500. The endorsers will probably pay it all though it is hard enough for him. M. Fox was badly injured by falling out of or upsetting in his sleigh on Saturday.

A sleighing party started off from here this evening for Skippack. Susie and Becker's went along and I hope they are satisfied now. Ulysses Hunsberger and others are the leaders.

Tuesday, February 9, 1886.   The sleighing party did not return till this morning at halfpast five. There were about 25 of them in two sleds. Weather is still warmer and snow is getting scarce through here.

I have been mending some the books of the Library this afternoon.

There was a riot out in Washington Territory against the Chinese. These were placed on a vessel. The militia let no one depart who did not do so willingly. It came to a crisis and the soldiers had to fire and one man was killed and three wounded.

There was a great riot in London yesterday. 15000 people assembled in Trafalgar Square and the Socialists taking them in hand led them through the streets and great damage was done to property. The police were powerless. The rioters had it all their own way.

Wednesday, February 10, 1886.   Gen. Hancock died suddenly yesterday on Governor's Island in the sixty-second year of his age.

There was another riot in Trafalgar Square London yesterday. But the police suceeded in dispersing the roughs. We received a report from the Topton Nat'l Bank of Feb. 1-86. It shows Bills Dis. 54000, Dept 24000, Undivided profits 1683. I think the Deposits are very low for the time the bank is open. The statement was printed on very fancy slips lithographed with an engraving in front.

The board of managers and book committee met this evening in the school house. It was decided to buy Chambers Encyclopedia, coal etc. was to be bought. John Swartley will go down on Saturday and buy the books. Took Gehman along home to stay over night.

Thursday, February 11, 1886.   Gen. Hancock will be buried in Norristown on Saturday.

Very windy and stormy all day. Rain.

They are at work on the book case in the shop.

These sleighers are still making a fuss about big and little and they will never stop. The young folks of the town are dividing off into classes each generally envying the others.

Have decided to stop correspondence with the Lansdale Reporter. Am tired of it and my time would be too much taken up by it.

It is said the railroad bridge at Sellersville has been rendered unsafe by the weather. Trains were delayed this evening.

Friday, February 12, 1886.   The weather continued to be very damp and moist rainy a little at intervals.

They are now well at work on the book case out in the shop. Was out this afternoon.

John & Swartley will go down tomorrow to buy the books. On Sunday is Valentine's Day so they will have to be sent tomorrow.

Saturday, February 13, 1886.   At last it has cleared off. It was foggy and raining all day. The water must have done great damage. The trestles at the Sellersville bridge were again washed out last night. Trains were not on time. The tracks were full of cars and engines this forenoon.

Swartley and John went down to buy the books today. John did not want to go on account of the weather. They bought the books at Perkin Pine & Higgins, 115 vols for 100 Dolls. Wanamaker was their closest competitor. They did not buy the encyclopedia. They report Chamber's for 1667 the best. Dr. Loux was here this evening and he insists Appleton's is the best. I wish the matter were settled.

Got a valentine from Phila. from F I suppose. Moyer's sash factory was not sold today. It was bid up to 2475 by Rosenberger of Lansdale.

Sunday, February 14, 1886.   Gen. Hancock was buried at Norristown yesterday.

Went to meeting this afternoon. Rev. Mack a brother of John Mack preached on the parable of the Prodigal Son. He is an excellent talker. I do not remember hearing him before. Many people have a great liking for him. The house was full and benches were brought in which were also filled.

Amelia and Maggie came down this evening to play and sing. I accompanied them home.

This was like a Spring day except the mud in the roads.

Monday, February 15, 1886. Ex. Gov. Seymour who died the other day will be buried tomorrow. He ran against Grant for President in 1868.

The weather today was pleasant. The book case is now nearing completion. Was out in the shop this afternoon and evening and helped a little.

It's going to be splendid. John said something about opening on Friday evening. I don't believe the books will all be here by that time.

Tuesday, February 16, 1886. Colder weather.

Fisher had a horse sale today and Becker bought a black horse four years old for 170 dollars.

Today is election day. There are two candidates for tax collector, six for school director two to be elected and two for Justice of the Peace.

For the latter, A. H. Gehman and M.D. Zendt are the candidates. For school directors, H. R. Bergey, Jos. F. Derstein, J. S. Rosenberger, Jno. H. Bergey Henry D. Wile and Geo. Rittenhouse. For collector, Dan Kratz, Dan E. Oberholtzer. There isn't much excitement here this time. It is supposed that this election will decide for six months school.

Was out in shop and helped a little on the book case till late this evening. Grandfather and Grandmother Hemsing had their pictures taken today.

Wednesday, February 17, 1886. At the election yesterday Dan Kratz received only 40 votes. D. E. Oberholtzer was elected Collector of Taxes, H. R. Bergey and Geo. Rittenhouse School Directors. Just the ones who are opposed to more than five mos. school. Joe Derstein was only 3 votes behind Rittenhouse. M.D. Zendt was 40 votes behind for Justice of the Peace, Abner Gehman being elected.

There were 388 votes polled.

One of these big engines came of the track up here at Ed's switch. They considerable trouble to get him on again which was done by the aid of another engine.

Stained the book case this afternoon and evening. It is now ready to take to the schoolhouse. Mother was out this evening to see it.

Thursday, February 18, 1886. Saw Jno Smith about painting a panel for the bookcase. He told me how Freed talked about our party to Quakertown. He swore and blasphemed fearful. Mentioned Smith and one fellow in town here as especial objects of his wrath. These things made me mad this afternoon. I have reason to suppose that I am the fellow he wants to see. I am sure Freed hurts himself in his business about this.

Will Haynes has been suspended for a week on account of a blunder made by a substitute last Sunday evening.

Mrs. Isaac R. Hartzel, (Kate Freed) died today. She had been suffering for a long time. She will be buried on Tuesday.

Friday, February 19, 1886.   Received today from Wm. D. Heebner 12 or 13 books containing reports of the different State Departments. One being Pamphlet Laws for 1885 and several others which will be of great value to the Library. They cost us nothing but the freight.

We expect to get some from I. Newton Evans yet. Received intelligence that the books would be forwarded in a few days from Perkinpine & Higgins. The bookcase was taken down to the school house this evening.

E. H. Souder and A. Lower have been serving as Jurors in the U.S. Court in Phila. The damage jury for the claimants against the Pike Co. was heard witnesses in the hall this afternoon. J. M. Shellenberger represented the Claimants and Rob't Yardely the Pike Co.

Saturday, February 20, 1886.   Another cold wave has reached us. The cold is not so intense as it has been this winter but there is a very sharp wind.

Mr. Saml Young had his sale today. His creditors were allowed to buy and so most things brought good prices.

Cousin Preston is down from Quakertown. Was sitting in Ed's office reading some war papers. One that struck me most was an editorial comment on the battle of Pittsburg Landing or Shiloh in which Grant Halleck and Buell were severely criticised. The latter though conceding him great ability and supposing the battle would not have been so disastrous had he been there in person. Yet blaming him for not being present in person. The second for his slowness in relieving Grant, and Grant for being "shamefully surprised" charging him with being asleep 16 miles from the field of battle. With criminal neglect for allowing a superior force to march on him unmolested. And that should he not be relieved from these charges he should be promptly led to execution. As his blood could be only though inadequate atonement for the blood shed.

Sunday, February 21, 1886.   Was at home all day reading Prescott's Conquest of Peru and Jules Verne's Around the World in 80 Days which I finished.

Preston was here for supper, after supper they looked at my books. Henry and Irwin had come down for him. He had intended to go home today but will not go till tomorrow.

Uriah was locked out again tonight.

Monday, February 22, 1886.   Today the second coat of varnish was put on the book case. The books did not come as we expected. We covered some of the old books with paper. Appenzeller, Miss Moyer Swartley Gehman and Mr. Moyer were there. It was decided to try and get the Rev. Mr. Sheif to lecture on "Up the Rhine", for the benefit of the Library.

W. D. Hunsberger would like to rent us a room on the third story at reasonable rates as he says. This would be well were the rates really reasonable. But it is not certain whether the book case could be got up there.

We had our pump fixed up again today. The water had had a disagreeable taste.

Tuesday, February 23, 1886.   Recommenced writing to Lansdale again today.

Wrote to J Wanamaker for Book News for one year. It is expected that tomorrow morning the greater portion of the books will arrive. I have quite a bad cold at present, am coughing all the time. Many persons are in the same condition.

Wednesday, February 24, 1886.   A portion of the books were received today. John and myself took them to the schoolhouse where Miss Moyer was still sweeping. The books are splendidly bound. A few being gilt tops and uncut edges. In this evening we went out to take a look at the books. I did not get home till half past ten.

Thursday, February 25, 1886.   My cold has grown worse till this evening I can hardly talk.

There is a great change in the weather. It was raining all day and it seems not to be over yet.

Made a triplicate key for the Library bookcase this afternoon.

Uriah Souder was in the city this week. He was at the Medical College with Jonathan Umsted was present at several lectures.

Rec'd a letter from Ed Donley this evening. He is a member of the Frenchtown Band. He says nothing about coming over.

Friday, February 26, 1886.   There was to have been a meeting of the board of managers in the school house this evening. But owing to the high wind nobody came. So we looked at the books again. The meeting was called to consider about the Sheif lectures.

I took Ten Nights in a Bar Room along and read a part this evening.

Saturday, February 27, 1886.   This evening I discovered that mother had bought a set of knives forks and spoons. She was trying to hide them from me but I heard them rattle as she was showing them to Miss Landis.

Knowing that a party was to come off here this evening I cleared out as soon as I could. About half past eight the party passed the store. Was over at the station, Haynes wanted to go down. So a quarter after nine Haynes, Jonathan, Auchey and myself came down. We gave them some songs and staid about 15 min. There were the Hunsberger boys the Price boys and the Blank boys, Miss Landis Hunsicker, Schwayer, Daub, Norah Hunsberger. About half past eleven Rufus and myself came down again. This broke up the party. The girls stopped playing immediately and made ready to depart. Ulysses H. staid awhile yet and Rufus and he didn't leave till the girls retired.

Sunday, February 28, 1886. Lay around sleeping all morning. Was reading Conquest of Peru part of the time. After dinner Little Emma and Clinton came over. Father and mother went up to Uncle Wm's. Miss Emma Landis (Becker's girl) came over. Afterwards Martha and little Eddie, and finally Katie Becker. After playing for them awhile I went up the street and went into the Hardware store where Mahlon Alderfer and Saml Alderfer with Morris Weil were together.

About half past seven there was a loud knock at the door which I opened and there stood Wm. Blank asking for Miss Daub. Rufus was at Becker's door at the same time. I told him where she was and away they went. They are now in the front room with the exception of Blank whose place is taken by Jonathan Hunsberger. He won't come here again. If these fellows only know what girls they had they'd be ashamed of them.

Monday, March 1, 1886. Today was very cold and this evening almost blew a blizzard. We were again to meet in the school house but again nobody came. So we stamped the books.

Received March number of Book News with an excellent portrait Edgar A. Poe.

Tuesday, March 2, 1886. The President has sent a long message to the Senator refusing to deliver to the Senate papers on file in the departments relating to suspensions from office. He takes the ground that they are his own papers. And that he alone was responsible for removals and that it was none of the Senate's business. It was small politics that asked such a thing from the President.

Was up in W.D. Hunsberger's steeple for the first time. The wind blew and whistled around there that was almost frightful.

We were down at the school house again posting the rules and regulations in the books.

Wednesday, March 3, 1886. The weather was on the whole warmer than yesterday though the wind did not yet leave off.

Bought a blank book today for the Library Ass'n for use as a Librarian's Record. Grandfather S came down this evening after supper and made father a very handsome present of a thousand dollars. Father was very grateful for it. He had intended reducing his load that am't but the good man was too quick for him. So much the better.

Was out at the school house again this evening. Classified the books and covered some. Rufus Landis was out. Milt Moyer too reading.

Thursday, March 4, 1886.   A great surgical operation was performed today on Mrs. Abe Snyder who has for three years not left her room, assisted by Drs. Wickert, Slifer and B Jonathan Umsted was also present.

It was done at her earnest desire. Loux told my mother that 30 out of a 100 died under the treatment. This was so far magnified by other people as to stand 1 successful out of a 1000. The multiplication table was applied pretty vigorously in this case.

Mr. Jacob G. Moyer a brother of Abe has taken Jno Smiths place as carriage painter. Smith remains to finish the work he has begun.

The wind has not subsided yet. It is now a week since it commensed. Old persons say they can not remember another such a long continuance.

Glued the book covers in the Library this evening.

Friday, March 5, 1886.   The Library was opened this evening. Got everything ready in a hurry before evening. The Chamber's Encyclopedia and three other books arrived today. Took the lamps over from the meeting house and fixed them in the school house. Hardly were the seven o'clock up than quite a crowd came all at once. The whole number of books that went out was 25. The total taken in from outsiders was 17 cts. A good start I think. We had a meeting of the board of managers on account of several matters.

Saturday, March 6, 1886.   This morning on my way to bank as I stopped in at Godshall's to return a key he prevailed on me to come in and listen to the plans of two Russians as they are called (Germans in reality) to form a syndicate to raise money for the poor farmers in Lansds who are compelled to pay as high as 24 per cent interest. For this purpose they have formed a company called the German Mennonite Loan & Trust Association. Capital 100,000, who will guarantee payment of all loans made through. They will pay 6% and loan at 7%. To me the plan seems feasible and good. But there are many that are very skeptical about it. The gentlemen are men of good address well dressed and come well recommended.

The minstrel show came off this evening. About 60 present.

Sunday, March 7, 1886.   Was reading "Last Days of Pompeii" almost all day. Have nearly finished it.

Was at meeting this afternoon. The house was packed. Rev. Jacob Moyer preached.

Mrs. Abe Snyder died this afternoon. Her case was hopeless.

Johnson the murderer of Sharpless has been found guilty of murder in the first degree.

It is probable father will convert the porch on the second floor into a room. This will be a good one for me and I should like it.

Aunt Sarah Sallie and Elwood were here this evening.

S. caught up a fellow again on the way home from Telford.

Monday, March 8, 1886.   Father did not lay a lien on Loux's property it seems as this was the last day to do so. He promised to pay him in April but he promises everything and will not be able to fulfill it. I think father will repent his benity.

Rec'd a picture of grandfather and grandmother Hemsing. Was up and wrote a letter sending a pair to Ohio. Mary Shellenberger also brought Susie's down.

She looks _____. Finished Last Days of Pompeii today. I think it is very good.

Tuesday, March 9, 1886.   The bank has again and finally won the Geisinger case in the Supreme Court after seven years of litigation. Don't know how much is left yet.

It will probably go hard with Curtis Gerhart in a short time. They can't go on very long any more at this rate and the bank will very likely push its judgment before long.

Mother is again abed sick. She is undergoing a course of treatment from the doctors. Grandmother comes down almost every afternoon to help pass the time.

Wednesday, March 10, 1886.   Grandmother H was here today. Uriah brot her down. They were upstairs all day.

The bank this afternoon took out a writ against Curtis Gerhart. The wonder is that it happened not before. They have been doing the worst kind of business all along which can never hold out. Jake was opposed to pushing them without first seeing. It seems so cold blooded he thinks. Isaac Gerhart and Jno S. Ruth went over to Doylestown today. The latter thought all fun. They suspect nothing at all. They sent money over twice today.

Thursday, March 11, 1886.   Have not yet heard whether the gun went off over at Fair Hill or not. I suppose it must however.

Eph F. Miller one of the endorsers of Seidel's notes came and who is also an endorser for C.G. came over today and fixed up one of Seidel's notes paying a hundred dollars on it and bringing a new note of 85 endorsed by W. H. Curtis. Jake told him it probably would not pass but he believed it was all right. Seidel refused to help him in anything. It is really too hard on these poor fellows that everything should slip beneath their feet.

Mother is still upstairs. It is a little lonely for her up there. Ed was down this evening.

Friday, March 12, 1886.   The crash did not come off till today. Have not heard anything yet.

The weather was cloudy. There was a slight rain fall.

Fixed up my flute this afternoon.

Were down at the school house making out a list of the Books for the printer.

Saturday, March 13, 1886.   The weather today was very threatening at least so it seemed to me for I took an unusual interest in the matter. The weather luckily was fair and we had a full house, another thing as unexpected.

At first I was afraid we could not make our expense but they continued to pour in till there were 16 Dollars in tickets sold.

Myself was the ticket agent, Rev. Mr. Sheif the lecturer had 75 views exhibited by means of a stereoscope.

C.G. Frick and Andrew were among the audience.

Mr. Jonas H. Freed had Susie up. This is the sixth young man for her inside of a year.

Sunday, March 14, 1886.   The am't taken in last evening was 16.05. Of this the Library makes half or somewhat over eight dollars.

Took Andrew along down to the school house and showed him the Library this morning.

Charley Frick did not call at all and I did not go over.

Andrew went down with this evening's train as he intends to go to the city tomorrow morning.

Monday, March 15, 1886.   The weather today was fair like a spring day.

The crash at Curtis Gerharts took place on Saturday afternoon.

Tuesday, March 16, 1886.   Today was another nice day. It creates quite a different feeling when spring approaches.

This evening there is a ball on Liberty Hall. It is said that Annie Moyer went to the city on purpose to buy a bouquet for this evening.

Had little Clintie fantastically dressed up in colored carpet rags and had him to act the part of a monkey which he was much pleased to do.

Wednesday, March 17, 1886. Mr. Curtis was over today to see the board. He is much affected. He would have his endorsers favored. He does not blame the bank for what has been done.

A sheriff sale has been advertised for store goods. Jno. S. Ruth is the asignee for the real estate.

The board had very much business today. We did not get done till five o'clock this afternoon.

Mrs. Don Bilger and her children with Sarah Amelia and Sallie were down this evening.

Thursday, March 18, 1886. We will receive the remainder of the books tomorrow excepting two: Hood's Up the Rhine & Southey's Nelson, which can not be obtained. I should have been doing much work but I did not get at it. Have been reading Cooper's Pioneer's and wanted to get through before tomorrow evening. So I sat up till midnight and read it through.

John Smith is sick I hear. His trouble is in the throat and is the effect of his trade. He stopped it seems in high time.

S.D. Hunsberger told Jake they were going to fight the bank on their judgment so as to cause an equal division. They are in for about 5 or 600 Dollars says rumor.

Friday, March 19, 1886. Felt very bad all day. Vomited a little in the afternoon. Took a good dose of Castor Oil this evening. Geo. Eaton also made an assignment of his property. The assignees are Lee M. Fluck and Gideon Appenzeller. Enos Cope will probably be the next man.

The remainder of the books arrived this morning all right.

Saturday, March 20, 1886. When I got up this morning I had no idea it was half past seven. Mother who had an idea that I was sick did not call me till then. The fact is I had lain half awake, suffering with a headache during a large part of the night hearing the rain pour and fancying I was lying in all sorts of shapes on a mountain of pillows. Had settled down in some comfort however and this was why I slept so late. I did not have much of an appetite yet. When I came to bank I found Mr. Landis feeling like an old rag too and so we dropped taking an account of the discount which we had set apart for today.

I hear that great distress results to the poor people from whom Curtis Gerhart had borrowed money who must now lose every cent.

Commenced reading Tom Brown at Oxford this afternoon.

Sunday, March 21, 1886. Continued reading Tom Brown at Oxford all forenoon. Grandfather H came down for the team and found father engaged in sharpening razors. Now if there is anything he takes a special pride in it is his ability to sharpen razors. He talked about his own good razor and excellent whet stone (which by the way he assured father were to be left to a descendant of the same name). So he took charge of the razors whose he ascertains by running them over his thumbnails that makes me shudder to look on.

Uncle Cornel's came down on a visit, C is in a very bad way. Sick nearly all the time and quite worn out. They will move on Tuesday a week.

Maggie was here for supper. Amelia brought down Cousin Katie and a sprig of a fellow Rickert a son of Valentine. They had rather a dull evening of it I was afraid, I'm such a dunce to entertain others.

Monday, March 22, 1886.   Today the sheriff sale at Curtis Gerhart's was to have come off. But this morning Enos Cope was sent over by Curtis to have it stopped as they were selling very fast so. But no one (to represent the Bk) from here went over. I.G.G. was over probably.

Clintie came over here for the first time with pants on. He is entirely too small for them.

Tuesday, March 23, 1886.   It used to be the fashion to wear them but I have seen him without it. Little Clintie came.

Wednesday, March 24, 1886.   This morning the barn of John Mininger was burned down while he was eating his breakfast. Two horses and eleven cows were burned.

Bought a new one horse bed for my prospective room. Mother is making comforts and quilts. And tomorrow what is called as a quilting is to come off.

Mr. Landes today asked the board to allow him to take in his son Rufus into the bank during the vacation. It was omitted and will be attended to next week.

Tomorrow is the last day of school.

Were over at Bakers with rags for the carpet in my room. Grandfather had old Jin killed today. She was over 20 yrs. old. She was long his favorite horse.

Thursday, March 25, 1886.   The address of Rev. H.G. Appenzeller son of Gideon Appenzeller who is a missionary in Korea is Seoul Korea.

The quilting party came off today. Grandmother, Mrs. Fred, Cousin Kate and Miss Landis were here and made a quilt and comfort for my bed.

Today was the last day of school. Most of them are glad of it.

Godshall is having his house painted.

C.H. Moyer's are getting ready to move into the barn preparatory to having two houses built.

Friday, March 26, 1886.   Jno. D. Souder of near Telford is writing a history of Franconia Township. So he wrote to Mr. Godshall for information about the Post Office the Hotel and the town in general. G. handed the letter to me and now I am to furnish the information.

Am deeply interested in Tom Brown at Oxford. I think it an excellent book for young men to read.

The great railroad strike on the Gould system in the States of Missouri Arkansas Kansas and Texas is assuming a serious aspect. The governors of the above States have each issued a proclamation warning all persons not to interfere with railway traffic.

Saturday, March 27, 1886.   Becker's girl has left them again so that they are in a new trouble. Finished Tom Brown today. Bismarck warned the Reichstag yesterday that if they would obstruct the countrys business they might be dissolved.

The weather was quite disagreeable today raining and turning to snow and the ground is now all white with snow.

The papers are now full of the Labor troubles throughout the country. Mr. Powderly Grand Master Workman of the Knights of Labor was out west trying to effect a settlement of the question. But Vice Pres. Hoxie would not listen to him and now he is in New York on the same errand.

Sunday, March 28, 1886.   F & M with grandfathers were over to Benj Fredericks today. Was in meeting this afternoon. Bomberger preached. The house was full. Took a walk with Uriah Souder up the railroad.

Was occupied most of the time in making clippings from the newspaper. This evening Sam and myself took a census of the town with the following result

No. of Dwelling houses	120
Population	611

The snow of last evening has all disappeared.

Monday, March 29, 1886.   Rainy disagreeable weather. The snow and rain have rendered the roads slushy.

 An end has been put to the Labor troubles it is to be hoped by referring the matter to arbitration. Mr. Powderly repeatedly wrote to Jay Gould to above effect but without success. So last evening he went to the latter's house. The result of the meeting was an order from Gould to employ all the Knights except such as had committed violence. Mr. Powderly is an able leader who has moderate opinions who is the opposite of such men as Martin Irons who ordered the present strike.

In Belgium the situation is more serious. There the military are constantly firing on the mob who are armed. They have already destroyed property to an immense amount.

Tuesday, March 30, 1886.   The rain continues. This is bad on the roads which were very good so far.

The great strike continues as Gould has refused to arbitrate. The order had been given for the men to resume work but on receiving news to this effect it was rescinded. It is only stubbornness in Gould or else it is done for speculation as Ed says.

John had trouble with Hunsicker's book again till he had it done. It had run over 3 mos. again. Now he will bal every mo.

Mother is very anxious that I should not go away from home. She will never let me do so. She thinks Rufus Landes is to take the place of one of us.

Wednesday, March 31, 1886.   It is now expected that the strike will soon be settled, Mr. Hoxie has consented to arbitration.

It rained hard this afternoon. The air is warm and unpleasant. Goettler is making the list of books for the Library. After making innumerable corrections it is quite a decent sheet.

This afternoon was Rufus Landes first day in bank. He got through the same way as I did the first few days.

We were rushed a little today and had a taste of April. We did not get out till after five o'clock.

Thursday, April 1, 1886.   A very fine day.

This afternoon they rushed on us again. We got through right well however. Rufus was not in except this morning.

Today Jesse Kline's moved away from the toll gate, Zuschnit taking their place.

Uncle Cornelius moved today also.

Saw John Smith this afternoon. He has been sick. He is troubled with a sore throat. He looks pale and haggard.

The grass beginning to turn green after the warm rain. The ground dried off rapidly today. Last nights heavy rain had rendered the roads bad.

Friday, April 2, 1886.   About 28 books went out from the Library this evening. There was to have been a stockholder's meeting this evening and a Librarian elected. But only a few members waited for the election and I was unanimously re-elected.

I worked all afternoon at covering books. And after the Library was closed I spent an hour and a half in the same way. I am determined to stop the freedom in which some members helped themselves in regard to the books. I did not open this evening till the time appointed and did not allow them to meddle with the books.

Saturday, April 3, 1886.   We were busier in bank yesterday than today. Yet we did not balance so well as yesterday, I can't see how it is. Some one or all of us are too careless or that is perhaps putting it too strong.

I felt tired out this afternoon. I did not have a full night's sleep last night and with the constant hustle it made me tired.

The labor troubles in the west still remain unsettled but trains are running on the Missouri Pacific Road. The strikers seem to have got the worst of it this time.

Sunday, April 4, 1886. This morning when I came down I was surprised to find the ground covered with snow. The fall had been about four inches and it continued to snow a little at intervals during the day.

Slept most of the forenoon. Was reading Richard Grant White's England Without and Within. Read about 90 pages today.

The situation in the East is again serious. Prince Alexander claims his governorship of Eastern Roumelia is for life while Russia contends it is only for 5 years. Greece also is impatient to fight and it is feared that war is imminent. A war which draw all the larger powers into the struggle.

Monday, April 5, 1886. Today was a cold rainy stormy day.

Wm. Trumbore, who works on the gravel train and boards at Funks' whose nephew he is, had his arm fractured at the wrist while coupling a car. The doctor thinks it will come all right again. Beckers have determined to get Jake Nase again. Jake visited them yesterday. We heard a great noise on this side of talking and laughing. Little innocently mentioned the fact that they were drinking whiskey.

After supper we heard a great din in the bakeroom and made out they were dancing. We could hear them sing. This morning Clintie informed mother that Jake was '**krank**' in the head and in the belly, that he had '**bauchweh**' and he '**hutz**'.

This is the way they are drawing him in. There was a fight on Saturday between some strikers who had ambushed a train and deputy sheriffs. One officer was killed and two wounded. One dead striker has been found and two are known to be wounded. The militia have been called out.

Tuesday, April 6, 1886. Very stormy and rain, the wind and rain have ceased this evening but the weather is not yet settled. B.S. Johnson has made an assignment. W.H.Keeler and J.H. Metzger both connected with Johnson have also kicked the bucket. The bank will very likely lose money through these scamps again.

Mother is out of patience with the cat who she suspects has killed a robin. I found it my duty to defend poor pussy on natural grounds, innocence. But mother says the second offence will be punishable by death.

Wednesday, April 7, 1886. Very doubtful weather still. Father and Ed went to the city together today and missed the train this evening. They telegraphed for a team and we sent Alonzo and Sam down through with Ed's and our horse. They came back about eleven o'clock all right.

Mary Shellenberger and her mother were here this evening to view the new carpet for my room.

Thursday, April 8, 1886.   The weather was about clear today, but quite cold.

The strike in the West continues. The railroads go on as before it seems. In East St. Louis a mob of a 1000 strikers marched through and forced all others who were working on the railroads to quit work. They were repulsed at only one point.

Today Mr. Gladstone is expected to make public his Irish scheme. It must have been a great time.

Sent in my statement to the Lansdale Reporter. This would leave 1.75 due me.

Friday, April 9, 1886.   Weather exceptionally fine. Railroad company is laying track to connect with the main track. They will work on Sunday and remove the switch house in Telford.

We will have my new room finished in a short time. Yesterday Mr. Gladstone made his promised speech in which made public his plans for the government of Ireland. He proposes to give them Home Rule and says it is the only remedy.

The House of Commons, the space before the Parliament Houses and the streets were crowded. Members secured their seats as early as 5.30 o'clock this morning. The speech did not begin till 4.35 this afternoon. Mr. Parnell made a speech approving and Mr. Trewlyan against it.

Saturday, April 10, 1886.   Was out in the school house covering books this evening. I wish I were through. I covered about 17.

Mrs. J.M. Slifer and child arrived this afternoon. She will stay about two or three weeks. Susie's sister was down here this evening.

Six or seven men were killed by the deputy marshals in East St. Louis yesterday. The mob became furious and was encouraged by a gambler and was with difficulty prevented from committing the gravest excesses by the earnest appeal Mr. Hayes a member of the Gen. Exec. Board of the N. of L.

He came over from St. Louis when he heard of the trouble and came just in time.

Sunday, April 11, 1886.   Was reading all morning. Took a long walk with Sam to Telford to see the men at work on the railroad. There must have been a hundred or more. There was one train from Bethlehem and one from Lansdale.

It was intended I believe to use the new track tomorrow but I don't believe they got through. Saw the historian J.D. Souder. He is the Secretary of the Telford S.S.

We came back about five o'clock. It was quite cold and I was glad that I had my overcoat.

There is at present a regular concert going on in the front room. A half dozen or more.

Monday, April 12, 1886.   There was a little rain in the morning but after that it cleared off and the weather was quite warm. There was a rumor this morning that J.G. Moyer of Perkasie A. T Cope of Hilltown had made assignments. These are probably both untrue as Father went up to Perkasie this afternoon and bought some lumber and he said he would send his check for the balance of his indebtedness to us. Helped to straighten fence on Godshalls line.

This afternoon the gravel trains threw carloads of cinders and the like down the enbankment to make it wider. Today the first gravel trains passed over the new track. Tomorrow the first regular trains will pass over.

Was down at the school house covering books. Leidy's school commenced today.

Tuesday, April 13, 1886.   Rec'd my Cert. of Stock of Lib. Ass'n today. Goettler made a neat job of it.

Today the regular trains ran for the first time over the new track. The through trains which before had to pass over the switch quite slowly now run past at full speed. The switch house and signal post were removed today. The light of the latter could be seen at a distance. The worst of it is that Haynes has to go to Telford and Souderton will no longer have a night operator.

Was down at the school house again glueing books.

There are still quite a number to be covered.

Wednesday, April 14, 1886.   Were very busy again today. O.L. Hartzel commenced painting my room this afternoon.

Wm. Trumbore's arm was amputated today. Several doctors from other places were here to assist Loux.

Saw Jonathan Umsted this evening.

Talked for a long while with Markly Hufnagel this evening. He is not always communicative.

Thursday, April 15, 1886.   W Trumbore is still under the influence of ether.

Miss Sallie Daub was here this evening. She left Freed's this morning with the expectation that she could get to Becker's here. But now Mrs. Becker has Susie Gentsch and will stick to her.

Friday, April 16, 1886.   Not so many books were taken out of the Library this evening as usual, only 16 went.

Messrs. Powderly and Gould are having a correspondence in which Powderly becomes personal with and threatens him thus giving Gould a hold.

Saturday, April 17, 1886.

Sunday, April 18, 1886.   Went down to North Wales this morning with the Buffalo; as it wast still very early I took walk around town then I came there he (Andrew) was still in bed.

We attended church at the Lutheran. Saw there, Mary Brunner, Carrie Shearer and two of those hateful Deisinger girls. Saw also Prof. Brunner there. In the afternoon I met Wesley Anders who accompanied me to the station. Andrew has quit school and is now working in Phila. making frames, coming home every evening.

Father and mother went up to Quakertown today.

Monday, April 19, 1886.   Yesterday a meeting was called to meet in the school house this evening for the purpose of re-organizing the Sunday School. I hurried to get my report ready went down to the school house and opened it and got every thing in readiness. The time came for the meeting to open, and not enough were there. When it was past eight o'clock therefore Mr. Godshall addressed the assemblage and told them it seemed as if no one took any interest in the movement and if this were the support we were to expect we had better stop. And so we went home. I think this bodes ill for a sunday school this summer. Should anybody start the movement we would be ready to take part again.

Tuesday, April 20, 1886.

Wednesday, April 21, 1886.   Milt Moyer and I went down to the school house this afternoon and took away the sunday school organ and cleaned it. We will leave it at Moyer's for the present.

Ben. Barndt has bought Sloop's property for 3500. They will move out in 2 mos. He has pulled down the barn and will build a new one 36 x 38. C.H. Moyer's house is also being pulled down. The fence has been removed and it begins to look a little dead.

Thursday, April 22, 1886.   We dug one patch of our garden this evening. It is still too wet. Our garden is always later than most others.

Hartzel commenced painting our house today. Becker still refuses to have his painted. It will have quite a onesided look. Becker is a queer fellow. He won't repair anything. He is pretty hard up for selling bread too or he wouldn't think of hiring Susie Gentsch just that reason when they could Sarah Daub who has left Freed's. He won't repair his tumbledown pavement just to show the people that he hadn't to do it.

It is now settled that Sunday school is to commence on Sunday. Have sent for the quarterlies today.

Friday, April 23, 1886.   Today was Good Friday. The bank was closed. We finished the organ by polishing it with Cassel's Furniture Polish. It looks quite new again.

People held their holiday by coming to town to do their shopping. The store was crowded all day. The streets were full of vehicles and this evening everybody seemed to be out promenading.

Mr. Landes was in bank awhile this afternoon.

Becker's have now hired Sarah Daub. Such indecision as theirs I never saw.

Was reading Uncle Tom's Cabin sometimes today.

Am feeling very much used up, tired or lazy the last few days. Slept in my new bed for the first time last night.

Saturday, April 24, 1886.   Charley Frick came up this evening. I met him on the road.

Becker has commenced selling ice cream now. It were a good plan if he would fix the pavement in front of his yard.

Sunday, April 25, 1886.   Sunday School commenced again this afternoon. Attendance good. Have a new class Ambrose, Penrose, Elwood and Saml Leidy. Don't know how it will work yet, must try and do my best.

Finished reading Uncle Tom's Cabin this afternoon. No wonder it made such a stir among the people at the time of its publication.

Frick was with Milt Moyer Schwenck & Bean this afternoon. Took a walk around with Uriah and was up in Hunsberger's steeple.

Was down at Zuschmitt's this evening and showed him about the Sunday School lesson. I found them pleasant people.

Monday, April 26, 1886.   Today was again kept as a holiday by many people. This has been the latest Easter for over a hundred years and will not happen again till some time in 1900.

The store etc. were again crowded today with shoppers.

I took a walk again this evening through town. It is very pleasant to do so in Spring. The shade trees with their richly colored leaves the green grass and everything makes it wonderfully pleasant. The people are either on the porch or walking. And it seems that you see only the pleasant side of life with the unsightly things left out.

Tuesday, April 27, 1886.   There was a meeting down at the meeting house this evening. Rev. John Funk editor of the Herald und Wahrheit of Elkhart Ind. Owing to the unsettled weather the attendance was not such as might have been expected.

Wednesday, April 28, 1886.   There is some trouble about but how it is or what it is I can not make out in the newspapers, Greece has armed herself and wants to fight Turkey, while the Powers won't let her. They have 74 Ironclads and 25 ships at Suday Bay.

We are sodding the embankment towards Godshall's yard. Will have everything new and pleasant after a while.

Sallie Daub came to Becker's on Tuesday. She moved this evening.

Tomorrow a sister of Mrs. C.H. Moyer will move into the lower part of Godshall's house.

Thursday, April 29, 1886.   Finished sodding the bank in the yard.

Scholl was here today and papered my room.

A new wardrobe has been made and is nearly finished. We laid the carpet in my room this evening.

I had a little argument with Uriah this evening in our yard. My temper got the better of me when he intimated that he wasn't allowed to go home to his mother. It was so utterly false that I went up to him and offered to strike him if he dared to repeat it. I would have done it too. But I am heartily ashamed of it now. We talked too loud People heard us. And it didn't do any good.

Friday, April 30, 1886.   The weather was somewhat cooler than yesterday.

Amelia was down this morning and I told her all about my affair with Uriah. She did not take his part at all.

Many persons made a mistake about the library this evening. As the four weeks were up many thought this must be the evening. But it is to open the first & third Fridays of each.

Mr. Appenzeller was here this evening too. I went down with him because he had come so far.

Saturday, May 1, 1886.   The weather was quite cool today.

F.G. Leidy has turned out to be a wholesale forger. Only a few of his notes are believed to be genuine. Mr. Landes wrote to three of the parties and they all reported in person or by letter that they had signed no notes for any one.

Mr. Landes went down and told his father about who has endorsed all the notes.

He is a very bold fellow and had everything well planned. He didn't own up to it yet. But he will have to one of these days. The signatures are all imitations of the genuine but there is the same stroke for them all and in this they are all similar. It is rather hard on his father who trusted him too well.

Sunday, May 2, 1886.   Took a walk through the woods where the trees have all been felled. Went into the school house and looked over the books. Here Uriah Souder found me and we together took a long walk through the fields. We climbed into the school house steeple and scratched our initials on the framing. The sunday school this afternoon was well attended. I have a class of five or six. They are Ambrose Hunsberger, P.H. Zendt, Elwood, Nelson Hunsberger Saml Leidy & Jesse Beaver who intends to come. Nelson is a little troublesome but I have gained confidence in them today.

Found cousins Mag & Amelia here after sunday school. Uncle Ed's were here for supper. Walked about in the evening. Was at Cornelius.' He was not so good today.

Misses Lillie & Kate were at Godshall's this evening singing. A great friendship has sprung up there since Charley comes.

Monday, May 3, 1886.   On Saturday the great strike for 8 hours work and 10 hours pay commenced in Chicago and other places. It is believed 35000 men are engaged in this strike in Chicago.

The cabinet makers who are mostly German Poles etc. are the most dangerous class. The Socialists take advantage of this strike of affairs and make incendiary speeches.

F.H. Leidy was up at bank today with his father. At first he wanted to deny that he forged the papers but he could not so he said not a word. He promised to pay 3500 by Saturday and give a new note for the balance.

Tuesday, May 4, 1886.   Weather warm and it commenced to rain a little several times.

At present everything looks beautiful. The trees are covered with blossoms the grass is not yet faded and retains its rich color.

Our house is looking very well I think. Geo. H. Swartz will have his painted the same color. Haynes the night operator is again at this place. The trains now run on the new track from near Perkasie and so he was no longer needed at Telford.

There is a meeting at Ed's office this evening to sign a petition and get the railroad Co. the stop the Buffalo in the evening at this place.

Wednesday, May 5, 1886.   At a meeting of the Anarchists numbering about 1500 men in Chicago the police attempted to disperse them. The Socialists threw dynamite bombs into the ranks of the police which instantly exploded and five policemen fell. The police fired on the crowd with revolvers and the helldogs replied. They were well provided with arms. It is impossible to get the true number of casualists. About 7 of the anarchists were killed and 50 wounded. Several police were killed and many wounded.

We sowed grass seed in the yard this afternoon.

Thursday, May 6, 1886.   A set of Indians selling medicine have pitched camp at Schwenk's hotel.

We dug our second patch in the garden.

A mob again assembled in Chicago yesterday morning and infested the drugstore of a Mr. Rosenfeld because they [believed] he had been giving information to the police. He was rescued but his store was pillaged. They then infested a liquor store rolled out the barrels of whiskey and drank the liquor. Afterwards they destroyed everything in the place. In the riots yesterday 2 officers were killed 4 fatally and 24 seriously wounded. The exact number of Anarchists killed or wounded would not be found out.

Most of the leaders have been arrested. They are most of them infidels foreigners Dead Dogs. In Milwaukee yesterday a number of rioters were killed and many hurt from a volley from the militia. The crowd fled.

Friday, May 7, 1886.   The weather today was rainy. The ground was already pretty dry.

There was a slim attendance at the library this evening owing to the wet weather.

Several attempts were made by the Anarchists to fire the lumber district in Chicago but were unsuccessful.

Saturday, May 8, 1886.   Raining again all day but cleared off this evening.

The answer of Greece to the ultimatum of the powers was not satisfactory and war is now imminent.

Russia will not take any action against Greece.

Went over the discounts today. Came within 18 cents. This may not be quite correct and yet it might and besides it is a great satisfaction.

Sunday, May 9, 1886.   Very pleasant day.

There was no Sunday school today owing to the meeting this afternoon and communion services at Franconia.

Was in meeting this afternoon. Very little interest. Rev. Detweiler preached. Finished reading R. Grant White's England Without and Within. Oswin Kline was up from the city. Took a walk to see the tents at Schwencks.

Saw a little Arab this morning. Talks English well. Resembles Jos. B Detweiler's boy very closely. Talked with quite a while. Is quite intelligent. Eleven years old. Lived in Alexandria Egypt. Lost their property in the bombardment. Has his father with him. Lived in Jerusalem. Wishes to return to his own country as his father cannot obtain employment. Learned English from the Missionaries.

Monday, May 10, 1886.   Weather has become quite cool.

The masons commenced work on C.H. Moyers cellar this morning.

Saw Jonathan Umstead a short time this afternoon.

J.L. Gehman came in this afternoon with the books which he failed to return last Friday.

Some of the Chicago rioters while pillaging the drug store drank carbolic acid in mistake for whiskey. Two of these have since died and others are not expected to recover.

Tuesday, May 11, 1886.   After bank hours went up to where they are at work upon the new road over which was formerly grandfather's lane. They have been tearing out the fine row of cherry trees which come nearly in the middle of the road with dynamite. I was there in time to see the last one torn out. It lifted it as it stood in the air about six feet. Then from all sides flew stones and mud and we had to look out for it when it came down. These stones flew a considerable distance.

Was up at the hill to see the Indian show. There were songs and speech whose chief object was to sell medicine by bold lying. There were some very comic songs. The Indians look like the portrait of Riel the French Canadian half breed who was hung during the North West Rebellion. There was also a most disgusting performance by mulatto athlete in tights. He pulled a hood over his body in various positions. Showed his body in various positions. And all in the presence of ladies. Then the insolent quadroon would bow with a triumphant smile after each performance. I was standing on a bench but got down immediately. Then some ignorant persons thought proper to applaud him. I was really ashamed of it. And the ladies too did not turn their eyes away. Had it been a woman who was performing such great (feats?) it would have been thought by them highly immoral. The truth is the people of the neighborhood are not well enought to discriminate a moral from an immoral entertaint.

Wednesday, May 12, 1886.   Painted the bird box this afternoon.

Godshall gave me a fine map of Europe which he received from P. Wright & Sons.

Some how or other I don't get much work done which I am at. I should have finished J. D. Souder's thing long ago but can't get it finished.[1]

The bank is pumping Wenhold. Something has to be done to get him more careful. He related how he tells his fellows that it is not the bank not himself who wants them to pay their notes but the 'goferment' by thunder.

The Buffalo train in the evening will stop here after time is changed. Eight have died and four are dying of drinking the wrong stuff in Chicago while pillaging the drug store.

[1]He was asked by J. D. Souder to contribute the history of Souderton to his planned publication, "History of Franconia Township."
[2]See also May 14, 15 also 22 (written by Henry Hemsing)

Thursday, May 13, 1886.   It has been raining all day and has not yet cleared off.

There was a terrible storm out west. Telegraph poles were thrown down. Houses thrown and people killed.

Friday, May 14, 1886.   Was up this evening in Hunsberger's office and took an account of their business for my sketch. I've not much more than M.B. Bergey to look for now.

Have been reading the Pathfinder when I had a chance.

Saturday, May 15, 1886.   Finished reading Pathfinder this evening.

John Souder was down to see me about business I promised to send up next week.

Sunday, May 16, 1886.   Went to Gehman's meeting house with mother and Sam. Communion. Started about half past seven. Father went down to Leidy's where the same services were going on. Susie was confirmed in Sellersville today. Was in Sunday School this afternoon, quite full.

Ina Snyder came into town this evening. I had a glance at her at the station. They say she is no good.

There was meeting this evening. It was overcrowded. I did not go out. Was with Haynes and Uriah. Took them up to see my room. Had an ice cream supper.

Hen Bilger's are here over night.

Monday, May 17, 1886.   A very pleasant day this. We have trimmed the trees in front of the yard. Becker should do the same.

Was up to see M.B. Bergey this evening. Will have to go again tomorrow evening.

The strike of the garment cutters has ended the men agreeing to work 9½ hrs. per day and 5½ hrs on Saturdays, with 10 hrs wages. There would have been great distress had it not been settled as many people in our neighborhood depend wholly upon it for a living.

Tuesday, May 18, 1886.   Trimmed the trees in front of the bank this morning. Fair weather. Cloudy this evening.

The second volume of Grant's Memoirs has been published. We did not get ours yet. And now Wanamaker will sell the same for $5.50 or 1.50 cheaper than the subscription price.

The Queen of Spain yesterday gave birth to a son. This child will nominally be a king as soon as he was born. King Alfonso died last winter.

Wednesday, May 19, 1886.   Pres. Gerhart did not come to bank today as he attended the funeral of his brother Hilary Gerhart.

I have marked Jonas Freed. He tried to make a fool of me this evening because I apologized for knocking off Morris Weil's hat. He saw fit to taunt me with being only a banker. I did not like it. He is going backward. He has been drunk severals times and some say he was so on Sunday evening.

Thursday, May 20, 1886.   A man named Al. Landis living in Hockertown was killed on the railroad above Quakertown today. He was flagman on the gravel train. He was sitting on a tie asleep and it is said he had been drinking. He leaves a wife and six children.

Friday, May 21, 1886.   This was library evening. Some again failed to put in an appearance and this makes me collect fines.

We decided on buying the Rollo Books for children.

I am now at work to finish the history of Souderton and will probably mail tomorrow some time.

Received second volume of Grant's Memoirs this afternoon.

Saturday, May 22, 1886.   Have at last finished notes to J.D. Souder for his history of Franconia. Was at work on it all the time I could spare today. I have nine pages of foolscap paper.

There was to be a festival at Telford this evening but a shower came up and the band returned home.

Sunday, May 23, 1886.   A fine day. Finished reading Last of the Mohicans this morning and read some in Grant's book. Jas. M. Slifer is down from Topton and I saw this morning before breakfast. He is probably down on business. He was over to see Groff and will go down to North Wales today yet. He will leave for home with the three o'clock train.

In Sunday School this afternoon, quite well filled. My boys still want Leidy out of the class. It shall not be.

Cousin Maggie was here this evening. Treated her with ice cream. Accompanied her home. Her father was not at all well today. Malaria. The nine o'clock train did not stop this evening. Time will not be changed till next Sunday as the road is not finished far enough.

Monday, May 24, 1886.   There was some rain last night and today.

Gladstone will appeal to the country if his Home Rule Bill does not pass.

There has been some fighting between the Turks and the Greeks in which the latter generally had the advantage.

Hartzel has commenced painting Wolford's house the same color as ours.

Have ordered the Rollo Books from Wanamaker. Must write Andrew and Ed Donley that there will be a festival June 5.

Jas. M. Slifer was down here in the interest of a Trust Co. which they are getting up at Allentown. I suppose it did not lay very well with their bank.

Tuesday, May 25, 1886.   Weather quite cool today. Cloudy unsettled.

Am reading the Deerslayer by Cooper.

Wednesday, May 26, 1886.   Got through quite early in bank today.

Did a little painting this afternoon.

Is very late and I should be in bed.

Thursday, May 27, 1886.   Was today what it has been all week. Rain this morning clearing off, rain at noon clearing off rain this afternoon and again, cleared off. It will get quite late for the farmers to plant corn. Commenced making a picture frame this afternoon.

The bank will be closed on Saturday Decoration Day being observed on that day. Mr. Landes made a card to hang on the door reading "Bank will be closed tomorrow, Legal Holiday."

The "Deerslayer" is occupying my time at present.

Friday, May 28, 1886.   The bank will be closed tomorrow.

Saturday, May 29, 1886.   We commenced cleaning the bank this morning and worked so well that we were done before dinner time. In the afternoon I brought up the lawn mower and cleaned the yard. Mr. Landes mowed away the grass for me. It is a great improvement. Landis & Moyer were in bank from one till three o'clock. I was not inside. They won't catch me setting such a bad example. After this I finished sundry painting jobs some of which Susie managed to spoil by sweeping dust against it.

When I came home this evening I found a great lot here. Among them Katie and Lillie Zendt whom I accompanied on their way home and spent a half hour with them not being very welcome I am afraid as they wanted to do some work yet.

Sunday, May 30, 1886.   Finished the "Deerslayer" this morning. After which I took a nap from which I awoke in time to get ready for Sunday School. Only three of my class were present.

Commenced the "Prairie" after dinner and again took nap.

When on my way to the station this evening I met Mrs. Ellis and carried her baby with me. I had it on the right arm when it should have been on the left. I dare say it was very awkwardly done. At eight o'clock made ready to go to bank to watch in Greaser's place who attended a funeral. Rufus Landes was with me. The new schedule goes into effect today. The 9 o'clock train stops here at precisely nine.

Monday, May 31, 1886.   It is officially announced that President Cleveland will be married on Wednesday to Miss Frances Folsom in the White House. This will be the first marriage of a president that was celebrated within its walls.

The Rollo Books have arrived. Books News is out today with a portrait on T.B. Aldrich.

Received a letter from J.D. Souder thanking me and announcing that the History of Souderton will be published in the "Independent" of this week.

The plate glass for W.D. Hunsbergers front will come to $240. Found out today that Mr. Landes knows all about my being at Wms. for a few ms. on Sat. eve. I did act foolishly I know. But this is a weakness they can't get over. It was so once before. They talk too much.

Tuesday, June 1, 1886.   Rec'd a letter from Ed Donley today saying he would come over on Saturday.

Was down at the school house this afternoon covering books. The general Conference of the Knights of Labor has been in session in Cleveland for some time.

Wednesday, June 2, 1886.   Pres. Cleveland is to be married this evening to Miss Frances Folsom. He is 49, she is 22. Newspaper correspondents have been making a great fuss about it for a long time.

John Kelly the head of Tammany Hall for a long time died yesterday aged 65 years. He was born in 1821.

Peter Benner who attends the night school at Spring Garden Institute has won the Silver Institute Medal for the best drawing and painting from a cast.

Uriah has been in the city since Saturday. He came home this evening and told me he was going down again tomorrow as he has obtained a job with Wm. B. Slifer.

We had Sallie Kline to help at house cleaning today. Was down at the school house covering books this afternoon. I am almost through now.

Thursday, June 3, 1886.   Pres't Cleveland was married last evening to Miss Frances Folsom. About 20 persons witnessed the ceremony. It took place in the Blue Room which with the other rooms were elaborately decorated with flowers and tropical plants. Attorney Gen. Garland was not present. Rev. Mr. Sunderland performed the ceremony. The party partook of a splendidly served dinner or supper in the East Room. The Pres't and his bride left foor Deer

Park the same evening where they will stay about a week.

Uriah went to his new home with the 1.25 train. He is glad to get off once.

Seth G. Bergey has been sheriffed by his wife. This will be another nice business.

Worked in the school house again this evening.

Friday, June 4, 1886.   Am nearly through covering books for the library.

There were not very many down this evening.

Saturday, June 5, 1886.   Ed Donley came over shortly before dinner. We went down to Lansdale with the 1²⁵ train to get chill medicine. Andrew came with him at three o'clock and together we walked through the town. Ed is a little taller than myself and is getting stouter. He plays the mouthorgan well. He plays that and the other organ together.

We went up to the festival this evening. There was a great crowd, L.M.Z. and Katie stood about. Ed tried to catch on to Lillie but she told him she guessed she was engaged and afterwards said she was. Which was not true however as they went home alone.

I found a relation of mine whom I had never seen before but who knew me Mary Hunsberger a daughter of Sam T. Hunsberger. She is real good looking and I am proud of the relationship.

Sunday, June 6, 1886.   Rufus was here last night. Andrew slept with me and Ed. & Rufus slept together. We took a walk to the school house and saw the Library. Ed. is a wilder boy than he was when he left here. I suppose he is pretty well at home where he is. It is a pretty rough neighborhood. He wanted to go home after dinner but we did not let him. We went to Sunday School which was well filled and Ed started off as soon as he could. He had 2 horses. Took a walk with Andrew this afternoon. He went down with the 6.19 train. He gets 2 Dollars a day at his job in the city.

Walked about with Haynes this evening. He is going to see Marietta Gerhart. He will go sometime after nine. Mike Bergey will try it too.

Monday, June 7, 1886.   Seth Bergey has again proved himself a cheat. He always enjoyed it and I think he will enjoy this in proportion. He has B.D. Alderfer and Wm. K. Moyer in for a 1000 Dollars which were found to be on the property after he sold it. Today Wenhold came down in behalf of Elias Barnd the holder of the judgment, and spoke so loud and with such authority that Mrs. Moyer took him for a constable and fell into a fit.

Planted cabbage this evening.

Tuesday, June 8, 1886.   The Home Rule bill was defeated last night for second reading in the House of Commons by a majority of 30 votes.

Parliament will now probably be dissolved and Gladstone will make an appeal to the country.

Walked around with Haynes awhile this evening. He is very open and frank.

Wednesday, June 9, 1886.   We had rain again today. Rec'd a letter from Uriah. He says he likes the city but will go for a wholesale house as soon as he gets a chance.

Ed Donley also wrote. He says he arrived home at 7.30 and went to church yet.

Wilson the murderer of A. Daly will probably be hung.

P Neatwell the St. Louis murderer will fare no better.

Thursday, June 10, 1886.   Mr. Gladstone intends to dissolve Parliament at the end of the present month. The Queen has given her consent to the measure. She had offered the Marquis of Hartington to form a Ministry. There had been much rioting in Belfast by the Orangemen.

There was some rain today and this evening.

Friday, June 11, 1886.   Last Saturday evening at the festival Freed sold liquor to minors to Jesse Benner to Ambrose and Penrose. People talk much about getting him into trouble but I think there is nothing in it. But this **should** be done. He should not be allowed to go on in this way. I do not know what to say to Penrose and Ambrose who are in my sunday school class.

The King of Bavaria has been deposed on account of insanity.

The bank will be calcimined on the 4th of July, and painted sometime in the fall.

Saturday, June 12, 1886.   There has been a great dispute about 4 cts between me and Henry Gerhart since Wednesday. He says he had 4 cts more Mr. Landis said for me it was not so. Gerhart wrote again and said he had a (nickle) ten cent piece and one cent. Mr. Landis wrote back that I was positive that it was short but that he could have the 4 ct if he was sure he was right. It makes me mad such a thing for I know I am right.

Sunday, June 13, 1886.   Dave Bryan's were here on a visit today.

Am reading life of Napolean Bonaparte. Was in Sunday School this afternoon. Old Herman was not present as he is sick. Borneman had his place. Sam R. Swartley was here to lead the singing. Was up with Oswin Kline who is up from the city.

Was out at uncle Cornelius' this evening. He is very weak and is going backwards, I did not know what to say to him. He said he was 42 years old but that he had been thinking more in these last two years than in the 40 before. He was visibly affected and almost broke into tears.

Took Amelia Maggie and Martha to Becker's for ice cream and took a walk through town.

Monday, June 14, 1886.   There was much rain this day. This morning it rained so hard that it woke me. Gared Landes came up from the city today and he and Jake together attended the funeral of Gared Clemens.

It is said that Mary Hackman is in an interesting condition since last Christmas.

Tuesday, June 15, 1886.   Ludwig king of Bavaria who was recently deposed committed suicide last evening by drowning himself in a lake. His physican who accompanied him in his walk rushed in to save him was also drowned. His brother Otto I has been declared king but he is also mentally incapable of governing. Prince Luitfrold uncle to the king therefore continues in the regency.

Wednesday, June 16, 1886.   Will Benner came back again from his travels yesterday. I saw him today. I don't think he has changed much for the better.

Was down at the library to look up the Napoleons. Have read his life looked at their pictures read Creasy's Waterloo and looked them up in the cyclopedia, the whole is discouraging. The unrivalled genius of Napoleon the abilities of his generals are all admirable. But their cruelty wickedness selfishness ambition &c are reprehensible.

Thursday, June 17, 1886.   It is said the rumored marriage takes place this evening. Most people pity their youth. Some of the young folks probably think it not much out of the way.

Mother was down in the city this afternoon to have her eyes examined. She needs wear no spectacles.

Friday, June 18, 1886.   Mr. Gladstone is making an election tour through Scotland. He was enthusiastically received all along the route.

Library was open again this evening. Must stop writing as it is late and I am sleepy.

Saturday, June 19, 1886.   Rufus Landes did not feel well today and went home.

There is a festival at Telford this evening.

Was up at grandfather H to have my razor sharpened. Saw Mr. Wm Freed and Mary Hackman the newly wedded couple drive past. Poor misguided creatures. Am reading Forney's Anecdotes of Public Men.

Sunday, June 20, 1886.   Felt quite bad last night. Took Caster Oil last evening. Woke up during the night. It was moonlight. A robin was singing probably mistaking the moon for the sun. Was almost late for Sunday School in the forenoon. Milt Moyer was not present so I took his place.

Henry Landes' were here today. Their daughter Lizzie and Jerome were along.

Did not go to meeting this afternoon.

Was up at Wms. There were Misses Lillie Kate and Annie, Rufus joined us afterward and then we came down to Becker's for ice cream.

Kate asked when alone why I did not go for Lillie. And afterwards when they left she tried to embarass me by telling me to take them home. The girls waited. But I kept my ground. I don't know if I was right or wrong. Walked about the town this evening.

Monday, June 21, 1886.

Tuesday, June 22, 1886.   Woke up late last evening and prepared to go to bed. Finding Sam was not in I asked Uriah who knew nothing and then I started to find him. Ran around awhile, for to me it was a puzzle that he was not in his place. I came home again when mother opened the window and told me to go to bed and that Sam was at home with his mother.

The Lansdale bank has declared a dividend of 3 instead of 4 per cent as formerly. This works hard on old Herman. He is the largest stockholder of the bank having between 70 and shares. The stock sold at about 200 is only worth 150 and this amount to several thousand dollars to him.

Cal. this afternoon filled out the chinks in the wall preparatory to calcimining on the 4th of July.

Wednesday, June 23, 1886.   The rain which commenced yesterday continued all last night till dinner. This is hard on the farmers. It interferes with their haymaking while at the same time they ought to work in the cornfields.

Felt very bad today. Have a trouble in the intestines. It is very painful.

Have received notice from Heebner of Lansdale that he has again sent us two books entitled Penna during the Revolution. This is very kind of Mr. Heebner and he seems to take an interest in our library.

Thursday, June 24, 1886.

Friday, June 25, 1886.   Felt very bad last evening and went to bed early. I slept well and this morning I felt all right but it comes on again in the evening.

Dreamt the other night that Miss Lillie was engaged to be married to C.G.F. and the ceremony was to come off this week. But on waking found all nothing.

Saturday, June 26, 1886.   There was rain last night and rain after dinner lasting only a few minutes.

The pain has not yet left me. But with the return of dry weather I hope to get better. Today it cleared off more than once and this evening there is not a cloud visible.

Becker has a festival this evening as Schwenck's, Mother said they would get me a carriage if I would go to bed earlier and not follow taverns.

Sunday, June 27, 1886.   Lay around sleeping most of the forenoon. Was in Sunday School this afternoon. New quarterlies were distributed.

Walked about town this evening with Haynes. He thrashed a fellow last evening at the festival. A fellow named Hemlock from Lansdale had been insulting the girls and among them Haynes' when he went for him and demolished him. He weighed about 200 pounds. This is just what the fellow wanted and he got it.

The weather today was delightful.

Monday, June 28, 1886.   The English elections will commence on July 2 and continue to July 14. Gladstone spoke last at Manchester. He has returned from a tour through Scotland.

Cousin Kate tells me there is to be a party at Moyers on Saturday evening in honor of Jennie's return.

Mowed the grass in the yard this afternoon.

Jonas Hangey spoke to me about a carriage of which father had spoken to him about. He has one ready and would like to sell it to me. It is one like Uriah's.

I hear Uriah is coming up on Saturday.

Tuesday, June 29, 1886.   Warm weather has set in now. Yesterday and today were excellent days for haymaking. This was what the farmers have been waiting for.

Got me a seersucker coat and vest this evening. The boys are already playing with firecrackers. It's only a nuisance.

The West Chester people are expected home shortly. Would like to go to Gettysburg at the latter part of the week.

The band will play in Quakertown on Saturday at the dedication of Uncle Hen's Hall. The upper part is to be occupied by lodges.

Wednesday, June 30, 1886.   Today was settlement day for the bank. A dividend of 2½ per cent has been declared a 1000 added to the surplus making it 23000 and some 4000 remaining undivided profits.

The sale of grass and grain belonging to the bank amounted to about $54.

Henry Ward Beecher is in England. He was present at a meeting in Liverpool where Gladstone spoke.

Thursday, July 1, 1886.   We hoed the corns and potatoes again this evening. There will be about 5000 bricks left for Moyer's house. Was ashamed of myself for making such a mistake.

Am reading Two years before the Mast.

The West Chesters will return tomorrow.

They are very busy shooting firecrackers &c at the station. This is the first year they had them for a long time.

Friday, July 2, 1886. The English elections have begun.

The President has signed the FitzJohn Porter Bill. After over 20 years this man has been vindicated. In 1863 he was cashiered and left the army. He has been asking for justice ever since and at last he has it. Pres. Arthur vetoed a similar bill.

Horace came home this afternoon. I saw him this evening at the library, Miss Moyer and Jonathan have not yet arrived. John Smith died this afternoon. He was about 28 years old. He has been gradually sinking ever since he left the paint shop. The last time I saw him was in bank sometime ago. He spoke very hoarse. He hopes of getting well. Chas. Schwenck was over yesterday and today. He gave himself up this morning. He was a gentleman and was respected by everybody who knew him.

Saturday, July 3, 1886. There was much shooting with fire crackers this evening. Was up at the store looking on. Shot off a few myself. The station was the head quarters.

The band went up to Quakertown today to take part in dedicating Hen's Hall. They came back before evening and went over to Earlington to the new race track.

The trains coming up today were very full. Am not decided what kind of carriage to get.

Spoke with father this evening about my future prospects. They always want me to stick my place. I explained that I could not do this if I wanted to and that if I could do better it was my duty to do so.

Sunday, July 4, 1886. Was in Sunday School this morning. Miss Moyer was in and taught a class of little girls. She came home last evening. Spoke with her a little. Andrew came up this forenoon. He was at C.H. Moyers for dinner. He came down in the afternoon. Martha and Amelia were here for supper. Andrew will move to the city tomorrow. He does not know how long he will have work but he expects it will be better in the fall. Were up at the station walked through town and sat up on the front porch till late.

Monday, July 5, 1886. Finished reading Life of Martin Luther today.

Andrew went down with the 9.41 train. He will go to town this afternoon.

They commenced kalsomining the bank walls today. They are only about half done. They have a terrible dust on the desks in there.

It was a very warm day. Kept in the house most of the time.

The doctor has his girl up. An old lady and gentlemen probably the girls parents were also up today.

This evening the officers of the lodge are to be installed. There is still firing going on.

Tuesday, July 6, 1886.   A very hot day. The kalsomining was not finished till this evening and we had to work under the scaffold all day. In the evening we got things a little in order. It looks quite well after it is done.

This evening Miss Lillie, Amelia and Kate came into the bank and soon after mother and grandmother followed. We were in there till Greaser came. Miss L is up at Morris' this week.

John Smith was buried today in Doylestown. There was no ceremony at the house it being against usage by the Catholics.

Wednesday, July 7, 1886.   A very hot day 91°. Had to pick cherries this afternoon.

The doctor advised mother today to take a trip for her health.

FitzJohn Porter has been nominated a Colonel by the President.

The English elections seem to be going against Mr. Gladstone. The Tories are gaining and the outlook is very uncertain. He will have to gain considerable before he has a majority.

The latest returns are Conservatives 210 Unionists 43 Gladstonians 99 and Parnellites 43, 253 against 142.

Thursday, July 8, 1886.   The English elections seems to be going against Gladstone. The latest returns are 250 Tories 47 Unionists 119 Liberals and 55 Parnellites. The English counties, the last hope of the Gladstonians are going Unionist.

John Smith was 28 yrs 8 m and 17 ds old when he died. He had been working here nearly six years.

Got a new seersucker this evening.

Was out target shooting with Ellis this afternoon. If I ever get me a gun I will get me a rifle like Ellis'.

Hoed the corn and potatoes this evening.

Friday, July 9, 1886.   The English elections stand 251 Tories 50 Unionists 130 Gladstonites and 65 Parnellites.

Russia has declared the port of Batoum closed and has been massing troops in Bessarabia. It is feared that this is the first step toward the breaking of the Berlin treaty.

Cooler weather today. Walked about town this evening with Horace and Haynes. Saw Jons for the first time this evening. They are again playing dominoes at the depot.

Saturday, July 10, 1886.   There was a splendid rain this morning. It was just the right time for it.

Was up at grandfather H's awhile this evening. Cornelius had been up there today. He walked up himself but grandfather brought him home. He felt very bad today and had an attack of the chills again this afternoon.

When I got home I fooled about with the boys &c and did not get to bed till half past eleven.

Sunday, July 11, 1886.   Did not get up till eight o'clock. Went to Sunday school in the morning. After dinner Rufus came down and wanted me to go to Lansdale Park with him. When we came up Horace was not dressed yet. We got down some time between 3 and 4 o'clock. White's Park is about 1 mile west of Lansdale. The 6th Reg. Penna. N.G. encamped here yesterday and will remain one week. They number about 400 men. Col. Jno. W. Schall commander. This was the first time I saw any soldiers. There was a dress parade at five o'clock. One of the men was discharged for conduct unbecoming a soldier and a gentleman. We met Miss Lillie and Amelia and of course had to escort them. We took a boat ride, walked out to Lansdale and there Rufus finding Morris Weil (the girls having more than hinted for us to take them home) took him in my stead, while we went home with the train. Of course, I felt bound to make attempt at calling Lillie and received permission to call again next Sunday evening.

Monday, July 12, 1886.   Sam'l Sorver met with a sad accident today. He got entangled in a belt that was hanging loose from the shaft. The belt wound itself up and pulled him against the shaft. His leg was broken and crushed. An amputation may be necessary. Two doctors were working at it this afternoon. He is in great pain.

I think I will have to suffer for my last evenings visit. They are at it already. Must help at raking hay this evening after supper.

A man named Graham has succeeded in the foolhardy attempt of going through whirlpool rapids at Niagara in a tub or barrel. It was 17 in. at one end and 26 at the other and seven feet ballasted with iron sandbags to keep it bottom up.

Tuesday, July 13, 1886.   Nothing worth recording took place today.

Wednesday, July 14, 1886.   Lords Salisbury and Hartington will probably form a coalition cabinet on the basis of local government for Ireland Scotland and Wales under the Supremacy of the Imperial Parliamant.

A great earthquake has taken place in New Zealand.

My carriage is already in the blacksmith's hands. It will be the kind known as the White chapel.

There was some rain this afternoon and evening.

Mother is quite out of humor with Susie and wants me to write somewhere else for another. Samuel Sorver is reported in a poor way for recovery.

Trade dollars were today reduced to 75 cts.

Thursday, July 15, 1886.   This morning on coming up to the bank Kate called to me that there would be a party tonight at Moyers' for Jennie. At noon I received an invitation through L.

Mrs. Frick was over here this afternoon. Charley is coming up over Sunday. I got ready about nine o'clock and went up to Wms'. Kate and the boys were ready. The weather looked threatening. We went out to Zendts' and found Schwenck Ellie Slifer Amelia Maggie and Mike Bergey already there. We started off L and myself bringing up the rear. We went into the room quietly. It was a complete surprise. Jennie had been over to see Kate who had been dressing for the party and sent down word she would be ready in a quarter of an hour. She was a little offended at this and went away. When she came into the room she did not know what to say. Soon however all was right. We went into the drawing room, Musselman came about 10 o'clock. Milt came down from bed. There were 14 of us. We partook of a standing collation. After that music various games and about half past one started home. I had written to L about coming up and coming for his things. Engaged to take her down to church on Sunday evening.

Friday, July 16, 1886.   Lord Salisbury is making overtures to the Marquis of Hartington for giving the Liberal Unionists 4 seats in the Cabinet and allowing him to become leader of the House of Commerce and to choose any office but that of Premier.

Felt rather sleepy at times during the day. Took a nap this afternoon.

The library was open again this evening. There were more books taken than for a while past. Jennie was down and took 4 books. She is studying up for examinations which will take place on the 24th or 29th.

There was rain last evening and today.

Saturday, July 17, 1886.   Cleared off today. Mowed the yard this afternoon. Engaged Reub's wagon for tomorrow evening. Looked at it and was a little disappointed. Charley Frick came up with the five o'clock train. I saw him after supper. He boards at Franklin St. He gets nine dollars a week and says this don't take him through. Old Herman will have to shell out sometimes I think. He says he is out nearly every evening to parties &c. We walked up toward the store. He had a package of books &c which he took out to Zendts' staying only about half an hour and returned with his own. We took ice cream. Were over at the station. Uriah came up with the train. Met Miss L & Annie Moyer. He praised her and said he couldn't do her justice, that he should have been up here every week and that he couldn't do. I kept as quiet as a mouse. Hen Alderfer tried to bother us up but he only created a little suspicion.

Bought a blanket.

Sam Sorver was reported to be very low today.

Sunday, July 18, 1886.   Uriah Souder came down this morning. We went over and ate ice cream. He says he likes the city. Frick came over after awhile. He had been sleeping all morning. He is out almost every night and is a regular society man. So he wanted to pick up a little. Frick and I went to Sunday school together. On our way home Frick congratulated me and then I found that Milt Moyer had betrayed me to him. He said he was glad to hear it. But that wouldn't talk girls to me anymore. I felt like splitting. Though he said nothing out of the way yet I told him to trust me. We promised to correspond. He went down in the six o'clock train. Uriah went along to Lansdale. Then I went and got a team ready for church. Had Reub's wagon. This was likewise my first essay. Arrived a little late. After we came home it rained. Spent a pleasant evening. Found out that the girls were anxious to let Charley know. They parted friendly. It had cleared off by the time I went home and it was quite chilly.

Monday, July 19, 1886.   Last night's storm made some ravages in the neighborhood. Trees were uprooted &c. Wrote a letter to Ed Donley and one to Cassel.

Wm. B. Freed and his Mary have become the happy parents of a baby.

My carriage is at present in the blacksmith shop.

Tuesday, July 20, 1886.   A very dull day at bank. The farmers and everybody were busy today harvesting. We got to disputing as to our height. So I brought a foot rule and at noon took all our measures. John measures 5 ft 6'4 in high in his shoes. Mr. Landes 5 ft 7½ in in low shoes and myself 5. 8 ⅛ in. John thought he was only 5 ft 5 in that I did not measure 5 ft 8 in. and that Charley Frick is a sixfooter. This last can also not be.

Painted the front porch floor this afternoon.

Was up at grandfather H's this evening.

Wednesday, July 21, 1886.   Rain again. There has been more rain this summer than for a long time. Am reading Prehistoric World.

The Gladstone Ministry has sent a message to the Queen bearing their resignations. The majority against was about 272,000.

Thursday, July 22, 1886.   The Queen has accepted the resignation of Mr. Gladstone. Was in the blacksmith shop this afternoon looking on. Am taking much interest in the building of my wagon.

Received a letter from Andrew this morning. He does not like his place. He talks about coming up to Campmeeting.

Horace was out riding Jacob Wile's horse this evening. I was to go with him but our horse is sick and so I could not go.

Was with Horace a while this evening.

Friday, July 23, 1886.   A.H. Leidy fell sick on Tuesday from inflammation of the bowels. He burst a bloodvessel and now there is little hope for his recovery. He was well on Monday.

Peter Benner is up from the city. He will be here some time.

The board for the bookcase at the library was finished today and I took it down and put it on.

Henry Hangey says our horse is about 19 yrs old, I told father and he refuses to listen to it. He is 13.

Father was out at uncle Cornelius'. He is sinking fast. Exchanged watches with father this evening. I like an open face better.

Saturday, July 24, 1886.   Aaron H. Leidy died today near midday. He leaves a wife and four children. He was in the full vigor of his health a week ago now he is dead. He has been doing an extensive business in manufacturing clothing. The examinations took place today at the square. Jennie Moyer has the primary again, Gerhart can have the Grammar if he wants it. Bean will not teach.

Was with Horace this evening. We met Jennie Moyer at their house and spent an hour or two there. Then we took a walk. He has been offered a good job by his father viz. to learn the spoke business and then to travel as a salesman with a good salary. We sat up on our porch till after midnight.

Sunday, July 25, 1886.   Mother felt very bad today. She was so very restless and weak.

Lay around sleeping and reading all forenoon. Commenced reading D'Aubignes' Hist. of the Reformation 1st vol. I am reading too many books at a time just now. This being the third.

Was in Sunday School this afternoon. Ambrose and Nelson were not there. Penrose and Samuel Leidy had perfect lessons. Went up with Milt Moyer after Sunday School to see the remains of Aaron Leidy but were informed we could not do so. Was at the station. Bill Slifers' went back to the city. Was out to L by eight. We took a promenade through town and had ice cream. Took her album with me. There is something said about going to Zeibers Park next Sunday. Don't know whether I will go or not.

Monday, July 26, 1886.   There was another heavy rain this afternoon. In Texas and some parts of the country there is a great drought and people are moving eastward to escape starvation.

There is already some rascally scandal got up about me to the effect that I did not start for home from Zs after the party till 5 o'clock in the morning.

Haynes and the Hunsberger's had ropes stretched across the walk all along. Mike Bergey cut them with his knife as he passed along. We passed over the platform and so escaped them. Rec'd a letter from Frick this morning. Wrote an answer and also to Andrew.

Mother staid upstairs most of the time today. She was better than yesterday.

Tuesday, July 27, 1886.   There was another shower today.

Mother felt worse again this afternoon. She is so dissatisfied with Susie. She is disobedient and will talk sharply every time she speaks. I told father how she acted and she got a lesson. The doctor was here this evening and he says she caught a cold.

Bought a pair of gloves this evening.

Heard that Ed Donley is coming over on Sunday a week. He will go to the Perkasie Campmeeting.

Wednesday, July 28, 1886.   An excursion today went to the shores of Connecticut. They will have a late time of it this evening. Schwenck and Miss Moyer went.

Ben. Barndt has commenced moving today.

Mother is still upstairs. She was better than yesterday.

Received letters from Andrew and Charley Frick. Andrew all at once grew tired of the city and has got a job at Lansdale. He will move on Saturday. Frick expects a great time on Saturday. He says if he can get a week off he will go for Jane Moyer just to make a couple and to keep in the crowd. He goes to Perkasie Campmeeting and I have a suspicion that he will start in with Jennie Moyer now. He wants it kept quiet. I had to laugh when I read it. See what will come of it.

Thursday, July 29, 1886.   A very warm day. The funeral of Aaron Leidy took place today. There must have been an immense number of persons present. Mr. Landes said that it was the largest funeral he had been to for a long time. He was widely known and respected.

Engaged Al Fretz's team for Sunday this afternoon. I hate to ask anyone for such a thing.

Friday, July 30, 1886.   Warmer if possible than yesterday.

Mr. Landis did not feel very well this morning so he came out late.

We have very much leisure at bank at present.

Mrs. Frick was over to see mother this afternoon.

Brought Fretz's team down and cleaned it this afternoon. It takes quite an amount of work to keep a team in order.

It is raining a little this evening.

Saturday, July 31, 1886. Was at work this afternoon cleaning Fretz's harness. Peter Benner and his partner were here for supper. He is getting on well. He will soon enter the Academy of Fine Arts. He showed me his silver medal. As they wanted to go over to Wm. G. Freed's for the night Uriah and I accompanied them to the upper end of the town. The band was serenading Moyer & Detweiler Geoff Tyson Geo. Swartz and Jacob Leidy. Everybody was out. Met Misses Jennie and Lillie and took them in at B's for icecream. Accompanied Miss L home and made arrangements for going to Zieber's Park tomorrow afternoon. Came home and shaved afterwards when it was quite late till I got to bed.

Sunday, August 1, 1886. Was in Sunday School this morning. It was announced that there would be no Sunday School next Sunday on account of the campmeeting at Perkasie as is the custom. Made ready to go to Ziebers after dinner. The weather looked threatening but yet we started. Bean and Kate took the lead. We drove on till below Hatfield when we turned again. Lillie took the lines once and drove ahead of Bean on a canter. I gave him the lead again. We spent the afternoon at Kate's and after some wrangling, for supper. Miss Tyson called though I don't believe she was very welcome. Rufus went into the parlor to entertain her and after supper we all followed. She had Jacob Leidy's little girl Agnes and Florence Price with her. The latter 9 yrs old plays well. After she left we took a walk through town. It was still damp and smoky. We went out to Z's on our return where I stayed till eleven. Will go to Perkasie campmeeting with the train next Sunday.

Monday, August 2, 1886. This morning Thos Scott residing between here and Telford was struck and killed by the 7.13 train up near Telford. He was first found by Isaac Hartzel at Becker's here. He was brought down by the 7.39 train to the station. I went over to see him. He was all cut up. A jury was held of which Ed. Borneman Goettler C H Moyer and H.K. Godshall were the members. Wrote to Uriah Frick and Andrew.

Was out to Cornelius' this afternoon. He is so weak. They are doctoring from Loux now.

Was up at grandfather's this evening.

Tuesday, August 3, 1886. The weather yesterday and today was quite cool. It was almost to cool for a seersucker this morning.

Lord Salisbury has formed a new ministry. The chief of which are Lord Randolph Churchill Chanceller of the Exchequer and leader of the House of Commons. The Earl of Iddesleigh Foreign Secretary. The Marquis of Londonderry Lord Lieutenant of Ireland. Michael Hicks Beach Chief secretary for Ireland &c.

These appointments are criticised.

Was working on the books this afternoon. Horace wanted me to go out riding but could not do it but promised for tomorrow evening.

Joe Derstein and little Joe stopped here this afternoon.

Wednesday, August 4, 1886.   Cool again today. Horace and I were out horse back riding this evening. He had Jack Wile's horse. We rode about six miles in all. Had a good long ride.

Received a letter from Frick. He is coming up on Saturday evening and will bring a friend along who wants to go to camp meeting.

Thursday, August 5, 1886.   Saml J Tilden died yesterday in the 73rd year of his age. The cause of his death was failure of the heart's action. He was about worn out.

We had old Shultz today to take out our potatoes. I hauled them home this evening. Mother was after me this evening about spending too much money. She says I spend too much for ice cream and so on. She is undoubtedly right but I don't see how a fellow can go out without spending anything. There is too much of it. But I'm no miser and never intend to be one. She never had the experience. I don't believe the girls ever have. Though some of these youngsters are downright extravagant for their means. But I think I don't deserve being rated in that category.

Friday, August 6, 1886.   Received a letter from Uriah. He says he was not along with the party last Saturday. He can't come up to campmeeting. He thought I was rather inquisitive. Cassel also wrote. He said only he couldn't come on Saturday evening and that he expected to meet me at the camp.

This was Library evening. The attendance was rather slim. Miss Jennie came down alone. Edwin Leidy brought home his and Newton's books. Newton is going to the city. He to his grandfathers', Rufus had brought two of his cousins.

Saturday, August 7, 1886.   Damp rainy weather. A dull prospect for campmeeting. Charley Frick did not come up this evening as I expected. Did not feel very well today. Suffering from diarrhea.

Received a letter from L. Souderton that she would be away today and if I expected to call this I should meet the 9 o'clock train. This I did. We made out to go with the morning train if the weather changed. This did not look very hopeful.

Gared Landes and his family are guests of Mr. Landes. They were along out to the bank this morning.

Sunday, August 8, 1886.   It cleared off quite unexpectedly during the night. I went out to _____ about 9.30. Stood around on the porch awhile. She did not get ready till near ten. When the train was almost due we started for the station. The platform was crowded. There we stood in the hot sun over one hour waiting for that train. Saw Ed Donley stop at Freeds'. He had a lady with him.

He came over on the platform and saw him go over with Rufus. Met him once in the afternoon and passed him. He did not stop to speak. He was afraid to show up I thought. At last the train came. And such a train! 15 cars and standing room only. Saw Mrs. Hunsberger get off the train. She saw me. All went well till Sellersville when the train got stuck. They fooled around quite a while and then gave it up. They first took up the front half and then the rest. We were among the latter. We did not get up till after noon. We went straight up to the auditorium and found seats. After we were rested we took dinner. Mr Yost of Cleveland O. probably of James & Yosts addressed the audience. Mike and Maggie were with all the time. We passed the line walking and sitting around. Saw Charley Frick. Had Miss Bossert along. Another set too. He came and spoke to us. In good spirits. Showed us photos of their party. Said he would be up for vacation the latter part of this month. Mike and Maggie were tired of it. They left with the extra. Met Miss Jennie Moyer and Rachel Stover. Saw Andrew on the platform spoke with him. Came down on the regular train. Met Charlie Stetson. Met Sylvester Jenkins and Mr. Freed of the Lansdale Bank. Spoke with the former. Standing room only. Was glad to get home. Saw Mrs. Hunsberger, helped to carry her trunk over. Florence gave me her picture. Saw little Emma Becker and Sally Keeler. Came out to about 8.30 Met her aunt Miss Hallman a young lady. Walked with them and her sister Anna. Felt very tired indolent And couldn't for the world ammuse myself. Left about eleven.

Monday, August 9, 1886. It is estimated that there were 12000 persons at the campmeeting yesterday, 1800 horse entered the grounds. Almost everybody seemed to be there.

We had intended to go out on horsback again this evening but our horse is in use and I will have to wait till tomorrow.

Tuesday, August 10, 1886. Splendid weather today. Went out on horseback with Horace this evening. The horse was not quite in order. He caught a cold somehow. We were through by eight o'clock.

Took a walk through the town. Met a number of young ladies whom at first I did not recognize. After I had passed them they saluted me and I was forced to turn back. I found them to be Miss L and her aunt, Miss Jennie Kate and Sallie Keeler. After talking we walked homeward I succeded in passing our place without being known. We went over to Moyer's and sat on the porch. Miss Jennie and Miss Hallman were full of the Chautauqua Literary Circle. Accompanied the girls home.

Mrs. Hunsberger and Florence came here this evening.

Wednesday, August 11, 1886. Isaac K. Zeigler who was seriously hurt the other day died last evening. The act was done by Geo. Sheif who in a drunken row was being put out of the room. He pushed Mr. Zeigler against a chair whereof he died.

Went up to the drugstore with Mrs. Hunsberger and Florence for a drink of soda water. We brought some along for mother too. She liked it pretty. But she can't drink her ale for anything. Florence and I walked up to grandfather H's and staid till nine o'clock.

Took them down to Delp's this afternoon. They told me that Lidy Crawford was already keeping company. I thought it couldn't be. She was only a little girl when she was up here.

Thursday, August 12, 1886.   This is the last day of campmeeting. Many went up from here. They will separate tomorrow morning. Am reading Dombey & Son.

H.G. Barnes' house is being moved further up and a new one erected on the site of the old one. The house is standing on rollers now.

Mrs. Hunsberger and I were up to the doctor's after nine o'clock. He didn't come home and we staied till eleven. Mother was getting anxious about us. I was thoroughly tired of it. Mrs. H. says she cant sleep if she didn't get medicine. Sam Benner was sitting round with his girl the doctor's housekeeper. She says the doctor will soon be married.

Friday, August 13, 1886.   A warm clear day. Mowed and cleaned the yard this afternoon and evening.

Liz and Florence went up to Enos Hagey's this evening.

Took a bath after I was through with my work. I was wet all through. A hand organ passed through town this afternoon. He had all the new pieces such as Seesaw, Sweet Violets, Golden Stairs and some others. He had 12 Dollars in change. There was one here the other day who had 20 Dollars.

Saturday, August 14, 1886.   Very little rain today. Had my hair cut this afternoon. Had my coat and vest pressed this evening.

Jennie Moyer will commence school on Monday.

Liz was here again this evening.

Sunday, August 15, 1886.   Lay around reading &c. Kate Stover came here and stayed for dinner. Was in Sunday School this afternoon. Was introduced to Mr. Moser by Milt Moyer. Took a walk with Rufus and Sam uptown. We stopped in at Mike Bergey's and saw the bees. Sam Detweilers' were here when I came home. Saw Dan Hunsberger. He had been up from the city. He is very tall. Well dressed, that is for him. Went out Tremper [?] St. about eight. Kate was there. W. D. Hunsberger's too. A host of little children. Anna was teaching school. Was bitten unexpectedly by their 12 yrs old cat. Accompanied Kate home. Felt very well. Had a good time. Went home at twelve.

Monday, August 16, 1886.   Changed hats again today. They were all mixed up in Sunday School yesterday. Planted celery this afternoon about 2 weeks too late. Expect it will rain. If not, too bad. Milt Moyer had 2200 plants out. Father got the contract for H.B. Freeds' house today for 1490 Dollars. There's nothing in it. Expected Gerhab would get it for certain. He was $65 higher. He can't understand.

The Congressional Convention at North Wales today nominated Rob't Yardly as the Republican candidate for Congressman. Bauman and Umsted were the candidates from here. Took a bottle of ale out to Cornelius' this eve. Did not see him.

Tuesday, August 17, 1886.   There was very little rain last night.

Took Dombey & Son along to bank today as I had not much to do. I like the book now very well.

Gave Miss Moyer the key to the lower room in the school room but which she could not open. She brought it down this evening accompanied by Miss Moser to whom I was introduced.

I promised to come down tomorrow and get the chair.

Wednesday, August 18, 1886.   Watered the celery plants this afternoon. They were doing better than I expected.

I stopped in at the schoolhouse to take up the chairs to the upper room. Had a pleasant talk with Miss Moyer. She says Miss Moser left this morning. She is a very pleasant person according to her.

Lib and Florence came down this evening to make arrangements to go to Landis' tomorrow. Could not help laughing when I found Miss L was in no favor with them at all. They call her the ribbon-girl. She said a young lady was going to cut her out and would see me this week yet. Could not get out of her who she meant.

Thursday, August 19, 1886.   Grandmother Lib Florence and mother went down to Landis' today. Went up to Grandfather H's this afternoon. Gets razor sharpened pockets filled with apples, and writes a letter for them to William Hemsing East Grantills Mill Wis.

Rec'd an invitation to Dr. Loux's wedding which is announced for Sept. 1st at 7 o'clock in the evening.

Were out on horesback with Horace this evening.

Friday, August 20, 1886.   Mr. Landes got an invitation to the wedding but Moyer did not. It is now rumored that he will make a trip to Europe.

Mowed the grass this afternoon. Kate told me a good one on Florence this afternoon, Miss L whom F calls the ribbon girl was with Kate last evening and F did not know her. The latter commenced making fun of her when Kate told her who she was. F was covered with confusion.

Library this evening. Misses Jennie and Annie Moyer were down till it was time to close and I accompanied them home. At Wm's gate we met Miss L. I hurried the others home and came over and did service again. I explained of course. The whole time was passed very pleasantly. Went straight home afterwards.

Saturday, August 21, 1886.   Seven of the Anarchist Murderers in Chicago were yesterday found guilty of murder penalty of hanging and one 15 years penitentiary. Efforts will be made for new trials. It is right that these vile dogs should hang. They have no business to live.

Was reading this afternoon. Expected Frick up but did not see him come.

Bought a new collar and white cravat this evening.

There was a celebration in Hilltown today A team of girls went over, K.J. A & L.

Cornelius is sinking. The band was not allowed to play in town.

Sunday, August 22, 1886.   Saw Frick this morning. He came up last evening with last train. Went together to Sunday School. Have a bad cold and could not sing well. F came home with me till dinner time. Went up to the photographer Pictures did not suit us. Took soda water and went to meeting. After meeting got the Guvnor to take us out with his new horse. Took supper at Godshall's. Went up through Telford. Stopped at Jos. R. Bergey's. Went up to the Lutheran Cemetery. On way down stopped at S.S.Kulp's. From there on home. Lib and Florence arrived just as I was brushing up. Frick was with me until I left. Spent evening pleasantly. Had fruit wine and cake. Went home a little before one. Met Horace who had been with Susie and Charley Price from parts unknown.

Monday, August 23, 1886.   Milt Moyer told me yesterday that he might leave soon and said, he would [tell] me all about it this evening. I did not see him but I heard he is going next Monday. Travel. Meehling Bros West.

Lib and Florence went away today. Wrote in her album. C.H. Moyer has commenced tearing up his old pavement. Ordered a new pair of shoes this evening. Frick went down early this morning. Bean was up yesterday.

Pres. Cleveland is in the Adirondacks.

Mother had a spat with the girls and came near sending them away.

Frick gets his vacation in 2 weeks.

Maggie and Mrs. Allebach came out for father this evening about a quarter after ten. The boys were and I were up yet. Father got up and accompanied them. He is probably dying. She says the doctor is out that the boys were at Perkasie. She did not say much else. She was much agitated. I did not say much. Father will probably stay all night.

Tuesday, August 24, 1886.   (Prince Alexander of Bulgaria has resigned, Aug 23).

Cornelius died this morning about eleven o'clock. Father came home about half past one this morning. He rested easier at that time. He was about 43 yrs. old. The boys were sent for this morning and came down with the first train.

It now appears that Prince Alexander was deposed probably through Russian intrigue or perhaps through the meeting of the Emperors William and Francis Joseph, a few weeks ago.

Wednesday, August 25, 1886.   Prince Alexander of Bulgaria was deposed by a conspiracy of a part of his people. This party seems not to be of the majority and it is mainly of due to the intrigues of Russia.

My carriage will be all ready by Saturday. I thought it would take one week longer.

Saw Harry Dettry this afternoon. Walked with him a short way. He seems to be a rough character. Drinks too much it seems by his talk.

Thursday, August 26, 1886.   There has been a counter-revolution in Bulgaria in favor of Prince Alexander. The revolutionists were put in prison.

Jos. G. Blaine made a speech at Sabago Maine Tuesday. He attacked Sec. Bayards policy, touched the labor question &c. He is probably getting ready for 1888.

Were out on horseback again this evening. We went very slow. My saddle was not in order. We stopped at Mrs. Landis's and she seemed glad to see us. We came a little after nine.

We noticed a meteor fall down over Leidy's churchyard. It looked like a skyrocket and burst the same way.

Friday, August 27, 1886.   Very warm today, 92 on our glass.

C.H. Moyer has his walk finished and they are at Barndt's now.

Cleaned the yard and washed wagon this afternoon.

Am reading 2nd vol D'Aubigne's Reformation.

Rec'd a letter from Uriah this morning. He says he will be up Sunday a week. I wrote to him about his harness. He paid 40 for his. Seems not to be too well satisfied with it.

I get disgusted with the talk of some of these young fellows. They seem to think it no sin to be act and talk impure. Foul talk and horses is all they know about. Smoking and drinking their only recreations. To be goaded by such fellows is almost unbearable.

Saturday, August 28, 1886.   Today was probably the hottest day of the year. It was 95 on our glass and some said 108 in the sun.

My carriage was not put together this afternoon. It will be done however at any time. There was harvest meeting this afternoon. Well attended.

Bilger's boys Jas & Will came up this evening. The old folks came up at nine o'clock.

Want to see the eclipse tomorrow morning.

Sunday, August 29, 1886.   The weather not being clear did not see anything of the eclipse this morning.

Cornelius' funeral being today I went out about half past nine. It was very warm. The coffin was brought out into the yard under the trees and the funeral discourse held there by Rev. Horning. The procession then moved on to the meeting house where Rev. Kuhn preached. A great crowd of people were present. The family all took it so hard especially the older ones. It seemed as if their hearts would break and it was a pity to see them. Went to Sunday School after the funeral which however was very thin, on account of the funeral. Miss Moyer is now acting as secretary. Milt was not in this afternoon.

Went out to the house after Sunday school where I met a great many friends. The Bilger boys went home with me to supper. We sat on the front porch till eight o'clock or after. They then left for grandfather's. Went out to Washington Ave. pretty late, took 'Scottish Chiefs' along. Went home half past eleven. It now seems to me almost clear that Haynes wants to pick a quarrel with me. He does not notice me anywhere. And now he wrote to Miss L a letter charging her with having scandalized him. And that he or she would get into trouble underlining 'he'. I see how it is. It is a challenge for me. But he is mistaken. He has spies out. I suspect H and R. I am watched. He wants me to begin. But he cawn't do it. I am not afraid of him or his set. I think I see through it. But he can't frighten me. It's all false I have never given him cause of offense.

Monday, August 30, 1886.   Milt Moyer left this morning. He will travel in Ohio &c. Will Bilger went home this morning and Jim this afternoon. The old folks also. The crossing at Chestnut St. is being paved with flagstones. This will make it fine.

Hen. Bilger's Sr. were here for dinner. Prince Alexander has returned to Bucharest and will probably resume the reins of government. Got a letter from Andrew who wants me to come down on Sunday. Don't know what to do. Says he will not come up before I come down.

The weather today was again very warm. More air than yesterday. Rain somewhere but not here.

Jos Slifer was buried today at Franconia Meeting House. He was nearly 88 yrs. old.

Dr. Slifer will soon start on a trip around the world.

Tuesday, August 31, 1886.   There was very little rain today. But it settles the dust if no more.

Aunt Mary Souder with Preston and Lillie were here at dinner. Preston is growing very fast and so is Lillie who is only in her 9th year almost as tall or stout as one of 10 or 11. I turned a baseball bat for Preston in the afternoon.

Dan Bilger's with their troublesome children of which they have four stopped in here this afternoon before leaving.

This evening Martha and Kate came in here being afraid of a dog which had followed them but who on examination was found to be Ed's. I accompanied them home.

Prince Alexander is returning to Bulgaria. The revolution is about at an end.

Wednesday, September 1, 1886.   A slight shock of earthquake was felt last evening in Phila. Pittsburg New York the South and other places. I have heard of no one around here who felt it. It happened at 9.55 last evening and lasted 30 seconds in New York and shorter and longer periods at other places. Rec'd a letter from Andrew desiring me to come down on Sunday. I have not decided what to do yet. Heard from Donley. He says watermelons are gone &c. Scarce this year.

Can't help bearing a grudge against Haynes for the way he acts. If I could only keep my mouth closed but I talk too much about. And it seems to me that everyone turns spy and goes and tells him. He is at Wm's almost every day now and is very thick with the boys.

Thursday, September 2, 1886.   The earthquake reported yesterday did more damage than was at first known. Charleston S.C. seems to have been the centre of the disturbance. The city is in ruins and about ¾ of it will have to be rebuilt. The extent of the damage is not known. 30 persons were killed and hundreds wounded. The people are encamped in the streets and public squares and are afraid to enter the houses. Great distress prevails. All communication was cut off. The people are in great terror. During the last 20 days there has been more than usual of these occurences. Earthquakes in Greece, Tangiers &c, Volcanic eruptions in the Mediteranean and Vesuvius, Water spouts and tornadoes in Central Russia, terrible cyclones in Texas, flooding of Mandelay, the renewed activity of the great geyser in Yellowstone Park the flooding by the artesian well at Belleplain, Iowa, &c &c.

Friday, September 3, 1886.   The damage to Charleston was found to be even greater than was at first supposed. About seven eighth of the houses were damaged or destroyed, 35 persons were killed and a 100 wounded. Mayor Smith is in a fix. His conduct is being investigated by Councils. He had not paid over moneys belonging to the city as required by law.

Prince Alexander on Aug 30 addressed a very submissive epistle to the Czar but the czar has replied in a menacing tone that augurs not well for him. My carriage is now completed. Saw it this afternoon. Saw Jennie Moyer this afternoon. She will go with Frick in our expedition to the Rocks. The Library was open this evening. Notice was posted up of the election on Oct 1. Took out, 'A Tale of Two Cities.'

Saturday, September 4, 1886.   Read an account of the wedding in the North Wales Record of Dr. Loux's wedding. Among the presents were a piano from the bride's mother and a bank check from the father amount not being stated. They went on a trip to Niagara and the St. Lawrence.

Got ready this afternoon and went down to Lansdale and ordered a harness of Tyson. Ordered the best for 43 Dolls. He wanted $45, can get it in a week.

Took a look at Rosenberger's and Sand's houses. These will be fine. Saw Charley Hendricks there. Walked around to the schoolhouse. This will be very costly. Estimated at $15,000. Got on train and went down to North Wales and found Andrew at home. We took a walk through the town in the evening. I was very tired.

Sunday, September 5, 1886. We got up quite late. Mrs. Cassel came home in the morning. Saw the new houses in course of erection near their place. Walked about town and then went to the Lutheran Church. The subject of the discourse was about the earthquake. Met Anders at the station. Went home with the milk train. Saw Frick and Uriah after the sunday school. We went into the carriage shop and took alook in at my carriage. Frick brought me Cuff Supporters and cravat. He brought Miss Bossert along up. We were up at the station after supper. Haynes and he made up a little as they were both going the same way. They left for Gerharts about half past seven. Left Uriah with Markly about eight. Reported about the intended expedition to the Rocks next Sunday. At about eleven I was nearly ready to go when she went out and brought in cake and wine to detain me. So I staid another half hour.

Monday, September 6, 1886. It is said Prince Alexander intends to abdicate. That he can't stay in Bulgaria in the face of the Czar. Prince Bismarck is believed to be the only person who knows whether there will be peace or war. It is a great muss seemingly.

Charleston is still having shocks of earthquake every day though they are constantly growing lighter.

Went with father down to Landis house where I picked crab apples. Frick went fishing today. He got five very small fish and is tired of it.

Uriah went down this morning. Was with Frick after supper. He saw Miss Bossert off at the station. We took a walk through town and went up to Alderfer's. After that home. Charley pumped Haynes last night he told him all. He says I interfered in his business and all that. That they were going to make me sick and all that. This is just what I thought it was. Everything was aimed at me right along. But let them go ahead. I am not afraid of them. They can't frighten me so easy.

Tuesday, September 7, 1886. Today was Rufus' last day at the bank.

John did not work yesterday. He was blessed with a little son yesterday morning. I did his posting for him. Was with Frick up to the cab this afternoon where we found a nice cool place. We then went down to the photographer's who was away. After supper we went over to the station. Haynes tried to thrust at me now and then but I did not notice it. He thinks he is sure of Frick. But there he is mistaken. I believe Frick will stick to me. He will try to raise a fuss next Sunday night but Frick will not be with him. I have taken him in my confidence. Haynes does not look strait at me. I think Frick knows better than to be fooled.

Wednesday, September 8, 1886.   The Czar has guaranteed the independence of Bulgaria. Prince Alexander has taken leave of the army. The Mayflower has beaten the English cutter Galatea in the race for the America's cup by 12 min 40 sec.

Went with Frick up to the cab again. From there we went to see Schwenck about the picnic. He is not sure whether he can go or not. After supper went to see Kate. She has no one to take her. She suggested Haynes and we went over to see him. He jumped at it but when he heard Schwenck was going he drew back. There is something between them. A terrible motley crowd. Then I have a talk with Haynes. I thought it no more than right to find out what it was. It was as I had suspected. Horace had reported what I had said to him a little wrong which though it only expressed my opinion of Haynes set it a going. That evening he wrote that letter to Lillie. He protested that he had all forgotten it but I confessed it was on my mind pretty much. He says he had not been drunk since and that much of that story about him was got up.

Thursday, September 9, 1886.   The doctor and his wife came home from their honeymoon this evening with the 9.00 train. The first we knew of it was when we heard a great noise of bells and horns. We knew what it meant. It was a Dutch Band. It lasted only half a minute. Saw some of the banders when coming. They said they had rec'd 3 Dollars. We were over at Moyer's this evening to arrange everything. Haynes says he can't go. He has to work at Hatfield. Charley Schwenck says he ain't sure yet whether he will go. He is a queer fellow. Because we didn't ask him first, he won't go. But we fixed it all right. The girls will get cakes and we get the fruit. Told L about Haynes. Horace lied about her to him. Got home late enough again.

Friday, September 10, 1886.   Frick tells me this morning that Schwenck won't go and that he can't get anybody to take Kate. So we will have to take it alone. Went up to Tyson's and engaged a horse for 1.25. He asked $2.00. He takes all he can get. Will have to get peaches at Lansdale. We saw all the girls tonight. Was at Wm's and took Lillie home. Met Susie on the way and told her to tell mother I'd be home soon. They tried to fool me afterwards. Frick felt a little discouraged this morning.

This afternoon a man came round and put up the telephone instrument. He will put up the wire tomorrow morning.

Saturday, September 11, 1886.   This afternoon the Guvnor Charley and I went to Lansdale to fetch my new harness. We started soon after two and got home at six. We bought peaches and pears for tomorrow. We made out to go to Old Goshenhoppen Church on Tuesday.

Charley and I worked hard after supper getting things ready. We cleaned the wagon bought a watermelon bananas &c. Will have a terrible lot of work tomorrow morning. I got to bed very late. Had to get ready and pressed my suit of clothes &c. Markly Huffnagel was in to see my new harness. It is fine.

The doctor gets serenaded tonight. The band is playing very late.

Sunday, September 12, 1886.   We got up at about half past five. There was a great am't of work to be done but we managed to get together a tolerable team after changing the horse, harness, and shaft. We had two horses, Landis's, Becker's harness and shaft, new. About half past eight we started in our yard. We had a watermelon, ¼ pk peaches, ¼ pears, 2 lemons, 1 doz bananas. The girls cakes &c. We went up by Dietz's mill. We got to the same place as we were last year. The stones of the old stove were there yet. Heffentrager's place deserted. So we took the horses half way up the hill and left the carriage at the Heffentrager's. We had 2 hammocks. We did not put up the swing. Had a fine dinner. Took a stroll over the mountain in the afternoon. Recognized many places of last year but could not find the Indian Rock anymore. A party of about 15 persons passed our encampment in the afternoon. Frick enjoyed it greatly. So did the girls. You don't know the inconveniences of such travel till you have the girls along. The bushes and all seemed to be much thicker. The distance greater than last year. At 4.25 we started off the mountain. When it commenced to rain only a little bit. The girls sought shelter under the trees while we got the team ready. It commenced to pour. Frick and I got wetter than we had ever been before. I enjoyed it and it was so. Was only sorry for the girls. We came home cheerfully though, after having a great time.

Monday, September 13, 1886.   We all got through our wetting better than could be expected. Charley had a little headache but he soon got over that. The only losses were a ring for the harness which cost 5¢ one of my cuffsupporters, a fan and the watermelon which was abandoned. We cleaned the harness this afternoon and put the things away. I pressed my suit again after supper. I could hardly get ready. Frick and I made our calls tonight to return hammocks &c. Frick and Jennie came out and we passed some time together. I was too sleepy. Lillie showed me the birthday presents they made to her father. They were all very nice. Schwenck is what he is. He belied us terribly. He was out driving yesterday. That shows he could have gone if he would. Was presented with a nice bouquet for tomorrow.

Tuesday, September 14, 1886.   We started this morning early at about seven o'clock sharp. We passed by Gilman's store, JB Moyer's, through Mechanicsville which has 11 dwelling houses 2 hotels 1 store and 2 smithies. We arrived at the Old Goshenhopper Church ½ mile south of Mechanicsville about 10.30. It was built in 1744 and rebuilt 1858, Luth & Ref. The monument over the grave of Jacob K Smith is 37 ft high, and is said to have cost 5 or 6000 Dollars. Could not find Mrs. Richards grave. Mr. Barndt who takes care of the premises and who is at once choir leader organist, monument maker &c looked up his records and found she was buried Jan 31-1879. His shop which was formerly a school house and teachers residence is a very old building. We ate our dinners in the woods opposite the church. We went down to Salford

Station where we had the horse fed. Charley and I went up the creek to Zeigler's dam where on trying to get a boat afloat a gust of wind blew my hat into the dam. It drifted quite a distance and I thought I had to swim for it. I got it however without doing so. We walked on up to a great ice house. We returned to the station when we started for home. We were very tired. We stopped off at Benj. K Alderfer's where we ate apples drank cider &c. We got home a quarter past five. After supper we were up to see Haynes for a short time.

While writing this I heard somebody outside when I got up and took a short walk with them after which I had to take Lillie home. I did it as secretly as possible to avoid being seen.

Wednesday, September 15, 1886. Frick was suffering from toothache today. He was not out of the house. Sam was down at the state fair today. Grandfather H. was down this afternoon. He wanted to know about our trip. I told him I could not find his aunt's grave. He thought it was not marked by a stone.

I showed him my new harness and he thought the leather was very good.

The telephone was finished yesterday. It was used between here and Telford several times and worked very well but between Sellersville there was something wrong.

Thursday, September 16, 1886. The report of the committee investigating the charges against Mayor reported in favor of impeachment on Monday. Maine went Republican by a reduced plurality. Wrote to Donley Uriah and Cassell last evening. Frick had his tooth pulled this morning. He feels broke up yet. He was in the house all day. Saw him this afternoon. He wishes his vacation lasted two wks longer. He will go down tomorrow morning. He was over with me in my room awhile this afternoon. The time passed by quickly and we both enjoyed it much. He had intended to call at the school house this afternoon but did not feel well enough. He went to bed early. He is a great society man down there. More than I could stand.

Friday, September 17, 1886. There was a meeting of the board of managers at the library this evening. I made my report for the last six months. Made a suggestion about a literary society. They are going to talk about it. Jennie did not want to stay at first. It soon came out that Lillie was the cause of it. Because I took them home the last time I suppose. I can't see how any one else had anything to do with it.

Rufus likes North Wales pretty well.

Frick went home this morning. He did not like to go to work again. He promised to come up next winter and enjoy sleighing.

Saturday, September 18, 1886. Talked over the telephone for the first time today. Uncle Hen was talking down from Quakertown. It works quite well and after you get used to it it will be easy.

Saw Alice Hendricks this afternoon. She was out with Horace and others this evening.

Susie went to town today and will stay till tomorrow evening.

There is some moving going on at the doctors. It is said Mrs. Lake is moving up.

Sunday, September 19, 1886.   Was around the house all morning. It was a very nice cool day and very tempting to go out driving as the dust was all nicely laid by Fridays rain.

Was in Sunday School this afternoon. Miss Lizzie Gerhart was down with Martha. When singing 'O let me cling to thee' the governor laughed and so did the girls as it reminded them of last Sunday. Miss Alice Hendricks was also there. Irwin Bean also. After Sunday School Sam and I took a walk and stopped in at Kate's where I found L. Ate some bananas. Tried to sleep after supper but couldn't. Had on a new pair of shoes which pinched me some. Arrived at eight. She sang 'Love comes' and 'I cawn't'. Found Fred Fluck had made some attempts but failed. Said some thing about Jennie but she wouldn't hear any thing of it. She said it was all right &c. But that's all put on. Came home 11.30.

Monday, September 20, 1886.   Was down in the lot this afternoon and tended the celery. Saw Emma Detweiler. Her baby's name is Bertha. Was in the cemetery. There are now about 14 graves. Made a cover for my carriage this evening. Wrote to Uriah today. Sent for Westlakes Letterwriter to Leary's 75 cts.

Tuesday, September 21, 1886.   Did not have much to do today. Read Dickens 'Tale of Two Cities' most of the time.

After bank worked on the books and made out the report of the library. Miss Jennie called on library business this afternoon.

Received a letter from Frick this morning. He was at home on Sunday and did not get up to Hatfield as he had intended. Wrote a reply.

Took our bottles home from the picnic. Went up to grandfather H's and was there till near ten.

Sallie was discharged at Becker's this afternoon. She will stay here over night.

Wednesday, September 22, 1886.   Received Westlakes' Letter Writer from Leary's this morning. Made out notices of the election of officers for the Library. Was down at the school house and saw J about it. She makes out her share and Mr. Moyer the rest. Pressed my pants this evening and bound some old quarterlies for the sunday school.

There was a kind of a revolution attempted in Spain on Sunday but was soon quelled. It was not well planned. A Brig. Gen. was concerned in it. Russia is all the time acting mean in regard to Bulgaria. She would like to see the conspirators go unpunished.

Thursday, September 23, 1886.   President Cleveland is returning to Washington.

Emma Detweiler, nee Hunsicker, was here today with her baby. The baby's name is Bertha. Mr. Detweiler came up this evening to fetch her and also to take Sallie Daub's things along. Was down in the field this afternoon plucking grass. Don't like it. When coming down from the P.O. this evening noticed somebody at Wm's so I dropped in by the back door and staid awhile. Had some noise with Rufus. Too bad.

Rec'd a letter from Uriah. He will come up Saturday.

Friday, September 24, 1886.   Mr. Landes and his brothers Abe and Gared went up to the rocks today on a pleasure trip.

C.H. Moyer had a sale this afternoon of fire wood stoves &c.

Bought a horse whip this evening for $1.40

Morris Landes and J.G.Godshall have rented the Franconiaville store. Have not much faith in this Godshall. He would suit better for a farmer.

Saturday, September 25, 1886.   Took my buggy home this afternoon cleaned it and made all ready for using tomorrow.

Received the History of Franconia today. It is covered only in paper. Have not read it yet.

Rec'd a letter from Frick this evening. He wants me to bring the girls down next Sunday. Don't think I will do it. Did not see Uriah yet. He was to come up today. Horace and Haynes went to Topton.

Mother said this evening that I looked sunburnt or yellow more than I used to. They made out that I was keeping too late hours. I think myself there is something in it. Must make a reform.

Sunday, September 26, 1886.   Started this morning about nine o'clock for the dedication at Leidy's Church. L was ready and we came down about half past. The church has been frescoed which a good appearance. Little too much of it perhaps. The change at the altar and the pulpit is a great improvement. Rev. Diehant preached in German. Rev. Rothrock of Lansdale in English. The former I liked but latter not. Revs. Sheif Dengler and Reiter were also there. Went down again in the afternoon. The roads very dusty and was some rain but I reached the shed before there was rain of any account. Rev. Dr. Mann of Phila preached in German and Rev. Becker in English. The former is a German and can talk. It is pleasant to hear him. The latter has a good delivery. There were present Revs. Dr. Mann, Balser Dengler Reiter Rothrock Sheif Kehon Huber and one or two others. The church was crowded both services. Had a seat in the aisle with Uriah and Os Kline in the morning and in the afternoon sat in the gallery. The Bridgetown Choir sang in the morning and the Ridge Road Choir in the afternoon. The latter had a cornet. Took a drive after church with Schwenck. Made out to go to Sellersville in the evening but gave it up on account of the threatning look of the weather. Was with Uriah till near eight. Kate and Jennie came in and we had a good time together. Went out quarter past eight. Teased about not coming anymore and she believed there was something wrong. Had to laugh. Went to bed at twelve.

Monday, September 27, 1886.   Met Jennie at noon and she asked me how it was about next Sunday. As I knew of nothing going on next Sunday. She didn't say what. Then I recollected Frick's invitation to come down with the girls. F must have written to her and I think he was a little too quick. Don't like the idea. Spoke to Uriah about it who promised to write. He went down with the afternoon mail 5.20.

Washed my carriage this afternoon and made a rack to put my harness on and have it now in my room.

Tuesday, September 28, 1886.   Wrote Frick this afternoon about next Sunday. Expected to hear from Uriah this evening but did not.

Was at carriage cleaning again this afternoon. Am over it now for awhile. Water is getting scarce and if it does not soon rain some wells will run dry. The one at the bank is used by the whole neighborhood.

The county conventions took place today in Norristown. Heard that W. D. Hunsberger had no chance for the nomination for Co. Treas. and he lost it.

Met L this evening. She still thought there had been something wrong on Sunday evening I assured her there was not. Today Penrose came over to the bank with a ck of 300. I gave him only a 100 on it by Mr. Landes' orders. She mentioned this too this evening. They did not like it at all I know but it can't be helped. She said she was to have come over for the money but that she sent Penrose. I am glad she did too for it would have gone the same way. We take no risks on M.D.Z.

Wednesday, September 29, 1886.   Heard from Uriah this morning. He says all arrangements have been made to meet us at Ninth and Green. From thence to Slifer's, up the Schuylkill and rowing on the Wissahickon. Met Miss Jennie this afternoon. She accepts this evening. She wanted to see if I were going. She told Lillie about it last evening. Got a lecture from mother when she heard it. She says I spend my money as fast as I earn it. She is not far wrong. But I hate to hear it. But this must not go on this way. Expected to hear from Frick today but did not.

Was out at Aunt Kits this afternoon. They are busy sewing. Maggie did not like Yardly very well. Was with Kate awhile this afternoon also.

Carried a letter up to grandfather's staid till nine o'clock and went home.

Thursday, September 30, 1886.   Received a letter from Frick this morning. He says he thought all was arranged. He expects us with the milk or Buffalo. Was out to see Miss Zendt about going. She is very willing as I could easily see. My parents do not like my going at all. But I am in for it and must. These girls have very little sympathy with you. This will be probably the beginning of the end. Wrote in her album this evening. Had it almost two months already.

This morning an excursion started for Valley Forge. Jennie and Kate went along.

Uriah was not at home again last night. Found out he was gone to Hatfield to a surprise party. He goes to see Katie Delp Eli Delp's daughter.

Friday, October 1, 1886.   There is a great sensation at Gwynedd on account of the mysterious happenings at F.D. Worley's house. A week ago the crockery and glassware commenced a series of antics which has drawn the attention of the whole neighborhood. The glass jars fell down and broke. The salt cellars &c spun round and flew through the windows &c. About $500 damages was done. Rufus Landes was down and saw the pieces. The mystery is unexplained.

The Library election took place this evening. Jennie sold two half shares one to Haynes and one to Lillie M. Zendt. The only change was in Secretary. Jennie declined to serve. Jonathan M. Hunsberger was chosen in her place. H.D. Detweiler and J.L. Gehman were tied as managers but after a second ballot Gehman was chosen. After the meeting was over took Jennie and Lillie home. Have arranged to go on the milk train Sunday morning.

Saturday, October 2, 1886.   Heard today that Lewis Keller's store and residence had all been burned down last night. Incendiarism is suspected. A man was arrested and taken before a Justice in Perkasie this afternoon. We heard the above through the telephone. Father and some others intend to go over tomorrow and see the ruins. He had a great shock and the damage must be great.

Nothing new about the Gwynedd sensation.

Am making ready for tomorrow. Will probably go to bed quite late.

Sunday, October 3, 1886.   Got ready this morning for the milk train but almost missed it. Bought a hat before going. Did not get to Zendt's even before starting but met L about half way. I hated this very much but its about the way it goes with me. Jennie was on the platform when we came. It was quite cold on the train going down. When we arrived at 3rd & Berks we did not meet Charley as I had expected and started for 9th & Green. He was not there. So we started for Slifer's. Had a little trouble in finding it for I had the number wrong. Found out at Kindig's. When we got to Slifer's Charley not being there Uriah and I started in quest of him. We found him at home and quite sick. He made ready and Uriah started to report after which he and I followed. It was now near dinner time and Aunt Kate insisted on our staying for dinner. After this we started for the park. Uriah and Allie leading Charley and Jennie next and Lillie and myself bringing up the rear. Saw the excavation for the B&O railroad. Saw the first brick house in Phila built by Penns 1683 and removed to the Park in 1883. Went up in the elevator and took a bird's eye view of the city. This was fine. Bricks, bricks with a huge pile of marble in the middle, and the Delaware in the distance. Had a field glass. Crossed Girard Ave. Bridge and walked over to the Art Gallery. How the walks and grounds are neglected and what a difference between now and the Centennial. The pictures, busts, antique furniture, relics &c were fine to look at and we enjoyed it very much. Left the building when it was closed. Returned on the River steamer 'Belmont'. Took a view of the Water works. Lunched at a restaurant near here. Went on out to the depot walking quite a distance. Saw the electric light for the first time this evening. Charley and Uriah went along to Columbia Ave. Said they were going to Church. We had a pleasant ride homeward. I think we were all pretty tired. Taking leave of Jennie took L home. She took me in the dining room where there was a stove. Left about 10:20. When I came home Jos Derstine's were here yet. Had some fun with them.

Monday, October 4, 1886.   Father, Ed, Sam and Alonzo were over to Bedminsterville yesterday. Everything is burned down. They stopped at Keller's. Saw Lewis who is crippled up. They will start up the store in the hall. Loss as placed by Lewis $35,000 at least. Ins. $20,000. The fire originated in the basement. It was discovered when but low but it spread and only a small portion could be saved.

Helped to haul two loads of water this afternoon from Wile's spring. Are wells are nearly dry. Made me feel very stale indeed.

Felt very tired from yesterday's expedition yet.

Kate and Haynes were out driving yesterday. Sunday School was very slim. Mr. Godshall intends closing the S.S. in two weeks. He is tired of it.

Tuesday, October 5, 1886.   Commenced reading 'David Copperfield' today. It promises to become interesting.

Wrote Ed. Donley, Cassel, Uriah, Frick and acknowledged receipt of Hist of Franconia to JD Souder. Ran around for quilters for tomorrow. They are going to make two comfortables for my bed.

Rec'd samples from Wanamakers of letter paper and envelopes. Very good and cheap.

Was up at grandfathers this evening. They were tired of their trip though pleased with the whole.

Saw last week that Lizzie Gerhart was down. Martha told me this evening that she was giving music lessons.

Was up at Kate's this evening. Teased her beyond all patience. Sorry for it afterward.

Wednesday, October 6, 1886.   Made all right with Kate again this morning.

Abram Keller father of Lewis came over today in his stead. He had about the same story as father. He says they will start again on the hall.

The quilting party came off today. Grandmothers H.&S. were here and Aunts Sarah, Lizzie and Kate Souder. With Old Polly. A good dinner. Some teasing as could be expected.

Heard from Andrew. He is coming up on Sunday. Heard from Frick too. He is full of Schwenck again.

Was in CH Moyer's house today. They are making ready for moving.

Was over at Godshall's this evening to take over a postal card when the Gov. and Mrs. Frick wanted to pay me for Charley about the fare. I would not take it. They kept me free and I would feel awkward if I should accept anything. Promised to help Jennie about the S.S. matter.

Thursday, October 7, 1886.   Went over to Moyers this evening with Mr. Godshall. Went to work with J on the Sunday School books. Mr. G left soon after. Jennies School will close on Saturday. Anna and Mrs. Moyer were in the room too. We had a pleasant time. Left quarter past ten.

Gen. Kanlbars the Russian agent in Bulgaria is evidently trying to stir up disorder to give Russian and excuse for occupying Bulgaria.

Friday, October 8, 1886.   Was down in the lot at work on the celerys. H.B.Freed's house is almost up at the square. H.B. has bought the Harleysville bakery and intends to go there. He tried to buy Becker's but he thinks it cant be done.

Commence D'Aubigne's Ref Vol III this afternoon. Am reading 'David Copperfield' at the bank.

Heard from Uriah today. He does not say where they were last Sunday night but says he'll tell me some other time. He and Charley did not do quite the right thing last Sunday that is they neglected the girls. If they did not want them why in the world did they make me bring them down.

Saturday, October 9, 1886.   Jennie Moyer's school closed today.

Andrew came up this evening. We took a walk up town. Met Jennie Annie and Kate with another lady a stranger. We stopped in at Hageys where Andrew ordered a pair of shoes. He will be up again in 4 weeks.

After we came home we found Amelia here. We had some music. We got to bed late enough.

Sunday, October 10, 1886.   We took a walk to Freed's new house this morning and from there up to the station. Saw Schwenck there and he asked me to join the choir. I refused because I have always done so and the same reasons hold good. Got the Record. The 7 Anarchists have been sentenced to be hanged on Dec. 3 in Chicago yesterday. Neche 15 yrs imprisonment.

Maggie and her mother and Penrose were here for dinner. Went to Sunday School. It was announced that next Sunday would be the last. Katie Derstine and her Rickert are in town today. They were with Martha in Sunday School. When we came home Aunt Kit told me Schwenck had said I had been at Zendt's as high as 6 times a week. It was a surprise. I am about done with him. The Hypocrite. I could not forget this all day.

Andrew went down with the train. He will go to school again next winter. Stopped at Kate's. Haynes was there. She gave me a bouquet of autumn leaves and pinned it on my coat. She wanted us to come out for a walk. Went out a quarter of eight. There is a change in the room. Stove put up and organ in the opposite corner. Talked savagely of Schwenck for awhile. Had a game or two of checkers and old maids. Heard that Bean was over at Kate's Thursday night to exchange letters. Left a little after 12.

Monday, October 11, 1886.   Saw Kate this morning. She was a little displeased because we did not come out last evening. She gave me to understand that Haynes would have to go shortly. He is expecting it too. Bean was over Thursday evening. He will be all right to come again. Kate has repented the step she took.

Heard a new Sunday School was to be started on Hunsberger's Hall and that Mr. Zendt would take ahold.

The Sunday School col. yesterday amounted to something over 6 Dolls. There is about 15 dollars in all to invest for books. Godshall is going on Wednesday.

They are making hay this evening over in the meadow. Grandfather H is down. I guess they would like to have me too, but said nothing and I have CH Moyers bill to make out.

The doctors performed another operation on Sam'l Sorver's leg today again.

Tuesday, October 12, 1886.   We were quite busy at bank today. I balanced JM Landis & Cos and several other books. Mr Moyer worked on HM Zeigler book of which a ck is lost. I got out about four. Moyer later. Had an appointment at Godshalls at four. Found Jennie there at work on the Sunday School books, list. Old Herman is going down tomorrow to buy them. Ordered letter paper and envelopes from Wanamaker through H.K. I teased Jennie a little and she said she'd get even with me. Bunting the telephone man was here today. He says the trouble was all at Lansdale. He spoke to Doylestown. He told the Lansdale man to press his pin tight and then it worked plain. John G Hunsicker and others will get a phone.

Wrote to Uriah and Charley. Gave each to understand about Schwenck.

Wednesday, October 13, 1886.   This morning when I came to bank John had a great fuss about a lost key to the safe. Mr. Landes had left them on the table and when he wanted to use it one of them was missing. We looked in every corner and have not found it yet.

Mr. John Ruth had his two boys along today. Mischievous fellows.

Old Herman came up with the books this afternoon. Was over this evening. Jennie came down too. He made out just as I expected. Cheap books and great big cards. He brought paper and envelopes for me from Wanamaker's. Walked home with Jennie. She was not quite pleased with Charley as I could see. She did not wish to let out.

BC Barndt must be happy. He has a little daughter.

Thursday, October 14, 1886.   Have not yet found the the key for the safe nor the ck of H.M. Zeigler. It is a mystery where it got to.

Mrs. Frick was over this afternoon. Grandmother S also. Mother was down stairs again while she had been up stairs yesterday and day before.

Was over at Godshall's to assort the Sunday School books. Jennie and the Gov. helped. It was a very pleasant to do it. It took from four to six. We made provision for 172 scholars. Godshall's supper was a little later than usual. Jennie is going to Doylestown tomorrow to attend the institute there. She will go to Pottstown in 2 weeks. I told her what I thought of Schwenck &c and she said she wouldn't care if she were me, But I do. Made CH Moyers bill this evening. It is about a yard long.

Friday, October 15, 1886.   The papers in European countries say that affairs in Bulgaria have reached a critical stage.

A.S. Hewitt has been nominated by the Tammanyites and endorsed by the Country Democracy for Mayor of NY City to run against Henry George the Labor candidate. The Statue of Liberty Enlightening the World is nearly completed and will be dedicated on the 28th. Library meeting this evening.

The new board of managers met and were inaugurated. Jennie was not present. Annie and Miss Ella Godshall from Lansdale came down from Lansdale. The Librarians salary was fixed at 5 Dollars for the ensuing year.

The doctor has been here twice today. Father gave him a lesson this evening. He was out of humor with him for not keeping his engagements.

Saturday, October 16, 1886.   Mr. Jonas M Freed and Kate Froehr were married today. They started away early this morning.

It is rumourd also of Hen Freed but nothing came of it.

Sunday, October 17, 1886.   I had promised to come up to the depot to see the excursion trains pass but as might be expected I did not get ready. Frick and Uriah went up on the first section. There were 45 cars.

Mr. Gehman brought the Nat Philosophy he bought in the city yesterday. He took his books along from the library.

Went down to the meeting house and arranged the old quarterlies &c which have not been used. Today was the last day of Sunday School for this year. The house was filled to overflowing. Presents were distributed. Revs. Horning and Clemmer addressed the school. Leidy had the most credits in my class. Did not have his books ready. Met Schwenck. Don't think he knows anything. Jennie asked me if I was cross yet. I must have spoken harshly on Thursday evening. Went home and read. Weather quite cold. Had overcoat. Was up at the station. Did not stay for the excursions. Called on Miss Zendt at about eight. She expected Kate. She did not come. The checkers cards &c had disappeared from the room. Had some music. L has something of malaria she says. She had a chill yesterday. She used Cologne as a restorative. Left at twelve.

Monday, October 18, 1886.
Mr. Blaine spoke in the Academy of Music in Phila to 6000 persons. Also in Horticultural Hall and before the Union League Club. He was enthuiastically received. This means something more than state affairs. It means that Mr. Blaine is still a candidate for the Presidency. He was introduced in Hort. Hall as the next President. He starts on his tour to Pittsburg today.

Mr. Moyer bought a lot at Leidy's sale on Saturday for 375 Dollars. 3⅜ acres. I think this is very cheap and should fetch more.

Sat in the bank this afternoon reading D Copperfield. Took a short nap. Was up at the doctor's and got some medicine. The first I use for a long time. Commenced to talk of going away to mother. I wished had not done so. For there is no convincing her and she will only worry herself about it.

Tuesday, October 19, 1886.
Sat in bank again this afternoon reading 'David Copperfield.' I was reading at home after supper when Irwin came down having been sent by Kate to tell me to come up immediately. I got ready and went having an idea what for. When I came up she asked me how I would like to go to Schwenk's husking. Lillie came in directly and I said I should be delighted. I went for Haynes who at first thought he couldn't but he got Markly to work for him and went along. When we came up we teased the girls about helping to play. They encouraged us and we didn't. Irwin Bean was there. Haynes was very quiet. He thought perhaps there were Lansdale fellows about with whom he is at variance. We got home about eleven instead of ten. Promised to take L down to the communion Sunday.

Wednesday, October 20, 1886.
Felt a little bit stale because of last evening. John thought I must have been out again. Susie was at the husking yesterday and I helped to make supper and moreover to wash dishes (helped). Heard last evening that Mary Stover and Mr. Wile were married but I don't believe it. They were at the husking as usual. Can't be true. There were two or three other huskings last evening and made the attendance rather slim.

The choir met at Zendt's on Monday evening. Mr. Schoch has joined it.

Schwenck was not yet quiet about that.

Tomorrow Hen. Freed and Mary Bergey will be married.

Heard from Uriah today. He says he will never go to Switchback in Oct again. He nearly froze. They were himself Frick and Erdin. Have not heard from F.

Thursday, October 21, 1886.   Was quarter of an hour late this morning. Too late in bed. It looked very much like rain this morning and it was a little moist but it's as clear again as ever. It is getting to be almost a drought. Water is scarce the roads rough and dusty and seeds won't grow.

Went up to Slifer's sale after bank. The upper property sold for 28.25 to H N Frederick, the middle for 825 to F W Kratz and E B Slifer the lower for 1480. I went up to buy books but none were sold. Spoke with aunt Kate a few minutes.

On my way home saw H B Freed's team standing ready at Bergeys and old Aaron hostler. The two Texas and a new Darrey wagon. Waited at the toll gate to see them start. Wish them peace and happiness.

Was reading D Copperfield this evening. Am getting interested in it.

It's ten and bed time.

Friday, October 22, 1886.   Was reading again most of my spare time today. Was up at the doctors for mother this evening.

Bought a new tie four in hand for 50 cts this evening.

Wrote to Uriah and Andrew this evening.

Saturday, October 23, 1886.   Henry B. Freed had a sale of his livery stock this afternoon. Mr. Landes left the bank to attend the sale.

When I came grandmother S was here. I was to clean the yard &c and with her aid I effected a compromise for about half.

There was a husking at Earlington this evening.

Kate was after me all day to come out to Zendt's this evening as the old folks were not at home and we'd have some fun. Not wishing to offend them I went out about half past eight and found Irwin Bean there. Kate was not there yet. He was there having brought L's album and she had planned a meeting with Kate. Kate being late he left before she came. When she came she took Anna and Sallie Hunsberger upstairs and when they came down they were all disguised. Kate being a man Anna the wife and Sallie a boy. We had a great time but a little too much noise. Before the boys came home they dressed round. About ten Elwood Ambrose and Penrose came in and then there was noise enough. I left a twelve. Met Mike Bergey going home at the same time.

Sunday, October 24, 1886.   Started a little after nine for church. Bought a lap robe and horse blanket last evening for 8.00. Roads are very dusty. Lillie had not been down since the dedication. Met Os Kline at the church. Lutheran Communion. Grandfather H. had asked for the horse and father had promised him not knowing I wanted him. So I had to run up to tell. So they waited till this afternoon. Went up the cowpath. Asked to be excused for this evening. Approved. Was in meeting this afternoon. Rev. Godshall preached.

Heard Ellis' baby was very sick. Read D Copperfield.

Was up at the station and saw off Os. Kline.

Coming home found Amelia and Miss Ellenberger here. Was introduced. Had a pleasant time. Kate came. Took a walk up town with the rest. I had Amelia and Miss Ellenberger. On the way home Kate, Sam, Susie.

Monday, October 25, 1886.   Took my carriage over to the carriage shop this morning without being clean. Water is too scarce just now and nothing would be gained by it. Cleaned my harness this afternoon. Saw Sheriff Stahlnecker this morning. He came in bank to have a check cashed.

The teacher's institute in Pottstown begins today. Miss Jennie will be up and Jonathan too the latter part of the week.

Brought the celery home. Of no account. Too dry.

Helped to pick hair for a settee cushion and this took all evening.

Tuesday, October 26, 1886.   It has been cloudy all day and this evening it began to rain. It rained pretty much and the dust is settled at last.

Went down to the school house and carried the books upstairs to lighten the bookcase as cleaning is in progress.

Horace was along. We wrote our compliments to Mary Stover and Annie Kulp on the black board.

Received a letter from C Frick today. He says he could not reply sooner being out every night. He will be up in about two weeks.

Rec'd a letter from Jennie from Pottstown this evening. She writes pleasantly about the great benefits she derives from the professor's lectures. Her chum who signs Countess Vere de Vere and who I take to be Miss Moser struck in some nonsense. Must reply.

Wednesday, October 27, 1886.   Was rather late at bank this morning. It was raining this morning and at intervals during the day. This time it is enough to settle the dust.

John Ruth is in the gold watch line. He showed me two samples a gentlemans and a ladies watch 10 carat 32 and 25 respectively. They look very nice. He wants a chance if I should want to have one.

Answered Jennie's letter this afternoon. I got it into the mail yet this afternoon. It is all very silly stuff I know and I daresay she'll think me foolish.

Also wrote to her friend who signed—Wilkins Micaw—ber—no, that what I signed, Countess Vere de Vere. I believe its Miss Moser and wrote under that supposition. Don't know if they'll answer though I don't expect it.

Thursday, October 28, 1886. 'Tom Brown's School Days' arrived this morning in excellent condition. Will send it down tomorrow. Was at work on the books and papers this afternoon and evening.

Finished 'David Copperfield' today. I call it one of the good ones.

It has been rainy and damp all day.

These candidates for the legislature come around pretty fast. Hebner was here sometime ago. Brown was here last evening and this morning another big fat fellow was here. Anti-discrimination fetches them out.

Beaver will be in Lansdale tomorrow afternoon.

Freed was to have a husking this evening.

Friday, October 29, 1886. Mr. Moyer went down to Lansdale and there saw shook hands with Gen. Beaver Col Stewart Messrs. Yardley Heebner and Col A Wilson Norris Republican candidates who were holding a reception there before going to Norristown. Went down to the school house this afternoon and made a fire to dry the bookcase and took down the books. The school house was cleaned this week to prepare for school on Monday. We put up the stove after I came home. I was very tired and lay on the settee and slept.

Saturday, October 30, 1886. Wampole had a sale for his property this afternoon. It was not sold being bid up to 2800 and something. Went down to the school house and made another fire this afternoon. Miss J must have come home last evening. When I came home Miss Allie Slifer was here. She left a little after eight and then went over to Jennie's. I had been teasing little Price past endurance and she feigned anger. Went up to the store and bought a pair of gloves for 1.75. Miss L came in just then and on going down I accompanied her to Wm's. They were at work on their dresses. As it was dark and rainy I staid till she left which was about eleven. She took Kate's gossamer and umbrella. Told her I could not get the horse for tomorrow and was excused.

Sunday, October 31, 1886. Went down to the school house to look after the bookcase. It was raining. Expected Andrew. But he did not come.

Sat around reading and sleeping and did not get dressed till four.

Grandfather Souder's were down part of the afternoon. I read a little of Oliver Twist today.

Jakey Moyer was in here awhile this afternoon. He related his experiences at the school house.

Went up to meet the train. Lillie Kate Jennie and Annie were there to see Miss Allie off. Spoke Miss J. She must have rec'd my letter I know.

Got out to Zendt's about eight. Kate was there and wanted to frighten me outside. She has given H the 'bounce'. She went out and brought the baby in and a dog. The baby was frightened and so was the dog. L.K. Allie and Ellie drove down to Lexington this afternoon. Rufus took them down to church in the morning. Home at 12.

Monday, November 1, 1886. Mr. Wampole sold his property today to a Mr. Kasinger of Lexington for 3000 dollars.

The political mass meetings receptions &c are now about over for this campaign and tomorrow is the election. There will be elections held in 34 states. In New York the great contest is for mayor. Three good men. Hewitt, Roosevelt, and George have been selected by the Democrats Reps. and Labor party. The latter's strength is unknown and will only come out at the elections. The Socialists and Anarchists take the latter's part. In Tennessee two brothers have been running for Governor. In Penna the Prohibitionist is the great uncertainty.

Was down to the school house this afternoon to see Jennie, deliver the key &c. She seems not at all pleased with Frick. I was mistaken in supposing her friend to have been Miss Moser. She said they had a good time up there. School commenced today. She refused to tell the name of the lady who wrote along.

Tuesday, November 2, 1886. Heard this morning that Dick Young's house was burnt last night. Dick was found in the barn. It is the belief that Dick did it for an unaccountable reason. He was in Norristown yesterday. I was asked half dozen times today whether I was of age and was going to vote. The Reps. are running a team all day to the square to carry voters. William was very busy and persuaded Fink to vote Rep. who had made up his mind to vote Democratic. Heard this evening that the votes did not turn out very well in Franconia.

Elias Freed wants to build a house in Harleysville this fall yet. We made an estimate for it this evening.

Wednesday, November 3, 1886. Beaver was elected Gov. by about 35000 majority. Montgomery went Republican between 4 and 500. All the county officers are Republican. Bucks went Democratic. In Phila. Gordon defeated Ex. Judge Briggs Rep. by 7000 majority. This is a good thing as Briggs was not a fit man. In New York Hewitt was elected Mayor. He received 90000 votes. Henry George received 67000 and Roosevelt 60000. George's vote is a surprise to the politicians. It shows the power of the Labor element and may be the rise of a new party.

Met Lillie this evening in front of Kate's place. Haynes is not pleased with the latter by his talk. L goes to Telford this winter to Leidy's to learn dressmaking.

Thursday, November 4, 1886.   Beaver's majority is now given at over 45,000.

Took the Stock certificate book around to several of the subscribers who had not taken them up.

After reading 'Oliver Twist' of which I do too much an neglect other things thereby.

Worked on the books as far as I could.

Horace came down and wanted me to go out on horseback with him this evening. Promised at eight o'clock. Saw a fire in the direction of Harleysville about 6.30 this evening.

Must now go up to the doctor's for medicine. And also to the post office. After which to the saddle. Saw a great meteor while at Telford this evening about 9.30 toward the east.

Friday, November 5, 1886.   Last evening found Penrose with Horace and we three went together to Telford. Met Lillie and Kate at the corner of Main & Chestnut. Spoke to them. Put our horses in Barndt's stables. Went over to Kuhn's where a husking party was in progress. Penrose went home. We acted up a little too much. Had to wait on Horace who took Marietta Gerhart home. Was a little out of humor. It was twelve o'clock when I went to bed. Slept very bad and I thought I must have been awake all night.

At the Library this evening the attendance was dull. Lillie and Jennie came out about a quarter of nine. Harry B Smith had John's share transferred to himself. Took charge of Lillie on the way home while Rufus had Jennie.

I was almost ashamed of myself before L on act of last evening. Swenk had told her this morning. Apologized as well as I could. I told her all. I know she did not like it.

Saturday, November 6, 1886.   Weather damp and foggy this morning which ended in rain this afternoon and evening.

C H Moyer commenced putting up his new fence today. Haynes was over to see Kate last evening. I suppose to settle accounts.

We balanced before dinner today as Mr. Landes went to a sale this afternoon.

Got excused from raking the yard this afternoon on account of the rain.

Read 'Oliver Twist' this afternoon.

Andrew came up this evening with the 6.37 train. Went up to Hagey's for his shoes and from there to the store where he ordered a new suit of clothes. Stopped in at Stover's and had oysters.

Sunday, November 7, 1886.   We got up very late this morning. Finished 'Oliver Twist' this morning.

Went up to Wm's after dinner. Uriah was there. Asked Kate whether Lillie could go. Finding this to be the case went over to Hangey's for the wagon. Hangey came along over and got it out for me. It was still a little dirty. There was some snow on the ground this morning.

Reiter preached on the meaning of the monogram back of the pulpit. J. H. S. **In hoc signo vireces or Jesum hominum salvato.** After we came home Andrew and I took a ride up to Telford. Stopped at Derstine's and no one at home. We stopped at grandfather's. We found Lillie and Kate there. Andrew went down with the 6.19. He ordered a new suit of clothes at Landis' for 23 dollars. Was up at the Station till 730. When I came home found Kate and Alonzo here. Went out Washington Ave at eight. Found Penrose and Sally Hunsberger there. Anna Zendt was also in the room. She looked very different from the other Sat. eve. Having made up my mind to tell Lillie that a stop should be made sometime I did it this evening. I made it the subject of the whole evening and made it very satisfactorily to us both as much as I know. I told her the plain truth as it is and she seemed to agree with me. Promised to come again next Sunday eve. On putting my hat found it had a new inside with my letter, H.

Monday, November 8, 1886.   The air is still very cold. A great change from last weeks. Cleaned my carriage this afternoon. Helped to make saurkraut this evening.

I believe the boys were out with their plug hats yesterday. When I came home last night Uriah wasn't abed. He was locked out. Heard he was going to see Maria Zeigler.

Couldn't help thinking of the conversation we had last evening. If Kate knew it she would go for me I know. She is going to Topton in two weeks. They have a little girl up there. Lillie is going to Telford on Wednesday to Leidy's to learn dressmaking. Her father is making preparations to build a tailor shop. At first L didn't say much and only said I must know what was good for me. But afterwards that she didn't expect anything else. She dreamed about it on Fri. night. I said it was because of the Husking but she said not. I am very glad we can part so friendly and I feel very kindly towards her.

Tuesday, November 9, 1886.   Mother went to town with the doctor this afternoon. They did not see Dr. Fox as he was away. So she stays till Thursday at Slifer's.

Met Milt Moyer this evening on our way to the ball. Shook hands with him but had no time to speak to him.

I had forgotten all about the ball on Sunday evening. Kate called me in this afternoon about it. She wants to go very bad I suppose to meet someone. So I wrote to Lillie and she (Kate) brought the answer back. So I dressed up and about half past eight went out. She was ready and then we fetched Kate. Went into the sitting room and brought in wine. Went out on the hall where the dancing was in progress. Soon after we came in one of the players fainted. He soon revived and after while took his place again. There was a few good dancers from Hockertown and thereabouts. One Springer was the best on the floor. Kate danced but Lillie would not do it. I wanted her to, but to no purpose. I did not dance myself for the reason that I can't dance and did not go there for that purpose. I got tired enough of it and will not soon go to such a ball again. Got home some time after twelve.

Wednesday, November 10, 1886.   Got a letter from Uriah today saying that mother was staying at Slifer's till tomorrow or Friday and that she was pretty tired when she came there yesterday afternoon.

Milt Moyer went down again this morning but returned this afternoon. He will stay here till the 29th. Saw the Gov. yesterday who had been in town and he says Charley will not be up till Sunday a week. Was up at grandfather H's this evening. They received a letter from Uncle Bill or rather his daughter Ella Scholl dated Oct. 31. The letter sent to them had been sent to the wrong address and it lay in the post office for a long time. They are well most of them and the old people are strong and hearty. I would like to go out there once if I could in some way.

Thursday, November 11, 1886.   The Bulgarian Sobrange yesterday elected Prince Waldemar of Denmark as sucessor to Prince Alexander. He is 28 yrs. old. It is thought Russia will object to this selection.

A son of Geo. W. Smith after running about town to borrow two dollars at last obtained them at Hunsberger's and bought a ticket for Bethlehem and ran up toward Telford. His father boarded the train and I think will catch him.

Mother came home this evening. She saw Dr. Fox today. Loux did not get there today. She did not get her glasses. She will have to go down again in three weeks. She was at Mrs. Frick's last evening, Charley was at Stetson's. She was with Mrs. Hunsberger today and last night. Florence's mother took her away and her whereabouts are not known.

Friday, November 12, 1886.   It is possible that Prince Waldemar will refuse the Bulgarian throne. The Czar's candidate was Prince Nicholas of Mingrelia. This may be all by play however.

It has been raining again today and is still at the present writing.

Some fellows are after C.H. Moyer about his house and fence. Such persons ought to be kicked.

Old Herman received a long letter from Jenkins cashier of the Lansdale Bk explaining why they don't 4 per cent div. anymore. There is abundant cause according to him. They should have stopped it long before. Evans gets 600 and Sylvester Jenkins 400 a year.

Saturday, November 13, 1886.   King Christian of Denmark has declined on behalf of his son the throne of Bulgaria.

It cleared off cold today. It has been very windy. I wanted to rake the yard this afternoon but I made but slow progress as the wind scattered the leaves.

Received a letter from Frick enclosing five or six of his cards very nice which I am to give to Lillie, Kate and Jennie. He says none for Schwenck. He will be up next Saturday. Kate called me in this afternoon and when I was in I found that L had run out of the room. She came in and I left soon.

Ben Barndt's fence has also been put up. Bought a pair of rubbers this evening.

Sunday, November 14, 1886.   The wind from yesterday has somewhat abated. Went to bed again about nine as I felt sleepy yet and lay in bed till dinner time. Made ready to go to church. Was too late for meeting. Was in church on the Hall. About 75 were present. Interesting. Old Hen Price was there too and very attentive, Schwenck and Jonathan were up to Perkasie dedication this afternoon. Calvin also, Kate and Lillie were to meeting. Sat around the depot and when I came home Martha had just left.

Went out a little after eight. She had just come home from an errand. We had a pleasant time. Had music and singing. Heard that Bean had started in at Hof's at Telford. This is bad for Kate. She had better left Haynes go away. I delivered one of the cards Charley sent me. We talked freely about the business in hand. She said she had many rivals and that there were some who did not wish her well &c &c. Of course this is all imagination. She brought a book and two handkerchiefs which she wanted to give me but I would not take them. She asked me if she were to invite me out in about 4 weeks whether I would come. Of course I would. She went out of the room and brought a very beatiful embroidered carriage blanket with my initials just commenced. I was very sorry and told her so. She said she had intended it for me and I should have it. But was not to think that it was to draw me back &c. I said I would pay her for it. And I had intended to make her a nice present. I am only sorry for the trouble it costs her. It was half past twelve when I gave her my hand and said good bye, and so ended a very happy time we were together.

Monday, November 15, 1886.   Got up in excellent spirits this morning. A very nice day. Such a whole week will settle Elias Freed's house. John B Detweiler has contracted a toll house on the Sellersville pike for 748 to be finished in two months.

The great pork packers strike for 8 hrs in Chicago has been declared off by Grand Masters Workman Powderly.

Becker in a fit of anger having threatened to sell out has actually posted up bills to that effect. Though it seems they have made up in the family everyone being cheerful.

Wrote to Charley and Uriah this afternoon.

Uriah was out again to see Maria last night.

Tuesday, November 16, 1886.   A very nice day. Wrote to Andrew this afternoon. Enclosed him one of Frick's cards. Gave one to Kate also.

Saw Horace this afternoon. He says he was at the husking at Telford last Thursday and took Lizzie Gerhart home. Andrew gave me away to him. But he says he don't believe it yet because in his opinion we think too much of each other. Saw L this evening in the store.

Went up to the doctors for my medicine. He got to talking about the Library and about getting up a literary society. He is full of theory but entirely impractical. He is also I think not the best judge of books. Though he is right about the cyclopedia. He showed me his. But it is too dear for one library. I told him this. But it seems to me that he never takes money into his calculations. And another thing. Though he may be right about a club room yet there would be too much prejudice against it. But I wish there was a society here. I must talk about it on Friday evening. He returned the book he had loaned from me a very long time ago. He also loaned me an essay he wrote a long time ago.

Wednesday, November 17, 1886.   A rainy day. Isaac H Moyer did not come today till we had balanced about 230 P.M. Lewis Keeler was expected but will come the latter part of the week.

Kate did not get off to Topton today it being too rainy. She will probably go tomorrow.

Prince Nicholas of Mingrelia the Russian candidate has been accepted by the Powers as Prince of Bulgaria. That is, if Bulgaria herself will have him.

Read D'Aubigne this afternoon.

Went up to grandfather H's this evening to write a letter to Wis. Took only a draft and will write it tomorrow afternoon. Can't understand Aunt Sarah right. Heard L praised up and Jennie and Annie Jennie especially described as too lazy to work. Mike Bergey had to suffer. I laid out Schwenck. Think I had better kept quiet about it.

Thursday, November 18, 1886.   It rained this morning but cleared off and is now getting colder. Kate started for Topton this morning.

Heard today that Eli Bergey was married on Saturday to Mary Miller a daughter of Eph. F. Miller.

Saw the goods this afternoon which Landis & Co brought for my suit. It is jet black. There is only enough for one suit. They say they cannot sell it. I like the stuff and will probably take it. A suit will cost 24 dollars. I asked father what he thought of it and he said it was 'fine goods that was certain.'

Friday, November 19, 1886.   Chester Allan Arthur ex-president of the U.S. died yesterday morning of a stroke of apoplexy. He had been sick for three years of a complication of diseases. He will be buried on Monday. Pres. Cleveland and Gov. Hill have issued proclamations proclaiming the fact.

Wrote to Ed Donley this afternoon. Also a letter for grandfather to Milwaukee Wis.

The library was open this evening. Jennie came down early as she had not the school house ready. L was not down. Penrose was. I spoke to the others about a literary society. John said today he could not take part in it. Gehman said he could not be present every time. Appenzeller however was much in favor of it and spoke about it a long time. I am to see the other people about it.

Saturday, November 20, 1886. A very nice day. Many people say that it will not last long. But, I think it will last till tomorrow. It will be excellent for driving by tomorrow. Got my carriage ready this afternoon.

As I was making ready this evening old Herman came over and wanted to see me. He showed me a letter which Frick had sent him saying he could not come on account of the death of a friend that evening. His name was Livzey. He is to help writing funeral service &c. He will come next Sunday instead.

Sunday, November 21, 1886. A repetition of yesterday. If Frick had only been up we would have had a good time. As it was Sam and I lay in bed till near nine Uriah not being at home. Was reading 'Nicholas Nickleby' till dinner when I made ready for meeting. A Russian from Dakota preached in a sing song way which prevented him from being plainly understood. Misses L & J were there. They passed our house before dinner. Was up at the station after meeting. When I came home found Maggie Amelia and Aunt Kit here. They staid for supper. Escorted Maggie home. Mike came soon after seven. He being not very talkative I left. They expected me to go the other way but I went home. Found Aunt Sarah & Kit. Sat around till little after eight when I put on my overcoat and went out. Walked about a little when I saw Sam come down the street when I made off then came in through the back gate and went to bed. Nobody found me out.

Monday, November 22, 1886. Geo. Eaton died yesterday of typhoid fever.

Was down at the school house this afternoon to look up the price of 'Vicar of Wakefield' for Jacob Shelly who damaged the book and wants to pay it. Must go again tomorrow to fix the curtain on the bookcase.

Was up at grandmothers and fixed her transom. Was in the store this evening and looked at my goods again. Milt Moyer was down there too. He is undecided whether he will get a Prince Albert or a cutaway. He told some stories about his travels.

Received a letter from Kate this afternoon. She don't like Topton. Says she will make an excellent nurse by the time she gets back.

Tuesday, November 23, 1886. Rain again today.

On Saturday we went over the discounts. Did not get it added till this afternoon. We must have made a mistake. For they are not near correct.

Answered Kate's letter this evening.

Did not get to the school house this afternoon. Was reading Nicholas Nickleby this evening and had just gone asleep when Mr. Beideman came in and woke me. This is the first time he came round this fall. He will stay overnight.

Wednesday, November 24, 1886.   Today they commencing the pavement in front of the bank and Wm's. C H Moyer is superintending it.

Mr. Beideman went away this morning. I left him at the breakfast table. His brother Henry is quite a politician and is an officer in the custom houses in Phila.

Mr. & Mrs. Greaser commenced the cleaning process this afternoon already at the bank. Went down to the school house this afternoon to fix the curtains. Jennie is yet under the impression that I go to see L as she expressed and desire to see the bank once and would like to do so in company with her. Cleared off today. Slifer will go at my suit week after next.

Thursday, November 25, 1886.   Got up pretty late this morning. Helped to clean the bank till half past three and that is how I kept my thanksgiving. It was raining quite fast all day. The pavement in front of the bank is all torn up and tomorrow the dirt will all be carried in again.

James wrote a postal inquiring how Topton Stock was sold. On inquiry I found that they sold for 111 and a fraction. I informed him by postal.

Friday, November 26, 1886.   A cold clear day. The ground was pretty near frozen all day. The pavement in front of the bank will probably be finished by tomorrow evening.

The Princess Beatrice wife of Prince Henry of Battenburg yesterday gave birth to a son. A great thing this. There is still a great fuss about the Bulgarian business. Dont know how it will end. Have caught a slight cold. Have a feeling in the throat which is uncomfortable. Bought a little licorice this evening.

Sam'l Sower's leg was amputated yesterday. They say it would not have healed so.

The telephone wires are being put up for Loux's phone. One post is placed right in front of us and Godshall. No great ornament.

Saturday, November 27, 1886.   The pavement in front of the bank was finished today. It makes a splendid walk. The telephone poles and wires were put up today to Loux's. The pole in front of our place was put on the other side on Godshall's account. Parvin looked at our phone. He thinks it wants readjustment and the ground is not very good.

Was up to grandfather H's to get my razor sharpened.

Received a letter from Kate. She seems to be surprised that we parted. She hints something about Miss Jennie or Miss Gerhart. I don't think L mentioned these. But they must have talked about them.

Frick came up this evening. Went over and spent part of the evening. He has not been up since the Rocks. He mentioned something about the prettiest girl-. He promised to come over tomorrow morning.

Sunday, November 28, 1886.   A nice day. Was reading Nicholas Nickleby all forenoon. Expected Frick over but he did not come. I don't know what business he had to stay away as he promised last evening he would come over this morning. Father and mother went down to H Landis. Frick went came over sometime after two o'clock. We started for church but changed our minds and went to the station and from there after the governor's horse. Receiving permission we drove through town to Telford and then through a roundabout way home. He says his present girls' name is Bitting. He changes company pretty often. He resigned from the social. He went down with the 619. We met Jennie and Annie at the station. We thought we saw a fire toward the south east. Did not see L all day. It must have been a dull day for him. Did not tell him anything. Haynes whipped another fellow on Friday evening who didn't behave. Mike Bergey came and told me he wasn't going out there anymore. When I came home Old Polly and the boys were here. When Sam came home in his new suit he was surprised to find me.

Monday, November 29, 1886.   Becker quite unexpectedly to me sold his property at public sale this afternoon to D.W. Kratz for 3800. Sold pretty well I think. Isaiah Moyer Jacob Allebach, and Daub were all bidders. Mrs. Becker was over this evening. They are well pleased with their sale.

Had my suit measured this afternoon. Guess it will have to be done over as I hadn't my undershirt on.

Received a letter from Ed Donley. He wants me to come over with my girl &c. By the way he talks he was in pretty deep with his as he says she would have been his within a year if it had not been for her father.

Read 'Nicholas Nickleby' till eleven this evening.

Tuesday, November 30, 1886.   Light rains and a little colder. Felt a little dull about the eyes from late reading last evening. Finished "Nicholas Nickleby," an excellent story. Was at work on the books this evening.

Ordered two diaries. One for Sam and one for myself. Milt Moyer gets the same goods as I have for a Prince Albert suit and an overcoat.

Met Sam Bergey in the store this afternoon. He travels for Geo. W. Yardley & Co Willoware Carpets &c. He feels very important and that is his great fault. He talked about the 300 dollar horse he has in use &c. He is as tall as I am.

Wednesday, December 1, 1886.   There was some snow today. Cleaned my harness this afternoon and worked on the books this evening. Wish my carriage were clean too and I would not go out very soon again. Too muddy. Rec'd a letter from Uriah today. He says how welcome are letters from Lexington &c. He had her to the theatre once. He seems to think the world of her. He will go and hear Patti sing. He says he is going to buy out Slifer on Jan 1st.

Met L in the store this evening. I expected she would hardly notice me but instead of that she smiled so sweetly that I felt like a brute. Uriah asked if I was still running her and said he hoped so. He must have had doubts however.

Thursday, December 2, 1886. A regular cold wave reached us last night. This has been the coldest day so far. Out at St Paul Minn. it reached 28 below zero yesterday. It was about 8 above here at some places.

Sallie Alderfer was married last Saturday to a Derstine.

Worked in the shop sawing scrolls for Sam Shrohm. Made money bags for the bank this evening.

Friday, December 3, 1886. The library was open this evening. Jonathan had his crowd up, eight or nine of his school boys taking books.

Swartley's school will give an entertainment on the hall tomorrow a week.

Did a good business this evening. Miss Lillie came down, alone. I told her to wait for Jennie who however did not come. She had not been home from Telford since Wednesday. There are six girls up there. Took her home after closing up. She has a very bad cold. Locked up mittens by mistake, so she made me take one of hers.

Haynes has been suspended until further notice for missing a train the other week &c.

Saturday, December 4, 1886. Everything indicates that there will be snow by tomorrow. I am not quite ready for cold weather for I wanted to clean my carriage first.

Amelia told me this afternoon that Andrew's suit did not get finished. I wrote him a postal. As he did not come I suppose he received it.

Kate came home again this evening. Spoke to Mike Bergey this evening at the station. He blame Amelia for her interference &c.

Sunday, December 5, 1886. It commenced to snow last night and continued to snow the greater part of the day.

Was at home all day reading DAubignes' Ref Vol IV. Did not get ready for meeting this afternoon. Only about 50 persons were present.

Martha was here part of the afternoon after meeting. Intended to go up to see Kate this evening but changed my mind and stayed at home.

The snow drifted a little else there would be enough for sleighing.

Monday, December 6, 1886. Still very cold but the snow has drifted too much for sleighing. Went over and saw Kate this morning. She thought I had made a great change &c.

Mr. Landes killed a hog today. Heard a few sleighs during the day. Was at home reading this afternoon.

Tuesday, December 7, 1886.   The last session of the Forty ninth Congress commenced yesterday. The Presidents message was read. It is a little weak in regard to the tariff. Otherwise well written.

Wrote to Uriah and Ed Donley. It snowed again this morning but cleared off this afternoon.

Went to meeting this evening. A Rev. Driver from Virginia preached. Escorted Kate home. L sent word she could not come I believe.

Wednesday, December 8, 1886.   People are out mostly with sleighs. This evening it was very pleasant to go and many were out. Met Miss L in the store this evening and she told me that Bean would take Kate out this evening. He was over here at meeting last evening.

Rec'd a letter from Andrew. He will come up on Sunday. He says he has a girl at last.

Was down at the school house for my mittens this afternoon and brought Phrenology along.

Thursday, December 9, 1886.   It was quite agreeable during the day though after sundown it turned colder.

Mother has a bad cold. Was up at grandfather S this afternoon. Mother sent me up to see why she did not come down.

She would have come except for visitors. She knows something about Bean's coming back again. Sam told me this evening that Uriah knew I had stopped. Can't imagine how he found out. Received a letter from Frick this evening. He pretends to have been too busy to write &c but take my time in answering. He think we up here believe anything. He says he was at a ball where he met Jon Umstead Ike Benner and Os. Kline, in Germantown. He will come on Christmas.

Friday, December 10, 1886.   The weather is very mild and the snow is going slowly. Acknowledged receipt of Frick's letter with a postal.

Fixed the lamp stand for the sunday school organ this afternoon. It was lying around about a year.

Met Miss L this evening. She was on her way to Kate's. She says Bean was here on Wednesday. Last evening he was at Hoffs for the last time. They must have made up some how.

Was reading Reformation Vol IV. It is very interesting where it gives an account of Zwingli's death.

Saturday, December 11, 1886.   The snow going fast now. No sleighing anymore. I missed it this time.

Looking out of the window a little before noon. I saw Miss L pass in and out to see Kate. She did not look up though she knew I was looking at her. I opened the window and spoke to Kate. Teased her about B &c. On learning that B was not coming this evening and that L would be there over night I offered to take them to the entertainment in the evening. Kate having also gone to Telford I met them at the station at eight and took them over. The Telford fair being opened this evening kept many away. There were some real good pieces although others were old and not well rendered. Milt had Miss Ellenberger there. She is down near Chalfont now. Martha was there with a Crouthamel from Lexington. After it was over I went along to Kate's L trimmed a bonnet for Kate. I got Kate's picture. Made L promise me one too. Kate wanted me to bring out L tomorrow evening. But I gave no answer. I knew what it meant. Had quite a good time. Left a little after eleven. When I came home the boys were not yet in bed.

Sunday, December 12, 1886.   We got up pretty late this morning. Sam had gone to Telford yet after the entertainment. He said it was not very good.

Andrew came up with the 10 o'clock train. We went over to Gerhart's for his suit. He put it on right away. It fits him pretty well. We went over to the store where he bought some other things. He commenced going to School on Thursday. He attended the lectures on Thursday and Sat evenings. In the afternoon we went up to church on the hall. Knobel preached. He left on the market train. Kate and L were in too. On the way home we got ourselves invited to stop in too. Sam Andrew and I went in accordingly. We acted up fearfully for a while. We then went into the other room for music. L played Dixie, &c Jennie Moyer came in after a while. Rufus too. We made a great deal of noise. We left about five. L had just preceded us but Jennie stayed. After supper we went up to meet the train. Met L alone on the platform waiting for a package. Went into the station and helped to make noise. The boys were doubtful about me and Horace said I should not forget myself tonight. We left there about a quarter of eight. Told them I was going home first. We went up to see Amelia. Noise again. Amelia had heard I had stopped off too and asked Sam how it was. Sam said I was there last night and she was satisfied. She says Katie Derstine will get married next Spring. We went home about half past ten.

Monday, December 13, 1886.   Andrew went down with the milk train. He talks of going to Florida. He went to see a young lady several times but who gave him the cold shoulder.

Weather today was foggy and thawing. Bad roads will follow.

Looked at some things they have out in the store windows for Christmas presents. That's one of the greatest puzzles. What to buy. Spoke to Milt Moyer about the Literary. He is in favor.

Lillie and Kate were in the store this evening. I suppose they are finishing the work they wanted to do on Saturday evening.

Tuesday, December 14, 1886.

Wednesday, December 15, 1886.   It has been snowing all day. Most of it melted as it came down but this evening it is colder and there are prospects of it lasting if it is not too windy.

Uriah had his photos taken. He showed one to us and mother asked him for it. He did not wish to do so at first but at last gave way unwillingly. Went to the school house and brought home DAubigne Vol V and Dicken's 'Old Curiosity Shop,' the last of which I began to read.

Looked in at the tailors shop this afternoon to see my new suit. Slifer was not there and they told me he was sick. My coat was just commenced. Perhaps I will have to wait another week.

Thursday, December 16, 1886.   Today it was very cold. Many roads are again shut up. Slifer is better but I don't think I'll get my suit this week.

Martha was here this afternoon making a coat for Alonzo. She likes to be teased about Crouthamel. She says Milt Moyer is to be married before Christmas. I believe this to be true although I never thought of it before. That's what his new suit is for. And Schwenck I'll bet he'll follow before Spring. He too has a very fine suit but doesn't wear it. She was sent away from Gehman's Milt being always there in the evenings. He had her at home over Sunday.

The greatest puzzle for me now is what to buy for a Christmas present. I have been racking my brain and yet I'll make a bad selection. I don't want anything too costly for that I can't afford and it would not be proper and not too cheap that would look miserly. Then I must consider my position &c. I wish it were over. Now for the girls it's all plain enough. Kate is at work all the time. Met L coming home from there this evening.

Friday, December 17, 1886.   This morning it was colder than yes-terday. Slightly warmer later. It was rumored that the Telford fair had been stopped but it has not yet. WM H Moyer was at the bottom of it.

Kate called me in this afternoon. She was at the window at work on a blanket with the letters I.B. thereon. It's very pretty and costly, too. She wanted me to go out sleighing with them on Sunday. Of course I didn't promise such a thing. She would like it if I would go back again but I told her how it was. I then asked her why she had mentioned Miss Gerhart and Jennie in her letter. She then told me that Miss Gerhart had been bragging she could take me away from L if she wanted to. That she had some one to help her &c. This is laughable. Haynes too is in great favor with her. It seems to me she must be a little weak.

Saw Ben Barndt about a literary society. He is in favor but is not very hopeful. He promised to come down to the Library. Jonas Freed insulted me while there. If I were only not so slow sometimes I would have acted different. Received a letter from Ed Donley this evening. He wants me to correspond with his former girl Minnie something.

At the Library this evening Appenzeller said I should get them together some evening next week and that I was to drop him a postal. Jennie came down with Milt and went home with J. She called on Kate but she went out to L with her work. We selected Wednesday evening for the literary.

Saturday, December 18, 1886. A light snow last night and rain all day take away all hope of good sleighing for tomorrow. Mr. Landes told me today that now about four weeks there has been no communication between them and their neighbors. They could not think what it meant till they found out I had stopped. Before that time there was some unnecessary talk. This is their weakness.

Pressed my pants this evening. My suit was not finished as I expected.

Sunday, December 19, 1886. Went up to the doctor this morning for mother. After that to the schoolhouse and made the fire that had gone out. Did not dress till near three this afternoon. Grandfather S's were down. Parents had just started to go out to Aunt Kit. Amelia and Maggie came. Uriah Souder came and called me out. He had no time to stop in. So I walked up with him to the watchmaker's. He got his watch and asked for a ring. He did not buy but I think he will. He seems to have grounded on that Barndt girl. He will go into business. Frick din't seem to understand my postal. Uriah will go to Lexington tonight and down tomorrow morning. He will go to Topton next Sunday.

Took Amelia and Maggie out home. Father and mother went out after supper. Met the train and went home and got a supper. Went out about half past seven to Maggie's. We were after Amelia about Mike Bergey. She says she will make up with him. Took Amelia home. Found Sam Freed with Susie when I came home.

Monday, December 20, 1886. Slifer commenced work this morning again. He sent word for me to fit on the coat. I did so. I looked in again this afternoon for a bottom. The coat was nearly done. Stood around the store this afternoon waiting for chance to order something. Fretz thinks a work box would do.

Was after Rufus to help get up the literary. He did not yet promise. Horace did. Read 'Old Curiosity Shop' Enos Frederick was here yesterday. He is a fugitive from his wife.

Wrote Ed Donley. Asked a great many questions. Don't know whether he will answer them.

Tuesday, December 21, 1886. Alderman McQuade was yesterday sentenced to 7 yrs at hard labor and $50.00 fine for accepting a bribe. Mother wanted to go to the city today but the doctor disappointed her again.

Wrote Frick a letter in German this afternoon.

Ordered a work box or something of that kind for a Xmas present.

Was up at the stocking factory this afternoon to see Milt Moyer and Mike. Milt wants to learn the business. Looked into Harvey Souder's shop. He has it fixed up nice. They run their sewing machines by steam.

Stopped in to see Kate this evening. Still at work on her blanket. She helped at butchering at grandfather S today.

Wednesday, December 22, 1886.   Today was a terrible day. The Bank Examiner came with the nine o'clock train. The Directors were and all crowded up. We worked like slaves to get through till the 1.25 train. Mr. Landis and I didn't get any dinner. We hadn't struck a balance when he left with the train. That is we did not find our mistake till near three o'clock. I was glad when it was over. He got after Mr. L and Mr Gerhart about our overdue paper.

Got a note this afternoon inviting me out for tomorrow evening. Accepted. Got the new work box all right this afternoon. The new literary society is a going. Nine of us met in the school house this evening. They were Appenzeller, Milt Moyer, Horace Souder, Jonathan Hunsberger, Rufus Landis, Mike Bergey, Lillie M Zendt Jennie Moyer and myself. I think it will be right nice. It is to be informal and no officers. We made out a program for next Wednesday evening. We will discuss the Constitution. Miss Moyer has a Select Reading and I have a recitation. Also a program for two weeks hence. Mr. Gehman wrote he could not come.

Took Lily home though I hardly had the chance. She will not be home tomorrow evening. Christmas evening instead.

Thursday, December 23, 1886.   Got my new suit this evening. I was really impatient to get it quite a while. I never had a long coat before. It is double breasted Prince Albert. I think it will fit well after being worn a little. One button is a little out of place.

Father and all our men were down at Towamensing meeting house putting new seats today.

Cut straw for the boys mattress this afternoon. Stopped at Kate's a little while this afternoon. Her blanket is looking beautiful.

While reading this evening I went to sleep and did not wake up till half past eleven when Uriah came home.

Friday, December 24, 1886.   This is the last day before Christmas. All the work has to be done today everywhere. Father got a turkey this morning. It was not at all cold today and rain toward evening.

Was up in Leidy's store this evening. They have their store fixed up beautifully. While there a number of masqueraders came in. Will Benner was an old negro woman. Will Hunsberger and Abe Price were the others. The boys each got a dollar for a present. He handed me a V with the remark that it would be the last I received from him in that way. Enough to make a fellow wild ain't it.

Saturday, December 25, 1886.   Contrary to expectation it cleared off this morning and became a little colder. It was a little too muddy to go out. Frick came up with the 8.55 train. He came over soon afterward. The scamp saved no picture for me. He had promised me one. That's the way it goes. Had on my new suit this afternoon and evening. Went over to see Frick in the afternoon. No girls came there. Fixed up went up to Kate's. Bean was there. They went out for a drive. We stayed with Horace, left about five. Told Frick I was going away this evening. He did not come over. Read 'Old Curiosity Shop.' Parents were away. Got ready till eight. Wanted to brush up the box a little. It fell down and the fastening came off. Had a great job to fix it. Had a pleasant time. She seemed to be pleased with the box. I was afraid she would not. It was but a trifle to the blanket she gave me. It is very beautiful. My initials with flower border. Came away some time after eleven. She promised to come to the Gov's this afternoon with Kate if invited. The boys were up at the Telford entertainment.

Sunday, December 26, 1886.   Did not have the best night' sleep I ever had. The later I get to bed the less I can sleep. Frick came over after ten. We sat around reading the paper till near dinner. After dinner we started off to meeting. Rev. Loux preached. Frick talked with Umsted awhile and I walked on. We went up to the station and from there back home. Amelia and Maggie were there. Had some everlasting music &c. A & M told how they had been to see L and had seen her Christmas present. Of course I denied all knowledge of it. Went up to the station to see Frick off. After that stopped in to see Kate. I found her well. She asked me how I felt and I said I was happy. I left just as Bean came in.

Went up to grandfather H's and saw their Christmas tree. Very pretty. Showed off my new suit. And now the Christmas holidays are over.

Monday, December 27, 1886.   Gen. John A. Logan died at Washington D.C. yesterday.

Father could not work today. He has had pains in his back a kind of rheumatism.

Rufus Landes got a gold watch for a Christmas present. Arthur a Waterbury. Commenced working on the books this afternoon. Committed part of Cowper's 'John Gilpin' to memory for Wednesday evening. Rufus, Elmer Weil and Sam Benner were summoned to testify in Norristown about the Deisinger case at Schwenck's. They hated it like sin. Rufus did not go. He will hardly slip through.

Tuesday, December 28, 1886.   The Temple theatre which was formerly the old Masonic Temple but which had lately been transformed into a theatre was yesterday totally destroyed by fire. The 'Little Tycoon' was being performed there for the greater part of its' (the theatres) existence. It was to have been succeed Jan 17 by an opera 'Phyllis,' the scenery of all which was destroyed. The loss am't to about 350000. Wm Singerly was the owner. The [fire] originated in a room in the Musée about 11 A.M. Two firemen lost their lives.

Horace called me in this afternoon. He told me that Jonas Freed and Anchy [?] would marry. He also says there is nothing in the report about Milt Moyer. He asked me why I stopped off &c. I said it was long enough &c. They all thought I was gone.

Wednesday, December 29, 1886.   Mother went down to the city this afternoon. She has been wanting to go for a long time. They are already raising a fund for Mrs. Logan. They expect to have a 100,000, before the funeral. If this goes on the big fellows don't care if they leave a cent or not.

The literary society met this evening. It seems to be doing right well. Some new members were added. We discussed the Constitution. But few took part as yet. Miss Moyer had a select reading. I recited John Gilpin was several times compelled to refer to the book. Not long enough in preparation. We sang two hymns. Took Lillie and Kate home. Asked L to get her father to join. She thinks he will. That will be a good thing for Appenzeller will be satisfied better.

Thursday, December 30, 1886.   Mother came home with the five o'clock train. She staid at Hunsbergers today and last night. They will come up on New Year's. Mother will have to go down again in about four weeks about glasses.

I found myself be the fortunate one. For she brought me just the pocketbook I wanted alligator skin, a match case and above all a silk umbrella with a gilt head.

Kate came down with her work. She came to ask parents to dinner on New Year's. She brought her work along. She is making a hat crown for Horace. She thinks Milt Moyer was married on Christmas. I believe it too. She insisted on seeing my blanket. I took her upstairs. They others wondered much what we wanted. I hid it well. Took her home.

Friday, December 31, 1886.   The year 1886 is already over. The bank today added 1000 to its surplus making it 24000. The dividend will not be paid till Jan 10 on account of the Washington authorities. Mr. Landes starts his new Ledger today and I will commence mine on Monday. We worked till near five this afternoon. I found the key which had been lost on Oct. 12 while assorting the cks.

Commenced work on the books this afternoon and evening. It is now half past eleven and the old year is near out. There is some snow on the ground with a thick crust over it. Sleighing is not so bad they say. It is raining this evening. Sam shot off the old house pistol this evening. The band intended to play at midnight but I think it's too rainy.

Sleighing parties—little Sallie Souder comes to visit—receives permission to court Jennie—Milt Moyer is married—literary society presents "Ten Nights in a Barroom"—begins business course by correspondence—travels to New York City in search of an immigrant servant girl—confesses love for Jennie—is jealous of the "Countess"

1887

Saturday, January 1, 1887.   Got up late this morning. Commenced to take stock account about nine. Got through with most of it by dinner time. We have about 67000 ft. lumber on hand.

The weather was very umpleasant. Cold and rainy. Parents went up to WMS for dinner. Mother got after me about that blanket. She had seen it before but kept quiet about it. I showed it to her. She thought it pretty. Showed my room to grand father H. in the afternoon. Becker's sale was in progress this afternoon. Did not get over. Was at work on the books. Lot of girls here with Susie. People went in and out on our side it was so much more convenient. Mrs. Badman had her stand in our barn. This evening Mahlon Hunsberger and Alfred Hagey's came up. They had a late supper. Hagey's seem to be nice people. They went up to their brother Enos. They others stay here. Was up to W D Hunsberger's with his bill. Did not get the accounts closed today.

Sunday, January 2, 1887.   Clear and cold. Mr H. as talkative as ever. If he has only one to talk to he is all right. Mostly about rich people. They went up to grand father's for dinner. So did parents. Saw Kate this morning. She asked me for something. So I gave her a bullet and a card for somebody else. They boys loaded the old pistol with bullets yesterday and shot with it. Going to hang it up in my room.

Messaros was acquitted yesterday. He was also censured for imprudence. Did not dress till this afternoon. Got the sleigh ready and went over to John Snovel's with Uriah. I was well blessed with our visit. They are good, honest, contented people. Around the stove we sat in the kitchen. Mr S. is very plain of speech and I like him. I was there once before while Uriah was there. They set wine before us with cake to warm us up. In fact I enjoyed it much. We went home flying. Had a better road and the horse was cold from standing. Came home just before the train went down.

Monday, January 3, 1887.   Colder probably than any day this winter. Down at zero. Started the New Ind. Liabilities today. It contains 1100 pages and will last about 4 years. The old one contains over 18000 notes and was started in May 1884. Went up to John Frederick for his bill this afternoon. He does not have it ready. He does not go out at present. This keeps me back very much and sours one's temper a little. I got J B Frederick's bill. Of course we must run after the doctor five or six times. Was in meeting this evening. An English preacher's visit from Maryland was the cause of the meeting. He preached on the text, "The just shall live by faith". The house was nearly full. Bean was there to take Kate home. It is very slippery and many people fell.

Tuesday, January 4, 1887.   Got to the bank after the milk train was down. Mr. Landes did not come out till after ten o'clock. He had an attack of this sick-headache again. It almost kills him sometimes. We worked this afternoon till five o'clock. Yesterday was not much better. It makes me so tired. John talks about a higher salary. If he gets 600 he is satisfied and will prepare to stay. If not he is going to jump.

Becker's & Kratz's moved today and yesterday. They had good days for it. The roads were as even as the floor and no mud or dust to bother with. Kratz's new baker ran away this morning and Geo Becker will take his place for tonight at least.

Wednesday, January 5, 1887.   Not as cold as yesterday. It commenced to snow toward evening and is still snowing.

We were very busy at bank today. Mr. Landes is rid of his headache. Got home at quarter of five.

This was the evening for the literary society. Appenzeller was not over. Milt Moyer Horace and Mike Bergey were not present. Some of the young fellows make too much noise. We had some exercises. Jonathan had a recitation. We made out a programme for two weeks. Jonathan took Jennie and I took Lillie home. Kate was not down. She was in Telford on Sunday evening with Lizzie Gerhart. Martha and she (the latter) fell out a little. Martha it seems talks to much.

Thursday, January 6, 1887.   Sleighing is almost perfect they say. Snowed only about three inches and this covers all the bare places. They are out pretty much tonight I think. Susie says Kate and Bean are out.

Mrs Henry K Kindig of Phila was buried today.

I am kept very busy all day. If I had time I would write to Uriah. Wonder that Ed Danley don't write once. Frick of course wants me to lick his feet. Andrew too does not report.

I don't know what's up but Jennie laughed about something last evening and said she wouldn't tell me else I'd think myself smart. Such things make me feel like a fool somehow.

Friday, January 7, 1887.   Three little boys of 9-11-15 years respectively started for Kansas yesterday afternoon from Franconia Square. They got as far as the tunnel when the little fellow gave out. They had an idea that if they had reached Bethleham half the journey was over. Sam has brought his accordeon down. Music will not be a rarity now. This was library evening. The books went pretty well this evening. I took L & Kate home again. Kate got a gold ring as present. It would be fine for coasting tonight.

Saturday, January 8, 1887.   Coldest day so far. 2 above zero at our glass this morning. Sleighing is so good and everybody praises it so with the merry jingling of the bell which say that every body else is out and enjoying it that a person can hardly keep within doors. I intended to go out this afternoon but did not get at it. This evening the same. I got to work on that old pistol polishing it and then Auchey came for the sleigh. I said I didn't use and he could have it. Amelia and Sally came down after supper about a sleighride for tomorrow. Now father and mother want to go they want to go I want to go. So I am to take A & S to church in the morning. The boys were on the pike today. Sleighing was never better.

Sunday, January 9, 1887.   Commenced snowing this morning. Got ready and took Amelia and Sallie down to church. There not many there. Dengler preached. The Prof. Dr & Mrs Cope Ben Alderfer and Emma Leidy were all of the choir present. Went down by the new road and home the other way. In the afternoon Uriah came down. He came up with 10 o'clock train. Started in business on the first. We took a sleigh ride. It was snowing all the time but we had an umbrella. We went over to Franconia Sq. down the Allentown road. When we passed Levi Hunsberger's Uriah wanted me to drive in there and see Isaiah. We called him out. He did not know Uriah at first but know me right away. He has a beard and moustache. He has taken up 160 acres of land in eastern Colorado as a timber claim. He says he likes the West. We talked of old times in school and he laughed as hearty as ever. He has changed for better. He will stay till spring. It was nearly six o'clock when we got home. Uriah went to Lexington soon after. Our new neighbors came over to see us this evening. Their little girl Katie plays well for her age.

Missed church this evening and afternoon. Uriah confirmed my suspicion that Frick played off when we were down. Why on earth he did it I don't know. He thinks he is smart enough to hide it. Bad sign.

Monday, January 10, 1887.   It snowed about six inches yesterday and last night. If this snow would only not drift it would be so much solider. But it did drift some today. Saw Uriah this morning. He said he drove to Springhouse 15 miles from here last night. He went down at 9:41. The Rev. Mr Grubb was in bank at dinner time. Wrote a letter to Andrew this afternoon and sure enough I received one from him this evening. Cousin Annie was down this afternoon. I made out to give her a sleighride some time this week. Commenced writing an outline on "Old Curiosity Shop" for Wednesday evening. The boys went up to Uncle Joe's this evening to make out a trip to Henning's tomorrow.

Bought two pr stockings this evening. This will be my last supply. This was my last day for H. F. H. Tomorrow I shall have to start for myself.

Tuesday, January 11, 1887.   Today an election for directors was held at the bank resulting in the re-election of the old board.

Isaiah Hunsberger was here for dinner. Father and mother both have a good opinion of him. He laughed when he mentioned Sunday evening. He was to take his brother Levi out West.

Young Smith belied me twice about that book so I went out this afternoon determined to get it. I got it.

Today I am one and twenty. That means shift for yourself. I have been looking to this time for a long period and now perhaps I will look back. There has been much teasing about of late and I have found myself chuckling at the thought. I remember last year there were so many things I wanted to do first which hardly received attention. Have not yet arranged for boarding as mother referred me to father about it.

A sleighing party starts from Telford tonight and another from Leidy's to Blooming Glen. Rufus is among the latter.

Wednesday, January 12, 1887.   Most of the directors were sworn in today. John's salary was raised to $550. today. I did not ask for more. It would have struck fire if they had not done something. Finished outline of Old Curiosity Shop this afternoon. Did not get it copied as I had intended. At the literary this evening Milt Mike Jonathen Jennie and Lillie were not present. Most of them were out sleighing. It is delightful to be out this evening. Not at all cold. A party went over to Blooming Glen this evening. Took Kate home after it was over. Appenzeller expressed himself well satisfied.

Thursday, January 13, 1887.   The weather today was again warm and the snow thawed. I was only afraid that it would rain before night and spoil my sleighride.

Prince Bismarck is urging the passage of the Army Bill with all his might. He says there must be no war.

John Roach the ship builder died on Monday.

This afternoon Uncle Joe's and grand parents passed here on a big sleigh on their way to Aunt Kit's.

Went up and told Annie that I would give her a sleigh ride this evening and she was much pleased. After supper took mother out to aunt Kit's and from there took up Annie. She was almost ready to go to bed. It was half past seven. We passed the band who were marching through town on account of their ball. We passed over to the cowpath and so around while it rained just a little all the time. We were out a little over an hour. Annie is very talkative. Will make a good girl some day if she keeps on. We got pretty wet on the outside. It rained faster soon after the team was put away.

Friday, January 14, 1887. John M Wilson was hanged in Norristown yesterday for the murder of Anthony Daly in Jan 1884 or 5. He was 30 yrs of age. Native of Nova Scotia. He spoke about half an hour confessing his crime and calling on his hearers to lead Christian lives. I hear Moyer's girls &c were not at the ball last night.

It is rumored today and is said to be true that Chas Price was married yesterday to Annie Frederick. He was there only once or twice sometime ago. It was a surprise to most people.

This morning it was still raining and everything was as slippery as could be. People were out in sleighs yet though at this rate the snow will soon disappear.

As I passed out of the shop this afternoon the school girls began to snow ball me. I returned the compliment. They are a wild set. Some of them too wild. They ought to bridle their tongues a little.

Received a letter from E Danly. He pretends not to know whose turn it was to write &c. He says he has a cold now. He is a reckless fellow. For now he talks of marrying again to a girl he goes to see a little over a month. This is going too fast and I will talk plain to him. He wants me to come over as usual and somebody has told him it is not true that L & myself had parted. Wonder who knows so much.

Saturday, January 15, 1887. The German Reichstag has rejected Prince Bismark's Military Bill. The house was immediately dissolved by decree of the emperor. Bismarck will appeal to the people.

All the talk is about Wilson now. Dr Bauman was not down to see it as the paper said. Chas Price and wife also have their full share of the gossip. Not half true I believe.

Sarah Amelia and Sally were here this evening. Was reading "Barnaby Rudge" this afternoon with no earthly care upon me. Grandmother S. was down this P.M.

Mary Boyer has been married a week or so ago to one Andrew Barndt. It was also rumored that Wm Ruth and Ellie Slifer had done likewise. This was as usual not true. The same has occurred several times.

Sunday, January 16, 1887. Got up pretty late this morning quarter past seven. Sat around all forenoon reading in the laziest manner possible. That is, it had that effect upon me.

Dressed after dinner and went to meeting. We were not quite the last who came in. The Rev. Jacob Moyer officiated. Young Crouthamel from Lexington was there with two fellows. Kate and Jennie, Ellie Slifer the wedding party Mr & [Bride?] Andrew Barndt (Mary Boyer) &c. After meeting Sam and I went up to the station. From there we started out on a walk with Jake Hunsberger up town down the cut and home again. A few sleighs were out today yet. Kate and Lillie escorted Ellie Slifer home toward evening. It is provoking how they dress up to break hearts &c. On the way home they swept past with speed of the wind. A sidelong glance was stolen by one of them at least. Was very sleepy this evening.

Monday, January 17, 1887.   B. F. Gerhat of Telford will be sold out by the sheriff next Tuesday. Israel Benner had an apoplectic stroke last evening and is not expected to recover. Mrs. Fentore Crouthamel died this morning.

Gen Hazen Chief Sig. Officer US Army is dead.

Last evening on going to bed Sam told me who my successor was. It is very delightful. Stopped in to see Kate this afternoon. He commenced yesterday a week. She thought nobody knew about. I told her I knew everything. She used to see him often at Telford. I laughed when I heard it. For his sister Lizzie recommended him very highly before. I am well pleased with the turn affairs have taken. Was reading "Barnaby Rudge" this evening. Spoke to father about board. He said he would give me the board for nothing if I would keep the books and help about the yard. I had always intended to pay for my board that I don't quite like this. I have thought of paying a 100 and half the books and then do some sawing out in the shop.

Tuesday, January 18, 1887.   Israel Benner died last evening. He was about 67 or 68 yrs of age.

It has been getting much colder. The roads are as even as they can be. It would be nice to go out. Rec'd a letter from Andrew last evening. He wants me to come down on Saturday. I think I'll have to do so. Wrote Ed. Danley a little cooly if he is not too thickheaded to under stand my meaning. We were pretty busy today. Read "Barnaby Rudge" this afternoon and evening. Thought today of plan which is perhaps possible. That is I may get the means to travel yet. I have been dreaming of such a thing since I was a boy. I am sure it would do me much good.

Wednesday, January 19, 1887.   Gen Beaver was inangurated Governor of Penna. yesterday with great pomp.

Saw Kate this afternoon. Was there nearly an hour. She is embroidering a schoolbag for Henry.

At the literary met Mr Harvey Clymer teacher of the Five Points School. We quite a little talk on Prohibition. Mr Clymer was against it.

Miss Jennie Emma Krupp and Kate were there. Lillie the foolish did not come again just I suppose because the Telford folks were not here. She was afraid perhaps she might give an atom of offense to Telford because of me. How strange. Really when I was left behind to close the school house I felt lonely. Forsaken by all the world, ha,ha, that's it. She was out to see Kate and I met her at the gate before going down.

Thursday, January 20, 1887.   Wrote Uriah and Andrew today. Promised the latter to come down on Saturday.

A man went round selling the auto-biography of the murderer Wilson written by himself. Sam got one and I read it this afternoon. I had intended not to look at it but after reading it was convinced that the man is sincere. Although he has over done the thing a little yet he meant well no doubt. And the example it gives of the effects of drink made me wonder why I have not sworn off entirely.

Read "Barnaby Rudge" after supper. It is very good I think. Old John Willet is entertaining. It made mother laugh although she thought must be a tedious book to read. Went to bed very late 11:30.

Friday, January 21, 1887. Weather quite warm today, and the water begins to run on the street. Finished reading "Barnaby Rudge" this afternoon. I liked it very much. Being very tired from late hours during the week I went up stairs this afternoon and laid down and slept about half an hour. I then went down to the school house to make ready for this evening. Spoke with Jennie for a while. Covered three books. Jennie said Lady Clara Vere deVere had asked about Mr Micawber.

There were not very many at the library this evening. Lillie came down about half past eight. Offered to take her home. On the way I teased her about Gerhart. She of course (she is going out with Cal. on horseback on Sunday she says) laughed very much and denied it. Found out however that she was out sleighing with him the other Wednesday night. And that she expected to go to Hoppenville with a party if there were more sleighing. She said if it were so I was in fault. When I saw her father come I started home. Sam and I carried Susie's trunk upstairs. We fixed up her room a little which made her very mad. Sam got pushed and I was slapped.

Saturday, January 22, 1887. Israel Benner was buried today. Derstine was buried yesterday. The funeral was on Thursday but they waited for his brother who came in from Nebraska. Barnes & Frederick had a horse sale at Tyson's this afternoon. Tried to make the 5.26 train for North Wales but missed it. Fixed up the old pistol nicely with father's aid. I had one screw too many.

At the station Haynes laughed and wondered what was up with me & L. He thought I was going down to hunt up something. Met Andrew at the station. We went down to the skating rink where the fair is held. It is a large building and is fixed up in splendid style. It was very full. Met Will Coar and talked awhile with him. Saw Carrie Shearer and Deisingers pests, Irwin Lukens Frank Ely Miss Roberts Wellington Rosenberry. Took chances on a few articles. It began to get noisy toward the end. Andrew thought they would be stopped for it. The fair is to continue every evening next week except Monday. We went to bed near midnight. Forgot to note down that John Musselman got married last Saturday. Andrew's sister had a beau on Saturday evening. A school boy Andrew said. He would not give me his photo for fear he would not get any.

Sunday, January 23, 1887.   Got up about half past seven. Took a walk about town and at half past ten went to the Methodist Church. Rev Hess is their pastor. Miss Connie Durrin plays the organ. Their windows are very ornamental with stained glass with the names of the donors. After dinner went to the Reformed Sunday School. Was very much surprised to see Dr Slifer walk in. Did not know he had arrived. Andrew neither. He has a beard growing. Arrived on Friday evening. They have a very orderly S.S. Good library. Walked about town up near Brunner's and got very muddy shoes. Avoided the Deisinger's. In the evening after again considerable walking we went to the Baptist Church. They have cushioned seats and carpeted floor. Plain otherwise. Good preacher. Described hell's horrors. Lillie Harley played the organ here. It is curious that most of the girls I know in North Wales are organists. Miss Durrin at the Methodist, Miss Shearer at the Lutheran and Miss Harley at the Baptist. Thought I could make the train yet after church and hurried to the station. Andrew tried to keep me back but I hurried on and bought a ticket when the operator told me the train had left. I was disappointed. Andrew laughed all evening. So I had to stay overnight again. Was very tired when we went to bed.

Monday, January 24, 1887.   Took the 7²⁶ train for home this morning. Andrew don't know where he will go in the spring. Met Markly Haffnagle on the train. He was down home and in the city. When I came home one asked me whether I was just coming home from Z's. It rained or snowed the greater part of the day and is very muddy. Rec'd a letter from Os Kline. He is full of music. That's all he does. He says he and Umsted go out sometimes. Subscribed for the N.Y. World today.

Old Herman was badly fooled today. He asked me where I was last evening. That my girl was there. Chris Moyer then told him I had long quit going.

Tuesday, January 25, 1887.   We were examined at bank today by a committee of the board of Directors. They were J.G. Gerhart, E.H. Souder and J.G. Metz. They came out on the cent.

This afternoon Kate called me in awhile and we talked a little. L was there Saturday night. Bean is sick. Saw L. this evening in the store. Was on her way to Kate.

Rec'd a letter from Uriah. He enclosed his card and bill head. He is very busy and works late. He was not used to this before. Was up at the doctor's for his bill again this evening. Not made out of course. Was at work on the books this afternoon and evening. Old Polly was down this afternoon.

Wednesday, January 26, 1887.   It rained then snowed and then cleared off cold. Got an invitation from Mr. Gerhart to come and see them once. "I had to spend my Sundays somewhere." I made answer I would come up to Sunday School once and &c. but it tickled me not a little.

Went down to the meeting house this afternoon and fetched away some singing books the old Garner's for this evening. There was a pretty good attendance this evening although they came late. Appenzeller always called me "Willie" and when I looked up I saw everybody laughed. Jennie burst out laughing once but she turned it off all right. Schwenk and Annie were there. Jonathan had an outline on "Pickwick". Very funny. Took Lillie home. Kate was not down. She says she had Gerhart only for fun but I see through that. She wants to hold out in inducement to me but I wish she would hold on to Gerhart. Got to bed late.

Thursday, January 27, 1887.   Wanamaker advertised 3 sets Waverly novels for 4^{50} a set. We wanted one for the library and so telephoned down about but got no answer. Of course they were all sold. Answered Os Klines letter this morning. He is full of music. Taking lessons, member of an orchestra and I think sings in a choir. Rec'd. a letter from S R Swartley asking about a dialogue we had on the hall during an institute. A map was enclosed signed Rosie Swartley. He takes great pride in this pupil it seems.

There is much in the newspapers about a war in Europe in the spring. One thing is certain. The Powers are all arming. And this may bring on a war in the near future. But perhaps this all talk.

Friday, January 28, 1887.   Received a letter from Frick this evening. Very short. He waited on me it seems. He enclosed a tintype in lieu of the cabinet he promised. Fisher & son sold a lot of horses at the hotel today. Jonas Landes has one for 200. They sold them all even the horses they took in.

Was very sleepy all evening yet did not get to bed till eleven.

Saturday, January 29, 1887.   Rainy and disagreeable. Then English Parliament has again assembled. The Queens speech was read yesterday. It refers but little to Ireland.

Read a little in "Edwin Drood."

Helped to estimate the cost of a house in Lansdale. It came so high that it is not probable that anyone he will build.

Sunday, January 30, 1887.   Susie went up home yesterday so mother was left alone with the work. We assisted her a little. Made my bed. Sam his and father theirs. Sam went to Hornings. Wanted to go to Telford but changed my mind.

Was at home and read "Edwin Drood." Mentioned something about 100 for board and keeping the books. Don't believe this to be final. Heard they were on the lookout for a lot to build a church yesterday but it was too wet. Father don't wish to stay in business he told me. He wants to keep Reub and let him have the thing &c. I asked him to insure for about $2000. Was up at the station. Gerhart came along down. He talked with Markly & Haynes. I felt a little awkward somehow. Went home to read again.

Monday, January 31, 1887.   Wrote to Frick and Uriah this afternoon. Was up in the store and talked with Ellis. He gave his experiences when he attained his majority. Read when I came home. Mother made me take her up to Nace's to ask for Emma. She did not get her. I was down at grand fathers' the while.

Mother is going to the city this week and wanted me to write a letter for Mrs Hunsberger to meet the train. I said I was going along if she went on Thursday. I don't know how it will come yet. I don't think it quite safe for her to go alone.

Tuesday, February 1, 1887.   Mother decided to go alone tomorrow morning and so wrote to Mrs Hunsberger to meet them at the depot. She replied this evening by telegraph. Drew my salary today for the first time.

Father is going to build an addition to the shop 24 x 24 and get a new moulding machine and a jointer.

Finished "Mystery of Edwin Drood" this evening at it remains a mystery still. This story was left unfinished by Dickens. There are some indications which way the wind blows with some of the characters but still remains unexplained while the outcome is uncertain.

Wished to go down to the schoolhouse this afternoon but did not get down. Fixed up some old track and put it in shape.

Wednesday, February 2, 1887.   The weather today was very unpleasant. Hail and sleet. Kate called me in this afternoon. She wanted to know the answer to her question. Went down to the schoolhouse this afternoon and did not get through till half past six.

At the Literary Mr Appenzeller was not present. We had our discussion and other exercises as if he were present. Mr Clymer had a recitation and Rufus Landes a select reading. Mentioned to L. that I had promised to see the girls home. Clymer staid and walked with me. K & L walked in front and at the corner K asked me if I had forgotten myself. I told her to shut up and at their gate was a little embarrassed for L commenced to walk faster and I left her go. I wasn't going to run after her so I went home.

Received another letter from Swartley and also from Uriah. He comes up on Saturday.

Thursday, February 3, 1887.   Damp and very slippery. Forgot last eve that it was L's birthday or I would have pulled her ears.

Sam Young got arrested yesterday morning and was taken to Norristown. Bortz's step daughter is the cause.

Did some bookbinding this afternoon and evening.

Friday, February 4, 1887.   A nice clear day.

Sam tells me that father and Uriah has a fall out this morning. Father struck him on the mouth. Uriah talks too big and does not always keep to the truth.

The Prohibition Amendment Bill has been passed by the Senate by a vote of 29 to 2. The Democrats abstained from voting. If it would only pass in the house then it would come before the people and then it could have a chance.

The library was pretty well attended this evening. Kate and L came down late. I pulled L's ears on account of her birthday on the 2nd. Told her I wasn't going to run after her on Wednesday evening. Took her and Kate home after it was over. She expected me to run after her on Wed. evening. Spoke about getting up an entertainment with Ten Nights in a Bar Room.

Saturday, February 5, 1887.   Heard through telephone from Doylestown that F.H. Leidy had failed. That his father was connected with it &c. Mr L thought that his name might be forged. In that case he will go to jail.

Jas and Hannah Slifer are down. She will stay for she brought the birdcage along.

Mrs Ellis was here about Susie when I came home. Father went after Annie Gunhardt this afternoon. She was not at home. Perhaps we shall get her.

Was in the depot this evening before the mail went up and saw Miss Gerhart there waiting. Went to the concert on the hall given by a Phila party. Good music. Some good acting but withal very rough. A rough set. One who seems to have been drunk last evening and fined 7^{10} at the station house. Gerhart and Bean were up with their respective ladies. I am afraid I'll set that G up and spoil her game. What surprised me most was to see Jennie alone in a seat and soon afterward Jonathan came in alone and sat down. He near the last came to a part where I sat and I asked him why he wasn't in his right place. Don't remember what he said but she went home alone. Something must be up. There was dancing after the performance.

Sunday, February 6, 1887.   Took a few rides on the sled this morning.

Went up to hunt Uriah up. Jas. saw me and called me in. Saw Dr Slifer who was telling about his travels. James goes away tomorrow morning. Hannah will stay here. Went away just before dinner. Went up again after dinner and found Rufus making ready to go away with Uriah's team. Uriah had to engage on at the livery for this evening. We went to church on the hall. Aker preached. He said it was probably the last time as he would be removed to another charge. From church we went down home. J M H. accompanied us. Cousin Annie came down and I wrote in her album. After supper went up to the station saw Gerhart, nodded and went over with Jonathan and Calvin for music. They played their horns. Ed Price came and we had a game of Casino. It seem there is something up between J & J. On the way home looked in at the station which was full of "bums." Haynes was away to the girls.

Monday, February 7, 1887.   Heard this morning that F H Leidy was off and had forged to the the amt of 9000. A N Leidy said he left last Tuesday already. His flight is all the talk around here. Don't know for certain yet how old Thomas stands. Uriah went down at 9:33. He is very merry. He bought a diamond studded ring from Hunsberger yesterday. Am sure of one thing now. He is going to take her.

Mr Landes told me that Z's commenced to talk all at once this morning. He thought perhaps I was out there yesterday. He says it's over two months now since they spoke last.

I believe Uriah and some of the boys went over to Blooming Glen to engage a hall to hold an entertainment. Funny ideas these boys have. The Lexington fellows are crowding the place. Three of my cousins and Mary Shellenberger.

Tuesday, February 8, 1887.   Foggy weather all day. This morning it was very slippery. Heard all sorts of stories about F H Leidy. Milt was over this afternoon and was closeted with Mr L for almost an hour. It is not so bad as it was reported at first. He has not endorsed any new papers.

Father failed to get Annie — from Kulpsville. We were a little too late.

Wednesday, February 9, 1887.   The prospects for the passage of the Prohibition Amendment Bill are good. The bill passed second reading last evening. Jacob Shelly a school teacher of Hilltown left home on Sunday and nothing is known of his whereabouts. He left home before once. Mother went down to the city this afternoon.

At the literary this evening I commenced to talk about an entertainment. As "Ten Nights in a Bar Room" did not arrive we could not act but it was decided to select one next Wednesday. The girls all went home by themselves. Ain't going to do it anymore. Almost forgot to mention it. Rec'd a valentine (cartoon) a terrible face from somebody. Burned it up.

Thursday, February 10, 1887.   Received the new history of the US from the 'World' this morning and also "Ten Nights in a Bar Room." Also received a letter from Andrew.

The Prohibition Amendment Bill was passed by the House yesterday. Now it has to be formally advertised again passed by the next Legislature again advertised and it is ready for the people.

Mother did not get home today.

Friday, February 11, 1887.   Very muddy. There was some rain. It is storming now 10 P.M. It was so dark part of the afternoon that we lighted a lamp at bank. Mother came home on the 5^{26} train. She will get her glasses tomorrow. It is full of valentines (cartoons) up at the store and the boys are sending them out.

Wm has a raccoon. He bought him from an old Rucksee [?].

Father commenced getting ready to build the new addition to the shop today. Will get no new carriage shop but will have an old one fixed up for my carriage.

Saturday, February 12, 1887. Cleared off and much colder.

Jas Slifer came home this afternoon. Saw him in the store this evening. Went over to the station. Went up with a set of fellows to Leidy's auction. We had a footrace going and coming. Stopped in at the stores for candy and oranges. Over to the station where we practised tumbling and jumping till about nine. The boys then went at dominoes. Saw Archie Reed at the auction. Spoke to Jonathan this afternoon about "Ten Nights in a Bar Room". He thinks its good and so does Moyer. Mr Godshall read part of it today and he wants the book. Mother got her spectacles today.

Sunday, February 13, 1887. Got ready this morning to go to Telford. Os Kline came in and went up to the station with me. I did not go on the train on this account. So I started to walk up. Stopped in at grand father's who told me that Jo's were coming down. So I staid there for dinner and in the afternoon father & mother came up. John Souder's were there too. Went down to Cornelius' and no one at home but Kit & Penrose. Maggie, Katie Derstein & Amelia dropped in. Afterwards Cal. Haynes Jonathan Henry & W F Hunsberger. Cousin Kate invited me to her wedding which is to take place on Saturday the 26th.

Went up to the station to meet the train. Haynes came down with me and we had some some music. Uriah W.F.H. Henry Hunsberger, Rufus, and Penrose Zendt came in afterward. We had a great time. Noise plenty of it. They all left except Rufus who was here after Susie came home. He stole her photos and Sam blew out the lights. We had a great time. Susie was much out of temper. Rufus gave me the pictures and left and she went to bed in a passion. Archie Reed is here over night. He sleeps with Uriah.

Monday, February 14, 1887. Tomorrow is the election. Dr Bauman and H D Detweiler have been placed in the field as Souderton and Telford's candidates for school directors. Geo H Ruth and Jacob D. Stover will run against them. Another pair were also nominated. In Phila. the fight is for the Mayoralty. E H Fitler the Republican nominee is said to be a very fit man and will undoubtedly be elected. Geo deB Keim a Republican nominated by the Democrats was formerly sheriff. He is said have made a bargain with Rowan the present sheriff to divide the income of the office with the latter on condition that he should work for him.

Mother scolded a little about the noise we had last evening. Heard from Frick today. Was up for Jonathan at the band room this evening. They have a nice room on W D Hunsberger's third floor.

Tuesday, February 15, 1887. Today was election day. They tried to get them out here and some said they turned out very heavy in the township. Some think Detweiler will go in while most of them believe Bauman and Detweiler will be defeated. They were after me too but I did not care to go as my name is not on the registry lists. Father and Mr Moyer went to Harleysville together but came too late to vote. Went down to the schoolhouse this afternoon and took the play to Miss J. Rec'd a letter from Ed Danley. He wants the marriage question answered. Ha ha! Wonder what he means. He must be a foolish fellow &c.

Andrew is coming up on Saturday. Read "Our Mutual Friend". Old Herman read "Ten Nights in a Bar Room". He was much interested in it.

Preston Lillie and their mother were here this afternoon. Did not see them.

Wednesday, February 16, 1887.   Both Telford and Souderton were beaten yesterday. Bauman had 167 and Detweiler 150. The other two had 204.

Fitler was elected Mayor by almost 30000 majority.

This morning early the people were indignant at the result of the election. Soon Ben Barndt and Detweiler went around for funds to employ an attorney. They raised $70 before dinner. This afternoon posters came out announcing a meeting on the hall this evening to discuss the borough question. The meeting was held and W D Hunsberger and Geo H Swartz are to go to Norristown to examine the law on the subject. Another meeting is to be held on Saturday evening. I think if pushed it'll go through this time. This evening there was but a slim meeting at the schoolhouse. But Appenzeller was there and we decided to try Ten Nights in a Bar Room. I will send for copies of the play. Appenzeller, Jonathan, myself Mike Bergey Milt Moyer Rufus Landis Rufus Souder Jennie Lillie Kate and Little Kate Moyer are the cast. It will take push.

Thursday, February 17, 1887.   Sent for 6 copies "Ten Nights in a Bar Room". Wrote Lillie this morning and went up and saw Milt and Mike. Mike said yes but Milt can't help being too busy. Think I'll have to take his place. Milt will perhaps take something else. I believe L. was sick last eve and so couldn't come last eve.

Spoke with Markley this evening. Gave him the play to read. He worked for Haynes who attended the lodge. Spoke about L &c. He said it made him mad to hear people speak about what they know nothing about. He said they talked the same way about me. A very nice fellow Markley is.

Friday, February 18, 1887.   Rained all day and the creek was flooded. Cleared off this evening.

Today the borough excitement is higher than ever. The opposition showed itself. Hunsberger and Swartz came back and reported that everything was in the hands of Councils. Swartz made use of this to blow up the business. He was about town all day talking against borough. They were out with a petition against it on that side of the creek. On this side they are just as firm the other way. And if they do not blunder we will get a borough on this side of the creek and leave the others go.

I was terribly disappointed this evening. Jennie and Annie came out early to the Library and said she couldn't help. Her father objects to the play. Now was the puzzle who to get. Ran after Jonathan and made out to apply to Telford for aid. The Gerharts saw Kate about it and thought I should wait till Monday.

Saturday, February 19, 1887. Father went to the city this morning. He bought a new style tin moulder and a jointing machine for 400.

Andrew did not come up till three. He brought his photo. Left again at eight. We wanted him to stay but he expects girls and wants to see about a job, &c.

Felt very blue this afternoon awhile for mother was after me about the entertainment. Kate sent down for me after supper and as I did not come right away she came down herself. Found Lillie in the parlor. Talked about the business till near train time when I ran over to see Andrew off. Came back and soon Bean came. L and I went into the back room. She hung back at first. But it pleased her all the same. Left the book with her. She will let me know.

Went over to the borough meeting. Ben Barndt was talking when I came in. Swartz talked against it. At last a committee of six was appointed to take it in charge. They are W D Hunsberger H D Detweiler F H Souder J H Moyer J D Moyer and M D Zendt. The great comedians started off at noon and have not yet returned.

Sunday, February 20, 1887. Sam Alderfer wanted me to get ready and go to meeting with him and mother. But I could not get ready. Hannah and old Polly came down and James and Wm soon followed. After dinner we went down and saw the library. There was a fire in the direction of Harleysville. He is at the Perkiomen temporarily.

Read "Our Mutual Friend." Went up to the station after supper. Saw Rufus talking with Gerhart. Went up to Tyson's Hall to church with Haynes &c. But we were too late. The seats were all taken and we went home again. Was up at the station pretty late.

The Great Comedians did pretty well last evening. They sold over 90 tickets. The band was down at North Wales last evening.

Monday, February 21, 1887. Snowed yesterday and today was very muddy again. Jas. M Slifer was in bank all morning. He will not go up till Wednesday.

Kate told me this morning that she too could not help. She did not wish to give a reason. I said I wanted to see her again. Rec'd. a letter from L this afternoon. She said Bean was the cause. I thought that must be it. Went down to the schoolhouse and saw Jennie. Saw Kate and Milt afterward. Didn't feel like giving up yet. Told Kate what I thought of it. Went out to Lillie's after supper and asked her about the business. She is all right. Took the play out to Jennie. L asked me to call around. Had a talk with Jennie and Annie. Their father would let them help if they wanted to. But he thinks it's wrong. Perhaps Annie would help. Went to Schwenck and saw him about it. He talked as if he would do it. But he is not to be depended on. He will come down on Wednesday evening.

Tuesday, February 22, 1887.   Washington's Birthday.

Intended to go to the city today. But the weather being unfavorable I staid at home. The Plays arrived this morning and I sent one to Appenzeller Schwenck and Jonathan.

Sat around doing nothing but reading "Our Mutual Friend" all day. Got sleepy and took a nap this afternoon. Was up at the barbers this afternoon.

The weather wasn't so bad that I might not have risked it. But I did not get off to the city. Don't know when I will go now.

The box over the telephone was put up this afternoon at the bank.

Wednesday, February 23, 1887.   The box over the phone works pretty well. Can't understand talking inside unless very quiet.

Aunt Sarah and Mrs. Jno. F. Souder and her children were here today.

This evening at the Literary we went over our programme in haste to commence on the play. Schwenck was down and said he could not help. Of course this would have spoiled it all. I think how ever he will take the part as he is very fond of it. That secured Jennie and Annie. Clymer acts as stage manager. Lillie's sister Anna is to be Mary Morgan. We read over about half of the piece. As it got late we went home. They are delighted with it. Lillie is not. She is afraid it wont take. Kate is not allowed to come it seems unless Mr Bean is around. I took L. Jonathan took Jennie and Charley took Annie. If it keeps on it will be all right.

Thursday, February 24, 1887.   Bismarck has been victorious in the German elections.

This afternoon Kate came out and wanted to know about the play. She said Mr Bean was not entirely opposed to it but it would hurt his feelings if she would. She is gone it seems or she wouldn't care.

Copied off two parts in Ten Nights in a Bar Room this afternoon. One remains to be copied. M K Bergey wants his to commence on.

Friday, February 25, 1887.   All the pieces in my hands "Frank Slade" "Willie Hammond" and "Mrs Slade" copied. Took them round today. Sent a book to Mike Bergey. Milton Moyer told me that Schwenck couldn't help. So I went over to see him. He pretended that it was all right. That he could get off during the week but not on Saturday evenings. As it takes only one Saturday evening he thought there was not much doubt about it. When Uriah came home he brought a book from Clymer which had been handed to him by Schwenck. I asked him what he said. He reported it uncertain again that he had not promised for sure &c &c.

Saturday, February 26, 1887.   Talked about Schwenk's wavering in bank today. I said it would be hard to be beaten by him &c. Moyer thought it were a good plan to prepare others in case of an emergency. As for instance get

Swartley to prepare one &c. Am going to watch him and would rather act on this than be beaten. Bought a whiskholder for cousin Kate this morning. She was married on Thursday evening. I was going to go up this afternoon but gave it up on account of the weather.

There was a deep snow today and now it is raining on top. Wonderful slush there'll be yet I believe. Read "Our Mutual Friend." Tried to finish it but did not get quite through. Too sleepy. No one was up to Telford to the wedding except Sarah.

Sunday, February 27, 1887.   Got up early as Susie went to Lansdale with the milk train to see her sister. Laid down and took a nap till nine o'clock when I went and dressed. After dinner Uriah came down. He gave me his picture. We went to meeting together. Allebach preached. From there we went up to the station to see Markly. From there down home again. We were not here long when Rufus came down about the team. Uriah soon afterward left. Aunt Kit was here with Penrose. Heard there were 40 at the wedding last evening. Dr Bauman and Bean's families were there, &c. Studied my part a little in the play. Uriah said his man was up from the city to the Great Comedians show and said it was the thinnest thing he ever saw. Sam and I sat around talking till late about our school days &c &c.

Monday, February 28, 1887.   Yesterday and today were cold days. It is very icy and rough. Did not see Uriah before he went down. The Telford entertainment has been postponed till Saturday evening.

Father is going to or did stop the Great Comedian's next show. He went up to Grandfather's this evening. Was at work a little in the shop this afternoon. It will make a fine work room.

Explained our play to father and mother. Mrs Kratz came over and spent the evening. There was a great earthquake in Europe last week one day. About 2000 persons were believed to be killed. Bismarck was victorious in the German elections.

Tuesday, March 1, 1887.   There was some snow today. Became a little warmer toward noon.

We were very busy balancing books today and did not get out till five this afternoon. Went down to the shop from bank. It is nearing completion. Reub can't wait for the new machines. Worked on the books. Practised on the play. Know three parts about it.

There was a great earthquake in the south of France and in Italy. About 2000 persons were killed.

Wednesday, March 2, 1887.   Tomorrow the survey of the borough will take place. Bean was down today and he thought a poor man had no business in this world. He would have liked to have the job.

Received a letter from Lillie this evening saying she could not come. So I went right out and fetched Anna out. L. fell last Thursday evening and hurt herself. Anna was to take Mary Morgan. Old Herman came down to see the literary society and we had pretty much singing. After we were over the piece we sent all the others home and proceeded with the piece. I heard Schwenck wouldn't help. Said nothing to Annie who knew nothing about it. When she found out she backed out too and then we gave Green to Clymer. Mehitable to Lillie, Mrs Slade to Anna And Mary Morgan to Flora Hunsberger. Took Anna home.

Thursday, March 3, 1887. Arthur Landes came out this morning and said his father could not come as he had a headache. He did not come till near three o'clock. He said he felt very bad. The surveyors were around today. It looked as if it were going to rain did not. They took Schock and those upper fellows in I believe.

Went over to see Mike in the stocking factory. Was down at the school house to see Jennie. Went over to see Jonathan and about Flora. Saw Rufus in the store this evening. They are all going to stick and it is high time too.

Friday, March 4, 1887. There was a little snow this morning but it cleared off this afternoon. Mother wanted me to take her to the carpet weavers but this afternoon when I came home I found that Sam had taken her. John D Moyer was out with the surveyors today.

Made some drafts for the play this afternoon after bank. Wanted to see Clymer but missed the train. At the library this evening I broke two chimneys in opening the book-case. Kate came down and I had a short talk with her. Soon after Jennie came. They left and soon after Lillie and Kate came back. L. wanted to be a little displeased the Schwenck's and Annie backed but I know better. On the way home she said that Milt Moyer had said something about herself and me. She said she would not tell me now but some other time. Stopped in at the station when I went home. Spoke with John and Will Hunsberger about furnishing the music for the entertainment. They seemed to be pleased. Heard that Schwenck had said that it was given up and that he had the chief part and came out in every scene.

Saturday, March 5, 1887. A cold day. It snowed a little this afternoon. I had intended to go to the Telford entertainment but gave it up again on account of the weather. Jonas Freed and Benj. Auchy were married this afternoon. There was quite a crowd at the station. I looked on from the store. The trade dollar bill has become a law without the president's signature. At the shop they are changing the position of the machinery. Was at work making charts for the play all evening. Cousin Amelia and Miss Maggie Souder and Sallie were here awhile this evening. Miss S. played on the organ and does it well too. Mr Zendt came in this evening to pay a little on his bill. He sat and talked a little. He is well pleased with being on the borough committee I think. It is very late again.

Sunday, March 6, 1887.   Cloudy and disagreeable. Father told me this morning that Frick was up. He did not come over. After dinner I went over on my way to meeting. I asked him to go along but he said he was all broke up and so I left him alone. Went up to the station and went along up to Telford with Horace, Haynes, Morris Weil & Elmer and Wm Blank. We walked about a little met the Sunday School Scholars the male portion of whom nearly all stopped in at Fenstermacher's. Saw Miss Gerhart who spoke Horace & Haynes. We then started home. The boys were a little wild and there was enough foul talk. Went over to see John Hunsberger about the music. He is a stupid I thought. He would not play for us. He promised to help at the entertainment.

Went home and took supper. Went over to Frick. Went up with him to the station. He is in love with the Bitting girl. But there is little constancy in him. Went away promising to write. Milt Moyer said something about attending Pierce's Business College in evening sessions. I got it into my head that I would like to do the same. Will write. Rufus come down home with me. We talked over the play &c.

Monday, March 7, 1887.   Very cloudy and foggy. Caught a bad cold somewhere. Wrote to Pierce's Business College about attending terms &c.

The new machines have not yet come. Don't know what's the matter. Did not see Clymer today so I sent him a note but he was away to a wedding. So we practiced without him and Appenzeller. Mike Bergey thought himself aggrieved I think and went home without saying anything. He wants to be coaxed I think. He is very touchy. Will take Ambrose if he won't do it. Jennie does her part well. Jonathan took her and I followed with L. She said she was up at Telford on Sunday. I did not see her though we passed her. Got through by ten o'clock.

Tuesday, March 8, 1887.   Today was a nice day. But it is very muddy. There is very beautiful moonlight this evening. Was very busy today. We went over the Ledger and I was at work balancing Cassel's book and others. The borough limits have at least been decided upon. Just above Schoch's line for the upper boundary. Received a circular from Pierce's Business College. Evening sessions are only from Sept to April. Practised over my part a little this evening.

Wednesday, March 9, 1887.   Henry Ward Beecher died yesterday morning at nine o'clock. He had a stroke of apoplexy last Saturday. He was nearly 74 years of age. The funeral will be tomorrow.

This evening Mike Bergey did not put in an appearance. He wanted to be coaxed. Markley Huffnagle and Frank Benner came down to the schoolhouse to hear our literary exercises. As we did not have any they soon left. We practised till half past ten. Clymer was here. He acts well. Jonathan said they asked $5.00 for music but we can't pay that much. It rained a little when we went home.

Kratz this afternoon cut down the great hickory tree in his backyard.

Thursday, March 10, 1887. This afternoon mother and myself went up to Telford. It was very muddy so that we determined to go home another way. We went to Derstine's to see them and how Mrs Jno F Souder was doing. She is recovering and will soon be all right. We offered to take little Sallie down for a week or two. But Peggy would not spare her. She is a very smart little girl and they want to keep her. Uncle Joe does not think much of the borough business. Went to bed early.

Friday, March 11, 1887. Today it was very windy. This morning we found that a note was missing. Mr Gerhart was down and he said he heard Barndt's note which was still standing open was paid. We looked the matter up and found there was no such thing. It was determined that I should go up this afternoon see M S Kulp and get him to get the note from Barndt. I went up on the three o'clock train but did not see Kulp. I went over to Gerhart's and went down with the next train. Went down to the school with a lot of papers. Went up to the station where Hen Price was disputing with the Methodist preacher Aker. He had his match. Saw Kulp and told him. Went up again with the mail train met Kulp at the station who told me he had it all fixed and went over to see Barndt. He was very tame and gave up the note and of course was very innocent. I got him fast several times. Kulp pitied him a little I think and wanted to shield him. Took the note over to Gerhart's who will hand them to Bean. Barndt is a rascal. Spoke with Abe Gerhart about our entertainment &c. Saw his sister just one moment. She did not notice me. Went to Mr Landes and reported.

Saturday, March 12, 1887. Today it was cold and stormy.

Sam'l S. Swartley father of S. R. Swartley died today. Fisher's had a horse sale this afternoon.

Read Scribner's new magazine today.

The band this evening serenaded Auchey.

Was up in the store this evening where I saw little Emma Becker and Sallie Keeler with cousin Annie. They promised to come down tomorrow morning.

Was out in the shop a while this afternoon. The new machines did not yet come. Father was down to Lansdale this afternoon.

Sunday, March 13, 1887. Fair day. The roads have dried off very much. Sam has a gold watch now. It is a beauty. Open face strong and warranted to last 21 yrs. It costs him 27 or 28 Dolls. Talked about getting one myself. Sallie Keeler and Emma Becker were here for about an hour. Teased them a little as of old. Very lively little girls.

Started for meeting this afternoon but was too early and so went home again. Little Hannah was here and amused us not a little. Grandmother was here a short time. Amelia and Maggie were here a few minutes. Walked with Mary to the station. Misses Becker and Keeler were at the window as I passed. Walked about town with Rufus. Many were out. It won't be long before promenading will be pleasant. Met Miss Annie and Jennie. We went in at our house and practiced our parts.

Monday, March 14, 1887. The long looked for machines at length arrived today. The moulding machine was started this evening. They are regular beauties polished up as they are. I started to go up to the watchmaker's this afternoon but met him on the way but will go up on Thursday evening and look at his stock. This evening Mike Bergey did not appear. Rufus Landes too was absent and he probably did not know. There has been some progress made. Flora is getting on well but she talks too fast. We had a good time together. Jennie says Kate promised to come down on Wednesday evening. Lillie says she had a bad cold last week. Jennie will have her last week school.

Tuesday, March 15, 1887. Harry Zeigler of Telford formerly a school teacher was drunk all last week and died last night from the effects of it. He was in the employ of Dr Bauman who discharged him on this account. He was down here and got some medicine of Loux and now it is a question whether it was the medicine or what. He took too much medicine. Dr Loux and Bauman had a consultation on the telephone and they agreed a blood vessel must have burst. He drank some horse medicine in mistake for brandy. Rum may be said to have been the cause of his death.

Wednesday, March 16, 1887. Wm B. Slifer came in bank this morning to see about his affairs. They will look the matter up.

Zeigler who died on Monday night did not of the medicine but a blood vessel is believed to have burst. They renewed Barndt's note again with $10 paid. He would find a harder customer in me I think.

Kate Slifer was here I believe a little before noon. Little Sallie Souder is here after all now. She came in from her cousin's funeral. She is a very good pretty little girl and I wish we could keep her. But she don't want to stay. I gave her books and did everything to amuse her I could. This evening they all came pretty late. Appenzeller did not come. Mike Bergey was here and all right. Lillie and Anna came first. Kate came down too. We cut up pretty much. It has improved much. Flora especially. Jonathan says we are to have the music for nothing. Clinton Souder and John Hunsberger with cornets and one Alderfer on the piano. On the way home caught on to L. but the boys didn't like it so when we came to our place L let go and down the lane I went. She thought I'd come back but I didn't. I ain't going to [be] made a fool of. Went to bed at eleven.

Thursday, March 17, 1887. Geo H Ruth had a trying experience in the city yesterday. He was locked up for reckless driving. He drove over a little child in the street and was taken into custody. After much trouble he was released yesterday morning after much trouble. Went up to the watchmaker's this afternoon and found he had just what I wanted. He was in the city today and so was prepared for me. He asked fifty for it and I got him to take $49. It makes me very short but it can't be helped. The others thought was a beauty. Little Sallie is pretty well at home.

Stopped in to see Uriah this afternoon. He was in bed. Dr Bauman talked about the Zeigler case this morning. He is not pleased with Loux of course.

Friday, March 18, 1887.   There was some snow last night and today. It is of no account and has nearly all disappeared.

Little Sallie did not feel very well at noon. She is longing for home. She does not want to stay here on that account. This afternoon I went up to the watchmaker and bought the watch at the price named. At the Library this evening Miss Moyer introduced me to a young man named Mack who is taking lesson in telegraphy. He seems to be a nice fellow. Miss L was not down. Had a meeting of the Board of Managers. Nothing done but orders passed for paying bills.

Saturday, March 19, 1887.   Went out to the shop this afternoon to see the new machine work. Father was away and Reub started it but soon gave it up. It did not work satisfactorily. Grandfather H was in. Showed him my watch. All saw it except Paul. Did not show it at bank.

Little Sallie is watching about going home. She wants to go. This evening I was up in the store when Jonathan wanted me to go along to the entertainment. We went over and found it pretty good. We looked at their stage arrangements. We want to copy some of it. The stage was enlarged somewhat and only one scene shown. Patriotic and humorous pieces. I think we can do as well if we try right hard. They had none of the best acting in some of the pieces. They had a full house.

Sunday, March 20, 1887.   Sam got the team ready this morning to go to meeting. The roads are very passable. We were pretty late as speaking had already commenced. They were the Quakers who are to preach here this afternoon. The house was crowded as I had to stand near the door. Saw Lillie and Kate sitting near me. I came near losing my gravity when in one of the long intervals of silence between the speaking, I looked at them and I sought to recover myself by thinking over my part in Ten Nights. Old Clemmer was a little impatient about the long silence. There was no singing. On the way home we managed to get after Kate and Lillie who were there with the little boys. Had a little fun with them. After dinner Uriah came down. We went to meeting together. Got a seat on one of the benches. Saw Martha and Lizzie Gerhart together. Took a long walk with Uriah. When we came back Martha and Maggie were here and Abram Licey. The girls helped to make supper. After supper the girls wanted to be taken home. Martha expecting something. She arrived home just in time. Maggie and I drove about anywhere. Went up to Telford and saw Sallie's parents. We have a little strategem. They are to go home and then write. She did not believe me at first. But I think it will work all right. Maggie gave me much in confidence. She is a sensible girl. She prefers J to L. We arrived home a little after nine.

Monday, March 21, 1887. Did not see Uriah this morning as I expected as he must have caught the Buffalo. Little Sallie is still here. Her parents must be home by this time. Mother took her up to the store this afternoon and bought her a doll. She is well pleased.

Wanted to write this afternoon but was so nervous from some cause or other that I shook like an old man. Gave it up. Showed my watch to Mr Moyer this afternoon. I was almost ashamed of it.

This evening at rehearsal Anna Zendt was sick and Mike Bergey wrote he could not be present. There was as much noise as usual. Had some fun on the way home. It rained just a little.

Tuesday, March 22, 1887. I was surprised to see snow on the ground this morning. It continued to snow and rain nearly all day. The roads will have a relapse.

Father hired David Moore today. He brought home a little bedstead for Sallie's doll. She said today she was not quite certain whether she would stay or not. She was very cheerful this evening. Susie is eighteen today. Pulled her ears.

Kaiser Wilhelm is ninety today. It is said that 85 royalties were to be present on the celebration.

Wednesday, March 23, 1887. The weather was very cold today for spring. The snow melted very little.

Heard today that Abe Barndt had been calling me a young upstart to Bean &c. It is a little provoking and if he had to deal with me he would have had more trouble.

This evening at rehearsal all were present. There was pretty much fooling again. Jonathan does his part very well. Appenzeller and Mike are most behind. Rufus gets some well. L. is very frolicsome. Anna talks too low and fast. We meet on the hall on Monday evening. On the way home the girls ran on before. It will come off probably on Apr 9.

Thursday, March 24, 1887. School closed today. Miss Moyer closed today. Gerhart, Clymer, Jonathan and others close today. Was at work making a sign for the Sickle and Sheaf this afternoon and evening.

Uriah came down yesterday.

Friday, March 25, 1887. When I came home for dinner Sallie was lying on the settee and crying. I soon found out what was the matter. Amelia had been in and had told her that her mother had gone home. I did not expect any thing else. This afternoon she was all right again except that she seemed to be a little lonely. I was almost certain that she suspected me of being the cause of all as she looked at me so queer. All this however disappeared as she got after me this evening and pulled my hair as they were never pulled before. Was at work on the books this afternoon and evening.

Saturday, March 26, 1887.   Went to work and cleaned my carriage this afternoon. It was almost too cold but I was glad when it was done. Almost froze my fingers.

Little Sallie wanted to go up to Grandfather H's but mother said it was too late in the evening. She was up at Christ Hunsberger's in the afternoon. Father bought her a pair of shoes.

I was tired and laid down to rest but she went for me pulled my hair and finally pushed me from the settee. I sat up after they went to bed and when I woke found it to be near twelve.

Sunday, March 27, 1887.   Sallie went up to Grandfathers. Father went up to see the horses. Mrs Zuschnitt came with her baby.

Mr & Mrs Allen Rickert (Katie Derstine) came about half past nine. I was not dressed yet. Mother gave her a half dozen tumblers while I gave the whisk holder. They had intended to go to Sunday School at Gehman's but gave it up. They went away about three. Went up to the station after supper hoping to meet Jonathen but did not see him till later. Went over on the hall with Rufus and Milt Moyer to see the arrangements. The curtain &c belonging to the Chalfont fellows are all there yet. Heard that another set had engaged the hall for the 7th. Very smart of them. Was at the station later. My watch had gained 5 min. the time I have it.

Monday, March 28, 1887.   This morning I was surprised to hear the news about Ed Price. He worked in Bethlehem last summer but did not pay his board. He wrote excuses once that he was married next that he had a child. On Saturday these people came down from Bethlehem to see about the matter. Finding it all false they publicly read the letters in the barroom. The effect was sweeping. He got the bounce from Norah and can't come near there. Everybody talks about him. He wanted to go off but had no money. He is in debt everywhere. He sneaked around the sawmill on Saturday and wanted Will Benner to run away with him. I believe Jonathan is much put out about it. No wonder.

This evening we rehearsed for the first time on the hall. We made a fire of pine wood. They were all present except Appenzeller. Clymer drove up from Lexington. Mike Bergey was a little rakish. They don't talk loud enought yet. The girls had not been pleased with us on Wednesday night. L. don't want to believe that it is anything but a dry piece. Got home at eleven. Sam is still home. He must be sick.

Tuesday, March 29, 1887.   There was a strong wind today and was very cold.

In the ocean yacht race the Coronet beat the Dauntless by about one day.

Mr Moyer Moyer did not buy a horse yesterday. They went too high. He is after another one today again.

This evening Derstine of Kratz's team found some man lying insensible on the pavement. They carried him into the hardware store where he came to. He had no food for over a day and half. The Doctor was called in who gave him medicine. He had no money and an amount was collected to send him on his way. Freed was asked to keep him overnight but did not. So they sent him on with the Buffalo. I talked awhile with him. He is 38 had been everywhere and seen everything. His name is Georgie.

Wednesday, March 30, 1887.   Very cold yet. We were very busy today. Work has commenced in earnest. Worked till six o'clock this evening on Hunsicker's book. Went up on the hall this evening and made a fire. I waited long but they did not come till near eight. They were all present. All went off well. Mike Bergey did well. Appenzeller is behind.

The price for admission was fixed at ten and twenty cts. I made a fearful mistake again with my forward mouth. In the last scene I did not behave and Jennie said she would not leave me in while I was drunk. I could not help myself and called out to the others that the old woman was mad. That settled it. I apologized. But she would not look at me any more. They all noticed it.

Saturday, April 2, 1887.   This morning the ground was again covered with snow. It snowed this morning and was very disagreeable but cleared off this afternoon and the snow all disappeared. I had promised to take little Sallie home this afternoon but we did not get through at bank before six o'clock. She came up about four and when I told her I could not go she turned away with tears in her eyes. She cried when she came home. Have arranged to go with the milk train tomorrow morning. Rec'd a very nice letter from Jennie this afternoon in reply to mine. I am forgiven. We hauled some new furniture down from Funk's for mothers bedroom. Funk complains of hard times. Went up to see Sam this evening. He is not well yet. Looks pale. Suffered from neuralgia.

Sunday, April 3, 1887.   The weather very clear. Sallie and I took the milk train for Yardly. Bought Scribner's at Jenkintown and read it to pass the time. Had a good train from there and arrived at Yardly at 9:20. We went to Bilger's. Everything was up and down there as they were making preparations for moving tomorrow. Got introduced to Will's & Jim's wives. They were both sick and considerably in the way. Will sat around with his all day. They are probably too lazy to work. It won't last. Sallie started for home as soon as she got there. Walked with Jim up to Dan's who had just got out of bed. A lazy good for nothing set. Was at Bilger's for dinner. Went down to John Souder's some time in the afternoon. They live near the canal. He has a shop in the cellar. He has been making a machine. Is always at something I believe. At the supper table they wanted to make Sallie ask me to go back again. I then explained that we could not take her as mother is ect. They would rather have her staid here. Took a walk to the river. John then told me that Bilger's goods had been seized and advertised on default of rent. He is in great trouble. Four of them fixed it up for him. It will go on so always. Left at 7:18 and came home 9 o'clock.

Monday, April 4, 1887.   We were very busy today again. All came for money. Guess it will come again by tomorrow and Wednesday. Got through about 4:30. Was hard at work till seven.

Went up on the hall and found the old curtain still there. Don't know when they will take it down. There was entirely too much fooling going on. We tore their canvas a little. Jennie was very gracious to me. We said not a word about it. I was thirsty and L was reading Slade when I said I was thirsty and next thing I knew she had sent for a glass of water. We tore down some of the canvas. There wasn't much order. Mike did not come at all. Got home late. Elwood was along up.

Tuesday, April 5, 1887.   It was considerably colder today than yesterday. A regular cold wave. Our figures ran highest today although we were not kept the busiest. But we worked till six o'clock or after balancing books. At this rate I can hardly see how we can get ready till Saturday. Nothing done with the stage yet, don't have my costume ready yet and nothing. They took down the curtain this evening. I helped them. Appenzeller & Clymer were absent. There was not much life in it. Kate and Annie Moyer came in and saw it through. It was almost eleven when we got through. If my cold don't get better soon I will be a failure. Uriah writes he can't come.

Wednesday, April 6, 1887.   Today was the terriblest day we had so far. We did not get to balancing before three and it was half past six when we went out. I was tired. Henry Ruth came and fetched away over 6000 dollars in cash for J.S. Ruth who is guardian for a Mrs Bishop who gets about 10,000. Worked on bills &c till eight when I went up on the hall. Met Lillie on the way over and they were not quite all there yet when I came over. Clymer had the sign ready. It looks well. Got over the piece pretty well. It is eleven when I write this. Fine weather. Moonlight. If this continues it's all right.

Thursday, April 7, 1887.   Got through first rate this afternoon. Went to the shop and finished the sign. Had a job to get a dagger made. The third one only passed. Made out some bills. A great crowd came up from Lansdale this afternoon I heard. Some said there were 29. Have not heard how it turned out. The general impression is that there won't be much.

Friday, April 8, 1887.   Went up on the hall this morning and began work on the stage. The fellows came in pretty well and we all worked pretty hard and we got through better than I expected. We asked for the Chalfont curtain and got it. This saved us much work. We worked hard all day and evening and have it nearly ready now. This afternoon the hall was full of people looking on and when we were ready to rehearse we cleared the hall except the players who furnished the music while we played. Andrew wrote he and another fellow from North Wales would be up. I have no doubt if the weather is nice we will have a crowd there.

Saturday, April 9, 1887.   Happily for us this was a fine day.

Did not get through today till 5:30. It was very provoking. Uriah made a trick bottle. Felt very stiff and tired this morning. Ran over on the hall to see how things looked there. Jonathan was there and had nearly ready. Ran up to the drug-store to get red paint for the face. The Doc not at home got none. Mrs Loux said they were coming down. Came home and found Andrew and young man by the name of Hargrave there. Welcomed them but excused myself and hurried to get ready. It was nearly eight before I got ready. Ran out to the shop and got together the first old hat and coat I could get. The hall was already nearly full and they commenced in about ten minutes. The orchestra was right in front of the stage. Dressed up in old clothes and was ready in good time. I looked like an old tramp. Swichel looked funny. They laughed a little when I first came in but were quiet right away. We finished the second scene in act II in splended style. Wasn't quite satisfied with my delirium in the latter part. The last scene was splended. Did not see it before I came in. After the curtain went down the people did not go home till Appenzeller went out and said good night. It was half past ten when we stopped. We took in $38.55. The girls were all in evening dress. They powdered my face as it was a little red. L. powdered also. A little too much of it I thought.

Sunday, April 10, 1887.   Another beatiful day. We got up pretty early as Andrew and Mr Hargrave wished to go home over Sunday. Went up to the station with them. Saw L. over at the Hall already. We went up and carried away most of the furniture. Ann Moyer wanted us to take it down last evening. I wouldn't do it. Carried some to Moyer's and some to Zendt's. Mehitable pinned a bouquet on my coat. Sat around the Hall at the station and down at Ed's where I did an errand for Miss Gerhart till about eleven. The people seem to have been pleased with our performance.

I was very tired and stiff this morning. Went to meeting this afternoon but could hardly keep my eyes open. Rev Mr Mack preached. Walked up to Ellis' and sat with them on the porch. They were not on the hall. Went home and sat on the porch. Asked Rufus in and he came. Kate and Mehitable passed some time later and they also sat down for a little chat. L. thinks we did well. I think she especially. Ego. Was up at the station. Talked awhile with James Slifer. He said we should get it up every once in a while. Walked up town to meeting at Tyson's which was crowded and stifling. Went home again. Tried to write but fell asleep.

Monday, April 11, 1887.   Another fine day. Almost too warm for the season. Many persons kept holiday today, that is made us in town here work.

Mrs Jacob Allebach died on Friday. They were only married a year and a half. Her child is two wks old. Worked till after six this evening. When I came home found Katie Moyer waiting for me with a note from Jennie inviting me to spend the evening there as Miss Moser was there. Accepted and went up at eight. Had an agreeable time. Milt was home. Schwenck came in but not into the same room. I was glad of it. Miss Moser lives at Norritonville. I met her first last summer in the evening. She was a school mate of Jennie's. Went home after ten.

Tuesday, April 12, 1887.   The Bank is now being painted. It was commenced last week. The colors are yellow and dark green. It will look well. Worked late again this afternoon.

We went up on the hall to take down the curtain. Willie Hamond came up to help carry down the organ to Moyer's. Jennie said she heard some people were quite affected by our play. We took down everything packed up the muslin &c. and I took it along home. Worked on my diary but fell asleep. It was 12:30 when I went to bed.

Wednesday, April 13, 1887.   It was more damp today and looked like rain.

Worked till five o'clock this afternoon. Met Jennie on the way home who told me Miss Moser had left for home. I had invited them to come down some evening. Thought a great deal of Mrs. Morgan the last few days. She is a good girl and these are scarce. We worked the lemon tree out of the celler last evening. Tough job. Am so sleepy that I can hardly write this. Ambrose Hunsberger started in with A G Stover yesterday in Elmer Wile's place.

Thursday, April 14, 1887.   Cloudy but cleared off this afternoon. Mr. Landes was at the funeral.

Got through this afternoon at half past three. Made a place ready for my harness this afternoon. The boys went over the yard this evening with a roller.

Mr Godshall was after me about the Sunday School this afternoon.

Friday, April 15, 1887.   John went away this forenoon. He did not say where he went but Mr Landes said he was going to join the church.

The bank walls are being painting. They stopped this afternoon [illegible]. Was up at the shoemaker's this afternoon. This evening's attendance at the library was very slim. And now the band must have a little too.

Saturday, April 16, 1887.   Mr Moyer did not come round all day. Rufus Landes was out balancing books. The Chalfont entertainment at Telford did not come off on account of some being sick.

Goettler gave us a pretty good piece in the paper. He stated the receipts, said the attendance was large and that there was more talent in the place than was perhaps expected &c.

Was up at Hagey's shoe shop this evening. Got talking about the library &c.

Stopped in at grandfather's on the way home.

Schwenck bought a lot from W D Hunsberger. Guess he is going to settle down once.

Sunday, April 17, 1887.   Parents went to Gehman's meeting and from there to Jos. Derstein's.

Sat around reading all morning and did not dress till after dinner. It was too late to go to church. Jennie, Kate and another girl passed this afternoon. It was a kind of a chilly day and not many were out. Went up to the station to see what was going on. Saw J. in the door. Went inside and talked with Jonathan and Markly Haynes also. I asked Jonathan why he did not go out and he said he'd be an old bachelor that is he'd wait five yrs. I said I would too and he made me give my hand on it. Five yrs at least from today Sam Alderfer witness.

Went home about 9:30.

Monday, April 18, 1887.   A most disagreeable day. There was rain sleet and hail. The trees were loaded down with ice and it was as bad as any day last winter. The telegraph wires broke down under the load. Horace and Morris Weil were badly fooled last night. Alonzo and they went over to Salfordville to a singing school. Horace and Morris both caught on to something and Alonzo getting tired went home without them. When they ret'd to Salfordville he was gone. So they started to walk home. Luckily for them Mike Bergey had not yet left Harleysville and they came home with him. They have been having a great time with them about it today. Alonzo I believe hates it a little. The Methodist were around here today looking for land to build a church.

Tuesday, April 19, 1887.   The trees were hung with ice this morning and as the sun shone on them gleamed like silver. The snow and ice disappeared before evening and the grass looked greener than before. The air is still cool. Am reading Dicken's "Little Dorrit."

Went down to the school house this to see J. mostly. Appointed Thursday evening for a meeting of the company. Told her of Frick's surprise on our coming down. She has lost all respect for him. I believe that she is a good kind girl. Cut out newspaper clippings for a scrapbook this evening.

Wednesday, April 20, 1887.   A fine day. There was sleighing on Monday in Northampton Co. There was no snow in the city only rain.

Jas M Slifer watched for some of the bank directors. He is selling stock for the new Trust Co. at Lansdale. The painters today resumed work at the bank.

When mother heard that Mr Moyer intended to build she thought I would have to leave the bank in the near future and was worrying herself about it. She is afraid of my going to the city. I told her I would not.

Fixed up the yard a little this afternoon. Sowed orchard grass seed.

Thursday, April 21, 1887.   No time of the year is more pleasant than a clear spring morning like today, while a hand-organ was playing "Home Sweet Home."

There is a great deal of humor when a worthless fellow has some money and pays his debts while half drunk merely to make a show. Such a case happened today. Planted a rose bush in front of the barn this afternoon. A number of strolling musicians passed through here this evening. A harp and two violins. It cost me a dime.

Went down to the schoolhouse this evening but not having the key I walked back. Followed Lillie down and Jennie came soon afterward. Rufus Landes, Mike, & Swichel were also there. Got a little mad when I couldn't get the others to vote. They were satisfied the way I'd make it &c. I didn't wish to decide and bear the blame. Talked with them awhile. I'd didn't wish to be called a boss. Was going to speak to Jennie but could not for several reasons.

Friday, April 22, 1887.   Fine day. Sent for Quarterlies &c. this afternoon.

Rec'd Goettler's Paper for the first time this evening. Found out that another Sunday School would be started on the hall.

Stopped in to see Jennie and asked for a private interview some time in the near future. Toward evening it became cloudy and rained a little.

Saturday, April 23, 1887.   A rainy disagreeable day. Mr Landes went to the sale at two o'clock this afternoon.

Went home at 3:30 and read "Little Dorrit." Took my razor up to grandfather's to sharpen it. He did so and is as proud of it as ever. He has a new razor strap of the very best of course.

This evening Henry and Preston came down. P. played on the organ a little. He stays all night. Henry went home not very well pleased I think. We tumbled about a little and Preston broke the glass on his watch. It formerly belonged to Fred. Frick is up. Went out and shook hands.

Sunday, April 24, 1887.   Preston went up to Wm's this forenoon. Went up to meet the train and saw it pass. Frick was at the station. We sat around awhile and started homewards. We saw Uriah over at the furniture store. Frick and he made out to go out this afternoon driving. Ellis, Preston & Milt Moyer were there too. After dinner came over a little before I started for Sunday School. Met Os. Kline. Mike Bergey was made Secretary in Milt's place. Old Herman kept on singing all the time while we arranged the classes. The attendance was fair. Walked about town till supper. Saw Harry Dettry with a lady walking. Took leave of Frick and Os Kline. Uriah left for Lexington. Treated the little girls with candy and crackers. It was rather cool walking. Took leave of Preston. He left on the Buffalo. Was very tired when I came home. My face burned and was very red. Used glycerine. Went to bed at nine.

Monday, April 25, 1887.   Got through my work very well today. Felt much better this morning. Kate and told me this morning that Schwenck and Milt Moyer would be married in splendid style on May 4. Two pastors. And such gossip. This agrees with Milt's talk. She asked me why I did not go out. She thought I could cut out Gerhart. Why not go for J also? I said I had given it all up. John and Jake were full of horses today. Jake went to the sale and bought moe for himself but did not get one for John. Walked over and looked at them myself. Jake has a nice horse.

Ging nach dem Schulhaus und sah J. wegen anstatten für besuchen bei ihr. Ich (illegible) es (illegible). Sie nahm es gnädiglich an aber sagte ich wär noch in Zeit gewesen da sie eine andern anbeitung absagen wird. Sie sagte mir nichts wer mein neblen (illegible) war. Ich sagte ich wollte es ein monat oder zwei abschieben und gab sehr ursachen. Ich sagte von Schwenck dasz keine liebe zwischen uns ware. Ich weiss nicht habe ich recht oder letz gethan. Hoffe ober recht.*

Didn't read much this evening. We were fooling all the time.

Tuesday, April 26, 1887.   It rained last night and was cloudy this forenoon.

Ellis drove Mr Landes' horse this afternoon. He behaves well. The painters are now putting the brick dust on the front. It's a dirty job.

Worked this afternoon till six o'clock. I balanced more than twenty books. Hunsicker's and Joe Ruth's were among them.

Rec'd a letter from Andrew this evening inviting me to come down to Dr Slifer's lectors on Saturday evening.

Wednesday, April 27, 1887.   Warm fair with alternate threatening weather.

After work went down to the shop to look at things. Horace came over and commenced to talk in the wagon house. He gets a carriage and harness. He will be one of the ushers at the wedding next Wednesday. Mike Bergey, Mack, Jonathan and Cal. Hunsberger will be the others. Milt was to be married Dec 16 but changed his mind on account of the talk. According to Ed. Price, Jonathan got the bounce on my acc't. How and why. Also that Ed Price thinks I feel big &c. That Haynes is going to try it again. And more to the same purpose. Asked me to go with him &c. And everything concerning himself. Took care that he didn't get anything out of me. Mr Landes said he heard everything was in readiness (satin dresses,) the guests invited and all.

Jakie Moyer was here this evening. He is despondent and wants to run away.

Thursday, April 28, 1887.   A little rain again this afternoon. Wrote little Sallie today. Expected a letter from her some time. Markly Huffnagle left here the beginning of this week. He went to Germantown. I did not expect it yet. Took some thing up to grandfather S's and went in and talked a while.

Friday, April 29, 1887.   Queer weather this week. A few drops of rain came down during the day. Cloudy and threatening all day. The painters have

*Eng. translation: I went to the schoolhouse and saw J. about beginning a courtship with her. (illegible). She accepted it graciously but said I was still in time since she was to decline another request. She said nothing to me as to who my [fellow-suitor?] was. I said I would postpone it a month or two, and gave very [illegible] reasons. I said, regarding Schwenck, that there was no love between us. I don't know whether I did right or wrong. Hope, though, right.

become used to it and worked on.

Mr Landes told me today that his neighbors were not very well pleased at not being invited to the wedding. She told me once that expected to be bridesmaid. A great disappointment of course. Glad I escaped. Would have been at a loss on account of my relations with Schwenck. Tackled old Herman about it today and he wanted to make me speak first but I wouldn't. He thought it was secret. Took a nap this afternoon. Felt very tired several days. Read "Little Dorritt." Interesting now. I hear Lizzie Gerhart is going to school on Monday to Allentown Female College.

Saturday, April 30, 1887. Very windy though clear. John went to Harleysville with Jacob Allebach to the horse sale. A. bought a nice horse for 191. Don't know what John made out. Jas Slifer came into bank today and spoke a few words with him. He said the only mistake I made was not going to school more. And more to the same purpose.

The bank is beginning to look quite gay under the new colors.

Talked with Ed. awhile this P.M. He asked me about the Salfordville trip. He would like to get Alonzo away from Horace. Was surprised that I had no invitation to the wedding. Thought I was stuffing him. He heard I was going there &c.

Saw Bill Slifer. They are up over Sunday. Isaiah Hunsberger being in the store we had a good laugh. Lillie passed through and smiled.

Sunday, May 1, 1887. Got up early for Sunday. Father went to communion at Leidy's and mother to communion at Gehman's. Got ready and went to Sunday School. Have a class of 6 to 8 yrs old. 8 in number. Mike was not present. L. was smiling. Schwenck was not present. Jennie was there. Didn't look at her.

Read Little Dorrit.

Same talked of going to Harleysville. Asked Rufus to go along and he did with Morris Wile. Got over about three. Dedicated the new blanket. When we came over we found Jonathan, Cal & Haynes with silk hats just arrived. We all went down to H B Freed's had ice cream and sat around there all afternoon. Saw Sunday school dismissed. Saw a distastefully dressed girl in red &c.

Went home the lower way. Saw Sallie Keeler. Got home 5:30. After supper went up to the station. It was crowded with people. Saw Jennie and Mack take a walk. I like to see this. Made them talk. Went over to Ellis. Talked nonsense. Walked through town once. It rained a little. Took ice cream. Went over to Zuschnitt's. Got sleepy and went home to bed.

Monday, May 2, 1887. A nice warm spring day. Heard this morning they had 53 signers for the borough petition. John was after a horse again. Bookhamer's. He tried her and liked her well. They struck a bargain in the afternoon. The price paid is $140. And if not as represented the money will be refunded.

Everyone is talking about the approaching wedding. It will be grand without a doubt. Jennie is to be brides maid and the little girls maids of honor. Trails, veils, dress, gloves and everything has been described. Jonathan will probably figure as best man. Had to laugh to myself often. Here everyone is troubling himself about it supposing this and that and now nothing. There was a talk that I was going to see Jennie, Lizzie Gerhart told Mrs Wolford &c &c. We joked in the bank at Schwenck's expense. Meanwhile the time is fast approaching. Worked till late on the books.

Tuesday, May 3, 1887.   Worked on my clothes this afternoon. It was warm work and very necessary.

The gossips and everybody else have a subject to talk about now. More is said than is true I think. There will be no school tomorrow. Susie has made the discovery that I do not belong to the upper class as I was not invited to the wedding.

Wednesday, May 4, 1887.   The bank today decided to pay interest on deposits left for 3 and 2% left for one year and six months respectively. The painters are done outside and will leave for about 2 weeks. Heard today that Dan Daub was invited to the wedding. Schwenck should keep such black sheep away. The stocking factory stopped work at three this afternoon. Teased Kate a little about it not being invited. Of course she and Lillie feel a little slighted. It does look so queer that none of the girls here are invited. After supper went up to store. Met Lillie and Kate. Had a little fun about it. In fact everybody is talking too much. Sat on the platform. Crowds were there. Stuff for band. Quinly [?] boys walked on their heads &c to amuse. They had horns. Older people encouraged them. They watched what was going on inside. They struck up again. Soon got a dollar. Were not satisfied and the big fellows took a hand in it. Every thing quiet till after nine o'clock. A great din then commenced. Bells, [unintelligible] which made no noise, horns, everything. Got another dollar. Struck up again. The whole party was on the porch looking on. Schwenck & Milt went up to the hotel and tapped a keg. I went home before this. Everybody was down to see it. More people were out than there have been for a long time. Couldn't help laughing. After I was home some time heard the noise again. They ought to be kicked. Miss Moser is up I believe.

Thursday, May 5, 1887.   Spoke with Horace this afternoon about the wedding. He said he wouldn't mind it much anymore. He had Miss Ellmberger for his partner Mike Emma Krupp, Mack Jennie and Jonathan, Miss Moser. Mike went for Miss Moser afterwards and took her off. He told me this evening that she was a very lively girl. He also said I couldn't go Jonathan.

Went up to Grandfather H's this afternoon and found Sarah sick in bed with neuralgia. Also went out to Aunt Kit's where they have the measles. Mag is pretty sick. They have a nice little dog.

Friday, May 6, 1887.   Rec'd a letter from Uriah saying he would come up next Saturday evening. So I have to change my plan of going. Will start on

Friday afternoon and come home with him. Went down to the schoolhouse this afternoon to fix up. Jennie came in and handed me the key as if she avoided me. Of course it's right. But it seems to me they are all avoiding me a little. Don't matter I'll only laugh more. This evening when putting down a book for Annie I said it was wrong that she was Mrs Schwenck now. Jennie blushed a little, smiled a little and said nothing. Kate was there and pushed me.

We were at work making out a list of books. Did not get through till half past ten. Decided I was to buy the books next Friday. The "Independent" has a short notice of the wedding.

Saturday, May 7, 1887.   Today being the last day on which a lien could be laid on the Herman property and father not having time to go down himself asked Mr Landes whether I couldn't go. He made some business ready.

So took the 9:41 train and went down. Wasn't acquainted in Norristown but walked on a venture. Found the courthouse and went into the treasurer's office where I left my umbrella. Went over to Weand's office which was closed. Went over in the courtroom where the court was in session. Boyer and Swartz were on the bench. This is the latter's first week. Boyer's face and hands are so blue that you expect him to die any moment. Spoke to Weand who sent another attorney who executed my lien. I took it back to Weand who looked over went over to the prothonotary's office to have it recorded. Went back for my umbrella which was put away and my name pinned on.

Walked along Main St a long distance. Got home with the three o'clock train.

Got to bed late. Sat around sleeping till Sus. Gentash and Sus. Daub came in with Christ & Levin Hunsberger.

Sunday, May 8, 1887.   Got up late. It was raining all morning. Lay around sleeping till almost noon. Dressed after dinner. Commenced reading the "Press" and noticed the name of Jeannette Ballou. It described her as she is. She is in Ludlow St jail. Has a baby having been betrayed by a lawyer named Anthony and sued by his wife for $50,000. I thought it could not be.

Went to Sunday School. Milt was not there. Helped Mike a little. Jennie passed me as if she knew me not. The boys said it was the same Jennie Ballou. Most of them blame the lawyer. Mack said JLM blamed her. The men are nearly always the cause of such things.

Was up at the station awhile. Went up again after supper. Haynes went down on the train to Phila.

The boys were singing and making a great noise at Kratz's this evening. Rain this morning.

Monday, May 9, 1887.   Threatening cloudy weather. Couldn't hear much now about Miss Ballou's case except that her grandfather died a short time ago worth $500,000. She got only 200 a yr and 5000 when 21. She is contesting the will. There was always some doubt about her origin which may have caused this. Pity for the poor girl. Such fellows as old Tremper are worst in such cases with young girl and are often the ruin of them.

Tuesday, May 10, 1887. It cleared off this evening. Mowed the yard this afternoon. Was done in a short time but got sweated a little. Rec'd a letter from Ed Danley last evening. He would like to get a job over here next spring. Wants to know all sorts things about the wedding &c.

Made an offer of 9.50 and $10 for Webster's Unabridged but did not get it from Ellis. Was very sleepy this evening and did not write in the diary.

Wednesday, May 11, 1887. A warm summer day. Everything is growing luxuriously. It is good that the heat has not penetrated the house yet.

Kate told me they made up a party to go to the Rocks on Sunday. Read "Taming of the Shrew." Got up early, that is at five o'clock. There were good reasons for it. It would be a good plan. It is lovely in the morning.

Heard from Uriah. He will go along to the theatre.

Jonas Landis was in a railroad accident this morning. No one was hurt.

Music at Kratz's this evening. Sat on their porch awhile. Jennie and Emma Krupp passed being out for a walk. Did not speak. Met Haynes. He talked about J. Had a notion to try there again but would not as he was afraid of the worst sack he ever had. Guess he'd get it too. He says Markly feels worse. He had been to Moyer's several times. Wonder what that was.

Thursday, May 12, 1887. Nice day. Not as hot as yesterday. More air. A high license bill has been passed by the Legislature making the license in cities 500. in boroughs 150 and in townships 75. In boroughs 3/5 goes to the borough, 1/5 to the county and 1/5 to the state.

Worked to get ready to go to the city tomorrow. I am hardly fit to go but it is time. Pressed my pants this afternoon. Put carpet on the back stairs in a hurry. Am making out a list of the books I want to buy. Must go and sponge my self.

Friday, May 13, 1887. Got ready till noon. Balance and all. Made the train and got down near three o'clock. Went for Perkinpine & Higgins first but could not please myself and went down to Leary's. Picked out a number of books and returned to P & H and ordered the rest. Arrived at Uriah's office about six o'clock. It is very small. We went for supper about 6:30. Met Slifer outside Uriah's. Kate and Allie were expecting me. After supper we started for the Chestnut St Opera House to see "Taming of the Shrew." We were among the first to arrive but could not get a seat. All the seats being sold in advance. So we paid 75 cts for the glorious privelege of standing. Uriah was tired right away but I didn't mind it. It was the first time I was ever in a threatre. I enjoyed it very much. It was performed by the Augustin Daly Co of New York. Katharine the Shrew was very spirited.

Petruchio and she divided the honors. The scenery was very beautiful. The music fine. In fact everything was beyond my expectations. On the way home we walked through the post office. We took an oyster stew and then went to Slifer's. It was twelve oclock when we came home. Couldn't sleep for a while longer.

Saturday, May 14, 1887.   Got up about six o'clock. After breakfast talked with Aunt Kate. She said Uriah's business was small and if would only increase a little faster. We went to see the Battle of Gettysburg. It is very natural and is a great painting. Walked through the Penna RR Dept. Through the public Buildings. To the European Museum. Uriah then went home and I went to Leary's and paid my bill. Bought a Webster's Unabridged. Went to the Dime Museum. So-so. Had my photos taken at 114 Ninth St. Started for Slifers and arrived 3:30. Kate and Allie were ready for a walk to the park. We went out for about a hour. The park was full of people. Very pleasant. Looking at the views of Pompeii. Hurried to make the train. Uriah gave the driver a quarter for extra time. Had five minutes left. Frick did not get on the train. Got tickets for Uriah. Was at the lecture. Sat beside Bean & Kate. Wesley Anders worked at the lantern. Was very sleepy. Uriah had his girl up. She looks well. They had a good house.

Sunday, May 15, 1887.   Frick came over early this morning having come on the Buffalo last evening. Mr Godshall came over and offered his horse for us to go out. Accordingly we made preparations to go. Uriah was down. We started about nine o'clock. Had a pleasant drive. Up the other side of Telford and through Franconia. After dinner went to S.S. Spoke Jennie. Helped Mike again. Milt wasn't about. Good attendance. Uriah went for a nap and we went down on the porch. Bubby Moyer furnished the fun. A set of roughs raised a fuss in front of our gate and threatened come and thrash us. It fairly raised me I threatened and had they come in one step I would have gone for them. They were from Lansdale. Was at the station to see every body off. Was at Kratz's afterward. A lot of boys and girls were there. They started for our place and we annoyd them so much that they could not rest. Mother came down and they cleared out soon. We sneaked to bed as quietly as we could.

Monday, May 16, 1887.   Contrary to expectation we escaped a lecture our place and we annoyd them so much that they could not rest. Mother came down and they cleared out soon. We sneaked to bed as quietly as we could.

Uriah came a minute before he left. I ordered paper from him. He wants to use the library. Of course for Miss Barndt. He don't read very much himself.

Found out today what kept Mr Moyer so busy all last winter. He is taking a course in bookkeeping and penmanship by correspondence with Bryant Stratton's Business College Buffalo. I think I will try it too. He wants to make use of it some way. Received the proof of the photos taken on Saturday. It is the tamest sickliest thing I ever saw. Bloated sensual ignorant it seems. I don't want such a picture. If he can't do better I don't want them.

Tuesday, May 17, 1887. Leary's books arrived this morning and Perkinpine & Higgins this afternoon. They were all delighted with them.

Cleaned harness in the afternoon. Looked at the books the rest of the day. Heard a noise of horns etc. and found that it was another dutch band at Sam Benner's wedding. After I had gone to bed the real band woke me up. Sent back the proof and gave instructions. Don't know much about and think it will do no good.

Wednesday, May 18, 1887. It looked as if it were about to rain this morning but cleared off again. Sam Benner was married to a "Magnet" by name. John B Moyer & Dr Acker did not come till this afternoon. John G. Barndt was in bank this afternoon. They after him to take a directorship. They were in yet when I left. Mowed the yard this afternoon. The machine is not in very good order.

Was at work covering the books the rest of the evening. It was ten o'clock when I went to bed.

Thursday, May 19, 1887. A nice clear warm day like it has been all week. I think I begin to feel better since I began to go to bed at ten or before and get up at five or a little after. I do my writing now in the morning and find I can do it as well as in the evening with no danger of falling asleep while at it.

Today many or most kept holiday in the usual fashion. They did their shopping and kept other people busy. They were all surprised that we had open. After we were through read Scribner's awhile till I feel asleep. Up to the store and home to "Little Dorrit". I'd like it better if I'd keep more at it. Frick wrote me and wants me to get up a party to the rocks. Don't believe we can do it. Will see J about it first. Couldn't do no work because other people didn't.

Friday, May 20, 1887. Father and most of the others have been going down to Mainland to put up a porch there two days. Mr L. having given J M Shellenberger to understand that there were good reasons for not reposing too much trust in him. Mr S. took offense and immediately sent a man up and paid off a note he had for collecting 8 years. I think it was right. Moyer thought not. Went down to the schoolhouse to make ready. Took some books down as samples. Picked out such as wanted covering and took them home. Had an interview with Jennie. The two months of course are not up yet. She talks of either going to school or going on a trip to New England. She won't go with any party where Frick is along.

This evening Mr Gehman was over to see the books. I think he was pleased. Jennie, Mrs Schwenck and Mrs Moyer came down. She had said she would not be down. Had a pleasant time with them. Mrs Schwenck was very gracious. I just kept on talking all the time. Jennie took "Taming of the Shrew." Ha. Wonder if the others know. Went home a little before nine. To bed at ten.

Saturday, May 21, 1887. Rec'd a letter from Uriah saying that he is in for a party to the rocks. His girl wants to go he says but he don't like Frick's plan of getting up city people.

The Legislature adjourned **sine die** this week. Among the last acts was the passage of the six mos. school term bill. This will make the township people mad. After the bank closed sat around with Rufus for a while. He showed me Horace's harness. He said he was going out this evening for sport. There was a tight rope performance at the hotel which attracted a great crowd. It is to be repeated Monday. There is very much walking done in the evening. I think it is favored much by the darkness. The town should be better lighted. The sixteen year olds are running after each other so as I never saw. Too much of it entirely. Ought to be stopped. Sat down at Zuschnitt's and saw the people pass. Kratz did a rushing business. Haynes and I sat on the hammock awhile. Mike Bergey's girl is over. He was with me awhile. Talked of Maggie. Don't know whether he means it but it's true all the same. He mentioned J. but I heeded not. Went to bed at ten.

Sunday, May 22, 1887. Made ready to go to Sunday School. Milt Moyer had charge. Jonathan led the responsive readings. My boys were all there. There are eight of them. After Sunday School met Cal. who was on his way to grandfathers. He asked me to go with him and we went. Stayed for dinner. While there word came that old Mr Geisinger had died. From there we went to meeting. We were both very sleepy. Went home then and put on seersuckers. Sat around reading. Martha and Maggie came. There was meeting on Tyson's hall. Went down to Zuschnitt's. Amelia and Maggie passed and came home with them. Had a little music. They left at nine. Went to bed at ten.

Monday, May 23, 1887. They took the fence away in front of the bank today and cut away from the embankment. They will move the fence in further about a foot.

Greaser's cleaned the windows at the bank this afternoon and this evening the weights were put in.

The tight rope walker performed the same feats as on Saturday evening. "He couldn't get ready." Wanted to see J this afternoon but had to help on the fence and she passed me there. They took a walk this evening. She never goes out alone. Always Emma Krupp or her relations.

Wrote Danley about festival. Wrote Frick about Rock party. Got an invitation to the "Grand Open Air Dance" at Tyson's next Monday eve. Ha ha. To bed at ten.

Tuesday, May 24, 1887. People were dissapointed about rain this morning. But about eleven oclock it rained splendidly till near noon.

Wolford is laying a conduit through his land to the creek for the water from the street. Bought a hammock yesterday. Went down to schoolhouse for stamp &c. Saw J. about writing U. She says she wouldn't be home that time. She hesitated about something and said she wanted time to say it. She would write. She asked me if I could call on Sunday evening &c. She showed me an envelope probably addressed by Schwenck which she wanted to answer and which caused her embarrassment. Of course I find the keenest pleasure in making a call Sunday evening. That will be walking over Schwenck's head. Perhaps there is a tinge of revenge in this? Went up to Hagey's and measured for a pair of shoes. Rufus was along. Took a ride to the cowpath with Mr Godshall.

Wednesday, May 25, 1887.   Heavy rain last night. Heard nothing of it myself.

Chas. Daub died yesterday.

Received my photos today. They are much better then the proof but the eyes look red and is all too deeply shaded.

Tried to fix the lawn mower this afternoon but got it too tight that it wouldn't work. The boys stood on it to make weight enough to drive the wheels. Didn't get my supper till half past eight. Was very tired. Must take it to Hange and if he can't do anything I am beaten.

Thursday, May 26, 1887.   Received a letter from Ed Danley saying he did not know whether he could be over on June 4 or not. He will let me know next week. The Lansdale Trust Co. have elected directors. They have W D Hunsberger. They elected J G Hunsicker but he will not act. Mr Landes was over to see him. They tried hard to get Metz to change. He wouldn't. Jno G Barndt will take Line Lexington for us. We can gain some that way. John S. Ruth is opposed to this. The people are being deceived a little by the new thing.

Rained a little this afternoon but got the mower fixed at last and mowed the yard. Read a little afterwards.

Friday, May 27, 1887.   Covered books this afternoon. Think I can finish on Monday.

Saturday, May 28, 1887.   Very uncertain weather. Jonas Hackman has made quite an improvement in front of the bank. The fence set in, new steps, and the embankment sodded. They commenced to clean the bank this morning so as to make a holiday on Monday. Helped after three. Made everything look nobby outside. Cleaned the sidewalk and everything.

Andrew came up with the mail train. I dressed and we went up to the store. He says Mr Hargrave is his chief comrade. He said he enjoyed himself when he was up.

During the last week the Opera Comique was burned in Paris in which almost 200 lives were lost.

Sunday, May 29, 1887.   Got up late. Andrew went up to C H Moyer's and staid for dinner. Uriah came up on the train and came down and brought me paper. Kate was down at the time and I had just shaved. Went out to the woods with and talked. Isaiah Hunsberger was there and told stories. U. thinks F is not pleased with him. They had an appointment and Uriah did not stay at home &c. He don't like his plan of going to the Rocks. Went home about dinner time and went to Sunday School with Cassel. After S S Andrew tried pretty hard to find out whether I had any engagements for the evening. I said not. He had intended to go home if I had. After supper we went up to the station and then saw Uriah off to Lexington. After we came home I told Andrew I had to leave him for the evening so he went out with Sam. Got ready and went over to Kratz's for ice cream. Milt & wife came in and saw me. Was received by J. Milt & wife came in soon afterward and drew back surprised. Mrs Schwenck first alone and then accompanied with Schwenck brought ice cream. They went out soon. Couldn't [help] laughing. J gave herself away very nicely. She told very innocently that the letter was from Cal. and that she thinks Chas F. wrote it. She was down to see Miss Moser yesterday and came home this morning. Went home at 11:30. Andrew was awake when I came in. The boys knew about it too.

Monday, May 30, 1887.   Went out to the shop with Andrew this morning. From there up to the store and then over to the train. He left with the 9:06. He wants me to come down to the lectures. Didn't promise. Hunted up Uriah. We walked up town over to the county line over to CDH's willow trees. Here we sat till dinner. We made a plan to go to the Rocks without Frick in three weeks. Told him about my going out last evening. After dinner went up to him and took the carriage and went down to Leidy's church to hear the Japanese student. The talk was chiefly on Home Missions and Foreign. Mr Appenzeller read a paper on Home Missions. Frank Hartzel on System in Church Work. Jos Proctor on the need of aid for religious institutions. Hartzel did well. IG Gerhart gave an account of the financial condition of the classes. And then the Japanese student spoke some time on Japan &c. He was hard to understand. He will be in Sellersville this evening. Kate and Lillie went up. We took a ride into the country after church and came back at six. Saw Uriah off on the train at eight. Walked up to Tyson's where there was to have been an Open Air dance but which was not yet in motion.

Tuesday, May 31, 1887.   The weather was very cool and windy.

There having been a Cabinet crisis in France there was great difficulty in making a cabinet. M Roveier had now formed one with Gen. Boulanger left out. He is the people's hero and there might be violence if he is not retained.

Got along with my work right well today. When I came home in the afternoon I commenced work on the books. After supper I got Rufus Landes to help on the new books. He stamped them etc while I glued the covers. I will soon be through with them now. Went to bed at 9:30 o'clock.

Wednesday, June 1, 1887.   There was rain last night and cold and damp this morning. It became quite warm later in the day.

Jno. G. Barndt came up today and was elected a director in place of Wm Souder who resigned. This afternoon they went for J G Hunsicker. He had been elected a director by the Lansdale Trust Co.

Am almost through with the new books. Only two to cover and a few to stamp.

Read "Little Dorrit." The story is becoming sad.

Jakey Moyer was along in this evening. He told how he was examined as to being sound during the war. The doctor said he was as sound as an acorn and chased him out. Uriah Stover, Ulysses, John Q. & Harry Hunsberger intend to join the church. Dengler wanted Elwood too. He asked about me I believe.

Thursday, June 2, 1887. The weather today was different. The painters commenced work inside. There is a very strong turpentine smell to undergo. Greaser brought three beautiful roses along the other day. Mowed the yard this afternoon. Father must have mowed it on Monday. Covered the remaining books and made everything ready for tomorrow evening.

Read Little Dorrit.

Beideman came about eight o'clock. I looked very shabby and so went up and dressed round. They are going to make a trip to the west next month.

Mrs Yocum and grandmother S were here this afternoon and for supper.

Friday, June 3, 1887. Nice day. Aunt Kitty was down today. She would have stayed over night had not the old folks been very anxious about her. Amelia came in first, Uriah next and finally grandfather came and fetched her. Beideman went away on the 6:50 train.

School left out today. When I brought down the books this afternoon there was nothing there. Wanted to see J. Rearranged all the books. The bookcase is filled pretty tight. Looks beautiful. Had hardly time to get round. Jennie was down pretty early. She'll go tomorrow evening. Had some fun with the boys. Lillie and Kate came late. After nine. Walked with as far as Kate's. Lillie was very cheerful. After L. left Kate and I sat on the porch. She told about Mrs Barndts troubles. We had so much queer noise that Polly came to the window.

Saturday, June 4, 1887. Mother got Elwood to fetch old aunty Kit down to see Aunt Kit. Came home early at noon to let Mr Moyer out to work on his hay. After I had my dinner Ed Danley came. He had a girl with by the name of Moore. I waited on them the best I could and Susie made the dinner. Left then and they went down to Lansdale with the 1.25 train. He came back with the 5:26 train. Ed was sick when he came home. He still has the chills. Miss More is a goodlooking girl. Kate invited them to come up. So after playing awhile we went up to her place. After being there awhile Ed asked Kate whether she couldn't stay there awhile. He isn't polite. So. we went out to the store and to the hardware store. While he was in there I slipped over and asked for J. She wasn't at home then so I left a message that I'd be there in half an hour. Joined Ed and we went up on the hall. Met Clymer and spoke to him. He will be up soon. Told Ed we had better go to the girls. So we went down. They had been out looking for us. Kate expected Lillie &c &c. I said I had to leave. Kate thought I would be afraid of them &c. Went over and found Jennie. She was undecided whether or not to go. At last we went. When the other parties came up they stood still and looked at us surprised. Kate sneaked halfway over and I made her come. Met Clymer. Went home half past eleven. J told me that they were all surprised. But Schwenck had expected it. Joined Ed and party. They now spoke. Clymer called me Morgan and I called him the darned shunk Green. Went home at a ten to twelve.

Sunday, June 5, 1887.   Got up at half past six. Miss Moore was up soon after five. She must not feel at home here. Gave one of my photos to Ed and she asked me to exchange with her. Ed will send them by mail. Had music. Went to Sunday School when Miss Moore joined L & Kate. Kate got us all to come up for dinner. Mrs Greaser gave me a fine rose on the way home. Gave it to Miss M afterward. Lillie too was there for dinner. We had a good time. Rufus went away after dinner. Horace helped to entertain. We went up to the store. Ed wanted to see about a blanket. They had a fire there last night in the front windows. It was soon quenched. Ed started for home about three. Kate and Lillie came along down to see them off. Horace and I went up to my room to sleep. I couldn't sleep much. Horace staid for supper. Went up to the station. Penrose Zendt was out driving this evening with Miss Maggie Souder. The children!

Miss J was practising on the organ when I came over. Her mother was in the room when I came in. Felt more at my ease than last Sunday. S has not yet returned the forged letter but returned her answer. This plainly shows that he was guilty. She says she believes that he does not approve of my coming there as he spoke in favor of another. Told her what I thought of him that I despised him and could not bend to him.

When I mentioned the rocks business she said she had half decided to go to school. So we will wait till July. We spent a very pleasant evening together. Jake Moyer came in at the front door to find out who was there. But J. closed the door. Went home at half past eleven.

Monday, June 6, 1887.   Got through tolerably well today. Read the Times in Ed's office. Went home and took a lunch, took my book and went upstairs. Slept soundly from six to eight o'clock. Went up to the store and from there to the bank. John was there at work on L Keller's book. Heard Ellis had a baby. A little blackhaired girl.

Asked L how she liked the festival. She said she was not there. She did not care to talk about it. When they were down at our place yesterday she did not come in with the other girls but sat on the porch. Mother asked me what it meant? She did not like it.

Tuesday, June 7, 1887.   Read Little Dorrit last night and finished it this morning. Was awake till half past two when I laid down and woke up at six this morning. Felt very well on it. Received a letter from Uriah concerning the

Rocks business. Am sorry I have to put him off. He says Miss Barndt wants Kate along. If Kate should go L would not be pleased. But I don't think they will go.

It rained hard last night and was raining a little all day. The ground is very wet.

A very painful operation was performed on Mr Zuschnitt today.

Wednesday, June 8, 1887.   Heard this morning that Haynes left here yesterday morning for Bound Brook. A new man is in his place.

Mr Zuschnitt is very ill. Father was down to see him this evening. Worked on the books this afternoon. Am dreadfully behind hand.

Went up to the post office this evening expecting to hear from J before she left when Jakey told me in a crowd of boys that she left for West Chester on the 1.25 train. She will probably write as soon as she arrives. Will have to tell Uriah about it.

Ordered a pair of pants this afternoon for five dollars.

Thursday, June 9, 1887.   A very warm fair day but there was rain this afternoon. Frank D Hartzel has won another prize in the University. It was for the best paper on Mental and Political Philosophy "The Platonic Ideas." He'll make something of himself. Worked on the books and made good progress. Mowed the yard this evening although it was almost too wet. Sent Elwood to the P.O. Nothing.

Mr Zuschnitt is doing well today. Rev. Dengler was in bank today. He is full of the microscope he has. The cost him about 100. He expects Mr Landes to come over this evening.

Mr Moyer and most of the borough committee were down to Norristown today on account of the borough application. It will probably be granted.

Friday, June 10, 1887.   A nice cool day.

Mr Landes and Morris Zendt to see Mr Dengler last evening. He has plans for building a church here and that is what he really wanted. He told Mr Landes to speak to Mr Godshall, father and others. I told father about it. I think he would do the fair thing about it. Let them build churches and go to work.

Worked on the books this afternoon. Am nearly through. Had a meeting of the Board of Managers at the schoolhouse. Bills were ordered to be paid and everything else put aside till fall. Gehman told the salaries of the teachers were lowered 2 a month. He was in a passion about it. I don't blame him. Rec'd Cabinet Cabinet Photos from Ed & Miss Moore. Rec'd a letter from Jennie. She says the school is full. She is afraid I'll laugh at her eccentricity. Queerness she calls it because she remembers Frick. Guess she'll laugh more at mine then I do at hers. The letter is dated June 9 and mailed on the 10th.

Saturday, June 11, 1887.   They are making preparations for a parade this evening of the Sons of Amer. of this place and a visiting organization. Two flags are hung across the street.

In response to Andrews invitation made ready to go to North Wales this afternoon. Got new pair of shoes from Hagey's. Am undecided when to use them day or week. Made the 4:40 train and went down to Lansdale where we have to change. Got down about 5:30. Saw a game of cricket bet. North W. and Norristown. Andrew came fr. the P.O. with my card dissappointed. After supper went over to Hargrave's and had a game of croquet. Had a introduction to his two sisters. Went up to the Academy which was soon crowded. Dr Slifer lectures on Chemistry. Interesting experiments. Brunner came and spoke to us when he saw me. Was introduced to Rev M Foust. Saw Carrie Shearer and Mary Brunner. Went to a Mr Miller's who has two sisters. Hargrave's sister was there. Music, singing. Saw a cornet worth 100 Dolls. Beautiful. Mr Miller goes to see Hargrave's sister. She is a nice girl. Fine voice. Miss Annie Miller is employed at Wanamaker's. Enjoyed the evening very much.

Sunday, June 12, 1887.   Got up a quarter after seven. Was very sleepy then yet. Mr Hargrave came in and we went to the Methodist church together. He sings in the choir. Saw Mr Miller and his sisters and Miss Hargrave. After dinner we went with Hargrave to the Reformed Sunday School. They wanted me to stay till evening but I didn't want to. So we went out of the school up to the station. Spoke to Wesley Anders. He's with Dr Slifer studying medicine. Was very sleepy when I came home. After supper walked around with Rufus. Went with Jonathan to church on the hall. A young man by the name of Mealseed preached.

Monday, June 13, 1887.   Was very sleepy this morning. It was very warm today. Did not get over all my work. Rec'd a letter from Uriah this evening. He will come up next Sunday.

Went to work on my wagon house. It will be hard work. Was up to the store where Ellis was hunting names for his baby. He made me choose one. Went to bed too late. Mike Bergey was telling me about the fellows &c &c.

Tuesday, June 14, 1887.   Was up at Dr Loux's this evening. He was not at home so I waited. Had a conversation with Jonathan Umsted. He told me about the examinations and so forth.

Wednesday, June 15, 1887.   Received a letter from Ed Danley. He says he is very busy. He says Miss Moore was well pleased with her visit. This warm weather makes a person sleepy. Dropped off several times today and yesterday.

Mr Bissel operator at Telford of whom L talked so much, is in trouble. He has been arrested.

Worked on the wagon house this and yesterday afternoon. Pretty hard work. Had Elwood to help this evening.

Henry told me this afternoon that Horace and his father had a fall out and that Horace would look for another job.

Thursday, June 16, 1887.   Another very warm day. Found it out in the afternoon when I worked on the wagon house.

Went in to Kate who was sitting on the front porch and chatted for about an hour.

The name of the girl in trouble about MrBis is Angie Hendricks the same who drove through here with Kate and L some time ago. Horace went to the city this morning looking for a job very likely. From Jennie. She has a prejudice against the diary and said she wished she were a mouse she'd gnaw it all up. She says she wants letters to prevent homesickness.

Some medicine Indian Show are up at Tyson's this week.

Friday, June 17, 1887.   Probably the warmest day we have had so far. Wrote Jennie this morning. Wrote Uriah for Scribner's. Wanted to work in the yard this afternoon but a shower came on and I had to leave it. So I worked on the wagon house. It is nearly finished.

Heard that Derstine & Bro's Hay house was struck by lighting and was burning.

This was Library evening. Mostly young people who were down.

Sam & Elwood were up to see Derstine's. The hay is burning yet.

Saturday, June 18, 1887.   Warm day. Rained last night. Took out "Kenilworth" for Uriah last evening. Commenced to read it and took it along to bank. Very interesting. Worked so much the faster because of it.

Mowed the yard this afternoon.

Took a warm bath this evening. Felt very well over it.

Got a very tastefully got up invitation to the North Wales commencement.

Uriah wrote this morning that Frick would be up this evening and he in the morning.

Sunday, June 19, 1887.   A very nice cool morning. Read "Kenilworth." Went up to meet the train this morning but came just a little late. Frick and his mother came up. Uriah got Scribner's for me. Nice number. He got his hammock and went down to the woods. I went home to get mine. Spoke with Frick awhile. Went out to the woods with "Kenilworth" and "Scribner." Uriah has the "Press." Went to Sunday School in the afternoon. Frick was not there. Joined Uriah in the woods. Frick and the Gov. came out some time after. He staid with us till five. The little boys were playing around there. Went up to the station to see Frick off. His vacation comes next month. Rode a short piece with Uriah. Went home and took it easy. Jake Moyer was in with Sam.

Monday, June 20, 1887.   A very hot day. Mother says the thermometer registered 104 in the sun.

Mr Fisher was buried today. The Sellersville Odd Fellows attended in a body.

Uriah left this morning. He says they can't go on the 10th July. He asked if I wouldn't take Jennie down one evening to see Miss Barndt. We spoke to Schwenck.

Horace tells me he is going to Ohio and that he will start tomorrow evening. Jake Reiff too has left Proctor and Cal Hunsberger will tomorrow take Kratz's team. Quite an upheaval. From Jennie. She writes quite a long letter dated Sunday. She told all about Horace's visit to West Chester etc. I asked him something about in the very words they used. He was surprised and wanted to know who told me. I didn't tell. Wrote a German letter signed Wilhelm Helmholtz which I will send to J for fun.

Tuesday, June 21, 1887.   A very hot day.

Enclosed the letter I wrote last eve to Uriah and told to mail it.

Wrote to Jennie this afternoon. I am afraid she is getting tired of my letters. I can't think of anything to amuse her.

Horace started for Ohio this afternoon. He came into the bank during the afternoon and bid me goodbye.

Read "Pickwick." There is some humor in it and I daresay I would have enjoyed it another time. My spirits are low sometimes it seems to me. I'd enjoy "Kenilworth" and I am almost tempted to begin another of Scott's.

Got to bed late on account of the heat.

Wednesday, June 22, 1887.   Yesterday was Queen Victoria's Jubilee. The procession from Buckingham Palace to Westminster Abbey was witnessed by hundreds of thousands of people. The ceremonies in Westminster Abbey were very impressive. Sam and Alonzo each bought a rifle. Fired a few shots with them and am delighted with it. The boys think I'm a pretty good marksman having hit the target pretty often. Rev. Mr Kehm was at Jake's place today. He came out with him to bank.

Thursday, June 23, 1887.   Rain more or less all day. Read "Scribner's" at bank and "Pickwick" at home. Finished wagon house except the lock this afternoon. Did not hear from J as I expected.

The Fidelity Nat Bk of Cincinnatti was broken a week or so ago by the Chicago Wheat deal and the officers are under arrest for misapplying the funds of the bank. It was a great fraud. The bank is only a year old.

Friday, June 24, 1887.   Mr Lake, the doctor's father-in-law died this morning. His sons came up and this evening the remains were taken to the city.

Mowed the yard this afternoon and cleaned my carriage this evening.

From J. She scolds me for writing the German letter for she suspects me right away. She suggests the Fourth of July as a good time for camping. Answered her letter and denied all knowledge of the German letter.

Got to bed after eleven and forgot to wind my watch.

Saturday, June 25, 1887.   Nice day. Was pretty sleepy. Wrote Uriah and desired an answer till this evening but none came.

Went out and saw Maggie whether she will go along to the Rocks tomorrow. She promised if her mother would be better. She to Amelia had kept Haynes before he left. This surprised me thorough I knew she liked him but I thought she thought more of herself.

Stopped in a little at grandfather S's on my way home. Bought a hammock for Uriah. After supper went up to Hunsberger's for Sam's rifle, on my way home met Os Kline who looks well. Stopped in at grandfathers who'll come down tommorow. Asked Amelia to go with me to Rickerts. Went out in the yard to practice target shooting. Grandfather was equal to any of us. I was a little disappointed. Something wrong with the rifle. Stopped in at Kate's. Annie Aschenbach Fred's hired girl was there and is very lively. Bean came and I asked him about the Rocks business. He says he'll go. He'd like the Fourth. Left at near ten.

Sunday, June 26, 1887.   Got up late. Sent Elwood up to grandfather's and had him hitch up for me. Started at half past eight an hour later than I expected. We went up through Earlington, passed Gerhart's hotel, Hunsicker's creamery. Pushed over towards Sumneytown by the least used roads under the impression that this made the distance shorter when in reality it made it longer. We pushed into the hill along a winding curving snakelike road where we couldn't see fifty ft a head. This was along the Swamp creek. Thinking it were high time to turn down I asked in English an old fellow who was driving cows the way to Heffentrager's. The answer I got was so unintelligible that was almost sure I would have to drive the first nice road up, over, a house through a garden and around a shire(barn). So the first house we drove in at the lane and a dirty woman directed us to drive into a hill where we found a terrible road. Soon the little boy came running after and asked whether we wanted to see the widow Heffentrager? This road ended there. We turned around and came out of this wilderness and drove south under our new directions till I saw the old place. Then home. The way seemed long. Maggie was heartily tired of the Rocks. I enjoyed it all. It threatened to rain. We came home at three, too late for Sunday School. Took grandfather home. After supper up at the station around there and home again. Read Pickwick a little. Kate, Amelia and Martha were here a little in the afternoon.

Monday, June 27, 1887.   Nice cool weather. Went home this afternoon and read "Pickwick" until I went to sleep. Went out to the shop to fetch wood.

After supper read "Pickwick" till about eight when I went to the post office. Saw a light in Kate's sewing room and got in at the window. Found Lillie there.

They were making a dress for Kate. Rufus came in soon afterward. They heard from Horace this morning. He got out on Thursday evening. Lizzie Gerhart came home on Saturday I think. Mr Beisel marries next Saturday. We much laughing and talking and noise generally.

Wednesday, June 29, 1887.   Very hot day. Felt very weak part of the day. Lewis Keller resigned today. He will go to Sellersville. He feels to under obligations to some Sellersville people. Worked on the books this afternoon. Did not hear from Uriah in answer to yesterdays letter about Lillie. As if to put me in a fix Frick must write and propose to the Rocks on Sunday. I wrote an evasive answer. Wrote Uriah about it. These letters will go tomorrow morning. Advised with Kate about it. She thinks I must ask L.

Thursday, June 30, 1887.   Did not hear from Uriah this morning as I expected. I did not know what to do about Lillie. Made up my mind to ask them anyhow. So I wrote to L requesting an immediate answer. She said it was all one to her, of course I knew better, and left all to Gerhart. Asked for him after bank but he wasn't around. After seven he wasn't home and he thought he could not but if he could arrange he would let me know. Saw L & K several times during the day. After supper went over to Irwin Bean to arrange matter. We made out what we'd want. When I got back L & K were on the road and I took them up and we had just a splendid ride. Moonlight and nice cool air.

Susie left this evening. She raised a racket about something and father went out and told her she could go and she went.

Friday, July 1, 1887.   One of the warmest days of the season. Uriah wrote this morning that L was welcome to go etc. Watched for Jennie and saw her get off the three o'clock train. Worked as hard as I could to get ready to go to Lexington to see Miss B. Wrote to J. and she said she'd go. It was a quarter of eight when I started. Went over to J first and took on Kate afterwards. Kate was the driver. It was just fine. The planet Venus is very bright just now. Got John Moyer to help Rufus at the Library. The first time I missed it. When we came down about half past eight Miss Barndt came out to meet us. She is a very agreeable person. We left at nearly ten. We had a fine time. The distance seemed very short. When I came home it was almost too warm to sleep.

Saturday, July 2, 1887.   Warm or rather hot again. Began to hear the effects of last evening's drive already. Old Herman of course had to make much of it and Ben Barndt hit me hard.

Went to work this afternoon and cleand my carriage and harness and tried to get all ready. I was surprised to see Frick. He came over and I asked him about Uriah. He said Uriah didn't know yet &c and that he was out to see him this afternoon. Of course he sees through it all but he is good enough to keep quiet about it. I did my errands and had him along. We went over to Kratz's and had ice cream. We met Jennie there. We sat at the same table. I don't know what she thought of it. He was kind enough to buy Scribner's for me. He couldn't read it. I'll be blamed if I didn't forget to eat supper this evening.

Sunday, July 3, 1887.   Very pleasant day. Could not get ready to go the Sunday School so I staid at home. Read Scribner's which F brought up for me. Frick came over after dinner and we went to meeting together. It was very hot and I was restless. I could hardly wait till it was over. Went up to look for Uriah after it was over. Found him at home. He pretended to Frick that he was sorry it was so &c. We got everything ready we could this afternoon.

Went over to Jennie in the evening. Had a pleasant time of it of course but at this distance (I write this on Thursday morning but it seems so many weeks) it is so faint in my memory that I know very little. We anticipated such a grand time tomorrow. Would to God it had been so unalloyed.

Tuesday, July 5, 1887.   It was raining when I got up this morning. It continued to rain all day at an amazing rate. It seemed to pour down somethimes. Uriah went down this morning. He told me Miss B. enjoyed herself very much. She was much disappointed with me. She expected to see a slim tall fellow. Was glad they all liked it. But I have wished that anything might have happened to prevent what it is too late to prevent. I was half angry all day and had a notion to write confessing my weakness and throwing up the sponge. D- this pride pushes me from one to the other. I couldn't bear having the world know that I gave up after such a wrangle. Concluded I had better wait. I may be too hasty. Rec'd first lessons from Buffalo, N.Y.

Frick went down with the Buffalo this morning. Did not get to see him. Schwenck's ballon was a failure. Burned up and everybody laughed.

Wednesday, July 6, 1887.   Very sultry this morning. There was rain several times in the day. Worked till six o'clock this afternoon on Landis & Co.s' book. Unloaded my carriage this evening. Saw Kate this morning. She did not see J. since that evening. She thought I had fixed it all up. She says she had a very pleasant time. I am glad of it. I can not reproach myself enough for doing what I have done. If I only never had read Baron Munchausen I should not have made the mistake. I am so sorry for — that I am afraid I can never atone for it.

Rec'd the books stationery etc from the college. I'll have plenty of work on hand. I would all be very well if I had someone to cheer me in it. Did not feel tired till today except last night when I slept like a log.

Thursday, July 7, 1887.   Warm disagreeable weather. Rec'd a letter from Cassel last evening. He says Hargrave and he will come up some time in August. He has joined the Reformed Church.

Made up my mind to write today and it had a cheering effect on me. Wrote a long letter the issue of which is very uncertain. Still it makes me hopeful that there is an end to it somehow.

Read "Kenilworth."

We have a new girl since yesterday named Crouthamel.

Friday, July 8, 1887.   Wrote letters to Frick and Cassel. Looked for a letter from J. but did not get it till evening. I had almost given up in despair and was thinking what to do in case I received no answer. But an answer came and a very kind one it was. I was excused as it had been an ordinary fault. Rufus asked me to go along to Harr's dam this evening. I said I could not go. I did not care to go with so many wild fellows. Read "Kenilworth." Can't keep off.

Rev. Mr Dengler was around here several times on account of a church they are going to build here. Mr Landes is interested in the project. He was down to see father about it. He has about a 1000 promised on it already.

Saturday, July 9, 1887.   Still warm sticky weather. There was rain this evening. Wrote J. this morning and rec'd a favorable reply this evening. Was over to Funk's yesterday afternoon and ordered a writing table for my bedroom. A nobby little thing it is going to be. Gave Kate one of my photos. She saw J. last evening. She laughs at it now. Mowed the yard this afternoon and had a splendid bath this evening. Read "Kenilworth" every minute I could spare.

Sunday, July 10, 1887.   Got up and dressed a little and read all morning. Finished "Kenilworth." A fine story. Somewhat disappointing. Took a nap and read D'Aubigne's Ref. last vol. There was a nice cool air all day which made it just splendid in the house. The roads were not dusty either. Went to Sunday School this afternoon. Only four of my scholars present. Jennie, Kate and all those came in late. I thought I was late. Took a book home from the Library. Took a draft of my desk over to Funk's. Markly Hufnagel was up but I did not see him though I was up at the station.

Had an excellent time this evening. Was ushered into the parlor where Mrs Schwenck was. S. himself came in afterward. Mrs S. showed me her presents, marriage certificate &c. A reclining chair, a Chmas. present. Also gold fish. We sang a little. Talked quite freely about our "spat" last week and laughed over it. She says none of the others know about it. I am glad of this. She took me out into the dining room for lunch. Stayed pretty late. Had an excuse. The time went by fast. Half past twelve when I left.

Monday, July 11, 1887.   A day like yesterday. Plenty of air and cool. Worked myself through well today. Went over to Funk this afternoon about the writing desk. Saw J. at work on the other side. (I think I'd have my ears boxed if she knew of this)

Talked awhile with Cal. this afternoon. He will leave Kratz's this week. F. Brey will take his place.

Commenced to study this afternoon a little. I miss that desk very much. Don't believe I can write downstairs.

Mother is out at the shop with father at present. We have pussy on the desk with us. She spilled the red ink and as punishment we daubed her paws and nose in red.

Thursday, July 14, 1887. The last three days have been very warm.

Had hardly any time to write. Have been at my lessons every evening. Got out the Penmanship lesson on Tuesday. Letter writing and Arithematic last evening. Bookkeeping and Business Forms this evening and part of Commercial Law. I think this is the hardest for me and the lessons are so long.

Finished "D'Aubigne's Reformation" yesterday afternoon and am now reading "Pickwick" a little again.

Uriah wrote on Tuesday morning. I answered. Wrote Frick. He answered with a postal saying his vacation commenced on the 23rd.

Friday, July 15, 1887. Finished the last last study in the first lessons that of Commercial Law. The first lesson will go in the morning's mail.

The attendance at the Library was up to the average. Jennie came down with Katie S. Moyer. She took Shakespeare, Ben Hur and Physiology. Gave her Scribner's magazine's containing Thackeray's letters.

Saturday, July 16, 1887. Very hot weather. The heat came through in the bank room yesterday and today. When I got through this afternoon I spoke with Kate awhile at her window. It was very cool inside. The air outside was so hot like that of a furnace. Did not mow the yard this afternoon. Took a bath after supper and enjoyed it immensely.There was a hand organ playing the while. By and by a storm came and it rained a little enough to cool off. Read "Pickwick."

Sunday, July 17, 1887. Got up pretty early this morning. Our girl wanted to go away at seven. As we expected company Amelia came down and made dinner. The papers say yesterday was the hottest day in eleven years. Today seemed to me almost as bad. Lay around reading the "Bride of Lammermoor" or playing with pussy. Henry Landes' came. I went up stairs but could not stand it long on account of the heat. Went to S School about two. The attendance was slim. Was with Uriah this morning and some this evening. Was a little late this evening but I worked to make time which made me sweat. She said "I thought you would never come." She was alone. We sat on the porch till after nine. Talked about books etc. Found out why Jonathan was so much in a hurry twice during rehearsals last winter. She thought I did wrong in deceiving people about Lillie. She wouldn't want to be pitied &c. I verily believe it wouldn't work either. But — I didn't say nothing.

Monday, July 18, 1887. Very warm this morning already. Was angry at old Greaser for not opening the windows earlier so that no air could come in.

At three Mr Gerhart, Mr Thomas Slifer and his lawyer Hunsicker came up to confer together about the sale of Slifer's properties. Don't know what came of it. Went up to the store and had my pants ordered remade. Went over to Funk's and looked after my table. Not commenced yet. Went home and commenced to study my lessons. They seem hard. It has not cooled off yet and I am in no hurry to go to bed.

Tuesday, July 19, 1887.   Very much cooler than of late. As I expected nothing came of the Slifer conference. They wouldn't agree to his unreasonable demands and he refused to listen to theirs. They are all foolish if they dont settle in some way.

Was very busy all day.

Worked out part of my lessons this evening.

Mrs. Frick came over. She brought the book she had read. She is going home tomorrow. Charley will come up on Saturday.

Mr Landes has his head full of building a creamery. Nothing will come of it very likely but he would like to have something to do for Rufus.

Wednesday, July 20, 1887.   Another cool day.

The board of directors today passed the most disgraceful resolution ever made by bank directors. Mr Ruth has been fighting against a compromise in the Slifer matter and now had a motion passed calling a meeting of the Stockholders on Saturday to decide the matter. This shows alarming weakness. If I had been in the board I would have fought it to the last. Ruth is trying to rule and has made some insulting remarks about Ed and Mr Gerhart. He says the talk is that this is the Souders' bank etc. Probably his own invention. We will have to notify all the stockholders by letter. We had company today. An old lady with grandmother S.

Worked on my lessons this afternoon. The others have not yet come in.

Thursday, July 21, 1887.   Cloudy and some rain. Received my first lesson from Buffalo this morning. They had most of them marked very good or excellent. They disagreed with my ruling in bookkeeping. As I expected I got no praise in penmanship. Had practiced from the wrong slip too.

Didn't have to write the notices to the stockholders today. Rufus Landes wrote them all out last evening. Worked hard at my lessons this afternoon but the two hardest are to get yet. Penmanship and Commercial Law. Went over to see Funk about the desk but he hadn't done anything at it today. He was out fishing. Rec'd a letter from Ed. Danley stating that he was married last Thursday. I don't know what he means but I always expected he'd marry early.

Friday, July 22, 1887.   A little rain this afternoon. Mowed the yard this afternoon. It had lain two weeks and was quite long.

Worked on my lessons till late. Very late. Thought I'd finish but I couldn't. Commercial Law was pretty tough this week. Went to bed at half past eleven.

Saturday, July 23, 1887.   Wet and rainy. The great Stockholder's meeting came off this morning. I was election officer. There were 188 votes cast all of which were for compromise. Not a single vote was cast for foreclosure. I think J.S.R. will hate it a little. Gus Thomas was up and worked hard. Didn't get my work done. Just kept up that's all. Worked on the lessons and sent them off this evening. Am always happy to get rid of them. Frick came up this evening on his vacation for 10 days. Spoke awhile with him. Saw Jennie with Kate but noticed them not. Read "Bride of Lammermoor."

Sunday, July 24, 1887.   Commenced to read "Bride of Lammermoor" this morning. Went to Sunday School with Frick, which was not full. Made out with Frick to put up a hammock this afternoon but at dinner a heavy thunderstorm came up. It rained fast. Under cover of this I finished my book. It is a very good story.

Wanted to sleep a little but Frick came over to go to meeting. So we went. I fell asleep but woke up when the preacher said, "Awake thou that sleepest." We walked up to Kate's after meeting. Lillie came out and had not expected to meet us. She invited us out to see Penrose. He is pretty sick. Erysipelas. Frick came over after supper but I excused myself and got away. Had a good time this evening. I thought feel tired but I got through all right. We talked about the books we read &c. She was reading Ben Hur. She has a good insight into character. She knows some people very well. Laughed when I went away. I said it was bedtime but corrected myself.

Monday, July 25, 1887.   Warm day. After bank went up to the store and got my pants. Hunted up Frick and we went over to Funk's together to see my new writing table. All done except the drawers. Very handy little thing. After supper we walked up the railroad and got a notion to go to Telford and came down with the 7:50 train. We walked as we did not have much time but missed it. A half a minute more would have been enough. So we walked about a little and got ice cream at Fenstermachers which was very good. We saw the Telephone Exchange too. Started for home where we arrived at quarter past nine pretty tired.

Tuesday, July 26, 1887.   I was still pretty tired this morning from last evening's walk. I could have worked on my lessons very well this afternoon for I thought Frick was gone fishing and did not see him. But I couldn't do anything. This must not come over me often as I will surely fail. Afterwards found that F. had not been away and that he had been at home sleeping.

Wednesday, July 27, 1887.   Warm day. Frick went fishing today instead of yesterday. He says it was fine. He came back about half past five. After bank met old Herman with whom I got to talking till Charley came. We talked about the creation unbelief baptism and fanaticism. Today John S Ruth acted as if he were well pleased with the result of the election on Saturday. A Thomas reports that Slifer is undecided.

After supper read "Pickwick." Then we went to the Post Office. Took a walk up town and then stood at our gate. We watched the people pass. Jennie and Emma Krupp passed us twice but did not look at us. Frick didn't know them and I didn't tell him who it was.

Thursday, July 28, 1887.   Did not get any return from Buffalo today. Went over to the barber this afternoon and had my hair cut. He found a white hair on my head. The first one. I think its rather early to begin. Wrapped it up in paper and took home to show.

Read "Pickwick."

After supper Frick and [I] went up to the post office from there to Funk's to look at my table. He was putting on the last coat. I'll get it on Monday. Had a little music on two organs not yet in the case. Funk worked the pedals and I the keys. One of 17 stops. Walked out Water St. and came back to see the camp meeting people off the train. Jennie and her mother were up it seems. She walked up town but came back soon. Martha's friend Miss Williams and Annie walked about town. Frick had an eye on her and they must have noticed us. We met them at every turn. Our girl not feeling well is away and cousin Sallie is here.

Friday, July 29, 1887.   This evening young Snyder brought me my bible. It is splendidly bound though I would prefer less gilding. The illustrations and everything are superb. Paid $14 for it. Worked on the books this afternoon.

Heard rumors that a newcomer had arrived over the railroad. Milt Moyer ought of course to be happy.

Many mistook this for a library evening.

Saturday, July 30, 1887.   Very hot. After bank went up to the tailor shop to get my coats. Frick was sitting on the bench there and talked about the Williams girl. Soon after we saw her and Annie come and they walked over to the office. Alonzo had to come over and Frick soon followed. I was sure he'd say something to her this time. I walked over too and we were weighed. On walking to the store she dropped something but Frick didn't pick it up. Got a letter from Jennie this afternoon which after referring to "sickness" in the family asked me to discontinue my visit for the present and asked for the schoolhouse keys to refer to the Library. She mentioned something about camp meeting but was afraid I would not like to call for her. I answered handing the keys to Kate and asked her to name the time for tomorrow. Saw her and Emma Krupp going down to the schoolhouse soon after. Got Elwood to clean my carriage. Met Jennie and Miss Krupp soon after on the street. We went in for ice cream at Kratz's and walked up to the end of the town. Miss K went in at Miss Moores and J and I walked on. Miss K joined us when we came back. Talked awhile with her at the gate. Two o'clock was the time appointed to go to camp.

A friend of Frick's came up this evening and will spend Sunday with him. Was introduced above to Trout.

Sunday, July 31, 1887.   Lay around reading "Pickwick" this morning. Thinking the train would again be behind time this year on account of the crowd for the camp meeting I did not get ready in time to see who left on the first train which was a special. The two trains were crowded to their fullest capacity. Uriah came up and went over to see him. Frick and his friend came there but left before we came out. I guess they were not pleased. Managed to get ready a few minutes after two. Jennie was ready when I drove to the door. Mr Moyer said there would be rain. The weather was almost unbearable. Drove wrong once. The Northern horizon was now black and its center seemed to be right over the tunnel. Jennie was afraid but I joked about it. At last a good wind struck us. Met Al Fretz on his way home. We thought we'd better do the same. I drove fast but was afraid we'd get caught. It was awful but Jennie was laughing now. We got home all right. Had my team away when it commenced. It must have been terrible up at the camp. As the trains came down it reminded one of a rout. The second train was so crowded that two trains of the same length could have be formed. Our boys were all right. Uriah was with me when I came back. Frick and he were with me on the front porch where we had fun.

Monday, August 1, 1887.   Uriah went down this morning. He says he'll come up again on Thursday evening to go to camp.

Spoke to Allie and Kate. Neither of them got wet. Allie will stay up for a week. Today was examination day. Jennie passed while I was talking to Kate and Allie. We had Mrs Greaser for washing today. The Doctor saw my Business Books and I told him about it. This evening it rained fast. I think we have the playfullest kitten I ever saw. Studied over my lessons. Ran over to see about the desk. Not finished. Jonathan has the Grammar School. Jennie I suppose the Primary, and so on.

Read "Pickwick" a little. Wrote a long letter to Jennie this evening. It was late when I got to bed.

Tuesday, August 2, 1887.   Hot again today. Rained this afternoon. Frick went up to Bethlehem this morning and says he had a good time. That is, he liked the place much. Worked on my lessons a little but don't have much heart in it yet as Funk hasn't the desk finished yet. I'm getting tired of waiting.

Ellis got a new gold watch open face figured or chased with the best kind of work. He paid $60.

Don't know what Jennie is thinking of the letter she must have got today. No doubt she thinks me foolish. Uncle Ed. came home yesterday afternoon well pleased with his trip. He was in bank this afternoon. See Miss B. yesterday. Her father and family passed this afternoon.

Wednesday, August 3, 1887.   A little cooler than yesterday. When I got to the post office this morning they told me that Lincoln Godshall had been looking for Frick and myself last evening. He wants to put daylight through Frick. He is down on me too. Was at work on my lessons this afternoon. Frick was away. Received a delightful letter from Jennie this afternoon. She says my letters are delightfully jolly and anticipates a good time for tomorrow evening.

Went over to Funk's after supper and found the desk had been ready the day before. Carried it home on my back. Frick met me and helped me to carried it up stairs. He is going down tomorrow evening. Told him about Godshall. He made it appear that it was our duty to make fun of them. He told me Ike Benner would be married the beginning of September.

Wrote Jennie appointing six o'clock as the time of starting tomorrow evening.

Thursday, August 4, 1887.   Weather was fair though cloudy. Watched it anxiously. Made ready to go this afternoon. Went over and saw Jennie about it. She didn't expect me as she thought it was all arranged. Waited on Uriah as he came off the train. He said he hoped we'd see each other at camp. We didn't though.

Jennie says her certificate is about as good as Jonathan's and that last year's was better. Then he isn't so high up after all. She says she wasn't satisfied at all with her certificate. On the way up as we were talking a fellow was trying to get ahead of me. Looking round I saw it was Rufus. Off I went and he staid back. He tried it several times and used his whip which frightened my horse. At last I couldn't control my horse. When we were through Sellersville Morris Weil tried it too and soon after I let him ahead. Then an old rattling machine came along and wanted to do it too. It made me mad but after awhile they went ahead on a run and a fellow lost his hat and they had to stop. When we got up there were many there and preaching was in progress. We couldn't see Uriah. Started home a quarter of nine. No one was leaving the woods yet and we had a delightful drive home. It took us over two hours. We both enjoyed it much I think. It was eleven when I came into the house.

Friday, August 5, 1887.   Warm day. Read Scribner's at bank. Mr Zendt got sick at camp meeting on Wednesday and was brought home yesterday. Worked like a slave to mow the yard this afternoon. Didn't get through till a little after six. Our girl Ida came in this evening and asked us to get some one else. We had some one already. Miss Shellenberger who comes next week.

At the library this evening the attendance was as usual. Jennie took "Waverley" and Scarlet Letter not being in I promised to see she'd get it. She promised to write as I am not allowed to come yet. Clymer came up this evening. He just reached us before nine. He took "Dombey & Son." I asked him up one Sunday and he promised to come. He is a dear little fellow.

Saturday, August 6, 1887.   Very warm this morning. In the afternoon a storm came on which cooled it off a little. Mother went along up with grandfathers to Quakertown. They have a baby up there. Preston came along down. Lillie too wanted to come. Went home this afternoon and went to work like a good fellow. Father made me a present of the bible I bought by giving me the money. He had told Snyder that he would pay it. Did some figuring for father. Came upstairs again and worked till twelve and got my lesson out contrary to expectation. Father handed me a letter from Jennie. Mother wanted to know why we were continually writing. It contains an account of a dream, a sermon on Cruelty to animals &c with the sweet part left out as she says.

Sunday, August 7, 1887.   Tried to sleep on awhile yet this morning but failed so I finished copying one of the lessons and made it all ready to mail tomorrow morning. Worked till twelve last night. Finished "Pickwick Papers" this morning. Took "Scarlet Letter" along to Sunday School for Jennie. She said she was anxious to have it last evening already. Mack and Markly Huffnagle were in Sunday School. Mike Bergey was not there so I took his place. Went over to the schoolhouse and took "Black Dwarf and Old Mortality" along home but couldn't read being too sleepy. Went up to the depot and spoke to Markly. Was up at grandfather H's. Amelia is doing well. Was at Kratz's a short time. Wrote part of a letter to Jennie but could not finish it.

Monday, August 8, 1887.   Elwood went down to Shellenberger's early this morning but did not get what he wanted. She said she could not come as she had malaria. Father was out all morning for a girl. At dinner we got to talking about going to New York for an immigrant and I said I would go on Thursday. Heard about one over at Blooming Glen. Sam went over this afternoon. She will send word this week. Had to help a little. Worked pretty well in my lessons this evening. Mailed a letter to Jennie. Cool like yesterday.

Tuesday, August 9, 1887.   Nice cool weather. Father was up for Sallie this morning and got her though she don't like to come. Aunt Sarah received a ck for back pension last evening for 2761.47. She will get 14 a month till Sallie is 16. From then on 12 a month. Mr Bean and Dr Bauman have been urging it on. Father told me this morning that Bean had advised her to deposit it in the Sellersville Bk for secrecy. The idea. They have their own private ends to gain. Bauman too told us not to say anything about it as he had been chiefly instrumental in bringing it on &c. I studied over this what he meant by it but could not make out. Mr L suggested that perhaps he would like to borrow the money. This is likely. I told father and he talked to Uriah about it. After dinner Uriah brought down the money and deposited 2500 took the rest along. She ought to pay off Bean and Bauman and then take her own way. They talk of building a house &c. If they would only take good care of it they could get on well.

We ordered Martin Moyer to look after the Blooming Glen girl.

Wednesday, August 10, 1887.   Finished my Bookkeeping Business Forms and Letter Writing lessons this afternoon. Have only Commercial Law and Penmanship to finish. Sam was over to see the Blooming Glen girl again this afternoon but reported that she would not come for less than 2.50.

Was up to see the folks. Took Sarah's bank book along. She has 2400 of it on interest for 6m. Bauman has his share. Bean has not been there yet. When I came home I found that it was decided that I should go to New York tomorrow. Ran out to Landes to say I couldn't be at bank tomorrow. If I could only hope to be successful. I'd hate it badly if it should turn out wrong.

Thursday, August 11, 1887.   Was ready this morning at six but the train was late. Gained nothing by this train as I had to wait long at Jenkintown. Some of the boarders at Beechwood got on the train there and went to Yardly for base ball or cricket. They were a merry set. Walked around on the hill and saw the new buildings there. It rained a little at this time. Train started at 8:53. Saw little Joe Bilger on the platform at Langhorne. He said they were all well but that Will was getting worse. James lived at Pennington. The rest at Yardly. Was puzzled with the geography of the country when we got near New York. Crossed the Passaic on a trestle bridge. Saw Newark in the distance way to the North. Could see the Liberty Statue when ten miles from N.Y. Got on the boat at Jersey City and arrived in N.Y. at 11:00 a.m. Struck east and south for the Battery at once. At first met nothing but foreigners Germans, Jews and all nationalities. An elevated road darkened the street. When I got on Broadway it was all changed. Saw terrible high buildings. Arrived at the Battery I picked out Castle Garden went in at a door marked Burea of Labor. Was asked what I wanted and was shown to the matron's room. Read the rules in front of her desk requiring New York references. I saw I was stuck. Found out sure enough when I asked her. To the left sat the emigrant women. Same marked "With Reference," "No Reference," "Recent Arrivals." Had to leave of course. Asked the way to the World Office. Went up Broadway and turned into Park Row. Saw the great Bank buildings, Post Office, City Hall, Newspaper Offices etc. Went up Eighth Ave to Central Park on the Horse cars. Walked through the lower park and down Fifth Ave. Watched for Vanderbuilts palace and saw it. One block below and opposite is the Cathedral. Went in and saw it. It is simply wonderful. Went down to the N.Y.C. & H.R.R. depot. Great building. Took the elevated down to the City Hall. Changed cars and went over the Brooklyn bridge. Took the boat and returned to N.Y. Saw the bridge from below etc. Took the street cars to Broadway. Were blocked up in Ann St. 10 min. Saw where Gen Montgomery is buried. Reached the boat in time which started at four. Talked to a man in business in the city while on the boat who said he had seen Vanderbilts place only once &c. Changed cars at Trenton Junction. At Neshaming Falls a lot of excursionists got on the train while it was raining and pressed me tight against the window. Met Andrew at Jenkintown. Had a long talk with him. Arrived home about eight. Mother didn't expect me to bring one but only wondered what could be the reason this time.

Friday, August 12, 1887.   Sallie got sick yesterday and father fetched Annie. Tomorrow Mrs Kohlschrieber will do the baking.

Landis & Co will build a warehouse shortly.

Mowed the yard this afternoon and did not get through till near eight o'clock. Wrote out part of Commercial Law after that.

Greaser asked me if it was true that Sarah got a pension yesterday. I said I was away yesterday. Of course everybody will be talking about it in a few days. Received a letter from Jennie this morning. She wasn't quite pleased with me for writing my last letter but said I might call again on Sunday evening.

Answered at once and said I'd come of course and glad I was to do so too. The boys left for home this evening as we can't keep them as long as we have no girl.

Saturday, August 13, 1887.   A nice cool day. The secret about Sarah's money is out. People begin to ask how about it? Milt Moyer and Mr Landes trimmed the trees at the schoolhouse today. Lesson from Buffalo returned this morning. Got No. 4 ready this afternoon. I'm always glad when the week is over and my lesson done. Met Miss Jennie on going up to the post office. Emma Krupp and she afterward took a walk up town. Plenty of music at Kratz's. Received a letter from the American Agency, Phila., offering to supply a good girl for $3 a week. Mother says we can't pay that much. Wm wrote to New York for a recommendation from Waterhouse. Went down and sat with Zuschnitt this evening.

Sunday, August 14, 1887.   Dressed this morning and went to Sunday School pretty late. Was tired of it. Mr Godshall's sick again and was not there. Jonathan led the singing and Mr Moyer did the rest. Kate and Lillie were not there. Heard this evening they were over to L's grandparents. Tried to read some in the afternoon. Elmer Weil was here while with Sam. Took a nap. Aunt Kit came in during the afternoon. Mrs Ellis and little Stella too were here a little while.

Dressed after supper and got up a quarter of eight. Emma Krupp was in the room but went out before I came in. Mrs Schwenck brought Milt's baby in. Mrs Milt came in soon after. Very little creature of course.

Had a right good time. Couldn't look serious for two minutes at a stretch. Jennie would have liked to box my ears for my letters. She has read Hawthorne's "Scarlet Letter." Before we knew it, it was after twelve. She told me something about a party at Miss Moore's in the near future. She will commence a short term of school tomorrow a week. Says she's going to graduate too yet.

Monday, August 15, 1887.   Received a letter from Horace this morning. He is in Acme O. a city with five dwellings &c. He will go to Wadsworth soon. I suppose it's a little lonely for him out there. The neighborhood is strictly temperance. He writes no dull letter.

It is curious how people can sometimes imagine that they only want to see justice done when it is really envy that is stirring them up. There is terrible talk out about Aunt Sarah's pension. That there was false swearing &c and that they intended to buy teams for the boys gold watches, bracelets, silk dresses, an organ &c. It's really ridiculous. People who ought to know much better talk so. CD Hunsberger and Isaac Benner are having a fuss. Isaac was drunk on Sat. eve. and made C.D. a black eye without provocation. Today CD had him arrested. It will perhaps go hard with Freed who sold him the liquor.

Tuesday, August 16, 1887.   Nice cool weather. Somebody is to be sent to New York again for a girl. I won't go this time. Don't have time. Wouldn't trust myself right either. Tough job.

The most outrageous talk is still in progress about Sarah's pension.

Worked on my lesson this afternoon and evening. Read "Old Mortality" a little. Seams to be pretty good.

Prince Ferdinand who was recently elected Prince of Bulgaria has assumed the throne without the consent of the Powers.

Friday, August 19, 1887.   Pretty warm day. Mailed my letter to Horace this morning. Mowed the yard this afternoon. Saw Mr Godshall out today for the first time since he was taken sick. Spoke a few words to him. The paper this evening has an account of the pension excitement. It says that Sarah got $2600 and that many thought not rightfully and that it had been reported in Washington for investigation. Goettler also says the project to build a church at this place has been given up. I don't think this is true as father went over to see Dengler at his own request.

The Library was not very well patronized this evening. Miss Jennie brought Hannah Roth along. She won't ask Kate any more.

Mowed the yard this afternoon.

Saturday, August 20, 1887.   Nice day. Rec'd returns from Buffalo this afternoon. Sent off No. 5 this evening.

Chas. Frick came up this evening. Saw him in the store a little.

There was a meeting on Tyson's Hall about the new church project this evening. It was decided to build.

Uncle Wm. started for Cape May this evening. From thence he will go to New York and try his luck. Hope he'll bring a good one.

Have wasted much time this week by sleep or else wanted to work too late. Fell asleep last evening before I was ready and had lamp burning till half past one. The windows were open and I think I caught a little cold. I had it so in my back twice today that I could hardly walk without groaning.

Sunday, August 21, 1887.   Lay around all morning reading "Old Mortality." Very interesting. Got ready in time to go to Sunday School. Mr G. was not present. He felt too weak. Frick wasn't out either. Jonathan took us through very creditably. An invitation for a surprise party at Reub Gerhart's was handed to me by Cal. It was written very poorly. I was disgusted with the place selected. Sat on Kratz's porch for about an hour. Read again. Went up to the station to see Frick off. The train was late so we went over to Uriah who had come up. Took a short ride with him. Ordered Scribner's. Father had come with the news that he had hired a girl. So I wrote a telegram for Wm to come home. Mother wanted me to take it up very badly. Came over to Jennies about

7:30 and shame to say it was 5 hrs later when I went to bed. The time slips away so fast that I almost forget myself. And her school commences tomorrow. Not decided whether to go to the party or not but rather not. Promised a long letter.

Monday, August 22, 1887.   Uriah went down with the Buffalo so I did not see him. Our new girl comes tomorrow. Mrs Greaser and Annie were here today.

Mr Moyer is very busy attending to his building. The bricklayers commenced today. He is very busy. Thought over what I would like to write to J. sometimes. Her school commences today. Felt almost jealous of Jonathan. I don't know why.

Worked on my lessons this afternoon and evening though I could not help spending about an hour and a half reading.

Got disgusted with the Arithmetic lesson as I got all the questions wrong.

Saw Kate and found out she wasn't going to the party. Must now try and write a little something yet.

Tuesday, August 23, 1887.   It was very warm today and this evening it looked as if it might rain. Between seven and eight the heaviest storm of wind and rain came up that we have had this summer. I did not mind it as I was at work upon my lesson till I came down stairs when I saw the grape frame had broken down right under my window. There were some terrible claps of thunder. Couldn't help staying down and finish reading "Old Mortality." Good story though just right for me just now. Borneman's child which died the other day will be taken to Boyertown tomorrow. Funeral services were to be held this evening. Our new girl arrived today. Her name is Stoves. Finished my letter to Jennie this afternoon and mailed it.

At the church meeting it was decided to at once commence work. Geo. H. Swartz wants to back out again. He tried to break it up. He don't care to pay his $250. He offered to pay a $100.

Wednesday, August 24, 1887.   Rain at different times today. This morning the position of the new church was staked off and work will begin soon. Jos Groff, Morris D Zendt, J.G. Leidy, W.G. Leidy and father are the Building Commission. Finished all lessons today except Penmanship and Commercial Law. Rec'd returns from Buffalo only this morning. Very much quicker work than usual. But the old fellows are having a vacation. A new man is in their place.

We heard this morning would go to the Trust Co. soon. The house of Jos Bergey was struck by lightning during the storm. The roof was damaged.

Elwood came back again today. Sam is at home yet.

Thursday, August 25, 1887. Finished Commercial Law No. 6 this evening. Am reading Early Days of Christianity by Farrar.

Received a short answer from Jennie. She is glad Kate does not go to the party. She don't want to be alone. She speaks in parables. I think she didn't wish to put much of what she thought on paper.

The party at Gerhart's will no doubt be a rousing success. (?)

Friday, August 26, 1887. Sent off Lesson 6 this evening. Went with Elwood up to Bauman's to fetch the new girl's things away. We didn't get them that's all. Mrs B. refusing to give them up because they were not packed. Elwood was very much displeased.

A man from Washington was around here today to investigate the case about Sarah's pension. He found Old Brey drunk and asked for Adam's old boss. John Frederick will soon have something to do with it now. Don't know what will become of it yet.

Saturday, August 27, 1887. Read over my lessons this afternoon. The girl was over to Apple's reunion and to Harleysville to a party. She said Alonzo had a girl there. Elwood was over too.

Worked on the books this evening.

Elwood told me today that Sam was paying attention to Miss Annie Johnson. That he was there last Sunday evening. He is great. Wouldn't wonder if he trembled a little. Went with Elwood up to Dr Bauman's. No — that was last evening. This was written on Aug. 31. This accounts for the error.

Sunday, August 28, 1887. Very cool this morning. Sat out on the porch awhile to sun myself. Commenced reading "Black Dwarf." Read 13 pages.

Sunday School was dry as usual. Mr G. took the lead again. Home from school to read.

Went over about half past seven. Milt was in the room when I came. He had been reading Shakespeare. He soon went out. No doubt I was myself in fault. Too much laughing and teasing again on my part. I never feel quite satisfied if I fool the time away in such a manner.

Monday, August 29, 1887. Finished "Black Dwarf" today. It's a very good short story.

Worked till late on my lessons this evening.

Tuesday, August 30, 1887. Read "Early Days of Christianity".

Very troublesome Arithmetic lesson this week. Partial payments.

Went down to the schoolhouse this afternoon to get some records at the Library with to make my semi annual report. Jennie was there yet and I walked along with her.

Friday, September 2, 1887.   Was so busy all week that I did not get time to write up. Rec'd a letter from Andrew stating that he and Mr Hargrave would be up on Sept 11.

Have my lessons all ready except that blamed sample letter.

Was very busy on the books on my lessons all week.

There was a meeting of the board of managers this evening. We presented our reports.

Jonathan told me there was another party going on next Wednesday for Mr Crouthamel at Lexington. He asked whether I had an invitation.

Jennie was down accompanied by little Kate. She said I might call tomorrow evening.

It is raining. Wish I could have cleaned the yard tomorrow.

Saturday, September 3, 1887.   Mr Moyer is much engaged with building now. We went over the discounts today but were terribly out of the way and will have to go over them again soon. Mowed the yard this afternoon. Mrs. Joe Benner was here for supper.

Got a start on a sample letter today once. Did not get it finished though. This is the first time I did not get off my lesson on Saturday with one exception I believe though. Got ready and came over to Jennie about eight. We had a very agreeable time of it. She has an invitation to a party at Lexington next Wednesday. I proposed a drive for tomorrow evening and she said she'd like to go but — I commenced to joke about and then she said she wouldn't go. It was only by doing everything in my power that I prevailed upon her to go. Had as-. Well we'll see.

Sunday, September 4, 1887.   Took a walk with Elwood out to the shop and so on this morning. Made ready and went to sunday school about 9:30. Mike wasn't there and Mr G. came out and said I must take his place. Jennie came at that moment and he told her she must have slept too long. She smiled but said nothing. Was on Kratz's porch reading the paper till dinner. Commenced "Thaddeus of Warsaw." Thought Uriah had come up so I went to look for him. Didn't find him and went over to the Evangelical S.S. But few there mostly girls. All who come are placed a class. Jennie too, was there. Finished my 7th lesson. There was very little to do but I could not bear to leave it till tomorrow. Started about a quarter of seven. Came home at ten. Drove around anywhere. Schwenck's were to Sellersville. Had a pleasant ride. She was well pleased with it and said she was glad she had promised to go. I intended to tell her something but did not. Yes I feel that I must tell her soon. Made out to go to the party at Crouthamel's on Wednesday night.

Monday, September 5, 1887.   Found old Lib. here this afternoon when I came home. Had plenty of fun with her. Was somewhat hindered in my lessons.

Felt very happy today somehow. Couldn't help being high spirits. Was up to grandfather H's after supper. Was looking for father. Grandfather is not well. He was in bed when I came. Amelia is high up for the party on Wednesday. She told me Miss Moore was disappointed with the Gerhart party. She told about a Mr Shellenberger who resembled me somewhat. I believe Jennie had talks about him sometimes. He is a Millersville graduate.

Tuesday, September 6, 1887.   We are having rollicking times with old Lib. Laughed a great deal at her queer talk. I was to have given them a ride this morning but father wanted to go away anyhow so he took them. Half expected a letter from Jennie as she is to write but have not been gratified.

This a little too much fun going on for the good of my lessons. But it won't last, that's one good thing. This evening while father was gone to fetch Ellis' horse mother and old Lib got on the carriage. We pushed a piece way up the lane, and back again in the yard. Then into the wagon house and closed the doors. They were entirely helpless.

Wednesday, September 7, 1887.   Got through very well this afternoon. Did some work on my lessons but not much. It looked very much like rain this afternoon and I was afraid we couldn't go to the party. It all cleared away however. Mother, Lib, Kate & Mrs Fred, went over to Rev Sam'l Detweiler on a visit today. Met Miss L. at noon. She said she couldn't go. Got Elwood to get the team ready and hardly got ready then. Jennie fixed a bouquet on my coat before we started. They were coming out of the house the time we arrived. Miss L was there after all. Started about eight. It was very dark. Arrived at Lexington about nine. There were excellent arrangements. Teams provided for. After waiting some time in the parlor Miss Crouthamel was introduced and afterwards Mrs Crouthamel. The games then commenced. Had plenty of them and enjoyed them very much. There were some there from Lexington. Among them Miss Barndt, Mr Clymer and Mr Fluck that I knew. Mr W.A. Crouthamel managed everything. That Miss Magargles, Miss Moore, Amelia, Maggie. Lillie and Gerhart. [Illegible] Jonathan, Cal, Mike, Alonzo Martha, Sam Musselman and perhaps a few others went down from here. The partners for the table were selected by means of ribbons or bows of which each took one and the two that matched were paired together. Mine matched Miss Barndt; Jennie, Mr Gerhart; Lillie, a Mr Krout, and so on. Cal had Old Mrs. C. Talked with Miss Barndt for awhile after the supper. Kept back from some of the games as I could not play them. Towards the last I took part again and liked it very much. We started to go home about half past one. Jennie was anxious to go before that time. The drive home was fine. Moonlight and quite different from going down. Jennie does not like Miss B as well as she did at first. I think myself she is a little heartless. J. must have guessed my secret. Indeed I spoke pretty plain so it was easy to understand. And what is best of all I think she loves me. I am almost afraid at this time to write these words but I know I love her. I am afraid if she ever reads this she will think I had better told her face to face then have scribbled them into "that diary."

Thursday, September 8, 1887.   Didn't sleep very well last night. Time too short. Made out very well during the day though I didn't feel like eating breakfast. The late supper last evening spoiled it. Tried to read my lessons this afternoon but soon fell asleep. Felt like writing to J. but changed my mind. A shocking murder was enacted at Blooming Glen yesterday afternoon. Geo H. Neff shot and fatally wounded a man by the name of Gänz whom he had accused of undue intimacy with his wife. He shot him four times and there is no hope for his recovery. One shot entered his head one the shoulder and two his arm. The murderer escaped over towards the Delaware. Neff was a son-in-law of Jacob Degel a very dirty fellow whom I have seen.

Friday, September 9, 1887.   This man Gänsend or what he is calld died yesterday afternoon. A reward of $300 has been offered for the arrest of the murderer.

Cleaned the yard this afternoon. Didn't get at my lessons. Rec'd lesson 7 this evening. There were so many errors in my letterwriting lesson that I am almost discouraged.

The Slifer matter is all settled now and Weand goes to the city tomorrow to end it.

We measured our height at the store. Cal measured 5ft 8½in. Jonathan 5ft 7. Rufus a little shorter Mike Bergey 5ft 5½in and Rufus Bergey 4ft 7in and myself 5ft 8¼in. Cal weighed 128 lbs. Rufus 132, Jonathan 133, Mike Bergey 134 or 5 and myself 154¼.

Saturday, September 10, 1887.   Felt very little like working this afternoon so I read Thaddeus of Warsaw.

Sam thought there'd be a lecture tonight but he was wrong. He cleaned my carriage this afternoon.

Saw Jennie this evening. Mrs Schwenck came in to show one of her presents a silver ice-pitcher all very pretty.

The wind whistled outside as in winter which made one feel very snug and comfortable.

Found out who it was that would have taken my place this spring. She made me guess it which I could never have done without hints. But when I found it was Markly didn't mind so much. For he is a good fellow and I was glad to know it wasn't some other good for nothing scamp.

Sunday, September 11, 1887.   Got up very late this morning as I did not wish to appear sleepy. Went up to meet the train. Andrew and Hargrave came. Uriah too came up. He came down to the house soon after. He brought Scribner's and paper I had ordered. We were much amused by the bird. He was very lively and not afraid of strangers. After dinner walked up to see the new church building. It rained a little. From there we went to Sunday School. Jennie wasn't there. Mrs Hunsberger came down and was here for supper.

Amelia was here to take the girl's place. We were very sorry we couldn't take the ride we had planned for this afternoon. After the boys left on the 6:17 train which was half an hour late I came home but not caring to read I wrote a letter to Jennie instead. Told her plainly I loved her. I wished to break the ice which it seemed could not be broken another way.

It is raining all evening.

Tuesday, September 13, 1887.   Caught a cold the other day and today it was very bad. Had a pain in the eyes and felt very dull.

Did not feel like working and passed the time the best I could by reading Thaddeus of Warsaw. I must confess another cause of not feeling very easy was in not having heard from J in answer to my letter. Of course she did not have time to write and will not write perhaps and that is what oppresses me. I sometimes blame myself for not seeing her about it and trusting something of such importance to a letter. It is said Sash Factory on the other side has been sold. Have not been able to learn at what price.

Wednesday, September 14, 1887.   Passed a very restless night. Was awake several times felt very dull this morning. It became better during the day and this evening I am much improved. My spirits were lightened very much by receiving at noon a letter from Jennie from which I am fain to take a very favorable meaning. I also feel justified in writing for owing to my foolishness she would have doubted me if I had spoken. She is afraid I will regret it. May God only make me worth of her!

Finished Thaddeus of Warsaw this afternoon. A very good story I think though I did not feel very well while reading it and frequently thought of other things.

The sale of the factory has it is thought gone to nothing. The fellow who wanted to buy is a rogue and ought to be punished. He talked big and was in bank, had plenty to drink and then wanted to borrow money of old Mr Moyer. That settled it.

Thursday, September 15, 1887.   Today was the commencement of the Constitutional Centennial at Philadelphia. Last evening the trains were full and this morning they were nearly all an hour or two behind time. It seemed as everybody was going. I would have liked to go but am afraid it will be crowed so that nothing could be seen.

Read the book Miss Barndt loaned me and was not much pleased with it. It is interesting enough if one has nothing else to do but you don't know more after you are through with it than before. Too sentimental, not descriptive and unreal. It is called "A Heart Twice Won."

Friday, September 16, 1887.   The Industrial Parade on Broad St., Phila. was the most imposing this country had ever seen. Col. A Louden Snowden was Chief Marshall. It took more than six hours to pass one point.

The Library this evening was neglected a little. Jennie came down with her brother Willis. She took I dont remember what along. Sent off Lesson 8 this afternoon.

Saturday, September 17, 1887. The military parade yesterday lasted nearly four hours. It was reviewed by Pres. Cleveland from the grand stand opposite the Lafayette Hotel. Mrs. Cleveland watched the procession from a balcony at the hotel. There were about 20,000 soldiers consisting of U.S. troops, the national guard of Penna. and other states, and the Grand Army of the Republic. The whole was led by Lieut. Gen. Sheridan. Gen. Hartranft was at the head of the Penna soldiers. Various governors took part in the parade at the head of their troops. Others sat on the grand stand behind the President. It was a grand sight. Sam and Elmer Weil went down this morning.

Went over to Jennie about eight. Talked over a subject this evening having an important bearing on the future of us both. Jennie I know loves me as I do her but she trembles for my constancy. May God help me and make me worthy of her who is far above in honor and virtue.

Sunday, September 18, 1887. Slept very little last night.

The cornerstone laying of the new church took place today. Walked up about ten. Quite a number of people there. Revs. Grubb and Dechant preached. Read the paper after dinner giving the concluding ceremonies in Phila yesterday. There was singing in Independance Square by 1000 boys and 200 men. Speech by Pres. Cleveland and oration by Justice Miller. The President was kept busy with receptions, banquets and so on. Mrs Cleveland was also much honored and some people went wild over her. They returned to Washington last evening.

Went up again about two. Met Clymer. Was with him most of the time. Dr Koplin preached the sermon. Dechant made an address. He is a great story teller. Very humorous. Dengler performed the ceremonies at the laying of the cornerstone. There was a great crowd. Jennie was up too in the afternoon. Went down to grandfathers from there. Staid for supper. Uncle Joes were there. And Aunt Kit. Came along down with the girls. They stopped in awhile.

Went over to Jennie. Arrived at an understanding. How fortunate am I in having won the love of a true girl who is just as I could have wished. I have often dreamed of such a happy condition though I scarcely hoped to realize it. Love is rare among women. It is rare among men. All look too much on individual gain or self regard.

Monday, September 19, 1887. Commenced Lesson 9 this afternoon. Finished Bookkeeping but could get no further as sleep rendered me powerless.

Am I not now the happiest lad in all these parts? And why should I not? Felt almost defiant at times. Yet it is wrong perhaps to rejoice much at what if it were God's will might be swept away.

Sam was a little angry with mother this evening for teasing him. She should not have been too rough on the boy. Yet he imagines himself wronged sometimes when no harm is intended. He cant help himself yet he is good at teasing others.

Tuesday, September 20, 1887.   A nice day. Very smoky. There must have been a fire somewhere.

Am not rid of my cold yet. Was at my lessons this afternoon and evening. It is about time that I go at it again in earnest. I must work now for I have something to work for.

Can't help wishing to read David Copperfield again. It is almost a year since I have read it and today it seems to be the best I have read. Some of its scenes and characters are so natural and true to life yet so pathetic that it is the height of enjoyment to think of it. I think nothing can equal Agnes the good and pure.

Wednesday, September 21, 1887.   Mrs Cleveland is said to have snubbed Gov & Mrs. Foraker of Ohio at the reception at the Academy of Music last Friday evening on account probably of the "battle flag" incident. I do not think this shows good breeding on her part.

After bank was up in the Hardware store where Jonathan and the others are at work on the stoves. Don't know how it is that I get so sleepy in the afternoons. Can't make much progress in my lessons in this way.

Elwood does not feel well and went home this morning. Grandfather H was here today. He was at work over in the field.

Received a short note from Jennie asking about a supposed introduction. Mrs Crouthamel wrote to her apologizing for having failed to recognize it. There was no such thing. Wrote her so and added some more.

Thursday, September 22, 1887.   It is very late having just got through with my lesson. I was terribly lazy about it today. I go to sleep before I think of it. Would have liked to send it off tomorrow morning but have to copy some yet. Rec'd a letter from Uriah this morning. Miss B. is down and keeps his pocket book low. I really begin to pity Uriah. He is spending his money for nothing. She is only making use of him. I think she has very little feeling for others.

Vina Ruth and Kate came down this evening. Vina stays over night. This kept me back but have made up again for it. Vina does not look well. Yet she is very cheerful.

Friday, September 23, 1887.   Weather very cold to what we have been accustomed.

Rec'd returns from Buffalo this morning. Sent off No. 9 this afternoon. Read some Titcombe's Letters. Wrote Uriah in answer to his of the 20th.

Vina Ruth here all day. She is gay as usual though there is a tinge of sadness about her. We talked over old times which she said were enjoyed by her very much indeed. I remember I used to watch them and wonder if I ever would enjoy life like they did. Now they are all scattered and could not be got together again. Some are dead, most of them married, some separated and so on.

Worked on the books awhile. It is very late 20 min of twelve. Time to go to bed.

Saturday, September 24, 1887. It was real cold today. Made a fire at the bank. It nearly smoked us out. Worked nearly two hours at it. Vina left this afternoon. Worked on the books. Emma Krupp was here with Vina this afternoon. Ellie Slifer came in for her this evening after she had left.

It is very late and I am tired and sleepy. Glad it's Sunday tomorrow.

Gave one of my pictures to Vina. Sent my watch to the watchmaker.

Sunday, September 25, 1887. Was very late for Sunday School this morning. Thought at first Jennie wasn't in but saw her toward the last. Went over to the Library with Jonathan and Mike. They think we ought to get up another play this winter. Took a short nap till dinner and read the Legend of Montrose. Henry Souder's came down soon after and grandfather S. They brought a little daughter along. Held her for about 15 min. She is named Mabel. Vina came in during the afternoon. They all staid for supper. Had a right good time. Preston and Lillie were down. Preston is very tall and Lillie stout and large for her age.

Got ready early. Heard Jennie was in meeting this afternoon. Went over before 7:30. Schwenck's had gone to meeting on the hall. She had been reading David Crockett and told me about it. I must read it too. Used to be prejudiced against the book. Curious but she still mistrusted me. She says I'm young and the chances are against it. But I know the reason. I am too cold. It is all too new to me and it'll take awhile to mould me into it. Could she only know that I am resolved to have her and no other. She said she **would** trust me at last.

Wednesday, September 28, 1887. The Volunteer was victorious over the Thistle in the first race yesterday. The Thistle was almost 20 min behind. The next race will be sailed on Thursday. The winds were light and it was pronounced a regular Thistle day.

Woodward was yesterday nominated for Prothonotary at the Republican county convention. Swartz received the nomination for Judge. It was a little rainy all day. Received returns from Buffalo this evening. He gets down on my writing. Almost discouraging but I don't practice enough.

Have a pretty hard lesson in Commercial Law this week.

Thursday, September 29, 1887.   Kate and the Gentsch girls were here last evening. She had come to ask Vina to go along to Lansdale. I told them the train was here at 9:33 and Kate said it was 9:06. I did not give up but today I found I was wrong.

Am retarded in my lessons by these blamed good books. Can't hardly keep away from the Legend of Montrose. Capt Dalgetty is very funny. It's a good thing I 'm almost through.

A G Stover had an auction last evening.

Friday, September 30, 1887.   Vina came back from Lansdale last evening. She was here during the day and went to several places on a short visit. She is very cheerful even gay at times. Sam and myself were shooting a little in the morning when she came out and laughed at us. Of course I tried to show her what I could do and no sparrows being in sight I fired at an apple and cut out a piece without the apple falling. She would not believe it though I showed her the piece and a caterpiller who had unfortunately been killed. We laughed long and loud at my marksmanship. She left this evening with her brother Will who took her to her sister's from whence they will go to Quakertown. It is still raining. The yacht race did not come off yesterday. Too foggy. Got a new suit this evening. Cutaway. First I had of the kind. Sam got a new suit and overcoat. Very fine. The overcoat does not fit too well.

Wanted to finish my lesson this evening but I couldn't do it. Clymer thought the Library was open this evening so I went down with him to get him another book. Had a pleasant talk with him. Worked pretty late. Am glad it's as far as it is.

Saturday, October 1, 1887.   The final yacht race came off yesterday and the Volunteer was again a winner. The wind blew half a gale and they were not bothered by excursion boats this time. The Volunteer crossed the finishing line 12 min before the Thistle being 2½ miles ahead of her. This time it is decisive.

There was a sale down at John C Moyer's for the farm and everything. Heard the farm was sold.

Saw the great frames for the new church today. They'll look grand. There was rain nearly all day but it cleared off this evening. Sent off Lesson 10 with this evening's mail. Have some copying to do yet this evening.

Must go down and work some on the books.

Sunday, October 2, 1887.   Tried to sleep very late this morning but couldn't. Missed breakfast, however. Uriah came up with the train and came down soon after. At noon Miss L and Rufus came down to fetch him to dinner. I was not dressed yet and had no collar on but didnt care much. We sang, "I'se gwine back to Dixie." Dressed after dinner. Uriah came down. Sam and myself went to Sunday School and Uriah, home. Sunday School very full. Milt Moyer and wife were there. Saw Jennie. She said Anna Lapp would be there. I could not go because the horse was taken by parents. Arranged to go to meeting this evening. Walked up to find Uriah. We took a walk uptown with him to see the new church. There were lots of girls with Kate; Lillie, Martha and the Magargles.

Went over a quarter of seven. Milt opened the door and talked with him a while. Jennie came down soon ready to go. It was full when we came but she chanced to find a seat yet. There were a great many outside. Rev Mr Funk from Indiana preached. Was glad when it was over. Never passed a more agreeable evening. Never until this evening could I feel that she is really mine. We are doing away with that reserve gradually which would have to be done away with sooner or later.

Monday, October 3, 1887.   Cleared off today or this evening rather. Fell back in my work today. Had so many notes to time. Wrote out the bookkeeping lesson and practised some writing. Did not trust myself to studing as I would be sure to fall asleep.

Uriah went down this morning. Ordered Scribner's for Oct. Poor little Robbie, our bird, got the slip today and flew off. He is not fit to be free. Too tame. Sure to be caught. Had much with him at times.

Tuesday, October 4, 1887.   Had a good sleep last night. Wasn't quite through this morning. Was pretty busy at bank today.

The Presidential party arrived at St Louis late on Saturday night. Yesterday he held a reception, went to the fair ground etc. Did my copying this afternoon. Work on the lesson goes slow. Mr. Godshall came over this evening with and old book written in the Hollandish language. We got to talking about things and it was eight before he left. He gave me the whole history of the New Mennonite Church.

Received Scribner's from Uriah.

Robbie was seen today. He flew on Mrs E B Slifer's head twice and ate some starch. He must have been very hungry. Wish we had the little fellow again.

Wednesday, October 5, 1887.   Mr Metz surprised me this morning by asking me to bring Jennie to their place some time. They had a teacher boarding with them by the name of Sadie Slough who would like to see her. He had brought her grandmother along over. I think she must have told about it.

Kate and Hannah were down this afternoon and for supper. Kate surprised me most off all by whispering that L. was "mashless" since Sunday evening. Adding in a general way that if I ever got tired of some one else I could &c. Ah, if Kate only knew she wouldn't talk that way. And if Jennie had heard it she wouldn't like Kate the better. But I wonder what it means. I sometimes think that Rufus is behind it all. I don't believe she would have made short work of him if she hadn't an eye on someone else. Finished my arithmetic this evening. It was a nuisance.

Thursday, October 6, 1887.   Pleasant weather today. Many went to the Doylestown Fair. Work was commenced on the church yesterday by the bricklayers.

Finished Titcombe's Letters yesterday and some other book Legend of Montrose last week I think. October's Scribner's had the last of the Thackeray Letters.

Am very unfortunate with my watch just now. Broke the main spring last evening.

Now I have it for certain. Met Rufus this afternoon and he told me he would stop any time down there, pointing to the cowpath. It's an understood thing between him and Lillie. I think it must be true that she put a stop to Gerhart for Mr. L says it's all right with them.

Have only the copying to do for the Commercial Law lesson and the Penmanship. Got returns today. The boys went to a husking.

Friday, October 7, 1887.   Was very busy all day. Fell behind with my work at bank but caught up again. Did some copying and then went up to the watchmaker's with my watch. Took a look at the new church. It'll make a very neat little church.

Went down to the schoolhouse and got things in order. Went down again a quarter after seven. It was the stockholder's meeting. All the old officers were re-elected with the exception of Jonathan who is succeded by Mike. Jennie was not down. She sent her sister Katie instead. She didn't like to stay long I suppose. Finished Comm. Law after I got home.

Saturday, October 8, 1887.   A very warm day for October. Finished lesson 11 this afternoon. Cleaned the yard afterwards.

Frick came up this evening. Spoke a few words with him.

Mr Wm K Moyer had a cornhusking today. They took a load of girls over to Blooming Glen. This evening they brought them back to Freed's Hotel where a frolic is now in progress.

Promised Aug. Thomas to go up to Tylersport next week to get the sizes for shutters for him. Didn't like it but couldn't get out of it; then I thought perhaps Jennie would go along. But I hardly expect she will. Read a little in Lessons in Life by Halland. Must write to Horace yet.

Sunday, October 9, 1887.   Got up pretty late all of us. Commenced reading the Heart of Midlothian. Took a nap in the forenoon and yet I was sleepy all day. Walked up to the new church with Sam before dinner. Frick came over after dinner and we fooled round on the organ till it was time to go to meeting. Went there. Not very full. Walked up town from there. Back again and over to the governor's. Promised the gov. to come over tomorrow evening to help arrange the Sunday School books. Started to go over about half past seven. Met Lillie and Amelia in front of out gate. Offered to escort L. home. Did so. She said I wasn't to tell J. This was the first thing I did. Told her about L and Rufus. She was surprised. They came back from their visit about six this evening. We had a very pleasant time though I think she was a little tired from her trip. She promised to go with me up to Tylersport on Tuesday afternoon. Very kind of her for I dont know what I would have done about it.

Tuesday, October 11, 1887. The weather today was cold and damp and very unpleasant. So wrote a note to Jennie saying we'd try it on Thursday. It was very disappointing.

Received a letter from Uriah. Answered it this evening. He says his eyes are very weak, and that the doctors say they will have to make him blind for two days to get them all right.

Mailed the letter to Horace I had commenced on Saturday evening.

Spoke to Rufus. He cant help referring to L. He says he will write his old one this week that he wont come any more. He said if he'd go for L it would be only for a while &c.

Wednesday, October 12, 1887. A new messenger for the bank, Wm. Baum, by name, was here today for the first time. He is a great talker.

The weather has cleared off but it is much colder. Adam Holly died yesterday of dropsy.

Recd returns from Buffalo this evening. Have all the lessons finished except Penmanship and Comm. Law.

Met Dr Slifer in the store this afternoon.

Thursday, October 13, 1887. Got through in good time this afternoon. Went over to Jennie's to see if she was ready. She was, and I went for the team. It was just fine for driving and it we enjoyed it I think. But I could feel that there was something wrong.

She didn't exactly approve of my taking Lillie home and yet she wouldn't say it was wrong. When we came up to Tylersport she said she'd stay on the carriage till I came out. Got through as soon as I could and we started home. Drove slow and didn't come home till seven. I think I understand what she means. I must do away with this secrecy. It must seem like reluctance to acknowledge her on my part. Gave mother to understand that I liked her and so but did not tell her we were engaged. Couldn't do any work any more. I was too sleepy.

Friday, October 14, 1887. Cold again this morning. O, what a hypocite I am. Saw Jennie while I was crossing the street and she over on the porch but I pretended not to see her. There's nothing in it at all and I must try and get rid of it.

This afternoon on going home from bank I saw Hen. Bilger walk out toward the shop. Went out and found that Will had died last evening. Poor boy! He has seen much trouble already. It was very sudden. I had not heard from him. Went up to Daub's to order his attendance and got the measure for the grave. Father will attend to that. The funeral will be on Monday. Finished my Penmanship and wrote out Commercial Law on the Slate ready for copying. It is 20 min past 11.

Saturday, October 15, 1887.   Got along very slow with my work today. After we were through this afternoon I finished my lesson and sent it off and afterwards cleaned the yard.

Read some afterward but did not accomplish much as I was too sleepy.

Sunday, October 16, 1887.   Lay in — I mean, I tried to sleep right long and for that purpose staid in bed to give myself a chance. But it seems I cant sleep late in the morning. But before I went down stairs father, mother and grandparents had left for Ephraim Stovers near Dublin. Elwood was still later. Read a little in Lessons in Life. Went up to the new church with Sam after dinner. From there to Sunday School. We were early. It soon filled up. When J came I thought I'd speak to her but she gave me no chance. The house was crowded.

When I came over this evening we soon got to talking over Thursday. I saw now where my fault lay. In public I seemed to avoid her while I felt under no restraint toward others. If Lillie ever thought I paid her more attentions than I would any other girl, she shall not hereafter for she'll find a difference. Jennie's school begins tomorrow.

Monday, October 17, 1887.   Got ready this morning for the funeral and went up to bank and worked till near nine. The body and mourners arrived at 8:53. The procession formed and proceeded immediately to the church. Dengler preached in English and German. I was surprised to hear that he was exactly a year older than myself. The body was wasted away to a skeleton and I would never have known him I think.

Did but little on my lessons today.

Was up at grandfather H's this evening. Spoke to lots of Bilgers. Most of them went home with the eight o'clock train. Was at the station to see them off.

Tuesday, October 18, 1887.   Mrs. John Souder and Will Bilger's widow were here today. I tried to talk a little but it didn't go. She is to be pitied. Little Sallie is very shy. She wanted to be coaxed a little. The noise of the children made mother very tired. Looked at the frame work for the church. Started in late at my lesson this afternoon. Arithmetic, those Equation of Accounts are very unpleasant.

Recd a letter from Uriah. He wants to go chestnutting on Sunday. His eyes are operated upon. It is very late. Must go to bed. Tomorrow Mr Landes and myself will be alone in bank.

Wednesday, October 19, 1887.   We were alone. I mean John was not at bank today but down at Norristown in connection with the Landis case which was settled today. She will move in two months and is allowed to take away the stuff belonging to her nursery.

We got through in good time. Rufus Landes was out to help a little.

Finished letterwriting and did my copying this afternoon. Saw Jennie pass from my window. She spoke to Mr Godshall.

Grandmother and little Stella were here this afternoon. Had her upstairs but couldn't work and so took her down. She keeps one busy.

Have to write Uriah yet.

Thursday, October 20, 1887.   Went up to the watchmaker's for my g. watch and left the other. He was surprised that the other mainspring was broke too. It was raining and as I did not yet get my lesson, I had nothing to do but study Comm. Law; this I found hard to do as I was continually thinking of something else. Went down to the schoolhouse to bring the Pres. report to Jonathan. Jennie was nearly through and I walked with her. She said the fire was all made and coal up on Monday morning when she came down. It is very kind of him but it wont last long I think. Read lessons in Life and slept most of the time.

Friday, October 21, 1887.   This morning Mr Gerhart, Mr Godshall, John, and Ed went out and decided what Mrs Landis may take away.

Didn't get anything done this afternoon again. Returns from Buffalo are not here and I wont get no lesson ready this week. Mrs Will Bilger and Sarah Ann were here this afternoon. I am to take them down to the church tomorrow afternoon. Read Heart of Mid Lothian.

Most of the officers were sworn in this evening excepting Appenzeller who was not here. Clymer was up. Gehman was here pretty early. J. dont come down herself. Mike was down and took charge of the Secretaryship.

Saturday, October 22, 1887.   Got through about half past two this afternoon. Elwood got the team ready and before three Mrs John Souder, Mrs Will Bilger and little Mary and myself were on our way to Leidy's cemetery to see Will's grave. We placed two beautiful bouquets on the grave. We reached home in time for them to make the 3:49 train.

Cleaned the yard and then went up to see how they were getting on at the church. Part of the frame work is up but it will take awhile before the roof is on.

Felt like going over to see Jennie and there was no reason why I should except other people's talk I concluded to set it at defiance and go. Met Mrs. Slifer on my way over but she didn't know me. I was unexpected but none the less welcome, I hope. Jennie has an invitation to a party to given Kate next Thursday evening. Arranged to go to church tomorrow evening. Left about ten.

Sunday, October 23, 1887.   Came down very late this morning. Went up to hunt Uriah. Found W. B Slifer's at Wm's. They promised to come down for dinner. Took a walk with Uriah to the new church, then to the Mennonite graveyard, and then to the schoolhouse for a book. Uriah wrote on the blackboard. He wanted to put my name on too but I didn't let him.

Found Slifer's here when I came home. They are cheerful. He has a new business, that of mirror-making. Father and Mr S went to meeting. I staid at home and tried to read a little of Heart of Midlothian but didn't get much done. Went up to Uriah after Slifer's left. Told him I'd be down at the church and he said he'd come too. Sam took the girl over to Harleysville this afternoon. He got the team ready for me. Was ready at seven. Got to the church at 7:30. Services had commenced. There must have been a mistake in the paper. Reiter preached on Preparing for Life in English. Uriah and Miss B were there, but did not see them till after the service. Jennie invited them along up and they accepted. Drove pretty fast coming home. Had a pleasant time. Had to laugh at Uriah. Then left about ten. Jennie was in meeting today. She heard Mr Bean was getting a suit made at Harleysville. I know what that means.

Tuesday, October 25, 1887.   Finished Bookkeeping No. 13 this evening late. Walked up and saw the new church. They are at work on the roof.

Finished Bookkeeping No. 13.

Wednesday, October 26, 1887.   Had first class luck with balancing today. Wasn't any thing too early however. Saw Miss Zendt this afternoon. She called to me from Wm's yard. She asked if we were coming to the party. I said we were. Asked her who all was invited. She said not many in town, some from Telford and so on.

Didnt get much done on my lesson. Read some Heart of Midlothian.

Thursday, October 27, 1887.   The weather today was foggy but it did not interfere with the party this evening. Went over to Jennie's about a quarter of eight. Mother chides me for pulling on my best suit in the evening and during the week. Jennie thought there was no hurry about going, so we waited till after eight when we went. The room was crowded and they were still waiting on Mr Crouthamel and Martha. Uriah, Clymer, Jonathan, Mike, Cal, Mr Gerhart, Mr Bean, Will Hunsberger and myself were in the parlor with the Magargles and Jennie. It was nine o'clock before we could start. Kate who must have heard of it before was dressed and laughed when we came in. The fires were speedily set a agoing and we settled down as well as we could. I was surprised to see the famous Gerhart girls there. Miss B. caught a cold on Sunday night and has it as bad as I. Mr Saml Musselman came about ten. He's a handy fellow at the games. Miss Lukens and Miss Maggie Souder gave some music. Afterwards we played fruit basket. Then drunken sailor. We had that going in two rooms. Then Bingo in two rooms. Miss Moore, Miss Zendt, Mr Gerhart and Jonathan then prepared the table. They brought in the bows and ribbons; Jennie drew Cal. I matched Amelia. Kate had Penrose, Miss Barndt, Rufus, Martha, Crouthamel, (foul play), Uriah I think had Maggie and so on. J. was at the first and I at the second table. We played Drunken Sailor like mad. It is exciting. I knew Jennie didn't care about staying so late. But we didn't get away till after one. I was a little too wild I know, but she said there was nothing wrong. If I only knew what she thinks. She is going away on Saturday morning. She promised to write on Sunday evening.

Friday, October 28, 1887.   Goettler came in this morning and wanted to know about the party. Told him there were about 35 or 40 present. Hadn't counted. Kate told me this afternoon there were 28. She knew all about it but tried to act as if she were surprised but had to laugh. She found out through appearances. Some teased her a little and little by little she knew all. Didn't feel a bit sleepy till this evening.

Dont know how it is but 13 **does** seem to be an unlucky number. I cant get through with this lesson 13. Got through Penmanship this afternoon. Watched for Jennie most of the time but watched in vain. She goes away tomorrow.

Saturday, October 29, 1887.   Was a little late this morning as I had to do a little writing for father. When the 7:39 went down I walked over to the station as I thought Jennie would perhaps go with that train; but she didn't. Went over again before the 9:06 and had the satisfaction almost unexpectedly of seeing her. Was tongue tied of course else I could have expressed my wish that should have a good time and so on. Grandmother was down when I came home. She thinks Martha too is settled on Crouthamel. Surprising that how all these people are mating. Sam and Zuschnitt were shooting sparrows this afternoon. I shot above and missed it. Worked out Lesson 14 in Bookkeeping and let Com Law alone. Will Benner and one Wampole were arrested for assault and battery today. They had to pay out to save themselves.

Sunday, October 30, 1887.   Charley Frick came up last evening. Read Heart of Midlothian. I could almost weep with Effie Deans on reading her trial.

Frick came over this afternoon. He is all wise as usual. Showed me how to set down a hat and other valuable information. We walked uptown to the new church. After that I got the carriage ready to go to Rickert's and he left me. Went out to aunt Kit's where Cal., Jonathan, Mike, Rufus and Morris Weil were playing cards. Took grandmother up home. She thought it rode easy in my carriage. Amelia was ready and off we started about five. It was quite cold. Found Kate at home. Rickert was milking. The old people weren't at home. They milk 15 cows. Very nice place. Rickert had two sisters and a younger brother. The beau of the younger of the two ladies came while we were at the supper table and took her away. We had a real good time. We sang and played my old pieces which passed for new with time. Was a little too jolly perhaps. When the young lady returned had to play again. Then the old folks came. Had to go at it again till I was really tired out. Wondered whether Jennie was writing something and thinking on [illegible] in bed. Wish she had been there.

Monday, October 31, 1887.   The weather is very much colder than it was of late. It felt like winter this morning. The teachers flocked to Doylestown and Norristown this morning as both institutes are in session this week.

Jonas Hackman was so drunk on Sat. eve that he would have perhaps killed his boy had he not been rescued.

Wenhold was down today and we mentioned something about the temperance question and he got nearly wild; no reason in him.

Uriah sent me the Nov. number of Scribner's today.

Worked on the books and did but little on my lessons.

Was sorely disappointed for I expected a letter from Jennie this eve but didn't get it. Perhaps she had no time to write. Must write Andrew and Uriah.

Tuesday, November 1, 1887.   I dont know why on earth Jennie dont write. Nothing this morning, nothing at nine, nothing at 1:25, and now Sam calls up after the last mail went, "Nothing but the Weekly News." Hang the Weekly News! No doubt she has good reasons and all that but I cant see them at this distance. I asked her to write more than once and she promised to write on Sunday evening. It dont take three days to carry a letter from Norristown. She'd feel very much hurt if I did so to her, and I'd just like to have her here to tell her so. It makes me almost too angry to study. Will write a few letters and so on and then go down and read Heart of Midlothian or something of the kind. Blame the thing. I don't want to be angry all the time. Perhaps it's because of the temperance question but if that's so I dont think this is the way to punish me for it. The letter might been lost but I dont believe it.

Wednesday, November 2, 1887.   Received the nicest little letter from Jennie this morning. It was written on Monday evening. She had written on Sunday evening but left the letter at Miss Mosers. She stays at a Mrs. Coe's. Enjoying herself. Answered her letter at noon. The mails between here and Norristown go slow I think. Got through with our work finely today thought I was late at noon. Read the Heart of Midlothian this afternoon and what is more remarkable I finished lesson 13, the greatest sticker I had yet. It wasn't any harder only I did not get at it.

A sad accident happened at Fair Hill today. Mr Curtis' little girl accidentally shot herself with a revoler that had been given her by her mother to play with. Mr Hollenbach had assured her it was not loaded. Mr H was at bank today and told the story allmost broke down.

Thursday, November 3, 1887.   The U.S. Supreme Court has refused the writ of error for the Chicago Anarchists and they must hang on the 11th.

Madame Jenny Lind Goldschmidt better known as Jenny Lind died yesterday, 66 yrs old. She was one the greatest singers who ever lived.

The Curtis girl is doing very well. The wound is but slight.

The bank examiner was here today and kept us busy. He went away at three.

Read Heart of Midlothian and studied but little.

Friday, November 4, 1887.   Weather was again very warm today but it changed to cold this evening.

Reviewed letter-writing — or rather punctuation this afternoon. Went to the schoolhouse and made fire and put things in order; but when I came down later the fire was out and it became cold.

Received a letter from Jennie this evening; she wrote most of it at the lecture last evening. She says she is glad it's nearly over. She expects to start for home tomorrow morning.

Sunday, November 6, 1887.   Read Heart of Midlothian and finished it this afternoon. Mr & Mrs Henry Shueck and their two boys paid us a visit today. Did not get to meeting this afternoon. Walked up to the church with Sam after I was through my book. The roof is finished and half of the floor is laid. Our girl made a change today; last evening Leidy stopped, I believe, and Harvey Sell started this evening.

Went over to Jennies about 7:30. She was glad to get home. She thought if I had cared much to come I might have come last evening. Had a good time. She has a cold. Am rid of mine, I think. She staid with Miss Moser two days Sat. and Sunday and at a Mrs Coe's the rest of the week. Miss Kate Hoffman (Countess Vere de Vere) was with her all the time.

Monday, November 7, 1887.   Felt a little sleepy this morning. Last night when I came home I got in through the window. Amanda came out the room rubbing her sleepy eyes to see what was the matter. She lighted the lamp for she had none before and I walked in and saw Sell just half awake rubbing his eyes. Had no business in there and hurried to bed. Elwood wasnt home till two. Too late for the boy.

Great excitement prevails on account of the Chicago Anarchists. Great pressure is placed on the Governor to commute the sentence. Dynamite bombs were found in the jail with them.

Didn't get much done this afternoon. Was engaged on a letter to Jennie containing nothing but nonsense.

Saw Jennie pass this morning and again this evening.

Tuesday, November 8, 1887.   Today was election day. Mr Landes went over before dinner. We went over about five. Davy and Reub went along. It was the first time I ever voted. Busy Bury was about when we came over. I avoided him and thought we could get tickets elsewhere. I hate these heelers at an election. Father went for tickets but by the time he returned Reub had got tickets from Bury. Voted the straight Republican ticket this time. It was as follows as near as I can remember: Hart, State Treas.; Williams, Supreme

Court; Swartz, Additional Law Judge; Woodward, Prothonotary; and so on. This is probably the last time Souderton votes at the Square.

One of the Anarchists had attempted suicide on Sat eve. They are now strictly guarded.

Wednesday, November 9, 1887.   Results of the elections: Swartz, Judge, 800 or so; Woodward defeated by 80; the rest of the Repub. ticket elected. Bucks, Repub by a small maj. except Register which is in doubt. Andrew Hartzel was running on the Dem. side.

Phila., Rep. as usual excepting Sheriff and Controller. Leeds one of the bosses was defeated. They did their best to slip him in. But the Independents were too much for him.

New York is Dem. by about 10 or 12000. Fred Grant for Sec. of State is defeated. In N.Y. City none but the Reg. Dem. were elected. A strong effert was made to elect Mr. Nicoll who was supported by Reps and Ind. Dems. George pulled a light vote.

Worked on the lessons this afternoon. The Anarchists have almost given up all hope. They are kept under the strictest surveillance.

Thursday, November 10, 1887.   I doubt if all the Anarchists will be hung. Judge Gary spoke a good word for Fielden I believe. They are trying to make out Linng insane.

Worked on my lessons. A little behind perhaps.

Recd a letter from Uriah. He hasn't any thing to say.

Jennie wrote about my sheet full of nonsense. She thought I was in earnest. Wrote it was all waste paper.

Friday, November 11, 1887.   The Gov. of Illinois commuted the sentences of Schwab and Fielden to life imprisonment. All the others must hang. Lingg committed suicide yesterday by means of a cap of eulminate of mercury I think they called it. He placed it in his mouth and lighted the fuse. It exploded and his face was all torn up into an unrecognizable mass. He died six hours afterward. He was conscious and wrote in German with his right hand what he wanted. There was an exciting time in Chicago today no doubt. These executions have been the topics of conversation for over a week.

It snowed a little today. Wrote for R Grant White's edition of Shakespeare to Perkinpine & Higgins. I intend it for a Christmas present for Jennie.

Am almost over my 14th lesson.

Saturday, November 12, 1887.   The four Chicago Anarchists were hanged yesterday as high as Haman. They died glorying in their murderous principle and showing no compunction for their terrible deed. Engel and Fisher shouted "Hurrah for Anachy," the latter adding; "This is the happiest moment of my life;" Parsons wanted to speak and shouted, "Hear the voice of the people," but before he could add more the crash came and all four were flung into eternity. Spies said something to the effect that they would be sorry for this. The jail was guarded by 300 armed policemen, and the militia and regular troops were ready to attack at a moments notice. No disturbance occured.

There is a rumor that Woodward was elected. Sent off lesson 14 this evening.

Received an invitation to a surprise party to be given to Martha on Thursday evening. The invitation comes from Line Lexington written, I think, by Clymer. We are going to have lots of them this winter if it keeps on in this way. Bought a new hat this evening. Cleaned the yard this afternoon. Was very tired and sleepy.

Sunday, November 13, 1887.   All the others went to Leidy's Church this morning where there were communion services by the Ref. Uriah came down about eleven and we walked up town to the church and then looked at Harvey Souder's concern. Ben Alderfer has bought the sash factory I hear. Walked on to J D Moyer's house but couldnt get in. Promised him to go to church this afternoon with him but dinner was too late. Hen. Bilger's and Will's widow, Sarah and grandparents were here this afternoon. Took grandmother home in the carriage. Read Washburne's Remiscenses of the "Downfall of the Empire" and the "Seige of Paris" in Scribner's.

Went over at 7:30. She was much vexed with me or herself for having misunderstood my letter this week. She'd like to have her letter back the letter I liked so well. She would rather not go to the party but there was no way of getting out of it so she thought we'd have to go. Had a good time. It seems a very short time to be together only once a week.

Monday, November 14, 1887.   Finished Bookkeeping No. 15. Was pretty sleepy this evening.

The German Crown Prince is said to have a similar throat disease to Gen Grant. The doctors say there is no hope for him. He is staying at St Remo in Italy. With the old Emperor on the brink of the grave and the death of the Crown Prince so near the attention of the world is drawn to young Prince William who will soon be at the head of the strongest nation in Europe. Received the new Shakespeare this morning. It is a nice set of books.

Tuesday, November 15, 1887.   Was very busy at bank today. Did not get out till half past four. Finished Letter Writing and Arithmetic. I would like to get my lesson off in spite of the fact that I will lose two evenings the latter part of the week.

Wednesday, November 16, 1887.   Finished all the lessons but Comm. Law. I think I'll get No 15 ready this week.

Spoke to Kate today a few minutes. She says she isn't certain whether she'll go to the party. Read the first part of Seth's Brother's Wife. That's as good as any.

The bank will have trouble with old Mrs Landes. She dug up 21 cherry trees which she had been forbidden to disturb. She will be dealt with according to law.

Thursday, November 17, 1887.   Went over to Jennie's soon after eight. We or I rather — would have preferred to stay there. But we started about half past nine eight? and were the last couple to arrive. There were some Lexington boys who came in late. It was after nine o'clock when the procession started at W A Crouthamel's. We met the Stocking factory boys who had been working late and who were going home at the time. When we came Martha was in bed. We had to wait awhile on the porch. We had a very good time afterwards. There were about 35 in all half of whom came from Lexington. It broke up a little before one.

Friday, November 18, 1887.   Of course I felt a little weaker than usual today. Finished lesson 15 and sent it off this evening. Spoke to Ed about the party. He was well pleased said they behaved well and so on. He compared us favorably to the time when he was young.

Library open this evening. Attendance slim. Spoke to Jonathan about a play or something. He said he wouldn't mind. Jennie brought Miss Heebner along down the teacher of the lower school.

Saturday, November 19, 1887.   Worked on the books a little this evening but near as much as I ought. Got to reading David Copperfield and couldn't stop. Of course I only read at random as I had read it before.

Sunday, November 20, 1887.   Read till dinner time. Dressed after dinner and went to meeting with Sam. Rev. Abram Moyer preached.

After that walked up to the new church. Stopped in at grandfather's on the way home.

Aunt Kit and Penrose came on a visit this evening.

Started away a little after 7:30. Jennie is much interested in 'Hypatia.' I fear I was a little too sleepy to be bright. Of course I didn't sleep nothing of the kind. When I was ready to go home Jennie with all her might tried to help me into Milt's overcout. Of course it was a mistake.

Monday, November 21, 1887.   Mother tells me Lillie and Maggie were here last evening to wait on Aunt Kit. Glad I wasn't at home.

Commenced lesson 16 with a heavy heart. Would much rather read instead.

Guess everybody is tired of "John Brown's Body" by this time.

Tuesday, November 22, 1887.   It is said that Will Ruth and Ellie Slifer, and Sam Brey and Hannah Roth are to be married on Thursday. Getting brisk. Mr Moyer is out of patience with his carpenters. He says they are a sorry set, or something to that effect.

There was a very noisy procession in the street this evening. Some medicine quack is around and he sent the boys with torch, banner, and bells around town to wake the people up. And they did so. Rev. Mr Aker was around today on account of their church collecting to pay the lot. Guess they want to build someday.

Wednesday, November 23, 1887.   Didnt get through till half past four this afternoon. Thought I'd slip through about cleaning tomorrow but Greaser asked me before I got quite home. It would have been fine if he hadnt said anything for then Id have the whole day. Didn't get anything done but reading. Was in the store this evening and spent some time there. Al Fretz leaves on New Years. He won't say where he is going.

Thursday, November 24, 1887.   Got up about half past eight being determined to be late about the bank cleaning. Then when I wanted to put on my old coat a mouse jumped out of it. I closed the door and window and told mother who said the mouse must be captured dead or alive. We went at it and when the mouse ran across the floor I saw mother dance for the first time. She got on the bed then till mousy was dead.

Helped up at the bank till one o'clock. Read the paper till two. (There is a cabinet crisis in France and they want the president to resign.) Found grandmother at home. Sat around till after three. Got dressed sometime after four. Walked up to the new church and climed up on the tower. They are putting on the roof. Then at my lessons.

Sam Brey and Will Ruth were married today. Ruth's went to Scranton.

Friday, November 25, 1887.   Was very busy at bank today. Got through very well however. The sheriff was today put on Mrs Landis on account of these trees. Mr Gerhart was in Norristown about the matter today.

Finished Letterwriting and Penmanship No. 16 today but went to sleep over the Comm. Law lesson.

Answered Uriah's letter of Tuesday. He is coming up on Dec. 21. He says Os. Kline is married to Maria Rondenbush. I was surprised to hear it. I thought he could do better. There is no doubt he has the best of them but then —

A most disgraceful thing occurred last night. There was plenty of beer at Freed's on account of the weddings and someone besmeared Ed's office door with filth. Ed was very angry this morning. He heard something about Elwood and went down and asked him about it. He only insulted him. I talked to Elwood, but it's all unfair.

Saturday, November 26, 1887.   I wanted Elwood to go and apolgize to Ed but he said he wouldn't. These blamed little Stovers think it beneath their dignity to apologize when wrong. These boys are getting to rough and they ought to be put down. I dont believe Elwood would do such dirty work but he is out too late entirely. They make nothing of them selves but unmannerly dogs.

Worked on my Com. Law this afternoon and got it written out but only half copied. It's 9:30 and Ill go to bed.

But the greatest event of all came off this afternoon. I believe. Sam Young was married to some foolish enough women.

Sunday, November 27, 1887.   Passed the laziest day for a long time. Finished copying my lesson this morning. It's a shame to work on Sunday but I cant get it ready else. Father and mother went to Fred Hunsberger's.

Amanda had a friend of hers for dinner. In the afternoon four more came but I did not see them being upstairs. Read just a little David Copperfield.

Sam and I walked uptown to the church. This was the only time we were out all day. It was a warm day for this time of the year. Went over at 7:30. Jennie had been along up to the Rocks with Milt and his wife. They had a good time. Ed's were there. Had a pleasant time but she called me a tease. I deserved it. Here I go to sleep while writing this on Monday evening.

Monday, November 28, 1887.   Rainy weather today. Very cold in the West. It's likely it'll be cold by tomorrow here.

Borneman said old John Binder would preach on Tyson's Hall this evening. Wenhold was in at the time and gave us one of his lectures; denouncing the the priests as he called them. He is a queer fellow. We complimented him and said he could beat old Binder all to pieces and so on. Mother told me this afternoon that Kate Souder would be married in a few weeks, though it's a secret yet.

The boys went to a show going on on the hall.

Worked on my lessons. Very sleepy toward the last and when I came to my senses I was down stairs at a loss what I wanted just as Sam came home. I made out that I had fallen asleep and when I woke my lamp was burned out and the room dark. Feeling cold I had come down to warm myself.

Tuesday, November 29, 1887.   Weather changed to very cold. There is a change of more than 30 degrees since yesterday. President Grevy of France has announced that he will resign. He will send in his message on Thursday. On Friday an election will be held for President. Meanwhile all parties are watching events. The Orleanists, for a chance of placing a king on the throne of France. The Bonapartists would like it too. The Anarchists and Communists would do away with government altogether. Anything might happen out there.

Worked on my lessons this afternoon.

Read some David Copperfield.

Wednesday, November 30, 1887.   Kate tapped the window this morning as I came out of bank. Turning I saw Ed Danley there. Ran over and found he had stopped here over night on a flying trip he had been making. Rufus had managed to put the blame on me for our failiure to come over. He went away on the 9:24 train. Half promised him to come sometime this winter. Jacob Sharp, the old rat, has been granted a new trial by the Court of Appeals.

Mother told me a little more of Kate's wedding arrangements. They will be married here at the house by Dengler. She will hardly get ready she thinks. When I expressed surprise that the wedding dress isn't to be white I was reproved by her. Lillie Zendt is to help make it. She is to take some part in the ceremony too.

A fellow from the city is to be bestman or something. Mrs. Ellis and Mrs Landis to be cooks. I am to be I don't know what and so on. Uriah and Miss B will be invited and so will Martha. That's all I'll write down for the present.

Rec'd a letter from Jennie this morning. She read "Taming of the Shrew" because I said she reminded me of one. Wrote an answer late tonight in fact it was half past twelve when I got to bed.

Worked on the books mostly this evening.

Thursday, December 1, 1887.   Very cold again today. We were alone in bank today. John moved into his new house. Mahlon Stover takes his place in the other. Lewis Wagner's moved in the Railroad Co's house opposite us, today.

We were very busy all day. I didn't get after with my work. Wenhold came and we balanced late.

Did a little on the lesson and a little on the books.

After supper went up to the watchmaker's. Sam went up with me and we arranged he should stop in on his way home. There was a young fellow there wanting to barter a gun. He wants to go shooting on Sat. and wants his own breech loader. But the best he could do was to borrow H's gun. He made a great to do. Don't know whether it was pride or what that he didn't want to use anyone else's gun. Sam came in before he was through and so I couldn't say what I wanted. I looked at some sleeve buttons and wrote on a card that I wanted to know about a ring and slipped it in his hands. He took the hint and called me into another room where I looked over a catalogue. Didn't choose but he said he's get some up. I guess Sam wondered what was up.

Friday, December 2, 1887.   President Grevy of France did not resign yesterday as he had announced. There is consequently great excitement in Paris. He changed his mind because he thought public opinion had changed.

He promised to announce his decision tomorrow.

Did some copying this afternoon and finished the writing lesson.

At the Library this evening were quite a number present. Appenzeller gave me a history of his wedding trip. Jennie was represented by her brother and sister. Took a look at Jonathan's room. It beats everything with old prints and flower pots. But it looks more homelike.

Read an account of Queen Christina of Sweden. Queer person she was.

Saturday, December 3, 1887. President Grevy of France resigned yesterday. He blames the Chamber and puts the responsibility on them. His successor will be elected today.

Got lesson 17 ready this evening. I hardly expected to though.

Elwood tells me Alicen Hendricks is down with consumption. She is following her mother.

Sunday, December 4, 1887. M. Sadi Carnot was yesterday elected President of France on the second ballot. M. Ferry and M de Freycinct withdrew in his favor. Finished Lessons in Life this morning. Dressed in the afternoon and did not get to meeting. Uriah came up at three o'clock. He came down told me Kate wanted me to come up to Ellis' for supper. We walked up to the church together. When we came back Morris Landis' were here. Toward five Rufus came down too from Kate. I managed to get off wondering what it was all about. We were ushered into the parlor by Ellis where Bean, Crouthamel, Kate, Martha, Miss Z. and Mr. Groff were assembled. After supper Mr Groff left, going down with the train. Bean, Kate and Miss Z saw him off. We smoked — that is Ellis and Rufus, and the girls couldn't stand it in the room so they went into the parlor upstairs. Uriah left first then Rufus and myself contrived to get off. Spoke a little with the Landis' and then ran over to Jennie. She received an unintelligible letter from Haynes this week about nothing written on their common office paper. She dont answer it. She wants to go on the hall to hear Prof Patton on Prohibition, Tuesday a week. She wished one of us was on the other side of the Atlantic. She wastes time thinking about me. Time wasted I know though I would not have her think so.

Monday, December 5, 1887. Blue Monday. Raining this morning and clear this afternoon. Got the Dec. number of Scribners from Uriah this morning. It is very fine. I asked him when he was coming up again and he said in a week and a half, and smiled. Queer answer if I didn't know anything about it. Worked on my lessons this afternoon.

Grandmother and her sister Salome were at dinner. Did some blowing on Temperance Prohibition and other topics in the store this evening.

Wednesday, December 7, 1887. Kate and Lillie are busy at work preparing for the wedding. Miss Barndt sent a note to Kate through me today which I took over. Kate brought an answer back and said she wanted to see me sometime. Horace has come back. He left his trunk here this morning and went to the city. He came back this evening.

Worked a little on the lesson today. Finished Letter Writing. Have a notion to write to Jennie yet.

The President's Message to Congress is severly criticized. It is confined to the tariff alone and advocates the next thing to free trade. Even the Ledger goes against it with all might.

Thursday, December 8, 1887. Rain this morning but cleared off this afternoon and is now cold.

Mailed a letter to Jennie this morning.

Horace came back last evening. Spoke with him at dinner for a few minutes. He said he had been out of work. He would have returned within a week after he started if he hadn't been ashamed. He stopped off at Niagara. They charged him at the rate of 2.50 an hour for 5 hrs riding.

Finished the Arithmetic lesson and practised writing.

Mr. Beideman came in this evening. Mother wasn't in so I went down and talked to him till father came during which I went to sleep awhile. Couldn't help it though.

Friday, December 9, 1887. This morning while standing in the store saw Jennie come across the railroad. I was going to come out when I saw her come toward the store. I retreated to the back end of the store while she posted a letter which knew must be for me. I felt a little embarrassed. Dont think she saw me. Came up for the letter afterward. It was written this morning. Says my letters always make her happy. Glad of it. She is reading Carlyle. Likes him.

Made out J D Morris bill this afternoon and finished my writing lesson. Had returns from Buffalo this evening. All well except a mistake or two in punctuating. Goettler says in the paper that it is rumored that one of our fairest daughters on Main St is to be married on Christmas. He wont have to wait so long.

Saturday, December 10, 1887. Rainy all day.

Finished Lesson 18 this evening.

Some people are not very well pleased that the election is to be held in the school house. Freed and some others among them. Nobody cares. Some thought they needn't go to the elections. The idea!

They were after me about Jennie this evening which I did not like though I was just as unjust to Amand right after but I wanted to get rid of it. I told mother afterward I did not like it and so on. I told her I would never stop going there. She opened her eyes and said "No wonder you dont like to hear such things." Yet she knows nothing of our engagement. Guess she'll tell father all I said.

Sunday, December 11, 1887.   Sat around reading and doodling on the organ all morning. In the afternoon Sam and talked up stairs and did not get dressed till after four. Tried to sleep a little after that but couldn't. Rested very well, however. Went over to Jennie this evening. Brought old Greaser's book along, "Three Eras of a Woman's Life" by T S Arthur. Dont know what she'll think of it. She was down to Norristown yesterday had a tooth fixed and her face was all swollen up. I fear I was a little dull this evening. I always am. Arranged to call Tuesday evening to attend the lecture.

Monday, December 12, 1887.   Kate called me in this afternoon on my way home. Horace was in the room and Lillie. The latter was at work on a dress for Kate. K then told me what she wanted. The wedding is to come off on Thursday at 6 P.M. Lillie is the brides maid, and Mr Groff groomsman. Rufus and I are to act as ushers. They will take a trip to Danley's and so on. I'm to be there by three. Uriah Miss Barndt and others will arrive on the three o'clock train. Martha is to be there and grandparents and so on.

Tuesday, December 13, 1887.   The Temperance lecture was postponed for unexplained reasons. Was disappointed very much. Would have liked to hear it.

Worked some on my lessons.

Went over to Jennie this evening. Her tooth is much better. We had a real nice time. Went home soon after nine. Thought afterward I might have detained her too long.

Went to work again after I came home. Folks didnt know where I was.

Wednesday, December 14, 1887.   The bank had an offer for the Slifer property from a Phila party. $5500. Not accepted.

The Prohibition lecture came off at Telford on Monday evening. Mr. Gerhart said it was good. He sold some tickets for the Fisher lecture tomorrow evening.

Kate was very busy today. The house had to be all torn up preparatory for tomorrow. L. I believe is very busy making her dress. Harry Hunsberger too is said to have matrimonial aspirations and that the affair is to come off shortly. Martha was here this afternoon sewing. She too is believed to marry soon. So it goes.

Did some on my lessons this morning again.

Thursday, December 15, 1887.   The weather this morning was very disagreeable. It rained the greater part of the day. This evening it cleared off. Got out of bank about 20 min of two. Ran up to the store to ask Ellis to help select a wedding present. Chose a set of colored glasses which were marked 3.50. Got them for 2.75. Wrote a card and had it sent down to the house. Came up a few minutes after three. Rufus wasn't around yet and Kate said I should meet the train. Mr. Groff, Uriah and Miss B. came along. I then entered on my duties as I understood them, asking advice of the women if I didn't know. I unpacked the presents and arranged them on the table; answered the doorbell and showed them into the room; — in short did the best I could, or understood how. Mrs. Ellis, Mrs Landis, and Miss Harr were in command of the kitchen and diningroom. The guests were; Mr & Mrs Jno B. Bean, grand parents, Mr & Mrs J. M. Slifer, Martha, Uriah and Miss B., the family and so on. Mr & Mrs Dengler arrived last. We rehearsed a little. Started the old clock at a quarter of six. Mr D. was called upstairs and gave instructions. Miss B. then played Mendelsohn's Wedding March. The procession formed at the head of the stairs. At Mr D's signal to me at the door they came down. Mr. Groff as groomsman and Miss Z. as bridesmaid came first. Then came the bridal couple and took the place in front of the minister. Rufus and I followed and stood back. Then the music ceased, and all arose. Then followed the ceremony which transformed Kate into Mrs. C. I. Bean. Just before the conclusion of the Lord's Prayer at the conclusion of the ceremony the clock struck six. Then Mr & Mrs Bean faced around and received the congratulations of every one in the room. We then went out and brought wine and cakes into the room. Rufus served the wine and I the cakes. Then the bride and groom led the way to the table; Mr & Mrs D followed and so on. Only fifteen could take seats. Rufus and I waited on the table. This was entirely new to me, and it kept us busy, but I liked it. There were eight or nine at the second table. The third and last saw Miss Harr and Will Benner the hostler, Mrs Landis and Rufus, and Mrs Ellis and myself seated together. I dare say it was the roughest of the lot for we had to help ourselves. Dengler's left before the third table. He asked me to join the Foreign Mission Society at Leidy's. Mrs D. was very kind. Soon after the band came and serenaded. We went out and stood in the hall or on the porch. In the background were many lookers on. A dutch band too was ready at this moment to strike up as we soon learned. We were at table when they commenced to play. Grandparents wanted to go home and I lighted them out. When they saw me with the lantern they stopped expecting something. I swung the lantern and ran in. They commenced again. Took Martha home. The sidewalk and street were crowded and I recognized many. When Mr Bean's were ready to go I again went out and they were quiet till they were off. There were only a few any more. Soon the other band marched past having serenaded Corn. Hunsberger who was also married today. The Dutchies commenced again and I went out and threatened them and then they slunk away. Uriah left with Miss B. after which I stood round awhile yet and they went home. The presents were: A clock, by Uriah; pincushion by Miss Zendt; silver cake dish, Mr Groff; silver teaspoons Mrs Bean; fancy tray, Mrs. W B Slifer; silver butter knife, Miss Barndt; water set, Martha; ditto, Mr & Mrs J.M.S.; set colored glass by myself.

Friday, December 16, 1887.   Slept very badly last night. Too much excited I guess. Mr & Mrs Bean started on a trip this morning. They sent wedding cake around today. There was some candy along in for me. The pike was strewn with tin cans and debris from last evening's noise. Saw Uriah this morning this morning. He'll come up on Sunday. Goettler has a piece in the paper this evening. Wonder who put it in. Little too high flown.

The Fisher lecture at Telford last evening was good Mr Gerhart says. Sixty seven dollars realized and not all paid in.

Did not feel like going to work this afternoon. The Library this evening was well attended. Jennie was down alone. I don't believe she is pleased with me about something. I tried to keep her as long as I could. What business had Jonathan to blush when he found she had taken a book he had recommended. She dont know it but I knew it. I tried to speak to her but she seemed to be in a hurry.

Saturday, December 17, 1887. Colder and it is snowing this evening. Have no returns from Buffalo yet. Think it is queer. Managed to finish Lesson 19.

Jos Knight a clerk in the Manuf Nat Bk has proved a defaulter to the amount of $67,500 dollars. He was in the service of the bank 36 yrs and has been stealing 23 yrs. He was lodged in jail.

Am very sleepy.

Sunday, December 18, 1887. Slept very late this morning as did Elwood. When we came down the others had been shovelling snow a long time. A snow 15 or 18 in deep had fallen during the night. Rufus came down to see about going over to Bean's. We decided to take the sleigh. He went up to get ready. Missed the train. Thought we couldn't go because father had given Horace the horse to ride through the snow. Went up to help get ready. All in confusion there. Horace came back and I got our team ready. Most of the others were gone. Roads very hard on a horse. We got over a little before twelve. Uriah didn't get there till one. Several there I didn't know. After dinner Rufus ordered the team. He wanted to be home by three. It looked five minutes of that time when we entered one yard. Met Amelia, Maggie and Mr. Allebach and went up with them to grandfather's. Stayed for supper. They have a new organ. Went home and dressed for the evening. At first Jennie seemed as usual. She had placed a chair at the stove and asked me to take it. I wanted her to take it but she sat on another one. I sat on the opposite side and removing the chair in dispute said, "We must not let anything come between us." I then asked why she was displeased with me on Friday evening. She wouldn't out with it first but soon told me she had been very angry with me and had in fact written a letter which she did not mail. I asked to see it. It was signed, "Yours as may be J— M—" without any address and ended with asking me to stay away this evening. What I feared had happened. She knew that she was aimed at at the time of the wedding and she blamed me for going to the reception. I explained all about it and how I was placed in a delicate position. I felt bitter towards some who had helped to stir it up—. I hope Kate is innocent. But Miss Z. — I'd like to wring her neck.

Went home much relieved.

Monday, December 19, 1887. Walked up to the church this afternoon. They are putting in wainscoting. Went up to the watchmaker's. Congratulated him on his marriage. He showed me some very nice rings set with a "rein stone." Too much like shams. He evidently thought I wanted a Xmas present. I told him I did not want it for that. He brought down the ring he bought for his wife. That was set with a diamond. I would like one but everybody would think me extravagant, (including the jeweler, for he hinted that way). I said I'd call again.

Received my 20th lesson from Buffalo. Sent off the 19th. The 20th takes me through Com Law and Arithmetic. Did very little on it and soon feel asleep.

Tuesday, December 20, 1887.   Instead of being cold it is warm and rains a little. Went out to the school house to get a book for Miss Barndt. Jennie was almost frightened when I came in. I said I was sorry, the weather was so disagreeable but she thought there would be chances yet. She was closing up and I walked home with her.

Got out my writing lesson this evening.

Wednesday, December 21, 1887.   The weather predict colder weather for tomorrow. It is time too for today the snow was going fast. All the better this if it gets cold.

Cant get a good hold on my lessons. The last Arithmetic lesson is a very hard one. There are many out sleighing tonight.

Worked till after eleven o'clock tonight.

Thursday, December 22, 1887.   Colder weather today.

Bought a pair of heavy mittens for sleighing. Went out to the school house. Jonathan was in the room. He talked about getting up a masquerade party at Mrs Hunsberger's. Helped Jennie sweep the room. Asked if she'd like a sleigh ride. She didn't say no but I soon found that she'd rather not and so gave up. She seemed to be relieved when I did so. Of course I was disappointed. She said the roads were rough but it seemed to me as if there were another reason. I tried to study but couldnt — my thoughts would always wander to one subject, so I went to work to write a letter asking her what was the matter, for I am convienced that something is wrong. I feel it. I was at about two hours, when father brought the mail up. My Buffalo letter showed that I was through with four of my studies. This pleased me so well that I came down stairs and sang and whistled away another half hour before I went to work. Worked till eleven again tonight. Tore the letter I had started to pieces. Took warm grid irons along to bed to make it warm.

Friday, December 23, 1887.   Still cold but nice for winter. It would be nicer to be out this evening but I hardly dare ask again. It seems to me that someone was working against me or that there was a reaction from last Sunday.

Finished all my lessons for the 20th letter except Comm. Law.

Mr Moyer talked of starting a business institute. He said I should teach Letter Writing etc but he didn't mean it and I couldn't do it.

Goettler says there are two marriages for tomorrow, Harry Hunsberger and Irwin Moll. There was to be a sleighing party to Harleysville tonight. I heard but was abandoned. It was Miss Z's getting up. She'll go crazy some day.

Saturday, December 24, 1887. Finished my 20th lesson at half past eight this evening. Was glad of it very.

Kratz's are having a party — an ice cream party this evening. There were only a few there. Rufus and Morris Weil came late and Rufus wasn't sober. Neither Elwood or Tom were invited.

Thought of going over to Jennies but it got too late.

Harry Hunsberger and Irwin Moll were married today.

Sunday, December 25, 1887. It being just right for sleighing this morning I went over to ask Jennie if she would like to go out. I was almost doubtful be said she would go although she was busy. We started at ten and she asked to be home at eleven. Sleighing is pretty good although in some places rather thin, but we had a right good time. She said she was going to church this afternoon. I resolved I would too. It was one minute of eleven when we got back. Grand parents were here for dinner. We had a great big turkey. Rufus came down for the sleigh in the afternoon. I said Elwood was going away. He took the girl over home. Went to church on the hill with Sam. Aker preached. I like to hear him. But I dont like to see him show his teeth. Of course that must be borne. Jennie was there and was much interested. "Bro Moll" was asked to pray but could not on account of his feelings.

Went up town to see the church. It was locked. Stopped in at grandfather H's.

Frick came over after supper. He will go down tomorrow afternoon. He promosed to send his photo. He went to meeting.

Dressed and went over to Jennie's. She looked better this afternoon I thought than I had seen her before. The fresh air had put a healthy glow upon her cheeks. I asked if there had been anything wrong this week but she said not. I told her I had written a letter. She said she had written one too that she was sorry she had said anything about the wedding. Time passed very fast. I opened my package containing Shakespeare. She seemed pleased. She took me in the other room to show what Annie gave her a plush stand cover. She then handed me a pretty box containing six white silk handkerchiefs and a muffler which she made me put on when I left.

Monday, December 26, 1887. Had to go to work again this morning though if we had known it it wasn't necessary. Lansdale Schwenksville and all others were closed. But it was too late.

Told Jennie of my plan of leaving the bank a year after this. She seemed to be afraid of my going away and forgetting her. (as if such a thing were possible). I wished I had said nothing. She pretended she did not wish to interfere with it in anyway. I asked by way of teasing if she'd care if I'd haul brick afterwards. She said if it was necessary but thought it wasnt. I asked the loan of a ring, why she right well understood and seemed to be reluctant to do it. She asked for time to consider. I named Tuesday evening but she didnt promise.

Did nothing in the world this afternoon when I came home. I dont believe there was any school today. Some kind of sleighing party started away here this evening. Our girl went along.

All the Reading hands are to go on a strike except the passenger men. The company is going to stick them out. It is said it will affect 65000 men.

Tuesday, December 27, 1887. The Reading hands all resumed work this morning. The officers of the company gave orders to the men to return to work this morning on penalty of dismissal. Most of them did so and those who did not were promptly discharged and new men employed. There is some dissatisfaction among the men. The crews at Port Richmond who originated the strike were discharged.

Worked on the books this afternoon. Sam was kind enough to help get the sleigh ready and by seven I reported to Jennie. Sam went along over. She was soon ready and away we sped toward Leidy's church. Very pleasant to be out this evening. Moonlight and cold though a little damp. The aid society of Leidy's Church was organized by electing J. G. Dengler, Pres.; Schwenck, Sec.; Appenzeller, E C Leidy and other were also elected to some office. Papers were read by Appenzeller and E C Leidy and J Proctor. Dengler was speaking to Jennie when I came in. We could not sit together. I was amused at some things. The way Dengler helped them along. "Do you make that motion Mr —?" A nod. "Do you second it, Mr —?" Another nod, and it was ready for adoption. Jonathan and Miss Magargal came down too. We took a short sleigh ride afterward. I went along in hoping to obtain her consent to my getting the ring. But she dont want the others to know. Oh, the sacred pleasure there is in being with a loving one. We decided not to go to the masquerade party on Sat. eve at Aunt Kit's. Left at half past ten.

Wednesday, December 28, 1887. There was rain all day. It will clear off colder. There was a report this afternoon that the Reading hands were again on strike on account of the treatment they received.

Answered Uriah's letter. He had proposed going to Quakertown on Sunday. I answered the snow was going and that put an end to it. Wrote to Andrew inviting him up on New Year's. Got through finely in bank today. Worked on books. Dont get to reading though I look into the Monastary, by Scott, occasionally.

Was up in the store this evening for over an hour. That's the way to waste precious time.

Thursday, December 29, 1887.   Received Frick's photo this morning. It's well taken but any one can see that he is thinking of himself mostly.

Very cold this morning and still colder predicted for tomorrow.

The Reading strike does not amount to much. At Richmond some men have left work but about a 1000 brakemen, engineers and conductors who had composed an assembly of the Knights of Labor disbanded and left the order. The company will win, I think.

Grandmother S was here this afternoon. Worked on the books this afternoon and evening. Met Jennie this afternoon as she went home from school. Saw her go down this morning.

Friday, December 30, 1887.   Worked on the books and was in the shop awhile this afternoon. Father will order down the rest from the church to finish the work here tomorrow.

In the store this evening Jonathan asked me if I was coming to the party. I said I couldn't promise as J. was going to Norristown. He said he talked to her and understood that she could go. I said I would if possible &c.

Saturday, December 31, 1887.   We will have a holiday on Monday. Was very busy today preparing for it. A general strike was ordered all over the Reading system. The passenger hands, trackmen and switchmen are excepted. Nothing will come of it except that many will lose their jobs. New men are being employed.

Was in the shop awhile this afternoon. Dressed after supper and worked on the books till half past eight. Found Jennie at home. She said **they** had come home from Norristown with the last train. She left the room as I was warming myself at the stove and suddenly returned with a young lady, to whom, to my surprise, I was presented as "Mr. Micawber." I was stunned. This was the "Countess Vere de Vere" (Miss Hoffman). I am sure I acted very foolish being unprepared to meet any one. The Countess too was surprised and said she had never expected to meet me. Jennie laughed and enjoyed it very much. They are very fond of each other and I really became quite jealous. But how quick and ready she is, and she talks! She kept Jennie laughing all day so that she thought she'd die of it. She left the room saying she wanted a drink, just to get away. Of course I felt she preferred her to me and so took my leave which she seemed right glad to see me do.

*Competition for school directorship—"speaks to" Jennie's
father—a tremendous blizzard—dreams of leaving bank and
Souderton—friends present "Lowva the Pauper" and defy
license ordinance—"graduates" from correspondence
course—a lovers' spat*

1888

Sunday, January 1, 1888.   Woke up early this morning to hear the rain
spattering on the roof. It had snowed last evening. I wished the others a
"Happy New Year" to which there was but a faint response. Found myself
thinking of last night, of Jennie, how she seems to prefer the Countess to me,
and the Countess what she must think of me. However, we contrived to pass
the time upstairs till late, and thereby missed breakfast. Elwood fetched
grandparents down. No Andrew. No Uriah. Too rainy I guess. Had turkey for
dinner. I shot him yesterday morning with Sam's rifle right through the ears on
the second shot. Wasn't far enough away to be too proud of it. It was a very
dreary day. The "Countess," being one of Jennie's best friends, should not
think me a boor. So I resolved to make amends tonight. But alas! she was gone.
I wasn't displeased either, for I was a little afraid of her. Contrived to displease
Jennie by being inattentive brute that I am. She forgave me and I think after
all she loves me as well or better than the "Countess."

Monday, January 2, 1888.   Lay abed very late this morning to prove
that I was keeping holiday. Went out to the shop about ten and we took stock
account. Uriah, Sam, and Elwood helped us. We were through by two. Found
we have on hand 98,000 ft Lumber, 12,000 more than last year. Walked up to
the church. It's looking nice but it will cost much I'm afraid. Worked on the
book this evening and went asleep on them. There were about twenty-eight at
the party. Irwin Moll and wife, Indians, Miss Magargal, "Martha Washington", and so on, cowboys, brides, grooms, negroes, queens and all sorts and
conditions of men were represented.

Tuesday, January 3, 1888.   Haven't slept sounder for a long time than I
did last night. It snowed just a little this morning. The miners have joined in
the strike. The company are more or less obstructed by it but they are
employing new hands.

Read in Scott's "Monastery" this afternoon.

Father's bills are not quite all in but it seems to me on figuring over the
accounts that he don't do as well as he might.

Mr. Landes was in bank most of the time yesterday.

There was a shooting match at Tyson's Saturday and yesterday for a hog weighing 600 to 700 lbs. She was killed today.

Wednesday, January 4, 1888.   John B. Moyer today resigned the directorship. He would have preferred to remain I think but he had no other way. His successor has not been named.

Read Scott's Monastery.

Made out a few bills. I feel very tired and worked-up this week.

Was amused at what Sam told me about the Magargal's. He was up at his grandmother's who told him: that the younger of them had received a letter which Mrs. C. wanted to open. They came to rolling on the rolling on the floor and shrieks. The elder is better. If Jonathan knew!

Thursday, January 5, 1888.   Did nothing but read Monastery after bank hours.

Was uncertain whether to go over to Jennie or not there being meeting at the Mennonite Meeting house this evening. Was afraid it would seem too officious. When Sam and I came up the lane Jennie and her mother came on behind us. A divine from Virginia preached excellently in both Eng. and Ger. He had a fine sonorous voice; his hair was dressed somewhat in the fashion of Henry Clay; and he was a very fluent speaker. I don't believe he has ready any good novels or he would believe in them.

Was ashamed of myself, for J. went home part of the way by herself, but as I had not brought her down I believed it improper to offer to take her home.

Friday, January 6, 1888.   Finished the Monastery this morning. It is none of the best books I have read; the spirit that is introduced makes it depend too much on the supernatural; but the characters of the sub prior and of Henry Warden are interesting.

A committee of three from the Board of Directors examined us today — that is — counted the money and found it correct.

There was a little rain today which froze as fast as it came down making it very slippery. Went down to the schoolhouse to make ready for tonight. Helped Jennie home for it was as smooth as a mirror and dangerous. I am afraid she wasn't very well-pleased for my not taking her to meeting.

The Library was but poorly attended. Commenced Rob Roy and read some in Knickerbocker's Hist. of New York. Choice humor.

Saturday, January 7, 1888.   Never so slippery as this morning. Walking about without a fall is almost impossible. Have escaped so far.

Went up to the doctor's to have two teeth pulled. Pretty tough work, but I'm glad it's done. Had no toothache and I don't want none. Have a clean mouth now I believe.

Went up to grandfather. He's to have my razor sharpened on his famous stone.

My mouth hurt a little this evening and bled more than necessary.

Sunday, January 8, 1888.   Damp and disagreeable. Read Rob Roy and The Press. Took a short nap this afternoon. My mouth bled last night and kept me awake for several hours. Did not dress till this evening. Expected Uriah but he did not appear.

Discussed religious topics with Jennie this evening. We had a very pleasant time together. Jake came over a few minutes. Went home about twelve.

Monday, January 9, 1888.   Was in bed yet when Mr. Gehman came for his book and asked if I was at home yet.

Amanda had a fellow last evening.

Read Rob Roy this afternoon. Very interesting.

Mr. Moyer will soon commence on his Letter Writing and Comm. Law.

Wednesday, January 11, 1888.   Very cold today. Received a letter from Andrew this morning. Thus am I assured that he is alive. Mr. Borneman this morning received the examination papers for John. He will prepare himself first.

Got out of bank late this afternoon. The new board was sworn in today. Two new directors, Wm. Souder and H. L. Kulp instead of J. B. Moyer and Henry Ruth. Read Rob Roy. It was my full intention to write to Jennie this evening but sleep has prevented me. This is my twenty-second birthday. If it were not for Jennie I should feel decidedly discouraged at the prospect. I never dreamed that I should be now where I was five years ago. I have perhaps made a little progress last year and I hope to make much more this year. But I have that which is worth more than silver or gold, the love of pure hearted girl.

Eddy Kohlschrieber was buried today. He died on Sunday evening. (Had a tussle with the boys.)

Thursday, January 12, 1888.   Cold, very cold.

Read Rob Roy. First rate.

Bound up my Arithmetic Penmanship Comm Law and Letter Writing for handy reference. Father sold Jim yesterday to Henry Landes. That is, he goes away in the spring. Poor old friend! I hate to lose him.

H. C. Landes has sold his house and lot to W. A. Crouthamel for 1050. Crouthamel will build some time. Landes will build a new house in the spring. J. H. Moyer is thinking of building two houses on Water St. The sale between Zendt and Fretz is not yet consummated. That would take the Zendt's away I guess.

Grandmother S. was here this afternoon. She made a kind remark of Jennie. Must prepare to go to work next week.

Friday, January 13, 1888.   Snow last night and rain today.

Answered Andrew's letter of Monday and Uriah's of this morning.

Made some progress on the books this evening. Finished Rob Roy this afternoon. A very good book indeed.

Sam caught a curious little mouse this morning. It's color is red with a white breast, large ears and eyes. He killed it this evening.

Saturday, January 14, 1888.   Worked on the books this afternoon.

Parents went up to Quakertown with grandparents, on a visit. Elwood went down to the city with Uriah yesterday.

Dressed and went over to Jennie to see if she wanted to go to some entertainment. She didn't and we passed a pleasant evening together. She is preparing a little for next Sunday but says if Dengler don't come round she wont go. She had no school on Wednesday on account of Eddie Kohlschrieber's funeral.

Wrote Andrew and Uriah. Al Fretz cant buy Zendt's place. The latter backed out.

Sunday, January 15, 1888.   Very disagreeable.

Read the papers most of the time. Was up at the new church with Sam. We went to meeting in the afternoon.

It became very stormy tonight. The windows rattled and the wind whistled. What fitter place to be in than with her I love. We did not mind the storm and were very happy together. She does not wish me to speak to her father yet. The storm had ceased when I went home. Crept into Sam's bed as it is warmer. Slept with him since Elwood went away. Uriah came back this afternoon.

Monday, January 16, 1888.   A cold wave has struck us again. There is a terrible blizzard out West. Many lives have been lost and trains delayed on account of the cold and snow.

Commenced work on the twenty-first lesson this afternoon and finished it.

The Manuf. Nat. Bk. has chosen W. H. Heisler of the 7th Nat. for their cashier instead of M. W. Woodward resigned.

Was glad to sleep tonight.

Elwood was expected home tonight but didn't come.

Tuesday, January 17, 1888.   As cold as yesterday. There was a little snow today.

An agent for the Yale and Sargent Time Locks was here today. An excellent talker. I believe the board has some idea of getting one.

Saw J. go down to school today.

Sent off 21 this afternoon. No. 22 nearly ready.

Heard they had some trouble at school yesterday. Jonathan whipped young Blank and Goettle last evening. They richly deserved it.

Wrote for Dicken's Dialogues.

Elwood hasn't come yet.

Our girl is boring mother terribly with her tiresome talk.

Wednesday, January 18, 1888.   There was some snow last night. The sleighs will go again. Cold weather. Terrible weather out west. One hundred and thirty-five lives were lost in the storm.

Mr. Baum of Bedminster was puzzled at my strange name and thought I must have been born abroad. It sounded so outlandish to him.

Finished Lesson 22 this afternoon. Worked on the books and did some copying.

Grandmother S was here.

Amelia stopped in and asked me to come up this evening. Went up about eight. Sarah thought her certificate was due but it wasn't. There is no decision about it yet. She says she has a place for it. Didn't ask where. Hope it aint Bauman. Elwood the little skinny aint home yet. All are getting anxious about him.

Friday, January 20, 1888.   Did some copying last evening but none today. Received Scribner's this morning. A fine number.

Went down to the school house this afternoon just as Jennie was about to close up. She says Dengler was to see her. So off we'll go on Sunday. The library draws but little attention. Clymer was up this evening. Received a new key from Jonathan.

Read Knickerbocker's New York.

Al Fretz has bought out Dettra's clothing establishment.

Saturday, January 21, 1888.   It was as cold today as at anytime.

Received Carpentry and Building this evening. Interesting number. Did some copying this afternoon.

Received letter from U. yesterday. He is coming up Sunday and will go sleighing. He wants to know why we dont go. Heard from Ed. Danley the other day. He wants to know everything. They had to kill old Jim in consequence of an accident. The "Buffalo" this evening was delayed here one of the steam pipes having burst. The engine was disabled. It was put on a sidetrack and a big hump who had been lying here took the train away. Had to stand around there till I was almost frozen.

Sunday, January 22, 1888.   When mother said the thermometer was down to zero this morning I concluded bed was the warmest place and stayed there. Uriah came down soon after the train. He did not come up last evening. We walked down to the schoolhouse for a book. It was bitter cold. He told me Horace had broken our sleigh. It made me very angry. Brought down Slifer's sleigh but did not take it as it is unsafe. Took my carriage to go down to Leidy's. Uriah went along over. It was a little late but Jennie wasn't at home. They told me she had walked down as I hadn't said I was coming. Was intensely disappointed and disposed to blame her though I knew I should have been earlier. Thought I'd go down anyway. Met Jonathan when about halfway whom I picked up. I didn't know yet what was going to happen before it was over. There she sat sure enough looking as if she did not need me at all. Then Dengler humiliated me yet by taking all the blame on himself because I hadn't prepared anything. Then she read her essay I heard very little and felt ashamed of myself. When it was over and we met she smiled. That settled it. I must surrender. She told me she had been very angry with me but wasn't anymore. In the evening she told me she had said to herself that she hated me. She thought I wasn't coming. It taught me a lesson.

Monday, January 23, 1888.   The cold this morning was severe. Yesterday it was 4 below and this morning 2 below.

Received Dialogues from Dickens this morning. They are good but had but little [time] to look over them. Had returns from two lessons from Buffalo. A letter from Bryant saying I should get examined while it was "fresh in my mind." That's satire. He couldn't have found me more unprepared. This makes me busy. Was at everything this evening. Copying, on the books, writing letters. Must work everything aside and get some one to superintend the operation. Have to study like a monk to catch up.

Wednesday, January 25, 1888.   Mailed my letter to Jennie this morning.

We were not very busy this morning. Two directors, Ruth and Barndt did not come until this afternoon. John wanted get out promply at three. He wants to finish this evening. Grandmother S. was here this afternoon. Finished the books this evening. Am now ready to begin, that is begin to study. Sent for Wilson's Treatise on Punctuation and Hart's Rhetoric. Mother found out about Dialogues from Dickens. She wanted to know what it was for. She does not want me to play on the stage. She says it is not proper. I told her with all deference to her parental authority that I ought to be old enough to judge for myself. Took the book down to the school house and laid it on Jennie's desk as I had promised. Was back again in a few minutes. It was snowing at the time. Had a discussion about dragons, hobgoblins, &c to the detriment of my time.

Thursday, January 26, 1888.   A six inch snow fell last night. Watched for her this morning but did not see her go. Received the Feb. number of Scribner's which is very interesting, and such a good letter from J. She does not doubt of my success in the examination.

Went up to the dentist's to have my teeth polished.

Read Commercial Law this evening. Spoke to Ed about acting for me at my examination. He did not know I was at it before. Brought him along down to show him my things. Sam had just dressed himself in Amanda's clothes and made a queer figure. He went out to have some fun. Ed talked about Ira. He was such a bright boy.

Friday, January 27, 1888.   Was at bank early this morning. Told Mr. Landes I was taking a business course. He wanted to know whether it wasn't humbug. I explained it all to him. He thought the method of teaching penmanship was better than any other. Received Hart's Rhetoric and Wilson's Composition. Valuable books. Don't know if they'll [help] me much now but I'll use them. John sent off his answers this evening. He is glad it's over. I wish I was so far. Sat in bank with him this afternoon while he copied his Ledger.

Read Commercial Law. Was so sleepy this evening that I could hardly do anything. Wrote Bryant this evening designating Ed as the person to hold my examination.

Had a curious dream last night. Dreamt I was an anarchist and wanted to blow up the school house but did not succeed. In revenge I wanted to murder someone. J. weaned me away from them. Stoned some anarchist who had come to see me.

Saturday, January 28, 1888.   The thermo. this morning showed 2 and 4 above zero. Many pronounced it the coldest day this winter. The air was keen, sharp, and biting. The sleighing party which went away last night came back after four this morning. They were half frozen. Very little pleasure in that. Our girl was along.

There is a concert on the hall this evening. The boys are up. Read a little Comm. Law. Am too sleepy this evening and have to give it up.

Grandmother S. was here this afternoon.

Schwenck has bought the Hatfield store property of H. M. Ziegler. I was sur-prised when I first heard of this last Wednesday. He had intended to build but that must be given up now. I always expected he'd watch for Hunsberger's store.

Tuesday, January 31, 1888.   Am so sleepy at this writing that I can hardly hold my head up. On Sunday I read Comm. Law, and studied Punctuation. Jennie went to meeting but I had no time. Sam handed me an invitation to a birthday party at Zendt's on Thursday evening. We wont go, of course. Sunday's meeting with J. was very agreeable. Yesterday Penrose Zendt asked to go with the sleighing party. I declined. But after school Jonathan came down and I couldn't back out. Ran over to J. to see what she'd say. She didn't like it, but we had no other way. Started for Harleysville about half past and got over before nine. The ride going and coming was very pleasant. I knew I'd be sleepy today. We got back about twelve but it was one before I got to bed.

Jonathan is all right for an entertainment. Believe Miss S. was disappointed. Was all right today till this evening. Jonathan said he'd go. This blamed party has thrown me back this evening.

Wednesday, February 1, 1888.   Was surprised to find Andrew here at noon. Thought of him during the morning and wondered when he'd come. When I came home from bank we walked up to the new church together. Showed him my work. He thought he wouldn't try it. He is still attending Spring Garden Institute two evenings in a week and studying architectural drawing. It's something that would suit me. We went up to the store together and stopped at Stover's and had oysters. It was eleven when we got to bed. He wanted to go down this evening but we wouldn't let him go. He was out with a sleighing party to Doylestown on Monday evening.

Friday, February 3, 1888.   Yesterday and today the snow had to go. Sleighing is poor now. They had a party out at Zendt's last evening. They had a pretty good time I heard. Some wanted to know why we didn't go. I said I hadn't time. (Which was true enough, though I slept like a log most of last evening). Mrs. W. P. Slifer and Allie were here yesterday when I came from bank. They went away today again. Mr. and Mrs. Henry Landes were here also. Andrew went home yesterday morning.

Examination papers arrived this morning, but the wrong ones. So we sent them back. They were the bookkeeping blanks.

Went down to the school house this afternoon. Did not see Jonathan. Walked home with Jennie. She says, Rufus and Cal. weren't sober on Monday evening.

This evening Appenzeller and Rufus were waiting when I came down. Jennie came down with Willis. Read "Book News".

Sunday, February 5, 1888.   Walked with Sam down to the schoolhouse to look for the quarterly I had mislaid on Friday evening. Found it this time and took it up to Jonathan. Was at the station when the train came up. Spoke to Mr. Metz. He seems to be very decent. Went home and read Com. Law. Couldn't stay at it all day. Am getting a little tired of it all. Mrs. Zuschnitt was here this afternoon. I seem fated to be always late. It was a quarter of eight before I got off. We had a pleasant time; we always have. The Miss Magargal and their dressmaker called on her today. She thinks they act very nicely whatever people say. She had been reading Dombey & Son. She heard Rufus and Cal. were drunk or had too much on Monday evening. She doesn't like the school directors proposed by her father; only two of whom have children.

Monday, February 6, 1888.   Was very late this morning. I was a little ashamed of it. No breakfast and yet late. Colder than yesterday. It had been too warm for several days. Met Jennie on her way to school. Mr. Moyer hasn't heard anything from Buffalo yet. He is getting impatient.

And now it appears that the "beateous" Miss Lillian went to the trouble of acting a part in order to appear surprised at her party on Thursday evening. "She suspected nothing and was away from home too"! If I saw much of it, it would make me sick.

Am going over the questions in Com. Law. Am over about two thirds of it.

There'll be plenty of candidates for office by Saturday evening. Mr. Godshall would take a school directorship and so would lots of others. To keep the schools down I suppose.

Thursday, February 9, 1888.   Colder again today. The soft snow of yesterday is frozen solid, and there were a few sleighs out. The people are all talking politics. There'll be plenty of candidates on Saturday evening. Mr. Landes, Mr. Godshall, and Wm. K. Moyer would take the school-directorship.

Mr. L. is pledged for only six months. We'll have enough men to take care of the schools, — that is keep them down.

Haven't heard from Buffalo yet. Wonder what in the world they mean by keeping me so long waiting. Am getting tired of the suspense.

Had a terrific spat with Elwood today. He insulted mother; father lectured him; and this evening I said something to him when he tried to provoke me by saying that a letter had been written by someone asking whether I had any money because I didn't spend any. It's rediculous.

He thinks that by barefacedness he can get through. And then to talk of being ill treated. It's exasperating.

Friday, February 10, 1888.   Very cold. Almost as cold as a few weeks ago.

Father spoke to Elwood this morning. I was not present. He is moody and says nothing.

I was placed in a very unpleasant position today at bank. Mr. Moyer felt hurt because he thought Mr. Landes was working in secret for the school directorship. He told me how felt about it when Mr. L. was out. When he came in and John had gone I found he was very angry with Mr. Moyer. His face was flushed and he told how he felt. It tried to smooth it down a little but kept very quiet. When John came I warned him that Mr. L. knew he was displeased. Of course, Mr. L. will not run and M. will not. So two candidates are gone. I agreed with Mr. M's policy and I am sorry for it.

Wrote to Buffalo this evening.

And now Sam talks of going away. To the city, for instance. He can certainly improve more in his trade.

Saturday, February 11, 1888.   Went up on the hall this evening where the nominating convention was in session to see what they were doing. Was there about ten minutes. They were nominating school directors when I was there. Mr. Moyer was not named. He declined the nomination before the convention met. Mr. Landes, H. K. Godshall, E. H. Souder, Wm. K. Moyer, C. M. Tyson, Jno. D. Hunsberger, M. B. Benner, Israel Ruth, A. G. Stover, were nominated for school directors; H. D. Detweiler, M. D. Zendt, M. B. Bergey, Justices of the Peace; J. G. Moyer constable; Israel Kline, declined; and so on. Went down to Jennie and told her who her masters would be. She thinks its too bad that Mr. Moyer is left out. She will not ask for a school, but will take it if offered. Promised to come over tomorrow to go to meeting. Rec'd a letter from G. Danly saying he had a baby two days old and weighing 8 pounds.

Sunday, February 12, 1888.   The girl got the sleigh today to take a ride. Sam and I had great fun sending her off. Uriah came down while we were getting the team ready. He has moved to his new store and expects more business. Went down to the schoolhouse to get a book; from there went up to the church. He thinks its very pretty. In the afternoon accompanied Jennie to meeting. After we came back Mrs. Moyer, Milt and his wife were in the room with us. Don't feel at home among them yet. From there went out to Mrs. Hunsberger's. They were angry with me for not coming sooner. Maggie would not come till I was there &c. Was glad I went out. Found out about the letter Elwood mentioned. Miss Z rec'd one from Alice Heany, a Harleysville girl.

This evening with J. was one of the happiest. She does not like to see her sister go away and says she will visit her once a week. I reminded her that she would have to leave home herself. She does not like to think of it. She is half afraid. Urged her to let me speak to her father. I think she'll let me. Traddles would say, "She's the dearest girl in all the world."

Monday, February 13, 1888.   Rec'd a letter this morning stating that other papers had been sent from Bryant & Stratton. Mr. Moyer is still sore. He says the committee would have gone back on him. It does appear so. But he'll be elected next year. Father will withdraw his name as a candidate for council. As he was nominated he would oppose such men as J. H. Moyer and J. S. Borneman. He is looking after a horse at Barnes & Frederick's. Saw Ed's papers this afternoon. There isn't very much, but perhaps enough to stick me. I am going up this evening to begin.

Wednesday, February 15, 1888.   Today it was much colder than yesterday.

Was so busy yesterday and this afternoon that I had no time to fill up this diary. I usually am in the office during the afternoon and down at the house in the evening. Wasn't there at the house this evening.

A man was killed at Rosenbergers bridge. He was standing on the top of a train when he was struck against the bridge. Felt very blue last evening about letter writing. Didn't feel like and could get no start. Had a notion to write to Jennie to cheer me up. I know it would.

Thursday, February 16, 1888.   Finished Arithmetic this afternoon. Ed was down this evening and I commenced copying. Ran down to the school house to fetch the lamp chimneys to clean. Jennie was there yet and I walked home with her. She will write to Miss Z. tomorrow about the meeting tomorrow evening. She was very cheerful which I was glad to note.

Father went to the horse sale at Blooming Glen today not with the intention of buying but when he came home he said he had bought one and a nice one by all accounts. He isn't quite satisfied with him as he wanted a larger horse. Did not see him yet.

Sam and I agreed to call him Prince.

Saturday, February 18, 1888.   We met in the School house last evening concerning an entertainment. Jennie sent word to Lillie and sure enough she came. At first she seemed a little shy. Miss Magargal the elder was there with Jonathan. We looked over a few plays but selected none. Jonathan wants rough and tumble and Jennie dont. Miss Z uses slang to a surprising extent. Jennie goes to North Wales today to attend institute.

The new horse is being exercised pretty well. He was taken out several times yesterday and today.

Did nothing on my examination yesterday but today I finished all except Letter Writing.

Politics. A number of names have been withdrawn from the borough ticket. Among them Swartz.

Beans is to have opposition in the township. Oh if I could only be there to cast a vote against him.

Sunday, February 19, 1888.   Sam and I went out with the new horse this morning. He is careless and you cant get him to go his best. He wants to see everything. But he carries his head high and looks well. Father said I might take him to go to church. So I did. But the mud! The horse and carriage was all besplashed. Read a piece. Changes in Japan. Jonathan had an abridgment of an article and Jennie the budget. After it was over Proctor told me I spoke too low. I thought it was none of his business. Rubbed the horse down after I came home.

Went over to Jennie about 7:30. We looked over some of "Thackeray's Letters" together. Wasn't she frightened when the curtain wasn't quite down. And now her father must be spoken to before long. She asked to see my diaries. The time passed very quickly. Saw that Haynes was up today.

Monday, February 20, 1888.   Very rainy and warm weather. Practised letter writing a little this afternoon. Am too sleepy to write much more. The great coalstrike is ended. The miners return to work pending arbitration. Pres. Corbin has donated 20,000 to distribute among the suffering mines.

Tuesday, February 21, 1888.   A nice day. Went to the election at noon. The schoolhouse is a beautiful place to keep it in. Don't know what any one can say against it. Finished my examination this evening. Am glad of it too.

Wednesday, February 22, 1888.   Holiday falls on Wednesday the first time for long. Tomorrow is our discount day. Greaser cleaned up the bank a little today. Worked at home on my 23d lesson all morning. After dinner went up town and learned the result of the election. W.D. Hunsberger, Burgess; J. H. Moyer, I. S. Borneman, F. H. Souder, Henry K. Landes and B. C. Barndt, Council. School directors, H. K. Godshall, M. B. Benner, E. H. Souder, J. D. Hunsberger, J. C. Landes and Israel Ruth, and so on. 112 votes were cast. Some were pretty well cut. Many stayed at home. Mailed my examination papers this afternoon. Cleaned my carriage afterwards. Was up at the store this evening. Mr. Metz talks well. Had I done one thing more I should have done a full days work. But I hadn't a chance.

Thursday, February 23, 1888.   We were through at bank about four o'clock today. Went over to Moyer's cellars where Davy is digging in one and Cal and Hen are masoning in the other. Dirty work in the well there. Grandfather H. came down to look on. The frost being about ten inches deep, Davy splits it off in blocks. Went up to Freed's with grandfather to look at Fisher's horses. Couldn't see very well but I wouldn't exchange for none of them. Grandf. thinks we should keep the new one but praises up old Jim as if his equal could not be found.

Jonathan did not come home from his trip. People, of course, talk as if Miss M had him in her toils. Cal thinks so. I understood. I am afraid I'll make a fool of myself before I get to speak to Mr. M. No doubt if he'd be near I'd run away for fear of having a good chance. Felt very sleepy this evening yet did not retire till eleven.

Friday, February 24, 1888.   Sent off Lesson 23 this afternoon. On my way to the post office I saw Jennie's father come and I believe I had some idea of running at first merely because this was the first chance I had to speak to him, and that on the street. I did not feel equal to it and was much relieved to find he had turned off. Finished most of Lesson 24. About eight went over to Jennie. We went down to the school house and found no one there. Jonathan came alone a quarter of nine and later Miss Z and Penrose. She had been down twice before. She seems to be anxious about it. After much ado we selected three farces instead of a play. Mike R.H.S. Penrose, Rufus Landes and the Magargals are to help. It was nearly eleven when we went home. Cant help finding fault with that Miss Z. I deserve a sharp reproof from J.

Saturday, February 25, 1888.   Mailed Lesson 24 this morning. Wrote a line to J. withdrawing a half-promise to come over tonight. It was late last night and besides it seems not quite the proper thing to say, "I will come" as leaving no alternative, or even "May I come" for she might not like to refuse. Promised her once she might read all this. Wonder if I'd not better fly for my life when she reads some.

Read some of Scribner's format. It is a good number. Mendellsohn's Letters are brought to a close. I can read a little now in between.Commenced Thackeray's "Newcomes." He uses so much Latin and French. Read only two chapters.

Sunday, February 26, 1888.   In the house all day reading Scribner's and the Press. Didn't get to meeting and mother was little pleased thereat. Sam's mother came in from meeting. Mr. & Mrs. Bean (Kate) came soon after. They had been here last Sunday and found no one at home. They were all here for supper. Mr. Bean has taken his father's business. He talks well and makes a good impression on the older people. Amanda's fellow came before seven and sat in the room with us without saying a word. I left at eight and so was a little late as Jennie thought. She intends to study bookkeeping some time. I asked her whose books she wanted to keep but she wouldn't say. Should I ever have need of a set she might keep mine. She thought would be nice. Twelve o'clock was here before we thought it and I had to leave.

Monday, February 27, 1888.   Colder again. Made some shelves for books in the window between mine and the boy's rooms this afternoon. Did little else but stand about in the factory looking on. Had an excellent chance to speak to Mr. M. this evening as I went to the post office. But, not thinking about it at the time, I forgot to avail myself of it. It makes me angry yet. Spoke to Mr. Appenzeller about our entertainment. We meet tomorrow evening at Jennie's. Told Rufus about it.

Heard that Miss Moore and Miss Z had rented Barne's cigar store and intended to start a dressmaking establishment. Don't believe it will be long-lived.

Tuesday, February 28, 1888.   Very cold again. Made out bills this afternoon and part of the evening.

There is a new strike on the Chicago Burlington-Quincy R.R. This time it is the Brotherhood of Locomotive Engineers. It is said the Knights of Labor will take their places in revenge for what the Brotherhood did in the Reading strike.

Went over to Jennie's about eight where we met to consult about the entertainment. Lowva the Pauper was chosen instead of the other three. Miss Magargal takes the title character. Jennie could do it best but she did not like it on account of some of the situations. She takes Mrs. Craft. I think her refusal to take the other is commendable. Lillie was just itching to have it but that would spoil the play. I think Aggie Farnham suits her well. She is allowed to dress. Jonathan takes Dick Langley, the villain of the play. Col. Farnham fell to my lot, a southern gentleman and J.B. Rufus, Mike, Miss Bertha Magargal, Miss Moore, R. H. Landes, Ambrose, Penrose, Horace and W. A. Crouthamel were also assigned parts. Horace, Rufus, Miss Moore, Miss B. Magargal, and W. A. C. were not present. Adjourned at 10:30. Meet at the same place next Tuesday. I left last. Jennie had been opposed to the piece before. She is reconciled to it now though. The boys were up yet. Hurried to bed.

Wednesday, February 29, 1888.   Thought I'd never fall asleep last night. Was so excited on account of the play; pictured it to myself though I had not read it yet. How to do it, where the weak places were and so on. And then I fancied J. must be angry with me for surely I did not leave her like a lover. These things pained me and I anticipated but a weary day.

John came late this morning, and is down with a very bad cold. At last he has received tidings about his examination. And they are glorious! Double Entry 95 per ct, Single Entry 98, Theory 99, Bus Forms 100. Average 98 per ct. He will leave me in the shade I'm sure. They had mislaid the papers. They are slow with my papers too. Read Lowva the Pauper this afternoon. Don't like the place where I have to embrace Miss Farnham; but that can be changed. Grandmother S was here today. Must now work on the books.

Thursday, March 1, 1888.   If I am not the greatest ass in existence (to use strong expressions as Wenhold did today) I'd like to see a greater. Last evening I had the best chance I can ever get to speak to Mr. M. privately, and in no danger of being observed. I met him on the street, but, instead of taking advantage thereof I stupidly passed him and then peered into the darkness after him, regretting it.

Was over to see the new building. One is under way. Stopped in at Funk's and looked at some furniture he is sending away to New York. Very beautiful. Poor Funk! He complained to me this morning about his business being ruined and so on. I'd like to help him if I could. Read Thackeray's Newcomes. Had Jake Moyer down here this evening but I went to sleep while he was here. Jonathan came in this evening to get the play. He goes up to Magargal's.

Friday, March 2, 1888.   Disappointed again with the non-arrival of my lessons this morning. Not until this evening did they come and then silent about the examination. Read Newcomes: Promising I think.

I have no doubt before long I'll be calling Bill Freed a good fellow and that sort of thing although I have abused him heavily already. I suppose everybody would a good fellow with me if they did me a favor even if I knew they were bad. And all this because Freed promised Jonathan and myself to fix up the stage for us and curtain complete. It's a good thing he sees his own interest in it any how.

At the Library, well I had to rid it of a number of boys who behaved badly.

Clymer was up and we had a long talk about Physiognomy till ten o'clock. He got me interested on the subject.

Saturday, March 3, 1888.   A very nice day. Only now and then a cloud obscured the sun. Quite cold though it looked like a spring day.

Grandfather S had his land surveyed today. He will throw his land into the market. Plenty of land to get now. Hunsberger has bought Milt Souder's place too. Worked on my lessons this afternoon and got out Nos 25 and 26 but did not send them yet.

Sam got a new set of tools last evening. I think today was his last day of apprenticeship.

Sunday, March 4, 1888.   No breakfast this morning. Too late in bed. Always manage to get the boys down and then lie awake.

Read Newcomes. It's long and I am only at page 180. Father told me Frick was up. Did not see him till this afternoon when I held the horse for father who went out to Aunt Kits. He happened to be out at the same time. Rather expected Uriah would come. Read the Press and an old story about a monk. An early supper and up to see Frick off. Come across Uriah, who came up this afternoon, and he accompanies me. Frick "broke up" as usual. Saw Uriah off. Went home and made ready for Jennie. And Miss Moser her friend is to be married next Thursday! Jennie is going down. Wanted her to tell me what her **beau** ideal was, but she wouldn't. She said I was "all right." Ha, Ha! I know it would do me good to know. How quickly the time passes. I had been here but a short time I thought when I had to go.

Monday, March 5, 1888.   Mr. Milt Moyer came back from a trip West yesterday morning. He had been away nearly two weeks. Jennie went out yesterday for the Autocrat of the Breakfast Table and read some. She is delighted with it. Sent off Lesson 25 at noon. And snow two or three inches! Looks just as if it were midwinter; but it will all end in mud.

Mailed No. 26 this evening. Hallelujah! tis done!

Met Mr. Moyer going home from the first meeting of Council. Saw him enter Stover's store and was on hand when he came out. Made a terrible bungle of it I know, and am ashamed of myself. But it wont have to be done again. He asked whether it was to be this spring. I said no time had been mentioned. He said she used to say she wouldn't marry yet. He had no objection. Am glad it's over. Jennie will be surprised.

Tuesday, March 6, 1888.   Read most of the time I had to spare. Ran up to the hardware and saw Jonathan about the play. He says Mr. C. will not help. So we gave that part to Ambrose and took in Sam. Told Sam and made ready and went along over. We were the first ones this evening. The books were distributed as we thought proper. Promised to copy for several. Miss Z and Horace were not present. We read over the piece. Will meet at same time and place. After they were all gone talked about the subject uppermost in our minds. She says her father hasn't said anything yet and that she was surprised when she received my note telling her about it. And now for a ring. No excuses! Too business like. Bosh! So she gave me one Milt gave her when she went to North Wales but which is broken. No matter, no excuse. So I kiss her goodnight and sent my best wishes to Miss Moser. Wrote Ed Danley.

Wednesday, March 7, 1888.   Feel quite light-hearted and dont mind hard work. Found time to read a little in the Abbot at bank. Read Newcomes at home. Am getting interested. Went up to Hunsberger and ordered a ring. He will go to the city tomorrow. Sooner than I expected. Mound a round of the town. Looked in at the church; the painters were there. Saw H. C. Landes cellar. It is full of water. Saw the two Moyers houses. Carpenters on the porch of one and mason's in the cellar of the other. Cold; quite cold.

Mother went a visiting today; down to Mrs. Becker this afternoon and to Zuschnitts this evening. Sam took her to Beckers in the carriage. Told her this evening I was engaged. She knew of course, as I supposed. She said little which pleased me well. That we did it for ourselves as everybody says. She always thought I wouldn't marry young and I said I wouldn't.

Thursday, March 8, 1888.   The papers this morning state that Emperor William is dying. He has been suffering from a slight cold which took a serious turn. It is said the Crown Prince will return to Berlin though he is not fit to travel. Told Funk, and he was affected a little I thought. The fact is, all Germans are for and proud of their Emperor Wilhelm. Funk has been in N.Y. putting up a bookcase. Enjoyed his trip very much.

Read Newcomes. Delightful.

Copied R. H. L.'s part in Lowva the Pauper.

Went up to Hunsberger's and fetched the ring I ordered last evening. It's beautiful. It's in a plush case. Inside the initials, "W.S.H. to M.J.M." "3 mo. 6, 1888". The "S" in my name is a little scratched but will soon wear off. I felt like dancing and am indeed very happy. Jennie had no school this afternoon. No doubt she is enjoying herself at the wedding. Hope she is having a good time of it.

Friday, March 9, 1888.   The old Kaiser is still sinking and his death is momentarily expected. Preparations are being made to remove the Crown Prince from San Remo to Berlin.

Returns from Buffalo this evening with comforting news that the teachers were very busy and had not yet looked over my examination papers but as soon as this is done they will let me know.

Jennie had no school yesterday afternoon and today. She is down at the wedding. Am tempted to look at the ring sometimes. Scratched the window of my room with it.

Mike Bergey was here this evening. He thought it was Library.

Spoke to Jonathan about the future &c.

Saturday, March 10, 1888.   Kaiser Wilheim died at 9:30 yesterday morning in the 91st of his age and 28th of his reign. The new emperor Frederick III was proclaimed and starts from San Remo today. He is not fit to travel. Got interested in these representative Germans.

Read Newcomes. Sent No. 27 and copied some. It's now ten and I am sleepy; therefore, to bed.

Zeigler in Harleysville is sheriffed. This settled him completely.

Sunday, March 11, 1888.   Rainy, wet weather. Read Newcomes all morning.

Went to meeting this afternoon in spite of the weather. Sam did not go. He is down with neuralgia. There were but few people at meeting. Jennie was there and that made it better. Sat on the top bench near the door. People looked at me perhaps but I did not wish to carry my umbrella far. Home to my book again. Did quite well today. Sam is a great deal worse. And now to Jennie while the winds whistle and roar we have a happy time together. I put the ring on her finger for which it is a trifle too large. She is pleased with it I think. She gave an account of Miss Moser's wedding at which she was present on Thursday evening. She came home on Friday afternoon. When the time comes for me to leave I am reluctant to go out in one of the fiercest snow storms we had this winter. There is such a sharp wind that it blinds you.

Monday, March 12, 1888.   The storm still continues. The snow is drifting everywhere. It is a regular blizzard. Business was interrupted. Only one mail came up in the morning about six. The telegraph wires were down and the local freight was delayed here all day. The roads are all closed. Shoemaker's four horse team came into town this morning and had to go through drifts as high as the horse. Three market men who go down on Tuesdays came over this afternoon and stay over night. The doctor was out on horseback with another man. No Blooming Glen or Gehman mail. The train which passes here at 10 A.M. with three parlor and sleeping coaches and two others, with two engines, one broken, reached here about six o'clock. I watched them as they passed up the road and soon heard that they were stuck in the cut. Put on my great coat and ran up. There they were fast in the snow six or eight feet deep. They tried to back out but couldn't. And oh! what a wind. We seem to live in the tropics down here in comparison to the biting air on the bank above the cut. The passenger cars were afterward successively drawn out by the freight engine which was also almost out of water. They shovelled in snow afterward. Ran up again after supper. Was better prepared for the cold. Waited in vain. Went down to the store where a young man wanted to sell his watch to raise money. Went over to the station and saw what was going on there.

Tuesday, March 13, 1888.   (Monday) Those fellows who were out last night had a hard time of it. They say Will Hunsberger isn't back yet. Rufus came home at five. Strasser, they say, is snowed in at Shellenberger's &c. They say Freed's is crowded with hungry people. Kratz sold bread and coffee in one of the cars. They'll stay all night and all next day perhaps. One car is an excursion to California. Another to the City of Mexico. Worst snowstorm I ever saw. Still snowing and drifting, 10 P.M.

(Tuesday) Thermometer almost down to zero this morning. Snow drifting nearly all day. We did **no** business at the bank today. People came to town across the fields. John and I went over the Ledger. I can't see how anyone can come tomorrow. No School, no mails, and nothing. Nothing was accomplished in getting away this train till this afternoon. Were it not for McCarthy the assistant roadmaster I don't believe they'd be through yet. But he brought 58 men from Lansdale and all he could get here and set them to shovelling and then ran his engine through at full speed. They got stuck at the upper end of the cut but soon got out and went up the road. He came back about 9:30 this evening with a south bound train. He is a man who will work without orders and disobey orders if need be. The belated train will start tomorrow morning. Three engines are stuck at Hatfield. Sam and I went over to Jennie's but no one else came. So we had a good time by ourselves. She says they've had a great time about her ring. All understand.

Wednesday, March 14, 1888.   At this writing 9:45 P.M. the last train came up, the second from the city. It had two engines. The unfortunate train at last started off in a snow-storm at 11:30 this morning nearly fifty hours late. The hucksters are over here waiting to go down. The Blooming Glen mail came over for the first time this week. Had a sorry time of it for Wednesday. Mr. Gerhart was the only director who was here. Having no papers and nothing I fetched me Newcomes to pass away the time which hung heavy on me. Had another snow this morning. Clear this evening. The roads in the borough were opened today. Schools were opened today again. I met the dearest girl in all the world on her way to school. A man on the snow bound train was taken sick this morning and Freed refused to take him, so Tyson came and took him up before Freed's own inhospitable door to his eternal shame. Oh, everybody is denouncing his selfishness and rapacity, and none louder than the writer but mother says mine don't count, that she thought I wasn't the ox I had shown myself &c &c. No doubt she is right in the main but I could not see my way clear to ask people here. Is it cowardice? I am afraid it is easier to make fine speeches about hospitality and such things, than to show oneself as such. Have just finished Newcomes. It is a very, very good story. Wish Jennie could have followed me. **Now**, I have read a good novel; next, I must go to work.

Thursday, March 15, 1888.   Today all the passenger trains are running nearly on time. They had two engines for every train this morning, but this evening it is better. At last we have heard from the outside world. We got all our papers today. The storm elsewhere seems to have been more severe than here. In New York travel and business were suspended. The wind reached a velocity of 66 miles an hour in Phila. A regular Western blizzard. Phila. and N.Y. were both completely cut off from the outside world. The storm reached over only a limited area. Eastern Penna N.J. and part of N.Y. Washington D.C., etc. Sent off No. 28. Am very sleepy. Am making a report for the library.

Friday, March 16, 1888.   Library this evening. Had a meeting of the board of managers. Jennie sent a note saying she'd like to go tomorrow evening if I pleased. Of course I please.

John spent the whole day with bourough councils. He is their clerk. They were considering bylaws. Sat in Ed's office when Jennie passed on her way home. Ed used to take Freed's part but he has given up. His unfeeling refusal to take the sick man awakens deepest indignation from Phila to Bethlehem. It destroys the reputation of the place. It is true that he charged 75¢ a meal and 3 eggs for 25 and even 10¢ apiece. Everybody, everywhere is talking about this extortion. Mr. Zendt, too, the agent made a regular ass of himself. He thinks one must be really be

Saturday March 17, 1888.   Goettler had to print his paper on one sheet only as his patent outside failed to come. And then he had to print them all over again as — so they say — Freed was not pleased with first issue. Don't know why as it contained nothing anyone need be ashamed of. It is smoothed off for Freed in both issues. A piece appeared in the Press the other day reflecting upon the people of the town. Jennie tells me a reply will shortly appear in the North American. It's to be M.B.M.

Was over to see J. this evening. She was a little angry with me a short time because I laughed while we were discussing temperance.

Sunday, March 18, 1888.   Got up very late this morning. Read The Abbot and His. of Germany all day. No church and nothing. Weather fine.

Herr Jacob Moyer was here part of the afternoon and evening.

The aid society met today. We did not go down as Jennie preferred to stay at home and I was glad of it. Was over last evening. Had intended to go to an entertainment but there was none.

When I came over there was a number of children singing. Miss Emma Krupp was there. Milt, his wife and Mrs. M. were in the room. J and I came in afterward. After they had all left the room I thought J was different. It is true she was kind and picked out selections from the Autocrat to show me, yet I felt different. We were silent a long time and I wished afterward I had gone home sooner. I am sure she was glad to see me go. Was very angry with everything after I got home.

Monday, March 19, 1888.   At last I have the result of my examination in a letter this morning. The result is Com Law, 99%, Letter writing, 95%; and Arithmetic, 95%. Better than I expected.

Received this evening an invitation to a birthday day social at Hessie Magargal's on Wednesday evening.

We had company today in Mrs. Enos Licey. Read but little. Did some copying and work on my lessons this afternoon.

Beautiful day.

A reply appeared in the North America of today signed by M.B.B. replying to the piece in the Press. It is good in some points. I think it is almost easier to write on the other side of the question.

Tuesday, March 20, 1888.   Wet, rainy weather. The snow has to go now. Felt so weak all day as if I had not my sleep out.

Worked at No. 29. Have it all ready except the questions.

Met to rehearse this evening. All there except R. H. L. and Penrose. Horace was there for the first time. We jogged over the piece slowly. Miss Magargal invited us again to the party. Jonathan was lively tonight. After they had left I showed the result of my examination to Jennie. She thought it was right good. Don't know why I feel so angry with her. There's something the matter let her say what she will. We go the party tomorrow night.

Wednesday, March 21, 1888.   Thursday — I have a dim recollection that it was about half past one when we got home from the party. And a snug little party it was, too. Mrs. Crouthamel, to whom I was introduced, Miss Ratzel, Ambrose, Ed Price and Norah, and Jennie and "mineselluf." It was raining all day and had not quite ceased last evening. This kept some away, but I believe some stayed away intentionally. Jennie told me on the way home it was Miss Hessie's eighteenth birthday. We had some pretty little games. Bingo was great fun the ladies being in the majority. And we boys never before stood such a chance. They have a wonderful snug little house. We had the inevitable dinner, supper, lunch, repast, or what on earth it's called. Mrs. C. gave some music on the piano while dinner was going on in the kitchen. We had cards afterwards. Can't play but would like to learn. Jennie does. When we went home it had cleared off cold. We went down the railroad being nearer and not so muddy.

Thursday, March 22, 1888.   I have the unheard of honor to be private secretary to our girl for I am to answer a fellow's letter and say that she will be pleased &c, &c.

Was sleepy and took a nap this afternoon. Tried to read the Abbot but didn't amount to anything. Commenced Lesson 30 this evening. Stood around the store pretty long. Wrote for a work on Arch. Drawing. Want to see what it's like. It is very cold this evening, viz — 22°.

Felt better towards J. than I did on Tuesday evening. Thought then there'd be an explosion soon.

Monday, March 26, 1888.   Today it rains again and it snowed last night. No end of winter! Felt a great deal better today, for the last two days I was half sick with toothache and a conglomeration of other aches. Lay around all day yesterday. It was better last evening and had a real good time with Jennie. My face is a little swollen though. Jennie had lots of company yesterday. Uriah was up. He was down twice. Read the Abbot and finished it today. Received a book on Building Construction. Must get another yet. Half a notion to go down to Cassel on Friday. Did some copying this afternoon. Mr. Kratz has sold the bakery to H. B. Freed who will run the two. He takes possession next week. Jennie tells me that the Countess knows of our engagement.

Wednesday, March 28, 1888.   We met last night at Moyer's. Lillie and Rufus were not present. Sam and I were a little late though not the latest.

Stayed a few min after the others left. She showed me the books of the teacher's reading circle.

April business is just now commencing. Had 1st notes today amting to 23,000. Not much cash. People are only getting ready. Did some ruling for my lessons this afternoon and attended to some other business. Rufus helped awhile at bank today.

Thursday, March 29, 1888.   And now the mud is so deep that people can't get through.

We met to rehearse this evening and all were present except Sam who had work up town. Miss Z. looked (or scarcley looked at me at all) very sour at me. Wonder if some one told her of one of my plain talks. There was much laughing all round. Mike and Horace left right after we were through which made JMH a little angry. We decided to try and get ready till Apr. 21, and get the Sellersville Orchestra. Then some one started a game and soon we were at blind man's buff and so on, and it was late before we broke up. We had lots of fun. And then I had to plague and tease my dear girl for awhile and it was half past twelve before I knew it. I did not tell her how late it was but ran home after stealing two or three kisses and bidding her goodnight.

Friday, March 30, 1888. Good Friday.   Got up at about eight o'clock this morning. Finished my 31st lesson and mailed it at noon. I believe John was in bank awhile this morning. Looked for Jonathan but did not see him. I was an hour late. Saw him after dinner in the barber shop. The band was on its way to Perkasie. Went down to North Wales with the 1:25 train. Didn't find Andrew at home but looked at his drawing instruments and talked to his mother and sister. He came home about half past six. Talked to him hurriedly and called at Hargrave's but did not find him at home. He followed us to the station soon after. They promised to come up on the 21st. Met Jonathan after I came home. We went into Freed's to see about supper for the Orchestra. He made a reduction of 50¢; he asked 25¢!

Sam moved this evening.

Told the others I was going to study drawing. That I wasn't going to work for 400 a year forever, &c, &c.

Saturday, March 31, 1888.   They are having huge fun on the other side (at Kratz's) They were going to have a brass band but that was all blow. And why are we not there. We have been invited it is true and specially too but it was only by an accident that they found out we had not been invited. It came late but we were immensely flattered. It was just five min of six. I was to bring my girl by all means. It was kind of them but we were unable to get ready. And so I set here writing to the tune of "What's to be done with drunken sailor?" while Sam is sleeping on the lounge. Took a peep through the window. I pity their dog who sits alone on the back porch unable to take part in the festivities and unable to understand what's going on. But I don't think I would like to see Jennie in such crowd. I dont think so. So Farewell! Fady [?] Watkins.

Sunday, April 1, 1888.   A fair day. Just a little rain in the afternoon lasting only a minute but enough to discourage me from going up to the new church where there was preaching and where a new Sunday school is to be organized next Sunday. Made a great mistake this morning. When mother was away I spoke to father about my plans and mother I think overheard me. This does not work well.

I passed a very pleasant evening with Jennie. Told her about my plans, troubles &c and said something that hurt her. She told me her ideal was to be one who would make her care for him and that I had done so. Left about twelve.

Monday, April 2, 1888.   Had a busy time of it today. Felt a little dull perhaps and it made me quite angry in the afternoon while balancing. April is upon us in good earnest. Got out at half past four but John stayed in.

Kratz's sale was just over when I came home. Went to work on the books. Sent for a work on drawing.

Kratz's had their sale this afternoon. They will move on Thursday to their house uptown. Hen. Bergeys will take their place.

Tuesday, April 3, 1888.   A fine day. The roads are drying off fast. Mutter ist noch bos. Sie sogt nichts zu mir.*

Rufus Landes helps at bank. We were not as busy today as yesterday.

This afternoon after the others had left John asked what good will I would pay for his position. I said I couldn't afford to pay a cent for it as I would soon be in the same position as he is in. He then told me he had an offer from some party in town and that he did not know what to do. He only wanted a little encouragement. But is my opinion that he is afraid to make the change. I think it would be better for me if he does not.

Could not get away this evening before eight. Jennie was ready to go when I came. Jonathan and others were down among them. Sam and Mike were not present. They both need it bad enough but don't care. We rehearsed in the schoolhouse. There was too much foolishness of course. Pictures on the board and so on. It was a quarter of eleven when we got home.

Wednesday, April 4, 1888.   Beautiful spring weather. We were not pushed as hard today as I supposed we would be. They had a racket upstairs again. John S. Ruth got off another of his speeches. It was aimed at John Barndt and Ed I think. He made a great noise, shouting and striking his fist on the table. F. J. Frick who had been sheriffed by the Doylestown Bk the other day was also mentioned. He succeeded in stopping the proceedings against him. Work will soon commence on a small addition to the house containing a range, bathroom &c. Have to go to work on my lessons. Got a letter from Uriah this morning. He wants to know about the entertainment. Today was the

*Eng. translation: Mother is still angry. She says nothing to me.

commencement of Jeff. Med. College. Umsted and Groff got through, I think. Groff goes to Bethlehem as resident physician in a hospital.

Monday, April 9, 1888.   Have been so busy that I found no time to write in the evenings. It rained on Thursday and I went out to the school house and arranged to have the rehearsal postponed to Friday. That night it rained very hard and woke me up. On Friday evening the Library election interfered a great deal and kept us late. Mike and Penrose were not present. Horace was disgusted with our order. Lillie was very angry with the Magargals. I actually behaved for once, and Jennie thought I was angry with her because she was a little wild. While the fact is it pleased me much to see her so full of spirits. It was very late when we went home. Sent off lessons 32 and 33 some time this week. On Saturday was the night of the entertainment. When I came over I found the Magargals already there. Jonathan came away from the band soon afterward and then we went up. He said he had front seats for us but they were gone. Jonathan was up in front with the band. They had some pretty good pieces but there was too much nigger show about it. We all agreed we had to [do] better or ours would be a failure. Met Horace and Mike on my way home and spoke to them about entertainments. Mike was away from home and could not be present. They agree that we have to beat them.

Lay in bed late yesterday morning. After dinner father asked me to come to the barn to speak to me about mother. He said it would drive her crazy if I persisted in my intention of leaving the bank. I promised not to leave this place next year but could not promise more. O how I wished I could have brothers and sisters that I would not be missed. Went up to the new Sunday School this afternoon. They did but little. Was surprised to see Jennie and her visitor come. Stopped in at grandfather's on my way home. In the evening I was introduced to Miss Cope of Norristown a friend of Jennie's (Schoolmate.) She is a pleasant person. After she went into the upper regions I poured my troubles into Jennie's ear. Told her of my plan in regard to Mr. Moyer. With this she disagreed and I have given it up as it would be stooping to obtain and end however much desired. And then to crown all, she laughed at me when I told her my salary was only 400. She thought I had nothing to worry about. But then she don't know how low this amount really is. Showed her my new books and she thinks that is the thing for me. Why did she herself four years younger and that she could live her life over again? Yet truly she loves me as I never deserve to be loved.

Tuesday, April 10, 1888.   Monday — A nice day. Rufus tells me Uriah was up yesterday. He is coming up in a team in two weeks. We decided this afternoon to go to work hard on our piece and get it out in two weeks. Will meet every night this week on the hall after tomorrow. Kohlschrieber asked me about the church organ and claimed that it belonged up to the new church. This induced me to speak to Mr. Godshall about it. He is not very well pleased and if he could get help he would start up again. He came over a short time this evening. I frankly told him that should there be two sunday schools I should take no active part in neither. Mother was present and she said something about my talk with father a week ago but not much. I think she has changed her manner toward me. She laughed when I told her of a trick of the new horse.

Tuesday — The paper says Roscoe Conkling is dying. He was caught in the great blizzard and has been sick since. Jacob Sharp the old briber is dead at last. There is a great fuss about Prince Alexander of Battenburg who wants to marry Victoria daughter of Kaiser Frederick. Prince Bismark is opposed to the match and does all in his power to prevent it. Dont know what will come of it.

It was raining today. Jonathan came in and we arranged to meet anyhow. So I went over and told Mike. Jennie did not expect me at all and wasn't ready. She had company. We met in the school house for the last time. Rufus Landes, RH Souder, and Sam were not present. We will meet on the hall tomorrow evening.

Wednesday, April 11, 1888.   We were not kept as busy as I expected today. Rufus I hear, is sick. There is something wrong with the directors. John S. has accused Ed of having been to Slifer's standing and having helped to get the bank in for it. He goads the others on and wants to provoke them. Thus far they have kept their heads. I believe that he would like to break off and go to Doylestown.

It was nice this evening and not too cold on the hall. Mike was angry half the time this evening and Jonathan says he cant bear him. I tried to keep composed but could not keep the dignity of a judge to hear Horace, and then Jennie taking him in hand and making him repeat his part till he had it right after the manner of a schoolboy. It was eleven o'clock again before we got through. I opened the hall and then went down for Jennie..

Thursday, April 12, 1888.   Looked like rain this morning but cleared off in the afternoon. Wrote to F. A. North & Co. about programmes in Mr. Landes' name. Met Jonathan this afternoon and we went over and ordered the hand bills. Spoke to Freed about a curtain. He says he'll put in another. There is a photographer at Freed's. He took the schools today. Saw the negatives. They look funny.

The masons commenced work at home yesterday but stopped off today. They've commenced tearing down inside. Dust everywhere. Jennie and I were first again. Jonathon & Co. second. Rufus is still abed but better. Roscoe Conkling is better too. Last evening I didn't speak loud enough. I spoke louder tonight but not better. Oh, if we could only get more action in it. They dont read out of the books much but its too tame. When I told Ambrose how to put on ring in the piece, Jonathan wanted to know where I had learnt it. He's suspicious.

Saturday, April 14, 1888.   We (J & I) came on the hall last evening as we thought, late, but there was no one there. Jonathan & Co soon followed and so on till, Horace & Mike, and R.H. L. were missing. It was too late to begin so we had a few games of "Pussy Wants a Corner" and succeeded in breaking a funnel for the photographer.

This morning the handbills came out and Jonathan and myself prepared them for the mail. John went away this afternoon at two. We're not so busy any more but John is. After bank we went over on the hall and began work. We found out there was to be a delegate meeting on the hall so we gave up our rehearsal tonight. Sent word all around except Sam. Went over to tell Jennie about half past eight. I'm not to write here what she told me but the hours passed so rapidly that it was half past one when I went home. I was ashamed of it but I think nobody heard me.

Sunday, April 15, 1888.   Got up very late this morning as late as nine o'clock. Helped to hitch up the horse for father. They went up to grandfather H's. Little Lillie Souder came down to say they should come up to grandfather S's as her parents were down. Went up to the new Sunday School on the hill. Dengler was there and had things in hand. He called upon Jonathan to help him. He asked me to teach a class and I promised for this Sunday. Stopped in at grandfather's on my way down. Went out to see Rufus Landes with Uriah. He is getting on well but we considered it best to set another studying in case he can't help. Set Elwood at it.

Went up to Jennie's about eight and instead of sending me home at ten as I had told her to, it was nearly twelve, because as she explained she wanted me to stay yet. Had a very happy time together.

Tuesday, April 17, 1888.   Yesterday afternoon at three Ed Danley came into bank. He said he was on the lookout for a job. We didn't get through at the bank till five, but we managed to do a little work on the hall. Took Ed along up and he was there the whole evening. We tried to have quiet but there was some noise, I think they were all a little angry. After it was over I hunted up Elwood and Danley in the station house.

Horace, Mike and Ambrose were there to pour out their complaints. When I came in they commenced. I said everybody was angry and that I was angry with Horace. I gave it to him pretty thick. He got angry, called me names, said I had insulted him, and swore he'd not come up any more. We went home and passed a very bad night. I was excited and could not sleep. Went over to Elwood where there was more room.

This morning wrote about programmes &c without success. Danley told me Horace said I had to apologize or he would not help. Danley went away on the 9:25 train. I think he has some promise of a job with Fred. At noon I asked Horace how and where I had insulted him. He said there was nothing only he had got angry, and he confessed he had been hasty, took back the "damned fool" phrase, said it was meant more for the others than for me, &c &c. Of course he got no apology from me. I had arranged with Jonathan to go down with me to Clymer to get him but Horace said that was not his intention to back out. We put up part of the frame for the stage. Freed put up something for a curtain. Everything was very quiet this evening till toward the last Horace, Mike, and Cranky got a little funny and I believe they were half full. Got home at eleven.

Wednesday, April 18, 1888.   Got to work on the hall soon after five. Soon after Jonathan came up. We worked till after seven and then went home for supper and get ready. The frame work is now all up and nothing remains to be done but putting the muslin on. It was half past eight when we came up and there was no one up then. We had some tinware for Horace and he did well. But it went slow.

Some of the boys were down in the bar room once and we had to wait awhile. Jennie thought they were half full again. Penrose came long after eleven. He ought to be shaken out once. It was 11:30 before it was over. Mike got angry at Jonathan when the question about boarding the orchestra came up. He wanted to pay for his. Jonathan said he'd he'd take more than his share rather than that they shouldn't be welcome at another place. That made Mike angry. Jennie wasn't pleased too. She had school examination today. That's it.

Thursday, April 19,1888.   This afternoon we finished the frame and nearly all of the canvas. Jonathan put up a curtain along the wall to guard against the paint. Also tacked on the matting on the floor. When Jennie and I came up this evening some of the Sellersville Orchestra men were already there. They were surprised at our late meetings. Mr. Dietz their leader explained how he is going to arrange the music. Jonathan came after awhile and so on. But Mike, Horace, and Rufus were still back. So I started out to hunt them up. Found Horace in the stable where a colt had seen the light of day but a short time before. Got Horace out but Rufus couldn't come. Mike didn't show his face. We went over the piece but it went miserably. I was ashamed of it. After we were through I told Mr. Dietz he could see we had plenty of work on hand. "Yes, you have work to get that through" was his honest answer. It was nearly eleven again. Mike stayed away out of spite no doubt and wants us to run after him.

Friday, April 20, 1888.   This afternoon the Misses Magargals were on hall and helped us along. Bert swept the hall cleaned the lamp chimneys and Hessie patched the canvas. Jennie had company and couldn't come. Freed is too stingy to do anything. We asked him for cord but he had none for us. So we got it ourselves. Felt blue about our performance last evening. If it goes that way will be a blown out failure.

And to crown all at their meeting last evening Councils passed an ordinance requiring every one to pay an licence of five dollars to hold entertainments &c on the hall. Goettler blew about it and this evening at another meeting it was changed to about 50cts for charitable, educational &c purposes. We dont think we come under this ordinance as everything had been advertised nearly a week.

This evening things went more in earnest. We had all the furniture there and all fixed. The boys were all in good time for once. Mike among the rest. They all did much better at rehearsals. Whenever anything was wrong we did it over. We want to go over it several times tomorrow. Tried the lightening. It didn't work very well. We must get a reflector. We used the cartridges to get the boys used to the shooting. Jonathan complained that Mike always shot him in the face. This is dangerous and we tried to get him to shoot another way but it was always the same. And now for the morrow.

Saturday, April 21, 1888.   At last the day has come. When we came to the printing office to get the programmes printed we found printing the new ordinance getting us in for 50 cts license. Goettler said it would hurt us more to be so favored than we would gain. We agreed not to pay the license and pay no attention to it. We had it so reported. Hunsberger told Jonathan we had to get a license. The girls thought we had better. But we thought not. In the evening the constable handed me a copy of the ordinance and said we'd better get a license. I said we'd rather pay the fine. Explained to Squire Beans who was present and he said we need not pay. When Jonathan came rushing up he slapped me on the shoulder and said, " O the darned license, we must get one." I comforted him with Squire Beans.

Went out of bank soon after dinner and on the hall about 1:30. Jonathan and the girls were numbering the chairs. He numbered 87. Made out diagrams. The others came one by one. Did the final touches among us. Found the reflector had been forgotten. So Mike and started for Wolford's a got a splendid piece of tin which we set on a frame. It was nearly five when we commenced to rehearse. Mr. Crouthamel was there as prompter. We went through it indifferently and had no high hopes for the evening. It was ten min of seven when we went off the hall. Had no usher and I was to act. Ran home ate a piece of cake and dressed. Andrew came. Left him and ran up and found people coming in. The constable was at the door. Squire Beans was willing to act as usher. Mr. Moyer at the window. People came in fast. It was a quarter of eight when the orchestra struck up. A ring. Up went the curtain and the play had begun. I went out among the audience during the first and second acts and looked on. It reassured me. Each was doing well and it looked fine. Commenced to whiten my hair during the second act. They said it looked natural. The third scene was fitted up handsomely. Horace did better than I expected. Mike too. Elwood was applauded. Ambrose was stiff. Rufus was excited. Sam got through pretty well. Jonathan went through without a flaw. Penrose passed. Jennie, why she made me afraid, that bold snappish woman. Aunt Charity seemed so in reality. Sonia deserved great credits. Lillie dressed fine. The lightning was natural. Thunder too low and continual. We omitted a great deal in the last act and made laughable mistakes but no one noticed. They seemed to be pleased. And when I said goodnight and hoped they were pleased, they applauded. I take this to mean yes. The receipts were $37.05. Had good music. Took Jennie home and talked it over for awhile.

Sunday, April 22, 1888.   Woke up somewhere between six and seven this morning. Couldnt sleep with so many things on the hall and everything open. After breakfast Andrew and I went up. Arranged things a little and then Miss Z came out and I helped to carry home her things. I then commenced on Jennie's and Milt came along up and helped take the furniture down the backway. Jennie wasn't up yet when I first came down. Miss "Lowva" Magargal was a little to quick for me or I would have brought hers down to

Jonathan's. I met her in the street with Miss Crouthamel. Took Jonathan's
things down. He was still in bed. He needs rest and so do we all. Went down to
hunt up Horace, Rufus and so on to distribute their watches, rings, chains, &c
which had been lying around last evening. Then started to hunt up Andrew
and Hargrave who had come up with the train. They were on the way out
toward the schoolhouse. He could not be up last evening on account of an
engagement at Brunner's. After dinner we started on a drive. Went up through
Telford to Sellersville and all around there, and came back down the pike and
home about four. Looked at Rufus' colt and then took a walk through town.
Supper was scarcely over when the train came. They had to run for it. Sam was
here awhile after supper and talking and getting ready took so much time that
it was nearly half past eight when I came over. It was too bad and she was
really a little angry though she did not choose to give it that name. And then
followed a short game of tit for tat which did no good. She told me about
Sunday school today and said there'd be a meeting on Wednesday evening,
and that if she wanted to go she'd go. She said it so much in earnest that I
could not help laughing and said the same for myself. In the end she said did
not want to go. We arranged to go to Sellersville next Sat.

Monday, April 23, 1888.   At last it is over! And I feel the effects of it
too. Tired, wornout describes my state pretty well. I have no desire for anything
but to lie down and rest. At noon I took a nap and overslept myself half an
hour. Heard rumors from last evening that we were to be arrested. That W.D.
took the train this morning presumably for Norristown. Expected, of course,
that the constable would be around after three. But none came. My plan was to
pay the fine under protest and if they found we did not owe it to return it to us.
It wouldn't pay to fight them. Posted for John this evening till six o'clock. He is
behind hand on account of his assessorship. Went up on the hall and fetched
down the tin used as a reflector. The photographer was working at a negative
of the planing mill. Did not see Jonathan. He was reported to be out. Nearly
everybody takes our part against that obnoxious ordinance. Glad to get to bed
soon after nine.

Tuesday, April 24, 1888.   Expected to hear from the Burgess this
morning but did not. John came in after ten (having work at home) and told
the result of the Burgess' trip to Norristown. He found out that the ordinance
had first to be advertised for **ten days** before it could be enforced.This will
reach till the first of May. This leaves us out and the Wrens also. This news
was so good that I could hardly contain myself. To be found right after taking a
stand is worth a great deal. Had we paid our license no more would have been
said about it.

Am wofully behind hand with my work. But sleep is the best thing I can do
and I get enough of it. Took two naps today and went to bed soon after nine.
Worked a little at Lesson 34 but it didnt amount to much. Jonathan's school
closed today and Jennie's yesterday. Saw her go home this afternoon from my
station on the housetop.

Wednesday, April 25, 1888.   It was quite cold for several mornings but became warmer during the day. Rec'd an invitation to an Apron and Necktie Party at Line Lexington from Miss Barndt. Sent my regrets this evening. Wrote Miss Z as requested by Miss B. inviting her to the party. Worked out lesson 34 and made ready for the mail. 33 & 32 were full of mistakes which the teacher had not seen.

Saw Jennie pass over the railroad this morning. I think she saw me. Took a nap this afternoon. I believe I could sleep any minute I'd try. The plasterers are nearly through upstairs. Went to bed at about half past ten.

Thursday, April 26, 1888.   And now for what happened in the world during the last week. Roscoe Conkling is dead and buried. Emperor Frederick's life was despaired of and is again recovering. Queen Victoria is at Berlin at present. The Battenburg marriage is no longer talked about. Gen. Boulanger has been elected to the House of Deputies in France. There is much agitation there on his account.

A nice day. Found some time to write up my diary and do some on the books. Saw Rufus' colt this afternoon. He is very lively and runs about the yard as if he enjoyed life as he probably does. And now for a surprise. Jonathan called upon me for an explanation about not having Jennie's name on the programmes. He said he felt slighted and thought it had been done in a sneaking sort of way. I explained why it was not put there but told him they could feel as they pleased about it. I would not run after any one &c, &c. This heated him a little, but I kept my balance. Am only sorry I can't return the favor he did me as I fear I can't.

Saturday, May 5, 1888.   All I remember about the last week is that last Saturday Jennie and I went up to the Sellersville entertainment enjoyed it and the ride home. Jonathan and his set and Penrose and his were up too. It was crowded. Didn't meet Jonathan. We put up at Binders, they at Harr's. Overtook them on the way home but went another way.

Next day I was in Sunday School. In the evening Jennie and I had our usual pleasant time together.

Building at home here, and being crowded with work and sleepiness prevented my writing up the diary and so no doubt much valuable history is lost.

Sunday, May 6, 1888.   Sam came home with me last night and it must have been after seven when we got up. Sam went home some time this forenoon. He intends going to the city tomorrow. I lay around all morning reading a little and sleeping more. Didn't feel any too well, having a bad cold and my throat is sore. Groomed myself up a little in the afternoon. Did not get ready for meeting where I had intended to go. Father and Mother went. Aunt Kit came with them. I was upstairs all afternoon. Took mother and Aunt Kit up to grandparents. Found a lot of young ladies on front porch and accompanied Norah Hunsberger down town till we met Price.

It was about eight before got to Jennie's. Aunt Charity was there. We accompanied her home and waited there till J.M.H. and Miss Hessie came back. Had lots of fun going home. It was just nice to be out. Jennie told me Mrs. Walton nee Moser and her husband were up today. They were in Sunday School and said I was naughty for not being there. I pleaded sickness. She says she had commenced a letter to me on Friday evening after I had left but threw it in the stove. She teased me with being spiteful and so on. She thinks I always get the better of her, one reason being because she loves me which she had not intended to do. I could not see it in the same light. Is it any wonder that it was half past twelve when I went home?

Monday, May 7, 1888. A beautiful spring day. Cool and clear. Have sore throat can't swallow very easy.

Jennie begins her summer term today.

Commenced Lesson 35 this afternoon.

Must go to bed.

Sam went to the city this afternoon.

Tuesday, May 8, 1888. Much colder and many expected rain. It is uncomfortable without a fire. We had none in back.

My cold is worse. A cough has been added. Swallowing anything takes an effort.

Finished Lesson 35 this evening and mailed it. That's the best place for me.

Thursday, May 10, 1888. Yesterday Jonathan was after me about going up to Perkasie with the play. He says the Sellersville fellows offered to leave the stage and all for us to play on. He will write about the matter but I hope nothing will come of it, for I know there is more work dissappointments and so on than appear on the surface. And then those blamed rehearsals, they take my time away.

Yesterday at three the man commenced putting in the range. He worked till 11:20 and at five this afternoon he was through. He's a good mechanic and makes money. He got $10.60. He says I have a weak throat. Don't know how that is but my cold is lodged in my throat chiefly and I wish I was rid of it.

I would like to get revenge on Jennie but don't know how so I put it on here in the hope that she will one day read this. Today, she kept holiday but never sent a letter. She might have done it before even though she **is** busy. I think it's all because of giving up to me. She is always saying something about me getting the better of her and while the truth is she is turning me round her fingers at her will almost. Would write but I can't otherwise than in a complaining way and that I won't do.

Worked out Lesson 36 in the rough. Have to copy part of it.

Friday, May 11, 1888.   A little rain last night and some today. There is over a foot of water in the tank. Have an error in Lesson 36 somewhere that I can't discover. Sent it off as it was. Fooled away an hour up at the store this evening.

Wrote Andrew, Uriah, Sam, Danley and Dr. Slifer and have to write to the College yet for publication wish that was over.

Moved upstairs this afternoon. Saw Jennie go home this afternoon. Am a little provoked at her. She'd like to tire me out and make me write. And then no doubt she laughs to herself when she thinks of my wishing it so bad.

Saturday, May 12, 1888.   Cloudy and rain which didn't amount to much.

Threw away a fortune this morning. Mr. Harmes of Hillsboro, Kansas, a prominent Russian whom I met about two years ago called at the bank to see me in company with Mr. Godshall and Mr. Stauffer of Quakertown. We went upstairs and Mr. G's suggestion. He wants an eastern partner to go to Kansas for the purpose of drawing money out there to invest among the poor fellows at from 10 to 18%. Of course he is sucking the blood out of the poor fellows there. He said a person could get rich easy &c. He offered me all this but of course I couldn't. He is a sharp one and would have to be watched. Said I couldn't go away so far from home on my parents account. Then too I don't want to become a Jewish money lender.

Jennie and I'll laugh at this tomorrow.

I'm sleepy.

Sunday, May 13, 1888.   Came down stairs at about half past eight. Read the paper, took a nap, and at half past two came to Sunday school. I was the last to come, of course.

There was a good attendance. Jennie was there and two girls with her. Mr Gerhart and his sister were present. She is getting stout. Went down to Sarah's from there and saw the excavation for the new addition to the house. A lot of girls were there as usual among them Maggie. After supper saw Jennie pass with the aforesaid girls. Ed's came in to pass the evening. Rang the bell at Jennie's at near eight. All had gone to church and [she] wanted to go. So did I, for Hess preached. We found scattered seats. The hall was crowded. Many had to stand outside. People admire Hess. After meeting was introduced to Jennie's cousins. Expected we'd talk over the sermon after we got home. But no, there was no talk at all soon. I couldn't help it brute that I am — — and made her suffer. I must tell her all how I felt and so on and teased and tantalized her. She could bear it no longer and begged me to stop. I don't know why I must make others suffer when I feel a little out of sorts. Well we made up and parted the best friends in the world. And what's best of all, (I'll get my ears boxed for writing it) she slyly imprinted a kiss on my lips and then hid her head on my breast. It was past one when I went away deceived by that blame old clock which struck twelve instead of one.

Monday, May 14, 1888. Didn't mind my short sleep much. Uriah was in bank this morning. He came up yesterday. Was down and I not at home. His eyes are weaker than ever.

There was sunshine and rain at different times today. Mowed the yard this afternoon. It should have been mowed over a week ago. Saw Jennie go home from school this afternoon. Was so stiff and tired when I was through with the yard. So I took a walk all over town and shake it off. Came home at eight.

Tuesday, May 15, 1888. Commenced reading Scott's "St. Ronan's Well". Guess I had best leave novels be.

A most disagreeable day this. It was cold chilly and cloudy. Cleared off this evening. This [violently?] the result of snow out West.

Brought down Reub Hangeys lawnroller on the wheelbarrow. It was heavy work and tired me.

Received Lesson 36 back from Buffalo. Had a monstrous error of over 3300. Overlooked the exact wording of one entry and this caused the error.

Thursday, May 17, 1888. Today the sun came out again for once. It was very cold last night. There was frost in some places. Watched Jennie as she went to school this morning. Knew she must have been up to the post office. Got her letter sometime this afternoon I was very glad to get it.

Wrote an answer this afternoon. Could not begin on it till I saw her pass, that is I was thinking so much of her that I could let slip the chance to see her on her way home from school. But I waited long in vain and I had already given her up when she passed later than usual.

Friday, May 18, 1888. Cold, damp and unpleasnt again today. I wish the weather would change once.

Read a little in "St. Ronan's Well" enough to set me asleep. Did some copying this afternoon. Jennie was as late again this evening.

It was dull at the Library, Jennie was not there.

It's late and I must to bed.

Saturday, May 19, 1888. There was a heavy rain last night — so people tell me — I would scarcely have found out. A little warmer perhaps than yesterday.

Mr. Randall made a speech on the Mills Tariff Bill in Congress yesterday opposing the bill. I am surprised at his boldness. That's not the way to find favor with the President.

Mr. & Mrs. Thompson were up again today. They seem very fond of their new place.

Saw Jennie several times today and passed her on the street. Guess she has been down to Hatfield.

They were surving the pike today. Van Ommeren does it.

Was up at Amelia's for my coat and vest. Met John Q Hunsberger Jos Benner and others. Ben Barndt was black drunk today. Jonathan spoke to me about camping on the 30th. He gave up the Perkasie trip.

Did some copying this afternoon.

Sunday, May 20, 1888.   The girl went away yesterday afternoon so we had to help mother with the work this morning. Read the paper and St. Ronan's Well in the afternoon. Sam came in the afternoon and as he cared little for going anywhere we stayed home. Some went to meeting and some to Sunday School. Saw Jennie go home from the latter. Sam was disappointed in his job and has had but little work since he's down. Sam accompanied me on my way to Jennie's as far as the bank, hatless.

We sat for awhile in the subdued light of the bay window while her parents occupied the other end of the room. We discussed the invitation to Jonathan's surprise on Thursday eve, and talked examinations. These the pleasantest hours of my life are so short and fleeting, and the time we wait for them seems so long. She was out in the evenings several times last week and saw me at work. She delights in teasing me now that she knows I won't tease her.

Monday, May 21, 1888.   A beautiful day though a little cold this morning they said. Many people kept holiday today again in the old way. And when others keep holiday I feel the same way. So I read "St. Ronan's Well" till late at night instead of going to work as I should have. (done)

Saml came in this evening. He wants to go down early in the morning. There was a fine musical concert on the hall by Sellers of Sellersville and Sam and went up for a quarter of an hour in a hurry. They had good music doubtless and some comic songs. A couple of ladies came out at Christ Moyer's and Sam thought one was Jennie. So after a few min at the concert we walked the town hoping to meet some on accidentally. But never a soul did we see worth seeing.

Tuesday, May 22, 1888.   Today beat yesterday. Pretty warm. Just right in the house. Knew pretty well I couldn't work before I was through with that blamed "St. Ronan's Well" that I read as hard as I could to get it out of the way as [illegible] did to cure himself of the liquor habit. It's much like drinking liquor, though this does some good if you keep at good books and does no more harm than loss of time and obliviousness of nearly everything else in the world. I'm glad I'm through with it anyway and did a little work in the yard besides. I must work now. Hightime. This evening yet. The paper hanger and three plumbers were here today.

Had a letter from Ed Danley. He is up at Bangor, Northampton Co. in a grocery.

Wednesday, May 23, 1888.   Rain again today. Instead of doing any work in the yard or working out my lesson I was put to work in the parlor to take off the old paper on the wall.

This seemed a terrible job to me but it did not prove so terrible after all for it came off easy after being soaked with warm water with a brush. It took no more than three hours and Elwood helped some at the finish. The papers plumbers and bummers were here again today, and will be here again tomorrow. I wish the thing were done.

Varnished part of the range this evening. Mother had done some of it.

Thursday, May 24, 1888.   There was no work to be done in the yard this afternoon on account of the rain. So I did a little on my lesson.

The trial of Geo. Neff the Blooming Glen murderer resulted in a verdict of murder in the second degree today. The trial of the other fellow Gettys commences right after.

Went over to Jennie's about half past eight ready for the party. Miss Hessie came in soon after and told me to take care of Jonathan who was outside. I did so but could not find any excuse for asking to go in.

Sunday, May 27, 1888.   Got up late and missed breakfast. A nice warm day and an exception.

Got the horse ready for parents to go to meeting.

Read Scribner's and the paper. Gen. Sheridan is reported dying of heart trouble. Gettys was found guilty of manslaughter.

Old Herman started a Sunday School today. Went to the upper one where Jennie was. Taught a class. Got disgusted with the ticket method. It's all a humbug. Took ice cream with Metz. Saw Haynes. Horace had him out driving. Mrs. Ellis came down after supper. She's got the prettiest little baby with black eyes.

Found Jennie alone. The Magargals had been around her a great deal the last week. She was not pleased when I recalled some incidents of last year. I had not treated her well and she feels it yet. I was puzzled at first because I only thought it matter to laugh at. It's true many of those things should be forgotten, and I'm just glad it has changed. How unwillingly we part is shown by it being always very late.

Monday, May 28, 1888.   Missed breakfast again this morning. Had enough to do to get to bank at all respectably. Gen. Sheridan is not expected to live 24 hrs. Emperor Frederick is much better and on Thursday attended the wedding of his son Prince Henry with Princess Irene of Hesse, his cousin.

Made some progress on my lessons and I expect to send two tomorrow afternoon.

Saw Jonathan and arranged to meet them at Magargal's tomorrow afternoon.

Expected Uriah up yesterday but he did not come. Should answer his and Sam's letters.

Must clean out my desk yet tonight. They want to clean my room tomorrow.

Today was warm and pleasant but it is raining now.

Tuesday, May 29, 1888.   Worked on lessons 38 & 39 but did not get through with them.

Saw a troop of 50 wild horses in front of the house this afternoon. They are to be sold at Harleysville tomorrow.

Went over to Jennie's. Told her I had promised Jonathan to come up to Magargal's. I thought she did not care very much to go. However, we went. They were playing croquet in the yard light by Chinese lanterns. Fooled about there awhile and we boys went and got a peach basket full of bananas oranges, lemons, and pineapples. Arranged to start between seven and eight.

Stayed awhile with Jennie after we came home and perhaps it was late when I left.

Wednesday, May 30, 1888.   Cloudy morning. Went up to see Jonathan about going. We decided to wait till ten and I went down to tell Jennie. Miss Magargal was coming down the railroad and this drew Jonathan to the spot. We fooled around there an hour or so. We afterward gave it up altogether as the weather looked threatening. About 11:30 Jon came down again and proposed camping in the woods somewhere. So I went over to Jennie and found she settled down to study a short time before. Went up to Magargal's and from there on up to the railroad to the woods above Daub's were we sat down. The ground was a little soft, but all went well though it was cloudy through the greater part of the afternoon. We had dinner and then hammocks. Jennie and I read a very funny story which had a fellow who'd say nothing but, "doose", "begad" and "by George." Ambrose had his rifle and so on. Jennie didn't care very much about and yet we did not start for home till half past seven. We took it slowly and were very tired indeed. Met Sam coming up. He did not know us. Rested awhile on the porch after we got home.

Thursday, May 31, 1888.   Was all broken up today. That racing yesterday did it. Had to sleep on the bed made on the floor last night. Mr. Landes was up to the Rocks yesterday. Finished Lessons 38 & 39 at last this afternoon.

The papers yesterday published Mr. Blaine's letter declining to have his name used as candidate for President.

A baseball match was played yesterday at Telford between the Telforders and the Ironclad from our borough. The Ironclads were beaten 18 to 12 and came home full of — the contents of a beer keg.

Greaser managed to clean yesterday and get through without me about as early as usual.

Friday, June 1, 1888. Barnes & Frederick were very much displeased with the bank for not collecting their note against Frank Hunsberger about which there is a fight. There'd be very little sense in the bank doing anything of the kind. Little Geo. Smith was at last arrested and brought before Justice Detweiler for stealing a watch yesterday. He ought to be put away.

Sheridan is reported dying.

Blaine has written a letter from Paris declining to take the nomination for President.

Had a racket about my room today. The girl wants to save work and get me out of it but that didn't go. The idea of having lived in a room two years and then be deprived of it.

Worked on books this afternoon.

The Library was tolerably well patronized this evening. Jennie sent down some remains from the picnic with a kind little note. Rufus and I feasted thereon when left alone.

Saturday, June 2, 1888. Cloudy again and looked like rain this afternoon. It did rain a little this evening. Mowed the yard this afternoon.

Got ready for the Lecture and it was a little late before I was through, and when I came up it had been put off on account of the weather. Only a few were up I believe. I believe Miss Z had Loux's student Kratz about her I heard.

Sunday, June 3, 1888. It was between eight and nine o'clock when I got up this morning.

Read the paper and "Scarlet Letter" commenced. Was sleepy after dinner and lay down and missed meeting, Sunday School both. Went down stairs near three. Martha and Annie were down. Sam came some time after meeting. He was here for supper. Grandmother S. was also down later.

Did not get over to Jennie till eight. We sat near the window in the gloom till her mother, looking in, remarked that it was rather dark.

Jennie was in Sunday School and from there accompanied the Magargals and Jonathan on a walk to Telford &c. I'd not be unwilling to cut the Magargals more. You can't get rid of them after awhile. Picnics, parties &c everlastingly.

We teased each other a little again though lightly but shouldn't be. One or the other might get savage.

Monday, June 4, 1888. A beautiful day.

The new school board organizes this evening.

Returns from Buffalo this morning. Worked on No. 40 this evening.

Read Scarlet Letter this afternoon. Took a short nap and could work better afterward. Saw Jennie pass this afternoon.

Carpentry commenced work on Sarah's addition to her house today.

Tuesday, June 5, 1888. This morning Gen Sheridan is reported to be dying. He had very severe hemorrhages which brought on another attack of heart failure, the severest so far.

The Dem. Nat Convention meets in St. Louis today. Cleveland will of course be nominated for Pres. and it is thought Thurman for Vice Pres. There is expected there will be a fight over the tariff plank. Scott is out there bossing in Cleveland's name.

And now three cheers and a tiger! Mailed my 40th lesson this evening. After copying and examination's over that hash is settled.

Finished Scarlet Letter today. It's a curious story and written different from any I have read yet.

Wednesday, June 6, 1888. Quite a hot day this. It seems nice this morning and there was a breeze through the day, but this evening it is all still. Worked on the books once this afternoon. It's a good thing I have no book started for I'm sure I'd waste away time now my lessons are over.

Thought I saw Jennie this evening but I must have been mistaken for I did not see her again. Listened a short time to some of Funk's reminiscences. He has a good stock of anecdotes about himself.

The Dem. Nat. Convention did nothing but organize, listen to a speech, waive red bandanna handherchiefs and then adjourn till today. What they will do with the tariff plank is interesting to know. No doubt they'll make a sort of straddle.

Gen. Sheridan was still living and slightly better perhaps. He dies hard.

Thursday, June 7, 1888. It was warm in the sun but there was good air. This evening it became quite cool.

The Democratic Nat. Convention has no platform &c yet. I believe they'll have hard fight over it yet. Having nothing else to do they nominated Cleveland by acclamation went wild over it and adjourned till today.

Did some copying this afternoon.

Friday, June 8, 1888. The Democrats yesterday completed their ticket by nominating Thurman candidate for Vice Pres.

The tariff plank in the platform may defeat the party in November.

It is in favor of free trade in so far as they go.

Saturday, June 9, 1888. The band had a festival tonight. Thought I'd wait till tomorrow and see Jennie but was up at the barber shop and so near that I walked down. She was on the porch where we sat a long time. Her mother wanted us to go in as it was to cool but we were in no hurry to obey. She seemed real glad to see me and I was glad I had come. We did not go to the festival. We had our festival at home. She is going to Lansdale tomorrow to see Miss Markley and stop off at Hatfield on her way home.

Mowed the yard this afternoon. Did no copying.

Sunday, June 10, 1888.   We were in bed till nine. Got up and dressed. When I came down Uriah and Mr. Godshall were waiting to to see me. Godshall wanted to know about giving out tickets in Sunday School. I am down on it and told him so. Don't know what he'll do. My intention was to go to Herman's Sunday School but Uriah hadn't seen the church so we went up there. Dengler was there and bossed everything. The church is to be dedicated next Sunday and the school is to sing. Had a class again. After it was nearly over and Dengler gone Milton made a speech. Dengler would have choked him for it and he deserved it too almost for it amounted to just nothing at all.

Lillie Minerva Zendt and a number of friends were up to the Rocks camping today.

Uriah and I sat in the yard after we came back. He was out in Washington for pleasure. It rained this evening for awhile like a torrent. Met Jennie at 9.11. She didn't stop at Lansdale. She had a good time, she said, but she was really quite sick when she came. She looked pale and had a greivous headache. It got better after awhile and we had a real good happy time of it. She teased me and enjoyed it greatly. I threatened to tell a dreadful story of my wickedness but she wouldn't hear of it and stopped my mouth. Was sorry when it was high time to go home.

Monday, June 11, 1888.   Cool today. Was over at Funk's this afternoon. He makes the pulpit for the church. Was out at the shop too. Paul makes the altar and reading desk.

Read "Bleak House." Here Dickens has the same odd characters again.

My last lesson was returned to me this morning. Wrote immediately to send the examination papers to Ed.

Was half asleep this evening when Mrs. Ed came in my room with Mother to look at it as I supposed but in reality to ask Jennie and me to Martha's wedding on Saturday.

We are to wait on the table if we pleased. This I think is meant as a great honor. Wrote to Jennie this evening which I must send to her tomorrow.

Tuesday, June 12, 1888.   Sent my letter to Jennie with little Mattie to school at noon. In the evening I received a reply as short as could possibly be. It said, "I shall be more pleased to have you come then I care to tell you."

There was a soap man at the hotel who had two niggers with him to draw the people together. Listened awhile to their singing and bone-rattling and then went down to Jennie. She had been up a short time too. She was surprised that Martha would marry now. Annie was over last evening to invite her and said the Magargals were coming. Amelia and so on. There'll be a big crowd no doubt. She'd prefer to be a guest. So would I. She will go to Hatfield this week. We agreed to go about four on Saturday. On my way home I found a drunken man in a great predicament in front of Wm's residence. He was hunting for a hotel but couldn't see no lights, queerist place he ever saw, no hotel around here &c &c.

Wednesday, June 13, 1888.   Was a little lazy this morning and didn't take any breakfast. Told Mr. L about Martha's wedding and he surprised me by giving me to understand that Maggie would be married on the same day.

Spoke to Mrs. Ellis this afternoon. She says there'll be a great crowd. Told here to ask for more help.

Went up to Hunsberger's this evening and ordered [illegible]. Butter knife in a case.

Stopped to see the niggers at Tysons on my way home.

Gen Sheridan is improving. The Emperor is not improving at all.

Thursday, June 14, 1888.   Nice day today. Looked like rain though.

Finished nearly all the copying this afternoon. Don't get to reading just now.

Got my present for Martha this evening. It's right nice I think. Got up there very late. He was just closing up.

Cut off the roots of the Lemon tree this afternoon.

Elmer Souder was very unlucky yesterday. His hand was caught the Planer and badly lacerated. He has a great pain.

Friday, June 15, 1888.   Emperor is said to be dying Dr. Mackenzie was unable to feed him with a tube. Sheridan is getting better. There seems to be a belief that Mr. Blaine will be nominee in spite of his letters.

Very hot today. Maggie was down to tell about her wedding tomorrow.

Sus. Gentsch is reported in trouble.

The library was slow this evening.

R. R. Cressman of Tylersport had an attack of apoplexy. Horace Bergey too had a few fits.

Saturday, June 16, 1888.   A very hot day. It was cloudy all day and we had a fine shower in the afternoon. Got a half an hour later out of bank than I wanted to and it was 2.30 before I could go. Then the barber kept me waiting. It was half past four when I came up to Jennie's. She was ready dressed and very becomingly, I thought. We found no one there yet except old Oberholzer's. We went out into the kitchen where I introduced Jennie to Kate (Mrs. Ellis). We then went to work preparing oranges, making lemonade and making bouquets for the table. After the table was ready we walked about the yard. The young people left at six and were back I think soon after seven. Jennie tended the front door. Not half as many came as I expected. Horace and his girl was there. None of the Crouthamels except the old people. Harry Hunsberger's, Henry Oberholtzers, et cetera. I was proud to have Jennie there for there was none like her there. Yet it made my own stupidity the more observable in comparison to her. Didn't like the idea of having her work there and after we were through I was for going home. Ellis went and we followed soon after. Jennie had some kind of silver bowl for a present. We left the table as it was. Jennie was very tired.

She said she liked it well. I suppose she thought my parents would be there. She is afraid of meeting them, I think. It was after ten when we went home. I remained with her yet awhile and everything was well till I left when she suddenly drew away and said she would not kiss me. It pleased me but little and was puzzled to know what it meant.

Sunday, June 17, 1888.   Very warm this morning got up reasonably early.

Went up to church as it is to be dedicated today. Got as cool a seat as could be had, on the backseat near the window. Dichant preached in German. Rev. Whitmer in English. I liked him well. There were many in the church. There are children's services in the afternoon. I expected we'd have company for dinner as they were so many people in town but there were none but two girls who are here to see Amanda.

Took a nap after dinner and came too late to get into the church.

I never saw so many people in Souderton as today. It was crowded to suffocation inside and many more outside where ever they could find shade. Was with Elmer Weil a great part of the afternoon. After it was over we went down to Reub Hangeys' to see the people pass. Up the street came Jennie and her company Miss Cope. I tried to be very angry with her and tried to persuade myself she didn't care for me. Went up to grandfather's to see the house. Home to supper and then over to Jennie's in time for church but she did not care to go, which agreed with me for I had forgotten my pocket book and was in quite a predicament on that account. So we walked in the yard and I put flowers in her hair (just think, for a fellow who wanted to scold) and then took a walk up the railroad with Milt's, and so on. So that I forgot to scold. And when she told me I had never spoken so harsh to her as last evening I was quite crushed and was sorry; for I had not remembered it. So we made up and I really believe she served me right. She said I seemed indifferent and that caused it.

Monday, June 18, 1888.   The weather was almost unbearably hot today.

There was a fine shower this evening. Met Jennie this afternoon going home from school and again this evening. Walked with her a short distance to her uncle Christ's. She says she is going to Hatfield tomorrow. Tried to study up a little for my examination but it amounted to about nothing.

Grandmother was down with little Stella this evening. Went to bed early.

The Republican Nat Convention meets tomorrow at Chicago. There are many candidates, almost every state having one but is thought that they may be forced to nominate Blaine even yet.

Tuesday, June 19, 1888.   A very pleasant day this. The rain last evening cooled the air and there was a fine breeze all day. Jennie went to Hatfield examination this morning. Saw her go enter the train this morning.

The remains of Emperor Frederick were yesterday laid to rest. There was no funeral sermon. The young Kaiser issued a proclamation to the German people. He issued proclamations to the army and navy on Saturday which are said by some to have a warlike tone.

Grandmother H's spent the day with us. She is coming down again when they paint the house.

Commenced my examination this afternoon. Jennie was on the porch for a short time and I could see her plainly. I'm afraid she ran in when she saw me.

Left the office after nine. Met Amelia and Maggie. Congratulated M on her marriage. Found Mr. Beideman at home. He stays over night.

Wednesday, June 20, 1888.   Warmer than yesterday. Mr. Beideman left this morning. He invited me up to Reading.

Received such a nice letter from Jennie this morning which wrote last evening. Wrote in reply this afternoon. Saw her go home this afternoon.

Continued my examination this afternoon and evening. Ed is away much of the time.

The Republican Nat. Convention met yesterday in Chicago. Nothing was done except to organize. The same confusion prevails. Everything in doubt.

Thursday, June 21, 1888.   Hot out at Chicago. The convention goes slow. They formed the permanent organization yesterday. Estee of California was chosen as permanent chairman.

Blaine — Blaine

Worked on examinations in Ed's office. Was very hot and went to bed soon after I came home.

Friday, June 22, 1888.   Hot weather. Yesterday the convention adopted a platform. This is a direct challenge to the Democrats. They go in for high tariff and reduction of internal revenues. Also reduction in postage rates &c.

Nominations were made yesterday and the following were nominated: Gresham, Hawley, Phelps, Sherman, Rusk, Alger, Titler, Depew and Allison and Ingalls. Three ballots were taken this afternoon. No results California must have voted Blaine in the beginning. Meanwhile Blaine is coaching in Scotland and seemingly indifferent as to the outcome of the Convention. Everybody thinks he will be nominated.

Worked on my examination. Met Jennie in the store this afternoon. She says her school left out yesterday.

Saturday, June 23, 1888.   This was the hottest day this year. It was over a hundred in the shade. The sun was terrible. I cannot see how people could stand it. The convention reached a ballot only yesterday and they were of not much significance all sticking to the favorite sons. Everybody still thinks that Blaine will be the nominee. It maybe that they will be compelled to take him. This afternoon the fourth and fifth ballots were taken. Sherman held his own. Harrison had 213 having lost two in the last ballot. Alger gained but little. Depew withdrew his name last evening and then the convention adjourned. They seem to want to obtain time to make deals. It's too slow for anything.

Worked at the examinations this afternoon and evening but could not finish as I had hoped. Thought several times I heard Jennie pass and this made me wish I could go out and walk. For it was hot as blazes. I had to have it closed partly and then the lamp. There was a shower this afternoon.

Sunday, June 24, 1888.   Hot this morning already. Read Bleak House awhile and then went out to Maggie's to return her album and something to help her in housekeeping. We sat in the front yard as it was the coolest place around there. Had the Press. There was a big picture of Blaine and smaller ones of all the others. The Convention took two ineffectual ballots yesterday and then met again only to adjourn until Monday. It looks now as if the nomination of Blaine were inevitable unless he withdraws again. They can't agree in no other name and they are all actually fighting him. He hangs like a great cloud over the convention. Saw Uriah. Went to Herman's Sunday School in the afternoon where Jennie happened also to be. She taught a class. Old Herman shook hands with me after it was over and said he was surprised to see me there.

Went up to Uriah afterward. Mr & Mrs Slifer were there and Bean's came afterward. It was half past seven when I got over to Jennie's. Father and mother had left for a drive. Milt Moyers' too, went out driving. It was too hot. Almost as hot as yesterday. We took a walk out Water St. up the railroad &c. Put wild flowers in her hair. I like to do it. They become her. She told me Charley had had some trouble on account of the note that was not discounted last Wednesday. I explained it to her.

While we sat in the room a gust of wind came and cooled the air but we had to close the shutters and so the room was necessarily hot. It was my pleasant task to fan her. We were very happy together. Trust nothing may occur to mar it.

Monday, June 25, 1888.   Hot again though an improvement on yesterday and Saturday.

News came this afternoon that Benj. Harrison had been nominated by the convention on the eighth ballot. It is rumored that Blaine had withdrawn his name by telegraph this morning.

Finished copying my examination papers late this evening. Was very tired after it was over.

Tuesday, June 26, 1888.   Very pleasant day. Not all hot. Harrison and Morton (Levi P. Morton of New York) were yesterday nominated by the Chicago Convention. Harrison was nominated on the eighth ballot. Morton on the first. Blaine sent two cablegrams in the morning desiring his friends not to vote for him. This turned the tide at last to Harrison. Sherman's friend's had great hopes but were deceived. Mr. Blaine when he heard of the nomination said "A good nomination." His wife owned to being a little disappointed as she had hoped he might be nominated by acclamation. Blaine probably could not have been nominated except by fighting Sherman &c and he did not want to do that. Elkins had prepared a trap for the others by putting forward McKinley as a dark horse. Sherman had withdrawn his name already but on discovering the trick went in again and fought to the last.

People seemed relieved that Blaine is not the nominee. They were doubtful of his strength.

The last act of the convention was to pass a resolution sympathizing with all wise and well directed efforts in for the promotion of temperance and morality.

Mailed my examination papers this evening. Hope for the best.

Wednesday, June 27, 1888.   It was cooler than yesterday today.

Pres. Cleveland was yesterday formally notified of his nomination for re-election. Read "Bleak House" a little this afternoon till I fell asleep.

Got a letter from Uriah this morning giving addresses where mathematical instruments could be obtained.

Started about six for Ben. Frederick's with mother and grandmother to visit old aunty Kit who is sick with neuralgia. The drive was very pleasant and we saw the farmers at work at their hay. Anticipate a good time for tomorrow evening.

It commenced raining on a very small scale this morning.

Thursday, June 28, 1888.   Rainy and cold.

Had to give up the drive we arranged for this evening and wrote Jennie to that effect this afternoon.

Read Bleak House. Very interesting. Did some writing &c. Wrote Uriah and Ed Danley.

Am getting restless and thought of going to the city on Saturday. Can't bear it any longer.

Friday, June 29, 1888.   Very cold today. Very little rain, but cold damp weather.

Mr. Barndt was after Mr. Landes about a teacher this afternoon. Don't know if he was a little full but he talked well. He favors Fulmer. Gehman it is said is also an applicant. I wouldn't teach the lower school if I were Jennie. Wouldn't do it.

Read Bleak House this afternoon. Too interesting for me. It takes up too much of my time. Worked at the books this evening.

Saturday, June 30, 1888.   Very much warmer than yesterday and gradually cleared off.

Received joyful news this morning. It made [me] dance a little. Averaged 98¾% at my last examination making my general average 97⁵⁄₇%. Will get my diploma middle of July as Mr. Davis is busy. Their letter contained lots of taffy.

Went over to Jennie's this afternoon and arranged to go out driving this evening. Went home mowed the yard and commenced putting rods on for the stair carpet. Had Elwood for hostler and started about 7:15. Went up through the town, everybody staring at us; stopped for some roses at Umsteds old ruin; when I came out the horse commenced to back and frightened Jennie; showed her my Buffalo; she was very glad of it; always knew I would do well. We stopped at Hackman's creamery; went in and saw it work; the separators were at work; Jennie thought it looked very clean. From there went on, little caring where we went it was so pleasant. Went further out and then down to Leidy's and from there on home. It's good that we have a faithful horse and I may even trust him too much.

A pleasanter drive one couldn't wish for. Came about 9:30.

Sunday, July 1, 1888.   Very nice and cool today. Was upstairs all day reading Bleak House. Enjoyed it as much as anything. Had intended to go to Sunday School but did not get ready on account of some work I had to do.

Saw Jennie go home from Herman's Sunday School.

Went over to Jennie about eight. Found her in the parlor the other room was full of people. Talked about school affairs. Went over to the other room afterward where her father was. She asked him to apply for the Telford School. Jennie is going to see Miss Cope on the Fourth and will start Tuesday evening.

Monday, July 2, 1888.   Got up pretty late this morning and was, on consequence, late at bank. First I heard was that Mr. Landes had sold his property to Isaiah K. Moyer and was to build.

Found a letter from Uriah saying he'd be pleased to see me on the Fourth. Also to my surprise, found my diploma there. Very fine penwork by Mr. Davis but the lithograph work could be finer I think.

Worked in bank till near six. Read Bleak House. Saw Frick who is up on his vacation. Showed my papers to him.

Tuesday, July 3, 1888.   A very nice day. Found Sam at home this morning. He had missed the train. So he went down with me on the 9.24. He got off at Columbia Avenue. I at once commenced a search for mathematical instruments but spent most of the time looking at the pictures hanging in the store fronts and at Jewelry. Bought a set at Queens', 924 Chestnut for $9.75 10.50 with extras. Went in at Porter and Coate's to take a look at the books. Bought a ever little on called "Don't" which I gave to Allie in the evening as she liked it. Was at Leary's. Hunted up Andrew's place but he had left already. Went out to old Lib's who insisted I must stay for supper and take her out to Slifer's. Mahlon is not very well. Lost over 30 lbs. Talks politics. Went out to Slifer's. Found Uriah in the hammock. Sent old Lib home. Allie went along out. We walked around the square. There was one house where she expected to be spoken to but they did not see her. We didn't get to sleep till one o'clock. Too much laughing about old Abe Hanes picture in Uriah's album.

Wednesday, July 4, 1888.   Wagons, gaily decorated with the national colors filled with people bound to seize on the best places in the park made the streets ring long before we were up. Artie was preparing to meet Henry and Irwin who were coming down. We went down to Uriah's office after breakfast. Started about ten for Independence Square with in his team. Met the First Regiment on parade on Broad St preceded by the Ringold Band. When we got to the Square I left the carriage to see the speaker. Saw Gen. Hawley the orator of the day but did not here what he read off his manuscript speech. Mayor Fitler who presided sat by his side. Uriah went down to look and while he was away the mailcarriers to the number of 552 paraded into that street and I had to drive out. After it was over we started out home. Allie was there yet and made dinner for us. Uriah could hardly eat as we thought the balloon would go up at one o'clock. Drove out as hard as we could and got there a quarter past one. The balloon wasn't nearly ready, but they were sending up paper balloons and dummies and all sorts of animals. We came back to the east side of the Schuylkill to see the races. Met the racer which was a single scull race between four. Turned back and saw the finish. Went back to the old balloon. Which wasn't ready. So we drove up to Belmont Mansion and Gen Drury Park and back and around the park. When we came back the balloon was nearly ready. Uriah left the carriage to see plain. I had to move out of the crowd on account of the horse. Uriah lost me as I had expected. Had a great time till I had him again. The balloon was called Eagle Ernie. Went up north easterly. Went up along the west side of the river to see another race. There were five starters Eight-oared race. We saw the start which was splendid but could not follow on account of the crowded road. Went home where I only stopped say goodbye as it was time to make the train. They wanted me to stay and see the fireworks.

Thursday, July 5, 1888. Very hot today. There was a shower this evening accompanied by heavy lightning. This cooled it off somewhat. Grandmother S and her would-be sister-in-law, "Old Nance" were here this afternoon and evening. Did nothing but read Bleak House this afternoon and evening instead of attending to other work much more pressing.

But I want it out of the way and be done with it.

Friday, July 6, 1888. Perhaps a little cooler than yesterday. The rain last night tempered it a little.

Had my drawing set along to bank today. I believe they think it's entirely too much for me and that I'll make nothing of it and so on. I am inclined to believe it too though Jennie wouldn't, but I am going to try and stick to it. But not as long as I am reading novels. This must stop or I'll never get anything done. Determined this afternoon that Bleak House must be finished today and get rid of it. I succeeded though it was twelve when I got through and was hardly conscious of what I read.

The library was tolerably well patronized tonight. There was a meeting of the board of managers about buying books though nothing was done. Walked a short distance with Jennie. She will take the primary. Mr. Godshall was to see her and says the salary will not be reduced. Asked to come over to see her tomorrow evening.

Saturday, July 7, 1888. Very hot today. Took a short nap at dinner. Worked in the yard in the afternoon and also at the books. Went over to Jennie about 8:30 to show my diploma and drawing instruments. She thought they were nice to have merely to look at. She says Mr. G. was over to see her about the school. He was surprised to hear that she had applied elsewhere and said they would not reduce her salary &c. She says she had a good time in Norristown especially on the 5th when she was with the Countess. Left about half past ten or eleven.

Sunday, July 8, 1888. Got up late, very late. Played with my drawing compasses a little and then went to Sunday School though it was late. Jennie came in right after me. Read along in the Ger. Testament class. After sunday school Uriah came down. I made him stay for dinner. There were only three of us. The girl, he and I. Parents were down to Landes'. After dinner went out to the shop for the police clubs after which we took to the woods and lay on the ground. Teased him about not coming down, although we had already arranged to go.

Started about 7:30. Had some trouble with the horse and whipped him. We didn't know the house but happened to get the right one. Miss Barndt came out to meet us. We were taken to the parlor where Uriah sat in state. Miss Barndt gave us some music. She plays very well. Stayed an hour and a half. Left at ten. Jennie was almost afraid to go and wanted me to let the horse walk. It was pitch dark and dangerous, but the horse was all right on the way home and we had no trouble with him. Jennie gained confidence after we were through the covered bridge at Unionville. She had a headache. Felt a drop or so of rain. It was eleven when got home and I did not go in but kissed good night.

Monday, July 9, 1888.   Commenced to rain last night about two and rained all day. Welcome, this rain was. There was a narrow escape for Moyers Co's hayhouse on Sat. afternoon I believe. The roof caught fire from a passing engine and was seen just in time to prevent its being burned down. Didn't know till last evening when Jennie told me. Today William got up a petition praying the railroads to fix a screen in their locomotives and had me write it off this afternoon.

Uriah went down with the 9.24. Am much interested in that drawing and would would like to play with them all the time.

Tuesday, July 10, 1888.   Last evening Jennie sent me her photograph by mail. It was a very agreeable surprise. It is an excellent likeness. Put it into a frame to see how it looked. I am going to frame it and hang it up in my room.

Wrote a note at noon thanking her for it. The back was all scribbled up with drawings.

Mother wants me to go up and see Frick.

Finished the blank books in my bookkeeping and prepared to put them away. Took me all evening. Told father how the horse acted on Sunday and got permission to ride him.

Rec'd a letter from Andrew. He says I promised him once to invite him to my wedding in bed. He must expect something of the kind shortly. I don't remember it.

Wednesday, July 11, 1888.   Nice day this.

Roeller Cressman of Tylersport was buried today.

Made a drawing board this afternoon. Wanted to ride out this evening but Elwood had to go to Franconiaville. He reports the horse wild.

Mother is not very well pleased with me for not seeing more of Frick. She urged me to go and see him this and last warning. She thinks I'm in fault.

Met him up at the furniture store. We arranged to go out driving tomorrow evening.

Thursday, July 12, 1888.   A lovely morning but his afternoon it rained enough to put a stop to harvesting for the present.

Stayed at drawing afternoon and evening.

The rained spoilt our intended drive. Frick says he can go Saturday evening.

I thought Jennie might write but she didn't.

Saturday, July 14, 1888.   Nice cool day. As previously arranged, drove out with Frick this evening around most everywhere. I am afraid I spoilt the pleasure of his ride somewhat. He had promised to call on a Miss Godshall this evening with no intention of doing it and it so happened that we had to pass the very house where she was staying. Frick was troubled all evening about it for he had intended to say he had been detained at home by company and now that wouldn't do. Of course I was very sorry but couldn't help laughing about it. Met Dr. Slifer this evening. He wants to see the Library &c. Found Sam at home when I returned.

Sunday, July 15, 1888.   Went out about eight and took Dr. Slifer down to the Library. He praised it, and we talked over his proposed lecture about China and Japan. He would like to give it here. I think we'd better have him come. Asked him to come to Sunday School but he wanted to leave with the 10 o'clock train. I was afterward surprised to see him walk in and sit down. He said he had changed his mind. He go up this afternoon. Mr. G. asked him to make an address which he did very appropriately. Jennie was in, too, early. Asked him home for dinner and promised to take him up to Telford if he'd like to go to the other Sunday School. He accepted. He talks about his travels in preference to anything else. He has been sick for sometime and is resting. After dinner Frick and his friend, Mr. Wil. Godshall of Lansdale came over. The latter has been in the Lansdale Bank since April. Went up to Sunday School with Dr. S. He was pleased with the church. He thought it was warm and asked me to go for the team. He waited in the school while I went home. Couldn't get the horse to go. When we got to Telford we didn't know the house and had to hunt it up. At last we found it at the opposite end of the town from where we looked for it. Stopped at Derstine's but found no one at home. Went home down the County Line and out Water St. because it was shady and because I thought I might find Jennie and give her a ride but Schwenk's were on the porch and she was not there. So I went home. Found Sam there. He told me some bearded fellow had been into Bergey's with Jennie, the Magargals and Jonathan for ice cream. It made me almost angry with them for it and I certainly felt a little jealous. Had Sam upstairs showing him my drawing set, &c. He don't look well at all. He ought to do something for himself.

Monday, July 16, 1888.   Sunday.

Went over Sunday to Jennie's about half past seven. Her mother showed me in the room. She came in immediately afterward. We took a walk as it was so nice out Water St. When we came back Milt teased her about being wild that day. She hated it and wanted to quiet him. We sat awhile on the porch. She told me about her visitors today. Dr. Snyder and a South American who had met the Magargals after Sunday School. Yet, I could help teasing her about the South American all evening. She thinks I really didn't care. But I couldn't help showing that I disliked the Magargals more and more. She intends going up to Sellersville with Bert to see the baseball. I threatened to go with Goettler. She don't want that. Asked her not to mind me. Left soon after twelve. She promised to write.

Monday — Nice day. Wrote Andrew this evening. Fixed up the hammock in the grape arbor this afternoon and took a nap, read Scribners' and Carpentery and Building there.

Played about little at drawing. Can't help thinking of last evening. Perhaps I am doing her a great injustice but I feel as if I had reason for complaint. I don't doubt her when she says she loves me, but her parents, her brother, and even that brother-in-law Schwenck have a better hold on her. Then she don't want to show that she cares for me. It's all secret on her part now. She wouldn't let me take her to and from Sunday School for fear of the talk; yet she is with the Magargals regularly as if she liked them better. Then they introduce her to South Americans whom nobody know more about than they are strangers. I am convinced that I don't mind all that. Will go with Bert to Sellersville to see baseball though it's as plain as day that Jonathan and Hessie will also go. But I don't want to say anything. I want her to see it herself. I don't want to seem a jealous tyrant. But brooding overs it make me unmannerly to her I know.

Tuesday, July 17, 1888.   Nice and cool today. Played at drawing this afternoon. Worked some at a frame for my diploma.

Rec'd a letter from Jennie this evening. She thinks I ought to be sorry for what I did Sunday. She thinks it would have made her angry if I had done what she did. I wrote an answer in which I think I am fully avenged. Hope she won't be angry.

Wednesday, July 18, 1888.   Mailed my letter to Jennie this morning. Wondered all day whether she had already read it.

Framed my diploma this afternoon and evening.

This evening I received another letter from Jennie about the contents of which I was so curious that I opened it in the store. It is a mercy she did not see me for I could not help to burst out laughing. I read over the letter many times. I think she was pretty angry when she wrote or wishes to seem so to me. The latter is most likely. There was no formality about it. She just commenced as if she would drown me with a volume of words, was very short all the same and simply signed "Jennie." I tried to think of an answer for it; but I was so overcome by the humor of the situation that I sometimes laughed aloud, which made my parents ask what was the matter. They said I acted as if I were turned crazy. Prepared an answer which I fear is little better than the former one, but ending seriously again. It was very late till I had finished half past eleven.

Thursday, July 19, 1888.   Rec'd a third letter from Jennie this evening. It is very agreeable to find a letter from one so dear awaiting you. But though I was glad for this one and felt as though I carried a treasure with me yet I was afraid to open this one at first. I think I saw her watching as I was on my way to the post office. I wondered what she must think of me. To put it off awhile I read Goettlers paper first though I hurried through it too. I then opened the letter and glanced first at the close where I saw, "Penitently yours" and I was surprised. I then read the letter. She says my letter had counteracted the effect the first had produced. I had not expected this at all. She could not tell how vexing the other one was. She says she is sorry for it all, and hoped this would end it. I am almost sorry now for what I did. If she knew how intensely I enjoyed it all since Tuesday evening she would pronounce me heartless. On Monday I felt bad over it and when the opportunity came I could not help revenging myself a little. I felt as if I had the lash and could not withstand the temptation to flourish it playfully if only to show my power.

Friday, July 20, 1888.   There was some rain yesterday and last night.

Gen. Boulanger is reported to be doing better from his duel with M. de.

Thursday, July 26, 1888.   To Perkasie Campmeeting with Jennie this evening. Didn't get home till twelve. A very pleasant drive.

Saturday, July 28, 1888.   Went over to see Jennie but did not find her at home. She was up at Magargal's again. Waited and soon saw them coming down the railroad. They met Jonathan. I kept out of the way when she stepped in the window. Told her I could not have the horse tomorrow and she prefers not to go with the train. So we gave it up.

Frick is up and had supper here this evening.

Sunday, July 29, 1888.   Went to Sunday School this morning. Frick was in too. Jennie came late. I suppose she slept too long. Lay about reading and sleeping all day. Took a walk in the evening. Went to church this evening in company with Jennie. Rev. Mr. Gross preached an interesting sermon. Perhaps I teased J a little this evening. The time passed very quickly.

Thursday, August 2, 1888.   This was a day, famous for mistakes, misunderstandings and good luck after all.

This afternoon after bank I received a letter from Jennie written last evening, changing the programme for today. Going with the train instead of the carriage and at three instead of six. As it was then past three I went over hoping to explain the matter but found she had gone with the three o'clock train with the rest. So I went home intending to go up at five. Then that train does not stop at Perkasie so I decided to go at half past six. Went up in time and as I was talking with grandmother I caught a glimpse of Jennie standing in the door. This was a surprise and I went over and explanations followed. She mailed the letter last evening and felt quite angry with me as is natural. She came back at five and stood on the porch while I was on the platform to go with the train. So she got ready and we went up. Found the services very interesting so that we missed the last train down. Had we hurried very much we might possibly have made it. But I thought there was time &c. Found M.H.Roth and wife in the same fix. Got a team of Cressman got home that way. Ulysses Barnes who boards up there was our driver. We had a good time and old "Rosy" brought us home till 11:20.

Saturday, August 4, 1888.   Baseball between Ironclads and Sellersville Jrs. this afternoon. Ironclads 14; Sellersville 12. First complete game I ever saw. Liked to look on but it was hot and had to borrow an umbrella. Jennie and the Mags. and their visitor were out too but I did not go near them till on the way home when I spoke to them. One young fellow was hit on the head and dropped down like one shot. But was soon all right but found he could not take part in the game longer.

Sam's here over night.

Wednesday, August 8, 1888.   Jennie left for Norristown or near there this afternoon. She will stay with Mrs. Walton a few days and will then bring the Countess, Miss Hoffman along back if she can. I did not expect her to go till tomorrow. I was over this evening to tell about an invitation I had from Jonathan to go to the Rocks with four horses on a big wagon &c. I was glad of an excuse for not going as I did not care to go.

Thursday, August 9, 1888.   The contract for Landes was given out this morning. We got it for $2275.

Our girl was fetched away this morning on account of the arrival of a baby in this world last night at Prices.

Mrs. Mininger our neighbor did the work for us. Miss Ellenberger will be here I believe tomorrow afternoon.

Saturday, August 11, 1888.   Our baseball team beat the Telfords by a score of 38 to 15 this afternoon.

Received a letter from Jennie this evening. She had written two, one to her Mother and the other to myself and had mixed them up so that her mother got my letter and I hers. Effected an exchange through Milt. She is not coming home till next Wednesday. Her friend Naomia will not let her go.

Monday, August 13, 1888.   Got up about half past five this morning and answered Jennie's letter.

Saturday, August 25, 1888.   Felt very bad all morning but got through well with my work about dinner time. Got Mr. Landes permission to go away. Wanted to start about half past one for the celebration but it was nearly two before we got off. It was held in John Press' woods. Everybody seemed to be there. Jennie looked for her sister Annie but did not find her. A baseball game was arranged in an adjoining field. We went to see it and took Mr. & Mrs. Irwin Bean along. Found the Mags, Amelia and Mrs. Milt under an apple tree. The game was uninteresting and stopped after three innings 14 to 1 in favor of Souderton. We went back to the woods and looked on. The Mags introduced us to a number of people I've forgotten who. The Lansdale Band furnished the music. Met Miss Barndt. We started away about six o'clock. On the way home we had what Jennie called a race and in which I was beaten thanks to my skill in handling a horse. Was furious at the fellows who did it. Jennie wasn't pleased. We made it all right immediately. Stopped at the house just as the train came up. The horse was frightened so that it took Milt and me to hold him.

Sunday, August 26, 1888.   Got up at seven, did a little reading, and got late to Sunday School. Sam wasn't there so I did not go into the class. Taught to a very bashful little girl instead. Took a nap after dinner and read a little of Josephus. Went up to Sunday School. Remarked how the influence of that powdered lady has gradually pushed out those she did not like and filled their places with her own set. There's Miss Tyson, Jonathan who is still Sec. however, Old Schock and so on. Found Aunt Kit at home. Mr. & Mrs. Allebach (Maggie) who had been in Sunday School paid us a visit. Went over to Jennie's about 7:45 and talked politics with Milt and her father for a while. Felt very bad all evening but and it must have been dull for her. She says she has not had time to do anything at bookkeeping and I am not to come over till Thursday evening.

Monday, August 27, 1888.   Slept badly last night and this morning I took a dose which spoilt my whole forenoon. I didn't get any work done this afternoon. Read Scribner's & c. Sam Musselman's condition is slowly improving. I was very glad to hear this as they had lost all hopes of his recovery.

Willie Moyer came over this evening with a note from Jennie asking me to come over. Miss Markley and Miss Barndt were there and she had invited the Mags. and their clan. They were there already and playing croquet with the help of lights placed in the windows. A wheelbarrow race, watermelons and various kinds of games followed. There was one young fellow there who is quite an athlete but wants to be too smart and I don't think Jennie liked him. Miss Markley is nice but I don't think she has much influence over Jennie like Miss Hoffman and Mrs. Walton. Left at ten.

*An ice storm—business trips to Philadelphia—epidemics
wrack town—Milt's son and daughter die—a daughter is
born—"that dreadful enemy Diphtheria has [entered] our
house"—the hired girl dies—the death of Daniel—scarlet
fever, and Jennie breaks down—Catherine dies—a coal
famine—father remarries*

1902

Tuesday, January 21, 1902.   Had Ellis to Ambler yesterday. He
examined all of Mattison's belongings. He seemed most impressed by the amt.
of money spent. Stopped at office and inquired about design for altar. He told
me he remarked to his wife it was a pity we were not situated in a more
progressive town. That we were worthy of a large business.

Found a message from G.R. Wallace this morning. Went to city at 10:15 by
trol. to Lans. Was at Burton's. Took a look at the Delaware all floating ice. Was
introduced to H.K. Wampole. Found him a Dutchman, says he is raised at
Salfordville. Found a green Irishman slightly tipsy on cars. He was all smiles.
Had to shake hands when I left the car.

On Chest. St. found the Lightning artist of ten yrs ago and got two of his pts.
framed all for 30 cts. each. I saw him painting the one in 5 minutes.

Wednesday, January 22, 1902.   Willis has Diphtheria in a mild form.
The house is quarantined. Met Dr. Oberholtzer and he says he may be over it
in four or 5 days. Grand F. Moyer boards at Willis'. He thinks it all queerness
of other folks to fuss so much, I suppose it is harder to submit yourself to
hardship than to see it in others.

The fellow who offered me oil stock yesterday at the picture sale wrote
already and seems to think I am an easy mark. Helen tells me she is best in
spelling. She has just entered the A class and is rapidly forging ahead. I wish
Amy would work as hard.

We have braced a new floor in 2nd story of mill. Makes it much stiffer.

Friday, January 24, 1902.   Daniel has such a bad cold if not worse that
we kept him from school this afternoon. This evening he was chilly and if it
were not for the fact that Willis sits with him at school I wouldn't think of
anything. I am very much afraid of diphtheria. They tell me Willis is better.

Rec'd a letter from 2nd Lieut. E.E. Hollenback Co. L 1st Reg. N.G.R.
ordering a company desk or chest. He asked how is that for a [illegible]? He is
back draughting and superintending at Otto C Wolfs.

The sensation in Washington now is the approching visit of Prince Henry of Prussia. England takes pains at this time to show that he was our friend during the war. The other nations are pointing out how they showed theirs.

Germany seems to go to great pains about the matter. We are nearly through repairing at the mill. Am taking stock account.

Saturday, January 25, 1902.   We are through taking stock but have not tabulated yet. On Monday I hope to start work in earnest. Have two jobs for the spring which I will start soon, besides some other work.

Daniel's cold is still very severe though I think now there is no diphtheria near. I hope sincerly we may escape that affliction. Willie is getting better I believe. Ida told Jennie that he was out of danger. That his heart was all right.

The treaty annexing St. Thomas and the other Danish Islands has been signed yesterday.

The girls had to be punished today and Helen bears a mark on her forehead. I wish they would once get so they had more sense. They fight so much and then there is tumult. If I were home more I would stop it if possible.

Sunday, January 26, 1902.   A rainy drizzly day. The Mennonites had baptism this afternoon 14 being baptized. 13 in meeting house and Annie Clymer of across the street was baptized in the creek. Jennie and the girls went to see it. I stayed with the smaller children as I did not care to crowd into the mud out of mere curiosity. The meeting house was so full that Jennie had to come home. There was no standing room.

I went to Sunday school this afternoon and to church tonight. Not very full.

Susan Derstine stopped in this afternoon. That Henry of ours is a useless creature, always in motion and hard to manage. Very strong and determined.

Monday, January 27, 1902.   Rain in afternoon. On Sat. eve J.B. Delp and Dan Gehman were nominated councilmen in place of Wm. Landes and Jonas Landis. J.G. Hunsberger being renominated. Delp was at the shop this afternoon and we talked about more efficient water service and road super-vision. I am in hopes he will push these matters should he get elected.

We have about the same amt. of lumber as last year 68 to $6900.00 worth. Father and I are going to the city tomorrow to see about a machine for cut off saw.

Tuesday, January 28, 1902.   Went to the city with father this morning. The house I was to bid on had been burned out and was certainly a wreck. The Millwork was about all gone. Some very good furniture beeing burnt up. We walked by the University and seeing the Museum I persuaded father to go in. There we saw cave dwellers relics, skeletons and pottery together. There were Egyptian Mummies and Central American skulls were there. Toys, tools, idols and arms and statues of very early times were there. Father was much interested.

We bout some machine repairs at L. Power & Co. I took him to the lightening artist. We forgot to take dinner through it all and I am afraid it wasn't good for father. I was very cold and the cars were cold coming home.

Wednesday, January 29, 1902. Weather very cold today. There was about 6" of snow.

Finished altar railing for Hat. Ref. church today. They think they will not have to borrow much money on it. They will dedicate in 3 weeks after Sunday. The Lutherans want to build too. That will leave Leidy's in bad shape. I think those congregations had best come to Souderton and keep Leidy's for a burying place. The Lutherans were talking of building here but they are very slow about it. J.M. Landes had promised them two lots on Broad St. but don't like the situation. The Ref. at Perkasie are also going to build. The Sellersville people are just completing theirs. There is too much cheap building going on and the consequence is that consistant rebuilding is necessary. There ought to be a return to the practice of olden times.

Thursday, January 30, 1902. At the consistory meeting Ellis in a joking way offered to buy a bell if someone will finish the church tower. Some of the others mentioned 20 and 10 offers toward the steeple. I think an effort will be made to complete the steeple and get the bell.

It has been very cold. Ida sent Hilda to Kutztown and the boys to Willis' when Willie got sick. Willie is better but quite thin she says. He has started to eat but his tongue is sore. He must have been quite sick. Spoke with Ida through the window this morning.

Sunday, February 2, 1902. There was rain yesterday, snow this afternoon and a fierce wind this afternoon and evening.

The offering today at church was for Bethany Orphan's Home. It amounted to $7.20 in the afternoon and in the evening I wasn't there. Hen. Godshall came out to see me and then it got too late for church. It is remarkable how warm storm sash will keep a house. The fierce wind did not affect us this year when we always had trouble.

Monday, February 3, 1902. A fierce wind storm began blowing yesterday afternoon and all night and has turned very cold. If the roads had not been so rough before the snow there would be sleighing now but so it wont do.

The blacksmith will have work now. It's been very dull for them so far.

Finished carpenter work in our new office today. When the painter gets through we can go on a little better with our work.

It is said that the new [illegible] building at the [illegible] was blown down last night.

Wednesday, February 5, 1902.   Still cold. We took down our shafting on upper floor in order to discover what was wrong with shake in it. We found it cracked and it must have been so when put in. We are lining up some of the pulleys with leather. Hartzel finished varnishing the office.

Framed some pictures last night and got to bed late. Have two more to put in. The frames look well but I am sadly stuck as to colors.

Ida told me Willie was still weak but over his diphtheria. He told me they expected to be able to wash things on Monday and that she wants her clothes [illegible] by that time.

Thursday, February 6, 1902.   My friend Willie is dead. He was my friend. I couldn't come there and sit down but he would crawl on my lap. I teased him much, but that was because I liked him. He was a good boy, brave I think he would have been, and though he had a temper that could have been controlled. What a companion he would have made for Daniel. He would have helped him guarded him for he was stronger, Daniel is tricky but Willis would not deign to use anything but strength and power.

I was never more surprised when Cal. told me Willie was dead after all. He died at three o'clock last night. He got weaker at 11 last night. They telegraphed for Milt and he answered this morning telegraphing several times during the day to encourage Willie not knowing he was dead. He arrived on the Black Diamond at nine this evening. We were at church to hear Pastor Bergey preach.

Friday, February 7, 1902.   We laid poor Willie to rest at 3:30 this afternoon. Mr. Luckenbill pronounced the burial service. Charley's were down and [illegible] Stimmels' were up from the city. Willis was not there. Grandpop Moyer said he was much afraid. He looked so beautiful in his glass coffin. No more of the dreadful disease that carried him off. A little thinner but not much, his own clothes on with a small wreath in his hand with "Suffer little children" on a card He looked to me like an ideal boy. Oh what a friend and protector Daniel has lost! but what a gain for Willie! Spoke with Milt this morning. He had hoped to find him alive. He told me to my surprise that Willie had made him worry more then the others as he did not know how to manage him. But that I think was because he was not around him so much. To me he certainly was a lovable child. His very faults were virtues.

If his brothers were punished he would attempt to defend them against his own father.

Saturday, February 8, 1902.   Went to Quakertown to meet C.M. Taylor. Did not get him till dinner time and then fooled all afternoon before we settled on the job. It was for one that I gave him a bid on Feb. 7 and a few changes have been made since which brought the price higher as well as the advance in lumber. It was this that caused the trouble. I had to give in a little. I have now about $3000. of work on hand which is pretty good for so early.

Saw Stoneback's new mill. It is at least 50 x 100 exclusive of engine room and drying room. It is a splendid building for the purpose, but I did not think from a lot I could see that they had their machinery arranged well. It seems he is going to tear down the old building. It is supposed he couldn't get any insurance on acct. of nearby buildings. That made him build.

Sunday, February 9, 1902. Father was here this forenoon. The others were in S.S. except Henry and I. At church this evening Ellis told me that he had been to Ridge Valley and saw the bell there and he was afraid that he was in for more than he had imagined.

Monday, February 10, 1902. Was at Farmer's Institute this evening. I found it very interesting. Amy went there after school and she was able to give a very good account of what she heard.

People who know things can be interesting. A farmer from Chester Co. was able to tell us what should be done in the way of nature study. He would like the schools to take it up only they are already over crowded. A Penna. Dutchman named Stout furnished the fun. A prof. from Washington talked about birds. I was surprised to hear that birds wintered in Brazil and nested in Alaska. The hall was full. I think others than farmers are taking an interest.

Tuesday, February 11, 1902. Wanted to go to the Farmers Institute during the day but could not get away. Took the Zelder children this evening and thought we were early but found everything packed. I put Daniel on top of a closet where he would see over the whole room and the girls and I gradually worked ourselves into the main room as others passed out.

The bad feature was the noise in the back part of the room. It stopped partly after one of the speakers threatened to stop the proceedings. Lectures by Dr. Tlifa which I couldn't hear, and by Prof. Cook on "Feeding the human animal." He had a chart of food values which I would have been glad to copy if I could. He made [illegible] at 25, 4 times as cheap as beef at 12, cornmeal cheapest of all. Pork cheaper than beef. Beef Tea indigestable vinegar & other spices no help sometimes harmful. Mrs Philip's spoke on the wife's share.

Wednesday, February 12, 1902. Expecting that Mr. Appenzeller and Miss Cope would be here this evening and having promised to come to Hatfield I wanted to go early, but this trolley schedule is of such a nature that it is absolutely impossible to guess when they run every half hour or when every hour. So I had to wait till 6:15 and coming home the same way, I walked about till I was thoroughly cold. Took an order for a reading desk for the church. They are pleased with the work.

Found Appenzeller here and Daniel and the other children questioning him about his cattle getting him to spell words &c. Miss Cope brought some Chataugua journals she wants me to get bound.

We are still finishing things at the factory. The office is completed but new saw bench and the fixture for drawing in the lumber is still months away.

Friday, February 14, 1902.   The Presidents son who was very sick with Pneumonia is recovering. Prices of lumber are very high. No. 3, 5/4 cuts are $28.00, No. 2 $41.00, No. 1 $51.00 or $52.00. It is only 4 yrs. when No. 1 cuts were $36, No. 2, $26. or $27. and No. 3, $18. or $19. Pine was quoted $24.50 and $25 and 1 x 12 $36. and 2 x 12 $40.00.

Milt came out this evening to have a sketch of his mine made. He is anxious to sell the two remaining block houses. He wants to get rid of it. I sincerely hope his mine venture will be a success.

Saturday, February 15, 1902.   We have our new cross cut saw about ready to set up. The only difficulty will be that we have to cross the belt.

Prince Henry sailed from Bremen for this country. He is expected to arrive next Saturday. He will be of course well treated but there is already a great deal of fuss about the matter. Some people seem to think that our country ought to make a point of insulting other nations.

Germany has just made another point against Great Britain in the controversy about the Spanish War. It seems that Ambassador Parncefotr will have to shoulder the responsibility and the Eng. Gov. says they had no knowledge of any interference and disavowed Parncefotr's act.

Sunday, February 16, 1902.   Took Amy and Helen to church with me this evening. Had Catherine with me this afternoon. Luckenbill had a good sermon about people putting off religion till a more convenient time. I received a report of Synod of last October.

Four funerals were announced for next week. Mrs. Francis Haring of Telford, a child of Musselman the local Expressman. Chas. Barndt of Telford and Henry C. Hartzel.

Monday, February 17, 1902.   This morning the ground was covered with snow and it continued snowing all day. There was a little drifting and in consequence rail road schedules were interfered with, and the trolleys kept busy keeping their line open. Nobody traveled today as it would be uncertain when you would get stuck. People are falling into the habit of calling a storm like today a blizzard but it is merely an old fashioned snow storm, not cold enough and the snow should be hard and cutting like ice. That is how they are out west and that is how it was here in '88.

John Alderfer was buried today.

Wednesday, February 19, 1902.   Yesterday the snow drifted badly and roads were closed up. The trolley did not run till noon today. I don't know even now whether they got all the way through. The steam cars were stuck in Derstines cut yesterday.

Today I started an interesting experiment. I raised Pen. and Hartman's wages for last year. It makes enough to pay Pen's subscription to church which I will hand to him and tell him I am going to keep the rest and save up for him.

Hartman as usual wanted me to advance him $5.00. I told him I would put $10.00 to his credit at J.M.L. & Co's and told him to get what he needed. He couldn't understand the situation but I did not tell him.

We were out at Cal's this evening taking out some lithia tablets. His back is giving him a lot of trouble.

Thursday, February 20, 1902.   Rec'd a letter from Wisconsin telling us that Mrs. Galloway who was here two or three yrs. ago has diabetes and weighs only 100 lbs. when she had weighed 160 lbs. last winter.

Pres. Roosevelt has decided the Sampson-Gehley controversy. He has decided that neither Sampson nor Gehley exercised any command during the battle. That it was a captains battle, that the loop was a great error. That the findings of the court were unanimous, he accepts their decisions, though not without examination. It is probable that after people all get to their [illegible] census.

Friday, February 21, 1902.   Moved batteries to Dynums room. Sam had taken the voltage of the battery I had been wanting to fire and there was still 19 ½ vol. with no acid in after standing in that condition 8 mos. I am anxious to see how it will show up after acid is in.

Audited Bldg. Ass'n accts this afternoon at the bank with Ellis and Jono Allem Ser. No 1 8528.

It has been snowing followed by sleet and rain. The water is unable to get away and it was impossible to get home without wet feet.

The trees are loaded with sleet and ice and I expect may break down. I never saw them bent worse than this time.

Saturday, February 22, 1902.   The storm yesterday and last night was in its way the most remarkable I ever saw or could hear of. The sleet on trees and other objects was thicker than I ever saw it. I picked plenty of pieces where the coating was ½" all around. Last night the elec. lights went out and we did not understand why. This morning the scene of havoc was great indeed. If the sun had been shinning it would have been very beautiful to see how the trees were breaking and glistening like diamonds. My shade trees suffered some but lost my apple and peach trees which broke away from the stem. On main street the weight of the wire had broken the two poles and the railroad crossing and at Grandfathers Souder's place. Such a tangle of wires I never saw. The trolleys did not run except to get their cars in. It was very dangerous. Some fires nearly resulted this afternoon. Last night Dr. Derstine's had a fire at Quakertown. At the shop one shade tree was badly damaged. We trimmed them to save them. The battery after having acid stayed at 14 volts.

Sunday, February 23, 1902.   This was a beautiful day. The sun came out in all his glory and with the ice glittering on the trees and the snow of yesterday on the ground made a glittering sight.

The damage stated by the evening paper of yesterday is greater than that of 1888. Certainly Phila. is cut off from the world as far as telegraph and telephone is concerned. The signal system is broken down so that railroad travel is dangerous. The trolley is not running yet though it is open from here to Quakertown. Was to sunday school this afternoon and to church this evening.

Monday, February 24, 1902.   Prince Henry arrived yesterday at 10 in New York harbor. They say New York presented a beautiful sight. A cloudless sky, bright sun and everything covered with ice. They were almost a day late. He sent a wireless telegram to Pres. Roosevelt yesterday when off the coast of Nantucket telling him he was sorry to arrive late. They had a stormy voyage. He went on board the Hohenzollern at once at one o'clock last night left for Washington. He was treated with some ceremony and met the Pres. at the White House. He will visit the Capitol this afternoon and there will be a banquet at the White House this evening. Last night they left for New York.

Wednesday, February 26, 1902.   Got word this morning I was to come to Phila. and take the job of H.K. Wampole Co.

The message had been late yesterday morning and it took 24 hrs. to reach us owing to the wires being down. Having promised to be in Perkasie I sent Elwood. The trolleys were all demoralized today. I just caught one that was nearly an hour behind but in effect was 5 minutes ahead of time. Took off Acuff's house at Ambler at Schermerhorn & Reinhold Thearchts of Montg. Co. Courthouse. One of them had seen Mattison's church and did not have a high opinion of it. As for the panelling he said it did not belong to our county. Took the job at H.K. Wampole Co. for $280.00. Wampole was talking Dutch with me again, he seems to enjoy it.

Friday, February 28, 1902.   Got vaccinated this morning. Have been wanting to do it all winter but never got at it. Telford has a regular epidemic of smallpox. They report from 12 to 18 cases. I don't know which is true. There must have been carelessness somewhere. Blank's Hotel had it sometime without being quarantined.

It was raining some all day and I got my dinner at the restaurant. While there it got so dark that I hurried to the mill. Then it poured. There was some thunder and lightning. The water catching up the broken twigs was ready to dam up. The creek was higher than for a long time. I was afraid the retaining wall against the mill would go, but we had stuck stone in it yesterday and it stood the test. The culvert under the railroad wasn't any too large at this end it must have been nearly full. It was against the elect. light cross bar on one side when I saw it.

Saturday, March 1, 1902.   The floods resulting from yesterdays rain and melting snows are worse than they have ever been known. The water in Manayunk was 32 feet above the usual level. The Reading and Penn Railroad are not running in the Schuykill Valley. Father was over to the shop for the first time this week. He is having the grippe. He felt very tired when he came over.

I hear Elsie Gerhart and Miltie Moyer got married today. The poor children are too young. He is scarcely 19 and she isn't 18. Mrs Liz. Moyer is not too well pleased at the match I hear. But I think she is a good girl and the only cause she may have is religion, of course her father is not one of the relations one would choose if such a thing was possible.

Sunday, March 2, 1902.   Went to sunday school and church this afternoon and to church again this evening.

Small Pox has again appeared in our town. Abr. Freed's child next to Cals was pronounced to have small pox this afternoon. Cal went right off and got himself vaccinated.

The Telford cases seem to have been almost criminally negligent. Wm. Blank had it and was not quarantined. They got it from Mrs. Freed's delivering beer. All of Freed's cigar makers got it. Willie Souder got it and the Dr. thought to be Typhoid Fever and so was not quarantined. His wife, his father and now his brother also have it. There is no telling where it will end.

Wednesday, March 5, 1902.   This morning it was snowing again. It continued most of the day and I decided not to go home for dinner. I stopped in at Grandfather Moyer's and took dinner there. Grandmother is in bed suffering from blood poisoning. She had a bunion which got sore and last week I saw her foot when her toe looked blue and I thought it would open. They have a doctor now. She was opposed to having a doctor at first. She is better than she had been. Hilda is sick too. I hope it will not be diptheria.

This evening I shoveled snow and it was the hardest work I have done this winter. It is so heavy and solid. It is blowing hard and there was still some snow. The trolleys were put out of service early in the day.

Thursday, March 6, 1902.   The trolley opened again to Quakertown today. From here to Hatfield it is still closed. Late tonight the snow plow went down and they may have opened during the night.

This afternoon we started to put up Landis & Co. cases for show windows. They have been so anxious about it and inquired so often that Father and Elwood hated to go to the store. We put both sides together roughly this afternoon and Jonas thought we had done much.

This evening Cal came out to fetch me to the Consistory meeting which I had forgotten all about. Morris Zendt reminded me in the morning and Cal in the forenoon but being at the store all afternoon it slipped my memory.

Saturday, March 8, 1902.   Grandmother Moyer's great toe was amputated on Thurs. morning. For some time she has had a sore foot. She had a sore bunion which turned into blood poisoning.

The toe commenced to turn blue. Being afraid of doctors in general she refused to have one until this week. Mortification or Gangrene has set in and the consequence was amputation.

She had been doing well since. This evening I stopped in to see about it and found them in an excitement about Hilda who had nearly died from croup. It appears she had some diptheria at Kutztown and this may be after effects. I went out after ten o'clock and found her much better apparently the doctor is there much and expects to come in again at 12 o'clock. It is probably membranous croup. She can't work the slime off and they are trying to work it downward. I hope they will succeed.

Sunday, March 9, 1902.   When I arrived at Grandfather Moyer's, Hilda was dead. She died at 7 o'clock this morning. She had membranous croup and it seems the doctors can't do anything with it. I sympathize very much with them. Ida has to be so much alone and her children would have been a great comfort to her. Now she has lost all.

Charly's came down to see grandmother, ignorant of Hilda's death. Kate Hollenback also came up in the same way.

This evening I went to church. They say there are two more cases of small pox developing. This makes 4. Freed's Frank, Milt Groff and old Mrs. Hen. Price.

Monday, March 10, 1902.   Dr. Hottenstein's came down this morning. They did not know Hilda was dead. Milt tried to telegraph Saturday but the Western Union wires are still down and they would not send the message over the R.R. wires. Mrs. Hottenstein was very much affected. Hilda was much thought of at Kutztown and I am told Mrs. Hottenstein wanted to adopt Hilda. Dr. Hottenstein said in my hearing that if Milt had not intended to go off he would have kept her at Kutztown.

The auditors met at our house tonight. We worked till eleven, but came out all right.

Today Prince Henry was in Phila. This finishes his tour. They rushed him over 4600 miles in 13 days and I am sure he was glad when it was over. They moved him from place to place at a gallop at break neck speed.

Tuesday, March 11, 1902.   Today Prince Henry sails for Germany on the Deutschland.

Wednesday, March 12, 1902.   Was in the city today taking off statein for Penlyn church in Phila. and a house at St. Davids. Was at Tourisons office. There they are getting quite aristocratic. They have a fine suite of rooms, and some nice old mantels taken out of old buildings.

Geo. Zendt was here this evening to bring the remaining items for the borough statement.

Thursday, March 13, 1902.   Hilda was buried today. It was a small funeral. She had darker eyelashes then her hair and her hair was light and very pretty. She had a mouth full of teeth that were made to bite. She was very popular at Kutztown. Willie was my favorite.

Hilda was 3 yrs. 8 mos. 16 days.

Friday, March 21, 1902.   Nice day.

Was in the city yesterday to take off work and stopped off at Norristown to satisfy a mortgage and pay Dannhour. This morning I felt a slight pain in my back and this has continued throughout the day. Hartman I hear is in a bad way. The poor fellow is suffering for past indiscretions. Stopped in the grave yard to see Willie's and Hilda's graves. Milt went to Canada last evening. Was in to see grandmother this afternoon. She is tired of doctoring.

Allen Landis left us today. Al Frederick moved on Thursday and will start in a week.

Rec'd a big car of lumber today which was unsatisfactory.

Sunday, March 23, 1902.   Not feeling any too well for a couple of days and as the weather was springlike I concluded to take a long walk with the children. So we went up to Indian Creek church. The children and I enjoyed it much. Had them in the cemetary and showed them the old graves. Rev. Abel Horning preached but he is old and feeble. Old Mrs. Luckenbill died this forenoon. She had been bed fast for 7 yrs.

This evening Rev M.R. Moyer preached in our church. He had a full house. I was surprised that the organ was not used, but found afterward that it was by request of Rev. Clemmer.

(The children above ref. to were Amy, Helen and Daniel. I was afraid it would be tiresome for Daniel, but he enjoyed it very much and this walk has become one of the happy day of my life (written Apr. 28) I wish now I had began this practice sooner.)

Monday, March 24, 1902.   About 9:45 this morning a little girl arrived at our house. This makes 5 girls and 2 boys. When Amy came to Mattie and Ellen, she said "seven is too many." And to Salome she said "now I'll have six kids running after me." When she saw the child she said "It's a cross looking thing." Salome told Catherine there was a little girl upstairs. "Why dont that girl come down"? "Has she no footys"? was what she asked me. When she saw the baby she looked at it a long time. Daniel wanted to know where the doctors got the babys. I said they grew. "Do they grow on stalks"? he asked. But Helen said they were too heavy for that. One of them, I think it was Mary asked why the doctor did not keep it for himself. But they suspect that the doctor wants to pick the nicest for himself.

Mother and child are doing well, the baby being very hungry, sucking its little fist soon after birth. It has very fat cheeks.

Wednesday, March 26, 1902.   Consistory met tonight. Passed bills, sent a committee to councils and put Cal, Frank Weil and Morris D. Zendt in nomination for Elders and Deacons.

Cal who felt hurt about some rebuffs wanted to refuse but was finally persuaded to go on. He thought I treated him curtly and I was short because I had no time to discuss things.

Was up to Quakertown to see Taylor. Took off a job and will send the bid tomorrow.

Thursday, March 27, 1902. Funeral services for old Mrs. Luckenbill were held this evening in the church Rev. Reiter and Rothrock preached. Rev. Fretz and Abel Horning were there too.

Was in the city today. The Lansdale station is going to be fine, also took off a lot of work for Tourison. A woman was in great danger of being killed stepping off the train at Lansdale before it stopped. She fell on her back and I was afraid she would roll under the wheels. She thought the train was stopping and said she didn't know what was the matter with her.

Friday, March 28, 1902. Ellis and Elwood went up to L. Lexington today on the trolley. I fixed up the church acc'ts. Mr. Wallace was up sometime this afternoon for some odds and ends and said that Wampole was very much pleased with our work.

Our baby cries much at night. The mother seems to be doing well.

Saturday, March 29, 1902. Wm. Hemsing of Wisconsin a brother of grandfather Hemsing died Mar. 25 and was buried yesterday according to a postal we recd. this morning. He suffered terribly the last four weeks. Sometime ago I rec'd. a letter from Mrs. Galloway one of his daughters saying he fell down stairs and hurt his head. He had a stroke of apoplexy or paralysis. That was probably the beginning.

We had our preparatory service tonight, a good attendance. A class of 6 were confirmed. Miss Hartzel, Grace Zendt, Edith Appenzeller, confirmed and Stella and Wa [?] Souder and Pearl Zendt baptized. Mrs. J.J. Harman was rec'd by letter.

Sunday, March 30, 1902. We had communion this morning. About 85 communed. Our membership increased by eight. There are some few that are always hanging back. If they would only come we would be strong.

This afternoon after practice Daniel fell down the cellarway, the door of which had been left open by Sallie Hunsicker and Sam Luckenbill. He was rushing for his cup and fell down. It is a wonder he did not break his neck but luckely he escaped hardly any bruises showing.

Was at the Easter festival this evening. Had a good attendance.

Written April 28. (Daniel never mentioned anything about his fall when he came. I was told by someone else and in the evening Sallie and Mrs. Hunsicker inquired particularly about him blaming Sallie for their carelessness. The little fellow did not mind it. He said his piece with the others enjoying it very much. Willi Stasser and Willie Vaughn were the others. At the Christmas festival Mary took Daniel's place as Daniel had been hurt. Wellie Moyer was in that piece and Willie Strasser.)

Monday, March 31, 1902.   The three consistories met at the church in joint session. Morris D. Zendt was elected delegate to classes at Hellertown. I think he was very much pleased.

Tomorrow is the first of Apr. I am glad I am almost over it. I have to pay Enos Moyer about $300, and couple of small bills and then I am through. Of course there are lumber bills but we have them always with us.

This evening Father came over to see the baby. Soon after Charleys came. He says they pay their pastor $800⁰⁰ and raise in all about $1300. He says when they started out alone they had 120 members. I dont see how they do it.

Friday, April 4, 1902.   Took little Henry to Lansdale to Dr. Moyer. His ear is very sore and it is spreading. They say Dr. Moyer can do more with children than some.

The little fellow enjoyed it all. When he saw a horse he had to shout and he was suspicious of chickens.

I had him at the shop before we went but he was not frightened.

The watchmens clocks &c arrived yesterday. We have not put them up yet but I dont suppose Israel is glad for them. He don't seem to realize exactly what he is there for.

Thursday, April 10, 1902.   At last that dreadful enemy Diphtheria has forced an entrance to our house. Helen has had a sore throat several days and yesterday Mary and Catherine were sleeping all day. Last evening I wanted to send for the doctor, but thought he could see better by daylight so I stayed up all night and watched. This morning I fetched Dr. Souder and after examining them he said he thought it was Diphtheria and that if I had anything to attend to I should do so. So I went to the factory and attended to everything possible. Went to Hatfield to finish altar drawing and came home about 5 o'clock.

Met Mattie on the way out in the forenoon and told her if she did not want to be quarantined she should stay away, but she concluded to stay thank God, and Mary our girl was nervous for awhile but finally she too stayed and now we are in for a battle with disease and death the outcome of which is known only by Him who watches over all.

Friday, April 11, 1902.   The children passed a good night. They are cheerful. Cath. was afraid of the doctor and it is quite a task to sprinkle her throat. Last evening the doctor used antitoxin. He said he had more faith in the atomizer. It certainly does bring the matter out wonderfully. Elwood bro't a bottle of whiskey last evening. I gave it to the children to husband their strength. Ida and Ella were out last evening. Henry was troublesome last night.

If only he does not get the disease. We have them separated in our old bedroom and I attend to them.

Reeder at this hour 6:30 A.M. has not quarantined us.

Reeder couldn't understand why I objected to having nails driven in my door. I sent him to the shop for a stand.

My patients were better this morning having little fever. They amuse themselves by trying to sing. They hate to have their throats syringed.

The improvement noted this morning continued this evening.

This evening Reeder acknowledged that the stand for the front was all right and thinks of using the same in future. Elwood and Father were out this evening. Elwood says Souder and Crouthamel want show cases like Landis and Co., I told him to make the plans.

Saturday, April 12, 1902. We passed a good night the children being slightly restless. Slept till 7 this morning and missed Reeder which annoyed me as I wanted to get some things. Elwood came out later and I told him. The Doctor says the fever has left Mary, and Catherine is slight. Mary's throat is practically clean. Amy and Mary (Stauffer) had their throats examined and the doctor left some medicine for each.

This afternoon Daniel said his throat hurt but we didn't believe it as he seemed to think he too had to have medicine.

These two evenings Cal whistles me up and inquires after the children.

Dr. Talmager is said to be dying in Washington.

Mary's temperature was 102 this afternoon. Catherine being only 99. Mary is costive and we gave her a physic. Have a good supply of disinfectants now. Used alchol for cresoline lamp but have to change to coal oil.

Sunday, April 13, 1902. Catherine said this morning "I wish I could get up," Stanly bro't some blue bells yesterday and Namon's today added geraniumas they are pleased to have them. Cath's temp is normal this morning and her throat nearly clean. Mary 102. He gave her a pill. They are cheerfull, Cath especially. Jennie found white spots in Daniels throat and he had to laugh. He has been anxious to have medicine and he told Mary afterward that "if he would get sick and die like Willie he wouldn't have to work" Amy has only a little tonsilitis and so has Daniel. Mary Stauffer is more diphtheria. I hope it can be checked.

I don't like the way Helen's throat is looking. The doctor passed her off with tonsilitis and never looked at her since, but I am concerned that she is a sick girl and wants attention. Mary Stauffers throat is badly swollen but I hope that it isn't bad.

Monday, April 14, 1902. Mary's temperature remains around 102, Helens 101 and something. He has not given Helen antitoxin. Catharine temperature is normal and she will probably be let out in a day or so. She is full of mischief and the paleness acquired makes her complexion fine.

I ran the washer this forenoon. Mary Stauffer's voice is husky today. Daniel is down this afternoon, This morning he wanted to put on his new suit and I made it a condition that he should stay in the house. He promised rather than take it off. Now 5 o'clock his throat is swollen and I think he'll be the next patient. I hope we will not have to lose any of our children. I don't care how long it takes if they will only get well.

Dr. Talmager died Sat. night. He will be buried in Brooklyn on Tuesday.

Tuesday, April 15, 1902.   My patients are all doing well. Cath and Dan'l have no fever. Mary is 100⅖ and Helen 100. They had a great time this forenoon. Cath getting up and leading the singing. Mary Stauffer is not so well and it is probable she had better be in bed.

I am so glad Henry's ecsema is healing. If it goes on the way it is now he will soon be free. I hope he will escape the diptheria. I am very thankful our cases are so mild. I am going to wash Catharine now and dress her.

The children are busy playing with paper making curls and hats and my todays paper barely escaped destruction.

I washed and dressed Catharine after dinner. She enjoyed being up so much she could hardly get enough to eat. We had oysters for supper. She wanted to have meat and ate some dry bread after she was through with her supper. The others had no fever this afternoon and the prospects are good for their recovery. Erb's were quarantined this morning. Kath and Raymond have it. Mild cases. Mary Stauffer is not so good.

Wednesday, April 16, 1902.   My patients are doing well. I find however that Helen has some very tough membrane on the one side which will not yield. I sprayed her 3 or 4 times and the doctor once. The doctor comes only once now. We are more anxious about Mary S. He kept her in bed today. She has a bad croupy cough and we are doing our best to stop it.

Erb's children are not so well. Raymond had a temperature of 104 Dr. O. told me. He said he was going to give them antitoxin this afternoon. I am much amused at the talk people have about us. They object to our having our windows open, the children ought not to be seen in the yard. They were re-ported to have been up to the school house. Mattie brot to our house and we gave it to Erb's. Someone complained to Dr. O. that Roy or Stan Moyer's children were wrestling with ours. I dont know what else and dont care except that it is not very flattering to our carefulness &c. I am sure no one else did more in the way of fumigating than we do.

Thursday, April 17, 1902.   We are having a great time with our girl Mary. She has membranous croup. We have to steam her with hot water and lime continously. I fetched the doctor tonight. Her temp. is 103⅖. He says he will give her antitoxin tomorrow morning. We sent for her mother and she had intended to stay at Moyers but after a while she could not stand it and came over. So we have a new inmate for our house. I hope it will all have a favorable ending. I think having her mother with her will have a good effect. My children are all getting along slowly Mary having a slight fever today. Daniel was to have got up but we had no time to dress him. Amy has a swollen throat but I could see nothing inside. She is very hard to spray. She can close up her throat completely. Little Mary has to cry a little at not being able to get up and I pitied her. Daniels throat is nearly clean but I think the doctor thinks it a good idea to keep him out of the others way.

Friday, April 18, 1902. Mary died a little after seven this afternoon. We are all feeling very sad tonight and the women are worn out. Mattie thought sometime this afternoon that she was dying but I felt her pulse and found it very rapid about 140 but regular. So I told them there would be no immediate danger of dissolution but about five o'clock her pulse was irregular and I knew that meant something. She mentioned to her mother that she would like a minister and we sent for Josiah Clemmer who came but did not baptize her as she was unconcious. I also sent for Luckenbill as I was uncertain wheather she could live long enough till Josiah came. As Josiah came I told Luckenbill to go home. She was as good a girl as we have ever had. Mattie did nobly. Nothing was too much trouble and she stuck to her place bravely. She is tired out now. My wife too forgot that she had a baby and worked too much I am afraid.

Saturday, April 19, 1902. We sent Mr. Moyer over to make the grave. Mary will be buried tomorrow about 12 o'clock at Franconia M.H. Dr Souder told me this evening that he had expected her to live longer but that the disease was fatal. Daniel's fever this morning was 101⅖ and this evening had dropped 2 deg. so that was only a trifle over normal. Mary and Helen are to take stronger food. They have no fever. Cath had a 100 But has no membrane.

Reports were out yesterday that Wm Nice's and Allebachs children had diphtheria and Reeder went there only to find the rumor false. Loux however dismissed the school. It isn't well to act on rumor. I was too sleepy to finish tonight. When Daniel realized that Mary was dead he said "If the doctor gives you medicine and people die anyway, what is the use of taking it." I told the doctor and he said he reason this official meaning logical I suppose.

Sunday, April 20, 1902. Our children were doing well this morning, Daniel being the only one with a slight trace of fever. The chief danger now is croup which would be fatal. Catharine coughed a little croupy the other evening but we can find nothing the matter except swollen tonsils. Mary was taken away about 11:30 this morning. I wrapped the children in a blanket and took them over to see her. She was in a closed coffin with a glass lid. Her mother went with Mr. Moyer who will take her home. It was a sad sight. Some of the neighbors came and looked at her when on the sidewalk. Her mother said she would be 20 in August. Only last Sunday when people were coming to meeting Mary said she had rejoiced over the chance of hearing Wangar and now she couldn't go. She was the humblest and best person to be around. She never got any trouble with the children simply because she let them go. There was no fighting with her. She

Monday, April 21, 1902.   Last evening both Daniel and Catharine had croupy coughs only a little but I was very anxious because his throat is bad. I fetched the doctor as late as 11:30 and he examined him closely and said he thought it would not develop into membranous croup. But there is the doubt. I sat up all night with him so he would not get uncovered. This morning he had a slight fever 99½ and while there was still some croupiness the doctor thought it was all right.

We sprayed his throat thoroughly today and have made a great improvement that way but there is the danger hanging over us all the time. This afternoon Catharine commenced to get tight and we are burning tar and turpentine. She has no membrane in her throat and apparently her chest is sound but I fear she is doomed. She has been such a good little girl taking her medicine and submitting so patiently to everything that she won my heart completely. She has such beautiful dark eyes and when she looks at you in such confidence you think she is too good to live. I wanted to help Mattie to wash, but was too busy around the children and this afternoon I fell asleep having lost considerable last night.

Tuesday, April 22, 1902.   We passed a good night contrary to expectation. Daniel did not sleep all the time but rested easy. Catharine who was very tight last evening slept well. The doctor was here late and we had to wake her up. Milt came home on Sunday and they were out here this morning. We had a few words with him. He is going away again soon.

We got more stuff out of Daniel's throat than before. A piece the thickness of my little finger and ½" long he coughed up. We are poulticing Daniel and Catharine to reduce the swelling. We took Helen out of the room and she and Cath. will be in my room. Mary had a temp of 101 and Daniel 102. It is very warm outside, a hot wave coming from the west. We expect rain in a day or two.

Wednesday, April 23, 1902.   The warm weather continues. Tonight it is windy. We dug the garden today.

This morning I was alarmed on finding spots on Daniel's hands legs and body. Ida came out and I asked her whether Willie had them. She said he had after he became unconscious. I told her to stop in at Dr Souders and hurry him up. When he came he said it wasn't smallpox or scarlet fever. He said it was certainly measles. So the poor fellow in addition to diphtheria has also measles. He needs much attention. It is so hard to spray him that I am sometimes afraid we are not making headway. If we could work on him like on Helen there would be no trouble. His fever this morning was 102⅗ this evening 102. We took Mary out of the room today. Now we have them all out but one. I hope God will spare us our children. It is all in His hands.

Thursday, April 24, 1902.   Daniel rested badly last night complaining of heat. This morning his measles were out more than ever. The others are doing well and the only trouble is to keep them upstairs. I hope he is not worse. He objects to taking nourishment. He is of a complaining disposition. We always have to limit the number of sprayings. Daniel's temperature is 102⅗ this morning the same as yesterday. He is costive. He loses his temper when we want to spray him. He is very angry with Mattie and does not want to speak to her. The doctor gave him a second injection of antitoxin today. I hope everything will tend to his recovery. Jennie seemed to think there was little the matter with him but measles but his diphtheria is bad and the doctor says he has held his own well since yesterday. His heart is rapid and he is giving him strychnine.

We are still poulticing. This is a very troublesome thing but it cannot be helped. D's temp was 103 this evening.

Friday, April 25, 1902.   Daniel's temperature is 102 this forenoon say 11 a.m. He did not sleep well last night and I gave him a powder at 3 o'clock this morning. I arranged to pay him 1 cent everytime we spray him. He then limits us to 6 times and I have to pay extra for more. I sprayed him this afternoon and find that the membrane has been gaining on us. His uvula seems to be embedded in membrane of course I almost despaired about the others but I never saw anything like this. His throat is full and it seems to choke him. The doctor says he is maintaining his strength but I do not clearly see what his strength amounts to with the disease making such progress. I still hope to see him well. This is two weeks quarantine for us and 1 week since Mary died. What will another week bring forth.

Saturday, April 26, 1902.   I feel better about Daniel this morning. We have sprayed his throat twice before ten and some came loose. The swelling of his tonsils is aslo reduced. He took nourishment and spoke of being hungry but did not know what he wanted. The spraying relieves him and he rests afterward. His bowels moved some and after the anxiety I had on that account the past few days I think that is favorable sign. He rested badly last night dreaming constantly. He spells words in his sleep. He thinks someone is in bed with him.

His temp. this morning was 101. This afternoon he was weaker and by 6 o'clock we could hardly spray his throat as he found it hard to expel the foam. He was delirious in his sleep. He asked me "Is there a city called Damascus?" which when I misunderstood owing to his inability to speak plain he shouted [illegible]. At 10 p.m. his temp was still 101 but he was still so weak that the doctor gave up spraying him. He gave direction how to give the medicine and left. At eleven we thought he was dying but he rallied and I soon found he would live beyond midnight. I lay down afterward but could not sleep. Mattie and Jennie were up too.

Sunday, April 27, 1902.   Daniel died at 5:26 this morning. He made a great struggle for life and in the end had to strangle. I expected heart failure but his heart was strong. He had a splendid vitality. It was only after his chest or lungs filled up tight with matter that it was absolutely impossible to breath that he gave up his life. Even then he made four efforts turning black and blue with clenched fists and muscles on the stretch. His eyes bulged out and his tongue protruded, only after life was extinct did his muscles relax. But he died the death of a Christian, little as he was. In the afternoon I told him to pray to the Good Man to make him well and he said all his little prayers, one that his mama taught him. "Now I lay me" and "Our Father". Perhaps an hour before his death his mother started a prayer which he repeated after her and then without prompting, repeated "Now I lay me down to sleep" three times till he went to sleep. Afterwards waking up he said "Give my money to the children" and his mother not understanding he exclaimed "my pennies to the children." Then he said "I am going off" and "tell them" and "say it" which we did not understand.

I gave him whiskey every hour which cleared his throat enough to speak. Also a strychnine pill every two hours to strengthen his heart. He tosed about and was very restless all night. Last evening he said "there is no Ella here" I asked him if he referred to the baby and receiving an affirmative answer I said the baby's name was Margaret.

I sent Mr. Moyer for the undertaker as well as for Gra. Hemsing and Moyer. We decided this afternoon to bury at Leidy's for numerous reasons the Moyers preferring here at the Mennonite Meeting House. And so we have a void that can never be filled. I am afraid his mother will sit around too much and I am of opinion that this is not good for her.

Monday, April 28, 1902.   Slept on 3rd floor with little Mary. It is a good room to get up early. The sun shines in at the windows and wakes you up. Father came out and heard Sam Moyer went to Leidys to look after the grave. I followed after I had breakfast. I think we have a nice lot and a nice situation (Schwenk's) Father and I looked over the graves in the old cemetery. That little boy as he lies stiff and cold looks so sweet I hardly can refrain from fondling him. I didn't know Daniel was so handsome.

This afternoon soon after five we started for the cemetery. Father with aunt Sarah, aunt Kit and Kate Scholl accompanied us. At the cemetery we found Milt, Cal Hunsberger, Charleys, Grandfather Moyers, Elwood Reub and Mr. Luckenbill. Enos has made a good o.s. coffin. It is certainly water tight and of cypress 1½" plank the corners of zinc. W.B. Slifer was also there. Daniel had on his new gray suit which he had on only once. The sunshine circle sent a bunch of flowers and Mattie took some white ones out of a bouquet that was sent out yesterday. He looked beautiful to me. His hair was more yellowish brown than during life. His face was marked where the skin was not healthy. Jennie, Amy and I went down. The others saw him here. When we used to ask little Henry "Where is Daniel" he would point to the door of the room where the body lay. So we laid all that was mortal of our darling boy to rest where in due time we will join him. We also hope to join him in the land beyond the grave. Adieu, Daniel.

Tuesday, April 29, 1902. I have been hunting some of Daniels play things together, but can find only his tool for his Testament and the horse and cart Grandfather Hemsing gave him. When I cut his hair on Saturday or Friday I forget which, why did I not keep a little, but I did not realize that he would never get well.

Yesterday after school was out possibly the whole primary school were waiting on the pavement to have a look at him. Then one of them came to ask me whether they could see him. I said I would gladly let them, but did not know whether Mr. Moyer would allow it. Miss Weil their teacher then came out and sent them home.

At nine o'clock they came to fumigate the house. We look downstairs the borough has a machine. They burned 2¼ [illegible] Our folks kept all well. They all lived upstairs while he was fumigating, they all complain of the smell I got some strong draughts.

I am very sleepy and can not write well. We did not get upstairs open till 8 p.m. Had the fumigator going for 3 hrs in the afternoon. They fumigated the small pox case uptown yesterday.

Wednesday, April 30, 1902. Ellis' were quarantined yesterday or the day before for Marion. They say this evening that she is better. I am glad if this hold true. They have a trained nurse. I wish we had one too. I think they must be worth more than the doctor. But it is too late. Our dear boy is gone and we can only go to him.

We had a big wash today. We boiled everything and then ran it through the washer. It took all day. Mattie was very tired. This afternoon I put up some shelving on the 3rd story. Tomorrow they say they will leave us out. I am glad of it. This was a beautiful spring day. The air is sweet with the odor of blossoms. I always think if Daniel was here to enjoy it. But he I hope is breathing a sweeter air.

Thursday, May 1, 1902. At last the quarantine has been taken off and we are free to go where we please. But what a fearful price we have paid. Two persons and one our dear boy has left us. I hardly know what we would not give to have kept him. Now we are only anxious to gather every little thing belonging to him and hold it in dear loving menory. I regret very much when I cut his hair that I did not keep a bunch but I threw them all away not realizing that he would soon be no more.

Friday, May 2, 1902. Found very pleasant spring like weather. The other evening every one remarked how sweet it smells. Ellis seems to think that Marion is all right now. I am glad if this is so.

We rec'd fr. school D's slate a card of embroidery on which he wrote his name and a paper on which he had drawn his umbrella and written a few lines on its uses. Everything else had been destroyed.

Went to Hatfield this afternoon, hoping to get a job fr. Snyder but Stoneback beat me. I do not see why he should work so cheap now after going to the expense he did building a new mill. Saw the new altar at the church. It was very well matched.

Just now 10:20 p.m. it is raining. This is unexpected to me. Mowed my yard this evening.

Saturday, May 3, 1902.   Went to the city today. Got a small order from H.K. Wampole and Co. and Tourisin promised me something if I'd come down Monday. They puttied the glass into the church windows and if the weather permits I hope to put them up next week.

Mattie went home this afternoon and does not expect to be back till Thursday. She wants to do the washing out there. It has been cloudy and unpleasant all day.

Met old Cass on the way to Lansdale this morning. She had heard on Thursday that Daniel died and said she thought it couldn't be. She said he always said to her "Won't you stay and bake some cakes for us."

Sunday, May 4, 1902.   A fair day. We spent most of the day quietly at home. Binden was here in the forenoon. In the afternoon Schwenck's came and Grandf. Moyers heard she, Grandf. Hemsing and J.L. Detweiler. Grandmother saw little Margaret for the first time. Grandf. H. took Henry along home in the coach and back again. We left the children out a little today. But their throats are still inflamed and probably sore.

After supper Amy and I went to the cemetary to D's grave for the first time since Monday. It is about a 15 min. walk. Was in church this evening. The Mennonites had communion this afternoon.

Miss Cope spoke to me about Daniel at church, "I miss him so much, yet it seems already so far away and yet it is only a week today that he died."

Monday, May 5, 1902.   Went to city this afternoon to see Tourisin. I thought he had a job for me as he told me on Sat. to come in on Monday. Took off a job that he already has. The Neilson job will not be ready for several days. Caught the train and reached Perkasie at 7 p.m. Stopped in at Charlies a few minutes. They are all well. Met Mr. Shultz and Mr. Allan at Detweilers, who expect to build a double house. Took theirs and another set of plans along home. Had to change cars near Clymers in Sellersville from narrow to the wide track. I think they'll get out of Sellersville today and after that they'll be coming fast this way.

We took the wash out to Granf. M's this morning where Mattie washed by machine. She'll come back here tomorrow to clean house.

Tuesday, May 6, 1902.   Was in Quakertown. Got some scattered orders.

Hen. Souder wants his bar room remodelled. He will furnish a lot of birch for it.

Wednesday, May 7, 1902.   Started putting clerestory windows in the church. The day was very cloudy and showers seemed near. We did not get up till after 10. I was afraid for a while we'd get soaked but I was justified in starting. It was just nice to work on a roof. If the sun had shown it would have been harder. We got one set up with the ceiling on and a roof over with paper. I am pretty sure they will ventilate all right. I think it will add to the appearance of the church. It seems to me that some people would prefer to tear down the church some day to improving it. I think such a course must be well justified. We ought to have a S.S. Room and I hope we will soon get it.

Thursday, May 8, 1902.   Erb papered the diphtheria room as the children call it. Had all the old paper taken off. We did not work it being ascension day. I did some estimating. After 5 o'clock I took the family down to the cemetery where we planted a few flowers on the plot.

Someone had been down and put a bouquet on the grave and put a chain formed of dandelion stems around the grave. Jennie took the baby along but a fellow like Henry is not convenient to take. He had to run after everything and falling got himself into trouble. This was the first time the children except Amy had seen the grave. I spread the ground over the plot and made things look a little better. Will have to put a lot of filling on yet.

Saturday, May 10, 1902.   A frightful earthquake occurred in Martinique Island Fr. W.I. or volcanic eruption. I should say, where by St. Pierre a city of 25,000 was entirely obliterated. It is supposed that 40,000 lost their lives. This is a mere guess but probably not excessive. The whole top of Mt. Relec is said to have been blown off and in the short space of 3 min. the whole thing is said to have happened. There was no way of escape for the inhabitants, even the shipping in the harbor being all destroyed except 1 vessel, which escaped nearly all its crew are dead or dying. 18 vessels were destroyed. The ashes a distance of 250 miles. The Island of St. Vincent a Brit. Island is also said to have suffered.

We have two of the clerestory windows on the church and safe from harm.

Sunday, May 11, 1902.   We all went out to grandfather Moyers spending the day there. The children enjoyed it much which is the main thing. Henry took a great interest in the horse, the chickens and the dog. He showed no sign of fear. He helped to carry in the eggs from the barn.

But for me the place wasn't what it used to be. Willie and Hilda are in Heaven with Daniel, Milt is away from home grandmother is crippled. Grandmother Lederach to whom the children used to go for candy is also gone. Ida and the boys went to church and to see Susie afterward. I thought it strange but she has been nothing but kind to us and doubtless meant it well. Ed. Hollenbachs stopped in a few moments but are afraid to bring the children. They went up to the old folks who also had diphtheria where they had not even been quarantined. I told Ed last evening.

Monday, May 12, 1902.   The volcanic disturbance in the West Indies is not over. The Island of St. Vincent has had eruptions and many people killed. St. Pierre has been utterly destroyed. The rest of the inhabitants are supposed to be destitute and relief is being sent with all speed. The Pres. sent a message to congress today I believe asking for an appropriation of 500,000.

Was in the city this afternoon. Was promised an 1800. job in Germantown. Went to Lansdale in an open car and caught in my teeth. Had toothache or more properly neuralgia all evening. Went to look at the church and found they had the 320 windows about in. Went to top of hill and found trolley track had been changed to schochs. A little work has yet to be done at the bridge. At Telford they had trouble getting the big cars around the corner. So they changed the curve. Stopped at father's Hen Bilger's were there. John Q's also.

Friday, May 17, 1902.   Went up to Sellersville this afternoon meeting Harry Hargrave. We took a look at the new Ref. church. This church standing on high ground and having a stone tower, has a dignified look and more or less massive appearance.

When we came into the auditorium we were disappointed. It has that slanting floor, pulpit in one corner which some people admire so and which I admit is convenient. But it destroys the dignity, and size of the room. The S.S. room was fine. I liked it. Stopped off at Telford to see Wampole.

Jennie and the girls took a walk to Leidy's cemetery.

Sunday, May 18, 1902.   At home nearly all the time. Taylor came this afternoon and I took Henry along to Mattie while we went to the factory. Grandf. Moyers took Jennie and the children to Leidy's cemetary after meeting.

Went to church tonight Rev. Dittmore formerly of Ft. Washington preached. He is Field Sec. of the Board of Home Missions. I had seen him before, but would not have known him. He has the necessary fire for his position.

It did me good to hear him. He preached on "We are laborers together with God."

Monday, May 19, 1902.   Our Heinrich is a queer fellow in some respects. He is more apt to talk when he is a little angry and then mingle it with crying, as I want to bed up, between sobs. or "I done." When he is put to bed however he will say "ing!," or "ding!," meaning sing. Then his mama will have to sing till he is asleep. He has now began to choose his hymns and will sometimes say "ing no not one." This morning he was singing himself, "Eus knows all about our doggle, no not one, no not one." He knows parts of the tunes of a number of hymns, "In the tee in the tee," he trys to sing for little birdie in the tree.

Tuesday, May 20, 1902.   Was in the city this forenoon to fetch plans and went to Orvilla to Howe's in the afternoon. He has quite a farm down there. A creamery, and a fine herd of Jersey cows.

He keeps an acct. of everything and everything seems to be done systematically.

The trolley people are working near Lansdale.

Wednesday, May 21, 1902.   This afternoon I fixed up the watchmen's clocks on the third floor and one down stairs.

We had just finished the last one when I found Israel standing and looking on. I told him to come, I had something to show him. When I told him it was intended for him he said at once he wouldn't tend it giving me no chance to explain it workings. I told him it would have to be used. He told me to get another man. I asked him whether he had previous information and he said he had and that his mind was made up.

So that settles him. Father is not sorry. He is hardly to be depended on.

Friday, May 23, 1902.   Was out to see father about various troubles. Told him about Cal's hint for more wages. About Israels leaving and Elwood's.

Cal asked last evening whether I would be offended if he got a job where he could do better. I said not and asked what job he had. He had none, I knew it was just his round about way of asking for more wages. I told him I would give him more but not much. Father said Reed ought to have more.

Saturday, May 24, 1902.   This evening Elwood stopped work. I told him I had another thing in mind but that he said he didn't like the business and so I thought there was no use. The idea of that was to get a cheaper bookkeeper and get a regular foreman. He thought the idea was good and that he would have liked it.

This evening I went over to Sam Moyers to see whether he wanted the job of watchman. He was in bed but as she is the manager I told her my business. She hardly knew as those watchman's clocks seem to haunt most people. I dont know what he will do but I do know I don't want him for driver any longer that I can help.

Bro't Tirsot's Life of Christ home or at least part of it.

Tuesday, May 27, 1902.   Was in Langhorne at Duffield's sale today trying to buy his millwork. It sold for 1055. My bid was 1050 and I think the next bid would have brought it to me. But I was doubtful what I would do with the numberless odds and ends. Cy. Smith wanted them bad but he was too slow or cautious to promise to take them so I let the thing slip.

Went to see Bilgers for a few minutes. Left on 6:02 train coming home 7:30.

Net result, loss of fare, time and an umbrella which I left at Wayne Junction on the way over. It has been raining for the past few days.

Wednesday, May 28, 1902.   The railroads and other mischievous combinations have conspired to get us into trouble. Last Thursday or Wed. a car coal came in. Next a car of lumber. Before we had started this another car lumber, on Monday morning another and this morning the fourth. We have two teams at work and would have caught up but for yesterdays rain. Roy wanted work so I gave him something. He is not what I want I think being too young and irresponsible. But they say he must have something today being 15 yrs. and it is true he should. I gave him some routine work at the office. May give him some at the shop as the sander &c &c.

I have had my dinner bro't out this week and Amy & Helen have each cleaned the office once.

Thursday, May 29, 1902.   The children of the Sunshine Circle are tomorrow going to decorate the graves of those that died. How I wish Daniel could take part with them and Willie too.

This evening the consistory desired to have the ceiling at the church fixed and gave me orders to attend to the same. I was also authorized to procure plans for a tower and report on the cost at next meeting.

We will get through with our lumber tomorrow noon.

A Mr. Diehl living in Ellis' house applied for the position of bookkeeper this afternoon.

Wednesday, June 11, 1902.   Old Quay today once more won a victory this time over his own Lieutenant Elkin.

Was in the city this afternoon taking off work.

The coal strike is a month old and no relief is in sight. Everyone is now using bituminous.

The stores are now closing Monday and Wed. evenings after seven.

Thursday, June 12, 1902.   Diptheria in town again this time at Abe Moyer's. Their Russel is very sick and they don't expect him to recover. He has had 4 doses of antitoxin. They have Dr. Albright. The only boy too.

The locusts have been keeping up their humming for over two weeks. One forgets much about them but I know when I was quite small I can have been only a little over 2½ years I heard the hum of the locust and that Mother told me it was the locust. I am sorry Daniel could not live to hear them. He would have been interested but none of the other children seem to ask any questions about them. At Wm. Henge's they seemed to have their greatest carnival. I don't see how they can stand it.

Have been having my dinner bro't to the shop ever since Elwood left and have Roy there. He is more useful than I thought he would be.

Friday, June 13, 1902.   Sent Roy to North Wales this afternoon with the team and was a little anxious about him as he could not get back till 6 o'clock and it looked very much as though there would be a storm. He had provided blankets and an umbrella. The storm broke loose after nine o'clock while I was in Hatfield to see Jacob off. When I went home the rain was pretty well over. Rain is good just now. Hay is short and the ground ought to have a good soaking.

Roy is active and can be made good use of. He is not much of a bookkeeper of course being too young.

I was surprised to see that Jott had a boy who is a good player on the violin. He is only about ten. They had practice at the church and he plays for the S.S. and the entertainment. I think there is music in him if developed. His face shows it I think.

Saturday, June 14, 1902.   I forgot to put down that last Sunday evening Will Kaufman and Petie left for parts unknown.

Kaufman had been selling stock for the Wheatsone Bridge Telephone Co. and having spent his time in dissipation was discharged and then persuaded Pete to go with him, and this foolish person having spent his wife's and her brothers little sums and being pressed on all sides for money leaves behind wife and four or five children and more to come. He had just opened a barber shop in Weikels store building having been compelled to sell out at Freed's.

Sam Alderfer who is treas. of the new Telephone Co. was after me to sell stock.

Pres. Roosevelt sent a special message to Congress in favor of Cuban reciprocity which the beet sugar senators oppose.

Went out and bo't a new hat, belt and shirt this evening.

Wednesday, June 18, 1902.   Paid county taxes this morning.

Had more or less toothache yesterday and today.

The brick layers strike on Monday came to nothing as it deserved.

Rec'd contract for Jos. R. Bergey house yesterday and some work for Mattison.

A telegram was rec'd this afternoon that Rev. Henry Appenzeller was drowned in Corea. No particulars were rec'd. Mrs. Ap. and her family have all been in this country for nearly two years, the children going to school here. It must be hard on them. Seperation by sea is nothing to seperation by death.

Thursday, June 19, 1902.   Was in Quakertown this afternoon. Old Hen is fixing his bar room and Taylor is putting in slate washboards. He filled out the back with plaster paris. Hen who is a candidate for sheriff is in good humor better than I expected.

Schlosser our new man has rented Peter's house. The paper says he is in St. Louis.

Went to the dentist hoping to get my tooth fixed, but some young lady was ahead of me so I have to wait till tomorrow.

Grandmother Moyer went to Perk. the other day and feeling bad on the way home vomited out her teeth. So she is minus her upper teeth just now.

Today the Canal bill was decided in the Senate. It is expected that Panama will win.

Henry fell today and had a deep gash across the bridge of his nose. I don't see how it happened.

Saturday, June 21, 1902.   Was at the commencement this evening. It was rather a cool day but still one felt a little warm when you came into church. But with all the crowd, everyone cooled off and it was very comfortable. I thought the ventilators were a great success.

Met Charlie White.

Mahlon Weil and Mamie Bergey were the graduates.

A Wm. Dengler from Kennet Square was the speaker instead of Mr. Green.

The order was not what it should be.

After it was over everyone left and I shut off the lights.

Sunday, June 22, 1902.   Grandfather Moyers went home with us from S.S. and Grandmother went along to church, but he would not go.

We rec'd a letter from Bilger's saying that Aunt Annie was very low. I forgot to deliver this letter till today when I was reminded of it by a telegram. I was ashamed of this neglect but I had intended to stop in last evening on my way to the commencement but left the letter in the wrong pocket.

Monday, June 23, 1902.   Rev. Anglemoyer was here this evening to sell Wenger's travels. I bought a copy. It is a good thing he wrote his book as a great many people get information that they would never have had and which they would have suspicions of others.

Today was Daniel's birthday. Oh if he could be with us to celebrate it.

Yesterday Bilger's telegraphed twice. Mrs Bilger's is very low. I got a letter on Sat. which I forgot to deliver till yesterday.

Cal. tells me that Hunsicker is well pleased with the church. He wants the wall fixed. Mrs. H. says the Ladies Aid Soc. has 250 and that they intend to buy a pipe organ and S.S. room and room for Ladies Aid in basement.

Tuesday, June 24, 1902.   What was my surprise to read this evening that an operation had to be performed on King Edward and that that there are doubts about his living. He was to be crowned on Thursday and the Coronation festivities had just began. He had given a dinner or banquet to the visiting royalties last evening. He had been seen driving the streets. He had gone through what was a rehearsal of the proceedings and now when all was ready he was stricken. What would have been joy will likely turn to woe and the soldiers who were to take part in the coronation procession may possibly remain for a funeral. It is possible that he will survive but it is likely that it was put off too long in the hope not to interfere with the coronation. He took a cold last week at Aldershot and it was said he had lumbago but nobody believed it serious. They said there was a plot against his life.

Monday, June 30, 1902.   My Aunt Mrs. Henry Bilger was buried at Leidy's today. She died on Wednesday. Father and Uncle Joe Derstine's went out to see her that very day, but they were too late. She had died an hour or so before they came. Aunt Sarah and aunt Kit were there since Monday. They telegraphed twice on Sunday.

The funeral came on the 9:10 train. We walked to the church.

Most of the relations were there. Old Herman was down too.

Abel Horning. Luckenbill preached.

We put a few flowers on Daniel's grave.

Aunt Annie looked very nice in death. She was 64 yrs. 8 mos. old. She had stomach trouble.

Tuesday, July 1, 1902.   The stuff for Moore's house in Germantown which we loaded on Sat. did not get off till this morning on account of rain. It was a great mistake not to go yesterday but the roads were wet. Today it was worse. Had 3 horses, Hen. Godshall as a leader. At Lansdale he frightened and broke the tongue and we were delayed 4 hrs. We sent Nat Moyer with other 2 horses to take the load. Rocks can hurt a little.

Tuesday, July 22, 1902.   It seems that we are getting all the trouble imaginable this year. Last evening Mary felt very sick and Jennie put her in the Bath Cabinet. During the night she vomited a number of times retaining nothing in her stomach. We cleaned her bowels with a suppository and still she was feverish 100⅘. In the morning 101⅖. Later 102, 102½. At one o'clock 103. During the night thinking of diphtheria I decided that I would get a trained nurse and board out believing I could do more good away from home. We sent the children to Gra. Moyers after dinner, that is Henry & Catharine. They were very happy and seemed to enjoy it. This morning Mary showed a red rash and we thought of Scarlet Fever. Her throat was sore and there was some membrane on her tonsils. We read up and believed it to be Scarlet Fever. Fetched the doctor after 4 o'clock who pronounced it Scarlet Fever. Tem. 102. Moved my clothes to G. Hemsing. I wanted to sleep in the barn tonight so I could be near if necessary but Jennie would not allow it.

Wednesday, July 23, 1902.   This morning Roy came over and told me Henry was sick. Went over and found his temp 101⅖. He was getting red. So I carried him home too. I hope God will spare my children. Last evening I telephoned for a trained nurse. I was promised the same one Ellis had. She did not come till 12:10. She was surprised to find two patients.

Mary's temperature this afternoon 103. At 8 P.M. 101. Henry 6 P.M. 101⅕. The cases seem to be mild but I am almost afraid to think so. I also tremble to think that the others may start too. If only Jennie does not break down.

I am beginning to suspect the water supply or my well as the cause of this sickness. I will have the water tested. I asked the doctor whether it was possible that Henry had it from Mary. He said not. The period of incubation was 6 or 8 days.

Thursday, July 24, 1902.   This morning Mary temp was 101 and Henry 101⅕. They passed a good night and Mary seemed brighter.

Went to the city this afternoon and saw Tourisin. Had to promise to come again tomorrow.

This evening Mary was 101. She must have been 103 during the day. Henry was normal.

Had to do a lot of figuring tonight but got sleepy.

Friday, July 25, 1902.   Was up at five this morning. There was much rain yesterday and again this morning. It was very dark. When I came out this morning both the children were normal. This evening Mary had 101 and Henry normal.

Was in the city again today. By a combination of unfortunate circumstances I failed to get to the city before about 1:30. Wanted to go on Scranton Exp. but the Trolly was late. Then I missed the next because it was late and we had gone on the local. But at Oreland we left the Express ahead.

I think I'll get Neilson the way Tourisin talked.

Was at Morre's House Germantown.

Saturday, July 26, 1902.   It is with thankfulness to God that I write down the fact that I saw my little boy through the window apparently happy and well. His attack was light but it was more than the rash as he says that has no fever.

Mary's temp tonight was 101. I saw the Dr. tonight and he says Mary's highest temp was 103⅗. He says her redness is beginning to fade.

I hope she will also soon be well.

Sunday, July 27, 1902.   This morning Mary's temp was 99. Henry was sitting on the steps crying. He knew he was not to come down. When he saw me he started to run out saying, "I want to go Papa."

This afternoon I went out and sat on the steps awhile with the others. Went with Milt to see Catharine. She seems to be a good girl if she can sit on someone's lap.

Went to church this evening. They gave me a bouquet which I took out to the children after church.

The camp meeting kept the trolleys busy today. Father went up this afternoon a short time. On the way back they rang up 227 fares. People are foolish and they like to crowd and see people. I don't know when they will all get home.

Monday, July 28, 1902.   Saw the nurse for the first time this evening. She was sitting on the front steps when I came. She says Mary's temp is 101⅕ this evening. She thinks things have gone remarkably well. She says Henry grew rebellious at the confinement. She had diptheria 3 times and has her tonsils removed.

Had to go to Hartzel's hotel on account of the addition about to be built.

Later on went out to see Jennie.

This has been a very warm day. Schlosser's child is very sick. He was away and did not get back till after six. It is hardly to be expected that the child will live over night.

Tuesday, July 29, 1902.   Was in the city today. Tourisin was too busy to talk to me about Neilson. Saw Pearson the arch't. He is a very nice man.

Went to Germantown to see the Manheim Club House. I don't want that job at all.

Got home 4:45. It rained fast at 6 o'clock. I waited pretty well till it was over as I did not get wet.

Mary has still 1% of heat,

Wednesday, July 30, 1902.   Mary had no fever this morning for the first time. At noon it was 99⅖ and she was bright. I hope this improvement will continue.

Had a spell of diarrhea last night and this forenoon. It made me careless about work.

Got a new house at Chalfont tonight from S. R. Cressman. I confess I was not anxious for it and thought my figure was high but he gave it. I hope there will be no trouble.

Am getting pretty busy. Unloaded car lumber today.

Thursday, July 31, 1902.   Mary's temperature is now normal. Jennie said they expect to fumigate on Saturday. She was a little indignant that they didn't do it right away, but I told her they did much the same thing the other time. They wish to keep on the safe side.

This evening they told me Mary was still in bed and that she is not to get up till it is all fumigated.

Amy has a sore throat. I am very much afraid she will get it too yet. That would be too bad. Jennie says she is such a help.

Friday, August 1, 1902. Amy has only 101 temp. this evening. The nurse says she is worse than Henry was though not so severe as Mary.

I bought some sheets and pillow cases tonight. Mr. Luckenbill came along from the store and sat with me on the porch a long time.

There was a riot yesterday in the coal region and the troops have been called out. Some say this will end the strike.

Saturday, August 2, 1902. Amy's temp is 100 and 101 in the evening. She is very hungry and thinks she must have something to eat. Mary was up yesterday a half hr. for the first time. She was up longer today. The trouble now is that Jennie is too much disturbed by the children. She does not get her rest. Henry and the baby are both troublesome which is no wonder and Helen is a poor worker. She does not stick.

Uncle Henry Bilger came this evening.

Last evening Henry used to walk around and say "My eyses! My eyses!" being sleepy.

Catharine watches the cows and Monday when the sale was she came in and said: "The man preached to the cows, and the cows made a noise"! The auctioneer reminded her of a preacher and it seemed to her that the cows were not behaving properly.

Sunday, August 3, 1902. Amy continues the same. Saw Mary through the window for the first time. She looks all right. Has cotton in one ear. She was very friendly. Was out home this morning. and fell asleep on the steps. Slept after dinner and they woke me up for church. Felt very tired and worn out somehow. I think Jennie must feel even worse. She has the worry of all those children.

A pipe blew up at the Power House, blowing out fire and steam. Two men were scalded. The trolley service under crowded conditions like today is wretched. They have no reserve power and a little mishap throws them out of gear. People went to camp today and crowded like crazy. There was a shower this evening and some must have got wet.

Took bouquet down home after church this afternoon.

Monday, August 4, 1902. Amy's temperature was normal this morning and only rose to 99⅕ this afternoon. She complains much of itching. The nurse says that it is a worse disease in some respects than diptheria.

Mary was up and dressed for the first time today.

Was up to Sellersville this afternoon to get someone to help. Enos has three funerals this week and we won't see him at the shop. Asked Amandus Daub. I don't know whether he will come or not. Measured up Jas. H. Nase's house.

Tuesday, August 5, 1902.   The children especially Henry and the baby make my wife too much trouble. I fear she is worrying. She tells me that on Thursday they are going to fumigate. This will be the second attempt and I hope none of them will catch it this time.

Was in the city this afternoon and took the contract for Mr. Neilson's house at St. Davids, Pa. With the stall I will get about $2300.00. I hope I can make it for that.

Wednesday, August 6, 1902.   Tomorrow at ten they are going to fumigate. I hope this will come true. It is quite time. Jennie's nerves are giving way and she is beginning to imagine things.

Today we put Frederick at some machine work and he did right well. He is proud of it.

I was up to Sellersville this evening for Amandus Daub but did not get him.

Today John Q's child Johnny was here for dinner and when came in fr. the shop —

Thursday, August 7, 1902.   At last we are officially over scarlet fever. That is we will be tomorrow. They fumigated our house this afternoon but the board will only come off tomorrow.

I was out this evening and Henry was very much pleased to sit on my lap. Amy looked so big. Her skin is peeling off. Mary smiled and wondered about the shirt I had on.

Loux's child, a boy died yesterday morning. About Henry's age according to the paper.

I asked whether I could sleep at home but they said I should wait till tomorrow.

Friday, August 8, 1902.   Quarantine taken off this morning. Found Jennie had not slept well. Henry had tried her hard. Amy looked big when I first saw her. Mary was a little thin. Henry looked very satisfied when I held him on my lap.

Saturday, August 9, 1902.   Jennie did not sleep last night as I expected. Mattie came out to do the work yesterday. She took Henry along out last evening. Jennie promised me she could sleep tonight.

Sunday, August 10, 1902.   I knew that if Jennie could not sleep tonight there would be a complete breakdown. And so there was. Sent Helen out for Mattie to fetch the baby away. She made breakfast. Told her to send Milt out. We then sent for a carriage and very much against her will took her to Telford to Dr. Bauman who gave us sulphura to put her to sleep containing neither morphine or opium.

Gave her some as soon as we came back. Ate dinner at Grandpop Moyer's where Ed's were. She slept this evening after the second dose and I felt much relieved.

Monday, August 11, 1902.   After Jennie woke about 11:30 I gave her a third dose but her sleep was interrupted after that.

This morning I noted a great improvement though the queer notions were not all gone. I was able to leave her alone.

At dinner time they told me Catharine had commenced to vomit. It troubled me and I stopped in to find out. I found as I had suspected that it was a probable case of scarlet fever again. Ida said Stanley was acting in the same way. So I did not worry so much.

This evening however the fever was very pronounced 101⅖ and Stanley was all right. Now I was in a fix. I can't leave the child out there. I can't leave my wife alone. I can't leave my business. It is the tightest position I have ever been in, and no one can help out.

Tuesday, August 12, 1902   I decided to take Catharine home. Jennie did not sleep well and I had only one dose. Sent Roy for more. Milt drove me and Cath. home in the carriage. She was very bright. The doctor pronounced it scarlet fever and I telegraphed for a nurse.

I told the doctor that in Phila the man of the house was allowed to go in and out under proper restrictions and I wanted the Board to change the rule according not for me only but for every body.

The board or 3 of the members met and I missed the meeting. They decided against it. Saw Dr. Souder and afterward had a talk with Crouthamel but could not see Dr. Vaughn but had a talk with his wife. I told them I would go in and that they should arrest me and collect the fine. Crouthamel said he thought there should be another meeting. Oberholtzer and Detweiler were in favor of my proposal but could not be present. Went home.

Wednesday, August 13, 1902.   This morning Dr. Vaughn came to the factory and told me that the Board of Health would let me go and come if I would get an affadavit that I had employed a nurse and that the case was isolated from the rest of the family and that we promised to remain out of the room.

I went to Ben Alderfer's this evening and we prepared it there.

Catharine's temperature was 101 this morning and 102 this evening. I regard this concession from the Board of Health as a great boon to others in my position.

Milt went west tonight. He will now drive that tunnel 800 ft.

Sent Mattie and Frank to Telford for sleeping potion.

Saturday, August 16, 1902.   Dr. Souder gave me a powder of salt called Chlorinal I think. This did more good than any thing we used to make her sleep.

Sunday, August 17, 1902.   Though she slept yet today she was very troublesome. I could hardly get her to eat as she got the idea that she ought to fast. This makes it bad.

Reference to J.

Tuesday, August 19, 1902.   Catharine I am afraid is very sick. Jennie was very down hearted today. I had to compel her to eat. In fact I had to do this since Sunday as she wants to fast. She thinks God will be more merciful if we fasted. I told her she had no right to let her baby suffer but arguments were vain and I threatened not to leave before she ate. This afternoon Mattie came out and things went better at supper time. I was afraid the nurse would not get waited on. We ate more "Force" and Shredded Wheat than ever before.

This evening the doctor took me into the sick room and showed Catharine to me. He says the Scarlet Fever is gone and that it is Typhoid now. I am very sorry for the child. How she has to suffer. Her fever was 103 yesterday and today somewhat over 102.

I am thinking of trying or adding another doctor. We gave Jennie a powder and she is very sleepy.

Am very busy at the shop. Am getting a load ready for Germantown.

Wednesday, August 20, 1902.   Jennie had a good night. She is sleepy yet. She can't hardly walk. She thinks its the medicine. But it is the reaction. Her nerves are unstrung. The baby makes trouble. It wouldn't sleep for a long time. I think there is gas forming in its stomach as it used to belch if I carried it. This did not even disturb Jennie much.

We got a load of stuff ready for Moore House Germantown. We worked like Beavers to get it ready. Now the trouble is we have no horse for certain. I am afraid our little Catharine will not recover. Her stomach is much swollen and she is having diarrhea. I want to speak to the doctor tonight about a consultation. Her temperature this afternoon was 103. I am afraid she can't stand this long.

Thursday, August 21, 1902.   Doctors met this afternoon. Asked Dr. Bauman and he thought there was a chance for her to get well. He advised the ice cap to be used as a pillow instead of the top of the head. Also recommended lemonade and albumen the white of an egg.

I couldn't understand their talk about medicines. Dr. Bauman said use plenty of Pepsin. Dr. S. had been using this in connection with others.

I relieved the nurse last night. This was not according to rule but I changed my clothes and fumigated afterward. Dr. Souder asked me to do it.

I had a little trouble giving her medicine but she passed a good night. Didn't have to give her powders. She has a diarrhea but Dr. Bauman said "Don't worry about that."

Friday, August 22, 1902.   Was surprised to find they were fumigating this evening. Reeder spoke about it this morning but I supposed they would not do it so I forgot about it.

The nurse thought the doctor was displeased and there was quite a breeze.

Mattie was here two days but went home again last night. Tomorrow night I am going to take care of Catharine. It is such a pity that Henry's ears are running and he is a little deaf. I only hope he will outgrow it.

Aug. 21. Rested all during night

Vomited after whiskey at 1 p. m.

Restless and talking this P. M.

22. Rested well

23. Very restless, slept very little

Restless most of the day.

Saturday, August 23, 1902.

Nurse's Record for Catharine

Aug. 12	6 P. M.	9 P. M.	12 P. M.			
	102	101⅗	100⅘			
Aug. 13	4 A. M.	8 A. M.	12 A. M.	4 P. M.	6 P.M.	
	100⅗	99⅗	99⅕	101	102	
					8 P. M.	
Aug. 14	101⅗	100	100⅗	101⅘	102⅕	12 P. M.
Aug. 15	100⅗	102	102⅖	102⅕	102⅗	102⅘
Aug. 16	101⅗	101	101⅘	101⅗	102	101⅕
Aug. 17	101⅗	101	100⅗	101⅗	102	101⅗
Aug. 18	102⅘	102⅗	101⅗	101⅖	101⅗	101
Aug. 19	103	102⅖	101⅖	101⅘	102	102
Aug. 20	102	101⅕	102	103	103	---
Aug. 21	---	103	102	102⅘	102	102
Aug. 22	102⅖	101⅘	102	103	102⅗	102
Aug. 23	102	102⅖	103	103⅗	103	102

Aug. 12. Some notes. Abdomen a little distended. Turp & Lard to abdomen.

Aug. 13. Quite restless during night. Slept little.

Aug. 14. Rested & slept better than before. Turp & Lard.

Aug. 15. Ate Oyster Broth. Quite restless. Did not sleep well. Abdomen much distended. Rheumatic Pains. Turp & Lard to abdomen.

Aug. 16. Restless. Turp & Lard. Did not sleep well. Delirious.

Aug. 17. Restless till 12m then rested and slept some. Ice to neck. Ice cap.

Aug. 18. Rested quietly all day. Very restless during night.

Aug. 19. Abd. much distended. Slept more this night. Very restless at times, talking in sleep. Vomited a little.

Aug. 20. Rested some better than before. Slept more. Rested quite well all day.

Sunday, August 24, 1902.   Catharine's temp. at 8 AM was 103⅖; at 12, 102⅗; at 4, 103. All these temperatures are taken under the armpits but at 4 PM she took a rectal temperature and that showed 104.

The doctor says she has meningitis. Read up on this subject a little and the consequence is that I have very little hope left according to the flesh. But He to whom all things are subject I know can help. _____

And now Catherine too is gone. — She died at ten o'clock this evening. The doctor had just been here and told me she couldn't live 24 hrs. She died less than half an hour after he left. How she reminded me of Daniel when she died. Jennie tried to apply hot bandages. I was afraid she would get out of her mind so I let her go. Sent for father and grandpop Moyers. Father came out. We got Amy and Helen up to see her die. She died peaceably.

Tuesday, August 26, 1902.   Mattie washed out home. Ellen and Naomi Moyer helped here at home. We were much at a loss what all to do. People expect to be asked. They thought we would call them together and so no one offered to do anything. I explained that we thought no one cared to come to our house on account of having so recently quarantined.

Went down with Moyer to have the grave located. I was surprised that the coffin would be almost as large as Daniel's only 3 in. difference Enos said.

Wednesday, August 27, 1902.   Funeral held this afternoon at 1:30 at the house. Rev. Moyer and Clemmer were to preach at the house but did not appear probably because the cards were marked private at the house. Rev. Clemmer was at the church. Trolleys stopped entirely on account of lack of water and this may have kept some away. Schwenck had to borrow a team. Then a rain came up while the services were in progress at the house. Still others were afraid. Many families were represented by one only. Luckinbill spoke German at the house, Eng. at the church and Clemmer some German.

Quite a number of people came on back to the house. I had hardly expected this but I was glad for Jennie wanted it and it was not so lonely. Catharine looked very nice and almost natural. Henry couldn't be kept quiet. He wanted to get on the wagon and called out during the service.

Sunday, August 31, 1902. Elias Nice fatherinlaw of Mr. Erb died this evening after seven. The last I saw him was on Tuesday morning and then he talked very hoarse. On Friday night he had a stroke of apoplexy and was unconscious to the end. They had seven sons & 1 daughter. He was a nice old man who never interfered with any one. I often thought while we had diphtheria and they also, and he was painting his wagon in the yard what a peaceable contented life they were having.

Thursday, September 4, 1902. Pres. Roosevelt came near losing his life yesterday or today. I don't remember which. A trolley car ran into their train and the secret service man Craig lost his life. The driver also being badly hurt.

The Pres. rec'd. a few bruises on the cheek and cuts on the lip.

Wednesday, September 10, 1902. Mr. Luckenbill was here this evening. He comes oftener than he used to. He tries his best to get these queer ideas out of Jennie. Somehow she can't help her self to say something about quarantine, the hardship or wrong of it. He told her the true Christian was willing to submit and gladly.

We are so busy at the shop I hardly know which way to turn. I just manage to get along and there is no catching up. I am behind hand on Hartzels Hotel. They are waiting at Nace's Sellersville. Just finishing Sholtz Home Perkasie. Not quite through with Reiff. Heckler is after me for some thing. Besides this Tourisin at Germantown and St. Davids.

Monday, September 22, 1902. Weighed Henry this afternoon at station. Weighs 29½ lbs. Mine was 184 ---. He is gaining weight rapidly.

Mary went to school for the first time today.

They have now missed 2 weeks of this term and 6 weeks I think of the last. And Daniel is no longer with us.

I think Yearick will lose his child. It is sick with menengitis and has been unconscious for 6 ds.

Sunday, October 5, 1902. We are in a coal famine now and I don't know what will happen later on. A few people have a little coal some enough for the winter but the great majority have none. We have been burning soft coal for two or three weeks but now I can't get soft coal and we have only fuel for 3 weeks. I bought my car a month ago at 2.10 at the mine and 1.55 freight but it is now 6.00 at the mines with prospects of going higher. I think they ship the high priced orders first and let ours stand.

Pres. Roosevelt called the operators and Mitchel to conference at Washington on Friday but it failed. The operators will have nothing to do with Mitchell saying a state of anarchy exists and calling on the Pres. to send troops to the coal regions.

I stopped off Shavings and wrote to Burten's for some but have no hope of getting any.

Sunday, October 12, 1902.   The coal situation is what fills the newspapers and is the general topic of conversation. The failure of the Pres.'s conference seems to have left things in worse shape than before.

Gov. Stone ordered the entire Nat. Guard to the Coal Regions this week.

Ed Hollenback as 2nd Lieut. of Co. L. 1st Reg is stationed at Latimer I think. Arthur Stover is in the same company. Another conference of politicians in New York failed on Friday. There are conferences every day both sides standing firm.

I have written again for my coal and have not given up yet but am getting cold comfort.

They claim they cannot get transportation but the fact remains that there is coal shipped. H. S. Souder got a car in nearly a week but he paid more.

This thing has to stop or matters will be serious soon. Both sides are stubborn as mules and it is all a question whether the union is to be recognized or not. The miners won't work as long as they are being supported.

Wednesday, October 15, 1902.   Today Reub. told me he was going to leave. It made me angry at once because he said he would leave in two weeks. He said he couldn't stand it any more &c. He was here 19 years.

I said more than I ought accusing him of wishing to leave us stick and telling him we would be doing business after he left. There was no use in saying this as it only made ill feelings. I don't know however what to do. I haven't anyone to take his place and probably can't get any one.

Spoke to Lew Hessler about it today. I think he would be all right but it wouldn't do to take him away from Wampole.

Thursday, October 23, 1902.   Today the miners go to work the convention on Monday and Tuesday voting unanimously to accept the arbitration commission appointed by the President. Thus is averted what would have been one of the greatest calamities this country ever suffered from. As it is there is sure to be trouble to get coal for sometime. There was a car shipped on Oct. 14 but did not get it. Another was shipped on the 21st the first having been wrecked or confiscated. We hope we will get the second car. We are nearly out of coal.

Reuben came to the shop this evening and I paid him the balance of what I owed him. Engaged him again for odds and ends. Told him to give Bordo notice and not leave him the way he did me. Pay him 16¼¢.

Saturday, October 25, 1902.   I am glad this week is over. We worked every evening for the last four days. I was almost encamped at the shop, taking two meals a day there. We made good progress though. On Thursday morning Davy Derstine did not turn up having gone to Harvey Souder. He doesn't stick anywhere.

Reuben is going to leave Tuesday evening. I was worried this evening as I did not notice him at church at first and thought perhaps he was not going to communion. But when the services were over I noticed him after all.

Sunday, October 26, 1902.   We had communion today. 85 partook.

Collection 45.03. More than ever before.

Norm Brunners and J. O. Snyders were down.

Was in Sunday School this afternoon.

We were in meeting this evening. Young Mack preached. He is not the equal of his father. We had the baby along this morning and evening. She is very good.

Luckenbill announced that he would soon preach a series of sermons based on Prof. Hilprecht's lectures on the excavations of Nippur.

Norman Zendt was taken as a member of the church. He was catechized and baptized privately.

Wednesday, November 5, 1902.   Pattison was defeated for Governor by about 170,000 plurality. I hoped Pennypacker would not be elected yet he was.

Uncle Henry Souder was running for Sheriff in Bucks. He was defeated by 800 votes.

Montgomery went Republican except for Gov. Pattison. Won by 500.

Monday, November 10, 1902.   Last night I was afraid Jennie would have Pneumonia again. Put her in Sweat Box and that did her good. She staid in bed till dinner time.

I am having the worst cold I have had for a long time. Had it all last week but it is steadily getting worse.

Father has rebuilt his stable and this evening I stopped in to see whether he wouldn't help us at the shop tomorrow when he told me he would get married on Saturday. This was not exactly a surprise as people had been talking enough about it. He had told me 3 mos. ago he had thoughts of doing this and I asked him who and he said Mrs. Ratzel. I told him I have nothing against it except that I wanted my interests safeguarded. He said this evening that neither is to interfere with the other. I want the thing more definite. Of course, I would have preferred him to remain single but I am willing to let him have his rights but stand for mine.

Friday, November 14, 1902.   Am getting more and more behind every day. I get so little done. There is so much for me to attend to that I don't get much of anything done.

Wrote letter to Dannehower about father the other day and this evening rec'd his reply. He says they must make their agreement before marriage. This is a fine time to find this out. Went out and hunted up father. He was at the store and bought himself a fall overcoat. I suppose he didn't like it much for he said "If every one were as solid as I there would be no need of agreements," but I told him that he must remember that the conditions might change entirely. That persons of whom we had no knowledge would probably have a say in the matter later on. I don't like to be at the mercy of any man. They are so heartless.

Saturday, November 15, 1902.   Telephoned to Dannehower this morning and he dictated an agreement over the telephone. It seemed to be long and it was hard work to write with only one hand free. This afternoon I had John M. Moyer Jennie's cousin to make a type written copy of same.

Took it in to Father this evening and he is to get it signed. We allowed her the $300.00 exemption allowed widows and 150 per annum as long as she remain unmarried after his decease. I think this is fair enough. She doesn't expect anything but I thought it would look bad and I found that father had intended to leave her his home but I told him in that case he couldn't even sell it so he made it a definite sum.

Sunday, November 16, 1902.   Father and his new wife my stepmother I suppose I have to regard her were here for dinner having been at Indian Creek Church. She seems to be a nice woman about the age of my mother. She seems to have known mother at school. Father tells me the agreement was satisfactory to her.

I am trying to cure my cold but am not very successful.

Didn't go to church tonight because nominations for Deacons were to be made and the Consistory chose me as a candidate so I didn't want to put anyone under constraint by my presence.

Wednesday, November 19, 1902.   We were at Cousin Ed Landis funeral today. He died on Friday night. Was sick only 9 days. He started with eryrsypelas and it turned to cerebral meningitis. He was born Feb. 17, 1866, about a month younger than I. He was a queer person. Had talents, but it seems to me he was to much of a speculator. He first studied medicine. Was manager of the High Tension Co. Had a saloon in Camden, N. J. Was ship doctor on a vessel sailed to Cuba. Seemed to be always looking for something to turn him rich. He was handling a patent for someone refrigerator down south. Was always experimenting. Was married to Kate Price 3 years.

Luckenbill baptized him on his deathbed. Luck. preached a powerful sermon but many didn't understand. He didn't preach quite simple enough for our people.

Thursday, November 27, 1902.   Today father was attending to the Ratzel Sale. Jennie was up and bought a lot of things. Parlor suit and alot of carpet.

We didn't work today but Ott and I fixed the Pulling gear for Truck.

The trolley had a terrible accident at Hatfield. A car containing 77 Passengers. John Essei, motorman and Will Sell conductor. The brakes refused to work and the car was overturned. 1 boy was killed. Jas. Detweiler son of Rev. J. B. Detweiler will probably die.

Sunday, December 14, 1902.   The whole country is covered with snow not deep but hard crust and no bare spaces. I don't believe I ever saw better sleighing. It is all ready no banks, but a good even surface to go over.

This evening was moonlight and the fellows who omitted to take out their girls tonight are guilty of neglect.

Ben Hackman died on Friday and will be buried on Wednesday. Old Benj. Moyer will be buried on Tuesday. Mrs. Andrew Benner was buried on Thursday.

Cal Hunsbergers were here this evening.

Monday, December 15, 1902.   I am at last through with Moores house at Germantown. Tiresome it was. Now they will be after me about Neilsons.

Mrs. W. S. Grant died of heart disease yesterday.

The British and Germans bombarded Portio Capella in Venezuela and the situation there is very grave. Owing to the position of the U. S. Gov. on the Monroe Doc. it may lead to acts on the part of both the combatants compelling us to interfere.

Pres. Castro is an adventurer and it is supposed would be glad to get the U. S. involved.

This will force the U. S. into a protectorate over such countries same as over Cuba. It will cause much trouble.

Sunday, December 28, 1902.   Emma Ratzel came out to ask us for dinner. Father had forgotten to tell. Jennie and the children were at Sunday School and did not come back till near dinner time so it was quite late when we came out. They had got hold of a turkey. Ed Souder's came as we left. On Christmas they had been at our place as well as Schwenck's and Grandpop Moyer's. We had Henry along but we could scarcely keep him satisfied. Took him home and started playing with his toys at once.

Had our Christmas Service tonight. On my way up I was afraid there was no one there everyone was coming down enough to fill a small church. When I came up I found out the cause. The crowd was so great that I too turned around and went home.

Wednesday, December 31, 1902.   Mattie was married today to Frank Sheetz. They went to Phila. and were united by Rev. Fluck an uncle of Mr. Scheetz.

They expect to live at home.

*Land dealings—personnel problems at mill—disagreements
with Jennie on matters of religion—shows Mrs. Roberts
around Philadelphia—Jennie miscarries—father and
bride take a trip West*

1903

Friday, January 30, 1903.   Watts got stubborn for me today because he
did not like the idea of having a second car of Buckwheat Coal. This last car
which had been ordered over a month and which was no longer expected is
very fine coal and I told Watts so but he would look at the samples I wanted to
show him said it was the same dirt and told me I should get some one else to
burn them. I said I would have to if he wouldn't. He commenced to swear and
surprised at the man I said "what kind of a fool (calf) are you. He threatened to
strike me and I repeated it as an assertion. He tried to hit me but I was on my
guard and not wishing to fight with the poor fellow I caught him somehow and
held him. I told him he could stay if he behaved but he said I should get
another man till Monday. Went to Telford for Jacob Groff this evening.

Saturday, January 31, 1903.   Somehow Watts had a pair of black eyes
this morning. Of course, every one believes I did it yet I think not at least not
intentionally. I know I pitied him and was not even angry when I found he was
powerless to hurt me. But no one will really believe me and I can't help it. I
was sorry today that I did not give him more time to think but it seemed to me
the matter could be settled at once. Groff was down this afternoon and
promised to come Monday.

Watts had nothing to say when he came for his money this evening.

If he had been as sorry for himself as I was for him he would have given in.

But a Watts thinks it a fine thing to be stubborn.

Monday, February 2, 1903.   Our new engineer started work this
morning.

The engine got very troublesome this afternoon and we had to stop off
toward evening to fix. One of the fero valves was out of order and I had to
make a new nob to hold spring. Did not get home till 8:30.

Tuesday, February 3, 1903.   Found the engine running very nicely this
morning with a great increase of speed. This affected the dynamo so that our
lights were too bright and they will have to be reduced in voltage. Fuses are
burning out one after the other.

Thursday, February 5, 1903. Was over to St. Davids this afternoon. Geo Stokes is foreman there now. He says it took 10 days to get millwork there.

Zendt put this on a R&R car and it had to be all unloaded at Wayne Junction and the consequence is that there are broken pcs.

Friday, February 6, 1903. Helen has been lying around several days this week with a severe cold. I was getting anxious for a doctor but J. never is.

Monroe Souder is quite low. He had pneumonia and hiccoughs later on that could not be stopped. Mr Luckenbill baptized him last week.

Got a Rheostat at the shop this afternoon. Owing to the increase of speed of our engine the voltage of the dynamo went too high and we had to reduce it. The moulder and planer do not affect it very much. Mr Groff our new engineer is unable to move to Souderton on account of his wife. I suppose I will have to look quietly for another man and use this one elsewhere.

Met Watts last evening but he did not answer my good evening.

Saturday, February 7, 1903. Slifer went to the city today and so did Mrs. Roberts, (Carrie Hemsing) They are getting so intimate that I am afraid the affair will have serious consequences. Jennie is worried and thinks Mrs Roberts has no right to remarry.

Read a funeral notice for Hiram Danley who will be buried on Monday. He died yesterday. They live at Flemington N.J.

Would very much like to go over.

Loaded stuff for St. Davids. Will send it on Monday with 4 horses.

Sunday, February 8, 1903. Henry Krupp and wife were here after S.S. and meeting. Enjoyed their visit very much. They took a collection for Missions in S.S. this morning and got over $20.00

Was in church this evening. The attendance was good.

This afternoon was rainy but has cleared off.

Very many people are coughing. Our children and the girl have bad colds.

Monday, February 9, 1903. Was in Perkasie late this afternoon to measure for a bulk window.

Stopped at Schwencks and learned about the new church. They were afraid Stoneback would back out if he knew the amount of the other bids.

I think there is a change in the situation with Slifer and Mrs R. someone asked him whether he knew he was sporting a grass widow. He said he knew what he was doing, but I thought I felt the difference. He is very easily influenced and H. K. Kindig got a hold of him in the city. He has someone for him and he wants to look that matter up now.

Tuesday, February 10, 1903.   Irwin Souder was the only one to go to Danleys funeral.

He had dropsy and heart failure. His body was placed in a receiving vault and will not be buried till the weather is better.

Today news arrived that Mrs. Galloway Mrs Roberts sister Sarah had died. I sent her some photos of the children not long ago and she wrote me two letters. She wanted me to send pictures of ourselves. I am very glad I wrote to her because last spring just before Daniel died she wanted a family group but Daniel never got on. She says she remembers Daniel and Catherine from the time she was here.

Wednesday, February 11, 1903.   This morning I made an offer for the Souder estate property.

I made two propositions, lst 8000 for all to remain without interest until sold and divided prorate as sales are made, nothing to be paid over until improvements are made. The second offer is for all the lots except those on North side of Broad St for 4000 each.

I don't suppose they will accept either of these offers, but Slifer seemed almost nervous about it.

Rainy today. We unloaded lumber but it was so wet that it did not hurt it.

Adam Crouthamel's and Jake Hunsbergers have scarlet Fever and are quarantined.

I believe Geo S Snyder has taken the Keeley cure. I wonder how it will hold out.

Thursday, February 12, 1903.   Today at noon Rein Clemmer's were quarantined for smallpox.

He came home Tuesday and the children kept coming to school yesterday. So today they stopped the school house and fumigated.

He ought not to have come home and expose his family and others so. I suppose I will try and get vaccinated again. Jennie is so opposed to vaccination that is not reasonable about it. I am for taking every possible precaution.

Friday, February 13, 1903.   This evening Ellis called me in and had a talk with me about the real estate. He wants me to increase my offer to 5000 and then he would talk like a Dutch Uncle. I told him I wasn't any too anxious to have it and that I would not give more.

Saturday, February 14, 1903.   When I came home tonight Emma Ratzel and Mrs Roberts were here and had a new dress for each of the three girls.

Helen's is Red, Amy's is blue and Mary's is a grayish green. They all look very well. Jennie is a little doubtful whether it is right. They are a present from Emma.

Rein Clemmer has a severe case. If only none of the others get infected.

We have about 325,000 ft of lumber instead of 211,000 last year.

Thursday, February 19, 1903.   The land deal seems to be coming to a focus. Ellis came over and wanted an offer on the plotted piece only as the others had taken the rest. This did not suit us but we offered 3000. This evening he offered this and the long field for 4000. There would remain only the 10 remaining lots which of course constitute the difference. We talked of offering 4500 for all of it. Elwood thinks we ought to get it. He would like to start building on the back lots.

Helped to audit accounts of Bldg Ass'n this evening. J.S. Moyer and J Landis were both there but I find they are poor friends. It's too bad. John told me a little but I didn't know what to say.

Saturday, February 21, 1903.   Monroe Souder was buried today at Leidy's. He was 60 yrs 8m and somedays old. Funeral at Ref. Ch. and Jennie was there.

We got our load off for St. Davids at last. I thought we would never get through.

Ott was up at the shop today. He is just out from sickness, having been in bed.

This evening we found that they had raised the price on us. Ellis asked me what I thought of it. I said it would make me pretty mad. We fetched Wm and Ed in the office and had it pretty hot for awhile. It seems that Fred came up this afternoon and they fixed the price at 5000 [illegible] our offer of 4500 or 7000 for all. Slifer is very much disappointed and so am I.

Ed got mad at me and he and Ellis had a tussel and Wm stood and said little.

We relaxed toward the end when Slifer talked to Wm about his soul. It seemed as though he never heard of anything of the kind. He is an agnostic.

Monday, February 23, 1903.   The land deal is complete. We went down to see Fred this afternoon made an offer and brought him along up — where he made his terms. That is sell the whole plot for 7000 for note of 1 year or $6650.00 cash which latter offer we try to accept. This evening we went to Quakertown and got Hen to sign the offer after which we brought it to Wm. and had a long talk about other matters and got to bed at 12 o'clock.

Our people all went to Telford to Jos. Derstein's after supper.

I think Fred is a little disappointed as he would have liked a slice of the land.

Tuesday, February 24, 1903.   We hear of offers for lots now and then. Elmer Souder wants corner lot opposite delp for 300 — and Cal has customer for one next to him for 200-. I am inclined to accept these offers if genuine and am in doubt about Laudenslager offer of 1100.

We haven't made an agreement yet but I told Wm to get it ready. Grandfather Moyer would like the ten lots on Front St for some purpose.

Mrs Clemmer and Wilmer have smallpox too and I am very anxious for them. Annie merely had varioloid but is not strong and then there is only Perry well and the small children to take care of. I hope he will soon be able to take care of them.

Friday, February 27, 1903.   Was in the city today. Looked at land level at Queens. It costs $25.00, must have it.

Was at Hoovers and took off 2 churches.

Old Mr Hoover is dead a year on Jan 28. Earle Hoover is getting as stout as his father.

Spent sometime at Leary's and bo't Rupp's 30,000 names and a Irving's Ahlambra nicely illustrated. Spent too much time there. Must stop this.

Saturday, February 28, 1903.   It was as warm as summer this morning and a great rain before dinner. The snow all disappeared and the roads are very muddy.

We blew off steam at the mill on Thursday. The inspector was here yesterday and today we closed up the boiler and babbited the engine. Cal is fixing his machine and Ott has made some changes on rip saw. I ordered the land level I saw in the city yesterday. This evening we ordered a double set of harness a triple tree and a road scraper which we expect to use for filling purposes.

This evening Aunt Kit, Mrs Allebach and her children were here. They expect to move to AB Benner's house next Thursday. Morris Hendricks was here this evening in response to my letter. We talked the matter of foremanship over. We did not come to any conclusion. I told him to think it over. He says he was badly treated by Bardo.

Tuesday, March 10, 1903.   Last Wednesday afternoon I came near losing the sight of my left eye. I poured Babbit metal into a box on the planer. Henry Rittenhouse got it ready and had left no vent hole but the one into which the babbit was poured. There must have been oil in. We heard it boil and just as it filled up it exploded into my face. My face and hair was full of it and my left eye was pasted shut. After removing the metal from my eyelids we found a piece inside next to the pupil. After this was removed the surface was burnt white. Went to Dr. Herman who thought it would come all right. Was down four times, the last time on Sunday morning. He put some belladonna in the eye on Thursday I think and this interferes a little with my sight. But he says in a couple of weeks this will be gone.

I have since realized how near I was to a catastrophe. It seems that we are often preserved from our follies without realizing it.

Wednesday, March 11, 1903.   It seems there is nothing but trouble. I think yesterday Noah Kramer came and told me this was his last week. I asked him where he went and he said to Bardo. I thought it good for him to find out.

This evening Penrose came to me with a letter from Bardo offering him 20¢ an hour. It seems Bardo's men are all running away to Weber and now he is after my men. This thing will make me trouble which ever way I regard it. If I let him go others will want to go. I don't think he wants to go but he wants more wages and I will of course give the others more.

If I only had an office boy and a competent foreman I would be willing to make a general advance.

Saturday, March 14, 1903.   My eye is all right again.

The effect of the belladonna is all gone. I have not worn a shade since Tuesday.

What an incredibly short time it took to get well.

And now Henry Bergey - next door to Clemmer's has smallpox too. This is too bad.

Started making drawing for Lutheran Church windows. This has made me very stiff. Must get pads for my knees.

Was down to Lansdale last evening to see Hendricks and he refused. Am entirely at a loss what to do now. Sent him an appeal to reconsider today.

Springer was here to ask me for job.

Noah stopped work last evening and settled his account today.

Sunday, March 15, 1903.   This proved a fine day spring like.

The girls and I walked down to Leidy's. It is nearly or quite a year when we took similar walks, once to Leidy's and once to Indian Creek when Daniel was along and enjoyed it so much. Today we visited his grave.

Dr. AR Bartholomew the Secretary of the Board of Home Missions preached there as well as at our Church in the afternoon. He is a powerful speaker and I believe filled with the Spirit.

His sermon confirmed me in some things. I remember that it isn't always a loss to spend money. It has not been in my experience. I am going to try once more. I hope I can be enabled to do much good.

Monday, March 16, 1903.   It is almost hearbreaking the way things are going. Ott didn't come around this morning till 9 o'clock and then said he was sick. I told him to go home and get well if it took 2 weeks or 4. But this afternoon he sent a letter from Dr. Cope saying he had to work in the open air.

So we have to go over it all again. I don't know where to look. Must have a foreman, a clerk and a cutter all at the same time.

Told Springer to come to work this morning.

Sent Rev. A R Bartholomew a check for $50. I hope it may do some good. I fear if some people knew they would think I was crazy. But I feel different.

We are in earnest about selling lots on Broad St. today. Slifer went to settle the matter this evening. They offered $1150. I think that is for the best.

Tuesday, March 17, 1903. Last evening Slifer sold the lots above Gehman for to Laudenslager and A.B. Benner for $1153.50. Slifer was determined that they should pay more than 1150 - which was evidently their limit. I told Ed Souder and he said we might have had $1200 - just as easy. I told him we intend on dispelling the idea that no one could buy lots from them. Ed resented this idea.

Was in St. Davids this afternoon. They are about done with our work but have none of 1st F finish there.

Friday, March 20, 1903. Today I hear that old Frank is going to be brought home. This will make a splendid horse for Slifer though he did not at first seem to think so. The man who had him sold out and of course had no right to sell Frank. He would have been glad to take Fr. to Lancaster with him.

Was in too see Elwood about the foremanship. He didn't want to give a definite answer as he doesn't like to leave Sam Alderfer stick.

Haven't done anything about the cutter problem. Slifer heard of a man at Quakertown whom I am going to look up. He also heard of a boy at Lansdale who is said to be very bright.

Kate Hollinback was here this evening. Mrs Allen Moyer also Jennie went out with her and I afterwards found that she had planned to get baptized to the River Br. this time. I cannot understand this and it worries me a great deal. How beautiful it would be if we could have agreed in matters of Faith.

Monday, March 23, 1903. Went up to Quakertown this afternoon to see the man Slifer told me about last week. Found Taylor on the front porch of the Bush House it being a rainy day.

He went with to hunt up the man. We found him engaged in making toys. They were certainly ingeniously put together.

I brought the man along down. We walked nearly all the way from near Richlandtown to Quakertown in the rain. Went through the mill and the man promised to come as soon as Taylor is through with him.

Tuesday, March 24, 1903. Little Margaret is one year old today. She has been a very good little girl so far. She has shown some signs of being spoilt a little.

This morning Springer came and reported that the men were all going to stop work if he commenced. That they had all signed a paper and are going to hand it to me this evening. He would prefer to wait till the trouble was over. Later Groff came in and said it was reported at Fran. Sq. that the men were all out. At the barber shop the men asked about our strike. I concluded that it was a hoax played on Schlosser and who talks too much. This afternoon Enos nearly lost his middle finger of the left hand. He got caught into the joints and cut it nearly off. He is always lucky and said he expected to remain so. Went out to Dr Souder with him who thinks it will heal together. He will have much pain.

Went to see Elwood to finish up. He said he would do it if he had the chance. Though he cant get away from his present job without putting Sam in a bad position.

I told him I would try John Freed next.

Wednesday, March 25, 1903. At last the foremanship is decided and John Freed is the man. He professed to have been better pleased to work under a stranger but I told him I wanted to put a premium on service.

Sunday, March 29, 1903. Did not get to Church today. Mr Abendstein and his son were here this afternoon. They came to see what kind of a place he would get should he come. I think he liked the office and most of the surroundings. I promised to come down on Tuesday evening to see whether we could get to an agreement. I told him he should have come on last evening but they said they wanted to see the shop.

The old man is a German and seemed pleased. The young man graduated first in his class of 30. He does not look handsome but that does not matter. He talks of a Trial Bal the first time but I told him the thing was impossible. I wish myself these people would not come on Sunday.

Read Washington Irving's Alhambra.

Henry is getting so spoilt he wants no one but his grand pop. We must take him home soon.

Wednesday, April 1, 1903. I think our new cutter is all right. The others like him and if he keeps on improving we will have to look for a house for him.

John is looking after things now. I think he will do all right.

Of course we will have to have a man to lay out work soon. Young Abendschein did not write and so that is the end of him. I sometimes believe and in fact I am almost convinced that these set backs are often if not always an advantage. If this cutter turns out better than Ott why shouldn't I be glad. So it may have been with the foreman, So it may be with the clerk.

Thursday, April 2, 1903. Rec'd the new scoop today. We tested it in the fields and found it worked all right.

Slifer also bought a horse from Geo Swartley for 170.

We went down to Lansdale this afternoon I to see Guthrie and then we looked at a plow cultivator and harrow.

He also went to see young Leidy for clerk.

Friday, April 3, 1903. Young Leidy was on hand this morning before I was out.

I set him to work experimentally to see how he would do.

Young Stauffer stopped work this morning. I set him to work under Reed Snyder and it seems that was more than he could stand. I hunted him up and told him how foolish he was and that I would tell his father the circumstances but he declared he did not like the trade and would stop.

Went over to see Erb about Elias. He asked me about him some time ago. He said he would find out over Sunday.

Saturday, April 4, 1903. Yesterday John told me that Deck the new man was going to stop. This morning he told me. He said he had an offer from the city for $3.00 per day. I told him I had intended to give him $2.25 per day. It made him think hard. This evening I talked again with him and tried to get at the real reason. I saw there was something the matter. It worried him. He said the thing was about the same only he could earn money faster in the city for a while. He said he was in debt to some extent and by pledging his tools he could raise the money in time while here he couldn't do it. I then promised to furnish this money and then he promised to report on Monday. I told him he had better bring his wife down and look it over.

Sunday, April 5, 1903. Heinrich came in from Sunday School and is here yet tonight. We will try and wean him home by and by.

Stayed home with the children this afternoon who slept. Appenzeller's stopped in on their way home from SS.

Heard that Mr Deck had his wife down today.

Archie Goettler died this morning quite suddenly and unexpectedly.

He must have been about 14.

The church bell tolled and I was at a loss to know who it could be.

Friday, April 10, 1903. We were at Appenzeller's today and had all along but the baby who was left home with Louisa. Jennie had compunctions about going but I put my foot on it. This disappointing people constantly and not knowing what is right and what is wrong is a nuisance. The last week has been a rainy one and the roads were muddy but the high winds during the day dryed them off. We went out into the woods. The trees are standing a little thin but there are a lot of young hickories coming up. There are some stout old trees. Instead of being on the highest it is on the lowest part of his farm. This was a mistake of the 1st settlers. We found the old road bed of the old Bethlehem road. Mattie and Frank were out this evening.

Sunday, April 12, 1903.   Today's Easter. We had Communion this morning. Counting the sick 87 communed. But there were some strangers among them Mrs Roberts, 4 were confirmed last evening. The misses Sallie and Emma Barndt. Miss Hendricks and Mr Walt.

The day was damp and unpleasant. It was better this afternoon. Easter service this evening. House was full.

Mrs Roberts came here after church this forenoon and stayed till after supper. She talks of going home soon.

Wednesday, April 15, 1903.   Elias Erb started work after all this morning. He was to start Monday but he had the boyish idea of being his own master and of staying out later. His father locked him out last Friday evening and so there was trouble. His mother worried so on Monday that she became hysterical. The boy promised to put his ideas aside and came to me last evening asking whether I would take him. I told him he would have to put his mind to what he was doing.

Today the last of them signed the deeds. We will soon be called on to settle. Yesterday and today were terrible stormy days. Raining and blowing continually.

Thursday, April 16, 1903.   Young Erb seems to be doing well so far. The rain is not yet settled. Tomorrow we hope it will be fair.

I am anxious to begin grading on Highland St.

Mrs John D. Moyer was reported dangerously sick from heart trouble.

Every church around here is getting a church organ and Andrew Carnegie stands half the cost. Now it seems we have caught the fever too. Mr Luckenbill proposed at the meeting on Easter Monday that the Ladies Aid society having 300 on hand they would borrow the balance and pay for it and Mr L to write to Carnegie for the other half. Perkasie, Sellersville North Wales South Bethlehem Allentown and all over they seem to be after him.

The Pipe organ people are busy I'll bet.

Friday, April 17, 1903.   Today we got the grade of Highland St plowed it in part and started scooping.

There is a great deal to learn in handling these machines. It was the first nice day for quite a while and we knew we would have to hurry if we did not want it to get too dry for us. There was a high wind and the instrument used to almost blow over. By evening what was mud in the morning was as hard as a brick.

Got our stuff from Chicago today. Corn Planter Potato Planter Rye [illegible] and all.

Friday, April 24, 1903.   Mrs. John Clymer died Tuesday morning after a lingering illness of dropsy. She will be buried tomorrow.

Jennie was over with her the last night she lived. She suffered very much.

Mr B.F. Hollenback, Ed's father died very unexpectedly on Tuesday. Ed was down at Richmond, Va. and Katie did not even get up till later next day.

Was up to Perkasie on Tuesday for the money for Reihl House. Saw Charley and agreed on price for cemetery lot.

Went to the city [illegible] and did but little business. The unrest about labor is causing some trouble. Carpenters want 50¢ an hour and put up no non-union millwork. They don't know when to stop. Building is at a standstill now around here.

Sunday, April 26, 1903.   Tomorrow it will be a year that Daniel died. I looked up his little belongings in the drawer where I put them and read the account of his sufferings. It is hard to believe that a year has gone by and soon after he died it seemed he was dead so long.

I still feel his loss keenly and I hope I shall ever feel it. Those boys of his age or who were his companions are always interesting to me.

May we all meet him in the beyond, where I hope he is waiting for us.

Friday, May 1, 1903.   Yesterday and a great part of April was quite warm, and the 1st of May started quite cold. I think there was ice. I heard of ice ½" thick.

Thursday, May 7, 1903.   The other evening Mary began to feel sick. We kept her from school yesturday and this morning I fetched the doctor. He said it was tonsilitis.

This is near enough to Diphtheria for me.

Very soon after the doctor left Jennie was taken with severe pains, probably caused by a strain of some kind and which may probably result in an upset. I was surprised to find her in bed at dinner time.

This evening Mrs Roberts was here and later grandpa Hemsing's came. They were surprised to find J. sick and J's father did not seem to know that Mary was sick.

Friday, May 8, 1903.   Sick folks up today at noon. Mrs Roberts was here this forenoon to help.

Saturday, May 9, 1903.   Started for the city at 8 o'clock with Mrs Roberts. Went in to Stephen Geiderd Bldg first, then into St Johns R.C. Church. From there to the City Hall to the Roof, where she wrote her name. Then lunched. Then to Independence Hall, Carpenters Hall, the Custom House (2nd US Bk) Girard Br. 1st US BK. The stock Exc. on 3rd & Dock. Then to Christ Church on 2nd above Market. Then to the River on the ferry to Camden. Then back took the cars for the Cathedral at 18th & Race.

Then to 18 & Diamond Episcopal Ch (Southe Memorial)

Then out to the Park on the Park trolly to Memorial Hall through which we took a glance but 6 o'clock came too quick. She was sorry we did not get there sooner. But we were tired and glad to get home. We arrived home at 9.30. She did not know how to thank me enough for no one had taken the trouble to show her much. I am glad I did this but she wanted to see the [illegible] and we forgot all about it.

Sunday, May 10, 1903.   Was tired out today. Didn't know I would get as tired. I am sure Mrs Roberts must be tired too. They are on a visit to Henry Hunsbergers at Silverdale today.

Got to Church this afternoon. Binkly preached.

He shouted and struck attitudes very funny looking and the young folks could hardly stand it. Wanted to go to Church this evening but Taylor and a Mr George arrived preventing it.

Monday, May 11, 1903.   Slifer and Mrs Roberts are at Luckenbills for supper.

Slifer told me today that last evening was the first time that he did not call on Sunday evening. Mrs R. did not like this because her time of going was so near. He told her he had expected to see her this evening again at least before she went. He said he found he had to cut his meetings short as they might be misunderstood. I think he was at one time nearly gone but he managed to keep strait.

Tuesday, May 12, 1903.   This morning at nine o'clock Mrs Roberts left for home.

She came out here early to give us goodbye. I was disappointed to have her go now. I wanted to take her along to Ambler and show her that Church. She had in fact expected to spend another day here but Morris Zendt got her ticket and told her if he was in her place he would start at once. In fact it would have been nice now. The weather was always bad while here or most of the time and her health is none of the best. In fact Aunt Kit said she didn't expect to see her again. She thinks she has consumption. She said she thought it was the mistake of her life to have come in the fall instead of the spring.

Slifer has completed Highland St.

I suppose he is relieved at Mrs R's departure.

Thursday, May 14, 1903. We are having a very dry spell. The roads are very dusty and the people are waiting with plowing for rain. The ground is in bad condition for plowing.

The petitions for opening Wile Alley and extend Penn Ave has been taken up by council and will be carried through.

Old Mrs Roger was buried today.

The uptown Co. is going to build 3 houses on Summit St. and two more blocks on R.R. Ave. Things are very quiet at this end just now, but the fact remains that we have the best lots in this town. Have a little Rheumatism in both knees.

Saturday, May 16, 1903. Rec'd a letter from Mrs Roberts saying she arrived safe and sound Wed afternoon in Elgin Ill.

Ich war zehr surprised wie ich zu hause kam und fand J. in bette liegen und grosse schmerzen leiden. Ich schickte fur der Doktor gerade. Am 6 uhr oder darnach hatte sie eine Misgeburt. Das Kind war ungefahr drei Monat auf dem weg. Es war ein Knabe gewesen. Ich beerdigte es auf meiners kleinen Bruders Grabe. Ich bedaure es. Die Frau hat viel Schmertzen und verliert viel Blut.*

We sent the children out to Granf Moyers.

Monday, May 18, 1903. Jennie was not as well this morning as one could wish. She had a slight fever. The doctor did not come till dinner time and found some matter had not been removed. Amy and Mary remained at home from school. Amy to help to wash and Mary to mind the baby. This afternoon I got Mrs Cath Hunsberger my aunt to wait on her.

She has no appetite and the medicine is not agreeing with her.

Monday, May 25, 1903. Walked with Cal up to Indian Creek Church to attend the meeting of classes. Dr. Koplin preached after which they partook of the Holy Communion.

Mr Luckenbill was elected President.

Tuesday, May 26, 1903. Drove up to Indian Creek and took Mrs Cal. Grace Amy and Helen along. There was a paper read by Dr Ferer on the Semi Centennial of F&M College. By W H Mader on the Education of Woman.

Father and his people went up on the coach.

Wednesday, May 27, 1903. Drove up to Indian Creek with Cal. The Papers read were How to retain the children in the S.S. by Rev Noss.

Bethany orphan's Home by F.J. Mobe.

---

*Eng. translation: I was very surprised as I came home and found J lying in bed and suffering great pain. I send for the doctor immediately. Around 6 o'clock or after she had a miscarriage. The child was three months on the way. It had been a boy. I buried it in my little brother's grave. I regret it. The woman has great pain and is losing much blood.

Mr Leidy Scholl and wife was with Father when I came back. Stopped in a little.

This evening it looked as if about to rain but did not.

I think there was no rain since Apr 16, and the ground is very hard and dry so that some are not through plowing and no one with corn planting.

This drought is unprecedented.

The hay crop is sure to be short. The dust on the roads is something terrible.

Thursday, May 28, 1903.   We had a nice little shower today. It settled the dust and things look very fresh. I am in hopes that the drought is over.

This evening we raised Mr. Luckenbills salary to $250. On going home from meeting Cal and I were talking when he noticed a fire in the direction of Telford. In order to find out we went up gradually. It proved to be Shelly's feed and hay press, the railroad station, some cars a number of barns blacksmith shop and Wampoles shop, all the Hotel sheds, lumber yard in part &c. It was the biggest fire I ever saw or wished to see. It was hard work to save the county line Hotel but the trees around it saved it and the workers. Mr Shelley's residence was also in great danger. The stables in back we stopped at Shellys or after that was burned. Egolf's tenant houses are also destroyed. There was absolutely no air stirring except the currents formed by the fire. If there had been a wind there is no telling where it would have stopped.

Friday, May 29, 1903.   Got home at 2.30 this morning. I had the key to the house and J had heard Harvey Souder's whistle but she of course thought I couldn't have been of much service at a fire in Telford. Was all broken up today. Went up again this afternoon. The coal and feed are burning and make great heat. The remarkable thing is that the contents of the ice house was the only thing that withstood the fire. They were hauling it away today. It is said that Shelly's insurance amounts to only $7000. I think the loss must be 4 times as much. The trolleys here were kept busy. And I understand the hotels too. Penrose did not show up at the shop today. Hartman was here very little this week. Blank kept open house for sometime last night and the thing commenced to tell. Some people don't know how to act when they have the chance.

Sunday, May 31, 1903.   The corner stone of the new Lutheran Church was laid today. Quite a number of people were here. The preaching was held on Freeds Hall. Mr Nickel and Mr Kline preached in the afternoon. Rev. Becker leading the other services. In the evening Rev. Chas Snyder from Hilltown preached.

Mr Luckenbill & Berkemeyer was also present the latter speaking a few words.

Monday, June 2, 1903.   When J. B. Delp came in the office I asked him whether we were to do the houses on Summit Ave. or not he told me I was to bid on them and the blocks together. Wampole had told me confidentially that this was the program in order to cut us out so I told him I would refuse to bid. If they wanted to give the work to Lukens they should do so at once. I was so angry that I hadn't control of my voice at first. Delp turned pale and said it was true, but that he couldn't help it. I read him a good lecture of course not blaming him as I might have not mentioning the North Wales case.

Tuesday, June 2, 1903.   Father's making preparations to start West tomorrow. I asked him for that ante nuptial agreement so I could get one copy of it. He brought it over this evening.

Hartman has left us.

I think the carpenters strike is going to lose in Phila as it deserves. But the textile strike is more serious. 75,000 to 90,000 went on strike yesterday, for 55 hrs instead of 60.

D.W. Sperry was up late this afternoon. He employs non union labor only or at least does not recognize the union.

Father's are going to Indianapolis first and from there they expect to stop in Ohio.

Sunday, June 7, 1903.   Had a good soaking rain last night and today. I hope the situation is relieved now. There was a shower over a week ago but it help much.

Many people have been unable to plow their corn.

Henry G Bilger was here for dinner coming with me from church this morning.

Frank and Mattie were here for supper though they did not wish to stay.

The Sunshine Circle has obtained a Piano at Church.

Thursday, June 11, 1903.   Rain plenty of it. Yesterday it got darker near noon than I ever saw it. We had the lights on at the shop for quite awhile. It rained considerable up country and also in the city.

Henry Beideman and wife came up on the trolley this afternoon. Jennie made dinner for them and he and I walked out to Slifer &c.

They were surprised that Father had got married and that they were out West.

Beideman's address is

1757 North 11th St.

He is still on the trolley.

Friday, June 12, 1903.   This morning the papers were full of the tragic murder of the Servian king Alexander and his wife Draga and a number of their followers. It was a horrible revolution. It is hard to say what the result will be. It may result in the long kept back Balkan War.

Monday, June 15, 1903.   The weather is cold and rain every day. The farmers now wish for a chance to get on their land. Slifer can't do any work. He is plowing for corn but he cant sow it.

Emma rec'd a letter from her brother. Father is about to start for Charlotte Mich I suppose to see Dan Wile.

He goes alone Mrs remaining with Perry Ratzel.

Rec'd a job from D.W. Sperry today. He rejoices over the the defeat of the carpenters unions. He says they are hurting for work.

Tuesday, June 16, 1903.   Jonas G. Hangey died today. He had been suffering from bladder trouble of some kind it seems. I did not know he was sick now. He will be buried on Saturday. I think he must have lived 25 yrs in Souderton. He was a good man. His brother Reuben lives at Telford.

A tramp was killed here on the railroad last night.

We are now nearly ready with 3 Sides for the Church.

Slifer did some hauling again today but the weather looks threatening again this evening. The farmers have a hard time getting their things out.

Bought a Beckens Duefar typewriter this afternoon for $35.00.

It seems writing is going out of fashion.

Thursday, June 25, 1903.   Was in the city this afternoon. Was in Germantown in Tourisin's office. Was much disappointed at getting a deduction of over $80.00 on Moore and Neilson. But the way they are treated is something wrong. Thousands of dollars held back for a mere trifle.

Was quite sick last night vomiting twice &c which weakened me very much. I staid in bed till 9.30 and then was very careful of what entered my stomach.

Met Will Haynes.

Friday, June 26, 1903.   Today was a nice warm day and almost clear at times.

This month of June has been the most remarkable I can remember. Cold and rainy people couldn't get on their land. Today Rosenberger pulled weeds on the land.

We delivered some of the church frames this afternoon and finished the big frame which will be taken over tomorrow.

The Mennonite Br. in Christ are holding services at the tent next to the Lutheran Ch. They are telling all kinds of stories which I don't believe are true.

Slifer says the land is too soft to get on. He has started on the lower lot.

Sunday, June 28, 1903. I was surprised this forenoon to see father coming in through the yard. I had not expected to see him for a week. They came home last evening. They enjoyed the trip but their passage through Ohio was short. Mrs. don't like to talk English. He says the condition of the crops is better here than in Indiana. of course there they are more advanced but now it is a little too dry.

We went to church this afternoon.

This evening to Grandfather Moyers though Jennie stopped off at Jos. Stovers and did not come over till 9 o'clock. I could hardly induce her to come. She thinks its wrong to visit anyone on Sunday. Milts had Henry along to Perkasie where he was bitten by something. He's lips are swollen. Milt thinks it was a snake. He took him to the Doctor.

Tuesday, June 30, 1903. We (Jennie and I and Milt and Ida) went to Kutztown today by trolley. Jennie couldn't stand the ride on the line to Allentown though that to Kutztown today she didn't mind. We started at 8:20 missed the car at Allentown so we didn't get to Kutztown till 12:30. Mrs. Hottenstein was expecting us for Ida had written her I rode out to the country with the Dr. When we came back we went upstairs. Jennie objected to being examined and so he looked at my back. I have had a mole on my back ever since I can remember. Jennie has been anxious a long time. There was a hard lump under the mole which made me suspicious there might be something wrong. The Doctor advised cutting it out but Jennie thought a plaster would do it. I have not sufficient patience for plasters so I decided to have it cut if his knives were sharp. I was disappointed that Milts had gone. Jennie dipped the blood out and made faces while doing it. I didn't take anything just to see whether I could stand it. It was not near as painful as I expected though the feeling was by no means pleasant. He said the opening was the size of about half dollar. He cut about ¾" deep near the muscle. The hurt didnt bother me much.

Wednesday, July 1, 1903. Today I expected to have a lame arm and very painful back.

But I felt it less than yesterday. Jennie says it is not inflamed or even red. I'll be very thankful to escape severe pain.

I found Slifer was interested somewhat in Kutztown. He is at present going to see a Miss Herman a maiden lady and a daughter of some old minister from up there.

In two weeks I am to go up there to have the stitches taken out of my back. I have four.

Thursday, July 2, 1903. I begin to feel a slight soreness but not enough to interfere with anything. I can write and in fact it does not affect the arm.

Jennie had to go to the Men. Breth in Christ tonight. I went up too later but couldn't hear much.

Yesterday and today have been rather hot. People can get on their land now.

It is time now that corn should be all planted yet there are many that have not.

We mowed our grass today.

We have Henry at home tonight.

The papers had quite a fuss about Henry as shown by slips posted on Monday, only half true.

Tuesday, July 14, 1903. Amy and Helen with Father went with me to Kutztown today. We had a good time everyone enjoying it. It was very novel to the girls. The hills, the rocks, the soldier's camp, the bridges. Allentown were the cause of many questions.

Father had never been out that way further than the Duck farm.

We arrived at Kutztown at two o'clock.

The doctor said it was a great pity that the stitches had not held. That it would take much longer to heal, but that it was healing nicely.

We walked around the town to the Norman School, and to the brick yard where we were during a shower.

Mr. Stimmel has things in better shape now than two weeks ago.

We got home after ten, I think, 10.30. They lost time on account of the trolley jumping the wire continually.

Monday, July 20, 1903. Pope Leo XIII died today at 4.04 Rome time after an illness of over two weeks, during all of which it was expected he could not live on account of his great age I suppose. But he always rallied and it seemed as though no calculations held true. He is praised very much on all sides. I suppose he made many friends by granting people an audience.

Was in the city today. Took off some work. Went to Radnor to measure a couple of mantels.

Went in to see the R.R. supt. about freight station I had written about. He promised to send some one and survey the land so as to have blue print made.

Tuesday, July 21, 1903. The wound on my back has healed very nicely. There is no scab on it and it takes a little time for skin to form over it.

Henry has been home now since Thursday when I took the children to the soldiers camp. He seems to get along well, except on Sunday and his grandpop couldn't get rid of him at S.S. So in the afternoon I went out to take him along but had no trouble at at first, afterward everything was all right.

He is somewhat self willed and yet not selfish. But he needs looking after and our influence over him is very little now.

How many questions he has to ask.

Friday, July 24, 1903.   Measured all the children except Margaret.

Amy grew 4 3/8" Helen 2 7/8 Mary 4" and Henry 7" since Nov. 1901. Had to wonder what the others would look like if alive.

Wednesday, August 19, 1903.   Since writing Cardinal Sarto of Venice was elected Pope and took the title Pius X.

Mr Luckenbill was at the shop this afternoon and we spent all afternoon talking of Jennies affairs &c.

We are very dull at the shop and we must pick up some work soon.

Work is dull all through the country.

The girls went up to Perkasie yesterday.

Mrs Katie Bean, Mrs Horace and Mrs Ellis, were here last evening.

Saturday, September 5, 1903.   I am having trouble with the cutting again. On Wednesday Deck left without notice and here I am without a cutter. I went up to see Reub. Next evening I sent up father. He promised to report last evening He came here and said they wouldn't let him go. He got a raise however and that was his entire object. I told him I wouldn't ask him again and this didn't please him. I also reminded him that we were keeping men after their time like old Jake and that we would have done as much for him.

I asked Elmer Souder and he promised providing Delp would not object.

Monday, September 7, 1903.   Today I picked out the lumber and Henry cut it. This works very well had I time to do it, any way this is the System I will eventually come to. Then I can get any amount of work through.

If I could only get some one to do my estimating this would be what I would like.

The two double houses I hoped to get from Perkasie we don't get and I feel that it wasn't quite fair. I wouldn't care but for the fact that work is getting scarce. I am going to the city tomorrow to see what I can do.

There was a terrible trolley accident at Ft Washington last evening by a head on collision. Bergstresser was badly hurt. Harvey Sell had the other car. His shoulder was dislocated. About 20 were taken to the hospital.

Sunday, October 4, 1903.   I suppose Deck is in St. Louis by this time. The other Saturday he sold his household goods paid us everything except ten dollars which he thinks I am to trust to his "oniesty." He is afraid he may not get work immediately when he gets to St Louis and so he wants money on hand. I wrote him a letter a few days before the sale advising him not to. But it did no good but at least I have cleared myself.

This evening we had for the first time a song service before church. I think the people will like something of the kind.

But our S.S. is not what it ought to be. Mr. L. said tonight that the consistory ought to have supervision over everything and it should though we have to proceed slow.

Monday, October 5, 1903.   H Alderfer the tinsmith's child died of Diphtheria this morning. They closed the schools today. Robinson's have it. Enos H Moyer's and they say Isaiah Moyer's too but that they refuse to be questioned. Others are mentioned. There has been a lot of tonsilitis in town and now it's full of diphtheria. Hen. Godshall's had it a week or two ago. I wish I had the power to destroy this disease.

Slifer had good building stone at the quarry. Last week we had given it up and then we found them. Slifer is nearly over grading Wile's alley. He will then go to Penn Ave. He told me today he thought he couldn't stand it. He can't stand the hard work.

He wants a Derrick now for the quarry.

Jennie thinks it her duty to write to people when sick or in trouble and these letters are not always appreciated. This makes her feel sad. I told her not to do any of it.

Tuesday, October 6, 1903.   They are having a great muddle in N.Y.C. politics. Mayor Lord has been renominated by the fusionists. Tammany has McClellan. Grout who had been Controller under Lord and also renominated by the fusionists accepted also the Tammany nomination and now the Fusionists want to get rid of him. Devery also is to run for Mayor. It is hard to say where it will end.

Monday, October 26, 1903.   Today Mininger was to commence our cement walks. He did send a man but did not come himself.

We started the work but did not put down any concrete. The day was very windy and cold. There were even a few flakes of snow this afternoon.

The 3rd Floor joists of father's House were laid this afternoon. Last Monday morning the Masons commenced the cellar wall. The work has gone forward very rapidly. He expects to get it all under roof this week.

Horace's are quarantined for Diphtheria and Strasser's also. The schools have again been closed since last Monday. We never had such an epidemic before. They are putting a cement floor in the school house cellar. They are busy making cement walks on Wile alley. So we will have some improvements at this end.

Monday, November 2, 1903.   Today it is two weeks since the cellar wall of father's house was started. Dan Rittenhouse put the last slate on the roof Saturday afternoon. Everything fitted well with this house and people think that father must know more about building than others.

Today Mininger wasn't here but last week we put 520 ft of walk down on

Franklin Ave. Many don't believe itll stay but I see no reason why it shouldn't except the concrete for the first day which contains too much sand. We had fine weather last week from Wednesday on.

Was over to Hatfield to see Cressman but he wasn't home yet so I will have to go again.

School started in again yesterday. Nath Moyer's buried their little girl today. She died of Diphtheria.

Friday, November 6, 1903.   The state of Panama has declared its independence and wants to secede from Columbia. The fuss is all about the canal. It is rumored that our gov. had recognized the new State. If so it looks like underhand business.

In New York Tammany has elected McClellan over Lord by 63000.

In Bucks Co. Judge Zerkas is defeated. Phila & Penna as usual. Maryland is Dem., bringing Gorman to the fore. He has been trying to get up a race issue, accusing Roosevelt of being the cause by breakfasting with Booker Washington. If the Dem. are green enough to take up such a candidate let them try it even if Wall St. helps.

For the first time in years I was not at the election.

We had snow flurries today. Put down only a little pavement but are prepared to finish up the lower end of Franklin ave. tomorrow.

Monday, November 9, 1903.   We had communion services yesterday. 87 of our members communed. 97 altogether. Willis was not present. JO Snyders were not down.

Israel Kline was buried today. There was a large funeral. The services were held in our church and from there to Leidy's.

Hen Bilger's was here for supper.

Saturday, November 14, 1903.   On Friday Pres. Roosevelt rec'd the Envoy of the new Panama Republic. The Democrats are going to fight a treaty with the new republic hoping thereby to gain a partisan issue.

In the senate they are opposing the nomination of Gen Wood as Maj. Gen. his record being attack. Such men as Rathbone whom he had convicted for postal funds in Cuba are of course opposing him. He may not have shown himself a great military man not having such opportunity but as Gov. of Santiago and Cuba he seemed the only man equal to the task. Gen. Brooke an old soldier failed.

Perry Ratzel is here. He had been traveling out West I had no opportunity to see him yet being away every evening.

Thursday, November 19, 1903.   Frank Moyers baby died of Diphtheria on Sat. and Beulah Zendt and Fred Zendt have diptheria now. Nice's

Mininger's and Shatz's are clear again but there are still 2 or 3 families quarantined in other parts of town. Perry Ratzel came to the shop Tuesday afternoon late so we went out in the evening. Rev. Luckenbill was there and they were discussing the dif. in church goverment. Jennie was out this evening and they will be here for dinner tomorrow. The weather has been interfering with our cement busines. He has nearly enough stone out but it is very cold. Out West there is a great cold 26 below in Montana.

A new treaty has been signed with Panama. The Democrats expect to oppose it for political effect.

Wednesday, December 2, 1903. The weather we are having is very unreasonable, last week it was very cold. The month of Nov was colder on the average than any month since 1808 I think the paper states. Nor have there been any such cold days since 1891 when it was a little colder a short time. So it wasn't strange that I should make the mistake of supposing we could finish our cement work easy.

Rec'd a letter from Mrs Roberts. She is in Milwaukee. Perry Ratzel reached Cambridge Nebraska last Friday morning.

Thursday, December 3, 1903. The snowstorm which commenced yesterday ended this morning. There was considerable snow to shovel.

Slifer was at the shop with sleigh early. Quite a number of Sleighs were out today. It seems that there is going to be no end of diphtheria on Chestnut St. E H Moyer, Hen Godshalls Hiram Mininger Robinson's Elias Nice's Shatz's twice and now Robinson's again. Strasser had it too at the other end.

Well this snow settles the cement business for this winter.

Father is not very well though much better. He was at the shop today. Gran. Moyer is failing rapidly I think. I saw her foot last evening and it is horrible to see the skin dead on almost half the foot. She is having two doctors but very little faith in none. Last week the whole set of us had diarrhea which we had trouble to get rid of I staid home on Sunday and it did some good.

Friday, December 25, 1903. Spent Christmas Day at Grandfather Moyer's. All were home but Milt and Hollenbacks.

We have a Christmas tree at home and the children think its great. Margaret has dolls in plenty and Henry engines cars and blocks. Mary a mirror, book & other things. Helen an umbrella sewing basket and so on, Amy a Mackintosh pocket book &c.

Saturday, December 26, 1903. We were at Grandfather Hemsing's for dinner. Turkey again. No one else there.

Henry got an engine and cars that move on a circular track. It is a great toy. Margaret got a rattle and the girls cups and saucers, and all of them new mittens.

Helen gave Emma the Autocrat of the Breakfast Table and father J sent the works of Menno Simon formerly grandfather Souder's.

In the afternoon father and I went down to Sell's quarry on the trolley but walked back. Such a cold wind I haven't been in a long time. You had to turn round to breathe. The Prog. Realty Co is erecting a stone crusher plant there. They have good stone but I dont understand what they want with such an outfit.

Thursday, December 31, 1903. The Iroquois Theatre in Chicago burned yesterday and 736 people lost their lives in the panic and flames less than half the audience of 1300 getting out. It was awful.

Japan and Russia are apparently on the verge of war. Neither of them it is said can retire without humilation. Japan's patience is nearly exhausted. It is to be hoped that peace can be maintained.

Slifer has decided now to stay in Souderton and accept the Street Commissionership. He thought for awhile he would go into the Laundry business.

We are not rid of the diptheria Scourge yet. Eva Souder is having it now. She started in very rapidly but is now rapidly improving. O when will be rid of this scourge. I believe that we have had 50 cases this year and quite a number of deaths.

We are not busy at the shop at all.

*The Russo-Japanese War—the depot is robbed—controversy
over school elections—a son is born—Italian street workers
imported from Philadelphia—Theodore Roosevelt elected*

1904

Saturday, April 16, 1904.   Admiral Skrydaloff commander of the Black
Sea fleet was appointed to succeed the ill-fated Admiral Makaroff who went
down with ship the Petrovalossky. This great disaster happened a few days ago.
The Japanese Admiral Togo had mines laid at night under cover of his torpedo
boats, in the course he observed they always took when coming out of the
harbor. Then he sent a weak fleet of cruisers to tempt the Russians out. This
they did and Togo tried outflank them with his battle ships, But the Russians
saw this and retired. On trying to reenter the harbor the admirals ship struck
the mine and sank in two minutes. Another battleship struck a mine but
reached the harbor safely. A torpedo boat was also sunk by the Japanese
torpedo attack. Very few of the crews of these two vessels were saved. Among
them was the Grand Duke Cyril the Czars cousin.

Sunday, April 17, 1904.   The Lutherans had Communion for the first
time in their new church.

We had Communion last Sunday. They have organized a Sunday School
and held their first session last Sunday I think.

Mr Luckenbill announced a German class for Wed. evening and also a
teachers meeting for the same evening. If we could only get our own members
to come out and work for work ought to be done.

Mr Luckenbill tried to impress this in his sermon this evening.

Monday, April 18, 1904.   It seems that the Democrats are going to
unite on Judge Parker of New York for their Pres. Candidate. Hearst the
newspaper man had made some stir and frightened them by a vigorous
campaign for delegates.

Tomorrow the New York Convention meets and it is expected that they will
instruct for Parker notwithstanding the opposition of Tammany who hoped to
bring forward McCllelland.

Bryan will make all the trouble he can, but if things continue he will be
obscured entirely.

Tuesday, April 19, 1904.   After waiting fully two weeks for a chance to stake off the new houses to be built on Adams Ave. I went out today and found I could not have chosen a worse day. The wind blew my tape so hard that we had to use an old stump and a stake for it to blow against. At least it blew over my instrument. Then I gave it up. It was the most unpleasant day for such a purpose I could have chosen.

Sold my bicycle today for $11.00 used it 2 yrs I think.

We are now pumping the water out of the quarry preparatory to laying the track for the new truck with which to draw out the stone. The ditch for the new culvert will require several days digging. We had to dig down fr. 4 to 6 ft for a distance of 150 ft. Joe Derstines moved today. Sam Detweilers moved some day last week Tuesday I think. Poor old Joe has to cry very easy.

Wednesday, April 20, 1904.   Went to the city today. Took the 8:40 trolley. Should have gone to Chest Hill to see Stokes but would have come too late for Teacher's meeting.

It is remarkably cold for the season and the ground was frozen too hard to plow. Slifer did some plowing yesterday and sowed some oats. Bo't this diary today a little late too but for awhile I had no idea of keeping one this year.

Hans Mueller our German engineer did not turn up till noon today. His apprentice Quinqar took his place. He had some money sent him from Germany I believe and without telling me he went off.

This evening the fuses were burnt out. Then I took supper and then went up to church where Mr Luckenbill was still teaching German. Afterward we went over to Luckenbills where Don went over the lesson. It was interesting but Taylor came and called me out so I missed much.

It was so cold and windy that I was afraid of fire. I think a fire had started at Dr Copes barn as we passed. They had a great fire in Toronto yesterday 5000,000 damage.

Friday, April 22, 1904.   Went to the city at 3 o'clock to Tourisin's first and then to Stokes out in Germantown.

I think I will get that last job. Came home on the trolley. Something happened to cut out the 9 o'clock car so I had to wait till 10 before I could leave Wheel Pump. I did not get home before 11.30.

Saturday, April 23, 1904.   Staked off the 6 Double Houses today. It was a nice day for it at last. But I found I had the 4 first on the wrong lots and so had to move them back. The digging of the culvert will be completed in a few days. The stone quarry is waiting for the track which we will put in Monday.

Slifer and father nearly had a fallout about the houses today. We exchanged Rock for the Swartley Houses and Slifer kicked about it to the others so father had a talk with him and it caused bad feeling.

This evening we settled for the Koffel lot on Penn Ave. Slifer sold it for 300 including pavement which is too low.

Ruff told me about a scheme of the trolley Co to get off Penn Ave. They have an option of an M R Norys land for 5000 and want to lay out a road through to Broad St. We will fight this idea.

Sunday, April 24, 1904.   Read Hawthorn's Blithedale Romance. I like the House of the Seven Gables better.

Was to S.S. & Church this afternoon and again this evening. Ellis asked me to be early in the evening as he might not be able to come. So I was the first one there and Ellis the second. The Lutherans had church also and it seemed to affect our attendance. Mr. L. said that just as it seemed his usefulness here would be at an end he would step aside. I told him he was pessimistic. He said Ellis helped to make him so. I if only our present members would be workers we would be strong.

Monday, April 25, 1904.   Slifer had another talk with father this morning. He said he didn't like to be talked to in that way.

He wants us now to buy a horse and use it if we like &c &c. We hauled the truck and track over today and I put part of it up. Tried to get a bargain with Joseph Clemmer for digging the cellars but he wanted 30¢ a cu yd and I did not want to pay more than 25. This evening Sam Moyer tackled me again about increases of wages. I was tired of it and told him so. He said he wanted to know this week or he'd leave. The poor man would find out what that would mean for him. But he seems to be too weak to realize his danger. If I give him more it will be in the nature of a present and not as a raise. If you once pay more you are expected to do it for all time.

Tuesday, April 26, 1904.   Rain last night. We put up our track today but did not quite finish.

Jennie Helen and Mary went to the city and came back about 9.20 tonight. She bought clothes for the children. Amy remained home from school to take care of Margaret and I had Henry with me all day. I took him along to North Wales to look at Swartley's house. He enjoyed himself but late in the afternoon he got cold and had to cry a little.

Hans cut his thumb today. He was very much afraid I would scold about it.

Wednesday, April 27, 1904.   Hunsicker called me upon the phone asking me and Slifer to come up as there was something in the wind. Slifer having gone to the city I went up alone expecting the talk to be about Mike Moyer's land. But it was about the new cigar factory. The Prog. Co. had undertaken to build one but it seems they are tired of it and now they want us to press the Imp. Co. to do it. I told Ellis and Slifer about it this evening. Ellis would have given them a short answer as he said Hartzel was talking big about the matter. Rain all today more or less and is raining quite fast at this time 10:30.

Saturday, April 30, 1904.   Worked on Quarry this afternoon fixing the track. We put the truck on but did not get the pulleys on. We drove up to see Harry Blank about starting the stone work for sewer. Delp promised to dig the cellars at 25 per cubic yrd. He will start Wednesday. Last evening we sold the lots J.M. Landis took 1st choice and took 1st lot on east side. Father got 2nd choice and took middle on West side. Ellis 3rd 1st on West side. W. H. Freed 4th 3rd on W side. Adam 5th mid on east side, and Slifer the last on East side. It was quite amusing. Yet everyone seems to be pleased at the outcome.

Sunday, May 1, 1904.   The new Ref Ch. at Perkasie was dedicated today. They had a nice day. Luckenbill was up this afternoon.

Was at S S & Church this evening.

Monday, May 2, 1904.   The Japanese defeated the Russians after 6 days fighting. Crossing the Yolu and driving the Russians back. It is thought 30000 Russians were engaged. The Russians attribute it to the superior artillery of the Japanese.

Delp started digging cellars this afternoon. He expects to keep his men at it all week.

We got the stone truck so that we pulled up two loads this evening. The horse pulled it very nicely and it dumps all right on the cart.

If only work at the shop wasn't so scarce. I am bidding but losing too much work. Delp has two North Wales houses were Lukens beat me by only about 22 dollars. I asked him for this work but he gave me no satisfaction. Guthrie would have given us the work if he had got it.

Tuesday, May 3, 1904.   The masons started the sewer this morning. They did very well today laying about 15 pieces of stone. This was pretty good for two men. Hen Price and Hen Nice are doing the work.

Fred Souder ordered the work for houses at Glenside which he expects to build of cement.

Emma Ratzel is here sewing. Elias Erb is digging mornings and evenings.

Wednesday, May 4, 1904.   Today we turned the first arch at the curve a piece of about 10 ft. It was the most difficult piece and I spent ¾ of a day here with the masons. I can't afford to put in as much time after this. We have the quarry at work all right now. We dump the stone right on the cart and have no trouble. If only this sewer wall is built then Slifer can start on the street which ought to be under way now.

The Japanese again made the attempt to close up the harbor of Port Arthur unsucessfully it is claimed by the Russians. 8 ships laden with stone being sunk.

The Russians suffered a bad defeat at the Yolu losing 3000 men it is said.

Took the whole family over to see the operations.

Thursday, May 5, 1904.   Went to the city on the noon train. Wanted to go on the Scranton Express but the trolley was too late.

Took off two jobs at Doughertys and then went out to Stokes Bros at Germantown and came home on the trolley.

Cressman and Nat Oberholtzer were waiting for me and I went out to Grandf. Moyers at ten oclock when O. paid his bill.

Cressman is figuring on the new hay house.

Friday, May 6, 1904.   This morning Slifer had the top of Adams Ave plowed and Elwood had two carts to haul the stuff.

They are getting on well with the cellars. They have the second nearly finished. Tonight there is about 60 ft. of culvert finished. This forenoon Slifer had Zeigler to take a photograph and all the men at work on the job. Harry Hunsicker and his automobile is on the picture. Hunsicker came over for me and I got a short ride. Was at the quarry two hours this afternoon. The stone is running out for the present and they are taking out the lower corner. Then there seems to be a 2 ft. layer of shell. It is a question whether it pays to go deeper.

Saturday, May 7, 1904.   Worked only till 12 o'clock at the shop.

Was at the culvert greater part of the afternoon. Put the east inlet of Adams Ave in this afternoon. In two more days they can finish.

Helped Milt to stake off Hay House late this afternoon.

Had teacher's meeting here this evening. The attendance was good though not quite so many old people as usual.

Sunday, May 8, 1904.   We went down to Leidy's church this morning, that is Amy, Helen and I. They had communion. 155 communed. Offering $41.+

Laid Daniel's and Catherine's tombstones for the first time. They were set up on Friday. The lot is still to be filled and graded. It ought to be done now.

It was a beautiful day. The trees are getting their leaves and beginning to make a little shade. The blossoms are out. Plums for several days Pears and apples just opening. My plum trees in the back yard looked so nice every branch and twig being white with blossoms. Christ Moyer said he never saw anything like it.

Was in S S & Church in the afternoon and in church in the evening. The Menn. and Lutherans also had services.

Monday, May 9, 1904.   Had a little shower this evening.

Stopped in at Grandf. Moyer's and they told me they had an offer for the Hay House lot. They would sell for not less than 5000. I offered to sell our lot back of Nyce's for 1500.

Milt told me he had been three times to see Sam Hunsberger to buy his property. He would sell part to the R.R. Co. He told me this as a private matter and asked me whether it was worth 1500 an acre. This would make 18000.

On the way home David Yeager told me Milt had offered 1000 an acre but that he had not yet reached their price. I don't know how this would affect us but I believe for awhile it would be a setback for our property. I would like to see the station moved over though.

Tuesday, May 10, 1904.   Was in the city today. It was very rainy. Left my umbrella on the car but got it again. I suppose it wasn't expensive enough to be stolen when not needed.

Wednesday, May 11, 1904.   We finished the sewer today as far as we intend to go until the houses are built.

Jacob Groff left yesterday while I was in the city. He told Leidy he had a better offer and wanted me to run after him. I told Leidy he should come to me if had anything to say. He went on the baker train at Telford.

Wrote for Harry Dancker today.

Thursday, May 12, 1904.   The Japanese it is claimed have now closed the harbor of Port Arthur. Have armies landed and investing it on the land side the railroad cut and an army or two threatening Kuropotkin. It seems they have managed everything wonderfully well. The Russians are destroying Dalny on which they had expended millions.

The Japanese lost a torpedo boat the first naval loss of the war. They were exploding mines at Dalny when one blew up this boat. The Russians are evacuating New Chwang.

Friday, May 13, 1904.   Cemented the top of the arch so as to strengthen it on Adams Ave.

Saturday, May 14, 1904.   Started to uncover at the quarry. The bottom has run out of good stone just as we had everything fixed. Was with the men this afternoon. Helped Wm Souder to get the lines on Penn Ave for the curb.

Got notice to come to the city on Monday on acc't of Telford Station. H.B. Shoemaker & Co. Contractors also to Stokes Bros for Shea House. Took also the contract for Ushenbrand House near Langhorne all this week. This makes things brighten up a little.

Harry Dancker is coming back Monday taking J. Groffs place.

Monday, May 16, 1904.   Was in the city today and took the contract for Telford Station.

Some of the others are bidding mighty low. I miss about everything I bid on. At Tourisins I was beaten on two jobs.

Bought Life of Columbus and Adam Bede 2nd hand of course, very cheap.

Tuesday, May 17, 1904.   Harry Dancker started work this morning.

Went to the city again this afternoon and measured up the Shea job.

Slifer was to the city today and this evening I saw him get on the train with the Bethlehem lady. I think he likes her pretty well.

The trouble with the man is that he wants a somewhat stylish woman with a little money and no children &c &c. This one has an invalid son.

Wednesday, May 18, 1904.   Started to write a letter to Mrs Roberts today but did not finish it. Wanted to write ever since November but never could get a good chance.

Thursday, May 19, 1904.   The Japanese lost a first class battle ship by striking a mine and 5000 ton cruiser by a collision.

The battle ship was the Hatuse and the Cruiser the Yoshino.

This happened last Sunday. Many lives were lost.

They also met with a slight repulse in Manchuria. The Russians used to report that they were going to retreat to Harbin but it is not likely that they will publish all their plans.

I am sorry for the Japs.

Friday, May 20, 1904.   Hans today had to stick his finger into the jointer in order to explain the width and breadth of board he wanted. The way John and Menno described it it wasn't a bad cut but he ran away to the doctor and Vaughn amputated the finger at the first joint. I didn't pity him much until he came back with a short finger probably needlessly cut. And now he is worried about his job and of course I can't lay him off now unless he can get something else. He don't suit me at all and causes nothing but worry. But I can't do him an injustice as it would seem.

Eddy Watts would like the job and I am going to give it to him the first chance.

Luckenbill came out to the quarry this after and asked me whether I had spoken to Sam. He knows a candidate. Habur [?] Ed Leidy mainland who would take it for 60 a m

Saturday, May 21, 1904.   Levelled off the St partly and also for filling the yards on Adams this afternoon.

This afternoon H. D. Detweiler tackled me about the School. He has a candidate Godshall from Schwenksville a nephew of preacher Godshall.

This evening he brought him around. He said he was particularly anxious to meet me as a former citizen of our town meaning J.D. Moyer probably had told him that if I were elected I would be one of the best members of the board &c. This wasn't meant for flattery of course &c. I told him I couldn't tie to any particular candidate that I had to be free to fight for other things.

Monday, May 23, 1904.   This morning I went to see Loux at the school house. I asked him whether he was a candidate and whether considered himself fit. He wanted particulars. I asked him about the hotels. He drinks no more than his business requires, &c & for his health under doctor's orders. He doesn't gamble because he does not play for money &c. Is, of course, a sinful man, but does not seem to be conscious of any gross sins.

I told him I couldn't agree with his standards. Told him it wasn't easy for me to do. He said he appreciated my coming but would not retire under fire.

Went to see Enos Moyer & Christ Alderfer this evening. Enos is doubtful. Have some hopes of Christ.

Snyder of Bean's Co. applied for Principalship today.

Tuesday, May 24, 1904.   Saw Wolford and Strasser this forenoon and Wm H Freed this evening. Freed is Loux's friend and Strasser non-committal.

I think we can get Wolford.

Went to the city and signed contract for D. Moyer House.

It was very hot today.

Wednesday, May 25, 1904.   Was at Hatboro with A. Oscar Martin to measure up for Reading Job. It was hot. Martin has a nice house of his own at Doylestown.

Friday, May 27, 1904.   The Japanese attacked and drove the Russians from Kinchan 12 miles or so fr. Port Arthur. They fought 16 hrs and lost 4500 men. The fighting being very desperate.

Saturday, May 28, 1904.   Ed Watts Jr will start work on Monday. Harry discharged. Ollin Watts too and another fellow fr. Telford. OP also asked for work.

This evening Prof Haber from Coatesville was to see me this evening. He says that if the Principal is qualified the boro can draw extra State appropriation for the High School. This is worth looking up.

A Mr Barndt from Sellersville was also here and made an application.

The Japanese followed up their defeat of the Russians at Kinchan by another at some hill 2200 ft high I forget what name.

Port Arthur is now closely invested by land and sea. Bloody fighting is expected.

Sunday, May 29, 1904.   This evening I hear that Sen Matthew S. Quay died yesterday at two o'clock. I hope he repented of his sins. In a way he was the greatest of his kind. The wrong kind I think. He has fastened a great evil on this state. But the people deserve it. They had the power and left these men tie them so that they seem helpless.

Was in S.S. this afternoon. In church this evening.

Luckenbill preached on Civic righteousness. I hope it will do some good.

Read Adam Bede.

The weather yesterday and today is cool but it is very dry.

Sallie Price my cousin is very sick. They can't move her to the country now.

Tuesday, May 31, 1904.   Milt Moyer told me Enos was undecided what to do with Loux. This is what I expected. He thinks he can't do much with him. He thought it a good plan to send Wm & Ellis to him. Accordingly I came out to see them this evening. Wm. promised to try it but Ellis thinks he had better leave it on acct of the church getting mixed. He may be right about it.

Wednesday, June 1, 1904.   On Monday afternoon it started to rain and it looks as if it wasn't through yet. The ground is now thoroughly soaked. It had been getting very dry and it seemed that now vegetation would suffer. The digging and grading will also be much easier now.

We have a load ready to go to Germantown but the weather does not permit a start.

The Japanese are following up their success at Nanshan Hill and Kinchan and have taken possession of Dalny which the Russians tried to destroy but did not quite succeed and now the Japs have an excellent naval back near Port Arthur. They talk of capturing the city by June 20. This calculation also a little low.

Today at 1 o'clock a young fellow fr. North Wales named Stone jumped over the Railing at the depot when the operator was out took what money he could get and being caught almost in the act by Wildonger was pursued by the latter down to our factory where the fellow dropped the money got out a revolver and shot. Wildonger dropped the bullet grazing his hand. Stone lost his hat made his way to Franconia where he bo't a cap and was near White's corner when he was captured by Wildonger accompanied by Henry Landis constable & Oscar Hunsberger, Milt and Frank Scheetz also went after.

Saturday, June 4, 1904.   Found out today that Mike Bergey was taking a hand in the school fight. It made me very angry at this and I was minded to go for him but thought better of it. Told Ellis and Adam and I think Adam at least is going for him. When a school director cannot be elected without politics things are at a low ebb. I am resolved that if his intrigues are successful I will publish the whole transaction in the paper. When he came to me to ask me whether I would take the office he said there ought to be someone in the board who wouldn't allow Loux to do as he pleased &c &c. Now he comes and wants to spoil everything. Was to see Alderfer and Wolford today and this evening I went to see old Sam Hunsberger. Got home late.

Gave out the painting for 6 houses this afternoon. Rein Clemmer has them at $40.00 each.

Sunday, June 5, 1904. Very hot day. Went to church twice and Sunday School once. This afternoon's sermon was more or less applicable to local affairs.

Monday, June 6, 1904. At last the school fight has come to a head. Got home late for supper with scarcely time to get to the school h. before 7:30 Asked Elwood this afternoon to take the reports if Goettler wouldn't. He went to Goettler and this evening after a little talk Goettler promised to come. He arrived early and contrary to my expectations no one said a word. Alderfer told me he didn't like it on acc't of the fuss. The old board cleared up all unfin. business among which was the selection of a place for the commencement. The grad. class sent in a petition to change to the Ref Ch. which was ignored and Lib. Hall chosen. The new board organized by choosing the old officers. The salaries were fixed the term also. When the time for electing a principal came I asked Loux to leave. He did. I moved to postpone the election of a principal. This was the [illegible] Vote a tie and the motion was lost. Strasser then nominated Loux and the vote was again a tie. We then reelected all the other teachers. I then moved to adjourn. Lost a tie. Strasser again nom Loux again a tie. Another motion to adjourn, a tie. A third motion for Loux, still a tie. At first the other side said they'd stay all night. We told them now we could stand it indefinitely. So Freed asked for a motion to adjourn. This carried. Freed, Strasser and Enos Moyer for Loux, and Alderfer, Wolford and I against. Outside it stormed fiercely raining in torrents. The thunder and lightening was very vivid and awful. Adjourned at 11.20. Loux came up and defended himself.

Tuesday, June 7, 1904. The rain last night was a torrent. It did a great deal of damage. Slifer had filled in to reach Broad St. fr. Adams Ave. This it swept away to the depth of 2 ft. This was stone and shell no soil. Up at the beginning of the new culvert he had not cut away enough and so the water dashed down the old channel also. The lower end of the culvert filled up to the extent of 18 or 20". At the factory our railroad tie lining was all right above the bridge but below it pushed the whole mess 2 ft down. I wouldn't have believed this if I hadn't seen it.

Loux told the children (it being their last day) that he had resigned. He talked about ingratitude about his dignity also in ref. to helping at commencement &c &c. He said it was church influenced &c. There was a great deal of talk today in town. I find though that he has some friends bobbing up where I least expected it. It seems some people are possessed of the idea that a teacher must be all right in the schoolroom and out of it being nobody's concern.

Talked with Ellis, Al. Reiff, H. Detweiler, Milt, Luckenbill Christ Hunsberger Ed Souder &c. who are all pleased. Loux went away early and was seen with Reub Geihart who fetched two pitchers of beer.

Wednesday, June 8, 1904.　Saw Chris Alderfer today. He seems very sober. He told me Freed had been to see him yesterday and told him it was all a scheme of the other business men to get him into trouble. He regrets now so much that he accepted the nomination. He did not want it and he says Bill Freed urged it upon him. I told him that if he lost business he would have to believe that Souderton did not wish its officers to do right. I told him that I liked praise better than blame and that I had been praised but that I thought this belonged to him and Wolford as it was comparatively easy for me to go into this while it was very hard for them. I think Alderfer is determined to do right but can't like the idea of suffering for it. Neither do I.

Thursday, June 9, 1904.　Went to the city this afternoon to see McLaughlin & Son about a job but did not see them. Took off some work at Tourisin. Gave out the plastering for the 6 houses on Tuesday. Conver and Frederick were both here. Conver's bid was $68 and Frederick's 57.00. I was afraid at first I had counted less but I found since I counted 80 each.

While in the city today I watched them tear off the first section of Wanamakers store. The front is down to the second story but in back they were taking down the sky light.

Took a look at the new subway they are building on Market St. They are east of 18th The western section is complete and I saw all its stages.

Friday, June 10, 1904.　Ron Goettler was at the office this morning and he tells me that great pressure is being made on C. Alderfer and that he is a very sick man. He says he knows parties that have been buying heavily there before the meeting that used to buy in the city before. That one person made the remark that they had expected this he would never have got on the ticket &c &c. Saw Wolford this morning and he says all the money in the town is not able to change him. Huber wrote me and Wolford that he did not wish to be considered if there were to be friction. I answered the letter. Got school laws and circular fr. Prof Schaffer this evening. J. L. Detweiler of Perkasie was here this evening took off some work for him and he missed one car.

Saturday, June 11, 1904.　A new applicant Hunsicker of Collegeville appeared this evening. He was a classmate of Hubers and was surprised that he was an applicant. Hunsicker said that he understood from Gehman that Loux would not teach. I hope this is true.

Sunday, June 12, 1904.　Went to Sunday School in the afternoon and to church in the evening. Mr. Luckenbill spoke on the hatred which Christ said his followers should have to bear.

Went to the BaccaLaureate service in the Lutheran Church. Loux took part despite his declaration that he would have nothing to do with the whole affair. It looks as if he expected something yet.

Monday, June 13, 1904.   Told Ellis to go and see Chris Alderfer and explain that there was nothing but lies in Freed's assertion. This afternoon Mr. Luckenbill sent a note that Ron had had overheard at the P.O. that Alderfer would flop. I got a little alarmed though I could not believe such a thing. Went to Adam Crouthamel and he promised to see him. He knows things which make it bad enough. At a quarter of five Freed came to the shop and announced a meeting for tonight. Now I was sure there was something wrong and I got excited. I went to Goettler to tell them of the meeting. Saw old Goettler get off the train and sent him to Alderfer. Reported to Ellis & Adam. They both saw him and reported they couldn't do anything. Wolford came over and told me. I went home and wrote out three amendments I intended to offer. At the meeting Strasser nominated Loux as usual. I offered an amendment. It was tied and lost. Alderfer voting with us. I offered another and for this they all voted. I offered a third and it was passed 4 to 2. Freed now asked for an adjournment and I made the motion and it was carried. I reminded them that they had not elected a principal when they recalled the motion to adjourn and Loux was elected 4 to 2 Alderfer flopping.

Tuesday, June 14, 1904.   Goettler told me last evening we had won and the others were too ignorant to know they had lost. I didn't agree with him I had talks with Fretz Luckenbill Milt, Detweiler, Ellis, today. Everyone was disappointed but seemed to be satisfied everything possible had been done.

Of course, we might have left them in ignorance for awhile but it would have done no good. It was a temptation but it would have angered them needlessly.

Went up to see Luckenbill tonight. They are having the commencement and Jennie wanted me to go. The girls went but I felt out of place.

Wrote out a statement for publication in the paper late tonight.

Wednesday, June 15, 1904.   Last night to my surprise my wife presented me with a son. He was born about 2^{45} A.M. as near as I can tell. He seems to be a hearty lusty fellow citizen though he slept nearly all the time or was at least quiet. Had no one in the house being quite alone. Fetched Bevy Hunsberger. Ida and Mattie were soon out. Jennie wants to name it after me so do others. The girls don't him called Jonas. When I showed the baby to Amy she asked, Is it a girl. We have nothing but girls.

Showed my paper to Elwood, Adam and Carl and they all said they would stand by me.

Had it typewritten and took it to Goettler this evening. Young Goettler hunted me up and was afraid I would let it drop.

Thursday, June 16, 1904.   Our boy did very well sleeping all night. The mother is doing very well.

Slifer is very busy scooping and digging. Helped to plow some this afternoon. It is getting quite stony.

Am getting back in my work. Wish this outside business were out of the way. Rev. Fretz was down and I told him I was in the fight for the betterment of the schools for the next three years.

I was told Freed said he would spend $25 to oppress my re-election. I am not working for that end. I am only trying to do right. But if he would try such a thing we would have quite an exciting time of it.

The paper came out tonight and many people could be seen reading it. I wonder what they make of it.

Friday, June 17, 1904.   I think we hit them pretty hard this time. It certainly was the talk of the town. Goettler told me that Mike would put in a denial in the paper next week. I hear Oscar said Enos Moyer was in the post office and asked for Mike and when he wasn't in he said I,I,I,!

H. B. Freed according to Elwood says it served Mike right because he lied so. I heard Will Crouthamel was very much pleased. J. C. Landes said something to Enos Moyer but he said he never heard anything against him.

Went to Telford this afternoon to pay Emmis Co. Then ordered some marble sills. Talked to Kuhn over fence on Lincoln Ave.

Saturday, June 18, 1904.   Kratz's baker was terribly hurt last evening. He got his arms into the dough worker. Some think he will have to lose his arm.

Slifer was away this afternoon.

Saw Ed Souder and had a talk with him about school matters. Mike Bergey passed and we spoke and I noticed a little smile. I wondered what it meant. This evening I went in to Wolford to see whether Loux had sent his certificate for examination. He had not done so. Mike had sent him a letter however telling him he expected to make an explanation at the proper time giving no hint when this would be.

We suppose he will have a meeting of the board called and have them vindicate himself as is so often done.

Sunday, June 19, 1904.   Was up all last night. That is I slept some but acted as nurse. Felt very badly as I had a pain over my bowels. The baby was very good and made little trouble. I did not sleep well. Lay around all forenoon and did not dress till ?

Tuesday, June 21, 1904.   Went to Langhorne this afternoon and measured up Asterbeand's house. Met Mr. Bilger and he took me up to Phares' House. The Republican Nat Convention met today. There is no opposition to Roosevelt and it is considered certain that Fairbanks of Indiana will be the Vice Pres. candidate.

Wednesday, June 22, 1904.   The convention met yesterday and organized by electing Elihu Root as temporary Chairman. His speech is said to be a brilliant one. Nothing else was done except to appoint committees. Everything having been decided upon the members are anxious to finish today. It may be things will be rushed through today instead of another session tomorrow. The Wisconsin people are having trouble. They have a fight between Shorner and the other leaders and Gov. Lafollette and his people. This may imperil Wisconsin.

We are going to get the stone masons tomorrow. They wanted to go to Laudenslagers but we wouldn't let them.

Thursday, June 23, 1904.   Was surprised to find nothing in the Independent from Mr. Bergey. Perhaps he means to put it off till next week to make sure of Hen. Freed's nomination but perhaps he feels too that discretion is the better part of valor.

Rec'd a letter fr. Perry Ratzal which pleased me very much. It is all about the school trouble. He says a drunkard has no business in the schoolroom. He says he went to a school where the principal was a drinking man and a large percentage of the students are today drinking men.

Friday, June 24, 1904.   Roosevelt & Fairbanks were nominated today. the former by acclamation.

Saturday, June 25, 1904.   Worked all day at the shop. It was the understanding when we stopped at 12 that every 4 weeks we would work till five. Am getting somewhat busy just at present.

This is Margerets' work [scribbing over the page] with Amy sitting by reading Last of the Mohicans and not seeing it until after the damage was done.

Sunday, June 26, 1904.   A very warm day. Horace brought Uriah here this forenoon and we had a talk for about an hour. Uriah was after mulberries at Hen Godshalls

Met Irwin Bean last evening and he talked about the school business. They seem to think that I was in the right and that we have taken the right course.

Was in Sunday School and church this afternoon. No church this evening on account of the service at Indian Creek.

A storm came up and we stopped in at Luckenbills until it was over.

Monday, June 27, 1904.   It seems that on Thursday the Russians having repaired their damaged ships and opened the passage of Port Arthur came out with 6 battleships 5 cruisers and 14 Torpedo craft. The Japanese tried to draw them out and give them battle but the Russians retreated but spent the night outside the harbor whereupon the Japanese torpedo boats were sent in and sank one battleship damaged a battle ship and a cruiser all with very little damage to themselves. The armies are gathering and a battle is expected in which probably 300000 men will participate.

Was up to Perkasie this evening and figured up DeVissel's house for Mr Lewis. Was also to see J. L. Detweiler. Couldn't go to Charley's as it was too late.

Tuesday, June 28, 1904.   Cloudy all day. We expected the masons yesterday but they did not come even today.

Loux has not yet paid any attention to Wolford's notice and today I prepared a contract and gave same to Wolford.

Started to rain this afternoon. Wolford just finished putting the tin on the main part of the new hayshed this afternoon.

Our baby is getting fat I think. I think he is growing. His Mother doesn't seem to be so strong.

Sunday, July 3, 1904.   Old Cath. Moyer came here yesterday afternoon and was here till this afternoon. She was with Jonathan Gulick but has now left him as she can no longer stand it. It is over 5 years that she was with us. One can hardly realize that time has passed so rapidly.

Went to church and S.S. this afternoon. No Chu. this evening. Milk cans out this evening.

Monday, July 4, 1904.   Nice day. The masons were working though they did not get through with the second cellar. I think they will finish tomorrow. I think we will get Hetrick to wall up the other cellars. Our stone is about all and we will try and get a couple of blasts off in the quarry. Heffentrager will do it.

We didn't work at the shop today. Father took in his hay. He had quite a good crop.

Briden was here this evening. He says he has his brother with him. He expects to keep him.

There were some fireworks but I didn't see them myself. I think the practice is dying out.

Elwood thinks something strange has happened to Mike. That he wants to go to church and did go once or twice of late. That he wants to join some church in town at least.

Wednesday, July 6, 1904.   School Board met last evening. Loux sent in his certificate last evening. On June 29, 1904 he added Algebra to complete the subject, that is fr. Qudeatics Equation, Phys Geog. Etymology, Drawing, and Literature. On 8/12, 1903, he had added 3 studies.

This accounts for his failure to report sooner. Freed said it was the best or one of the best Certif— in the county. I copied it. It is good till 1906. Freed said Loux would sign the contract if the others would. I said they would each one sign on their own responsibility. The sec. is to give ten days notice.

Went down to Ambler this afternoon. Heckler says he got $19000 notes fr. Dr. M.--- I couldn't get any money out of him however.

Went to Devine who gave me an order for wm fes. to change Dr. M's stable practically rebuilding the same.

Rained very much last this evening when I came off the train.

Thursday, July 7, 1904.   The bricklayers started on the first house yesterday. They got half way up the windows today but the rain stopped them around four o'clock or earlier. Hetrick's stone masons started yesterday morning on the 3rd cellar. Heffentrager made a blast in the quarry but Slifer doesn't seem to think it satisfactory. He says so far the stone is no good. Hilger was hurt falling off a tree on the 4th of July.

I expected to go to the city today but put it off till tomorrow. Rain this afternoon and evening.

Today the lot between Sames and the church was sold. Pres. Sames taking the lower half and J.M. Landis the upper half each paying 500-.

Goettler who wasn't present at School Bd on Tuesday evening goes for Council a little this week. They laid trolley ordinance to Trooper on the table. He also says the Co. Treas. is taking money that does not belong to him by deducting 5% fr. hotel licenses.

Saturday, July 9, 1904.   The Democratic Convention which met on Wednesday had not finished their work this morning. When the papers went to press the nominating speeches had been made and they were apparently ready to vote. The nomination of Judge Parker seems assured. They have had such a long fight over the platform. Hill wanted a gold plank and Bryan fought this so that the money plank was left out altogether. This is the way the platform was adopted.

We have now sold the two lots between the church and Sames. Pres. Sames paid $500 for the lower lot and Jonas Landis is to pay the same for the next one.

Was up at the quarry this afternoon and find the stone has run out altogether. It is all shell and is no account. We will have to take the top off.

Sunday, July 10, 1904.   Rain this morning. Cloudy all day. In Sunday School this afternoon and church this evening.

Stopped in at fathers a little this afternoon. Our horse Topsy has influenza. Father and I were very angry yesterday and I am sorry about it. He has such a contemptuous way about him when he differs with you that I got angry. He doesn't believe that Ellis' house is set 6" lower than Landis'.

I now hear that Judge Parker telegraphed that he wouldn't stand unless a gold standard money plank be inserted in the platform and that the convention had taken a recess for three days in consequence. I can imagine what an excitement such an unheard of thing caused. Hitherto he has been silent and no one was able to draw an expression of opinion from him. It seems he can speak with decision if necessary. I like his pluck.

Monday, July 11, 1904.   It seems the Democratic Convention finished their work at about 1.40 yesterday morning by nominating Henry G. Davis of West Va. for Vice Pres. a man 81 yrs. old and rich.

Judge Parker telegraphed that the gold standard was irrevocably established and that if elected he would act accordingly. That if this did not meet with view of the majority of the convention his name should be withdrawn and another chosen. After great excitement and confusion the convention sent a telegram in reply that the money question was a settled matter and that only live issues were in the platform. Some of the delegates were in an ugly mood and Mr Bryan rose from a sick bed to oppose a gold plk. in the platform. Parker gets great credit for his independence though he hurt some of those Democrats out there. Bryan said it was manly to give his opinion before the convention adjourns but it would have been more manly to have said the same thing before the convention met.

Tuesday, July 12, 1904.   We are getting real busy at the mill and I find I have to watch the work very close in order to get it through.

We have over 25 buildings contracted for or underway with several more in prospect. Bo't a car chestnut this afternoon that Bardo was to have had but could not meet. I hope the lumber is good. Ben Alderfer is having cement sills and lintels made for his house. They are quite expensive on acc't of the labor involved.

The Russians are gradually being driven back at every point. Kinchan being the Japs last capture.

The Democrats seem to be very confident of Parkers election. Some betting men are betting 10 to 7 on Roosevelt while Parker men are asking 2 to 1--

Wednesday, July 13, 1904.   We are getting very busy at the mill but I think by close management I can get it through. Bought slate for the houses from Jake Delp. We have the third cellar nearly finished and the second house nearly to second floor. The second story joists are laid on 1st house. Met at the school house for looking up repairs. After we were through I had a little talk with Christ. Alderfer the first time after the fuss. He says that after Loux promised him he couldn't do otherwise than he did. I told him that after Louxs' promise to him we must hold him to it. He says he is going to talk to Loux.

Saturday, July 16, 1904.   The hottest day so far. McLaughlin of Phila. was here about the Allen Stable. Told him I had just promised some work for

Doylestown that had to be done next week.

Started for Doylestown this afternoon but did not get down till about 5.30. Couldn't leave till 1.36 and got home late. Went to Rotzel & Raike's office and there met Mrs Raike. She is the whole firm, very stately &c &c. Mr. R. likes beer I found. They are going to fit up a room at the school house. They have quite instructive exhibits in the school house halls. Things are made quite attractive for the student.

Sunday, July 17, 1904.   A very warm day.

Went to S.S. & Church this afternoon. No ch. this evening. Charley Schwenck's were here this afternoon. C is a little stiff yet but is getting along very well.

Cal Hunsberger's came after supper.

Tuesday, July 19, 1904.   Worked at the mill till 9.30. Did not get home for dinner or supper. We got done with some of Tourisons and all of Shea House stuff. We loaded it in the dark and it was quite late after 11 when I got home.

Slifer and I went over to Price's brickyard and he arranged to have brick here to keep them going. Harry has promised a whole lot of work for next Monday plainly showing that he intends to leave but we don't want to let him. Benner started putting in the water pipes on Wednesday.

The Russians were badly defeated in an attack on Motica Pass.

Saturday, July 23, 1904.   Got our frames for Doylestown loaded. We did right well this week but next week promises to be worse.

Sent a part of Shea House and Tourison's stores on Tuesday. On Wednesday we shipped Asherbrand.

Kept Geo Rittenhouse going all the time he sent sash to Telford yesterday and also the o.s. Doors. And today Doylestown. We worked two evenings this week but not this afternoon.

Monday, August 1, 1904.   Board met tonight. We came near having a riot again. Strasser got up and talked against recording the maker and seconder of a motion. While doing this he looked at me and asked what it meant. I told him I thought everything was to be recorded. E.H. Moyer then said it ought to go on the minutes but not in the paper. Strasser then again took the cue saying that it had never been done before and asked what it all meant. He said it was none of the people's business. I told him a man that made a remark like that wasn't fit to be a school director. I was sorry afterward I spoke so bluntly but that is what I meant. E.H.M. too thought it ought to be done behind closed doors &c &c. Freed smoothed it over a little. I was very angry. So were the others. We bought supplies tonight. A man by the name of Kern sold them. I found he had seen Loux and given him the prices first. We

cut his prices a little. We bought only 25 seats where Loux recommended 30.

Tuesday, August 2, 1904. Today it rained most of the time. We have had such an amount of rain this year. It is hard to get the hay or oats in. The bricklayers and masons couldn't work and have lost much time of late.

Rev Fretz was down to ask about the school business. He heard something about Goettler.

Wednesday, August 3, 1904. J.K. Allebach came over to see about sending his children to school. He agreed to pay $72⁰⁰ for the five. This is below the regular rate but it was reduced on account of the number.

Was at the church tonight. Penrose wasn't at the shop but saw him tonight at Hartzel's. If that boy only knew what was good for him. I am afraid he is fast going to the dogs.

Thursday, August 4, 1904. We are again getting pinched for getting work ready. Yesterday Pen & Harry did not work and Harry did not turn up today even. Penrose seems to be drinking. It is too bad. This morning father had another tussel with Hans. Hans wanted a chair downstairs and they made him bring it back. He is trying hard to get another job but I am afraid he won't succeed quick enough for we must be rid of him soon. He is too careless and we had one fire already.

In tonights' paper Goettler tears up the Council and School Bd. members properly who oppose having the reports in the paper. He came over on Adams Ave. and I asked him whether he had anything and he said he wouldn't be surprised if they were arrested tomorrow. I then read it. It appears that they attacked him in Council at the same time as the school board. Henry Souder declaring that either Goettler would have to go or he would. Hen Freed suggested executive sessions. Romander had to defend himself no one else will.

Sunday, August 7, 1904. Went to Sunday School this afternoon and stopped a little at Grandfather Hemsings on the way home. Found Calvin Musselmans soninlaw of Allen Freed at our place when I came home. They expected to go to Teachers meeting at Clemmens in the evening. Went to church with Amy, Naomi Shellenberger. Agnes Leidy's husband preached. This I believe was one of his first attempts. His matter was all right. He wants more confidence and learn to preach extemporaneous. He wants also more earnestness but that will come when he feels surer of himself.

Monday, August 8, 1904. Ellis told me last night that W. H. Freed had been to see Christ Freed about keeping Goettler out of Council promising to keep him out of the school board. I urged Ellis to make a determined stand against this. This evening I went out to see Wolford and he says he'll back me up. Went up to see Adam Crouthamel and found Goettler had just come in to see him about the same thing. Had quite a talk with him. He said he would resign if they would go into executive sessions. Had quite a talk with

Romander Goettler afterward. He still had an idea that Wm. H. Freed was siding with them or at least would not do anything against them. I told him different. They are going to give them another push this week. I find Goettler really has an idea of defeating H. B. Freed for Co. Treas. I think I could not do this if I had it in my power unless I thought I was really doing a public service.

Tuesday, August 9, 1904.   The bricklayers started the 4th house on Franklin Ave yesterday. The masons are on the 5th house and will get it ready for the bricklayers in time. Elwood's house the rafters are being put on.

The Japanese seem to gradually be working around the Russians so that in the end they may be surrounded. It is said they are approaching Mucken from the east and west. This would cut Kuropotkin's communications. The remarkable thing is how quickly they are doing these things. From Port Arthur no reliable news came except that they are gradually approaching nearer. All sorts of rumors come but generally without foundation.

Wednesday, August 10, 1904.   Went down to Gwynedd this afternoon to measure up the Wood House. I was to meet Guthrie but he had just left when I came. I think I was just as well off too. I prefer to measure up a building myself and quite alone.

Abel was to go to Germantown today but it started to rain and he came back. Slifer decided to take it down and started soon after dinner. He expects to stay over night.

On our way home from Gwynedd it commenced to rain and got worse and worse till we got to South Hatfield when they took off the poles the lightening burning out some thing. A light went out and commenced to burn on outside. It was a fearful storm. They trolly men thought it was the worst one for lightening this summer. This has been a remarkable summer. One man told me that July had only 4 clear days.

Thursday, August 11, 1904.   A sea fight occurred at Port Arthur yesterday but we cannot learn the result. It is supposed that the bombardment made it too hot for the fleet inside so they endeavored to escape but were engaged by Ad. Togo till nightfall. Two of the ships were seen to return to Port Arthur. A gunboat reached Chefon. Of the rest of the fleet nothing is known. It is reported that the Japs lost the Cruiser Kasogi.

Was in Norristown this afternoon and did not get home till near nine o'clock. Measured up Buchanan house. Went in to see Dannenhower about excluding Goettler and he is of opinion it can be done but thought it mighty poor policy. He is going to look it up. He does not think the question was ever raised. Goettler came out again today with a lot of digs at the councilmen. Every once in a while he has "nobody's business" mixed in with the news. I am sorry that he mentioned Jake Delp for stopping his paper.

Friday, August 12, 1904.   The news about the sea fight are still indefinite. Five vessels are accounted for. Two were seen returning to Port

Arthur and 2 cruisers and a torpedo boat took refuge in German Territory. The Japanese believe the rest were sunk destroyed or captured while the Russians hope they escaped Vladivostok. The Japanese took possession of the gunboat that reached Chefon.

Goettler came down to see me this forenoon. He says if Council decides for executive sessions he will publish the minutes and issue legal proceedings and have H.B. Freed, Harvey Landes or J.B. Delp removed from office.

Staked off or gave the lines for the cellar walls of the 6th house this evening. I am glad this is the case. I am tired of it. That is the expenses especially.

Amy Helen and Mary went to Highland Park Camp meeting with Sam Moyer and Martha. They enjoyed it much.

Saturday, August 13, 1904.   Admiral Withoft the commander of the Port Arthur fleet was killed having both legs shot off. About 200 were lost on board the Czarevitch which with the Askold & a torpedo boat put into a German port at Kiasu Chiau. The greater part of the fleet returned to Port Arthur and it seems to be effectually crippled. A son was born to the Czarina and is therefore heir to the Russian throne. This has caused great rejoicing in Russia and the Czar in a proclamation said it gave him greater joy than a victory in the field would.

The teachers meeting was held at our house tonight. Old Binder was also present.

Sunday, August 14,1904.   Went to S S this afternoon. Had a talk with Dan Luckenbill after school. He told me how he read 200 pages of some theological work this morning. I can't understand how he can do it. He must be able to fix his mind on the book wonderfully well.

Aunt Sarah came in just before we went to S S & meeting and told how Oscar Bilgers 2nd son of Dan Bilger had died of typhoid fever on Friday.

Monday, August 15, 1904.   Some how I get angry when I find Slifer has an idea of postponing till next year the very things I was most anxious to do this year. When I talked off cement walks he put it aside as impossible. When I talked of the hole to be filled he didn't seem to think that was important. He seems to think that he is building the houses &c. He is certainly running up the expenses. I know these things sound mean but I think he has the wrong idea even and it makes me angry.

The Japanese have now defeated the Vladivostok squadron and sunk the Rurik while the Rossia and Geomobol escaped badly damaged. The Russians have now only four cruisers free as the Port Arthur Squadron is all battered and they are unable to repair it as the Japanese batteries are said to command the harbor. Admiral Kamiraice who had before been unable to get near this.

Wednesday, August 17, 1904.   Slifer talks of getting married now to Mrs. Cooper of Bethlehem. He used to talk about the objection of her having a son but that I believe has been overcome. He talks of moving into the Adams Ave house and selling the other half to his sister. I don't care what he does about it.

The stone at the quarry is nearly all gone. The masons are however nearly finished and he is now hauling stone to the culvert again but we had more stone on hand there this spring than we are likely to have when he is done with the houses.

I am sorry this is so but these men dont seem to care much some of them what it costs.

Thursday, August 18, 1904.   It appears that the Battle ship Pallada was sunk in the fight of Aug 10 as the Japs claim and she has not been heard of since. The two ships have returned to Vladivostok. The Japs saved 600 men from the Rurik. The other two were on fire several times. The Novik and Diana have not yet been accounted for though it is said the Novik was sighted several times making for Vladivostok.

The Jap commander at Port Arthur has called on the garrison to surrender. The harbor is swept by the Jap guns and the Russian ships made a sortie to escape their fire. The final assault is expected to begin.

We worked tonight. It seems every Tom Dick and Harry wants their work this week. The bricklayers are to start Ben Alderfer on Saturday and Koffels on Tuesday. We have at least finished Thomas first story. If we were only done with Dr. Reading.

Friday, August 19, 1904.   Worked tonight. Noah Kramer was in and also Rob Funk. Noah says Bardo is very busy.

Saturday, August 20, 1904.   Rained last night. Bricklayers did not work today though they might have worked in the afternoon. Carpenters have studded up the first house almost. The lathers can start in Monday.

John Springer told me this afternoon they had quite a flood at Fort Washington and Jenkintown tracks flooded the north bound track being the only one in use for awhile. Father has not been well for the last few days. He was at the shop yesterday and today but his hands and eyes are swollen and I took some Lithic tablets in for him. I think his kidneys must be out of order. He says he has some medicine from the doctor now.

We sent Guthries porch posts away this afternoon. He has been waiting for several weeks. Shipped Dinger Cornice which was also a couple of weeks overdue. Also the balance of Torisan as far as we know. We are getting ready for Ben Alderfer and Mrs. Koffel house.

Monday, August 22, 1904.   We had quite a shower again this evening. There was rain Saturday night and on Friday night. Such a summer as we had is very remarkable for rain at least.

Frederick started on the basement at the school house. Slifer and I went to Telford to see basement at Hoff's and at the school house. We found them in good condition and decided that this was the thing for us too.

Went to Lansdale to measure up Fred Souder's next cement block house. It looks very well.

The Russian Cruiser Novik after escaping the battle at Sea and leaving Kinon Chiaou before the 24 hr limit sailed aroung the East coast of Japan and tried to make Vladivostok from the N.E. but was caught by two cruisers of the Jap. Navy and had to be beached. All the ships of the Port Arthur squadron are now accounted for. The Diana is in a French possession.

Tuesday, August 23, 1904.   A journal on the main shaft in the cellar got hot today so that in some mysterious way a pulley commenced to burn some 18' away. It burned nearly through about 1½" in diameter before we it was seen. When I saw what was the matter I decided to have it fixed at once, stopped at 5.30 and worked after an interval for supper until nearly three o'clock. I reached home some time around three A.M. Hans Menno and Ed Watts helped. We fetched Henry Alderfer to solder some brass on the shaft but this was a failure that delayed us several hours.

Wednesday, August 24, 1904.   Felt very tired today. I wished very much I could lie down and take a good nap this afternoon.

Our journal worked all right today though it got quite warm.

I almost got a disagreement with Slifer today. I made some suggestion but he waived it aside and I told him I knew he didn't like me to say much but as long as I paid half of the expenses. This evening went up to church to teachers' meeting. Only about half a dozen there. On the way home stopped at Grauley's factory and Mr Rosen showed me and Amy the whold factory. Enos and some of his men were building new tables. Went to the tent of the M.Bn. Ch. Jennie had gone there and we thought we would help take the children home. Was surprised to find Jennie out and they praying over her. She is too excitable to go to any such place.

Thursday, August 25, 1904.   Felt very tired today.

The bicycles arrived today. It was quite a surprise. The new Columbia is a delight. It has a 56x72 Gear and is easy to change from one to another. There is no jar to it having cushion front and back. The Hartford is also a very nice bicycle. I got Stanley to bring it down for me. Amy smiled and said little. She never does. Though I know she is pleased for at noon I asked her whether she wanted to ride mine she said no but she would like to ride a bicycle.

Went out to hunt Hen Godshall tonight but he wasn't home. I had to show it to quite a number and all thought it was a fine machine. Took Ben Alderfer's bid over and he didn't seem to mind it as much as I expected he would.

Saturday, August 27, 1904.   Henry Rittenhouse ordered a Hartford

Bicycle this morning. He can hardly wait now till he gets it.

Mike Moyer sold the land from his lane on up to Stover of Perkasie for 10000-- He certainly is a lucky man. He still has about 22 acres of his own. It is rumored that this is to be cut in to the boro and to have electric lts and water furnished. This I think will be a little slow coming. I do not think however that we will be hurt by it. I expect to be benefitted.

Monday, August 29, 1904.   School commenced today. Was in the high school rooms this morning to see Loux about Stanley Springer. It was very full of children, or it seemed so.

Went down to Kulpsville this afternoon to measure up Becker's house. It went all right down but my legs got a little tired on the way home. I am not used to it. I tried my wheel thoroughly for hill climbing and it is all right. Yesterday I climed up by Holly's and twice at Binder's hill and it worked all right.

The roads are getting a little dusty now for the first time since early spring. It was quite warm today. It had been real cool the last few days.

Thursday, September 1, 1904.   The greatest battle of the present war is being fought at Laouyung. For two days the Japanese having been pushing an army estimated at fully 250000 men on the Russian position without success. Yesterday's fighting resulted in favor of the Russians. The division under Gen Kuroki has taken a small part in the battle and it is believed that today he will make an attempt to cut the railroad. If he would succeed in this Kuropotkin's position would be desperate indeed.

Today John M Moyer, E O Souder and Rom. Goettler started for the World's Fair. As a consequence Penrose did not turn up. It is very provoking this of him. He cares no more for himself than a tramp does.

Friday, September 2, 1904.   The Japanese General Kuroki by a flank movement compelled the Russians to evacuate Laouyung after a battle lasting almost a week. No details of the losses are obtainable. And whether the Russians succeeded in making good their escape is still in doubt. They undoubtedly must have lost most of their stores. And if so they will not be able to make another stand, and if not it is not hard to believe that the Japs will catch them yet. Some of the papers call it one of the greatest battles of history. I am going to wait for more detail before I would say that. In the number of men engaged and desperate fighting it may equal the most sanguinary. But it is hard to get an adequate idea of a battle from newspaper accounts.

Monday, September 5, 1904.   The school board met tonight and not a word was said about excluding reporters. Romandes Goettler having gone to the World's Fair Goettler sent a Mr Keller out. He himself attended the council meeting where he expected trouble. Strasser and Enos Moyer were not present. The only trouble seems to be Shellenberger who is going to prove something of a barnacle. He had a bill for 11 days work to help the house cleaning.

Tuesday, September 6, 1904.   Last night sometime after two oclock 2[15] I think we heard the fire whistle for a short time. I thought of fire at the shop looked out and could see nothing. I didn't believe there was fire on acc't of the short whistle. Took the bicycle and went out to the fire co's place. A lot of boys were there who didn't seem to know what it meant. Hans who was among them suggested that there might be a robbery at the car shed and that it should be looked into. I didn't believe it but thought I would go over and scold those firemen for disturbing the town. When I arrived at the power house I went all through it but found no one in there. Josiah Moore and H. Ritten came and I told them there was no one around and that they ought to be kicked. Went up to the train shed and found there had been a robbery indeed. A man Hoffman by name was still bound with picture wire his face bloody and someone trying to loosen the wire. One safe was blown open and the money amting to 929.25 taken. The big safe was ready for blowing up but the whistle frightened them off. A man called Hickory told how they tied him on a chair. Jake Zeigler was eating lunch and was tied and hit on the head three times. It seems there were five or six of the robbers and they stole Wm. Hengs horse and an old milk wagon with wooden axles and made off. Harry Hunsicker followed them up below Willow Grove with H Landes Constables, detectives, trolly officials, reporters swarmed the town. A distorted account of it was published in the paper this afternoon. Was at the trolly shed this forenoon listening to the acc'ts of the dif. news. The detectives from Allentown had an idea who it was but Ziegler couldn't remember what they looked like.

Tuesday, September 13, 1904.   Pres Roosevelle wrote his letter of acceptance the other day. To me it seemed ably written and to the point avoiding nothing, but of course the Democrates can see no good in it and so they condemn it.

The battle of Laouyung while it was a triumph for the Japs yet the Russians seem to have withdrawn their army without the loss of a gun or equipment carrying their wounded and about half their dead. The Russians loss is given at 16000 and the Jap at 17,500. These are the reports of the Commanders of each army.

Wednesday, September 14, 1904.   We had a rain this afternoon that was not equalled for years. I was feeling a little badly so I did not leave home promptly at dinner time but soon it rained so I couldn't easily. At last I thought I had to go. I neglected to put on rubber boots so my feet and legs got wet through and through in spite of rain coat and umbrella. Our lining of RR ties for the creek all tore loose and went down the creek about 400 of them. I saw some go down Groffs meadow. It must have been a sight to see them start. The water played in back of them and lifted them. A great many of them remained in the meadow below us.

We worked after supper and the rain had stopped a little when we went home.

Thursday, September 15, 1904.   The rain continued tonight accompanied by wind. I often thought of Harvey Souders factory on which the roof had been lifted up for a 3rd floor and was all open. Was up this morning and it seemed to me as though the wind could easily have carried it off. Went down the creek and counted 52 ties in Groff's meadow and about a dozen below but father said there were about 25 or so at the lower end of Allebach's. I couldn't discover any at Sol Krupp's where the bridge was washed away. Eph Freed had not seen any. In the culvert they were jammed together in a way that would have caused a flood if it had happened earlier. Geottler was flooded a little.

Hunsicker's store too had a sewer burst in at the side and the water rushed in. At Sellersville considerable damage was done.

Sunday, September 18, 1904.   We were at grandfather Moyer's for supper, the first time for over a year.

Went to church tonight. Mr. Luckenbill preached on Unmortality. After next Sunday he will preach every Sunday night.

Read Tillie a Mennonite maid which I borrowed from Emma last Sunday. Read and also finished Oliver Twist.

Monday, September 19, 1904.   Measured the children tonight and find that Amy is exactly the height of her mother 5' 2.8, Amy grew 3¾" Henry 3⅝, Mary 3⅜ and Helen 3" since July 24 - 1903.

On Saturday afternoon Slifer started for Bethlehem and said he could not return till Monday evening. He has a fine harness and team in general.

Levelled off on Sat. and found the deepest cut to be made is 24'. I cut down 20' the depth above Freed's house and found not a stone in it. This made me feel good. The stony part is really only 75ft wide and we will cut it down somehow.

Thursday, September 22, 1904.   Weather cold. Ice this morning. It makes one very much afraid of winter already and here is only the beginning of fall. Plasters started to white coat the first house. We are pointing the cellar walls, the first house being finished. The lather is working on the third house and the carpenters are laying floor in the same on the other side which Slifer will occupy.

The street is going down gradually and I am surprised at the amount of filling it takes. It is something awful. We worked at the shop tonight. Yesterday 3 or 4 went to the Allentown Fair. Today Penrose went with such fellows as Peter's and Jesse Benner. I am afraid and almost sure he will not get back sober.

Nothing but rumors from the seat of war.

Sunday, September 25, 1904.   Warmer again.

Garret Souder's boy Isaac was buried today. He had cancer at the bone of his leg above the knee. It was a very large funeral.

Had a short talk with John Moyer.

Was in church in the afternoon and evening. Had a talk with Luckenbill after church about Penrose and Menno. I am going to talk with both of them. Jennie is having dreams again. I dont know what about but she is all excited about religion and of course thinks she has to right some imaginary wrong and has started to write letters. She wants to be baptized again. &c. She imagines I think that after having done these things she will have peace.

Saturday, October 1, 1904.   Today we laid part of the frame for cement pavement. Very little filling is now required. The east side is nearly all dug away. Slifer was in the city today and most of his men worked only till dinner time. We had a carpenter to lay the frame. Slifer is sick of it and I wish he would get away. All I ask is to have the pavements dug down as far as they are to go and the rest we will do while he is gone. If only the plasterers cementer and carpenters will stick and keep the thing going.

Monday, October 3, 1904.   This morning we decided to get Italians to finish our street work. We have only 3 men left and they can't do the work. So I went down to see the railroad bosses who told me to go to 8th & Fitzwater St where I could get any number. As I have to go to the city anyhow I thought I might as well look it up. We have either to stop entirely soon or force matters.

Tuesday, October 4, 1904.   Went down on the 8 o'clock train this morning. Went to see Mr. McLaughton first about the ceder posts we are in trouble about.

Then went down to 8th & Catherine asked a policeman who got me into an office from whence a young man started out with me to hunt men. After considerable trouble he said he had them. I paid him a dollar for his trouble but he could not bring them to the station as they said they couldn't get ready. So I promised to be down in the morning again for them.

Went down to Lear's this afternoon and found they were very [illegible]. Did not see Lear himself.

Wednesday, October 5, 1904.   This morning they started in earnest on the Adams Ave pavement. He laid I should say about 70 ft till this evening. They are now finishing in the first house. Delp had taken men away again. It made me mad as there was no reason for it. Went down and fetched up 7 Italians. Got back at 3 o'clock. The lot I had engaged yesterday did not turn up with the exception of one man. So we had to get new ones. I had to pay a dollar a piece for getting them to a fat contractor. It was a very interesting experience.

This afternoon Hen Freed tackled me and asked me to do something for him. I told him I would neither do anything for him or against him. We had a long talk. I told him I wanted to keep out of politics and I wanted the politicians to keep out of the school board. I told him I was responsible for Goettlers being on the school board. Told him my theory of politics.

Thursday, October 6, 1904.   Our Italians seem to be good workers. The work made good progress today and Slifer is pleased. The cementers stopped work again and so the finishers. It is very provoking.

The weather is cool and it makes one very anxious to get done.

We worked this evening in an another effort to catch up but it seems we are slipping behind every day.

Goettler was rough on H B Freed this week. He accuses him of not paying the minimum rates for electric lights paying only 64 cts the last 5 mos. where others paid 2.50

Sunday, October 9, 1904.   Went to S.S. this afternoon and to church twice.

Read a book given by Isaiah Stover giving a history of the Church of God from their standpoint. Holdeman the Author traces the lineage to the days of the apostles through the Waldenses. He claims Menno joined the Waldenses. That the Thessalonians a church founded by St. Paul were still in existance in 1540 and pronounced the Mennonites the only church which agreed with the word of God.

Of late or since 1840 or so the church had fallen into decay so that in 1859 he and a few followers left the church. All the other breaks or schisms were not from God. But his is and the lineage he calls it is with them. He seems to think that God can only recognize one church and has always done so from the beginning of the world.

Monday, October 10, 1904.   This morning things looked lively on Adams Ave. There were ten or eleven men working on the street, 6 or 7 carpenters and about 8 plasters cementers and helpers. Nearly 300 ft of cement walk is now laid on the east side. We had the men all digging on the east side grading up for the pavement and digging ditches for the pipes.

Slifer gets a little excited when things go like this and would be willing to make things by guess just so it goes. I spent half my time over there today although I was badly needed at the shop where everything is behind time. We had two cars of lumber in this morning. One was shipped without orders.

Thursday, October 13, 1904.   Worked tonight and Tuesday night. Got a load of stuff off to Norristown. How glad I would be to be done with a few jobs. The rain yesterday stopped work these two days on the cement work.

Friday, October 14, 1904.   Goettler gave a cutting reply to a communication in the Harleysville News signed Justice in which the writer defended H.B. Freed and sneered at Goettler's defeat for school Director Council & Romandes for J.P.

He said as to school director that they wanted a man they could control even though he had not behaved properly a few weeks before the election rather than take one who would look out for the interests of the taxpayers and turn out a Hemsing. I wished he hadn't mentioned me. People think he means to flatter me and while I think he meant to say he would have done just as I did, yet most people may not understand it in that way.

Have about 650 ft cement walk finished.

Saturday, October 15, 1904. The attack of the Russians seems to have been signally defeated. The Russians loss being more than at the battle of Laouyung. No very accurate reports have yet appeared except that the fighting lasted four days and that the Russians lost 15000.

Went over to Kulpsville to get the list of the balance of the stuff.

Got 200 in money and a little from Tourisan. I have the greatest trouble to raise enough money to make ends meet at present. In fact I had to borrow money.

Becker took me through his clothing factory. It is very interesting and is run on a large scale. I had never seen cutting done before.

Father helped me stake off some side walks this afternoon.

One of Dan Bilger's boys is here on a visit.

Thursday, October 20, 1904. Goettler had practically nothing to say this week in answer to another communication in the Harleysville News which abused Goettler in every way possible.

I think he realized that a thing can easily be over done.

Nothing authoritative can yet be learned about the battle around Shakhe. It was asserted that the Russians lost as high as 50000 the Japs having buried 10000. Yet the Russians were not routed as they have been standing their ground of late. The fighting lasted about 9 or 10 days. The armies are resting now.

Friday, October 21, 1904. Tonight and this morning there was a heavy rain.

After dinner the Italians dug across the hump on Adams Ave all having picks as it was too soft to haul. This softened up the stony soil and it will not take long to cut it down. Slifer is anxious to dig the trench for the water pipe. He is afraid it will not be done if he don't do it. We are now nearly ready to lay the cement walk on the west side. Slifer asked father the other day to take his place as he can't wait any longer about going west and getting married. He tried to get his house finished before the rest but he only succeeded in putting the others back as I told him it would be impossible to get the finish ready.

Am having trouble with Mrs. H. who wants to draw her Bldg Assn and return her salary when she taught because of some imagined shortcoming as a teacher.

Thursday, October 27, 1904. Made all arrangements at the shop and went to Norristown this morning. Missed the trolley on which the others went so I took the 8 o'clock train and caught the Norristown trolley at Lansdale. Loux and 16 of his scholars were on the car too. He took them all over Norristown showing them the court house, the jail, the asylum, the charity hospital, across the run to Bridgeport the High School &c. They enjoyed it very much of course.

Directors met in the court H. A man by the name of Cyrus Caley presided a witty cute old fellow. The Franconia Directors were all down. I thought I was alone from here but Wm H Freed & Chris Alderfer came too. The session lasted till noon. The subjects discussed were are the teachers institute, paying for the time and money spent on them. What is the best way of enforcing the compulsory school law. Is any new school legislation needed. The uniform standard of high school values were postponed to next meeting.

The new court H. is a very fine buildg. Marble stairway. 2 to oak finish. I liked it very much.

Friday, October 28, 1904. The wanton attack on fishing boats by the Baltic Squadron is causing great excitement in the world. At first I thought it was the result of fear. Afraid that saw a spook torpedo boat in every thing that floats. Some still think so. Others think that the Russians were drunk. Adm. Rodenjersky says they were attacked by torpedo boats. The fishermen say that two torpedo boats approached them and went toward the fleet. The Adm. says there were no torpedo boats of theirs with the fleet. Meanwhile England is concentrating her fleets and the report is that the Russians are not to be allowed to pass Gibraltar. They are now at Vigo Spain where they coaled and are making repairs. It is a very dangerous situation indeed. The English demand the punishment of the Russians, who were the cause of the trouble and this the Russians do not wish to do.

Saturday, October 29, 1904. Christian D Hunsberger died sometime early this morning. He had a stroke of paralysis on Monday I think. He was hauling corn and fell while on the wagon. Wm Henge was coming one way around the farm and Chris the other way. By the time Henge reached him he had fallen over. He was lame on his right side and at first I hoped he might recover. He was the youngest of the Hunsberger brothers, about 64 yrs. old.

He was a peculiar man. He could always point out a way for someone else but he never did the thing himself. He had some money to start with about 7000 I am told but it is a question whether he is worth anything now. He had a farm and lived in town. How he ever managed to get his work done I don't know. He had only one horse. His sons are Jonathan Ambrose Howard and Oscar. The daughters Mrs. Ed Price Miss Flora, Mrs Alice -- and Bertha.

Sunday, October 30, 1904. Cal and I went up to Perkasie last evening and attended a meeting of synod. It was the first time I was in the new church. They have things arranged very well but I don't like the style of those churches.

Too much like a theater. They have a good organ a fine sunday school room and the rest of the church I did not see.

Went to Indian Creek to hear Rev. T.C. Liesbach preach. He was Luckenbills old pastor. It was very windy going up.

To S.S. in the afternoon and to church in the evening where Rev. Hoffman of Catawissa preached. He was a classmate of Luckenbills.

Saturday, November 5, 1904. Pres. Roosevelt came out in a statement to the public denouncing Parker's statement that Cortelyn was blackmailing the trusts. He says such a statement is a wicked lie.

Slifer paid off the Italians today. They stopped work last evening. I came over and gave them goodbye. When I shook hands Schepz said. "Nica Monne."

They gave me their names and all asked me to write my name for them.

Their names as I remember them. Francisco Schepz, Paoli Laspada, Bernardo Labaito, Franzioni Guiseppe, Antonino Ponzio, Orazia Mendella, Orlando Solontore.

Sunday, November 6, 1904. Had communion this morning. There were 91 members present. This was a good number, 3 or 4 could not be present.

Went to S.S. this afternoon and to church in the evening.

Monday, November 7, 1904. Tonight before the election it looks like Roosevelt according to all the estimates I could see. I think the Ledger Wash. Correspondent gives Roosevelt 314 — Parker 162. The Republicans do not expect to elect Higgins Gov. of New York.

The schoolboard met tonight. Everything was peacable.

Slifer expects to get married on Wednesday

Tuesday, November 8, 1904. Nice day though frosted this morning. Our cement men started work again today though it is almost too cold.

Harry Hunsicker was busy hauling old and crippled voters to the polls. Voted early in the afternoon. Cut my ticket terribly. Voted for Dem. Justice of Supreme Court instead of Elkin. Voted for Dem. Assemblymen except Rev Fretz who was on as a prohibitionist. I couldn't swallow that other gang. Voted for neither Freed nor Albright. I was afraid I couldn't separate my principles from my passions. Voted the rest of the Repub. ticket.

Was in Perkasie this afternoon. They are very close after us there.

This evening at 11 o'clock called up the Ledger for election news and the answer was. "Roosevelt has swept the country. Has 317 Electoral votes, carried 31 states. New York 22800, N Y City Parker 37000." I was satisfied with this.

Saw Sam Hunsberger was getting the news from the North American. They got all the dispatches which were too tiresome for me. The barber shop was also getting news. Was at Standard Hay Co office.

Wednesday, November 9, 1904.   It was a glorious victory.

The papers late this afternoon say 343 to 133 — It was a landslide, a surprise. This campaign was so quiet, so unusual that it looked as if people were indifferent. There were no political meetings here. A little affair at Morwood but that didn't amt to much. But when the voting came the apathy was all gone and all over the nation is the same story. If it hadn't been for the unfortunate wage fuss in the S. he would probably have carried more of the South.

We worked tonight instead of last night. Saw Goettler tonight and he was feeling bad. He said he thought I had been avoiding him of late. He didn't know whether to stop reporting or not. I said this would be a surrender. He hardly knew who his friends were it seemed to me. He said I was the cause of his

Thursday, November 10, 1904.   Roosevelt's victory was so overwhelming that it is not hard to believe that the Democrats are almost as well pleased as the Republicans. Missouri has also been carried by R. The Electoral vote is 343 and Parker 133. The poplar plurality is supposed to be about 1,900,000. — Where McKinley's was 849,000. Mr Beyer made a few remarks. He calls attention to the fact that in 1896 & 1900 he was opposed by the Gold Democrats while this year these G.D. were all back in the party and he and his people were all working for the ticket and yet the defeat was the worst in history. He expects to take a hand in reorganizing the party. He says it must be agression instead of retreating.

H.B. Freed was only 3 wks. short of Roosevelt in this town. Goettler says tonight he is in the fight for Reform in the borough.

Penna has a majority of 490,000. N Y 170,000, Mass 70,000 and yet elects a Democratic Govt. Douglass the shoeman

Sunday, November 13, 1904.   This morning I found it raining which later turned to snow but melted. In the afternoon the ground began to get white and when I went home from Luckenbills after S.S. people were shovelling snow. My shovel soon broke for me and I used the garden rake which was a poor way to do. At this hour 9 o'clock it is still snowing.

The attendance at church was slim.

There was to be a Home Missionary Service but it was postponed till next Sunday evening.

We were entirely taken by surprise this time. Same's house is one story high and so is Godshall house at Hatfield. I am not sure that the Lutheran Ch. is quite under roof. We have a lot of filling to do on Franklin Ave. and this makes the ground too wet.

I suppose tomorrow I will be in trouble again from every direction.

Monday, November 14, 1904. The remarkable storm of yesterday caused great damage throughout the country. Telegraph wires downed.

This morning the plasterers came but could only white coat as it wasn't fit to carry mortar. Plenty of carpenters today. The floors in at last and the other houses nearly ready for plastering. A lather came too.

Had letter from McDevitt & C Lewis. Phone from Thomas of Langhorne, visits fr. B.B. Alderfer C Lewis & J.L. Detweiler & Dr. Oberholtzer. Also letter from Devine & Russell all pushing for work. If anyone can be happy under such circumstances I would like to know it. Young Cressman started work this morning. Lewis was so mad his voice trembled and he could hardly control himself.

Saturday, November 19, 1904. Got a letter from Slifer today. He wasn't well since he went away having a bad cold. He was in bed one day while at St Louis. I don't think he has had much pleasure out of his trip so far. They stopped at Washington on the way out and arrived at St Louis last Saturday. He had been to the fair only one day the time he wrote. He said they had expected to get back by Thanksgiving but didn't think they could do so now.

Wednesday, November 23, 1904. We made 8 deliveries today four by wagon and the rest by freight.

Our men worked well and I was glad to get these things off before taking a holiday. Even then I had to disappoint Russell and will not get through with Wood House and Guthrie as intended.

I feel very tired and so do the men no doubt. It would do us all good to have a week off. Was up at church after supper where Mr Luckenbill explained the lesson.

Thursday, November 24, 1904. This is Thanksgiving Day. The weather continues nice and we will not have any better. The carpenters and plasterers are working. Adam Crouthamel's house is nearly through plastering they expecting to finish tomorrow. Slifer's furniture came yesterday. I don't expect them now before Sunday or Monday. Had to go up to Perkasie this forenoon to see about J L Detweiler's house. We have had a busy time for the last two months and I was glad for a holiday.

Was at home this afternoon. Jennie and the children went to River BR. Meeting. We had Mrs Cass Moyer and Grandfather H' & Emma here for supper. After supper Appenzeller came. We had a very nice evening. There was meeting at the Mennonite Meeting House. Appenzeller brought some pears and nuts along for the children.

Sunday, November 27, 1904. Today the weather turned very cold. This afternoon the Mennonites baptized a number at the Meeting house. Among them were Henry Rittenhouse and wife. Alpheus Allebach & wife Horace Rosenberger & w.

Wm. Clymer and Katie Moyer were baptized at the creek above the shop back of the lumber pile. It didn't look like a likely place for a baptism but Christ Moyer and Henry Krupp made a dam and though there had been a little ice on he took it off and a great crowd witnessed the ceremony. We had most of the children there to see it.

We were at Grandpop Moyers for supper from where I went to church, after carrying Margaret home.

Our attendance isn't as good as it used to be. I can't quite grasp this unless it be the Lutherans but that cannot be either I think.

Thursday, December 8, 1904.   Conver sent men yesterday again after having discharged Stoll and Detweiler on Saturday. It is time too for we would have put someone to work to finish it if he had not.

Went to the city today. Failed to see Tourisan but saw Boyd's men and got information I sought. Took off one job at Sperry's.

Bo't some paper and Dynamo brushes.

Wanamaker's store is progressing slowly. The roof is on and the wall is above the second story.

Bo't a lot of books and pictures for Christmas.

The Japanese claim to have sunk at least three of the Russian Battleships with their guns from 203 metre hill which they recently captured. If so this will release Togo's fleet for work against the Baltic fleet on its way to the Indian Ocean now.

Wednesday, December 14, 1904.   At last we are rid of Hans and that is something to be thankful for.

I was never so disappointed with a man before. Here I expected he would have things in good order because he pretended to be a machinist. Everything is in disorder. tools lost broken and others here not belonging to us. He had time till Saturday but he got a job at Sellersville and then he stopped at once.

Menno is engineer.

Thursday, December 15, 1904.   Snow which fell on Monday had made good sleighing. Weather has been cold all week.

At Port Arthur the Russians fleet has all been destroyed, with the exception of the battleship Sebastapol. The Baltic fleet is slowly approaching some being near Cape of Good Hope others in the Indian Ocean.

Wednesday, December 21, 1904.   The boil that I thought I had at the back of my neck had turned out to be a carbuncle. Yesterday I met Dr. Oberholtzer and he told me to have it out. So I stopped in last evening and he ripped it open and burned it out with nitrate of silver. This evening I went in again and he opened two other pockets. I am in hopes that he can check it. It would be an awful thing to be laid up on that account.

We are doing night work again trying to get done with Thomas' stuff. We had nothing but bad luck with this. Cutters breaking. Hans substituting lead for Babbit also causing a day's delay. It is reported that the battleship Sebastapol has been wiped out and that the Jap fleet has sailed to meet the Baltic Fleet. This is not likely to be actually the case. I should think they would spend all possible time refitting although it is reported they have already done so.

Friday, December 23, 1904. We worked every night this week in order to get done with Thomas' House. We will load the stuff tomorrow unless rain prevents which I hope it will not.

Hired Noah Kramer this morning at 17½¢ an hour. He wanted 20 last week but I wouldn't give it to him. So this morning he said he was willing to work.

Dan Luckenbill was here this evening. He came down just as I went out to the shop and was here yet when I returned. He wanted my mileage book.

Sunday, December 25, 1904. Took the children to grandfather Hemsings but Jennie wouldn't go because it is Sunday. Not on her own account but because others keep Sunday she doesn't want to cause them work.

Joe Derstines were also there. Gave them a dollar and gave Emma a Golden Censer and Vicar of Wakefield and also a picture. Jennie had some things which she expects to take tomorrow. Emma made dresses for the girls and grandfather H. gave leggings & rubbers for the little ones.

Gave Amy a Golden Censer, Helen some Poet and Mary Alice in Wonderland. Gave the neighbors such books as Grandfather's Chain Legends of the Prov. House. &c

Father fetched the children out in the sleigh.

Monday, December 26, 1904. All went to Grandfather Moyer's. Roy fetched the children in the sleigh. Charley's and Willis were also there. Katie couldn't come on account of a sick baby. Leon has grown to be as tall as his father and is only 15.-

Had a good time. Gave the boys books and the women pictures.

Had our Christmas service tonight.

Mrs. Roberts dies—attempt on life of Czar—the distractions of politics—Rev. Luckenbill is criticized—Principal Loux accused of drunkenness—rumor of syphilis causes panic— Jennie baptized by immersion—Loux shot by robbers

1905

Sunday, January 1, 1905.   Spent the day quietly going to S S & church this afternoon. No church this evening. Had my new boil lanced this evening by Dr. O. I hope I may now be rid of these bothersome visitors.

Monday, January 2, 1905.   Went over to Appenzellers today. Helen & Amy couldn't go on account of examinations at school. Weather was very mild and consequently the roads were getting sloppy. The children enjoyed the ride very much. Drove Topsy for the first time this afternoon after having him nearly nine months. Had Kratz's carriage and had a little bad luck with it. Tore the cover and broke off the lantern. Had a good time. Fetched the girls over after school and stayed for supper. Mrs. H. did not want to go. She thinks it's wrong.

Appenzeller has been appointed executor of an estate netting 100,000 commission. This together with the share will amount to over 3000. I am very glad for him indeed. He has 3 horses, seven cows 4 calves and three steers at present.

Tuesday, January 3, 1905.   Port Arthur has fallen at last. After a seige perhaps the most wonderful on record. It took eleven months to subdue one of the best fortified (both by nature and art) position on earth. And people are beginning to realize that no people but the Japanese could have done it. The highest skill together with a fanatical bravery that has no fear of death were combinations that nothing could withstand. While the Russians under Gen Hoessel seem to outdone the defenders of Sebastahol. The surrender followed immediately on the capture of some of the main forts. Golden Hill and Liaotashan were still in the possession of the Russians but would ultimately have to yield.

The Russian Gen Hoessel asked for terms, Gen. Nogi who had been empowered to make terms since Nov. appointed a commission. What the terms were is not yet known.

The Japs marched in today.

A snow storm is raging. Getting colder.

Monday, January 9, 1905.   Went down to Hatboro this afternoon to settle the Dr. Reading bill.

Tuesday, January 10, 1905.   Ellis came over and offered us 1500 for the corner lot provided that we would build new of cement pavement along Penn Ave. He says the culvert needs repairs &c. I told him I would see Slifer. Went off to Perkasie to see J. L. Detweiler for money. Got 400. When I came back the boiler was leaking badly. Had to blow off and put in new backing. It took all afternoon and all evening.

Exchanged Mrs. H's original Standard Hay D. stock 20 shares for 52 new shares of Standard Hay Co. 25 each. The old were 50.

Wednesday, January 11, 1905.   Sold the lot at Broad & Penn Ave to Ellis for $1550.00 subject to Slifer's approval. We are to put cement pavements on two sides and fix the culvert which he alleges is out of repair. I asked him whether I might have it published in the paper but he objected to the announcement because the said it would hurt his business.

It got too late for me to go up to the church tonight.

We have now sold 18 lots for a total of 6500, nearly as much as we paid for the land, of course we spent nearly 4000 for improvements. It is time that some of the money should be paid back.

39 years old today.

Thursday, January 12, 1905.   Rainy and slippery.

With Slifer completed the deal about Ellis' lot.

Visited the school for the first time this year or for that matter in all my life. Started with Loux's room and was there two hours. After dinner Hackman's till recess. After recess Miss Kirk's room. It was very interesting to me. Loux is undoubtedly a good teacher. I don't take much stock in their literature. They learn a lot of data but the question is does it make lovers of good literature. I don't think much of Hackman's teaching though he has some poor material to work on. Miss Kirk I think is very good in her place. She knows how to manage. Mary cried when she thought I wasn't coming. Hackman hasn't enough language to explain even what he knows. Then I don't think he reads as Loux said he advised him to read to overcome his deficiencies.

Saturday, January 14, 1905.   Rec'd a letter this morning from Mrs. Robert's daughter Grace saying that she died last Sunday evening. She had been suffering from Bronchitis ever since she was here and she seemed to be getting gradually weaker though this fall she had been better except her cough. This evening tried to get someone to run for council. Ellis wants Jonas.

Sunday, January 15, 1905.   Went to church this afternoon and evening. We had two good sermons and a slim attendance. Mr. & Mrs. Slifer were at church this evening. The offering was for the orphans. It was $3 or 4.00 less than last year.

Robby Luskerbill was down on a visit this afternoon.

We looked over books. He was amused at the definition of a passive verb which said "a passive verb is one which betokeneth suffering"; as I am loved. This he showed to Dan.

Thursday, January 19, 1905.   There was an attempt to assasinate the Czar of Russia while he was blessing the Waters of the Neva by loading a cannon with grape shot and firing it through the little chapel on the ice and the windows of the Winter Palace instead of firing a salute as was intended. A policeman was killed but the Czar and his family was unhurt. There is a great strike going on in St. Petersburg and on Sunday they want to petition the Czar to address their grievances..

Saturday, January 21, 1905.   Ellis and some of us have been planning to have a reform in the council and in the school board. I proposed Dan Zeigler for school director and then Ellis asked him for Councils. It seems very difficult to get any one or the right kind. I went to see Wolford the other night if he would be willing to take the nomination He, I think, will not refuse. I don't think the Democrats will nominate him and the Republicans will have to do it.

Sunday, January 22, 1905.   Went to S.S. this afternoon and after S.S. Cal's came with their baby named Irwin, with Grace and little Paul.

Went to church tonight with Cal early as Ellis sent word he couldn't go.

Luckenbill had a good sermon but not as good as last Sunday.

Dan was in the city and said there was fighting in St. Petersburg today 150 being killed.

Old Mr. Franconi is dead.

Monday, January 23, 1905.   The strikers in St. Petersburg in their effort to reach the Winter Palace to petition the Czar were stopped by bullets. They were lead on by a priest Gopin who strange to say was unhurt though hundreds around him fell. Some papers think that as high as 2100 were killed and 5000 wounded. The Ledger had only 250 killed.

It is hard to say just what happened. What would have happened had the mob been armed is easy to guess. As it was the slaughter was all one sided.

A few soldiers refused to fire on the mob and but nearly all obeyed. The Czar had left the Palaze.

If the soldiers are true to the Czar I do not see that the insurrection is over.

Tuesday, January 24, 1905.   It now appears that the authorities tried to drown the discontent of the working classes in blood.

It appears that the whole empire is excited and that a similar strike is proceeding in Moscow. Meanwhile the Czar is in hiding at Czarskov Selo.

The Revolutionists are active and the revolt seemed to be spreading. Hope liberty will win.

Went to J H M's tonight but he refuses to run for council.

This forenoon Ellis and went to O. Sam Hunsberger for advice. He will be with us.

Went over to see him again tonight on acc't of J B Delp. Wolford we will try to put on and it is said the other side has Ed Alderfer.

Wednesday, January 25, 1905.   The snow storm which started last night became a blizzard this morning. It had drifted so that roads almost impassible. Milt and I had intended to go to Franconi's funeral but I concluded I wasn't nearly enough related to risk going. It was hard work going out with the snow driving in your face. It snowed furiously all day. There was no school. The trolleys soon stopped running. Only part of our men were present and in the afternoon only five were here. We stopped at 3 o'clock as we thought it would not do to be out when dark. Franconi's funeral was postponed as they couldn't get through. There was a funeral here at the meeting house attended by 14 persons, a sister of old Benj Kruph. It got colder and is near zero tonight and blowing tonight.

I don't remember seeing so much snow at one time. It seems to me there must be 18 inches.

Thursday, January 26, 1905.   Last night there was a fierce wind and the cold this morning was down to zero. The sun shone brightly all day. Everybody had his share of shovelling to do and Chestnut St. looks picturesque. In some places you can not see the road as you walk along notably in Wm. Souder's field. Where the banks are thrown up 7 or 8 ft. on Main St. the trolleys have plowed a lane through and all other Trans. had to pass through the same and watch the trolley's. In front of Landis' store the pavement was clear. It was not till this afternoon that the 4 trains stuck below Rosenberger's were released. The south bound track was in use all day and late this afternoon the snow plow went through clearing to the last track. Only 5 of our men turned out today and they were all out clearing snow except for Watts. who was to fix the engine but found one of Han's mistakes and had to ship the crank to Lansdale to get a bolt out. Milt's have a little boy. He was born just a little before dinner.

Gave Katie a picture for a present. She reminded me of my neglect.

Saturday, January 28, 1905.   We were unmercifully beaten at the primaries tonight. I had been running around all week trying to help gather force for the forming a ticket. My especial care was the school and Ellis' Councils. When I picked Dan Zeigler Ellis went and asked him for councils. This afternoon I asked Elavon to nominate Wolford and Charly Hunsberger was agreed on to nominate either J.B. Delp or Hen. Detweiler. Christ Moyer nominated Mahlon Derstine for councils. This was our ticket. The other side had Ed Alderfer, J.B. Delp, councils. Dr. Souder & Chris Alderfer for school directors. Mike Bergey wanted to shut Wolford out because he was a Democrat saying it was against the rules of the party and calling on the chairman to strike off the name. But Frank Moyer didn't have the nerve to do that and so I made a motion to proceed with the voting. They scraped the hotel people and all together and beat us. Ed Alderfer leading with 95 Delp 77 or so Derstine 55 Zeigler 53.

Wolford got 39 and Detweiler 49. They preferred the changeable Alderfer to Wolford. Of course we folks did not feel good.

Sunday, January 29, 1905. I am pretty certain that Christ Moyer and his people did not vote for Wolford last evening. I can't forgive that. They relied on our support for Derstine and then took advantage. Wolford is to be punished for his vote last summer.

Hager's child was buried today. There was no church this afternoon. Spoke to Dan Lukenbill about the Democratic primaries. He went down to see Andrew Benner and they are going to try and put Wolford on the ticket.

Went in to Ellis a little after Sunday School. He had been reading last days of Pompei and is much interested therein.

Monday, January 30, 1905. The Democrats will have their primaries tonight and Andrew Benner thinks they will nominate Wolford. He says Gerhart's influence amounts to very little. I am glad if this is so. This morning I stopped in to see Wolford. He seems to be very grateful for whatever was done. Talked to Noah Kramer and got him interested. Went to Ambler to measure up for Wainscoting Railing &c.

When I came back Fred Souder was here and set a block of his cement on the shelf before our door. He is enthusiastic over his cement blocks.

Noah Kramer told me that Gerhart planned to put Wolford on the ticket for Councils so he could not be used for school director. I went and told him and he said he would see to it that his name would not get on that ticket that way.

Ellis is much disappointed. He thinks there is no hope of doing anything. That he cannot be nominated by the Democrats and that he will be defeated. He thinks nothing can be accomplished by running an independent ticket &c. I did not agree with him.

Tuesday, January 31, 1905. The Democrats nominated Wolford by 30 votes to 7 for Pierce Woeman. Gerhart's total strength. Gerhart was completely floored. I came up to the store this morning Dr. Oberholtzer Wm. Souder and J. M. Landis being there. Gerhart came in and Ellis went for him for making an agreement with Mike. Gerhart hated it but he couldn't defend himself. Noah Kramer told me that they circulated the story that we wanted to throw out Loux and put in Lucinda Lukenbill. The Democrats also put on H. Dietz

D. Yerger and Will Nase for Council. Jacob Allem was also nominated for school board. This evening I stopped in with Ellis at the Hardware store. I found the Zendt boys and Milt in there too. I found the idea prevailed that Wolford and I were engaged in a fight to oust Loux for revenge.

It makes one almost desperate to think how one is misconceived. I told them then that I knew. I was regarded as mean and revengeful but that I wished I could throw on a canvas to these people a picture of what I could and would do if I had been revengeful or mean or any of the other wiseness.

Wednesday, February 1, 1905.   A little snow fell this evening. Was up at Horace Shellenbergers this evening where Mr. Luckenbill was teaching Roy and the girls German. No one else was there. We went over the lesson after Roy and the girls had left.

We discussed the political situation. Poor Horace Shellenberger is in a dilemma. He is told to support Will Nase J B Delp and Ed Alderfer and to offset Wolford and he didn't see why he should. I told him support the whole Democratic ticket if he thought it was a good one as it wasn't the Democrats but the Republicans who would decide the fight.

Was at Goettler's this afternoon and handed him a paper to be published.

Thursday, February 2, 1905.   David R. Stover an uncle of Elwood's was here today stopping with father overnight. He is a great talker. Talks about religion mostly. Your Stover is generally an extremist either the one way or the other. Elwood says he can't make him out. He talks religion to him every opportunity he has and Elwood gives him no satisfaction.

Friday, February 3, 1905.   This school fight is going to be a hot one this time. Everybody seems to be determined. I hear that Mary Alderfer is on Wolford's side. Milt came over this afternoon with a proposition to divide the town among workers. He had been to see Ellis about. I think this is the right thing to do. Spoke with Elwood and he suggested the same thing. It comes in line with Wm. Souder's plan to organize a non-partisan league for taking an interest in town politics. I put a little piece in the paper signed "One of the Rickers". Someone else suggested that the school director should read "Tilly the Mennonite Maid". It was evidently a stab at Loux.

Went in to see Menno today. He had been a very sick boy and I hadn't known it.

Thursday, February 9, 1905.   Two communications in the Independent this week. One by Elwood reproving the writer of last week for giving a stab at Loux. The other by myself in Penna. Dutch I thought we could keep the people stirred up a little and not forget what was going on.

Monday, Febraury 13, 1905.   Met this evening in Ellis' office with Milt, Goettler, Elwood, H. Detweiler, Adam Crouthamel. Ellis found the registry list and the town was divided among those we thought we could do the most good.

We decided to vote for Derstine and Yerger for council and Wolford and Allem for school directors.

There are 423 names on the voter's list and quite a number of names I had never heard. Young Goettler told me he was going to see Loux this evening and was going to tell him to keep his hands off the town.

Tuesday, February 14, 1905.   Was with Ellis and the two Goettlers this evening. We went over the names that we were doubtful about who to send and among which were those we didn't know. There were 38 on the list. Young Goettler told me that his visit to Loux was a success. That he thanked him for coming. That he said he has nothing against Ben Wolford and that he is suspicious of me. That he believes I want to get him out of there by fair means or foul. Goettler told him if he did what was right I would be the first to try and raise his wages.

Wednesday, February 15, 1905.   Met with Andrew Benner tonight at Ellis'. He seemed a little dubious at first but when he found that we were pretty well organized he thought the work could be done. He promised for himself and Yeager to do what he could to turn the Democrats to Derstine and get them to cut Nace.

Thursday, February 16, 1905.   Goettler's paper came out very moderate. I think he felt he might do more harm than good. There were two communications one in some kind of rhyme giving the politicians a hit. The other was by Mrs. H. in her usual style.

Friday, February 17, 1905.   Went to see Wolford about supporting Derstine. Bill Freed came in at this time to see us about getting a lot of 325 specimens of commercial products free from the commercial museums provided we could furnish a suitable case to put them in. We were both in favor.

Told Chris Moyer I was trying to get Wolford to support Derstine. He asked me in surprise, Do you think Wolford would vote for a Republican? In the evening I went to Wolford and he authorized me to say that he would do all he could for Derstine. Went and told Milt at once. Was over to see old Sam this evening. He is all right. He said that a vote for the old order is a vote of approval and that of course he can't give them.

Saturday, February 18, 1905.   Was up to see Elwood today. Went up to Jerry Alderfer's this evening. He is all right. He thinks he can get the Kratz's and will speak to others M. S. Landis & c. From there went off to Morris Landis. Threshed out the whole story and left him favorably impressed. He showed me his heater which is superior to mine in that no dust can come in. I think he gets more heat up than I do. Met Morris D. Zendt and he is all right for Wolford. Tackled Sam Sell and he is all right for Wolford.

Monday, February 20, 1905. Pierce Worman's baby died. This I think is the 4th child they bury. Finished up a hard day's work. Saw old Sam but he is unable to see how Christians can mix in these matters. Was with Freddie Hasky and he is all right. Was with Slifer who is to take care of Henry Moyer. Saw Jacob Landis uptown. Went in to see John M. Morgan on this forenoon and told him plainly we wanted help for Wolford in return for the favors we were giving to Derstine. We discussed the Loux matter and he said they had the idea that Luckenbill had influenced Wolford and me. I told him I would rather be influenced by Luckenbill than by W. H. Freed. This evening the whole set got together in the store and made reports. We hope we have the gang whipped. At least very discouraged. It looks very favorable. Met at Landis & Co. late. Jerry Alderfer proposed Harry Kratz for watcher. He also promised

Tuesday, February 21, 1905. Went down to Binder's this morning and convinced him that it was his duty to come to vote. Promised to send tram. After dinner to John Clymer who was almost angry at first supposing that I was against Derstine. He had an idea Freed was supportive of Derstine. Finally induced him to come. Had sleigh to fetch Binder, J. Derstine, and old Mr. Goettler. We had Harry Kratz there checking off the votes. The voters came out slow at first and I was afraid people were not taking the interest they should, but late in the afternoon they kept coming faster and when the polls closed 326 votes were polled. There are 423 in all. I expected 350 to come. After it was over we went to Landis & Co. where we went over the list and tried to make an estimate. We found it was very close in everything except Yerger I was sure was elected. We waited. Goettler going out for the news. There were present Ellis, Jonas Landis, Milt Moyer, Penrose Zendt, Harry Kratz Sr., Cal, Wm. Souder. It was about 12 o'clock when Goettler rushed in breathlessly saying there was bad luck but we had licked the whole business. Yerger and Nace were tied. The election board decided the matter by lot and Nace took office.

Wednesday, February 22, 1905. Went in and congratulated Wolford this morning. Horace Heller said Loux was down and was the first one to announce the result in the fire co.s room. He mentioned Wolford and Allem first. Where ever I went people saw I was pleased and others seemed pleased too. Mahlon Derstine was waiting for me to see about some sash. Milt came after and said didn't the Democrats turn out for you? I told you they would. Davy Yerger naturally is sore. Old Dan Kratz didn't come home to vote. Geo. Kratz was too stubborn to do anything on account of some grudge.

We people (our side) certainly gave the winning votes for every candidate. I know I turned in 7 for Nace myself. I know the Moyer people voted for Alderfer where they should have voted Yerger. The neatest part of all was the rebuke Gerhart got for trying to down Horace Shellenberger. Their people really tried to have Jonas Greaser elected inspector instead of Shellenberger. Goettler found it out and was turned in for Shellenberger making him majority inspector. They defeated Willis for assessor. Was up to Luckenbill this evening.

Thursday, February 23, 1905.   Goettler said little except to claim a vindication of his stand last summer. Were in L&Co's office when we talked it over. Goettler, Penrose, Elwood, Ellis, Jonas Landis were there. They reported that the other side was very much in distress It appears that they expected to win easy. Harvey Souder reproached Hen. Freed for not minding his business. Hen said he was completely beaten that was all. Morris Zendt is so much put out about it. He thought everyone should resign. He says the borough cannot buy any more stone from Prg. Realty Co. &c. He got ten votes for constable.

Went down to Edgewater Park, NJ with Delp this afternoon to take some measurements. Was at Worman's funeral this forenoon.

Friday, February 24, 1905.   It is hard to get down to work again. This being a politician is exciting if there is opposition, but it is somewhat de-moralizing too. You enjoy immensely the stories of the discomfiture of the other side. We resolved not to show any elation on getting the news Tuesday night. I suppose we do not in public but when we get together there is always something to say. This takes the time from your work. Ellis had a talk with Freed. He congratulated Ellis and asked him what he had against the Prg. Co. Ellis told him about stone and they argued for a while but did not get it finished. Heard that some wonder whether I [illegible] to take Mike's place now but another thought I didn't have that disposition.

Saturday, February 25, 1905.   Didn't get over my election fever until today. I wasn't any good for any work for quite a while.

Tuesday, February 28, 1905.   Was in the city this afternoon and took off one job. The work seems to be coming in now and bidding is lively. Wanamaker's building is up about eight stories all granite. I thought they would be using bricks.

Saw Ellis' floor plans made by Elwood. He didn't have Martin's plan with him and I hadn't seen it yet.

Bo't Ely and Gloucester Cathedral and Forster's Life of Dickens at Leary's today. Had a talk with John S. Ruth and introduced him to Dan Luckenbill on the way home. This evening Yerger came into Ellis office and reported there seemed to be no chance for him unless he made a fight. We were very glad to hear this as the fuss will now have a chance to subside.

Wednesday, March 1, 1905.   Went to see Dr. Oberholtzer about Water Rent and to Bldg. Association from there and then up to Luckenbill's.

Thursday, March 2, 1905.   Was in the city this afternoon and took off two jobs.

Dan Zeigler's came out this evening and we had a very pleasant evening together. The two girls Anna and Edna are jumbos compared to ours. Edna is only a little over three and is taller than our Henry.

Ellis showed me Martin's plan for his house. I don't think it is so awful as they made it. I would have some changes made but on the whole I think it looks well. Some of the interior arrangement ought to be changed.

Met Oswin Kline on Arch St. this afternoon. He has eight children living and says his wife died from heart disease. I pitied the poor man. She used to be Maria Roudenbush.

Friday, March 3, 1905.   The weather today is beautiful. The sun shining so clearly makes some impression on the snow. There were some sleighs left the last few days and indeed I saw a few today but around here I should say it didn't pay to use them. Jake Delp says over in Jersey there is no snow left. If it were all over like it is on Chestnut St. there would fair sledding.

The Russians and Japanese have been in battle all week over a line 100 miles long and the indications are that the Japanese are getting the best of it and that the Russians as heretofore will have to fall back.

Mary came home at noon with a sore throat. I hope it will be nothing worse.

Saturday, March 4, 1905.   This morning it is snowing furiously and Roosevelt is likely to have a disagreeable inauguration day. They have so often talked of changing the date till Apr. 30 but it never comes to any head.

The snow ceased about noon after it had snowed about four inches. They had no bad weather in Washington and everything went off fine there. This was said to be the 42nd snow this winter.

Roosevelt's inaugural address was quite short but full of meaning as is everything he says.

This evening D. Yerger got a letter from Donnehower stating that he could make a contest for the seat in council and he says he is going to do so. I had hoped that this was the last of it but it seems not.

Sunday, March 5, 1905.   Went to S. S. and to church in the evening. Clear but cold. Betsy Souder was with us for dinner and said there was a fire near Lansdale this morning. This evening I heard the fire was Fred Souder's hay barns and cement sheds at Lansdale. The feed store was also damaged. Fred seemed to be in hard luck. Ellis was down this afternoon he said.

Monday, March 6, 1905.   Father was down to Lansdale this morning. Fred thinks it must have been an incendiary as there was no possibility of fire where it started seemingly. He has 3500 insurance.

The Japs are pounding away at the Russians who were unexpectly surprised by Gen. Nogi and his Port Arthur veterans marching on Mukdan. If the Russians are not in retreat they seem to be in danger of being surrounded.

Elwood came over to see if D. Yerger could be induced to let the matter of a contest drop. I went to see Andrew Benner and Elwood. To Ellis and William

S. Ellis went to A. B. Benner again this evening.

This evening meeting of the school board was as fine as silk. Bill Freed was very nice indeed. The collection from the Commercial Museums was accepted. Allum came down thinking his term had commenced. Christ Alderfer wasn't there. I don't know whether he doesn't feel like coming but I was glad since Allum made the mistake.

Tuesday, March 7, 1905. Went to the city this afternoon. There was snow again this afternoon followed by rain. The battle around Mukdan seems now to be going against the Russians. Kuropotkin was going to break through the Japanese lines but has enough to do to hold his communications and it is thought that he will attempt a retreat.

Prof. Hilpreath is in trouble. The papers are full of it. The other men like Rorke, Peters, Haupt are criticizing some statements he made in his book. Dan Luskenbill also goes against him. Clay says he believes he is incapable of making a true statement. &c &c.

Met Dan on the train this evening and he talked all the way on the matter.

Thursday, March 9, 1905. The Russians are giving way at all points and the only question is whether they will be able to get away. They are said to be practically surrounded and it is certain that they cannot all get away. This great battle has already lasted 17 days and it may be sometime before it is finished. If Ogama succeeds in making this a Sedan he will be regarded as the greatest captain of the age. But Kuropotkin is a master of retreats as was shown more than once.

Friday, March 10, 1905. Tonight Ellis informed me of a new complication as to councils. In the eyes of the law the present council is an illegal body. Neither Yerger or Nace is elected. Nace and Alderfer are ineligible having been in the election room and acting as election officers. Derstine was elected but the old councils can hold over but which one is to go out. The old councilmen must resign and the council must elect new ones. Ellis asked me what to do. I told him have a frank talk with Freed and lay the case before him and get him to use his influence to get the others to resign. Ellis thought the same. He was down to see today about the matter.

Saturday, March 11, 1905. This morning the Ledger announced a dispatch from Kuropotkin admitting that he was surrounded. There is a corps of Japanese somewhere that did not take part in the fighting which is supposed to be making efforts to get to the rear of the Russians. If this move succeeds there seems to be no hope for even a part of the army escaping. The Russians are terribly routed. I read Senator Beveridges Russian advance in the light of the present some parts are very amusing. Everyone is interested in the fighting. Even father seems to be reading the paper every morning.

Sunday, March 12, 1905. Went to Sunday School and church this afternoon and again to church this evening. Milts had their baby in church this afternoon. It is now six weeks old.

Mrs. H. went to the River Brethren meeting, of course.

I notice Amy is reading Hame's Hist. of English 2 vol. having read the first. Helen is reading magazines. Both the girls have been at these magazines for a long time so I have decided to lock the bookcase. For they neglect their work and the little ones. Henry and Margaret think they must have them too and the consequence is that they will be worn out soon.

Saturday, March 18, 1905.   The Russians were driven out of Tir Pass and are now being pursued and attacked by the Japanese. Kuropotkin has been dismissed in disgrace and Linevitch takes his place.

We did not get the boiler closed today. There is still a little work to do on Monday morning.

Sunday, March 19, 1905.   There was a warm rain this morning that was just the thing to take the frost out of the ground. It makes the grass look green already and spring will probably be on time this year after all.

You can see a little snow in heaps and along Chest. St. but the country in sight here is bare. However, they say some of the roads up county are still almost impassable with snow.

To Sunday School this afternoon and to church this evening. Harry Groff is said to be very sick.

Thursday, March 23, 1905.   Wolford and I went down to West Point this morning where the Montg. Co. Directors Association met. The subjects discussed were "What is the best method for conducting examinations for graduates." "In the employment of teachers should experience be recognized with additional salary." "Should the Rudiments of agriculture be introduced into our rural school studies." These were well discussed. We took dinner at the hotel. While we were waiting Schaffer came in and we all shook hands with him. Supt. Coughlin of Wilkesbarre spoke in the afternoon followed by Supt. Schaffer who spoke only a few words. Schaffer was to speak in the evening but we did not stay.

Wednesday, March 29, 1905.   The weather has been springlike for several days. I had my shade trees trimmed today. Will have my yard cleaned tomorrow. Slifer started digging sewer yesterday. Rickert had his lot laid out and is digging foundations for his stable. Am not through [illegible] acc't yet. Terms I can't get through. Went to Luckenbill's this evening. There were four present.

Thursday, April 6, 1905.   Heard only today that Hen Godshall had been operated upon for appendicitis at the German Hospital about Tuesday. Old Sam Moyer told me that he was very home sick but this evening Ellis said he better [illegible] and that it was the unexpected that was hard on him. He is still however to remain quiet and do very little talking. I hope he will soon be able to come home.

The consistory met tonight. There is a shortage this year that is hard to understand. We talked the matter over. I thought the school matter might have something to do, also the Lutherans. Morris Zendt thinks that Mr. L. talks too much about education. That he offends people. Decided to issue a circular letter appealing for funds. This thing cannot go on like this.

Saturday, April 8, 1905. Quite a snow storm today for about a half an hour. It came down fast but melted and the ground did not get white. Talked with father over the change in ownership of the factory. I am to have the factory and he all the other property except the Land Co.

Sunday, April 9, 1905. Henry Krupp's were here for dinner.

Menno Clemmer has Scarlet Fever and their little Eva is very sick having got Bright's Disease and Croup. She is not expected to survive.

Menno Moyer died yesterday. [Illegible] was here today to [illegible] the funeral. Was in Church this afternoon and Evening.

Monday, April 10, 1905. The Russian fleet has passed Singapore but the four best vessels in the fleet are missing. It seems that Rojestoensky will try and make a dash for Vladivastok with as many ships as he can and sacrifice the others. It is not known where Togo is.

The mason are nearly after our diggers and I don't see how they are to work tomorrow.

Today they buried little Eva Clemmer who died as a result of Scarlet Fever.

Wednesday, April 12, 1905. Today we did not work. We hired Moyer Bros. big wagons and went to Menno's funeral. There were twenty on the wagon. Joe Derstine's & Grandmom Hemsing and Mrs. Clemens, and old Cass went along.

Penrose went with another tram. Noah Kramer did not go.

It turned out a very nice day. The little meeting house at Delp's burying ground did not hold all the people. Rev. Bergstresser preached. Menno's hair was long and curly. His face looked thin. He was 17 years, 4 months and some days old.

Thursday, April 13, 1905. Some time ago Mike Bergey asked Slifer to bid for carrying the mail to Morwood. He did not want to at first but at last sent in a bid and was successful. This does not suit Mike and he refused to have the contract executed say there was a mistake and that he had to see Wanger. This evening Slifer made a demand for the papers but Mike again refused saying he had sent it to Wanger. Slifer had a letter prepared asking the 2nd ass't. P.M. Gen. what to do. It is interesting to see how it will turn out.

Saturday, April 15, 1905.   The Russian fleet seems to be all together and sailing straight for Formosa where the Japanese are supposed to be. It looks as though there would be a battle any day. If the Russians should win it would be a great disaster for Japan. This Russian fleet is supposed to be stronger in battle ships to the Japanese. Their foolish firing on each other at Hall last fall gave one the idea that they were excited or drunk.

Sunday, April 16, 1905.   Quite a snow again. More than the other Saturday and lasting longer. Some of the leaves of Mrs. Moyer's raspberries were just opening and these caught the snow and it looked exactly as if they were in blossom.

Annie Clemmer is not so well but her mother is better.

Tuesday, April 18, 1905.   I was down to Ambler this afternoon and went to K & M Co. first. Mr. Rise [?] at once started to talk about the poor work we had sent and I was surprised. We went up and looked at it and he said he did not blame us about the Mahogany as the painters had spoiled that and they did. But the office Partition and oak doors were in bad condition and I had to say so. Dr. Mattison came in and said he had always intended that we should do his house when he would change it but now we would receive not preference. He said he told his wife this. I couldn't help feeling hurt. This was the first I heard of it and to be condemned so sternly even though justly was hard.

Wednesday, April 19, 1905.   Slifer now had his contract and Mike is anxious that they should be signed. Slifer showed me the papers this evening. We met Mike on the street and Slifer always greets him with "How are you Mr. Bergey." The masons are nearly through now with the sewer. They have some 20 ft and then about 24 ft. beyond the other side. They won't get through tomorrow but I wish they would.

His men will tomorrow start to dig for planting trees. Then a couple of the yards will have to be graded. And then the digging for the cement curb.

Thursday, April 20, 1905.   Today the last section of the sewer between Franklin and Adams Ave. was completed. The stone man failed to deliver the stone in good time or they would have been able to put in the remaining section to Broad St. on Saturday. But as it is there scarely a load left.

Stokes was up from the city and Taylor was down from Quakertown. I went with him to Lansdale to see Fred. He thinks Hen's job will go ahead.

Delp has decided to bid on Ellis' house after all. I guess he thought he couldn't make capital out of it.

The Bldg. Ass'n are going to build 4 double houses like ours on Second St. Wm. H. Freed had some lots to sell. But the situation is good for the purpose.

Saturday, April 22, 1905.   We had preparatory services tonight. Jonas

Freed was elected Deacon instead of Ellis who goes out. Mr. Luckenbill had a good sermon. Rob't Luckenbill, Jesse Underkoffler, Lillie Schwenk and Alvertan Auchy were confirmed.

Sunday, April 23, 1905.   A beautiful day.

Ed Hollerback came out this morning but I could talk only a little with him as I had to get ready to go to church.

We had communion this morning. About 84 communed. Mr. & Mrs. Wm. Y. Kline became members. Also Theo Haag and Mrs. Curly, nephew & nieces of Mr. Luskenbill.

On my way home found Uriah Souder waiting with his automobile at Main St. with Helen and Mary in the back seats. Ellis and Cal were wondering what he was waiting for but I saw my children. I said it was for me.

Went to S.S. this afternoon and to church tonight. Slim attendance tonight on account of the other churches having their Easter services.

Monday, April 24, 1905.   Lots of people did not work today.

We had our Easter festival tonight. Though it was crowded yet it did not seem to me like the crowds we used to have. The Russians have left Kamrach Bay. The Japanese government complained to France about break of neutrality and the French government at once notified Russia and by order of the Czar the fleet left. Nothing is known of Togo's whereabouts. A battle may now be fought at any time. Everything seems to be waiting on the outcome. Even the armies are doing nothing.

Tuesday, April 25, 1905.   Was in the city today. We are going to get the Knight Bldg. at Ambler. Spery has the contract. At Wanamaker's new store they are turning the arches over the last windows in the front. It is all granite but I notice it contains iron or something for the stone turns yellow.

Wednesday, April 26, 1905.   Today we completed our sewer all the way to Broad St. and I am ever so glad of it. Tomorrow Slifer will get the shade trees for Adams if it does not rain. He is grading the lot being nearly through with Wm. H. Freed's.

Thursday, May 11, 1905.   Tonight Jerry Thomas and his wife were here again and I sold them the lot on Penn Ave. between Highland St. and John Freed's place. In fact, there are 3 lots. I sold the whole for $1000. This leaves us only one full lot on Penn Ave. We have now sold over $7500 of ground. I wish the lots on Franklin Ave would go better. That worries me a little.

The Russian fleet is said to finally have left French Indo China, and their two fleets are said have united. The crisis between France and Japan is still at its height and it is a question whether Japan will not call on England for help. In such a case the war would become something terrible.

Tuesday, May 23, 1905.   Visited the schools for the last time for this term.

Wednesday, May 24, 1905.   Mayor Weaver has dismissed his Directors who are under control of the machine and has thereby struck terror into the machine. One by one councilmen are coming over on the Mayor's side. It has caused great excitement. Went to Mabel Hunsberger's funeral. She died on Friday or Saturday and was 11 years, 4 months old. She was buried at Hillside. She looked like a skeleton.

Thursday, May 25, 1905.   Visisted the school today. Two left out today Miss Kirk's and Miss Weil's. Miss Frey's tomorrow and Hackman's Monday. Loux and Miss Shelley will close a week later.

Had quite a talk with Loux. He would like the cabinet of Physics but I told him I would like it but we had no room and there was not time to teach it. I told him I was disappointed in his opposition to housing the museum collection properly.

Friday, May 26, 1905.   Went down to Lansdale this morning in reference to my appointment as appraiser for Bardo's estate. Came too early as it was to be at 10 and I came at 8. Weber was to help but he didn't turn up so John Detweiler was appointed. We got over the books and machinery. His books consist mostly of bad debts. He owes everybody and has nothing to get.

Went to see Dr. Moyer about Loux. He couldn't recollect and asked Dr. Crouthamel who did but did not care to say much as he wants to move to Souderton. But he told me when I promised not to use his name that he was so drunk at a political meeting last fall that he could scarcely walk.

Saturday, May 27, 1905.   It is said that the Russian Fleet was seen near Shanghai and if this is so they must be headed for the straits of Korea. I am sometimes afraid they have eluded Togo as it looks as though they went east of Formosa and may have fooled him. If not, there will be a battle soon. It is thought by many that Togo's fleet may be much weaker than the Russian and of course if the Rus. should win the whole course of the war would change.

Mr. Wolford and I went to see Mr. Allem about effecting a change in the organization of the board. Mr. Allem seems to be with us so far and will work with us though I don't believe he would have gone against Loux entirely.

Sunday, May 28, 1905.   Very warm today. Was in SS this afternoon and brought Chas. Bergey along home. Went to church this evening where Mr. Frantz a student preached. He is doing well.

Monday, May 29, 1905.   Admiral Rojestoensky's fleet is said to be completely defeated by Togo. 13 ships sunk and seven captured with 2000 prisoners is the report. The battle occurred Saturday and Sunday. They sank 2 battleships, 5 cruisers, 3 destroyers, 2 special service ships, 1 coast Def. armor clad. They captured 3 battleships, 1 destroyer, two coast Def. ships, 1 special service ship.

Was down in Lansdale again to finish Bardo appraisement. Went over the lumber today. His stock consists mostly of trash except the Y.R. of which he has a good stock. Am glad I am over it. They had long list of stuff which didn't amount to anything. I suppose to make it look as though they had a large stock. They are a fraud and his creditors will lose. He didn't worry about that. They have 6 good horses.

Wednesday, May 31, 1905.   It appears that the defeat of the Russian fleet was as complete as possible. Only one small cruiser and a torpedo boat have reached Vladivostok so far. All the rest seem to have been sunk or taken. Admiral Rojestoensky and Nebatagoff were captured, the former being wounded. The Japs have battleships Orel and Nicholas I and 3 or 4 cruisers in port. Yet it is said the Czar is for the war to go on. If that is the case it is probable that he does not dare give his people a chance to think about their own matters and fear revolution. But revolution is bound to come, it seems to me.

The gang has completely surrendered to Mayor Weaver and are pleading for mercy. This ought to be given but the fight carried on until the whole city government is cleaned out.

Thursday, June 1, 1905.   Had the children's hair cut today. Now Mary and Margaret both have short hair and I think it improves their looks. We put the hair away.

We kept this (Ascension Day) as another holiday in the same week. Went down to Leidy's this afternoon to fix the graves and on the way back had quite a talk with Milt Leidy. He says there is considerable dissatisfaction with Luckenbill though not open out. Leidy said that everyone was wondering that things went so slowly at Souderton. He says Telford has sent a petition to Classis for a separate charge and that Tohickon and Bridgton also want to unite. In that case there is going to be a break up in our charge.

Friday, June 2, 1905.   Was in Norristown this afternoon to finish the Bardo appraisement. Bardo's creditors had a meeting and he was over there looking not a bit worried. He said he looked on the sunny side of things &c.

Am gathering quite a lot of work in just now. Got the four double homes on 2nd St., a house in Lansdale. Snyder from Delp and another in North Wales from Detweiler all this week. Then Kindig and McReam last week &c.

A stab at Loux appeared in the Independent this week again. I wish the thing was over. Landis examined the classes today. W. H. Freed was at the school I believe. Mrs. Moyer wanted to go and asked if I would go but it wasn't possible. Amy came out first as usual with 93.4 average. She has 100 in Literature and [illegible]. 99 in History. 93 in Geogr., 92 in Physiology, 95 Grammar and Spelling 98. I think she drops most of their [illegible]. Helen is third with 89. She was poor in Physiology. History 84 Geography 85 all the other subjects she had 90 and over.

Sunday, June 4, 1905. Went to SS and church this afternoon. Rev. Horn preached both this afternoon and evening.

I wonder where Luckenbill has been these two Sundays. Milt Leidy says he is preaching a trial sermon somewhere though he said this was in strict confidence.

Classis meets the coming week and it would be interesting to go. We discussed the situation after church and I asked the question what would we do in case Indian Creek would go alone? Would we unite with Leidy's? Ellis said we would go it alone. I don't know whether this would be best or not. I think our church ought to use that as our burying ground.

Monday, June 5, 1905. Work is coming in on us at a great rate. Last week I got about 4600 worth and this morning two jobs making 1200 making over 10,000 worth in all.

This week's meeting of the school board lasted until after one o'clock. The old board meeting consumed a long time in settling up old matters so it was toward ten o'clock when the new board opened. When Freed was nominated I asked for yea's and nay's and the vote stood tie. Then I said I preferred to give my reasons in private and had a resolution to offer asking for private sessions. All voting to be done publicly. This found favor and was passed. Then we held a private session in which I told them that Loux had not been doing right and that we demanded a new president to keep him straight. After a long deliberation and after offering the chair to everyone and being refused, I had to take it. We then elected Mr. Loux. Reelected the old teachers except Miss Weil and Mr. Hackman and elected Sallie Barndt in Miss Weil's place. The German school and the assistant principal being left open.

Wednesday, June 7, 1905. Was up to Sellersville tonight with Cal. to hear Dr. Hay our missionary to China. I was surprised as the small audience. That is I expected the building would be full. But it goes to show that our people really care very little about missions. They care mostly for themselves. To have nice churches &c. I like a beautiful church too, but not at the expense of every benevolent undertaking.

Dr Hay told of what had been accomplished in Japan first. He says the Gospel of Christ has taken a firm hold on Japan and that if the missionaries would go away the work would continue. And he is of opinion that in time to come Japan would put us to shame in loyalty to Christ. But poor poor China. Rich in resources but poor in its religion, its government, its morality & superstition.

Thursday, June 8, 1905. The Russian emperor is willing to know what terms the Japs have to offer for Peace. This may or may not be the beginning of peace.

Stopped in to see Goettler yesterday about the Monday evening meeting. He seemed to think it was a great triumph for Loux but I told him he was in a tighter place now than ever before. He must reform or quit. Was in to see Wolford Tuesday morning. He seemed to feel very well. When I passed Strasser he commenced to talk about the matter and said that this was just what they had been trying to do all along. He said he would speak to Loux and if he didn't do better now he should be thrown out. That he would vote against him and that if he wasn't in councils we should throw him out. That he had chances enough now. I hear that some of our friends are not satisfied. They seem to think we have the power and ought to have used it. But they will have to admit later, I think, that they were wrong.

Sunday, June 25, 1905.   Harry Hargrove came in just before I was ready to go to SS. Took him along and kept him for supper and church. Harry is the same old fellow, gentlemanly. As we were sitting on father's porch Henry Hair and Chas. Gerhart passed by and returned when they saw me and wanted me to go to Enos Moyer with them. They said it was about the church matter. I told them it was all talk but they said that Mr. L had an opportunity to go to 2 or 3 places and that Indian Creek would like to hold him.

Wednesday, June 28, 1905.   Received a letter from Dan Luckenbill. Was surprised and thought at first it had a cent stamp and contained advertising matter. He described his sea voyage and his first impression of Germany. He said you can't get rid of the smell of beer as long as you are in Germany.

Thursday, June 29, 1905.   The carpenters started work on the new porch.

Consistory met tonight. Mr. Luckenbill was present and we had an interchange of views. Mr. L. feels much hurt as so many people are gossiping and he, it seems, has several chances to go elsewhere. We told him we did not want him to go but someday we would expect to go it alone. We had told him before and he said this is right. After the meeting he felt better and I think expects to stay. He really does not wish to leave as he says it would mean the breaking up of his family. Here he could have Dan at home and also Rob. Lucinda was married this afternoon to Dr. Hottenstein.

Sunday, July 2, 1905.   Tonight Mr. Luckenbill made some reference to the trouble by saying he did not know how long he would stay. We thought he was settled but he said someone had told him that he did not preach sharp enough. And yet he said others said he preached too sharp and he said he intended to preach as Christ would have him.

Monday, July 3, 1905.   Mr. L came down this morning and told me Wm. K. Shellenberger had asked him to resign. I told him he shouldn't do it at the request of such a man as Shellenberger. But he said he couldn't stand these things forever. He said he doesn't wish to be driven out. He said he wants everything kept quiet and will stand for an election up country. I am sorry things have come to this.

This afternoon I went to buy tickets for fathers'. They cost $63.20 each and are good to Denver till Oct. 31.

Tuesday, July 4, 1905.   Did not work at the shop but Cassel worked and finished the cement pavements. The carpenters worked on the porch on Adams Ave. and I am beginning to see what it looks like. I am pleased with it so far.

Father, Mrs. H. and Emma were out for supper. They are going away tomorrow at noon. The fireworks tonight did not amount to very much.

The Russians are in a bad way. They have at last appointed a peace commission to meet Aug. 1. But the whole empire is in disorder. The rebels have the battleship Potemkin while the whole fleet is interned for fear of further meeting. There were troubles of this kind at Cranstadt and the Black Sea fleet was to put down the rebels but it seemed nothing could be done.

Wednesday, July 5, 1905.   Today our folks started for the west by way of Niagara Falls. They expect to go to Cambridge, Nebraska and from there to Colorado. I expect they will stay 6 weeks or so. They left on the 11:45 train.

Tuesday, July 18, 1905.   Elwood told me this morning that Loux was on a fishing trip and both he and John Allem were drunk. He says Jerry Alderfer had seen them. I went up to Jerry this evening and he told me it was so and also that he would testify to this before the board. He induced Price to take a drink he says. He says Aaron Moyer also saw him.

Friday, July 21, 1905.   Got Hen. Godshall to see Aaron Moyer about the fishing trip. Moyer told Hen. that they were drunk. This settles the matter. I am satisfied now that it is true.

Saturday, July 22, 1905.   Saw all the directors during the week. Wm. Freed was away all week.

Called Loux up on the phone and told him I wanted to see him. We met at the school and I asked him to resign. This he said he wouldn't do as it would be an admission of guilt. I told him in that case he would have to have a hearing. He said a hearing would ruin him. He said that Aaron Moyer would testify that he was sober. He told me he had four drinks and a pocketful of cigars all day. He offered to sign a paper that he would resign if he was caught taking more than a soft drink.

Tuesday, July 25, 1905.   Went over to Dublin tonight with Hen. Godshall to see Milt Stover, but he knew nothing. We had a nice drive.

Friday, July 28, 1905.   Saw Benner Simmons this evening asking him to come and testify to what he saw at Franconia Square but he said he believed we were right but he did not like to interfere as it would cause enmity in his family. He told me some valuable things however.

Saturday, July 29, 1905.   Hen Godshall and I went over the fishing route this evening. We went to Franconia Square where we found a very disconnected story but found that they were there at 11 o'clock. They had first forgotten their fish and started to drive toward Souderton. At Morwood they seem to have been about 6 or thereabouts. At Salfordville they were about 5 o'clock &c. We did not go as far as Salford Station as we were told they had a row over there and as we were told they were sober here we went home.

Wednesday, August 9, 1905.   The Japanese Russian Peace Commission met at Portsmouth yesterday or today forget which. It is to be hoped that an agreement can be reached. M. Witte, Baron Riser are the Russians and Noinister [?] Takahira and Burm [?] Kamura are the Jap commissioners.

Monday, August 14, 1905.   Today I got a new camera and took a few lessons from Dan Zeigler in focusing and timing pictures. He took one and I took three. They were all successful and one photo I took of Dan himself made him say that I had a very good camera. I am glad this is so because I would like to take a picture of some work we do to preserve it for reference.

Tuesday, August 15, 1905.   Am sorry but some of the most interesting things have happened in the last two months which I have not put down. I have not been as well as usual and my nerves have been on a tension. This Loux business. This Luckenbill excitement in addition to my regular business seems to be responsible. Mr. Dan Sperry is also in the same condition. Leidy Heckly is said to be in bad shape. Here Ellis has been very sick with catarrhal appendicitis but I know he was very nervous.

Wednesday, August 16, 1905.   Herman Godshall died between 1 & 2.

We expect our folks back today but it seems that they are not quite ready. Wolford and I were down to see the Co. Sup't today about the Loux matter. I was told he wouldn't say anything but he tells me he will. I was told to notify Loux that I had laid the facts before Sup't Landis and that he (Loux) would probably hear from him inside of a week.

Went from Norristown to Ambler where I measured up the Knight Bldg. and also took off an estimate for Bartleson. When I came home I found old Herman had died and that our folks had not come home as I expected. Wrote to Loux and put letter in drop box.

Thursday, August 17, 1905.   Our folks returned home at three o'clock this afternoon. Father was well and grandmom has a little cold. They seem to have enjoyed themselves but were glad to get home. Father came over to the shop about 5:30. I was almost surprised. I helped carry down his trunk. We picked corn and Elderberries when he came. We pulled out a couple of Potato stalks and found potatoes just beginning to grow. They brought a couple of SaltCellars silver from Niagara Falls. A nickle watch and knife for Henry and souvenirs for me and the girls. I am glad they are back.

Saturday, August 26, 1905.   President Roosevelt's appeals to the Czar have resulted in that poor man declaring that they will not pay indemnity in any form however disguised. He is willing to divide Saghalin.

It is strange to me that these Russians can never realize their position. And it seemed to me I would not have the patience to go on with them.

In Manchuria they would stand no chance it is thought against Ogama. It would cost untold suffering such another battle between the greatest armies ever confronting each other. But it seems they do not care.

Monday, August 28, 1905.   Yesterday Takahira visited Mr. Witte proposing that the meeting of the peace conference meeting for today be postponed till tomorrow. Witte accepted.

This evenings papers stated that the elder statesmen were holding a meeting in Tokio with the Emperor.

Schools started today. Was at the schoolhouse this morning with Wolford. Loux was not very cordial.

Tuesday, August 29, 1905.   The meeting yesterday of the Elder statemen with the Mikado and the statements that new propositions will be offered makes me believe that the Japs will offer such terms that the Russians will not dare to refuse. I told this to Oscar and again to Jennie. Yet the papers all seem to believe that the conference will break up and that peace is impossible and really the Russians don't deserve it. If it wasn't for the poor fellows who have to suffer — I would say they ought to have another licking.

Wednesday, August 30, 1905.   Was in the city today. Took off some plans and measured up Clark's cottages. Bought 10 vols. Froades History of England for 1.00. They are in fine condition. Only two volumes missing and that doesn't so much matter as it is partial any how.

Well there is peace at last. Japan did the surprising thing waived an indemnity. It is called a great victory for Russia, the only one she got. It is true she doesn't have to pay 600,000,000 but Japan gains everything she fought for and more. It is said some of the Japs wept but they will think better of it. They have acted as a Christian nation should and not as the Christian nations do. Pres. Roosevelt gets the greatest amount of credit out of it. He is hailed as the Pacificator and in fact I believe peace would have been impossible but for him.

Thursday, August 31, 1905.   Met Ed Danley with Horace this evening. He is in poor health. He says he will see me tomorrow. He hasn't done any work since March. He says his family is well. Has two children now. George and a little girl 1½ years old.

Went to meeting tonight. A man by the name of John Blosser from Ohio preached. Has powerful voice and fluent but speaks too fast.

Friday, September 1, 1905.   Ed Danley came home with me tonight and stayed all night. He has been sick and he is taking time to see all his friends.

Saturday, September 2, 1905.   Ed had telegraphed for his camera but it rained all morning. After dinner we took a few pictures but it was too dark for satisfactory work.

He went down to Hatfield with me later in the afternoon where I measured up Jonas Ott's house. We took a long walk through Hatfield though it rained more or less.

Sunday, September 3, 1905.   Ed left about nine o'clock to go Lansdale to church. His boy George is now 18 years old and he has a little girl named Ruth 1½ years old.

He told me the first night I saw him that he would lay down a thousand dollars to have a pair of twins.

Attendance at church this evening was very good, there being no other services in town.

Monday, September 4, 1905.   School Board meeting tonight. The man with the Physical cabinet was here again, but we told him it was decided. Miss Shelly complained this morning about the size of her school and also about buying supplies. The supplies were granted and a rule made to exclude children not six before Dec. until January. Those becoming six during the remainer of the term to be admitted in January.

We had contracts with all the teachers except Loux and with him we said there was no use making a contract as the other directors would not back it up. They said he would have to behave from now on &c and when Freed said he believed the town would vote for Loux I told him they had last Spring. That Wolford was elected in spite of great odds. The politicians &c all fought him. This made them angry again but I couldn't help it. I told them I didn't blame Loux I blamed the Board.

Tuesday, September 5, 1905.   It is said the Peace Treaty is to be signed at three o'clock this afternoon. That ends at last the most disastrous war of modern times.

This morning the cementers came. I had three men to dig and three or four in Cassel's gang. They made the gutter at Broad and Franklin and started a good stretch at the lower corner. I expect them to do a good bit tomorrow. Was at Herman Godshall's sale yesterday. Jennie bought a lot of things amounting to $5.32. Cornelius Hunsberger bought the property for $3035. I guess that means he will move down here with his jewerly business. Some think that Harry Hunsicker wants the property up town. It is said a book publishing firm will be located up town.

Monday, September 11, 1905.   There was about 25 feet of cement pavement left that we attempted to lay this morning at the corner of Broad and Franklin in front of Rickert's house. It rained too soon and we covered it up getting wet during the process.

Tuesday, September 12, 1905.   With considerable trouble the pavement was finished looking tolerably well. They put down part of the gutters today. The other set are about finished with their curbing. After that we will have some digging and filling to do and then it will all be done except the sewer part which they have also promised in a week or so.

I heard this morning Jake Frederick was in trouble having been arrested for embezzlement. Loux and Dr. Vaughn are said to have been his advisers. According to what Dr. Oberholtzer tells me it is a bad enough case. He took money from people after allowing their policies to lapse. Dr. Vaughn did much of his doctoring and they drew out the cases as long as possible. Loux has now lost two half days on account of these things. Perhaps this last half day was for another purpose.

Wednesday, September 13, 1905.   All the cementing except that over the sewer is complete except a little gutter at the corner of Adams Ave. and Broad. I am very glad this is so. I saw Hetrick who is to do the mason work and he said he would do it in about a week.

The battleship Mikasa, Togo's flagship, caught fire yesterday or the day before and blew up in Sasrbo [?] harbor with a loss of 599 men. This is a tragic end to a famous vessel, one of the most powerful afloat. It is strange this should happen after the war is over. What might have happened if such an accident had occurred during the war is hard to know.

Was at Joe Derstine's tonight. Things are looking well there. Uncle Joe and Clement had already gone to bed.

Thursday, September 14, 1905.   We are getting to be very busy at the shop and I fear are running behind. I will have to spend all my time at the shop now if I can. I am glad things are in such shape that I will be able to give my whole attention to the shop.

Ellis' house is rough coated and we have done very little with the finish. We are keeping the other jobs under way but there will be trouble. This is too much.

Saturday, September 16, 1905.   Saw Ed and Katie who came back from Indianapolis last week. Katie says she enjoyed her trip very much though she said it cost a barrel of money. Ed had a plant to measure up and make plans of same which took him something like six weeks.

Saw Fred Bowers the other day who came back from Germany the other week. He said he often thought of me when he was looking at the fine buildings.

Sunday, September 17, 1905.   Cut off my moustache this morning. Jennie and the children all thought I looked very strange. Margaret looked in surprise but the baby didn't know me. He looked and when I approached him he turned from me and hid his face. He was always very ready to come to me but this time he shrank back in fear. When I spoke to him he recognized me and allowed me to take him up, but put his hand where my moustache had been. When I went out everyone had to laugh because I looked so strange. Mr. Luckenbill had done the same thing and walked up to SS with me. He had just heard from Dan who will have to come home by way of Paris on account of the Cholera in Germany. He expects to start for home next Saturday. Was in SS and church tonight. Ellis' were there and I said Stovers' were at our place. They brought Menno Simon's [illegible] to him.

Tuesday, September 19, 1905.   Mrs. Slifer brought out Slifer's plans for his house. It is very nice I think and will likely suit them. While Mrs. S. was there John came in and said Elias was hurt. That he cut off two fingers. He had already started for the doctor's. Met them coming back from Oberholtzer who wasn't home; to Dr. Souder's who wasn't home; to the drug store who wouldn't undertake it; to Dr. Rahn's who wasn't home, toDr. Vaughn whose team was out. When we arrived at Dr. Crouthamel's he had just come home. They are off at the first joint or not quite so far. A vein was cut and the blood squirted out.

Mrs. Erb was waiting for us and cried when he came home. Mr. Erb was home and not well. This evening he went out again to have the doctor look at it as it pained him. The poor boy never knew what pain was till now. I'm afraid he will have a bad night of it.

Thursday, September 28, 1905.   Rec'd an invitation to Lillian Hunsicker's wedding. She will be married in church next Thursday afternoon. I suppose it will be quite an affair. As far as I know this is the first one to be married in church.

We are very busy in the shop. Elias' fingers are healing nicely.

Loux stopped off the high school in order to serve as a juror. He seems still to think that the world would wait for him. If he doesn't report the names of o.s. scholars soon he will get a calling down. I told him four weeks ago and again last week and he hasn't done it yet.

Hiram Hartzel has bought Wm. Henge's farm for 4500 it is said.

Sunday, October 1, 1905.   When I left for SS Cal told me that there seemed to be something the matter with Dan as Mr. L. had rec'd a telegram. When I came up to church I was surprised to see Dan there all right. I was very glad to see him. He arrived here late last evening and the telegram had arrived too late for his father to meet him at the wharf as the ship had landed at 4 o'clock and when Mr. L. arrived Dan had gone. He looks a little thinner and well bronzed. He says he met so many nice people and that he has friends over the whole world with whom he expects to correspond in German. Saw him again this evening at church.

Monday, October 2, 1905. This afternoon Dr. Oberholtzer came over to the office and told me that Christ Hunsberger had a bad disease and that Will Sell's children had it too and that he had taken the responsibility of sending them home from school. Penrose Zendt called me up on the phone about the same matter and afterward came over to tell me more about the matter. He was excited about the matter and I never knew what a terrible thing it all was till now. This evening the matter came up before the Board and W. Freed who had also been posted by Penrose and Dr. Oberholtzer also urged every precaution. I told them of Loux's stopping school without permission and Enos Moyer especially condemned it. He didn't have the o.s. school reports ready even now. He had not been very careful to obey my instructions to him a month ago. They told me to tell him these things must not happen again.

Tuesday, October 3, 1905. Went to school this morning and attended to the syphilis and itch cases. Told the teachers to burn the books and Shellenberger got new books. Miss Shelly told me Mrs. Will Sell wanted to see her but she was afraid to go nearer than the fence. I went over and had a long talk with her. I was very sorry for her. She tried to explain that they were not the cause and I told her no one blamed her.

This evening went to Dr. O. to tell him that if he didn't report the man Shelly who caused the trouble I would. He promised he would do so tomorrow. On the way home met Christ and Penrose talking. They stopped over and told me that Chr. had been in the city with 3 Drs. and that they pronounced them simply boils and no syphilis. I told them I was glad but that I wanted Dr. O. to know right away but Chr. did not want to tell him. He promised to call him up on the phone to tell him to see me before he went to Telford. Saw Dr. O. at the hardware store playing cards. Told him. He felt bad. Said there was a diagnosis at stake &c &c.

Wednesday, October 4, 1905. On Monday they started on Slifer's cement blocks. Saw them make the blocks this morning. Saw Christ who said he was in to see Dr. O. — and it looks as if there is going to be a mess. Heard during the day that people are keeping children out of school. That others were sick &c.

On the way home Dr. Ace was talking to Dr. O. and said it seemed to him the schools ought to close. I told him there was nothing to fear and that the schools could not close. Mike Bergey said it was all nothing and that we should not take hasty action.

Went over to Erb's and found there is nothing the matter with Raymond. People are very easy to fall into a panic, unreasonably so. They talk too much.

Mrs. H. went to Riv. Bro. meeting taking the girls and I am taking care of the children. She is very anxious to draw her building assn. money and put it into the bank. She is certainly cranky on this subject and impossible to handle.

Thursday, October 12, 1905.   Rev. Detweiler was here this evening about Jennie's baptism business. He talked to her about the Sabbath and interest but I don't think anything can be done. He then started with me about baptism giving me a tract giving the verses about it. I said I was acquainted with them. Told him it was unnecessary. That there were different ways of understanding these things. He claimed the Bible as his authority but I told him they all did and misunderstood it all. I told him I could not approve of it though as to consent I would not refuse as I couldn't say yes or no. With this he had to be content. I told him what I found fault with in them. Their closed ceremonies their non voting &c & ceremonies. He left later.

They will announce it about next Wed. and the ceremony will follow the following Sunday.

Sunday, October 22, 1905.   Started for Silverdale at 8:45. Got there at 9:30. Jonas Frederick gave me some advice. Said I was in his position and that he had said he would take his wife home for such a thing &c. They were singing when I came in. Rev. Bowers & Tyson & Detweiler gave short talks. Bowers proving that Anabaptists had always been persecuted. Rev. Detweiler asked her whether she believed in God &c. Whether she renounced the flesh & the devil and accepted the authority of the church and whether she would if she had a fault to find first speak to the person herself and be willing to receive reproof.

We started for the water at Kilmer's Dam near Blooming Glen and Perkasie. The weather was cold enough to wear overcoats. Mrs. shivered at first. They immersed them thrice. When she came out the women threw a shawl over her and I a horse blanket. I then drove to the nearest house where we had to wait a little. I was afraid we were in the wrong place. The others came up and then they went in and changed clothes. We then drove home and I got back about 12:45. She was chilly on the way home. She is coughing some tonight but I hope now she will be satisfied and find peace. Was in S.S. & church this afternoon and evening.

Tuesday, October 31, 1905.   As a result of a great railroad strike in Russia covering practically all railroads as well as many of the other industries with the Army and Navy doubtful Czar Nicholas yesterday issued a manifesto granting a universal ballot, free speech and press and a responsible ministry, for which M. Witte is chosen with the title of Minister President.

This is the deathblow of the autocracy. Everyone is pleased except the socialists and such who won't be satisfied with anything. But it is a great step forward. M. Witte in his delight issued an address to the Amer. people. When he was over here making peace he handled the reporters and he knows the influence of the press.

We finished the cement walk over the culvert on Broad St. although the gutter is still to be made. It is a little cold at night but we keep it covered up.

Wednesday, November 1, 1905.　Baby Willie is learning to walk. He can stand alone and sometimes makes a rush of 3 or 4 steps but he is afraid to walk deliberately. Loux is very saucy. When I told him the other morning he is not to stop school again he said he would do it when he pleased. That the court was above the school board. I told him about two half days that he missed but he was defiant; claiming that I had done a couple of dirty tricks, &c. I tried to keep my temper and told him if that was his answer I would tell the School Board. Yesterday however he asked me to have off on election day saying he would get a substitute. We are so busy at the shop I don't know what to do. Everything is dropping behind.

Wednesday, November 8, 1905.　The election yesterday was a great victory for reform. The city party swept Phila. and Mayor Weaver is sustained and can now complete his work.

Berry is elected State Treas. of Pa. and says the lid will now be lifted entirely. The failure of the Enterprise Bank last month gave the people a glimpse of what was happening under the surface. In New York Jerome is elected by 11,000. He was on no party ticket and every man who voted for him had to cut his ticket. McClellan has a small majority and Hearst it is said is going to contest on the charge of fraud. In Ohio the Cox machine in Ohio is put out of business.

Cut out doors for Bldg. Assn. houses. We ought to be further advanced with this work. Lang & Thomas at N. Wales are also getting desperate.

Wednesday, December 6, 1905.　I was called up on the phone twice from Halmeville on account of Cal Bilger who they said had run away with a 15 or 16 yr. old girl and inquiring whether he was here. On inquiring I found they had been at Joe Derstine's Monday night and left in the forenoon on receipt of a telegram from home. It seems the father of the girl is trying to locate them and I don't know whether trouble will follow.

Russia which has been tied up for weeks by strikes rebellions &c is still in the throes of anarchy. No news of any account reaching the o.s. world. The telegraphs railroads, everything tied up, soldiers & sailors mutinied, no one knows what will happen.

Monday, December 11, 1905.　Yesterday part of the Hudson Peak building blew down. 9 bays fell over and three windows were completely smashed. All the others were damaged. The north wall was exposed to the full force of the wind though curiously enough the part where there is no angle wall which stood alone is the part still standing.

Thursday, December 14, 1905.　Today we put in the concrete for part of the new addition to the shop. Chas. Price hauled some of the bricks and if this glorious whether holds a little longer we will be all right.

John Binder died last night. His son Samuel was there but neither he nor

Mommy noticed anything until he seemed to be sleeping so long. When they looked right they found him dead. Poor man! He, I always thought, was one of my best friends. I believe he died happy.

He was a wonderful old man. A great memory and he had some great thoughts. There were few memories to match his knowledge of scripture. He arranged everything for his funeral himself. Was down to his house tonight. I saw his corpse this morning and again tonight. I am sorry for old Mommy. She will be very lonely. He did me great favors and was really a great help to me. I will be one of the pall bearers. Funeral next Tuesday.

Friday, December 15, 1905. The weather became colder. The paper again predicted rain or snow and it was very cloudy and gray all day but there were only a few flurries around six o'clock. We kept on cementing all day in spite of the cold as we could do it. Under eves and indoors practically as the old shed we built to make Mattison's frames we left stand until the foundations are all in. It started to freeze but we began to use hot water for mixing the concrete. The brick layers could not go on at the Hudson Peak Bldg. it was too cold. I wish I had my storm sash in the house. It is time for them.

Tuesday, December 19, 1905. Today Binder was buried. Allebach and Detweiler preached as he intended. I went out to the shop in the morning as I had some things to look after. I had no idea they would have such a short service at the house and I had just started to go when they came out and so I missed carrying him. Dan Rittenhouse taking my place. He looked very natural. Had quite a large funeral. Jake Allebach thought it would have made proud had he known it.

But I miss the poor old man. He was a true friend to me and it seems sometimes to everyone though he had a rough manner. Most people give him credit for trying sincerely to lead a Christian life. He had a quick temper and could not control it but he was soon friends again. As Mommy expressed it it seems lonely without him.

Friday, December 22, 1905. The borough is having Main St. fixed up with a steam roller. It is amusing the expression you hear about. Most people don't believe in it. All condemn one kind of stone or another. Others say council men are not fit, &c. &c.

Willie's vocabulary to date: "along" to go visiting or even to bed. "Det down" for get down from your lap, "dop" for stop that, "da lie" or "lys" for light electric or coal oil, "wawa" for water, "baby" for his shadow on the wall, pictures &c., "minny" may be for cake or something to eat, "Bolla" his bottle, "Mamie" for Amy "Bapa" & "Mama". He can say girl plainly though I doubt he knows the meaning.

Saturday, December 23, 1905. Didn't get all the work done I wanted done. I expected to finish Ellis, Hens Souder and such things by this time. The rain this morning frightened me as we had a load of stuff for Germantown uncovered. Abel however had it covered when I came out. The season this year is much later than the two last. Here we have been having mild weather up to Christmas. They had a snow storm in the city last week but we didn't get it. Were in the store buying things for Christmas. Bo't an express for Henry, washtub &c for Margaret, ball for Willie, chain for Mary, pocketbook for Helen. In addition Mrs. has books &c. Gave each of my men a dollar. It took 25 of them to reach around.

Monday, December 25, 1905.   At Grandfather Moyer's for dinner. Grandmother is almost blind. Schwenck's were down and Willis' were also there. Milt's were in Kutztown. Willis got up a shooting match. I fetched my camera and took six snaps with what luck the future will show. Stayed for supper also Willis. The girls went to Christmas festival but I did not.

Tuesday, December 26, 1905.   Were at Grandfather's house for supper. Had another turkey. The children enjoyed it. Worked today at the shop.

Wednesday, December 27, 1905.   We started a choir at the church tonight. The members so far are Ellis, Cal, Jordan Allem, Irvin Yocum, John Bossert and myself and the girls that always have been in. Eva & Stella Jordan, Grace Zendt, Liz Hunsicker, Liz Underkoffler, Mrs. Bossert, Sallie Hunsicker &c.

Thursday, December 28, 1905.   Mr. Loux was shot tonight. There have been so many robberies of late that when he saw a light at Rosenberger's school he was suspicious and took a posse down. He had Constable Landis & Mathias and a number of others. He was shot in the body about 3 inches below the navel. I was at Al Reiff's when I first heard of it. Ron Goettler went down to the shop with me where I phoned to Dr. Vaughn who told me it was a very serious wound and that they were ready to operate on him there. Coming from the shop we met Milt when we went up town to Dr. Vaughn's. There was Mr. Luckenbill, Dan and Morris Zendt and quite a number of people. Went in. Dr. Souder etherized him. Dr. V. and Oberholtzer were dressed for operating. Loux had taken communion. When he lost conciousness Dr. Vaughn cut him open large enough to get his hand in. It looked like butchering. Just as we left they found the bullet in one of the intestines. Got home about one o'clock. First heard it about 20 min. after eleven. Men are down at Rosenberger's watching where they think two men remain. It is raining fast and I can't believe they can keep it up all night.

Friday, December 29, 1905.   At three o'clock this morning I put on my rubber boots and raincoat and started up town for more news. Met Dr. Oberholtzer who told me all the thieves had escaped and that all had gone home.

Visits Loux—buys an Invincible Sander—a son is born—San Francisco earthquake—Jennie's mother dies—plans made for new church

1906

Friday, January 12, 1906.   The High School children were admitted to Mr. Loux's room this afternoon. He shook hands with each but they were not allowed to speak to him. They sang for him however downstairs.

He had sent them a very affecting letter after hearing that they were not behaving as well as they ought. It is now reported that visitors will be admitted from two to four each day.

Saturday, January 13, 1906.   Strasser asked me this morning whether I had seen Loux. I told him I thought of going up this afternoon. He said there was now an opportunity for seeing him and he thought he would tell me. I took this almost for an invitation. In the afternoon I went up but understood from Mrs. Vaughn that he was worse probably from the excitement of yesterday and that the doctor would prefer not to have anyone see him. Soon after I saw Morris Landis at the shop and he told me they were already making preparations for operating on him tonight. The second bullet is causing the trouble. His temperature is rising and pus formed.

Sunday, January 14, 1906.   From what I can hear the operation last night was successful so far. The second bullet had cut the rectum so that his stool came out through the wound partly.

Monday, January 15, 1906.   Was in the city today to see Tourisin and also tried to see Mr. Medary but could not find him. Bought a couple of books on Genesis. This is the first I had seen of what is known as the Higher Criticism outside of what Lymon Abbot writes in the Outlook.

The Legislature today meets in special session to carry out the reform program outlined by the Govenor. How good they all are now.

Wednesday, January 17, 1906.   Was in the city again today went down by trolley as I had to go to Germantown to measure up Newhall's house. Got back at 7:30.

H. Rev. Smith who is holding revival services at the Brethren Church was here for supper but as I wasn't home I couldn't meet him.

Friday, January 19, 1906. Was up to Sellersville to see Newbold's new sander. He has an H. B. Smith Machine which he claims is the best. He says this machine was gotten up by the inventor of the Royal Invincible. The machine looks to me as though it might be all right.

Saturday, January 20, 1906. We have now the new addition at the shop closed in and are laying floor. It darkens the shop considerably as it is but hope it will be better after it is finished. Was at the Br. Church to hear this Smith preach. He is a good preacher.

Have a bad cough and did not go out all last week. Jennie went up every evening. She even believes it would be good for my cold to go.

This afternoon I bought the Josiah Clemmer property on Water St. for $865 for Jennie. This is considered very cheap. She has the money in the Bldg. Ass'n. and thinks that is wrong so I thought I would fix it this way.

Mrs. Kratz and daughter of Silverdale were here for supper.

Sunday, January 21, 1906. Read the World before Abraham. Very interesting.

In Sunday School this afternoon and Church this evening.

Was at Grandfather Moyer's this afternoon. Talked about the political situation this afternoon. They all think something ought to be done. Ellis thought he wouldn't do much this time &c. Hen Freed sent him and me an announcement of primaries for next Saturday night.

Tuesday, January 23, 1906. This has been a remarkable winter so far. The last five or six days have been so warm as to be uncomfortable. The thermo. today at 1:30 in Phila. registered 71°. There was a cold wave to come here last evening but lost itself. This evening it rains after threatening all day. We had the dynamo going all day because it was too dark where we built the new addition. The tin roof is now on and the sash in and floor laid.

Saw Ellis yesterday and Adam this evening about the political situation. Ellis can't stand the excitement and Adam won't do much. Saw young Goettler and he can't see much either.

Thursday, January 25, 1906. Was in Glenside this afternoon, to look up the Luetgen House. Found that Miss Luetgen was a sister of the Luetgen that built a house at Ambler. Mr. Bean was down too.

After I came back, I went to see Adam Crouthamel. I found he had no fight in him at all. Was willing to let Harvey Souder go back to Council but said he could support us in school fight and be over at the primaries.

Friday, January 26, 1906. Went to Ambler this afternoon to see Dr. Mattison for money but he didn't give me any. Wanted an itemized statement,

&c. I'm bound to get it out of him soon. Went also to see Heckler. Heckler is quite well again. Talked about his sickness and says its the hardest thing in the world to let things go.

Talked with J. B. Alderfer on the way home. He says they have no one up town for school director. Went to see Goettler after I came back. He tried his best to knock Dr. Crouthamel on the head, but had no one to substitute. Found they had ambitions but did not think they could be elected. They promised however to support whoever would be taken up.

Saturday, January 27, 1906.   Went to Hatfield Institute this morning but too late to see Miss Kirk's class drill. Was in a discussion about the parents' part in the discipline of the school. H. Z. Wampole of Telford opened the discussion and Jonas S. Moyer followed after which I spoke my little piece. It made a little nervous to face all those people and I had to walk up to the platform from the back of the room. Supt. Ruttof spoke on geographical influences on History and Benj. Franklin, Miss Nible spoke on Literature and Penmanship. I had to go home after three o'clock. Saw Rev. Fretz this morning and he said Abner Moyer wanted to be school director. Found out he would take it. Saw Cal. Penrose Zendt, Wm. Souder, Dan Zeigler, father, g. f. Moyer, Sam Hunsberger, and Elwood. Sam Hunsberger saw to it that Ben Gehman was to nominate Rev. Fretz. Elwood promised to nominate Dr. Crouthamel. Heard Wm. Souder &c. talk above W. A Crouthamel for Council and also Hen Detweiler had told them Detweiler could not take it. Told Hen Detweiler to nominate W. A. C. which he did. They could hardly get the second name for councilman's nomination. At last W. H. Freed was persuaded to take it. The results of the contest for school director was Dr. Crouthamel 41, M. L. Landis 29, Rev. Fretz 30, Abner Moyer 19.

Monday, January 29, 1906.   This morning sometime someone telephoned from Vaughn's that Mr. Loux wanted to see me. I did not get a good chance to go till after dinner. At dinner time I had a talk with Jonas Freed who had really been feeling badly against me. I found he misunderstood much and regarded me as sensational to say the least.

Mr. Loux was very glad to see me it seemed. He was able to talk quite well and has been allowed to read for several days. Tomorrow he says he is to sit up for awhile. He looks well in his face though his hands are white and his legs thin. He says that only 3 out of 1000 hurt as badly as he was recover. He attributes his recovery to 1st the grace of God, 2nd the skill &c of Dr. Vaughn and 3rd to his strong constitution. He says if he gets well, he expects to devote himself to his family. He says he has laid aside all old animosities when he entered that room. He seems to think highly of Amy. He says she seems to have a boy's mind. She, he says, has a remarkable memory and also great reasoning powers in mathematics. Came away when I found he was getting more tired. Mr. Luckenbill was there when I came down.

Tuesday, January 30, 1906.   The Democrats last evening couldn't get any one to run for Burgess and only a Mr. Smith for Councils. They put up Andrew Benner and Harry Weil for school directors and it is undoubtedly the intention of such men as Gerhart and Shellenberger to defeat Rev. Fretz if possible. Saw Gerhart and Shellenberger standing together and talking and laughing. I suppose, of course, that a man like Fretz is too suitable and must be defeated.

Wednesday, January 31, 1906.   Went to Perkasie this afternoon to see Coeson Lewis and also Charly Schwenck. The latter wants a porch and I advised him to get Martin.

Lewis is bidding on a block of 10 houses. I put in a bid for stock work. I'd like to sell that as I might do it as well as anyone else.

Thursday, February 1, 1906.   Went to Ambler this morning and got a note out of Dr. Mattison at last. He was just ready to go to N. Y.

Stopped off at Lansdale and saw Bardo's Invincible Sander. They have a 48" machine and it works fine.

We have now finished the new addition with the exception of cutting through the partition in the basement. Weikel will whitewash it tomorrow.

Sunday, February 4, 1906.   On the way to church Hiram Hartzel told me that Loux's case has not been satisfactory. Some solid matter passed from him on Wednesday or Thursday and tore out the stitches so that it may take another operation. [Illegible] Hartzel said the doctor does not know what to do.

Monday, February 5, 1906.   School Board met tonight. Everything peaceable. Wolford and Strasser only visited school today. Went there too this afternoon. Was in Miss Shelly's, Miss Kirk's, Miss Barndt's and the High School room.

The weather is quite cold now. A cold wave to arrive tonight. This may give the icemen some ice at last. There has been no ice so far this winter. It has been a hard winter on the blacksmiths who had little sharpening to do.

The great Torrey Alexander Mission was started yesterday in the Sec Reg Armory. 6000 people listened to him twice yesterday with overflow meeting in the street. The Ledger gave his first sermon in full.

Jennie was up to see Susie's little girl who broke her collar bone.

Tuesday, February 6, 1906.   Very cold last night and today. I think they may get a little ice this time. Froze some pipes on acc't of the ignorance of the men.

It is said they will have to operate on Loux again.

They are getting up a benefit for him. Irene Hartzel is to recite and so is Joe Kratz. The Octette is to sing &c. Mrs. H. does not approve. It does seem to be mixing pleasure and amusement with charity.

This business is getting very expensive for Mr. L. He told me last week it was going to cost him upward of 500.00.

Monday, February 12, 1906.   Rev. Fretz was down to see me about the election. He said he had heard nothing, neither had I. I can't judge whether the split in the Democratic Party is enough to make some of them wish to defeat their ticket or whether the hatred of the whisky people is great enough to make them forget their differences and fight Mr. Fretz.

Wednesday, February 14, 1906.   Was in the city this afternoon taking off some work at Tomison's.

They have begun tearing down the second section of Wanamakers old building. It is done in such a hurry it seems to me that only the heavier timbers and iron are saved.

Thursday, February 15, 1906.   Mattie today became the mother of another little girl.

Black haired this one. Sorry it wasn't a boy.

They call it Catherine.

Friday, February 16, 1906.   The special session of the Legislature adjourned yesterday after having accomplished more in the way of Reform than any one session ever had. The Personal Registration Act for cities, the Uniform Primaries Act, the Repeal of the Rippert bills, the change in the salary of the Insurance Com & Sect of Int Affairs refers to salary and a number of other bills were passed and enacted into law. It also passed an apportionment bill which had not been done since 1880 I believe.

Was in the city today and took off some work. Saw Mr. Medary about the church. He will draw a sketch plan and perspective for about the bare cost of the office work about 25 or 30 dollars. After that he will make regular charges. He thinks however that the superintending should be done by someone up here.

Monday, February 19, 1906.   Met at the church tonight about plans for the future. Told them about Mr. Medary and Mr. Hunsicker thought we might try him and see what he would get out for us. Wrote Mr. Medary to set a time when he could come to Souderton.

Tuesday, February 20, 1906.   Went to Glenside with Slifer today to see the Luttgen House. It is stained dark green and black and dark brown. He liked the finish. Got back about 6:30.

This was election day. Didn't find much electioneering going on so we did nothing but remind a few persons of the existence of an election.

Went up to the choir practice tonight.

On the way back got the result of the election. Dr Oberholtzer was elected Burgess without opposition. W. A. Crouthamel & W. H. Freed were elected councilmen with practically no opposition. Dr. Crouthamel got about 138 votes Rev. Fretz 118 to H. Weil 92 & Andrew Benner's 84 or so.

I am glad they are elected though they were cut considerably. We are now I believe getting fit men into the school board.

Wednesday, February 21, 1906. Was to Quakertown today and took dinner at the Bush House. They are putting finish on the new part of the Bush House now.

Thursday, February 22, 1906. Mr. Appenzeller, Edith and Miss Cope were here for supper and spent the evening. Miss Cope brought her Chautauquans to be bound.

Weather mild. Mr. A. talks of plowing soon.

Saturday, February 24, 1906. Dr. Torrey's work at the second Reg Armory was finished yesterday. They will begin in a week from now at the 3rd Reg. at Broad & Wharton Sts. in a week from now. Yesterday a 1000 children came out to confess Christ at the call of Dr. Torrey.

Susie Ellenberger died on Thursday of Pneumonia and will be buried on Tuesday. She was Milt's sister-in-law. Old Mommy is now quite alone with only Roy and Stanley left. She had six children and they are all dead now.

Sunday, February 25, 1906. To S S & Church this afternoon. It rained quite a great deal today.

This evening to church. No Rain. We made a great failure in our bass solo in the choir tonight. One or the other got wrong and we were all mixed up.

Tuesday, February 27, 1906. Susan Ellenberger was buried today. The Lutheran Church was full. Milt was home at the funeral.

Thursday, March 1, 1906. Went up to see Mr. Loux this evening. He expects to go home Saturday. He was very cheerful. He was able to walk about and sat in his chair and smoked the pipe. They had three operations. After the last one he lived a week on Champagne so that all his drainage was through the kidneys as his rectum was stuffed with cotton. This lasted a week and was a great annoyance.

Friday, March 2, 1906. Went to the city this afternoon. Took off two jobs at Sperry's and then went out to Germantown to measure up Mostels. On the way home had a talk with old Squire Bean. He is getting old. He says he preached to Loux last week when he was there to see him and told him they had both drank to much. He says he believes Loux is a converted man. I hope he is.

Ordered a suit and rain coat from Reub. Gerhart today.

Monday, March 12, 1906.   Many years ago I remember the Gilbert family (colored) came around here and I remember the old man's bass was something wonderful. This man now 74 years old came to ask permission to lecture and sing to the scholars and any one that would come.

Went to the school house tonight and took Amy Helen and Mary along. He talked of his life as a slave and of his escape. Also he sang some but owing to the want of an organ he did not sing so much as his neck is much swollen from a swelling of the glands due to singing. The Doctors Reed Snyder and Cal. were there and a great many school children. He took a collection and got some five dollars though he did not count it.

Tuesday, March 13, 1906.   Bought an Invincible Sander yesterday. It is a 48 inch machine and costs me $1050 — though I am getting it $50 under price through an arrangement with Grammes & Son of Allentown.

Am taking estimates for Exhaust Fan Pipes. These things are all very nice but they cost so much money. I bought pretty much lumber and it leaves me a little short. I hope to get through some how however.

Wednesday, March 14, 1906.   About an inch of snow on the ground this morning. It looked more like winter than any time for 2 mos. it seems to me.

Thursday, March 15, 1906.   Today we had the nearest approach to a blizzard all winter. There was a fierce wind and at least 6 inches of snow which is packed so tight that you can almost walk on top. I heard some sleighs to-night. Figured on some work in Quakertown today. I wish I could get it but I hardly expect it. Would like to ad a little business in stock work. This is a block of 12 houses and the work amounts to 3450.

Friday, March 16, 1906.   This morning the snow was harder to shovel than any this winter. Of course there was little snow all winter. I had to take the garden spade and plow it low before I could shovel it. The sun came up bright the early part of the day which thawed up the hard crust but the sleighs were out to some extent and tonight Leidy expects to go on a sleighing party.

Mr. Loux was brought down to the school house today and listened to their singing it being Friday afternoon. They had him sit in a rocker in the music room.

It was a surprise to the children.

Saturday, March 17, 1906.   Still snow on the ground and I saw a sleigh go this afternoon.

This afternoon Uriah came over and asked whether he could have work all summer and I told him I wouldn't promise. I was really glad he talked of going away because he is getting troublesome again. He has his head full of fantasies and thinks he somehow can bring about a change in society. He is a Socialist and of course it seems to me those people are bound to be unhappy. He will go to Bardo's.

Ed Hollenback came to the office this afternoon. He says he is getting 1200 a year.

Got a new overcoat this afternoon. It is rain proof and cost me 25.00. Get it from Gerhart.

Sunday, March 18, 1906.   Went out to Grandfather Moyer's this afternoon as I missed Sunday School through some people coming here. Ed says my coat sleeves are too tight and I believe that he is right. I don't see why Gerhart can't make a fit or why he can't make clothing loose enough.

Was at church tonight.

Ed thinks and so does Katey that Torrey is making money and that that is object. But they have not been there to see or to hear.

Monday, March 19, 1906.   Great snow storm all day. This afternoon the snow became coarse and afterward turned into rain. But this was the heaviest fall of snow we had this winter. This was quite a storm and one is almost reminded of the blizzard 18 years ago.

Tuesday, March 20, 1906.   There was quite a lot of snow shovelling last night and this morning the pavements were very slippery.

Today Hendricks our new engineer moved up from Chalfont.

There was sleighing by some people today.

Wednesday, March 21, 1906.   It doesn't look like spring today. The snow melted but little today. Leidy was out with a sleighing party last night. Rob. Funk moved to Lansdale today. They had diphtheria only a short time ago. Went to the city to buy some turned mouldings &c. at Fressenden Hall's who have veneers and any kind of turned and carved mldg. you can think of. Was also at some Italian firm for composition mldgs. where I saw them making models for designs.

Saw Dr Torrey for the first time but heard only ten minutes of his talk. Went in to the Academy of Music to find out how the thing was going and found the first floor at least well filled. Every thing was so nice and quiet that you could hear very well at the back end. I want to hear him right now soon. Went up to choir meeting tonight but was too hoarse to sing well.

Monday, March 26, 1906.   The ground is still white with snow except the streets and walks it is gone. A sort of fog is covering us tonight and I think it will now be soon all gone.

Our new engineer Wm. Hendricks started in on Friday. Ambrose helped him Stauffer [illegible] on Saturday. Cal and I went up to Groffs tonight to tell him about the church building or the employment of an architect. He seemed to be pleased but said he couldn't use it much any more.

Wednesday, March 28, 1906.   Grandmother Moyer is very low and is not hardly expected to live. We didn't know any thing about until last Thursday when we heard both grandpop and she was sick. But we thought nothing of it until Saturday grandfather came out to ask if Amy couldn't come out so he could get away.

Hollenback's were up Sunday. Saw her Monday yesterday and today. Charley was down last evening. Both Willis and Milt are out West. I don't believe they will see her alive again. She is very weak indeed. She can't see hardly anything. The trouble is with her heart. She had taken a bad cold and they had been afraid of pneumonia, but that she passed safely but is so weak. Ida came out this afternoon to fetch Jennie.

Saturday, April 14, 1906.   Grandfather Moyer was taken with Pneumonia last night. Jennie was out at the time. Willis sent for the doctor this morning. Had him down again this evening. We took one of our single beds out this afternoon. Charly Schwenck was down this evening and stayed all night.

Annie was down in the afternoon and we talked about getting a nurse. Jennie and Mattie were more or less opposed to it but Annie & Willis had already talked about it.

We worked only till noon for the first time this year.

Sunday, April 15, 1906.   Jennie says her father is almost well and that if he did not have the nurse would probably get up today. This evening his temperature was 102½ and he feels pretty sick. Was out to see him this evening. He says he does not remember how he got to bed.

Was to Sunday School this afternoon and to church this evening. Will have our Easter festival tomorrow night. Mr. Luckenbill announced church for the forenoon next Sunday at 10:45 and Sunday School also. I am afraid this will not work well. Many of our S. S. belong also to other S. S. and we will lose a good many.

Monday, April 16, 1906.   Grandfather Moyer's temperature was 101 this morning, 99 at noon and 102½ this evening.

He feels very weak.

The consistory met this afternoon, that is the joint consistories. Mr. Luckenbill asked about the new building and I told him we had decided to go ahead provided the money could be raised, and that I thought it could be raised if no work be done before the money was procured.

We had our Easter festival tonight. Church was full. John B. Swartz of

Perkasie made a short address and I thought it was good perhaps better to the point than if Mr. L. had made it. On the whole I think our festival passed off creditably.

Got a telephone in the house and it was finished today.

Tuesday, April 17, 1906.   A son was born to us late this afternoon between five and six o'clock. Remained around home helping to fix the house and yard till three o'clock when I took Henry along the shop. I felt that with the telephone I was safe to go away. We sent Mary and Margaret to Grandfather Hemsings. Henry was there too in the forenoon. When I came home the baby had arrived! He is a fat chubby looking fellow like Margaret. We do not have a nurse. Mrs. Ed Moyer is helping out and Mrs. Erb doing some of the housework.

Fetched Margaret and Mary home and the first thing Mary said she hoped we wouldn't call it Jonas. The girls are all opposed to Jonas and I don't admire it myself for the name Hemsing.

Grandfather Moyer's temperature was 103⅕ this evening. Schwenck's were down this evening.

Wednesday, April 18, 1906.   Beautiful day. Arranged with Eddie Souder to take me over to Harleysville this afternoon.

Jennie rested well and the baby cried a little sometimes. Had Henry at the shop. Ed Souder has a secondhand Reo Touring Car and Harry Hunsicker wanted to give it an over hauling. We started about three o'clock taking Henry along. I got them to take our over coats but we did not need them. Harry Hunsicker went along and it almost seemed dangerous the rate we went sometimes. He sent a 20 mile an hour gate for awhile. The roads are too rough. We stopped at Geo Fredericks where I engaged the daughter to come as long as we could. We then went to Dunkard Meeting House where I didn't get anyone. We went to Harleysville where Harry H. wanted to fix a broken machine. We came home about six o'clock. Enjoyed the ride much though I sometimes thought they would throw Henry out. He enjoyed it much.

Didn't go to ch. tonight. Grandfather Moyer is very weak and his heart is causing anxiety.

Thursday, April 19, 1906.   Terrible earthquake in San Francisco and vicinity. Fires started and the water mains being all broken the fire unchecked is burning up the town. Thousands are trying to get away. They are dynamiting buildings to stop the fire.

Grandfather Moyer was supposed to be dying last evening and was very low this morning. Mrs. Franconi is here this week but will leave Friday.

Baby does seem so well. Does a great deal of crying.

Friday, April 20, 1906. ⅔ of San Francisco is gone and the remainder there is little hope to save the remainder. The property loss is supposed to be five hundred million. The number of lives lost has not been ascertained.

Grandfather Moyer was very low this morning but they moved grandmother upstairs for the doctor said he couldn't recover if she wouldn't be taken out of the room. He rested five hours during the day and seemed to be better this evening. Milt telegraphed he would start for home today.

Saturday, April 21, 1906. Fire in San Francisco under control. ¾ of the city is burned up. 300,000 people homeless. 200,000 encamped in Golden Gate Park. Danger of famine. Water supply inadequate.

They are rushing tents and supplies with fire trucks across the continent. Contributions from all over the country are being sent to the sufferers. Congress appropriated 1,000,000 and will probably another million will be appropriated.

Grandfather was probably better today but is very weak. They had such a time getting help but now Mollie Priesten has promised to come as long as she can stand it.

Jennie is doing well and the baby has improved.

Sunday, April 22, 1906. Grandfather Moyer was very low last night. They thought he was dying. But they kept working at him and this morning the doctor said he now had some hopes for him. He said if he could last a few days the fight was won.

We had church in the morning at 10:45 for the first time. The Sunday school at 9:45. The church was well attended but the S. S. dropped 52. I told Mr. L that we would have heavy losses but these young people are not willing to make sacrifices. It keeps the children off the street. There seems nothing for them to do.

Church this evening was well attended.

Monday, April 23, 1906. Was surprised to hear that grandfather M was very low again last night and that his temperature had fallen as low as 90 during the day. It is a virtual collapse and if God wills not otherwise his chances of life are poor. Went out at nine this evening and the Dr found his temp. normal which is a good thing. The Dr. said that if he had no more of these sinking spells he would pull through.

Was in Quakertown this afternoon estimating &c.

Friday, April 27, 1906. Was in the city today expecting to go to the Torrey Meeting. In the afternoon they did not leave me because it was for children only.

Went to Andrew Cassel's. Saw 18th & Diamond St. Church. Went home with Andrew. He is building a new laundry almost 3 times as large as the present.

At supper I found I couldn't get back till 7 o'clock but Andrew said there was plenty of time but when I got out Broad Street was full and the doors shut. Bo't hymn book and then went to Beth Pres. Ch. where Moody's son-in-law preached. Enjoyed the service much. Was surprised at the no. of people. Heard Chas. Butler sing. He certainly can. But it is my fate not to be able to get near Torrey. The meetings will now close and I will not get near. Got home in the last car.

Tuesday, May 1, 1906.   Milt told me today that no one should be surprised if mother died any time. He said she had changed very much. Went up to see her and saw her condition was pitiable. Her face is swollen and her jaw was trembling. It looked as though she must be in great pain. Milt asked her whether she wanted any thing but she managed to say she did not.

Thursday, May 3, 1906.   Grandmother Moyer died last night at 25 min. of ten. She is thus released from sufferings to great to bear. She had a wonderful vitality to bear up so long against disease. She was often so they thought she was dying.

Grandfather took the news cooly. He is improving fast and the doctor declared he was over his disease and was safe if no complications set in.

The time for the funeral was set for Tuesday afternoon at two o'clock in the afternoon. The service at the house is private.

Saturday, May 5, 1906.   Was in with grandfather Moyer and had quite a long talk with him. He realizes how near death he was. He believes that if he had not had the nurse he might have died. Jennie went out late this afternoon. She says she would not have known her mother but thinks she is the most beautiful dead person she ever saw.

Planted a quince tree today a little late perhaps. Moyer's boys were working in the garden. Very warm. Had quite a shower toward evening.

Was a little bit late for church but they had been waiting. I hurried but [illegible] to get there. Church was full. Ten were confirmed. Abe Alderfer & wife, Hiltebeitel & wife, Mrs. Morris Hunsberger, Mahlon Benner, Carroll Souder, Webster Snyder, Aug. Underkoffler, and Mrs. Jacob Alderfer — nee Lizzie Nice.

A sad accident occured today at Godshalls dam 3 boys were drowned. Two sons (all he had) of Rev. Abe Clemmer, and one son of John Clemens of Moorwood. Rev. Clemmer was at Berks Co. when the accident occurred.

Sunday, May 6, 1906.   Communion at church this morning. 145 communed at the church. The offering was $80.27.

Tom. Benner & wife, J. O. Snyder and wife were present among those from a distance.

Everyone seemed pleased and happy. I hope this state of affairs will continue.

The services in the evening were not so well attended on acc't of the weather.

Handed a copy of the statement of the church to each member as they passed out. This shows an increase in receipts over last year of $210.00 and all debts paid all apportionment met and only 1.53 short.

Tuesday, May 8, 1906.   Grandmother Moyer buried this afternoon. No one was allowed at the house except the children. Jennie and the children came to the meeting house only. Rev. Mininger delivered a short prayer when grandfather had seen her. Rev. Mininger and Mike Moyer preached, the latter in English. There were a great many people present.

Schlegel & Mans were at our house before and after the funeral. Kuhn's of Grater Ford were with us for supper. We six carried the coffin. Did not have any handles as grandfather wanted everything in the Mennonite order.

Wednesday, May 9, 1906.   Father's cousin David W. Wile from Ashland Ohio arrived yesterday. He is a man about 56 and his wife is perhaps older. He was at the shop this morning but I had gone to Richlandtown with Henry to measure a house for J. H. Shelley. Henry enjoyed this trip very much. Got back in the 1.36 train.

Mrs. Wile I met in the afternoon. Emma bro't her to the shop. She is a lively talker.

Friday, May 11, 1906.   Rec'd sketches for a new church from Mr. Medary this morning. One plan shows an L shaped structure quite a high building and tower in front. The other is a cruciform structure with two arms and a tower where the transepts cross the nave. There is a spire on top 103 ft. high. Showed it to Cal, Hunsicker, Luckenbill, Morris Zendt. They all liked the last. It think it is a great building and hope it will be built in my time.

Wile's were with us for supper and evening. They are very nice people. She used to be a music teacher and he sells pianos. He was originally a blacksmith.

Saturday, May 12, 1906.   Father took Wiles to Aunt Sarah this morning and I took them in at Hartzel's where he tried to sell a piano. I showed Hartzel the new church and he seemed delighted with it. Showed the plan to Mr. Groff. He said he was willing to abide by what the others would do. Didn't get the address from Beideman I wrote for yesterday.

The nurse left Grandfather Moyer's this evening. He is considered in good condition and she is fulfilling a previous engagement.

Sunday, May 13, 1906.   Showed Mr. & Mrs. Wile the old records of the Hemsings. He took them down and seemed interested. He said he was 34 yrs. old when his mother died and she was 34 yrs. old when he was born. They went up to Joe Fredericks. This afternoon at 2:54 they left for Phila. He expects to go to Washington to the piano dealers convention. After they had left Beideman phoned from Phila. and he will meet them at Wayne Junction. This afternoon 18 were baptized by the Mennonites. 7 in the creek near the factory. Probably a 1000 people were there to see. Charly Hunsberger & W. Nice's, Ulysses' & such were among those baptized in the water.

Rev. Anglemoyer preached this evening in Mr. Luckenbill's stead. It pleased the Mennonites much. Mrs. Moyer was there and a number of Mennonites.

Monday, May 14, 1906. Weather yesterday was fine. Nice to be out. Today the weather was threatening but did not rain right.

Got another house at Lansdale today and also Zeigler's addition. He is going to spend about 2000 on his place.

Tore up the walk in front for cement pavement. Have Ed Moyer at work for several days to fix up the yard.

Ends term as Burgess—war makes coal scarce—bids on ship work—children contribute to diary—considers church separating from Indian Creek—visits Andrew Cassel in Philadelphia—Jonas Harold ill—father killed by train—the armistice

1918

January 7, 1918.   This evening closed my term as Burgess. I have served the town in this capacity for four years and it is a great relief to lay the work aside. For over two weeks I have spent practically all my time getting out the water bills for Mr. Groff in making my report. This with the assistance of Crouthamel was finished only about 8 o'clock this evening when Council was already in session. We neither of us had any supper and so I went home as soon as I got thru or about 9 o'clock.

I think it is too much to expect that any one should escape criticism while holding public office. In fact honest criticism is helpful. But unjust charges behind your back which I experienced make you feel grateful that the ordeal is over.

I hope Mr. Groff will have better success than I had in every way. I did the best I could with the means at hand, and I really feel that some things were accomplished that will be of service in the future.

January 11, 1918.   Am 52 today. Am especially well this winter. Not bothered with rheumatism so far.

January 18, 1918.   Today we used up our last coal at the factory and we will be forced to close until we get some. We ordered coal from the Reading thru Moyer & Son but cannot get it.

We ordered two cars from Hoffman at N Wales, but these were confiscated by the Fuel Adm. and went to New England. One of these was shipped Dec 7 and the other on Dec. 19. We had them trace the car for us but all in vain.

It seems to me that there has been some terrible blundering somewhere.

January 24, 1918.   Got some coal from Snyders at Hatfield. Eight tons or so. But it will not do us any good for the present. Fuel Adm Garfield will close all industries tomorrow for 5 days except war industries & food. This was a shock to the whole country. It is a confession of failure on the part of the administration.

In addition to these five fuelless days there are to be 9 fuelless Mondays up to sometime in March.

This will mean 14 days lost. All this is very discouraging especially to those who have plenty to do and are not permitted. To such as we who cannot get coal or lumber anyway it makes little dif. But how we are going to keep our men together I cannot see.

January 30, 1918.   Started up again today with the coal from Snyders. It turns out to be very poor stuff. These coal operators are certainly guilty of sending out anything black for coal. We could not have turned the engine if there had been heavy work.

February 2, 1918.   Wilmot Allebach got notice to go to Camp Meade next Wed. Hastings Crouthamel and three or 4 others will have to go too.

February 4, 1918.   11° below zero here. Official 1 or two below in Phila.

Third Muddle Monday. Too cold to work if we had coal.

We managed to get thru with oil stoves and hot water heater in old office.

Completed work on estimate for ship work on which we had been working about 3 weeks.

Work till 9 P.M. without supper.

February 5, 1918.   Clear.

Weather much more moderate for the first time.

Went to Phila to submit bid for Joiner Work for 40 ships to be built at Bristol by Merchant ship Bldg Co. Working with F.L. Hoover & Son, who will do the erecting.

Got news that we are to have half car of coal tomorrow. H.S. Frederick Fuel Com here told me they commandeered their cars at Abram's and some other places.

February 6, 1918.   Cloudy much warmer. Steady 46° first time this winter.

First U S transport sank on way over Steamer Tuscania, over 1000 lost.

Weather quite mild.

Got coal ½ car, good quality.

Today Wilmot Allebach left for Camp Meade.

This is the first of our men to leave. If we get the ships I will try to get him back as I will need men and ship work is the most important work in the country today.

February 7, 1918.   Started up again today.

Geo Gerhart left yesterday. He supposed we would not be able to get coal for a while yet. I wish I could get something that would make these fellows feel they had made a mistake by leaving.

News of Tuscania much better this evening. A great many more were saved than first reports showed.

Arranged with Rev Boehm to preach at church during the period when no candidate is at hand.

February 8, 1918.   Clear. Weather mild, Pavements slippery this morning on acc't of melting ice and snow.

Lots of water connections frozen. They opened 23 yesterday I was told. Sometimes it takes quite a while.

They are charging $3.00 for this service. People kick.

About 200 or thereabouts were killed aboard the Tuscania. It happened Tuesday evening on N.W. Coast of Ireland.

The coalless Mondays continue here though this has been changed south of Virginia. They have had no school for over two weeks at North Wales.

February 9, 1918.   Rain.

Mary got a letter from Harold tonight and she is quite happy — Jonas.

Took a music lesson.

Bought a fountain pen.

Fell in front of Landis & Co's store. Was safely piloted to street in front of garage by Jerry Alderfer — A.M.H.

Tried to straiten out books this P.M. I will have to fill out income tax blank soon. Even tho I know I haven't really made any money. It is so complicated a process I asked Frank Moyers advice this evening.

February 10, 1918.   Mary and Miss Sutliff were here for a while they are going to leave tomorrow. — Jonas

School starts tomorrow after an enforced vacation of two & a half weeks. I'm mighty glad. Wonder if we'll have to make it up later on. After all, we accomplished something. Ella finished her dress and I've mine well on the way so time wasn't lost. — Mary

I shall never forget pleasant time and kindness shown me by the Hemsings during our vacation. I felt at home. — Ella

Rev. Franz preached tonight at the Ref Ch. Church was practically filled. He has many friends from the surroundings who were present I understand he would be willing. I wish our people would come to a decision.

February 11, 1918. This is great weather. For Fuelless Monday or any day to have it. Weather very moderate. The snow and ice melt but it will take several weeks at this rate to get rid of it.

I am paying Pens full wages but he doesn't turn up on a day like this.

I had some men at work on Dry Kiln.

This P.M. Sam D. Moyer called up to inform his parents that he would bring his wife home tomorrow. This was a surprise to me. I am told she is a school teacher of 15 yrs experience. She is from Danboro and is a second cousin both on the fathers and mothers side.

Pres. Wilson appeared before Congress again today and made a direct answer to Hertlings speech in the Reichstag and also to Count [Egarmin]. Wilson talks well and he seems to think talk will win the war.

The Germans have concluded a peace with Ukrania, a part of Russia.

The Bolshevik government is said to have given orders to demobilize its armies and will probably exchange prisoners. Yet they will not sign a peace. This serves the German purpose.

February 12, 1918. At Teachers meeting W.A. Crouthamel's this evening. Talked some in ref. to getting a new minister.

Many favor Rev Frantz.

Got a letter from Dr. Bowman in ref. to choosing minister. He thinks we are pursuing the wrong method. He says dispose of one before you ask another to preach. I think he is right.

Hoover called up and said he had three interviews with Mr. Cort the purchasing agt of the Merchants. He says he is very noncommunicative. He says he doesn't know the man but that it might not be a good sign. But the matter is not decided.

I felt however that one might as well try to forget it. Yet it is hard to give up.

February 13, 1918. Clear. Weather very mild today and yesterday. Snow going very fast, Am glad it is going this way. Less danger of floods. A great coal saver this is. Our shop cat has disappeared. Pens says she was sick when he saw her last. We had her four or more years and she had raised a number of families.

This evening Evans of Hoovers called up and asked me and Cr. to come down tomorrow morning and later to meet the Merchants ship people. They will want to examine our factory next week. This is encouraging. Will go down and see what it means.

Jacob B Landis called up from Lancaster saying that he would be entirely at our services. I told him we had Rev Boehm for Sunday. He said he would be guided by us as to what to do. I told him to wait a little.

February 14, 1918. Cloudy.

Crouthamel and I went to city today to Hoover's first. At ten Hoover, Evans, Crouthamel and myself went to Ward the naval architect of the Merchants. He asked us a number of questions in ref to the work to make sure that everything was understood. Also he asked some that were not his business to ask.

He told us he would call us up early next week and come up and look over our mill.

After we were out Hoover asked what I thot our prospects were. I said I thot we were about as far as when we started. He will come and look us over at least. He evidently has a leaning toward the big fellows.

He says it will be 3 mos before a vessel will be launched after laying the keel. A month later she ought to be ready to sail. They will lay the first keel next week.

February 15, 1918. Went to Ambler this morning to see Dr Mattison but did not find him in. Went on to Elkins Park to look at Pauls houses. Had to go to Wayne Junction and come back. In the evening I had to make two changes to get home.

They have House No 15 ready for Cornice. The wall is half way up the first floor the whole structure resting on 2x3 furring.

The stone masons were working for the first time today after the cold spell.

House No 8 is not started.

Warm weather the last few days and the snow which seemed so solid has thawed and largely disappeared.

Some ice crust on west side of Main Street and in fact all our Sts have it. Some fields and yards are still coated with ice.

I was told that they had ice 32" thick in the Perkiomen. It was too thick for their conveyers. They had to plane it off.

Henry and Margaret and I saw a robin this morning sitting on the ash tree.

February 16, 1918. Received a letter from J.B. Landis this morning. He tells us that in the settlement of this question we are to consider only the good of the charge. The man is nothing to be considered if he is likely to be any detriment. &c. The letter is very creditable to him.

Got bill from Elwood today. It is awful. He has been letting the thing go for 4 years. I owe him $300. He says he has been thinking of building a house but of course at present nothing will be done.

Mary says the school Board pays them for their lost time. That is only fair.

The first keel was laid at Bristol this afternoon according to the Admiral Bowles.

Colder today. Some people thought spring was here but it is too early. The boys saw or heard a robin this week.

February 17, 1918. Cloudy.

Rev Boehm preached this evening on the valley of the shadow in the 22nd Psalm. It was a fine sermon.

It is a pity that talents like his are not put to use.

We formed a committee this P.M. and evening to canvass the membership in ref. to separating from the Indian Creek people and raising money for our own pastor. If we can do this it will be the making of our church.

February 18, 1918. Clear.

Pens says he received a letter from Wilmot Allebach that he did not pass the physical exam.

This may mean that he is coming back.

Heard this evening that our coal shipped on Jan 31 had been again seized by the Fuel Administrator. even tho it was shipped in the name of the Souderton Water Co.

February 19, 1918. Rain.

Had a talk with J D Moyer this P.M. about Ship Contract. He seems to be greatly interested. He said he tho't Mr. Reiff could help us thru the Lit. Loan Com.

I think this a capital idea and went in to Mr Reiff this evening but he appeared to see difficulties. In fact at first he thot we couldn't build ships. We were too small &c. I explained that we would furnish only the house trim. Then he understood. I don't know whether Mr M can induce him to do any thing.

Missed Teachers meeting at Bennetts.

Rev. Hoffman phoned that Barndt had induced Mr. Antone had siezed a car for us at Rutherford. So we are likely to get coal after all.

February 20, 1918. Cloudy.

Mr Ward of the Ship Co has not yet made a move to come and visit our plant.

Mr Hoover called up this morning and stated the matter was yet undecided. That some one is coming in a few days. That Mr Thompson told him it didn't look so promising as some time ago. While he does not know what this means he thought it looked as though a lower bid had been rec'd. He says there is still hope. He wants to have a private talk with Mr. Thomson if possible to get more information.

Got a letter from Helen. She talks of hiring out for $4.00 per week on a farm near Doylestown. A great scheme. I would prefer to have her home.

February 21, 1918.   Cloudy.

Mr Reiff called me up this morning to say that if I wanted him to do anything I should come along to the city. At first I thot LNC could attend but changed mind. He told me he still could not see how. We went to the Girard Natl where he does bus. Introduced me to Mr Ashton, the Cashier, The Pres. Mr Wayne who he wanted to see being out of city. Mr. A. tho't that as Hoover was the principal we should not interfere &c. I took Reiff to Hoovers office. S.E.H. was in Princeton but got him on phone. He said, by all means take him up to Mr. Cort Ask for Mr Thompson who can get you an interview. But like all the others Thompson was not in. We got into Mr Cort anyway. Introduced R as pres. of our bank. R. told him we were good for whatever we would undertake. This Cort said was very important and explained that an 800,000 contract required some financial backing. However he said it was made easy on a/c of 80% payments as the work progressed. The 20% being paid as soon as boat was accepted. He asked about Labor. I told him we had no labor trouble, that the men to a large extent owned their own homes which they did not like to leave &c. on the whole I thing the interview did some good.

Went down to see Mr Kroll. He is coming up Saturday.

February 22, 1918.   Snow. Did not work today.

Unloaded lumber. Two cars in. Car coal commandeered by Barndt also in. Made arrangement with S & C to haul it.

This evening some entertainment at school. It was good.

—————

I was at the entertainment at the High School it was called "Somewhere in France." It was very good. — Jonas

I sang tonight at the entertainment. No casualities reported. — Margaret

Met Anna Moore at the school house tonight and we both sure enjoyed the performance as long as we could see it (That is, when we weren't in danger of having the shoes torn off our feet by some youngster's clumsiness.) I'll make Ella feel sorry she didn't come along up. "The minuet" was great, but then Amy trained them and it couldn't be else. — Mary

February 23, 1918.   Clear.

Mr Kroll was up this afternoon. Left an order for 8 Refrig. He says McCracken is looking for another factory but does not expect him to find one.

Finished my canvas for church today. Willis, Elwood & Pens were my share. They all did well.

Finished up my reports this week. Class as a whole is much better though exams were a good deal stiffer. It pays to keep their noses on the grindstone, tho' the wear and tear on nerves and temper are considerable. Have been learning to knit. A washrag is my trial piece and Jonas is catching the fever. Wonder how long it will last with him? They've changed passing mark from 70% to 80%. It bothers me a good deal, for it lessens the chance for a goodly number of my young hopefuls ever getting through. We got a new flag this week and are exceedingly proud of ourselves as we're the only grade with a big flag. We salute every morning and can do it quite smartly now. — Mary.

February 24, 1918. Clear.

Amy and Papa are in church. I didnt get ready. The usual round of two Sunday Schools, dinner and Supper completed and I'm none the worse for it. Saw the Sgt. Henry Alderfer in Sunday School as he said he would be. Visited Aunt Ida with Carrie Himmelwright. Wonder if they have sold the place as they had expected to? Also I wonder if Ben Alderfers' being there was merely a friendly visit or something on business? — Mary.

After a splendid sermon this evening by Rev. Boehm the Committee appointed last Sunday to canvass the membership reported.

They visited 173 members who were in favor of an independent congregation. 13 who had been on their list were not seen. The remainder were too far away and could not be reached.

This was a ⅔ vote of the whole membership. They promised to increase their contributions $742.60. This proved to be sufficient as it will leave us at least $200. to spare.

This will mean a great change and will be a surprise to Indian Creek I have no doubt.

There is to be a meeting at Jas. H. Gerhart's tomorrow night when this matter will be brought up. Everyone is rejoicing.

February 25, 1918. Cloudy, rain.

Weather today was warm, clear this morning and partly cloudy this afternoon. Small shower this evening.

This **is our wedding anniversary** 27 years. How the time flies. Last fall Wilton Appenzeller said it was 24 yrs since we had joined the church and taken our first communion.

How changed things are now.

Tonight the Joint Consistory met at the home of Jos. Gerhart. The news we had to tell them was hard for them. Jos Gerhart was excited. I did not like it for he is not a well man.

I was asked to explain what had taken place. I tried to do so and to make it plain that the consistory had not started the trouble.

Mr. G. couldn't understand that an irresponsible committee would be allowed to rule. That they did not even consult with the elders. Morris said that was true.

But Morris was nice tonight and he is entirely reconciled to things as they are.

The Indian Creek people were very quiet and sober. I told them there was all the work a man could look after in our congregation. I hope we have succeeded in our efforts to see things in our light.

February 26, 1918.   Clear.

Wrote student Landis today and explained the altered situation in our church. Also wrote to Dr Boaran asking him to read the Landis letter.

At teachers meeting, (M.D.Zendt's) this evening.

Wednesday, February 27, 1918.   Consistory met at Hunsickers this evening to take measures to bring about a separation from Indian Creek charge.

It is strange how harmonious everything is. Morris seems to enjoy it and Hunsicker is satisfied.

Prepared a request to Classis for detaching our congregation from Indian Creek.

Crouthamel was in the city yesterday but did not get any word from ship. Hoover was in Washington yesterday.

February 28, 1918.   The last of Feb. I am glad of it.

The nearer we approach Spring the better for this winter was the severest I ever experienced.

Finished my books and Tax return at last. If I had not put extra pressure on this time it would have next June. I find our inventory runs 2000 higher than last year. No wonder we are short in money now. We were short last year but it is worse now.

Sent formal request to Rev. Lindeman to convene special session of Classis in order to have our congregation separated from Indian Creek charge.

Read an article in Colliers this morning "Wake up." If this is really true then the situation is indeed alarming and all for lack of ships. The Germans have sunk ¼ of the world's mercantile fleet. The most hopeful estimates will enable us to build as fast as the present sinkings a year from now. Then it will be too late. Fore they are barely able to supply Eng Fran & Italy now let alone sending a larger army.

In Australia there is a surplus of wheat piled up 10 miles long. A plague of mice followed by disease. All for lack of ships. Sounds like the plagues of Pharoah.

I wrote to Hoover & Son asking him to read this. I said we had made at least an effort to help. That I did not feel like making mill work or D.R. furniture in such a crisis.

March 1, 1918.   This morning Hoover called up and stated that he had bad news. That Jas Elgar Co. of 849 Broadway NY had landed the ship contract at 16000 a piece. As our price was 20000 each they will do this work for $16000 less than we. We certainly did not expect to make such a profit, I am sure. Mr. Hoover cannot see how it can be done for the money. He told us to go for them. We wrote them but I dont expect any results there from. Too bad we cannot land something big. I would have felt that we were doing some thing to help the country in our war program. But it was not so to be.

March 2, 1918.   Rec'd letter from Rev. Lindiman that he had called classis in special session for Monday Mar 18th at our church. This is acting promptly and I am glad of it.

Hoped Mr Kroll would come up but he did not come.

Was at Riv Bro meeting. Mary Kinding and Miss Wenger will go to S. Africa as missionaries. They both spoke and sang and Mary's was especially good.

March 3, 1918.   To SS. this P.M. Rev. Boehm preached this eve. People are very fond of his preaching and many would like to have him called but I am afraid he would not suit as we must have one all to ourselves to get the best results.

March 4, 1918.   Father was 79 years old today. I did not get a chance to speak to him about it. He is busy with a new grape arbor. Because his old one lasted over 40 years he is making this just like it.

Rec'd letter from Rev. Lindiman stating that Classis would meet in forenoon instead of P.M. He suggested that he come down and preach for us and then talk it over.

We will have him come on Sun. Mar 17 and ask him to stay overnight to the Classis next day.

March 5, 1918.   Went down to Ambler to see Dr Mattison about a bill which he disputes on because he says the first sash we made leak. We have had quite some correspondence about this and today I went down to talk it over. It is a shame to have a fuss after so long and pleasant business as we had together. I made a deduction of 50 from a $215 bill and all is well.

He took me thru the shingle plant where he says they have piled up about $800000 worth of shingles. He says they will go on until they have a million dollars worth. They are borrowing the money. Their equipment is expensive. Very heavy machinery.

Enjoyed my experience very much.

They tell me Mr Luckenbill was in town day. Too bad I didn't see him. He bro't his Henry Ford and goes home tomorrow.

Teachers meeting at Gehmans this evening. Crouthamel met Mr Elgar at the Merch Ship Corp. He says it looks as though our fig were being considered at first but that this concern slipped in later. Too bad.

March 6, 1918.   Was in the city today. Went down with Rev. Brown Dr. C's brotherinlaw.

Rev Luckenbill was at Dr's for supper and at Ellis over night.

Phoned for Dr. C. this morning for Jonas has rheumatism. Stays in bed. Very stiff.

Went with Rev. Brown to Acad. of Fine Art. Enjoyed looking the pictures over. Saw one of Pres Wilson by Sargent, Painted for Dublin University.

Settled acc't with F.G. Stewart for Cresson. Went to Sash & Door Manf. meeting. It now becomes a chapter (D) of Lumberman's Exc.

There was just a quorum present.

Went down to 11th & Walnut to meet Krall. He says McCracken has to leave by May. They are at the last cutting.

I proposed to offer McCracken a chance to participate in profit of Furn. Manufr. for use of name. He said no. That his name doesn't count. He still has his head full of Refrig. I find. He is coming up Sat.

Went to see I T Shoemaker. He is running a job again for White Motor Co. He will make out well evidently. Took the order for millwork at $1250. Shoemaker used us and others well and I believe is honest.

Met Brown (H.L.) on the street. He does not look well. He has nothing to do.

March 7, 1918.   Mabel told me today she would leave on the 1st of April. I had known about it thru Horace to whom Pens and she had told on Tuesday. On Monday she bo't a house on Derstine ave in Lansdale. I am indeed very sorry to see her go. She has been very faithful and I felt I could trust her to anything. There was no danger of her talking too much away from home. I told her I appreciated her services very much and hoped she would stay awhile longer.

Of course I cannot blame her. She has been married several years and would like to have her own home. I understand she does not get along well with her mother.

March 8, 1918.   Perc. Barndt will also leave on Apr. 1st. This means that I will have to look for a new man in his place. He will take his father's farm. I cannot blame him for going but it is hard to replace all these people.

Planted onion seed in hot bed. Also cabbage beets, & tomatoes. Had planted radishes, peppers and early tomatoes last Saturday.

Rec'd some cuts of DR Sultrs [?] together with price list of same as requested from Krall.

March 9, 1918.   Mr Krall came up this afternoon. This is his proposal. He will ask a drawing account of 35 per week. As soon as furniture is being sold. This same is to be deducted from a com. of 10% on total sales. This is to include all expenses travel and hotel or agents com.

My total cost of selling including designing would be 10%.

I think this is reasonable. The only question to determine is whether he can sell as much as he claims and this can only be shown by experiment. The second is whether I will be able to finance such a thing.

There was some rain tonight.

March 10, 1918.   Very high wind all day. Colder tonight freezing, wind still strong. To Sunday School this P.M.

At Milt Moyers after S.S. He sent for me. He has the opportunity to sell half of the house, the side toward Funks including the barn for 3000 to Warren Moyer for his auto trucks. Ida was opposed saying that 3000 was not enough. Milt declared he can get 2500 for the other side but I do not believe this. He must have 1800 to come out. He declares he is compelled to do something for he cannot keep it up. After Ida had considered the matter right she decided to give in.

At Church tonight Rev. Boehm preached on the Power of the Spirit, or the influence we exert on others whether for good or evil. People are greatly taken by his sermons. Wish we could get him but his business relations will probably make it impossible.

March 11, 1918.   Was surprised to receive a visit from Dr Bowman Lancaster Theolog Seminary today. He was here just a short time between trains, leaving for Perkasie on the 1:24 train. I had been reading the paper and was taking a nap when he walked in and introduced himself. I woke up at once. He noticed my pictures of cathedrals and was deeply interested. In fact our talk on these threatened to cut out the business on which he came.

He had the subscriptions for Theolog Seminary with him, some from Souderton and the bal Indian Creek. He asked me to take charge of them and collect same.

Then we talked of our changes. Walked up to the station with him. Introduced him to Morris. It was comical to see Morris surprise. "How did he find you &c."

He thinks Rev Frantz ought to stay where he is. He offered to come here sometime in 5 or 6 weeks. He is a fine old fellow. Hair white as snow. Must be 65 yrs old probably 68 yrs old. A fine conversationalist. When I told him of the need of a vigorous minister he said he long known of this &c. I told him we did not blame Luckenbill for he had not the time. He said it was nice to draw the Veil of charity &c.

March 12, 1918.   Was down at Chester today getting sizes for Resurrection School. They have certainly lost a lot of time this winter. They are just completing the roof.

Went down on the trolley and back on the steam Load.

March 14, 1918.   Rain.

Went to city this P.M. to see Andrew Cassel. Am getting so restless that I must talk things over with someone.

Was surprised to find Andrew talk of retiring from bus. Of his lack of energy, &c. In other words he finds he is getting old gradually.

Undoubtedly I am getting there too in some ways, but I do not wish to lose courage on account of dissappointments.

He says he has nothing to worry about yet he often can not sleep &c.

Stopped in at his house a few min. after leaving the office. Rained.

He thinks that if I close my mill I will have a loss and if this goes bad my loss will be slight. He believes it safe and sensible to try it experimentally.

Saturday, March 16, 1918.   Clear.

I asked Adam Crouthamel over and showed him the data about the furniture business, also my bus. statement. He seemed to think it all right. He wants to bring H.H. Freed to see it. He says that will help me to get my matters arranged.

Harvey Souder came down to see. I had invited him yesterday. He of course is very optimistic about it.

Mr. Krall came up this P.M. We went over to the Hunsberger Feed store. We found a lot of fellows upstairs who sneaked out before I came up. Krall saw them. They were probably gambling as I heard there was such doings here.

We think the building will do well for the purpose intended. The roof will need some fixing &c.

Told K. that I would go in the thing if I can arrange the finances.

Cold today. Day Light Saving Bill is passed. This means the clock will be turned back on March 1.

Saw Reiff tonight about Seminary subscriptions.

At Hardware Store rather late. Adam tells me confide in Reiff.

March 18, 1918. Went to hear San Small in Zion Men. ch tonight. He certainly is witty. And how confident of victory for Prohibition. He says even beer will be stopped before the 4th July. That next yr. enough of States will ratify the Prob. Amendment. This PM. Delaware became the 9th State to ratify. Very few State Leg. meet this year. Already three or four of the nine who ratified were wet states. The house was not as well filled as four yrs ago, somehow. That was advertised better. House to house. This thru the churches but I guess ours was the only one to do it. The others refused.

March 19, 1918. Mabel asked whether I had any one in her place. I said not. She then offered to stay providing she could leave at 4:30 in the P.M. I asked her whether she tho't she could get the work thru. She said she could. I guess I will have to do this. I would rather have her with her experience 8 hrs than a new one who knew nothing for a longer time.

March 20, 1918. Had Mr Reiff over and showed him the furniture, &c. Told him I wanted a dif arrangement for financing. He advised me to go to Trust Co. Said if I couldn't arrange here I should come to him and he would take me to Wallace. Keeley is a Director in Mortg Trust I believe.

He was very nice indeed. Feel much better after unburdening.

March 21, 1918. First day of Spring. Fine day. Went to city this P.M. to attend a creditors meeting. Devin School is in trouble and I stand a good chance of losing some hard earned money. Big names Statesburg, and a lot of others connectd with it. A big fraud it seems to me.

Saw 39 Pierce Arrow Trucks on the north Plaza of City Hall. They had been brought from Buffalo, 40 started on the 14th and one dropped out. They came from Newark today. Will go on to Baltimore tomorrow morning. One of the men told me there were 700 men waiting their turn to bring Pierce Arrow as fast as they are finished. He says they give them trouble as they are not tested out thoroly at factory.

These are for French Gov.

Krall was on the phone and wanted to know what the prospects were as he did not want to spend money with a lawyer unless it would go thru. Told him I tho't it all right.

March 22, 1918. Henry and I saw two bluebirds today in our yard. They are the first bluebirds that I remember to have seen in our yard. I am going to make a wireless and put it up when the war is over. — Entry by Wm M Hemsing, Son of WSH

Adam told me this morning the loan would go thru. He saw HH Freed. Hunsicker and Mike Fore. He said I could count on it.

Am glad of it. Can now act.

Wrote the RR. Co. or Klink to rent the Hunsberger Feed Store.

Sent Perc. up to see John Frey and feel him whether he can be had. Would like to get him. Must have some one as Perc. will leave this week.

Jonie continues weak. Took him in to the Dr this evening and he found his temp was 103 and pulse 120. He told him to go to bed. Don't know what ails the boy.

March 23, 1918. Mr. Krall was up this P.M. He bro't sketch of an agreement with him. Now that the thing is coming to a head I note he has some misgivings, about the war for instance.

Jonie is still in bed. Henry sat with him all day.

Local Institute here today.

A lecture by Dr. Geo. Raignel on 3½ yrs of the Great War.

He gave a very interesting review of the war up to this time.

The Great German Drive is on a 60 mile front. They have driven back the English, captured 25000 prisoners they claim.

They report shells falling into Paris 240 millimeter about 10%. If this is true they must come 62 miles at least. This is hard to believe though. If this is true what can be done with these Germans.

I cannot believe that Providence will permit such a people or God to win this war.

March 24, 1918. The Doctor told me this morning that Jonie is a very sick boy.

I gather that his lungs are affected as well as his heart. His temp is 101½ but his appetite is good. I hope with fresh air and nourishing food we may be able to help him if thru Gods mercy. I had noticed for a long time that he was very thin but attributed it to his rapid growth. I am afraid we have neglected him and that the matter is more serious than we realize.

To Sunday Sch. this afternoon. Rev Boehm preached tonight. Asked him about Rev. Ditzler. He says he is a fine fellow good voice and believes he would be active though this he does not know of his own knowledge.

Arthur Landis is coming to Church. Quite a number of people are interested that had not been before.

I was sixteen today — Margaret

April 10, 1918. Consistory met at Hunsickers. Mr Ditzler writes he cannot leave Frederick, but will visit in this neighborhood and is willing to talk to us next Wed Eve.

Have writen him an invite to come.

April 12, 1918. Snow all day. Melted or it would have been deep. Bad weather all week. Great wind storm yesterday. Telephone wires bet. here and Norristown & Phila down. One wire to Lansdale.

Trolley car burnt down completely early this morning. High Tension wire on track and car ran into it and burnt up, Trolley men lucky to escape.

I am afraid some peach & plum trees suffered damage for they had buds almost ready to open.

Jonas still in bed. Temp this eve 102½. This morning 99½. Pulse 126. His pulse yesterday was 140. Don't know what to think. In bed now since Tuesday.

The Germans have opened a drive in Flanders on a 18 mile front and driven the English & Portuguese back two or three miles.

Quiet in other portion where the advance was 40 miles.

Situation serious. English to take men from 18 to 50. Conscription in Ireland. The Irish are fighting this. They certainly want special privelege. Lloyd George wants to give them Home Rule, but they are thinking more of the draft.

It is certainly hard to believe that Spring was here. It looked like summer and we had a perfect Easter.

April 14, 1918. John Fry started work today as foreman and [illegible]. Hope he will not get into the draft right away. He is not 21 yet but will be soon and they are passing a bill drawing all coming of age.

April 17, 1918. Clear. J Harold was 12 years old today. He was quite excited about it. A deportation from his room, 6th grade came in and bro't him a beautiful bouquet of carnations & other flowers, a flashlight and ten cents left over. I understand they raised over 2.00. He was very happy over his presents. He got some candy, and three very big oranges. I promised him 1.00 of thrift stamps.

He was a little feverish 101 and pulse 112.

Rev. John A Ditzler of Frederick Md. arrived this P.M. and came to my office. He is a stout man with a big head.

He preached tonight on the Just shall live by faith. There were about a 100 in Church. One trouble we will have is comparing him with Boehm. Took him all around the building. He seemed to like the building. He was at Gehman's over night.

The battle-South Ypres still very hot. The British in the main holding firm.

They retired east of Ypres to shorten their line and also avoid a flank attack.

April 19, 1918. Went down to Hatboro to see about a mantel that has gone bad at Mr Reading's house. We are unable to get a settlement out of the Contractor Mr Ramsey of Ivyland. Am afraid we will have trouble getting our money. Did a great deal of walking and found myself stiff with Rheumatism this evening. On the way home found Mary and Henry on train.

April 20, 1918.   Cold & Damp. My rheumatism did not get better. So I went to Dr. C. and got a little med. Also got Lithia at the Drug S.

Mr. Krall came up this after. Says he has his second suite on the board. Not thru with the tables. Am anxious to see what they will be like.

April 21, 1918.   Rain all day. Being stiff with rheumatism in left knee I decided to stay home from Sunday School and Church.

Grandfather H. was out to see Jonie. He says Aunt Kit is in a bad way. Sore from lying. Enos H. Moyer is helpless from Rheumatism. So is H A Groff Burgess. He has been out of bed little since new years.

John Clymer is down with Cancer and Dropsey.

Jonie was sitting up part of the time. He is slowly getting better. His temp is normal and pulse about 90.

Father told us many interesting things about the town. For instance Main St was once called Possum Lane and hit the Cowpath by a zigzag rout near Haldeman's below Indian Creek Church. Church Road to Appenzellers was called Bull Lane and Chestnut St was Cressman's Lane. Water St. was evidently the first laid out street in the present boro Limits. Dan'l Hemsing (my grandfather) had Reliance Road extended to Cowpath before the Pike ran across.

Sam Souder (bro of Henry my grandfather) being a deacon in the Men. Ch. asked him to do it and he paid the expenses.

April 27, 1918.   Helen came home today. The term ended yesterday or Thursday. She had expected to stay with Sarah or Iva but came home on account of Jonas. She did stay at Sara's over night.

May 16, 1918.   Learned that Classis had stopped Boehm from preaching. He had been dismissed to Lancaster Classis. Jas Gerhart however asked permission to have B. preach indefinitely This they could grant. The matter should not have been bro't up and then perhaps they would have taken no notice. Our people will feel bad and ascribe it to **jealousy.**

Met at School House to organize for War chest, Red Cross YMCA YWCA &c. combination

Wanted to go up to Church and hear Dr Moore of   at the W Missionary Society of Tohickon which met today.

May 17, 1918.   Father and I went to HS Beideman's funeral this P.M. 2 o'clock at the house. Met Kate (Kline) Shirm there. Few people. Went along to Cemetery on N. E. Boulevard. K of R. Cem. Had quite a talk with Mrs H and Mrs Arnold afterward. Missed train by only a few minutes which provoked me for I wanted to do some work on War Chest. Prepared map of district this morning.

May 18, 1918.   Received card this morning that the vessel Ed sailed on arrived safely beyond seas. It was signed by Ed himself and I was glad he thought of us here. Chris Freed recd a postal too Pen too bad.

Mrs. Mich K Bergey was buried this P.M. only a little over 45 and 8 children survive. Sad.

Krall tried to get a house on the Co Line but the man wants to sell for 2100.

Finished up my organization for the War Chest Campaign next week. Have 13 solicitors and the district bet. Hillside & Broad. Wish it was over.

May 19, 1918.   Learned this P.M. that Mrs Barney Rubin had bought the Kline property opp. the Church for 1195. We had a meeting of Consistory on Wed night. to consider this but Morris said it would bring more money 2200 perhaps and Hunsicker was afraid to tackle it. We wanted a price fixed 10 or 1200 and buy it if sold at a bargain but no. At the price sold it would be possible to pay it off with income and it would be a splendid site for a parsonage. Rev. Spotts preached.

June 10, 1918   Funeral, Nice Day. Heavy Rain in evening.

June 11, 1918.   Too wet for plowing now. Had intended to go at it this morning but last nights rain spoiled it.

Horace brought in father's hat and one shoe. It was a congress shoe and showed the cut where his leg was broken. Also marks on the sole where he was push along the track probably. I have been wondering what has become of the watch case. Much of the works of watch were found, the main spring, the pinion, the

Too wet for ploughing

Found fathers 1 shoe & Hat

Wheres case of watch?

Some nice letters of sympathy

June 12, 1918.   Rain this morning Ground very wet. Sun came out in P.M. and good wind.

Crouthamel's grandmother and Mrs. Arnold went to city after rain. To hospital, to eye specialist and some business.

They brot us some eggs 12 doz to do up. Paid 20¢. They were big ones.

Rec'd letters of sympath fr. Dannehour, H.H. Bridler, Lear, Coolbough, Fistar and Underhill.

Milt Barndt's barn burned down this morning. Lightening. These people will have trouble getting the lumber.

June 13, 1918.   Weather cleared off at last. Hope for a chance to plow tomorrow.

Received a letter from Dave Wile's today. Wondered very much why we did not hear from them before.

Mrs Arnold, grandmother and Crouthamels' were at the house for supper. They bro't 24 doz eggs which we put up with water glass This is the first time I ever tried this. They cost me 36¢ per doz. This used to be the high price years ago when they would come as low as 12¢ But last winter they went up to 60¢ and higher.

The Food Adm. is asking people to limit to 1½ lbs of Beef per person and to eat pork instead. Well we do not reach this limit for we eat practically none. The bread shortage hits us harder. We have only 56 million bushel of wheat in the country and 30 millions must be exported. This leaves 26 mil bus. for 2 mos where 80 mil is the normal supply.

The fuel question however is by far the most serious.

Class Day exercises tonight. Did not go.

June 14, 1918.   Rain again during night. Ground too heavy to work. This evening another shower. This year is remarkable for Electric storms. Last year there were notably few.

We hauled some coal and three loads of Mahogany shorts from H.L. Souder. This is the car I bought from Thompson.

Rec'd letter of condolence from Hayman and John Schofield.

School Commencement tonight. Cant go home until the rain stops

July 10, 1918.   Tonight we went up to see the aeroplane at Sellersville. It is a biplane of medium size and also is an instructors plane.

July 21, 1918.   Rev L. E. Bair from Millersburg preached. Is not a candidate but evidently could fit us very well and I think everyone liked him. Spent some time with him. Took him to S.S. in the morning. Kinsay took him to Telford.

On the afternoon at Schlessars Hunsicker was there. Went to Ellis'.

Preached a good sermon

August 4, 1918.   Rev Gerhard preached. He is from Jefferson Md.

August 6, 1918.   This morning it became very warm. In fact last night was warm. But today was a record breaker. Temp. 103.2 in Phila. Hog Island it was 113 I think. They had to quit work. So many industries. Here Shoenenman, Zendt Souder H S & W A Crouthamel sent their people home.

We got thru but our men showed the effects. I do not think one place is quite as hot as some.

The iron on machines felt hot. Rain is very necessary.

Unloading walnut from Ohio.

Humidity was very high

August 7, 1918.   Hotter than yesterday. Temp 105 in Phila at two this P.M. perhaps it will be higher.

We felt more of a breeze.

Tonight a breeze came up and I do hope it will end in rain.

Took a bed home and some photos (old ones). The bed is the one father made for himself. It looks nice on or 3rd Floor rear room.

November 7, 1918.   FALSE ARMISTICE Armistice signed today at 11 A.M. Fighting stopped at two.

It was around three or a little before 2.30 perhaps when we heard whistles in the distance. Tho't there was a fire.

Then Harvey's siren began. After awhile I was curious to know where the fire was. Started for office.

Tele. was ringing. Girl said Goettler wanted me. I asked where was the fire. She said there is no fire, its peace. Goettler said start your whistle armistice signed.

Sent the men home at 4.30

November 8, 1918.   It turned out that the report of signing the armistice was all a mistake.

November 11, 1918.   Today is the real end of war. War ended at 6 this morning. Signed 5 hrs previously.

Men would stay at work. Had to declare a holiday.

Had a parade in town. Firemen, school children. Red Cross, and others. Did not see it. Remained at shop as I had a lot to attend to. Am glad it is over at last.

Appendix

Mary Jane ("Jennie") Moyer Hemsing (1865-1923)
Married William S. Hemsing, 1891
Photograph taken 1890.

Henry Frederick Hemsing (1839-1918)
Father of William Hemsing. Operated a planing mill in Souderton.
Married Mary Hunsberger Souder in 1863

Mary Hunsberger Souder (1843-1897)
Mother of William Hemsing.

Daniel and Sarah Frederick Hemsing
Grandparents of William Hemsing
Daniel was a cooper. Photograph taken 1886.

Henry F. Hemsing planing mill. Hemsing and Henry H. Souder opened this planing mill on Chestnut Street, Souderton, in 1871. Souder sold his interest to Hemsing in 1880, after which Hemsing continued to operate a mill on the site until moving to Water Street (now East Chestnut) in 1892.

Charles Godshall ("Goody") Frick
Friend and neighbor of William Hemsing

Andrew S. Cassel
Apprentice to Henry F. Hemsing
Following custom, he lived with his employer, served two years, and
then received a set of tools. He later went into the laundry business in
Philadelphia. Photograph taken 1884.

Uriah Souder
William Hemsing's cousin and next-door neighbor. Son of William and Susan Souder.

Partial listing of relatives and other persons mentioned frequently in the diaries, listed in the order in which they are introduced.

The name by which Hemsing refers to each person is printed in capital letters

ANDREW Cassel — apprentice to William's father, lived with the Hemsings.

MOTHER and FATHER — Mary Souder Hemsing (1843-1897) and Henry F. Hemsing (1839-1918). The aftermath of Henry F.'s accidental death is related in the diary.

PENROSE Zendt — brother of Lillie Zendt.

MARTHA Souder (Mrs. Adam Crouthamel, 1870-1941) — William's cousin, daughter of Edmund H. and Elizabeth Oberholtzer Souder. Sister of Alonzo.

MR. LANDES — Jacob C. Landes, cashier of Union National Bank from 1876-1915.

URIAH Souder (b. 1862) — William Hemsing's cousin and next-door neighbor on Main Street. Son of Wm. H. and Susan Hackman Souder. Brother to Kate.

KATE Souder (Mrs. Irwin Bean, 1868-1917) — William Hemsing's cousin and neighbor, sister of Uriah Souder.

SUSIE Daub — hired girl in William's parents' household, employed in 1885.

"OLD HERMAN," "THE GOVERNOR" — Herman K. Godshall, a director of Union National Bank from 1876-1881, as well as a founding father of the Souderton Mennonite church and first superintendent of the German Sunday School organized there.

MILT Moyer — brother of Jennie Moyer.

"JENNIE" MOYER (1866-1923) — Given name Mary Jane. Called "Jennie" after Jennie Lind, popular singer. Daughter of Jonas D. Moyer. Married William Hemsing on Feb. 25, 1891. Siblings include Milton, Willis, Mattie (Mrs. Frank Scheetz), Annie (Mrs. Charles Schwenk), Katie (Hollenbach)

LILLIE ZENDT — daughter of M.D. Zendt. Object of William Hemsing's first courtship. Became his second wife after Jennie's death.

ELLIS Souder — uncle of William Hemsing. Youngest son of Henry Souder. Partner with Jonas Landis in Landis & Co. general store.

ALONZO Souder (1868-1890) — cousin of William Hemsing. Son of Edmund and Elizabeth Oberholtzer Souder. Brother of Martha.

SAM Alderfer — successor to Andrew Cassel as Henry Hemsing's apprentice.

Charley SCHWENK — brother-in-law of Jennie Moyer.

AMY (b. 1891) HELEN (b. 1893) DANIEL (1895-1902) MARY (b. 1896) CATHARINE (1898-1902) HENRY (b. 1900) MARGARET (b. 1902) WILLIAM (b. 1904) JONAS HAROLD (b. 1906). Children of William and Jennie Hemsing.

IDA, WILLIE (1896-1902) and HILDA (1899-1902) Moyer. Wife and children, respectively, of Milt Moyer.

MARY Stauffer — hired girl in William and Jennie's household.

MATTIE Moyer Scheetz — sister of Jennie Moyer.

EMMA RATZEL Hemsing (Mrs. Henry Hemsing). William's stepmother.

William SLIFER — husband of William's cousin Catherine H. Souder (1851-1901). William's partner in development of Souder land, 1903-1904.

Family of Souderton founder Henry O. Souder, grandfather of William Souder Hemsing

(Compiled primarily by Henry Souder Landes, grandson of Henry O. Souder)

HENRY O. SOUDER (1807-1897) married Hannah Hunsberger (1814-1890) on Nov. 23, 1834. They had eight children:

1. WILLIAM (1835-1915) married Susan Hackman (b. 1841) and later married Emma Rosenberger. Seven children:
    - Hannah (b. 1860), married James M. Slifer
    - Uriah (b. 1862), married Valeria Barndt
    - Horace (b. 1864), married Minnie Sellers
    - Rufus (?-?), married Lizzie Cassel
    - Katie (1868-1917), married Irwin Bean
    - Irwin (b. 1872), married _____ Long
    - Henry (b. 1873)

2. EDMUND (1838-1916), a hardware dealer, married Elizabeth Oberholtzer (1847-1929). Nine children:
    - Alonzo (1868-1890)
    - Martha (1870-1941), married Adam Crouthamel
    - Ira (?-?)
    - Anna (b. 1874), married Menno Moyer
    - Morris (b. 1876)
    - Hannah (b. 1878), married Willis L. Moyer
    - Edmund (b. 1881), married Anna _____
    - Ida Elizabeth (?-?)
    - Oscar (b. 1889)
    - Sylvia (b. 1891), married Vincent S. Clymer

3. ELIZABETH (1841-1914). Married Henry C. Landes (1836-1893). Six children:
    - Emma (b. 1862), married Jacob K. Clemmer
    - Morris (b. 1864), married Emma Hackman
    - Edwin (b. 1866), married Katie Price
    - Henry (b. 1871), married Mary E. Hause
    - Elizabeth (b. 1875), married Russel W. Dewey
    - Jerome (b. 1879), married Magdalena Fox

4. MARY (1843-1897). Married Henry F. Hemsing (1839-1918). Two children:
    - Harrison (?-?) died in infancy
    - WILLIAM SOUDER (1866-1940), married Mary Jane ("Jennie") Moyer, later married Lillie Zendt. William and Jennie had nine children:
        - Amy (b. 1891)
        - Helen (b. 1893), married Felix Norrison
        - Daniel (1895-1902)
        - Mary (b. 1896), married Harry Frank
        - Catharine (1898-1902)
        - Henry (b. 1900), married Marion Summerill
        - Margaret (b. 1902), married Oswald Moore
        - William (b. 1904), married Mildred Willard
        - Jonas Harold (b. 1906)

5. FREDERICK (1846-1927), a feed and coal dealer at Telford and Lansdale.
   Married Mary C. Allebach (1849-1906). Four children:
   > Artemus (b. 1880), married Sarah Gamble, later married
   > Anna Wislon
   > Laura (?-?), married Wilson Stauffer
   > Alvin (?-?), died in infancy
   > Eugene (?-?), died in infancy

6. HENRY (1849-1919), kept "Bush House" hotel in Quakertown. Married
   Mary Ruth (d. 1920). Three children:
   > Preston (b. 1873)
   > Lillie (1878-1921)
   > Mabel (b. 1888)

7. CATHARINE (1851-1901), married William B. Slifer, a Souderton merchant
   who became William Hemsing's partner in developing Souder land in
   1903-1904. One adopted child:
   > Arthur Voorhees, renamed Artemas Slifer (?-?).

8. ELLIS (1858-1933). Partner with Jonas M. Landis in Landis & Co. Married
   Catharine Ziegler Keeler (1862-1945). Five children:
   > Stella Luella (b. 1885), married John G. Yocum
   > Eva Lillian (b. 1887), married Henry C. Bergey
   > Florence (?-?), died in infancy
   > Marion (b. 1895), married E. Stanley Godshalk
   > Edna Kathryn (b. 1898), died in infancy

SOUDERTON INDEPENDENT

PUBLISHED AT
SOUDERTON, Montgomery Co., Pa.
EVERY SATURDAY.

W. F. GOETTLER, Proprietor.

April 16, 1887.

The dramatic play "Ten Nights in a Bar Room" given under the auspices of the Souderton Library Association, in Freed's hall, last Saturday evening, was largely attended. The manner in which the play was rendered spoke words of praise to the participants, and proved that after all Souderton had better talent than many expected. To say the least, every character knew his part well, and went through the whole play without a flaw. They netted the handsome sum of $38.55.

SOUDERTON INDEPENDENT

PUBLISHED AT
SOUDERTON, Montgomery Co., Pa.
EVERY SATURDAY.

W. F. GOETTLER, Proprietor.

April 27, 1902

DANIEL HEMSING.

Daniel, oldest son of Mr. and Mrs. William S. Hemsing, Chestnut street, Souderton, died last Sunday morning from the effects of diphtheria. The child's age was nearly 7 years and his departure is sadly missed by the family. This is the second death that has occurred in this house within two weeks. Miss Mary Stover, a domestic, having died from the same disease. The community sympathizes with the family. Private interment was made on Monday afternoon at Leidy's church cemetery.

SOUDERTON INDEPENDENT

PUBLISHED AT
SOUDERTON, Montgomery Co., Pa.
EVERY SATURDAY.

W. F. GOETTLER, Proprietor.

May 1, 1902

MISS MARY STAUFFER.

Miss Mary Stauffer, who was employed as a domestic in the family of William S. Hemsing, Chestnut street, Souderton, died last Friday evening, aged about 20 years. She had been suffering with an attack of diphtheria. Deceased was a daughter of the late Abraham Stauffer, of Bergey. Interment was made at the Franconia Mennonite meetinghouse last Sunday.

SOUDERTON INDEPENDENT

PUBLISHED AT
SOUDERTON, Montgomery Co., Pa.
EVERY SATURDAY.

W. F. GOETTLER, Proprietor.

August 29, 1902

CATHARINE EUNICE HEMSING.

Catharine Eunice, daughter of Mr. and Mrs. William S. and Jane Hemsing, residing on Chestnut street, Souderton, died last Sunday, after an illness of several weeks with brain fever, aged 4 years and 4 days. The deceased was an attractive child and her sweet face will be greatly missed by the family, as well as the neighbors, who deeply sympathize.

The funeral was held on Wednesday afternoon. Services at the house were private. Interment at Leidy's church cemetery.

SOUDERTON INDEPENDENT

PUBLISHED AT
SOUDERTON, Montgomery Co., Pa.
EVERY SATURDAY.

W. F. GOETTLER, Proprietor.

1887
History of Souderton

The first settlers who emigrated to this section of the country were Welshmen. The first building erected by them, was on the premises of Ephriam Freed, on the upper Skippack below this place. Where the greater part of the town is now located, a few hundred yards east of the railroad depot there stood an old fashioned log house and a "swiss" barn, then owned and occupied by Jonathan Hunsberger who also owned all the ground where now the depot of the North Pennsylvania Railroad is located, and where most of the business is now transacted. Thence along Church Road a few hundred yards north-west of the depot, on the right hand of the road was the residence of Henry Souder, Sr., and on the left his carpenter shop and lumberyard. Still further up on the north-west side of the Skippack creek, stood an old log cabin, formerly owned by George Henge, deceased, the ancestor of the Henge's family of this place and vicinity, thence due north, about one-third mile north-west of the railroad depot, was the residence of Michael Henge, lately deceased, now owned by William Henge. This was all the inhabitants of the town in its infancy, would say prior to 1850. It is now probably more than 150 years since the first settlers set foot on this section of the country. We find many of their decendants living near the original settlement of their ancestors, and still a great number kept moving westward from time to time, and we now hear of them from places on the Pacific coast, or more than three thousand miles away from the homes of their ancestors.

Fifty years ago, what is now the principal street of Souderton, was a narrow lane, having a low washed out bed, with high sloping banks; on one side of which was a forest and on the other lay barren fields. This road originally extended to the Cowpath road, near the Indian Creek church, the upper part of which has been abandoned since 1865. What is now known as Water street, was its only branch.

There were only a few houses in the surrounding country, traces of which still remain.

The oldest house in Souderton was built in 1837, by Henry Souder, Sr., at the corner of Water street and what is now known as Main street. This property is now owned by the railroad company, was bought to avoid bridging Water street at this point.

About 1848 Henry Souder, Sr., established a lumber yard at this place. The lumber was hauled from Point Pleasant, on the Delaware River, a distance of eighteen miles.

In the Fall of 1855 S. D. Hunsberger & Bro's. commenced the flour and feed business opposite the place where the depot now stands. The present building was erected in 1864.

The North Pennsylvania railroad was completed in 1856. Although no depot was built the place was known as Franconia Station, Wm. Souder acting as agent for the company. The present depot was built in 1865. J. C. Landis, was the first agent who received a regular salary from the company. Upon the organization of the National Bank, he being elected its cashier, resigned and Morris D. Zendt, the present incumbent was appointed in 1876 to succeed him.

The railroad gave a new impetus to business and from this time the growth of the town was rapid.

In 1864 Jesse and Joseph Huber came into the village and built several houses and established a cigar factory which gave employment for a time to many persons, but we are sorry to state that it suffered the fate of many others who were engaged in the same business.

A post office named New Harbor was established May 12th, 1860, Wm. Souder was appointed postmaster. Its name was changed January 13, 1864, making it agree with the name of the station which was now Souders. William B. Slifer was appointed postmaster June 22, 1869, who moved the post office from Wm. Souder's office to his store. It was again removed after the appointment of Milton D. Zendt as postmaster, February 28, 1876. The name of the post office and station were changed to Souderton, in March 1876. Postmaster Zendt resigned June 4, 1885, and was succeeded on November 6, 1885, by William K. Shellenberger, whose appointment dates from October 28, 1885. The post office was again removed from Hunsberger's store to its present location, in the store of Landis & Co.

The Harleysville and Souders turnpike was chartered June 2, 1863, but was not completed till 1866. A stage route was established between this place and Green Lane, but was soon abandoned.

The Souderton Hotel was built by Jonathan Hunsberger, in 1858. It was occupied by Franklin Zepp, two years, Alex Sellers, six years, Frank F. Hendricks, seven years, Elias Snyder, six years, W. D. Hunsberger, three years, W. B. Slifer, two years, and Wm. H. Freed, the present landlord took possession in 1885.

Liberty Hall, a spacious building connected with the hotel, was built by W. D. Hunsberger, in 1881.

The store known as Landis & Co's, was built in 1860. Souder and Bergey occupied it four years, Henry Souder, Jr., two years, W. B. Slifer fifteen years and Landis & Co. since 1882.

Hunsberger's store was built in 1860, and occupied by Wm. D. Hunsberger one year. The next occupant was Milton D. Zendt, who took possession in March 1870. He was succeeded by S. D. Hunsberger & Bro, June 1st, 1885.

The first hardware store was founded in 1861 by E. H. Souder. It was enlarged as business increased to its present size. It is now one of the largest hardware stores in Eastern Pennsylvania outside of Philadelphia. E. H. Souder carried on the business for sixteen years. In 1877 he formed a partnership with B. C. Barndt, and the firm was known as E. H. Souder & Co. In 1883 E. H. Souder retired and Danley & Barndt succeeded. B. C. Barndt took possession in 1884.

Moyer's feed store was founded by H. K. Godshall in 1864, who continued in business three years and A. K. Frick two years. Moyer & Bro. took possession in 1869. The building was enlarged in 1871 and in 1882. In the latter year a chopping mill was added to the business.

M. B. Bergey erected a planing mill on Main street in 1865. It passed into J. M. Souder's hands in 1872. It was removed to Green street its present site, in 1874. It was destroyed by fire in 1884, but was rebuilt the same year. It was leased in 1888 by John Gerhab, agent, who still carries on the business.

In 1871 another planing mill was erected on Chestnut street by Hemsing & Souder. On the erection of Souder's steam saw mill in 1872 adjoining the place, horse power was superseded by steam. In 1880 the partnership was dissolved and since that time the business was continued by H. F. Hemsing, the present proprietor.

The Union National Bank was incorporated May 12, 1876, and opened June 10, 1876, in Henry Souder's store house, opposite the depot. It was moved into its present building, January 1, 1877. It has a capital of $90,000.00 with a surplus and undivided profits amounting to $30,000.00. Its deposits on May 22, 1886, amounted to $171,304.97, discounts $192,718.95. The first board of directors were I. G. Gerhart, A. Sorver, C. D. Loch, Henry Ruth, John S. Moyer, Chas. Godshall, Aug. Thomas, H. K. Godshall, G. H. Swartz and M. B. Bergey. The present board consists of I. G. Gerhart, A. Sorver, John S. Ruth, Henry Ruth, E. H. Souder, John B. Moyer, Wm. Souder, Isaac H. Moyer, J. G. Metz and Aug. Thomas. I. G. Gerhart has been president and J. C. Landis cashier since the organization of the bank. Jas. M. Slifer was the first teller appointed January 2, 1877, and served until 1883 when he resigned to accept the position of cashier of the Farmers' National Bank, Pennsburg, Pa. but is now cashier of the Topton National Bank. He was succeeded by J. D. Moyer.

On August 2, 1878, Peale & Goettler, established a printing office, on Main street, in the building of Mrs. Barbara Price. On the 4th day of August the first sale bill was printed in Souderton, for the sale of real estate and personal property of Henry Yoder, near Franconia Square. On the 16th of August the *Germania Gazette,* a seven column paper, printed in the German language made its appearance weekly until April 23, 1881, when its publication was suspended, and the German type sold to John Shupe, at Telford. In Jan. 1879, prior to the suspension of the German paper, Charles L. Peale withdrew from the firm and W. F. Goettler, the present proprietor succeeded. On April 16, 1881, the *Souderton Independent,* then only a five column folio made its appearance for public favors. On June 4, of the same year it was enlarged to six columns, and again on October 28, 1882, to its present size.

The printing office was moved from the building of Mrs. Price, in the spring of 1880, to the hotel hall, then owned by W. D. Hunsberger, and which was torn down in the summer of 1881. From the hall the printing office was moved into the open shed, then located on the site of the new hall. The printing material was removed from the shed in order to move the building to where it now stands, and then it was again occupied. On November 26, 1881, the office was moved to its present location.

J. G. Leidy's store was opened in September, 1882. It is known as the Central Store. The business was for a short time carried on by Leidy & Alderfer, but since 1888 Mr. Leidy is the only proprietor.

M. B. Bergey's hosiery mill was started January 1, 1885, and moved into the new building, September 1, 1885. It gives employment to fifty-seven persons, forty in the factory and seventeen outside.

A school house was built on Chestnut street in 1875. Prior to this time the children attended Five Points and Rosenberger's schools. The teachers who taught here during the winter terms were F. G. Wile, one term, Jacob A Bucher, one term and J. H. Leidy, three terms. Those that taught subscription schools were F. G. Wile John A. Wile, D. B. Detweiler, J. H. Leidy, Rev. Henry Gerhart, Albert Miller and A. M. Alderfer.

As the population of the town increased more school accommodations were required. In 1880 the old school building gave way to the present two story structure. It would be an injustice to the citizens of Souderton, should we fail to state that they voluntarily raised a considerable amount of money toward the new building. The line of teachers of this school is as follows. The principals of the Grammar school were: I. L. Gehman, one term, Enos C. Beans, four terms, C. N. Gerhart, one term; of the Primary, D. S. Harr, one term, Chas. White, two terms, Miss Connie Durrin, one term and Miss Jennie Moyer, two terms. Those that taught subscription schools were F. G. Wile, J. H. Leidy, Albert Shitler, Jacob K. Moyer and Enos C. Beans.

The Souderton Library, located in the school house was opened March 5, 1886. It is open for the exchange of books the first and third Friday of each month. The Library contains over two hundred volumes of travel and adventure, reference, scientific, biographical and historical works.

There is only one church in Souderton, built by the Old Mennonites. It was dedicated on Christmas Day, 1879. There is tri-weekly worship and occasionally at other times. It is also used by the Sunday school for about nine months in the year.

The business of the place may be summed up as follows: Three general stores, one grocery store, two furniture stores, two feed stores, two hardware stores, two shoe stores, one jewelry store, one drug store, one tinware store, two steam hay baling establishments, two planing mills, one saw mill rim and spoke factory, one hosiery mill, two steam mills, one cigar factory, two cigar-box factories, one carriage factory, one furniture and organ manufactory, one harness manufactory, two clothing establishments, two lumber yards, two coal yards, two blacksmith shops, one barber shop, two tailor shops, one repair shop, one bakery, one printing office, one national bank, two telegraph offices, one post office and two hotels. The population of the town in 1886 was 611. It contained 125 dwelling houses, or one for every five inhabitants.

W. S. HEMSING

Letter to Employer, Union National Bank

To the Board of Directors,

        You will perhaps be surprised on the appearance of another paper from me. Last Wednesday's proposal was very unsatisfactory to me. When I asked for Four hundred, I did not ask to have more, nor mean to have less, than Four hundred. I did not ask this amt with a view to fall back 25 or 30 Dollrs. Had I that in view I would have asked for 425 or so, and so land safe at Four hundred. Therefore, I suspect that you had a wrong idea of what I meant.

If, however, the above is not true, and you understood me to ask for Four hundred Dollars; and that you knew I had not used the above number in disguise for some other number, then I can only conclude that some of you were dissatisfied with my services, and that while you did not wish to directly inform by word of mouth, you chose to do so by making my salary $22 less than what I asked.

There is something else to confirm me in the above. (You must pardon me for bringing Mr Moyer's case in here, but I must do it.) In the first place Mr Moyer asked for Five hundred, I have no fault to find with this. You granted it, because you thought it was reasonable, and to show your appreciation of his services.

I asked for One hundred less, (And I still believe that, as his services are worth Five hundred

mine, are worth Four,) and you showed your
displeasure by giving me $25 less,
   When your proposals were made known
to us, you expressed yourselves as
highly pleased with Mr Moyer's services,
for which I know you have good reason;
but, your silence on this point to me
betrayed the fact that you were not satisfied
with me, Now I would not have you ~~feel~~
understand that I felt hurt out of envy to
Mr Moyer, who I know deserves praise, or
that I wanted to be praised, a weakness
I would be ashamed of; but it was
your unwillingness to openly express your
disapprobation of my services, preferring to
do so by an obscure hint, which only
deepens the sting,
   If then the above is true, it is my wish that
you would inform thereof, and I am willing
to at once resign, conscious, however, of having
done my duty while in your employ,
   If, however, I am mistaken in the above
conjectures, and you earnestly believed
that my services were not worth Four hundred
Dollars, then, and then only, will I accede
to your estimate,

                     Your humble servant,
                        Wm. S. Heming

This letter was written around 1885
and was probably never sent.

SOUDERTON INDEPENDENT

PUBLISHED AT
SOUDERTON, Montgomery Co., Pa.
EVERY SATURDAY.

W. F. GOETTLER, Proprietor.

FRIDAY, OCT. the 11th, 1889.

TOWN NOTES.

William Hemsing is building a fine brick house on Chestnut street. It will be something new in architecture for this place.

CHESTNUT ST
FROM MEETING HOUSE GROUNDS

Home at 118 Chestnut St., Souderton (on right)
Built as an investment by Henry F. Hemsing

SOUDERTON INDEPENDENT

PUBLISHED AT
SOUDERTON, Montgomery Co., Pa.
EVERY SATURDAY.

W. F. GOETTLER, Proprietor.

Saturday March 17th, 1888

The Great Storm.

Railroad Travel between this Place Philadelphia and Bethlehem Blockaded for 52 Hours.

All the Mails were Delayed from Monday Morning until Wednesday Evening — The Roads were all Closed.

The Railroad is again open for Travel and all Trains are running but are from 20 to 30 Minutes Late.

On Sunday last about noon a rain storm visited us and rain poured down in torrents the greater part of the afternoon and evening until about ten o'clock when very unexpectedly a genuine snow storm, or rather a western blizzard struck us and by morning the railroads and wagon roads were so completely blocked that travel was almost impeded. The Buffalo express and the milk train south and the early mail train north reached their destinations with much difficulty several hours late. After ten o'clock on Monday morning the blockade was complete, the only train reaching here was the western express with three Pullman sleepers, one reclining chair car, one regular passenger car, and a double header, or two engines, which left Ninth and Green streets, Philadelphia, at 10.50, nearly two hours late and landed in a deep snow drift in the cut north of this place about six o'clock in the evening. A freight engine which was side-tracked here followed up and brought all the passenger cars back to the depot where the passengers were compelled to make the best of it until Wednesday forenoon at 11:40. The passengers consisted of two theatrical troupes, salesmen, and some forty Raymond excursionist en route for California and New Mexico, among the number, it was said, were George W. Childs of the Philadelphia *Ledger,* and family. Many of the passengers were quartered at W. H. Freed's hotel, and at private houses, while others were supplied with meals in the cars by baker, Daniel W. Kratz, and his assistants.

Although, as usual, some of the passengers were penniless, none went hungry, as all were well cared for by our open-hearted and generous citizens who invited such persons to share with them at their homes.

The two engines and express car of the express train stuck in the snow drift until Tuesday evening, and the engineers, firemen, express messenger, and baggage master were well cared for with good coffee and eatables by the generosity of Jacob G. Leidy, of the General Store.

Conductor Eli Linn, well-known by almost everybody along the line of the North Penn, being on this road the past thirty-one years, and who is a perfect gentleman in every respect, together with all the passenger train hands, boarded at Freed's hotel, but were compelled to lodge during the night on the seats of a passenger car which stood opposite the depot on Souder's track.

Allen Magargle, conductor of the north bound local freight train and crew were side-tracked here until Wednesday a.m. This crew boarded themselves with the best eatables obtainable in the town, which was by no means poor grub. Al. Diehl was the chief caterer and prepared a royal good dish.

On Tuesday afternoon a crew of some forty men from Lansdale came up the road and soon cleared the north-bound track to this place. The two engines and express car which were almost snowed under were extricated and the crew worked their way with great difficulty to Perkasie where they received orders to return. In the meanwhile the two engines that were taken out of the snow drift here proceeded towards Lansdale to get water and fuel, but when near Hatfield Station they again stuck in a drift. An engine from Sellersville was sent for to help them out but he too got stuck there. The crew from Lansdale by this time with forty shovelers and an extra engine arrived, but they could not get the other engines out so the five engines and crews were detained in the drift all of Tuesday night until early on Wednesday morning.

By Wednesday morning about ten o'clock a crew had worked its way south from Bethlehem to Perkasie. Now the road was cleared from Lansdale north, and conductor Linn received orders to get ready to go ahead. An engine was sent from Lansdale and the train was ready to start out at 11.00 o'clock, but "misfortunes never come single and alone." A sick man was on board the train under the care of Dr. Hiram R. Loux, and who during the previous night was paralyzed and by the order of the doctor had to be removed. Mr. Freed the landlord opposite the depot was asked for a room which he had to refuse, his rooms all having been engaged, and the unfortunate man had to be taken to C. M. Tyson's hotel, about one-fourth mile from the depot. The man was alone and no one on the train seemed to know him. His name has since been learned, and is Chandilier P. Williamson, of Vineland, N. J., has a wife and four children, and was en route for Pittston, Pa. He is rapidly recovering and may in a few days be removed to his home. The train left here with delighted passengers at 11.40.

Telegraphic communications were entirely cut off between this place and Philadelphia and could not get any further south than to Lansdale until Tuesday, and then only for a short time. The passengers that were delayed here took advantage of the Bankers and Merchants lines to communicate with their sweet-hearts, wives and daughters, that line being in working order, north and south. Had the railroad company's lines been working the blockaded road would have been opened for travel much sooner, but as it was the officials did not know where the trains were and consequently were completely at a loss where to begin. There were plenty of engines on the road that could probably had kept the road open but certainly could not run without orders.

There was no mail south from Saturday, March 10th, at 5 p.m., until Wednesday, March 14th, at 3.10 p.m., nor north from Monday, March 12th, at 5.30 a.m., until Thursday, March 15th at 8 a.m. The Star Route mails to and from Gehman and Blooming Glen did not go or come until Wednesday forenoon. The roads were so badly drifted that traveling on them was impossible and to cut down fences and go through the fields was the only way to get along at all. All mails, north, south, east and west, are now, Friday morning, coming in and going out on schedule time.

The south-bound track which was entirely closed with huge snow drifts was opened for travel by a large force of men on Friday. But few freight trains have moved over the road this week. Everything is expected to be in good running by this Saturday morning.

The Bound Brook Route from Philadelphia to New York was still blockaded with snow and wrecked engines on Friday, and all trains to New York went over the North Penn. railroad via Bethlehem.

IN OTHER PLACES

The storm extended over New York, the New England states, New Jersey, Delaware, Ohio, Virginia, as well as over the whole area of this State. No trains entered New York City on Tuesday and Wednesday, and many people were frozen to death in that city and Brooklyn, as well as in other places within the territory covered by the storm. All the railroads leading to Philadelphia, were blocked and the trains were in the snow from 24 to 48 hours. The passengers suffered considerable from the cold and for the want of food. In many places the larders of the hotels and private houses were thrown open. Such a storm was never experienced in this section of the country and the saying that "no true blizzard ventures East" became obsolete popular expression on the 12th of March 1888. The storm which raged on that day had all the characteristics of that combination of fierce gale, bitter cold and flying sleet and snow to describe which the word "blizzard" was first coined fifteen years ago. It was preceded by the same remarkably fine weather which tempts the Dakota settler a long distance from home, and it came as suddenly and unexpectedly as the blizzards which bewilder, benumb and freeze the Western traveler. It left the great cities of the East with their matchless railroad communications and telegraphic facilities as completely cut off from the world as if they were isolate farm houses on the trekless prairies of Dakota or Montana. Many ship wrecks at the Delaware breakwater and off Sandy Hook are reported. More than 25 lives are reported lost. Eighteen pilot boats are missing and many tugs and schooners have been wrecked and the worst is feared yet.

Lewis K. Haas, conductor of train No. 306 and crew were snowbound at Sellersville, on Monday, Tuesday, and Wednesday, boarded at Harr's hotel. All the passengers on his train, which were quite a number, speak highly of the good accommodations and reasonable prices. When the train arrived at that place and Mr. Harr learned that it would probably be detained for an indefinite time he invited all to his hotel, saying he had accommodation for them all. Soon all proceeded to the hotel and those not having any money to pay for board and lodging were boarded and lodged at the railroad company's expense.

The Doylestown branch was not opened for travel until Thursday evening, and the Stony Creek road was still blockaded on Friday afternoon.

SOUDERTON INDEPENDENT

PUBLISHED AT
SOUDERTON, Montgomery Co., Pa.
EVERY SATURDAY.

W. F. GOETTLER, Proprietor.

JANUARY 16, 1914.

NEW TOWN COUNCIL.
BURGESS HEMSING'S MESSAGE.

After the Burgess and the new members of Council had taken the oath of office, administered by 'Squire M. D. Zendt, Burgess Hemsing called the meeting to order. At this time M. Hemsing made introductory remarks as follows:

"In assuming the office of Burgess I wish to express the hope that the relations between the several members of the governing body will be cordial. That we may all act in a spirit of helpfulness. That we may be able to co-operate in everything that relates to the good of the town as a whole. That wherever differences occur as they will occur wherever men have minds of their own, we will not allow anything to stand in the way of getting together and work for the best interests of all.

"I have not at this time decided on any permanent course as to the Burgess' dealing with the Council. But it seems to me that for the present, at least, the best method would be not to present at the sessions of Council, except in the following manner: At the opening of each regular session present a written report together with such recommendations as it seems desirable to bring before Council for their consideration. If requested by the Council I shall then be glad to explain in detail any matter thus brought forward.

"After this I expect to retire leaving the matter in the hands of Council for discussion and action.

"At this time I wish to ask your consideration of only one matter on which it seems to me prompt action ought to be taken.

"My attention has been repeatedly called to the fact that no bond is at present required to be given by the Treasurer of the Water Committee. This officer collects, I am told, over $5,000 a year and it seems to me that it would be no reflection on any one's honor for Council to require bond from all officers who handle any of the public money.

"It seems to me that it were well to make a beginning now with what may in the future prove to have been a wise precaution."

Mr. Hemsing named Wm. H. Freed as temporary chairman which was followed by re-election of Henry A. Groff as President.

SOUDERTON INDEPENDENT

PUBLISHED AT
SOUDERTON, Montgomery Co., Pa.
EVERY SATURDAY.

W. F. GOETTLER, Proprietor.

JANUARY 11, 1918

Former Burgess Hemsing Reviews Work of Past Four Years

REVIEW.

In the four years just elapsed we have worked together in a commendable manner, and I believe for the best interest of the Borough. We did not accomplish as much as we might have perhaps, certainly not as much as we hoped to do, but if I enumerate some of the things we did accomplish it is not done in a boastful spirit but with regret that we did not succeed in doing more.

Altogether 17 Ordinances were passed.

Ordinance No. 56 was renewal of the Electric Light contract with the Excelsior Electric Light & Power Co.

Ordinance No. 60 makes provision for changing building lines on any street or portion of a street in the Borough. One attempt was made to carry this into effect on one street but owing to the opposition of two persons the matter was dropped. This Ordinance enables the residents of any street or part of a street to prevent future buildings beyond the present building line. As unanimous consent is needed for this, advantage should be taken of the time when unanimity exists and before a street is spoiled by some short-sighted act of some owner.

One of the most important matters of legislation was the passage of Ordinance No. 63, regulating the erection of buildings. This defines a fire limits in the more congested parts of the Borough, roughly defined as follows — Summit street on the North, the railroad and Third street on the East, Highland on the South, Adams and Wile avenue on the West. The more stringent requirements apply only to this section. Some other matters like the prohibition of shingle roofs applies to all parts of the Borough. As time passes and changes made in accordance with the requirements of this Ordinance will its value be realized. There are several fire traps in this section which will sooner or later cause trouble unless remedied. Under this Ordinance, Council has the power to change this and therefore in some sense the responsibility is placed upon them.

Ordinance No. 64 regulates the laying of drain pipes and prohibits any one except the Borough employees from digging in the streets.

Ordinances Nos. 65, 72, and 73 open North Second street, Railroad avenue and Highland street.

Ordinance No. 66 places on the Borough plan all streets not yet opened and preventing the use of such streets for other purposes. It would be well to have these streets extended in the new annexation and placed on the Borough map.

Ordinance No. 67 annexes the tract East of the railroad from Fairmount avenue (Reliance road) to Franconia avenue (Second street, Telford), down to Central avenue. This is a tract of about 110 acres with an assessed valuation of $49,370 and a population of 140.

Ordinance No. 68 gave a franchise to the Philadelphia Suburban Gas & Electric Co. for supplying gas to the inhabitants of the Borough. This has been partly done and is a great convenience.

Ordinance No. 69 regulates the use of water and requires the use of meters. Elsewhere I go into details as to this matter.

Ordinance No. 70 regulates the use of the public highways. Anyone familiarizing himself with this Ordinance and living up to its provisions will help to prevent accidents and will be able to travel in any city without fear of violating the traffic rules.

Ordinance No. 71 annexes about 375 acres of land, assessed at $227,640.00, and a population of about 586. This makes our present population over 3,000 as shown by a census last summer.

There is one difficulty in apportioning money for the new sections of the Borough. The streets were in such bad shape that something had to be done at once and a great deal remains to be done. Second street has been graded at the lower end and north of Summit street it was graded and macadamized. After this work is completed this street will be used very much more than heretofore. Much work has also been done on Water street, partly by arrangement with Franconia township before annexation. Stone has also been placed on Price avenue. These improvements have cost $2,943.34, yet we had not collected a cent of taxes before these improvements were made. It is true that these sections will bring something over a thousand dollars into the Borough treasury as their share of the township's assets. The annexed district will net about $2,300 in Borough taxes of all kinds, and this amount should be spent on this section for all purposes. They are entitled to all of this but not any more. This will be the first time any such amount was spent on their section and yet they have always paid nearly $1,700 in road taxes and one year over $2,300 without complaint. Now they get all their money's worth and surely they should be satisfied.

The new sections of the Borough are expecting street lighting. This should be given them as soon as possible wherever sufficient buildings exist to warrant it. It will also be necessary in the northern section to make some arrangements with the Excelsior Electric Light & Power Co. the owners of the existing light line.

As to water, practically all who are served by the Telford Water Co. appear to be satisfied so there does not seem to be any hurry in making a change in this for the present. The silk mill can be served from Central avenue, if necessary.

Owing to the coal famine, which seems to be getting worse instead of better, would it not be advisable to turn off the street lights after 12 o'clock or even later. It may not seem to amount to much since their coal are saved in Allentown, but if we all do our part it will amount to a great deal in the aggregate. I make this suggestion now for I feel that it may become compulsory soon in which case we will have no choice in the matter. If we do it because we want to help we can feel that we too are doing our share in whatever way it lies in our power to assist in this crisis.

I have been acting Building Inspector ever since Ordinance No. 63 was passed. The reason for this was that no one seemed to be available at the time and after that the matter was not taken up. I hope, however, that this responsibility will not be placed on the Burgess for he cannot legally hold any office, and if he could do so he should not be asked to do something which requires a great deal of time and for which he cannot be paid.

One of the most important duties that Council has to perform is the making of appropriations for the different departments. To do this properly estimates of the costs or fixed expenses must be made; after these are provided for then the money still available can be used for such purposes as are most urgent. We have been making efforts to do this thing for several years but I always felt that not sufficient time and consideration had been given. Money was set aside for certain purposes and not used therefor, other matters were taken up for which no provisions had been made simply because not sufficient time had been devoted to the matter in the first place.

Signing the Resolutions making these appropriations is the only part the Burgess has in spending the peoples' money-so therefore he should not be held responsible for any expenditures except to those to which he has given his approval.

There is one matter as to the power of the Burgess that I want to call attention to.

Sec. 6 of Article VI. Chapter VII of the Borough Code, provides that "the Police shall be under the direction of the Burgess as to the time during which the place, where and the manner in which they shall perform their duties." He may for cause and without pay suspend any policeman until the next regular meeting of Council. I mention this matter, and I mention it now so that the matter is clearly understood that my successor be not accused of assuming power not belonging to him. It is necessary that the Burgess should exercise this power for only in this way can he enforce order and obedience to the Borough Ordinances which is his duty to enforce. It is the duty of Council to appoint or discharge a policeman but the inference is that the policeman has to report to the Burgess for orders, the latter should have fuller knowledge as to fitness or faithfulness of the same and therefore his [illegible] should be taken in order to act intelligently.

Last summer I recommended the division of the Borough into three wards, one north of Hillside avenue, another south of same and both west of the railroad, the third all east of the railroad, this would make three wards of nearly equal population.

Each ward could have their representation in Council. Adequate facilities for voting could then be provided. I am aware that any 20 citizens of the Borough by petition to the Court of Quarter Session could obtain action in this and that Council is without jurisdiction in the matter. But it would not be just to put the expense of such action on the petitioners for it is clearly in the interest of the Borough. In this respect Council could, and in my opinion should help. There would be no other expense for the Borough involved.

One of the matters that I had hoped to induce in Council to consider is "Garbage disposal." Most people have no place for their garbage so it is on the manure pile if they have any, or on the ash heap which is often dumped in the alleys where it is a nuisance, obstructing surface drainage and taking up room needed for traffic; wherever placed, the garbage mixed with manure, ashes, tin cans, etc., becomes a breeding place for flies and mosquitoes, unbearable stenches and a menace to the public health. Now it seems to me that if the Borough would require the garbage, ashes and tin cans be kept separate, the garbage being placed in closed cans and removed at regular periods, the ashes too after a sufficient amount had accumulated all this could be moved with the minimum expense to the householder and at no cost to the Borough. For this garbage, if properly handled, is valuable for feeding hogs and if some one with a keen eye to profit would take a hold of this proposition he would be doing a double service — increase the food supply, rid us of a nuisance and at the same time making a good living. Ashes too have a value providing they are not mixed with everything else under the sun. By making stated trips for ashes and these placed so as to be convenient to load they could be moved very cheaply. Tin cans do not seem to have a market value on account of the little tin on them so they would have to be placed on some dump. If some one would devote some time and effort to this I feel sure it would bring results. For the Borough to spend a lot of money for this when it ought to be practically self-sustaining would not be right.

WATER DEPARTMENT

This is the first year that all the water used in the Borough has been metered. For a long time a few places were metered. Early in 1915 a meter was placed in the pumping station. This enabled us to learn the amount of water being pumped and to get some idea of what the cost of pumping amounted to in relation to quantity. In 1916 all the business places were metered and the next year meters were placed everywhere. We have 525 water connections, practically all of which are metered. In the old Borough limits there are 39 houses that are not using Borough water; several of them have asked to have water but as there are no mains in their neighborhood it was found impractical at present.

The amount of water pumped in 1916 was 5,803,602 cu. ft. In 1915 6,107,312 cu. ft. while in 1917 4,165,430 cu. ft. was pumped. During 1917, 2,170,130 cu. ft. was pumped at the catch basin, or slightly over half. This amount, however, is not very reliable as it is based on the number of strokes of the pump which may or may not be right. 1,895,300 cu. ft. was pumped at the pumping station on Main street, and, being metered, is reliable.

This shows 33⅓% less water pumped this year than last. This difference is so great that one man is now able to pump all the water required in 10 hours except under exceptional conditions. Before the installation of meters we had to pump day and night when all the water had to be pumped from the wells. I think I am safe to say that but for the saving in water we would now be looking for an additional supply.

The total amount of water revenue properly belonging to the year 1917 is $6,231.85. This does not include water supplied to the schools, which, if paid for, would have cost $332.84; the water used at the water plant, etc., for flush-ing the streets and cleaning the reservoir, I have no means of determining. Taking the total of all meters registered 2,478,056 cu. ft. and making proper allowance for the above unmetered water there is still a million cu. ft. unaccounted for. Some of this is due to leakage, and a constant watch must be kept for any signs of leaks in order that this may be repaired as quickly as possible.

The total water revenues are as follows:

1910	....	$4,181.24
1911	....	4,354.65
1912	....	4,854.48
1913	....	5,211.22
1914	....	5,336.78
1915	....	5,664.16
1916	....	6,273.39
1917	....	6,231.85

From 1910 to 1914 were years of great building activities; since then there has been comparatively little building and consequently there has been but little increase in the amount of water used. The amount of revenue required to take care of all the expense included the redemption of bonds, extensions, etc., in the average year is about $7,300.00 per year, pumping at one-seventh cents per cu. ft. is therefore done at a loss. If there were no minimum charge of $7.50 for the first 1,500 cu. ft., we would have to charge for the water actually registered on the meter and including that used for the schools at the rate of nearly one-third cent per cu. ft. in order to meet the cost per year. If the rate were one-sixth of a cent as last year it would have produced about $350.00 additional revenue. If the Lansdale rate were in force it would have produced $7,129.00. Leaving the rates as they are and without any reduction, for they cannot be reduced at this time, it will be necessary to raise about $1,000 or $1,200 by taxation to pay for the bonds falling due.

It is impossible to get reliable figures as to the amount of water pumped unless the water at the catch basin is also metered.

Some instrument which enables one to locate a leak of any account should be used from time to time. Meter readings should not be taken less than four times a year and the readings watched very closely as there are always some likely to stop for if a little dirt gets into the mechanism it is likely to stop and still allow the water to flow through. No doubt a great deal of loss results from this |illegible| meters are liable to be |illegible| should by this time be understood to be false. The Public Service Commission requires that meters be adjusted to within 4% slow or fast, but there is nothing so convincing as a meter testing machine which will enable every one to see for himself just what the meter is doing under all conditions.

Comparing the receipts from water rents from householders and excluding business people in 1916 and 1917 we have the following result, to wit:

All water users paid $4,081.37 in 1916 (flat rates).

All water users paid $4,444.29 in 1917 (meter service), or an increase of $326.92 or 9%.

Of these 411—272 paid more water rent under the meter system than under the flat rate or a total of $3,136.40 as against $2,493.90, an increase of $642.50 or 25%. On the other hand 139 paid less than before or a total of $1,307.89 in 1917 as against $1,587.47 in 1916, a decrease of $279.48 or 17½%.

———

I herewith submit a statement showing the indebtedness of the Borough from 1913 to the present time.

1913
Water	..............$24,566.60
Borough	.... 22,000.00
Light	.... 18,300.00
	$64,866.60

1914
Water	..............$23,140.33
Borough	.... 23,000.00
Light	.... 18,532.76
	$64,673.09

1915
Water	..............$19,911.79
Borough	.... 21,900.00
Light	.... 17,500.00
	$59,311.79

1916
Water	..............$21,517.79
Borough	.... 22,100.00
Light	.... 17,000.00
	$60,617.79

1917
Water	..............$20,411.79
Borough	.... 20,400.00
Light	.... 16,500.00
	$57,311.79

The actual outstanding debt is really only $55,900, because $1,411.79 represents a debt due the Electric Light Account by the Water Account. The net debt reduction in four years has been $7,554.81. We had extraordinary expenditures of about $2,500 due to work in annexed district from which no taxes have been received.

Taking these facts into consideration there would seem to be no reason for raising the tax rate.

The debt reduction of last year of $3,306 being only exceeded in 1915 when the reduction was $5,361.30. There was an increase of debt in 1916 owing to the installation of water meters, etc.

Our country being engaged in the war all it resources are needed and all its energies exerted in order to win, labor being scarce and materials high in price, only the most necessary work should be undertaken in the Borough. Of course, the streets must be maintained in good condition and even improved where possible, but no construction work of any moment should be undertaken.

We have had plans prepared for a sewage disposal system—nothing is more necessary than this and yet it will be impossible to do anything further in this matter until things become normal. Rapid reduction of the debt from now on will bring us nearer to its realization when the time comes, for we may then be in a position to borrow the necessary money which is impossible now. Our present

borrowing capacity is $40,000 in addition to our present debt, but in a few years this can materially be increased.

We have long been asking for better railroad facilities in this town. While we have not yet succeeded in getting them we have at least, through the action of the Borough authorities, succeeded in inducing the Railroad Co. to buy the land for such improvements. Here again the war has interfered with this improvement for the Railroad Co. would undoubtedly be building a new depot at this time under ordinary conditions.

—————

And now the time has come for me to hand over to my successor

the various duties with which I have been entrusted. I am proud of our Borough and feel that it has been a great honor to have had a share in its service, yet it means sacrifice of time, it requires patience, it is easier to make enemies than friends, and the reward of a good conscience is the only reward you can expect to attain. Of the public I ask for my successor that spirit of fairness due to all and especially to one which gives his time and talents often at a sacrifice for the public welfare.

W. S. HEMSING.

Drawings of Homes on Main Street, 1890, by William S. Hemsing

These homes stood where the Souderton Furniture Mart stands today.